Angus Calder was born in 1942. He [...]
Cambridge, and co-edited *Granta*, t[...]
research in the School of Social Stu[...]
where he completed a doctoral thes[...]
1942–1945. From 1968 to 1971 he le[...]
College, Nairobi. For several years he was a freelance author, and
he is now Staff Tutor in Arts with the Open University in Scotland.
His latest book is *Revolutionary Empire: The Rise of the English-
Speaking Empires from the 15th Century to the 1780s*.

THE PEOPLE'S WAR

'Admirably readable, evoking the very smell of high explosives and
charred wood after an "incident", with the weariness, the boredom,
the cups of tea and often the humour of life in Britain during the
war'
Oxford Mail

'Rationing and bombing and ENSA and cod-liver oil without
cloying nostalgia'
Evening Standard

'Most fascinating of all are his vivid accounts of the blitz and his
shrewd and well-informed analysis of political developments ...
His book cannot be skipped. It forces you to read right through'
The Tribune

'For the British, this was not so much a war of pitched battles
between armies as it was of ersatz eggs, smashed plumbing, maimed
children and 'austerity' – general misery orchestrated by enemy
bombs and British bureaucrats ... Angus Calder ably combines the
methods of the journalist, historian, sociologist, researcher, poll-
ster and commentator to tell you how it was to be a British civilian
in Hitler's war. The cumulative effect is overwhelming'
Time Magazine

ANGUS CALDER

The People's War

Britain 1939–45

GRANADA
London Toronto Sydney New York

Published by Granada Publishing Limited in 1971
Reprinted 1982

ISBN 0 586 03523 0

First published by Jonathan Cape Limited 1969
Copyright © Angus Calder 1969

Granada Publishing Limited
Frogmore, St Albans, Herts AL2 2NF
and
36 Golden Square, London W1R 4AH
866 United Nations Plaza, New York, NY 10017, USA
117 York Street, Sydney, NSW 2000, Australia
100 Skyway Avenue, Rexdale, Ontario, M9W 3A6, Canada
61 Beach Road, Auckland, New Zealand

Printed and bound in Great Britain by
Cox & Wyman Ltd, Reading
Set in Monotype Times

Granada ®
Granada Publishing ®

To my parents

Contents

Illustrations

Acknowledgements

The author and publishers gratefully acknowledge permission to reproduce Bertolt Brecht's poem, "General, that Tank", from *Modern German Poetry*, translated by Michael Hamburger and Christopher Middleton (MacGibbon & Kee); an extract from Brecht's play *The Caucasian Chalk Circle*, translated by James Stern and W. H. Auden (Methuen & Co. Ltd); and passages from Winston S. Churchill's *War Speeches* (Cassell & Co. Ltd and McClelland and Stewart Ltd, Toronto).

For permission to reproduce the illustrations, acknowledgements are due to the following:
Associated Newspapers Ltd (Pls. 12, 13); Associated Press Ltd (Pls. 3, 57); Cecil Beaton (Pls. 6, 25*b*); G. H. Bodle (Pl. 32); the British Broadcasting Corporation (Pls. 45, 46, 47, 48, 49); Common Wealth (Pl. 62); Faber & Faber Ltd (Pl. 50, from *Alamein to Zem Zem* by Keith Douglas); Hawker-Siddeley Group Ltd (Pl. 31); Michael Hillary (Pl. 51); Imperial War Museum (Pls. 2, 5, 8, 9, 10, 14, 17, 18, 22, 25*a*, 26, 30, 35, 36, 43, 52, 55, 56, 57, 59, 63, 65, 67); *Jersey Evening Post* (Pl. 54); Keystone Press Agency Ltd (Pls. 11, 23); London News Agency Photos Ltd (Pl. 40); London Transport Board (Pl. 20); R. G. MacNeill (Pl. 34); The Mansell Collection (Pl. 60); Paul Popper Ltd (Pls. 1, 21, 33); Pictorial Press Ltd (Pl. 7); *Radio Times* Hulton Picture Library (Pls. 4, 27, 28, 38, 39*a* 39*b*, 41, 61); the Raymond Mander & Joe Mitcheson Theatre Collection (Pl. 44); Sport & General Press Agency Ltd (Pl. 19); Syndication International (Pls. 42, 53, 66); Vickers Ltd (Pl. 29). The cartoon by David Low (Pl. 24) is reproduced by arrangement with the Trustees and the *Evening Standard* and the cartoon by Giles (Pl. 58) appears as published in the *Sunday Express*, February 24th, 1944. Pl. 37 appears by permission of the Controller of H.M.S.O.

Select List of Abbreviations

AA	Anti-Aircraft (also abbreviated to "Ack Ack")
ABCA	Army Bureau of Current Affairs
AEU	Amalgamated Engineering Union
AFS	Auxiliary Fire Service
ARP	Air Raid Precautions
BEF	British Expeditionary Force
CD	Civil Defence
CO	Conscientious Objector
CP	Communist Party
CPGB	Communist Party of Great Britain
CW	Common Wealth Party
CWAEC	County War Agricultural Executive Committee
DA	Delayed Action (bomb)
DC	District (War Agricultural) Committee
DSIR	Department of Scientific and Industrial Research
EEF	Engineering Employers' Federation
ENSA	Entertainments National Service Association
EWO	Essential Work Order
GP	General Practitioner
GTC	Government Training Centre
HE	High Explosive
HG	Home Guard
IB	Incendiary Bomb
ICI	Imperial Chemical Industries Ltd
ILP	Independent Labour Party
JPC	Joint Production Committee
LCC	London County Council
LDV	Local Defence Volunteer(s)
LEA	Local Education Authority
MAP	Ministry of Aircraft Production
MOI	Ministry of Information
NBBS	New British Broadcasting Station
NEC	National Executive Committee
NFS	National Fire Service
NIESR	National Institute of Economic and Social Research
PAYE	"Pay As You Earn" (taxation)
PEP	Political and Economic Planning

ROF	Royal Ordnance Factory
SCNE	Select Committee on National Expenditure
SFP	Supplementary Fire Party
TRE	Telecommunications Research Establishment (Radar)
TUC	Trades Union Congress
UXB	Unexploded Bomb
WI	Women's Institute
WLA	Women's Land Army
WVS	Women's Voluntary Service

General, that tank of yours is some car.
It can wreck a forest, crush a hundred men.
But it has one failing:
It needs a driver.

General, you've got a good bomber there.
It can fly faster than the wind, carry more than an elephant can.
But it has one failing:
It needs a mechanic.

General, a man is a useful creature.
He can fly, and he can kill.
But he has one failing:
He can think.

Bertolt Brecht

Preface to the Second (Panther) Edition

IT is self-evident that if I were writing this book now, I would write it differently; one gets a little less stupid, perhaps, each year. I would certainly have striven to present in some more astringent way the sentimental-cosy kinds of detail which enabled one critic (in approval, alas) to describe the book as "an essay in almost unadulterated nostalgia." And I would have tried to integrate my socialist understanding of life more fully into the text: I suppose I am surer of it now.

But the conditions of modern publishing prohibit leisurely rewriting, and it wouldn't be wise anyway – when would one stop? All I have done is to touch up the style in one or two places and correct errors of fact or emphasis noted by critics and correspondents. Amongst the latter I must thank in particular Horace Alexander, Margaret Cole, Frank Phillips and John Yates for their kind efforts to rescue me from my own negligence.

It was Mrs. Cole who raised the question of my use of Mass Observation reports (also challenged by Henry Pelling in *History*). They were, indeed, produced by inexperienced people in very difficult conditions. But for me they were an indispensable aid to tracing popular views and reactions in all kinds of fields, from aerial bombardment to greyhound racing. The statistics produced by M-O pools aren't definitive (which statistics of that time are?) but they generally conform, where comparison is possible, with Gallup Polls, which Mr. Pelling prefers, and the fact that they are consistent with each other means that even if the absolute percentages are too high or too low, the trends and variations must surely be real. M-O reports must indeed be used with caution, as I recognized when I was handling them, but their biasses and shortcomings are so evident that it should be easy to allow for them. I stick to my idea that they are probably the richest source of material available to the social historian of the period, and repeat my thanks to the M-O staff for letting me use them.

I must also take this opportunity to thank Sir Richard Acland, Kay Allsop, Robert Best, Freda Clegg, the National Committee of Common Wealth, Hugh Lawson, Charles McRonald, Jack Parker and J. Rodney Waite, who lent me private papers to assist me in my study of the Common Wealth party. I left them out before because I hoped shortly to get my thesis into shape for publication, but I have had no time to do so, and must make amends now.

Nor have I been in a position to revise my bibliography, except in a couple of small instances. I must note here, however, the recent publication of two books overlapping greatly in scope with this one and complementing it in other respects. Henry Pelling's *Britain and the Second World War* (1970) is the best attempt so far to relate the military and political aspects of the war. Norman Longmate's *How We Lived Then* (1971) is an exhaustive survey of the conditions of everyday life during the war, based chiefly on information privately supplied, but including a bibliography which lists many specialized and ephemeral sources not to be found in my own.

Nairobi, April 1971

The People's War

Foreword

THE chief aim of this book is to describe, as accurately as possible, the effect of the war on civilian life in Britain. While several good books have been published about the period from 1939 to 1941, the latter years of the war, when the war economy emerged in its full rigour, have been neglected. So I hope, firstly, that this book fills a gap.

But merely to arrange facts on paper in a certain order is to interpret them. If my interpretation has any novelty, this must lie primarily in the range of topics which I have tried to cover, and in my assumption that each kind of human activity, in total war, is interdependent with every other kind of activity; for instance, one cannot separate the increase in book reading from the restrictions upon other forms of entertainment, and from the shortage of consumer goods. When this book was first projected, I proposed to make of it a series of independent chapters each dealing with a single topic. This notion was discarded firstly because it prohibited any overall narrative flow, but secondly because I felt increasingly that any arrangement which divides topics too neatly from each other is bound to falsify social history. Hence, the reader who comes to this book seeking information about, say, food rationing or the mobilization of women will find that he has to consult not one chapter, but three or more. I have sorted out different aspects in each case and have juxtaposed them to parallel material drawn from other topics. In case this sounds forbidding, I should add that I hope that the general reader with time to follow the book from cover to cover will find that each topic flows naturally into the next.

No doubt I shall be accused of wilful "debunking". But I have not tried to explode received ideas merely for the sake of the bang. Nor can I claim much credit for uncovering falsehoods long concealed. If a mythical version of the war still holds sway in school textbooks and television documentaries, every person who lived through those years knows that those parts of the myth which concern his or her own activities are false. The facts which destroy the legends are not hard to come by; the official histories, which inevitably provide a backbone for this book, are full of piquant and surprising statistics.

Anyone writing a book of this kind owes an immense debt to those other writers whose work provides facts, arguments or quotations. The best way in which I can express my sense of obligation is to urge readers not to skip the bibliography which they will find at the end of this book; though unfortunately much of the best documentary writing about the home front has long been out of print. The creator of Hyman Kaplan has written wrily of "the three vows of scholarship – Poverty, Bibliography and Jargon"; while I have avoided the first, and have striven to avoid the third, Bibliography seems to me a matter of common courtesy to the general reader who may wish to explore particular topics further, as well as to those authors whose books I have discreetly pillaged. For the student's sake I have provided full references, but for the general reader's sake, these are segregated at the end.

Besides these scholarly acknowledgments, I have many personal acknowledgments to make. I must thank my agent, Michael Sissons, and my publishers, André Schiffrin and Tom Rivers of Pantheon and Ed Victor of Cape, for their patience with a project which has swollen far beyond its original scope, and for their helpful comments at many points in my writing and rewriting. To Paul Addison, of Edinburgh University, I owe conversations and assistance over several years of convergent work, amounting at times almost to collaboration, and thanks for taking great pains with my completed manuscript. I must thank him also for introducing me to the collection of typescript reports from the war years filed at the offices of Mass Observation. Leonard England of Mass Observation has allowed me to spend many days at work with them, and to quote freely from them here, and his staff have always been helpful and considerate.

Professor Asa Briggs supervised the postgraduate study on which several sections of this book are based, and volunteered to read a nasty carbon copy of my manuscript. My father, Lord Ritchie-Calder, has taught me a great deal through his conversation over the years, and has criticized my chapters on the blitz and on science. Others who have given their time to criticizing individual chapters are my brother, Nigel Calder; Paul Cheshire of N.I.E.S.R. and Robert Milsom of the T.U.C.'s education department; and Kay Allsop who also lent me a diary quoted here.

The forty-odd ex-members of the Common Wealth Party who gave me interviews or lent me papers are acknowledged in my thesis on the subject. Tom Driberg, M.P., Jock Haston, J. B. Priestley and D. N. Pritt are others whose help has been valuable in interpreting wartime politics. D. E. Farwell, Douglas Gill, Arthur Marwick and Kenneth Richards have provided me with books, memories, conversation and, at times, consolation. Mrs. Margaret McKnight retyped an especially nasty chapter.

Above all, my wife Jenni has criticized and assisted my work time and again, has created the conditions in which I could keep going, and gave up her own work while the manuscript was completed. I hope the book will seem worth it.

Introduction

"THIS is a war of the unknown warriors," Churchill told the world in the summer of 1940. Subsequently, he contrasted this Second World War with the First. "The whole of the warring nations are engaged, not only soldiers, but the entire population, men, women and children. The fronts are everywhere. The trenches are dug in the towns and streets. Every village is fortified. Every road is barred. The front lines run through the factories. The workmen are soldiers with different weapons but the same courage."* In 1940 and the years which followed, the people of Britain were protagonists in their own history in a fashion never known before; hence the title of this book, *The People's War*.

Those who made the "People's War" a slogan argued that the war could promote a revolution in British society. After 1945, it was for a long time fashionable to talk as if something like a revolution had in fact occurred. But at this distance, we see clearly enough that the effect of the war was not to sweep society on to a new course, but to hasten its progress along the old grooves.

In the shocked Britain which faced defeat between 1940 and 1942 there were very obviously the seeds of a new democracy. Between them, the threat of invasion and the actuality of aerial bombardment had exaggerated a tendency already noted in the previous world war. In a conflict on such a scale, as 1914–18 had shown, the nation's rulers, whether they liked it or not, depended on the willing co-operation of the ruled, including even scorned and underprivileged sections of society, manual workers and women. This co-operation must be paid for by concessions in the direction of a higher standard of living for the poor, greater social equality and improved welfare services. For the conscripts in the armed forces were dangerous enemies to the old social order; jolted out of their acceptance of it by communal travel, hardship and danger. The rifle aimed at the enemy might be turned on the ruling classes, as it was in Russia.

In 1939–45 the people of Britain were called into a participation which was wider, deeper and longer. It embraced veterans on the

* Churchill, *War Speeches* I (Cassell, 1951), pp. 233, 235.

one hand and even children on the other. As for the armed forces themselves, the new techniques of warfare centring on the tank and the aeroplane ensured that the best educated and most socially conscious generation of young men in Britain's history was increasingly courted as well as bullied by the military hierarchies, cajoled into a more skilled, a more conscious role than their fathers had played in the First World War.

With parliament muted, with the traditional system of local government patently inadequate, with the army conceding the soldier's right to reason why, with the traditional basis of industrial discipline swept away by full employment, the people increasingly led itself. Its nameless leaders in the bombed streets, on the factory floor, in the Home Guard drill hall, asserted a new and radical popular spirit. The air raid warden and the shop steward were men of destiny, for without their ungrudging support for the war it might be lost; morale was in danger.

"Morale" – that word which haunted the politicians, the civil servants and the generals. What the people demanded, they must now be given. Had they taken the tubes as deep shelters? Oh well, they must keep them. Did they demand fairer shares in food? Tinned salmon must be rationed "on points". Were they puzzled by set-backs in production? Let them elect representatives to joint production committees. Were they depressed by their conviction that victory would be the prelude to a new slump? Then plans must be made to ensure that life really would be better for them after the war

So the people surged forward to fight their own war, forcing their masters into retreat, rejecting their nominal leaders and representatives and paying homage to leaders almost of their own imagination – to Churchill, to Cripps, to Beveridge, to Archbishop Temple and to Uncle Joe Stalin. The war was fought with the willing brains and hearts of the most vigorous elements in the community, the educated, the skilled, the bold, the active, the young, who worked more and more consciously towards a transformed post-war world.

Thanks to their energy, the forces of wealth, bureaucracy and privilege survived with little inconvenience, recovered from their shock, and began to proceed with their old business of manoeuvre, concession and studied betrayal. Indeed, this war, which had set off a ferment of participatory democracy, was strengthening meanwhile the forces of tyranny, pressing Britain forwards towards *1984*. The new capitalism of paternalist corporations meshed with the state bureaucracy was emerging clearly, along with the managerial ideology which would support it. As the brilliant scientist willingly devoted his creative energy to military purposes he was working, not for the people, but for those few who would control the atomic bomb.

And at the very moment that the British people had become leading actors in their own history, power was withdrawing itself from their reach, across the Atlantic. As the war ended, the giant corporations of the U.S.A. were dividing world power with the cruel and hypocritical bureaucracy of the Soviet Union. Better armed than ever with bombs, promises and arguments, they would soon have to reckon with new enemies, those to whom they showed their visage of brutality without their mask of humane condescension, the poor of the colonial world.

If the countries of Asia and the southern hemisphere are rarely mentioned in this book, it is because people in Britain found it so easy to forget that their relative prosperity depended on them. India was bullied into participation against the wishes of its own leaders, and when Britain "stood alone" in 1940, she stood on the shoulders of several hundred million Asians. Conscripts from Africa fighting in Britain's armies had their eyes opened to the possibilities of defeating the very power which they supported. The fall of Singapore showed how easily a paper tiger might be torn to shreds. The British called it a "world war", yet thought of it essentially as a European squabble in which the Japs had irrelevantly intervened; so the most vigorous debates of the war years are now archaic, lacking a dimension which only hindsight can supply. But if current events in the western countries indicate that a younger generation is consciously resuming the quest for democratic community which was thwarted in the later years of the war, that generation at least is aware that it must find allies among the wretched of the earth, and that a war for one people must now imply a war for the world.

Chapter One

Prelude: Munich in the 'Thirties

Oh, blindness of the great! They wander like gods,
Great over bent backs, sure
Of hired fists, trusting
In their power, which has already lasted so long.
But long is for ever.
Oh, Wheel of Fortune! Hope of the people!

Bertolt Brecht

"... Everybody knows or else should know
That if nothing drastic is done
Aeroplane and Zeppelin will come out,
Pitch like King Billy bomb-balls in
Until the town lie beaten flat."

W. B. Yeats, *Lapiz Lazuli*[1]

I

IN the First World War, the "Great War", "the war to end wars",
Britain had been raided by zeppelins, and later by twin-engined
bombers. No shelters had been prepared against this novel
barbarity, and frightened Londoners had invaded the underground railway stations. In London, and elsewhere, there had
been mass panics and near riots. Over the whole country 1,413
people had been killed in just over a hundred raids, and this
modest total would have represented only one night's work for
the Luftwaffe in the winter of 1940–41; but two major raids on

London in the summer of 1917 had produced an average of 121 casualties per ton of bombs dropped.[2]

The theory of air war, as the major powers developed it in the 1920s, laid great stress on a swift and tremendous initial assault, which could only be parried by counter-bombing. Speculation also confronted the terror of poison gas, which had been used on the Western Front in the First World War, and was employed by the Italians in Abyssinia in 1936.

In 1937, British experts estimated that in a new war the enemy, now presumed to be Hitler's Germany, would bomb Britain at once and continue his attack for sixty days. On the basis of misleading and inadequate figures of the effects of bombing in 1917–18, it was assumed that each ton of high explosive dropped would cause fifty casualties, killed and wounded. It was further assumed that the enemy had a massive fleet of suitable bombers, all of which could be used at the same time, and all of which would aim accurately at populous areas. So, in this first terrible blow, six hundred thousand people would be killed and twice that number injured. One Briton in twenty-five would become a casualty, and in London, the main target, the proportion would of course be much higher. Exaggerated reports of raids on Barcelona in 1938 provided the still more terrifying multiplier of seventy-two casualties per ton.

These calculations are now notorious for their inaccuracy. The actual rate experienced in Britain during the Second World War proved to be no more than fifteen to twenty casualties per ton, and sustained and accurate attack of the type imagined proved impossible. But the civil servants who laid plans on the basis of these errors should not be credited with preternatural stupidity. "Thinking about the unthinkable", they were right to be pessimistic.[3]

Baldwin's National Government issued the first circular on "Air Raid Precautions" to Britain's local authorities in September 1935, inviting them to shoulder voluntarily the responsibility for protecting their people. Some boroughs went vigorously ahead; others dallied, and continued to dally even after compulsion was introduced in 1937. In April 1937, an Air Raid Wardens' Service was created; by the middle of the following year, this had recruited some two hundred thousand citizens. Meanwhile, scores of thousands of police and local government employees received training in anti-gas measures.[4] So the fears of the authorities were publicized. When the intelligent citizen thought about war, he saw in his mind's eye, not the noble if heart-rending scenes of 1915, not the flower of the nation marching away to fight in a foreign land, but his own living-room smashed, his mother crushed, his children maimed, corpses in familiar streets, a sky black with bombers, the air itself poisoned with gas.

In September 1938, it seemed almost certain that Britain would fight in defence of Czechoslovakia. A new social survey organization, Mass Observation, which had recruited voluntary "observers" amongst people all over the country and in many walks of life, discovered that a surprising number of Britons contemplated killing their families if war broke out. "I'd sooner see kids dead than see them bombed like they are in some places," said one woman, thinking of Abyssinia and Spain.[5]

II

Neville Chamberlain, hero and villain of that "Munich crisis", had been Prime Minister of Britain since May 1937. He had previously been a "reforming" Minister of Health in the Conservative Government of 1924–29, and more recently, as Chancellor of the Exchequer, had apparently done much to steer Britain's recent recovery from slump. Upright, after the old Victorian mode, arrogant in a fashion peculiar to himself, Chamberlain was nearly seventy, an old man craving peace in an age destined to war. But a meanness in him denies him any claim to the dignity of tragedy.

Auden, in a famous phrase, called the 1930s "the low dishonest decade". They were also the golden years of David Low, the cartoonist. Chamberlain, with his winged collar, with his rolled umbrella, with the face of a nervous eagle, was only one of nature's gifts to Low. After all the reassessments, all the "facts" then taken for granted which have turned out to be dubious or false, Low can still evoke for us the political creatures of that time as a worried, radical contemporary saw them. Mussolini's puffed-out chest; Hitler's mean mouth and satanic forelock; porcine farmer Baldwin; the dapper, boyish Eden; Franco, afflicted with five o'clock shadow; and fouler still the odious little Laval and the swollen, bemedalled Goering. In the background, Churchill, but not yet the British bulldog, merely another grotesque aberration of history.

From the horrors of the First War, Europe drove pell-mell towards the worse horrors of the Second. The Russian Revolution, a threat to the rich, an example to the poor, hung over the internal and external politics of the nations which assembled to "make peace" at Versailles in 1919; even then, it seemed wise to appease Germany, for the sake of another ally against Leninism. The League of Nations, then fathered, groped towards failure from the start. Soon, Mussolini made his disenchanted Italy a prototype for barbarism. In 1931, Japan shredded the pretences of the League, attacking China with impunity. Fifteen years of economic and political chaos in Germany culminated with Hitler's rise to power in 1933. In 1935, Mussolini assaulted Abyssinia; in 1936, Hitler's forces occupied the "demilitarized" Rhineland, and Franco raised his revolt against the Spanish Republic. While Fascism and Nazism tested their soldiers and weapons in Franco's support, Britain and France pursued the mirage of "non-intervention". Chamberlain, when he became Prime Minister, accepted that the notion of "collective security" through the League was a walking corpse, and followed what he called a "general scheme of appeasement", mindful of the Red demons lurking in the East. High society in London showered its favours on the German ambassador, Herr von Ribbentrop; Tory M.P.s blurted out their admiration for the "new spirit" which Hitler had given to Germany. The left was confused and divided. While a small section of the Labour Party had remained pacifist, another section, to the right, had hoped against hope for collective security through the League, and a third, to the left, led by Sir Stafford Cripps, had pursued the possibility of war against the ruling class at home, in alliance with the Communist Party. But in any case, Labour was remote from power.

In 1931, confronted by financial crisis, the Labour Prime Minister, Ramsay MacDonald, had deserted his party to head a "National" Government including a few of the few remaining Liberals, but also Baldwin's overwhelmingly more numerous Conservatives. A confused election had followed, and Labour had lost five-sixths of its seats. The "National" majority was five hundred. Labour's weakness, and the belief that the party had been beaten down by a "banker's ramp", encouraged the celebrated political extremism of the decade.

One of the ablest Labour leaders, Sir Oswald Mosley, turned to Fascism, and at its peak in 1934 his party may have had more than thirty thousand adherents. Another, Cripps, declared that Labour must be prepared to use dictatorial methods if it was to achieve its socialist ends. The small Communist Party cast a spell over many of the best minds in the universities, where pacifism also flourished. In 1933, the Oxford Union passed its famous resolution that it would "under no circumstances fight for its King and Country". A little later, Canon Dick Sheppard's Peace Pledge Union boasted a hundred thousand members. If only a small minority went to such political extremes, the quality of many of those found in it made its gestures profoundly significant. "Breathes there a man with soul so dead/Who was not, in the 'thirties, Red?"

And their protest was echoed, less raucously, in the heart of British politics. Baldwin's massive majority had brought the two- or three-party system near to death, and alignments at the centre were as confused and fluid as those on the left (where efforts were made, towards the end of the decade, for a "popular front" which would embrace Communists, Labour, Liberals and even anti-Fascist Conservatives). An influential body of "middle opinion" (to take Arthur Marwick's phrase) had espoused the ideals of the League of Nations, and men of all parties and none clung desperately to the last hopes of peace.

In the summer of 1935, eleven and a half million Britons voted in a "Peace Ballot" conducted by supporters of the League, and recorded a ten to one majority in favour of all-round disarmament and "collective security". In September, Sir Samuel Hoare, the Foreign Secretary, affirmed Britain's support for "collective security" in the context of Mussolini's aggression in Abyssinia. It seemed that Baldwin's Conservatives had niftily stolen the foreign policy of their Liberal and Labour opponents, and cries of "cheat" followed the election which Baldwin called in November.

The opposition parties received nearly ten million votes to Baldwin's eleven and a half million, but the Conservatives and their "Liberal National" and "National Labour" allies retained four hundred and thirty-two seats in the new parliament, to Labour's one hundred and fifty-four. The Liberal Party – in power a bare two decades before – now had only twenty-one representatives, and the remaining seats were taken by four members of the Independent Labour Party, which had broken with Labour in 1932, four Independents, and a lone Communist. This remarkably unrepresentative parliament was destined to survive for ten years, and twenty-seven defeats in by-elections before 1945 merely chipped the immense block of Conservative strength.

The new Government, still styling itself "National", at once turned round and betrayed the League. In December, Hoare and his French opposite Laval came out with a plan whereby two-thirds of Abyssinia would have been ceded to Italy. Even *The Times*, a hot supporter of "appeasement", was outraged. Baldwin sacked Hoare, temporarily, to save his own bacon, and renounced the proposals. But when the Government abandoned its sanctions against Italy in the following June, the League was in ruins.

Civil war in Spain broke down pacifism on the left and helped to clarify political alignments. Both "Red" and "middle" opinion were anti-Franco. The Left Book Club, founded in 1936 by Victor Gollancz, became one centre of a broad campaign in support of the Spanish Republic, and within three years it gained nearly sixty thousand members.[6] Meanwhile, Catholic and right-wing opinion acclaimed Franco as a Christian Gentleman.

After his annexation of Austria in the spring of 1938, Czechoslovakia was the next target for Hitler, and by September a new crisis had reached boiling point. On September 15th, as fear mounted, Chamberlain flew dramatically to see Hitler, and even the Labour *Daily Herald* applauded him, an old man braving the monster in his den. But when news came that Chamberlain was willing to give Hitler what he wanted, there was an immediate and startling revulsion of feeling; for the first time, the issues began to clarify for the "men in the street", two-thirds of whom, Mass Observation found, felt that the Prime Minister should have defied the Fuehrer; though women, racked by visions of bombardment, were much more inclined to favour Chamberlain.[7]

Hitler was not appeased, and Chamberlain flew to him again. At Godesburg on the 22nd, Hitler was still unsatisfied with the speed at which Britain and France were ready to give him the German-speaking areas of Czechoslovakia. Yet the notion of "selling the Czechs" was now less offensive to public opinion in Britain, which had swung back towards Chamberlain. For the day of the bombers, Armageddon, was palpably at hand.

On the 25th, the A.R.P. services were mobilized and they soon enlisted a horde of eager new volunteers. The following days saw a hectic spate of activity. Cellars and basements were requisitioned for air raid shelters. Trenches were dug, by day and night, in the parks of the big towns, for the same purpose. Some two score "blimps", barrage balloons, appeared in the sky over London. On the 29th, the Government published hastily concocted plans for the evacuation of two million people from the capital.

Thirty-eight million gas masks were issued to men, women and children – but none were available for babies. Fitting on these grotesque combinations of pig-snout and death's-head, sniffing the gas-like odour of rubber and disinfectant inside them, millions imagined the dangers ahead more clearly. Symptoms of panic appeared: a flood of hasty marriages, a boom in the sales of wills, signs that people were hoarding sugar and petrol. A great many people planned, and some made, their getaways from the cities; Wales and the West Country entertained a spate of refugees.[8]

Addressing the nation on the 27th, Chamberlain expressed what his fainter hearted countrymen were thinking. "How horrible, fantastic, incredible, it is that we should be digging trenches and trying on gas masks here because of a quarrel in a far away country between people of whom we know nothing."[9]

Parliament assembled on the 28th, to hear Chamberlain dilate on his efforts for peace. After he had been speaking sombrely for over an hour, he was handed a note. Hitler, he exclaimed, had invited him to Germany once more. Hysteria swept through the chamber. Chamberlain sped towards his rendezvous with infamy at Munich. The Czechs were briskly sold out and by two thirty on the 30th the crisis was over.

When Chamberlain stepped from his plane next day, he held up a piece of paper for the cameras. Hitler, according to this document, renounced all war-like intentions against Great Britain. "I believe it is peace for our time," the Prime Minister told a cheering crowd in Downing Street that evening. "No conqueror returning from a victory on the battlefield," proclaimed *The Times*, "has come home adorned with nobler laurels."[10]

Only one member of the Government, Duff Cooper, saw fit to resign in protest at the Munich betrayal, though some thirty Conservatives, led by Churchill, abstained when the settlement came up for a vote in the House of Commons. But once their gasp of relief had subsided, the British people felt uneasy once more. Shame on the one hand, fear on the other, had not been appeased.

III

It was the best of times, it was the worst of times. It was a time of intense political activity for the few, and apathy for the many; of derelict shipyards and packed super-cinemas; of neglected farmland and pluperfect batting wickets.

In 1934, J. B. Priestley, the novelist, made an *English Journey*. He found, he said, not one England, but three. There was the "Old England" of thatched cottages and castles, still a green and pleasant land. There was the England of nineteenth-century industrialism, of coal, steel, pottery, cotton and wool. And there was a new England of glossy filling stations, giant dance halls, Woolworth's stores, "motor coaches, wireless, hiking, factory girls looking like actresses", belonging, he observed, "far more to the age itself than to this particular island. America, I supposed, was its real birthplace."[11]

All three were affected by the world economic crisis. The countryside suffered behind a lovely façade. In 1936, when the Government made a long list of places which should be given priority in the allocation of official contracts, some of the most beautiful parts of Britain found their way into the tragic catalogue; Fowey in Cornwall, Ross-on-Wye, Harlech and Portmadoc in North Wales, Keswick in the Lake District stood there amongst the industrial eyesores – Liverpool, Wigan, Hartlepool, Glasgow, Dundee. All these were areas in which the rate of unemployment among men over eighteen years of age had averaged at least twenty-five per cent over the previous twelve months. And the worst of the depression was now over.[12]

In 1932, an average of 2,750,000 insured workers had been unemployed in Great Britain. The south-east of England, around London, had fared best, with only about one worker in eight out of a job. For the south-west it had been one in six, for the midlands one in five, for the north one in four, for Scotland one in four – and for Wales more than one in three. Even in 1937, one Scot in six, one Welshman in four was unemployed. A line drawn from the Severn to the Humber, through the midlands, would have marked with rough accuracy the division between a relatively prosperous "New" Britain in the south and east and an afflicted and demoralized "Nineteenth-century Britain", where a generation had been tortured on the Procrustean bed of industrial decline.[13]

Coal, steel, heavy engineering, shipbuilding, textiles had grown up together and were going down together as their export markets shrivelled. Clydeside, Tyneside, Lancashire, South Wales had made Britain "Great". Theirs had been the heroic age of the industrial revolution. In the coalfields, they still had a composite epic hero – known variously as Temple the Big Hewer, Bob Towers the Durham County Coal Cutter, Jackie Torr, Big Isaac Lewis – who could drill with his nose and cut coal with his teeth while he held up the roof of the seam with one hand. His age was over – let him hew all he could, there was no sale for it. The buoyancy had gone; the meanness of the houses, the arduousness of the conditions, and the defiled landscape endured.

To refine the meaning of "mass unemployment" still further; between 1931 and 1938, while the population of England increased by an estimated 3·7 per cent, that of Wales fell by 4·9 per cent; that of Merthyr Tydfil, on the South Wales coalfield, by 12·5 per cent. The bolder spirits left the "depressed areas"; as well they might, since in 1934 three workers in five in Merthyr were unemployed, and two out of three in the Tyneside shipbuilding town of Jarrow, which became a symbol for the ugliest features of the decade. "There is no escape anywhere in Jarrow," wrote J. B. Priestley, "from its prevailing misery, for it is entirely a working-class town. One little street may be rather more wretched than another, but to the outsider they all look alike. One out of every two shops appeared to be permanently closed. Wherever we went there were men hanging about, not scores of them but hundreds and thousands of them."[14]

It was in the depressed areas that the problem of long-term, hopeless unemployment was most acute. The older men suffered worst:

> I am an old miner aged fifty an' six.
> If Aa could get lots, wey, Aa'd raffle me picks.
> Aa'd raffle 'em, Aa'd sell 'em, Aa'd hoy 'em awey,
> For Aa can't get employment, for me hair it's torned grey.[15]

Life became an indignity. The street corner and the public library were the habitat of the hopeless. After unemployment insurance ran out, men fell back on "transitional payments" or on "public assistance", on "the dole". To draw the full dole, they had to prove need, and from 1934 onwards the authorities operated the infamous "Household Means Test", whereby the earnings, savings and other assets of all members of the family were assumed to be available to support an unemployed man. "Thrift was penalized and improvidence rewarded," writes C. L. Mowat. "Family solidarity was undermined ... The test was an encouragement to the tattle-tale and the informer, the writer of anonymous letters and the local blackmailer ..."[16]

The harried, penny-pinching spirit of the dole was by no means confined, however, to Nineteenth-century Britain. Unemployment struck at middle-class families who had thought themselves immune from the tribulations of the poor; in 1934 it was estimated that some three hundred thousand *uninsured* blackcoated workers (who did not appear in the general statistics) were unemployed – clerks, office managers, engineers, chemists, architects. Young men just down from university took up teaching as a last resort and turned to Communism. But even teaching, so notoriously "safe", was affected; temporary unemployment among newly qualified teachers persisted until 1938. No sensitive nose, anywhere in Britain, could escape the rotten smell of waste.[17]

And yet, in so many ways, it was the best of times, so far. Britons did well from the plight of the poor in colonial countries, which meant that prices for primary products fell while wages remained relatively steady. The increase in real income was not, of course, evenly distributed, but "even the unemployed man with a family was better off in the 'thirties than the unskilled labourer in full work in 1913." Various indices show that the general health of the nation improved. The death rate and the infant mortality rate fell significantly, and a dramatic comparison has been drawn between the medical reports on men examined for military service in 1917–18, when only one-third were adjudged Grade 1, "perfectly fit and healthy", and in 1939–46, when seven out of ten fell in this category.[18]

The improvement, of course, was least felt in the depressed areas. In 1937, Surrey had an infant mortality rate of 41 per thousand, while the town of Jarrow's stood at 114. But an increasing proportion of the nation's people lived in the relatively prosperous areas. Around London, the counties of Middlesex, Surrey and Hertford gained population at five or seven times the national rate, while "boom towns", like Luton and Coventry, grew at the same sort of pace.[19]

Such places were strongholds of the consumer goods industries and of the new, lighter engineering which made, inter alia, cars, cycles and wireless sets. If the island still lagged far behind America in spreading such goods as motor cars and refrigerators over the counties and classes, the New Britain already showed the main features of the post-war "Affluent Society", where industry relied on producing attractive things for the home market, to be bought in the big new chain stores which more and more undercut and drove out the small shopkeeper. In place of the old coke boiler, the new electric fire; in place of the big ship, the family motor car; it was a shift from power to comfort, from expansive Great Britain to inward-turning, hedonistic Little England.

The New Britain paid good wages and relied on its workers to buy its own products. It would be straining language to suggest that the working class, now that it was courted so sedulously by the expanding advertising industry and the brash, new-style mass circulation press, was arriving at economic dominance. But along with the shift to home markets came a new cultural style, profoundly affected by superficially "democratic" gales from across the Atlantic, and strongly marked in the new mass entertainments, the radio, and, more notably still, the cinema. In the New Britain, the immigrant worker from Scotland and his manager, perhaps only recently arrived in the middle class by a daring ascent of the flimsy educational ladder, danced to the same tunes and watched the same films. "There are wide gradations of income," observed George Orwell, "but it is the same kind of life that is being lived at different levels, in labour-saving flats or Council houses, along the concrete roads and in the naked democracy of the swimming pools. It is a rather restless, cultureless life, centring round tinned food, *Picture Post*, the radio and the internal combustion engine. It is a civilization in which children grow up with an intimate knowledge of magnetoes and in complete ignorance of the Bible."[20]

This new style was inseparable from a new kind of economy. The First World War had not ended war, but it had comprehensively transformed the economic life of Britain. By the time it had ended, the old ideology of laissez faire which had served the British ruling class so well in the nineteenth century had been on its last legs – so obviously that the "Anti-Socialist Union" had decided to change its name to the "Reconstruction Society". The Government had stepped in to protect some key industries, to rationalize, or even nationalize others, to control what was produced and to decide what should be consumed. After the war, the momentum created by the vastly expanded state apparatus had carried on even through an atavistic and misguided effort to restore Free Trade and laissez faire, symbolized by the nostalgic return to the Gold Standard in 1925. By the time of Munich, the state had reorganized the railways so that four companies now worked where a hundred and thirty had worked before; had created nationally owned corporations in the new fields of radio and air passenger transport; had organized and partially nationalized electricity supply; had regulated prices and output in agriculture; had forged a powerful cartel in iron and steel; and had striven, with limited success, to rationalize the coal mines. While much of this activity was a defensive response to the slump, it still marked an irreversible break with the past. In the 1930s, businessmen themselves clamoured for protection from the rigours of the free market, and the state obliged.

For the moment, men were reluctant to admit that the old days of the bold, independent entrepreneur had gone for good, and still more reluctant to reason out the new role which the state was, willynilly, playing. Yet the onward march of monopoly was clear enough. Before 1914, very little had been produced under monopoly; but in 1935, "at an absolute minimum" (Eric Hobsbawn points out) "upwards of a hundred and seventy products were produced substantially by one, two or three firms." From having been perhaps the least concentrated of the great industrial economies in 1914, Britain was, in 1939, one of the most.[21] The controversial doctrines of J. M. Keynes, who preached the virtues of strong state intervention, were on the verge of becoming the economic orthodoxy of the centrist politicians of all parties; they would make of the state, not an instrument of socialism, but a key component of a new capital- ism, dominated by home-grown giants like I.C.I., Anglo-European enterprises like Unilever, and American invaders like Ford.

By the mid 'thirties, what might be called a "young man's consensus" had been achieved in the centre of British politics. Right-wing Labour men like Herbert Morrison, advanced Liberals like David Lloyd George, and progressive Conservatives like Harold Macmillan could agree among themselves that a "mixed economy", with a state-owned section supporting, rather than threatening, private industry, was the pattern for the future. The most famous products of this all-party drift of thought were perhaps P.E.P. (Political and Economic Planning), a research organization set up in 1931, and a book called *The Next Five Years; an Essay in Political Agreement*, published in 1935.

It was in the latter year that a new direction in state activity came as a clear harbinger of the immense apparatus of control which would be necessary in the next world war. Rearmament began in earnest. Hence, A. J. P. Taylor reads two different stories from the 1930s. "One is the story of steadily accelerating preparations for an inevitable war. The other is of groping attempts to prevent war – attempts which failed regretfully and by mistake."[22]

For the New Britain, rearmament meant a gay boom in aircraft production. In 1936, motor-car manufacturers were brought into this field by the "shadow factory" scheme; in 1938, the Air Ministry's "Scheme L" provided for the production of twelve thousand new military aircraft in three years. For Nineteenth-century Britain, rearmament brought a boost for shipbuilding, and the creation of large new arms factories in the depressed areas. For the well-to-do, rearmament meant premonitory increases in income tax, surtax and death duty; in 1938, well over a quarter of the nation's budget was allocated to "defence".

At the time of Munich, air raid precautions were manifestly inadequate, Britain had only six squadrons of first-rate fighters and her army, relatively starved of funds, could not have sent more than two divisions across the Channel. But the plans had already been laid which, soon after Munich, sent the British rate of aircraft production creeping past the German. The Czech crisis created a new sense of urgency. Expenditure on A.R.P. was hastily tripled. The financial limitations on rearmament were largely, though not wholly, lifted. The doctrine of "limited liability", which had previously restricted the army to no more than five regular divisions, was scrapped, and plans for expansion to thirty-two divisions were made.[23]

For any illusions that Munich had meant "peace in our time" had rapidly withered. Men flocked to join the rapidly inflating Territorial Army. In March, the German Reich digested what was left of Czechoslovakia. In the same month, Britain promised to support Poland in the event of a German attack. April saw the announcement of military conscription in peace, for the first time in British history.

IV

On the night of August 9th, as the expected crisis boiled up in eastern Europe, London was thrown into darkness by a trial run for the "blackout" which would come into force if war broke out. On August 21st, British negotiations with Russia, which had been pursued with the utmost lack of vigour for several months, finally broke down. On the same day, the German foreign minister was invited to Moscow. On the 22nd, the British Government announced that it stood by its promise to Poland. On the 23rd, the Nazi-Soviet pact was signed.

On the 24th, members of parliament, who had been called back from their holidays, passed the Emergency Powers (Defence) Act, by which the Government was empowered to make such regulations as appeared necessary or expedient to secure public safety, the defence of the realm, the maintenance of public order, the efficient prosecution of the war, or the maintenance of supplies and services essential to the life of the community; in short, to act as it liked without reference to parliament. The first hundred-odd new regulations under the Act were issued five days later.

Also on the 24th, military reservists were called up and the A.R.P. services were warned to stand ready. On the 25th, a treaty of alliance was signed between Britain and Poland. Yet, six days later, only one person in five admitted to Mass Observation that he or she expected war – a far lower percentage than eighteen months before, when Anthony Eden had resigned as Foreign Secretary after disagreements with Chamberlain. Even now one person in three was of the opinion that "anything" (even a second Munich) would be better than war.[24] Such timid souls were comforted by the testimony of astrologers and spiritualists, who asserted confidently and unanimously that peace would be preserved.

In the small hours of September 1st, German troops moved into Poland. By six a.m., Warsaw was being bombed. John Lehmann, the writer, when he heard the news, "had the feeling that I was slipping down into a pit, clutching at grass on the ledges but failing to stay the accelerating descent into darkness." In one cotton mill in Bolton, Lancashire, the news was heard "through a woman hairdresser in Derby Street coming into the mill to tell the manager, who told an oiler and greaser, who came round telling various weavers . . . Some believed the news, and some didn't. Then one or two went out of the mill and bought a special. Then they all believed it. One weaver had hysterics. She had a son. A few were crying, but on the whole they didn't bother much, till about four o'clock, when the boys got their calling papers at the mill. At four o'clock they were all working. At five they were in uniform waiting for their pay. The oldest was only twenty-four. They were all given a hearty send-off. They had a mixture of bravado and fear on their faces."[25]

That day, the official evacuation of mothers, children and cripples from London and other major centres began; an endless stream of people swept through the main line stations and flooded out over the rural counties. Only about twenty thousand viewers, all in the London area, had television sets. On Friday, September 1st, the B.B.C. was transmitting a Mickey Mouse cartoon to prospective buyers at the Radiolympia exhibition. "A caricatured Greta Garbo had just said 'Ay tank Ay go home' when the long-awaited order came and the world's first television service closed down."[26]

At sunset, the blackout began in earnest. That evening, the

Labour Party brusquely rejected Neville Chamberlain's suggestion that its leaders should join his new War Cabinet; but Winston Churchill, kept out of office for ten years by his unpopular stands for imperialism, rearmament and King Edward VIII, accepted an invitation to enter it when the moment came.

If the moment came. Chamberlain continued to appeal to German reasonableness and to place hopes on peace moves by Mussolini. By the 2nd, the people were mostly convinced that war must come, and a mood of "Let's get it over with" was setting in. When Chamberlain appeared in the House of Commons that evening, its members expected him to announce war. Instead, his speech seemed to foreshadow a second Munich. As Arthur Greenwood, acting Labour leader during the illness of Clement Attlee, rose to reply, little Leo Amery, a veteran Tory imperialist and confirmed anti-appeaser, shouted "Speak for England, Arthur." Other Conservatives, ashamed at this temporizing, took up the call, and from the Labour benches came cries of "Speak for the workers" and "Speak for Britain", a pertinent reminder that Scotland and Wales were also involved. Greenwood seized his moment of history with a sturdy speech. ". . . I wonder how long we are prepared to vacillate," he asked, "at a time when Britain and all Britain stands for, and human civilization, are in peril." And the Tories cheered.[27]

That night, the worm turned; Chamberlain's cabinet revolted. A group of mutineers were called to Downing Street, and told the Prime Minister they were on a "sit-down strike" until war was declared. At last Chamberlain said quietly, "Right, gentlemen, this means war." Almost at once, there was a tremendous clap of thunder. A dramatic storm, a "regular Old Testament hundred-percenter," as one journalist called it, flogged London with a faint premonition of floggings to come.[28]

September 3rd was a Sunday. At eleven o'clock, the British ultimatum expired. At eleven fifteen, the metallic voice of Chamberlain was heard on the radio, and querulously he told the people that his work for peace had failed.

After the strain of the last few days, this announcement brought relief to many. But the eerie feeling of relaxation, even of elation, was dispelled at eleven twenty-seven, as the sirens sounded over London, a banshee wail. Civilians in the streets were brusquely shepherded into the shelters by steel-helmeted police and A.R.P. wardens; the congregation in St. Paul's Cathedral filed calmly into the crypt. Here it was; Armageddon, a dryness in the mouth, a pricking in the bladder. A joke.

The "all clear" soon sounded. A single French plane, arriving
unheralded, had provoked the first, but not the last, phoney
alert of the Phoney War. As if in grim counterpoint, an air battle
had occurred. A technical fault in the defence system had sent
two groups of British fighters into the air over the Thames.
When they had engaged each other, two planes had been shot
down, and a pilot had died.[29]

Chamberlain assembled his new War Cabinet of nine.
Churchill returned to his old "Great War" position as First Lord
of the Admiralty – to the fleet went the signal, "Winston is back"
– and another critical Conservative, Eden, was given the
Dominions Office. Otherwise the faces were the same, those of
the "men of Munich". A string of new ministries was set up – for
Home Security, Economic Warfare, Food, Shipping, Information – following lessons learnt in the First War.

All commentators marvelled at the contrast between the
hysteria of August 1914 and the absence of hatred and high
spirits now. This time, there was no stoning of dachshunds in the
streets. But a holocaust of pets occurred as homes were disrupted;
outside vets' surgeries "the slain lay in heaps." Everyone seemed
to be on the move, in transition. August and September 1939
saw the "greatest flood of marriages ever counted in British
statistics", while two powerful forces tore fiercely at everyday
life, the home, the family, the office, the factory.[30] Young men,
and older ones, were swept into uniform, while the threat of
bombardment swelled a mighty exodus from the cities. The
second force, for the moment, was more powerful.

And yet there were no bombs, there was very little war. As a
disrupted nation settled down to weeks and months when it
seemed that almost no Briton anywhere was striking a blow in
anger, evacuation dramatized its disunities. It showed how far
out of touch was Chamberlain's government with the conditions
and opinions of those whom it "represented". It exposed the
inadequacy of Britain's social services, both in town and country.
It offered experimental proof that the poor were hideously poor,
in the south-east as well as in Nineteenth-century Britain. It thrust
a better standard of living in front of small townschildren, and a
far worse one against the noses of middle-class householders.

But while it exposed the diversity of sorts and conditions of
people in this nation which had stumbled into war, it was the
first of those social developments from the imperatives of
military and civil defence which scrambled the people together
and acquainted them with each other as never before. During the

first weeks of war, observers were impressed with a bizarre phenomenon. In the buses, the trains and the pubs of Britain, strangers were speaking to one another.

Chapter Two

"This Strangest of Wars": September 1939 to April 1940

A blackout warden passin' yelled, "Ma, pull down that blind;
Just look what you're showin'," and we shouted, "Never mind."
OOH!
KNEES UP, MOTHER BROWN! Well, KNEES UP, MOTHER BROWN . . .

An old song, rewritten, autumn 1939

EVACUATION

"They call this spring, Mum, and they have one down here every year."

Evacuated child[1]

I

IT is estimated that between the end of June 1939 and the first week of September some 3,500,000 or 3,750,000 people moved from the areas thought vulnerable to those considered safe. Population movements in September alone affected a quarter to a third of the population.[2]

When war began, large sections of various Government offices were due to leave London under a plan called the "Yellow". If the worst came, the Government itself would evacuate under the "Black Move". Some twenty to twenty-five thousand civil servants, with their records, went to spas and seaside resorts where large hotels provided plenty of accommodation. Meanwhile, hotel keepers in several spa towns were given notice, sometimes no more than one hour, to clear out their guests and make way for the "Black Move". Weeks after the outbreak, such hotels were still empty and there were loud attacks from the press on the officials responsible. There was a further instalment of "Yellow" in 1940 but the idea of a "Black Move" was finally abandoned in the following summer, when, in any case, no part of England was safe from air attack.[3]

The B.B.C. sent its Variety department to Bristol and established its main centre at a country house near Evesham in Worcestershire. The National Gallery evacuated its treasures, which found their wartime home in a cave in a disused slate quarry in North Wales. The Bank of England dignified the hitherto obscure village of Overton in Hampshire. For a brief period, an abortive dispersal of Billingsgate Fish Market spread stinking fish and profane language widely over the nation. Private firms, where they could, followed the official example and removed their headquarters from London, so that Herstmonceux Castle in Sussex (for instance) became the address of the Hearts of Oak Benefit Society.

Some five thousand, six hundred prisoners and Borstal boys were freed. The hundred and forty thousand patients sent home from hospitals to make way for air raid casualties included tubercular cases, patients in an early, operable stage of cancer who now went untreated, bedridden patients discharged to the care of relations who might, for all the authorities knew, have evacuated.[4]

About two million people privately evacuated themselves – to Wales, Devon, Scotland and other quiet spots. It was reported from Southampton that five thousand people left for America in forty-eight hours. Constantine Fitzgibbon recalls:

> . . . a constant stream of private cars and London taxis driving up to his mother's front door in the Thames valley in the September of '39, filled with men and women of all ages and in various stages of hunger, exhaustion and fear, offering absurd sums for accommodation in her already overcrowded house, and even for food. This horde of satin-clad, pin-striped refugees poured through for two or three days, eating everything that was for sale, downing all the spirits in the pubs, and then vanished.[5]

For it was, of course, above all the well-to-do who could afford to quit their homes and flee. The newspapers were full of advertisements from country hotels proposing, none too bashfully, what bolder spirits called "funkholes". In the hills of the west and north, rich ladies settled down to a quiet war, and some stayed, with little access of discomfort, for six years. One actress who stopped at a luxury hotel in North Wales in 1940 found it harbouring women "whose sole occupation seemed to be backgammon, a lot of drinking, and a little knitting for the troops".[6]

II

The Government saw the official evacuation "simply and solely as a military expedient, a counter-move to the enemy's objective of attacking and demoralizing the civilian population. The Government thought that a large exodus from London and other cities was inevitable; panic would send the people out and unless the Government took firm control chaos and confusion were bound to ensue."[7]

Under the principles laid down by an official committee which had reported in the summer of 1938, official evacuation would be restricted to "priority classes", and would involve the billeting of millions of townspeople on country householders. There was no way out of this, though the authorities who prepared the official scheme after Munich would dearly have liked to find one. One M.P. from a rural district wrote to Sir John Anderson (who, as Lord Privy Seal, was the minister in charge of the scheme) and told him that "compulsory billeting would be far worse than war."[8] In the event, there were compulsory powers to enforce billeting at a pinch, but the basis of the billeting actually carried out was quasi-voluntary.

Britain was divided into "evacuation", "neutral" and "reception" areas, with current populations, roughly, of thirteen, fourteen and eighteen million respectively. The former were the urban districts where heavy raids could be expected. (But certain towns later heavily bombed – notably Plymouth, Bristol and Swansea – were not designated "evacuation areas".) "Neutral" areas would neither send nor take evacuees.

From the beginning of 1939 onwards the local authorities in the reception areas took stock of the available billets. Volunteers carried out house-to-house checks. There was found to be "surplus accommodation" in the reception areas for 4,800,000 people – but even in February 1939, one million billets had already been privately booked. The Government also set about building a number of camps, which would hold a fraction of the expected influx.

But the response to official publicity in the summer of 1939 showed that the demand for evacuation would fall far short of potential. At the time of Munich, over eighty per cent of London parents had said that they would want their children to be evacuated. Yet, in August 1939, whether from added courage or greater apathy, only just over two-thirds were of the same mind.[9]

In the event, under half of London's schoolchildren went. There were very great regional differences in the response. In the great Lancashire conurbations, the proportion was about two-thirds, and this was the highest in the country. But the Black Country sent only a quarter of its schoolchildren. Only eight per cent left Rotherham and only fifteen per cent went from Sheffield. These differences must have been due chiefly to the varying degrees of vigour and flair with which local authorities had publicized the scheme. (In the case of Sheffield, however, the low proportion reflected the fact that the Government had turned down the city's own scheme to send its children to neighbouring, and familiar, areas of Derbyshire, and had insisted they must go to Lincolnshire – further from Sheffield and nearer to Hitler. Over the county boroughs of England and Wales and London County, taken together, the proportion of schoolchildren evacuated was forty-eight per cent; from all Scottish evacuation areas, it was thirty-seven per cent.[10]

The evacuation scheme had three parts. First, those eligible must be encouraged to go. Then, they must be transported. The relative failure of the first part meant that the transport scheme, otherwise the most efficient part of the authorities' preparations, did not work properly. When the children poured on to the railway platforms on September 1st, 1939, they were marched into whatever trains happened to be waiting until these were filled, in many cases with little or no attempt to control their destinations.

It was, on the surface, a triumph of calm and order. The parties, clutching gas masks and emergency rations, shepherded by their teachers, were guided and controlled by an elaborate system of banners, armlets and labels. In three days, nearly one and a half million people were decanted into the countryside; from London and its suburbs; from Portsmouth and Southampton; from Birmingham, Coventry, Walsall, West Bromwich and Smethwick; from Derby and Nottingham; from Liverpool, Wallasey, Bootle and Birkenhead; from Manchester and Salford; from Sheffield and Rotherham; from Grimsby and Hull, Bradford and Leeds, Middlesbrough, West Hartlepool, Sunderland, South

Shields, Tynemouth, Newcastle and Gateshead; from Glasgow and Clydebank, Edinburgh, Rosyth and Dundee. If a relatively small number are included who left soon after this first evacuation, there were 827,000 schoolchildren; 524,000 mothers and children under school age going together; nearly 13,000 expectant mothers, 7,000 blind, crippled or otherwise handicapped people; and 103,000 teachers and helpers.[11] Most of the parties managed to raise a cheer as they left. There was not a single accident or casualty.

Nevertheless, one teacher called his twelve-and-a-half-hour trip from Glasgow to Aberdeenshire "the most depressing, deplorable and disgusting journey I have ever had the misfortune to make". The evacuees arrived after midnight without having eaten for twelve hours.[12]

Such lack of food and conveniences was fairly general. Many of the trains had no corridors. In one case at least, a train which had started off from London for the south-west deposited its charges in Berkshire – the calls of nature were too strong. The children had, in most cases, assembled in a state of high excitement at seven or eight in the morning. They arrived dirty, tearful and exhausted. Normally clean children were at their worst, and the condition of the really scruffy ones was unspeakable.

Schools were scattered over large, unfamiliar areas. One boys' school from London, which had taken especial care to ensure that friends travelled with friends, brothers with brothers, in carefully demarcated groups, had them broken up in the course of changes from train to train, then from train to buses, until the buses eventually deposited the boys in various villages over an area of fifty square miles. Parties from the east London suburb of Dagenham were evacuated, exceptionally, by boat. Arriving in ports in East Anglia, they found the reception authorities aghast at the numbers. "No organization existed for dealing with them. Schools and other buildings were opened, but bedding and blankets did not exist. In some cases for four days they lived – teachers, mothers and children – on an official diet of milk, apples and cheese, sleeping on straw covered by grain bags."[13] But other towns and villages were taken aback, meanwhile, to find that only a fraction of the expected horde had arrived. Worse, many communities which had been looking forward to entertaining children and had been told to expect them, were invaded instead by busloads of mothers and babies, or pregnant women. The first part of the evacuation scheme had largely failed. The cities were still loud with children. The second part of the scheme had misfired. The third part involved looking after the evacuees when they reached the reception areas. On August 29th, the Board of Education sent out a circular to local authorities which blandly observed, "The extensive preparations for evacuation being well forward, it is time to consider what is to happen to children after evacuation."[14]

III

Of course, if the great cities had been devastated at the outbreak of war, most of the defects of the evacuation scheme would have seemed unimportant. But, as two critics put it early in 1940, "Evacuation had been primarily conceived as an emergency measure; it has now become a social question of some magnitude and of uncertain duration."[15] Local authorities in the reception areas, as Richard Titmuss reveals, "had been asking for months to be allowed to spend money on preparing maternity homes and hostels, and for the purchase of various items of equipment. All these applications had been refused until six days before the outbreak of war." The Government's ban on spending reinforced the feeling current amongst many in the reception areas that evacuation would never happen. The social services in the country were in any case generally inferior, both in quality and quantity, to those of the towns, where, as country dwellers were soon to learn the hard way, the need was more intensive. In some cases, an influx of evacuees taxed the most basic amenities of modern life. One seaside town in Wales, called upon to receive sixteen hundred evacuees, was "at its wits' end to cope with a serious shortage of water".[16]

In the towns, a local government official was usually given the job of billeting officer. In rural areas, the chief billeting officer was usually a volunteer, with local volunteers in charge of individual villages and districts. Such people naturally varied enormously in status, competence, integrity and compassion. It fell upon them to organize a social experiment of unprecedented size and difficulty.

In every area, there were fewer evacuees than had been expected. The most put-upon counties – Sussex, Cumberland and Westmorland, for instance – received half, or little more than half, of the numbers they had been told to expect. At the other extreme, Cornwall had only three per cent, Kesteven only seven per cent.[17] This from one angle reduced the problem of billeting;

from another, it at once gave every householder who was called upon to find room for evacuees a legitimate cause of grievance – "Why me?" Even where a whole village was swamped with evacuees, it might soon learn, to its outrage, that one of its neighbours had hardly had any at all.

Methods of billeting varied greatly. In the well organized city of Cambridge, volunteers were waiting on the station platforms as each train came in to take the evacuees to "dispersal centres" organized in different wards, and efforts were made to keep school parties together. In many areas, however, local house-holders had assembled to pick their evacuees when the trains or buses arrived, and "Scenes reminiscent of a cross between an early Roman slave market and Selfridge's bargain basement ensued."[18] Potato farmers selected husky lads; girls of ten or twelve who could lend a hand in the house were naturally much in demand; nicely dressed children were whisked away by local bigwigs. Those who got "second pick" were often resentful, and there was likely to be a residue of unwholesome looking waifs whom nobody wanted, but whom somebody would have to take when the billeting officer began to mutter about compulsory powers. The alternative was usually a more or less haphazard distribution of children by the billeting officer and his helpers.

Social mismatching was inherent in the scheme. The official evacuees came disproportionately from the poorest strata of urban society, for several reasons. Firstly, the well-to-do were more likely to have made their own arrangements. Secondly, the evacuation areas were mostly areas of high population density, where overcrowding was at its worst, while the wealthier sub-urbs were often classified as "neutral" areas. Thirdly, the poorer classes had maintained a higher birth rate than their social superiors. Social surveys of several provincial towns in the 1930s had suggested that while twelve to fifteen per cent of families were living below the poverty line, they included twenty-two to thirty per cent of the children. Large families, then as always, were a contributory cause of much poverty.[19] And it is clear from detailed studies of evacuation in several areas that parents with only one or two children were less likely to send them away, and swifter to bring them back, than those with five or six; the smaller the family, the more it clung together.

As for the other half of the experiment, there was a shortage of housing, sometimes very acute, in the country as well as in the towns. Those with room to spare would be found disproportion-ately among the well-to-do. A Scottish survey suggested that only four out of ten evacuees from the overwhelmingly working-class town of Clydebank went to families judged to be working-class, and a third went to homes which were assessed as "wealthy".[20] In many cases, like was matched with like, and working-class families took working-class children into environments much like those which they had known at home. But rural Britain was electrified by every sort of tragi-comic confrontation. Elderly gentlemen found their retirement invaded by half a dozen urchins from the slums of London or Liverpool. Neat spinsters who had agreed to take a schoolchild might be gifted instead with a sluttish mother who arrived smoking a cigarette over her baby's head and disappeared with her offspring as soon as the pubs opened. Sensitive, withdrawn children were thrust upon rough farmers. With quite incomprehensible obtuseness, Catholic families from Liverpool (with its rich underworld of Irish immigrants) were dispatched to rural Wales, where a narrow Calvinism still held sway and there were no Roman Catholic churches. On the first Sunday of war, God-fearing Welsh house-wives had to decide whether to miss the chapel service, to take their charges with them, or to let them run wild. "One priest felt it necessary to call upon the parents of the evacuees to insist upon their return home, alleging that any physical danger they might incur thereby was trifling when compared with the spiritual dangers they ran by remaining."[21]

A thirteen-year-old Jewish boy, used to the friendly warmth of Stepney, was billeted in Buckinghamshire with his young sister. Because they had refused to be separated, no house was found for them before it was close to midnight. "Rose whispered," he writes. "She whispered for days. Everything was so clean in the room. We were even given flannels and toothbrushes. We'd never cleaned our teeth up till then. And hot water came from the tap. And there was a lavatory upstairs. And carpets. And something called an eiderdown. And clean sheets. This was all very odd. And rather scaring."[22]

On the other hand, some children who were used to running water and flush lavatories were billeted in agricultural labourers' cottages where the fields provided the sanitary facilities and water was drawn from a well. Because they had bottled themselves up in the train, or because they were upset at being parted from their parents, or because they thought the country darkness must harbour ghosts and were afraid to move, at the beginning of September, from Aberdeenshire to Devon, countless numbers of children wet their beds.

IV

Oliver Lyttelton, who would, within a few months, become a
leading member of Churchill's Government, had volunteered to
put up ten evacuees in his spacious country house, and received
thirty-one. "I got a shock," he writes. "I had little dreamt that
English children could be so completely ignorant of the simplest
rules of hygiene, and that they would regard the floors and
carpets as suitable places upon which to relieve themselves."[23]

If sophisticated public men were surprised, the average middle-
class householder was stupefied.

> The state of the children was such that the school had to be
> fumigated after the reception.
> Except for a small number the children were filthy, and in
> this district we have never seen so many verminous children
> lacking any knowledge of clean and hygienic habits. Further-
> more, it appeared they were unbathed for months. One
> child was suffering from scabies and the majority had it in
> their hair and the others had dirty septic sores all over
> their bodies.
> Their clothing was in a deplorable condition, some of the
> children being literally sewn into their ragged little
> garments . . .
> Condition of their boots and shoes – there was hardly a child
> with a whole pair and most of the children were walking on
> the ground – no soles, and just uppers hanging together . . .
> Many of the mothers and children were bed-wetters and were
> not in the habit of doing anything else . . .
> The appalling apathy of the mothers was terrible to see.

These remarks were taken, "at random", from reports submitted
to their headquarters by seventeen hundred Women's Institutes
in England and Wales.[24]

A torrent of protests on these lines surged upon newspapers,
billeting authorities and members of parliament. Five days after
the outbreak of war, a meeting of Chamberlain's ministers,
mainly influenced by reports of the condition and behaviour of
mothers and children from Liverpool, decided that the Government could no longer assist the evacuation of mothers with small
children under five, and schoolchildren would be moved only on
a small scale after raids had actually started.[25] The peril of the

city dweller receded from sight as the anguish of the householders in many a safe Conservative rural stronghold loomed hugely. On September 14th, the Government's supporters made bed-wetting and lousy heads their theme; Labour M.P.s intemperately denounced their remarks as slanders on the working class, and sniped at the billetors themselves. The press, with little news, and no great carnage, to report, reaped a heavy harvest of evacuee stories.

What were the facts? The Women's Institutes claimed at this stage that "in practically every batch of children there were some who suffered from head-lice, skin diseases and bed-wetting." A more dispassionate survey which the W.I.s prompted concluded much later that the complaints "related to only a small proportion of the evacuees", but added that they had been "nationwide and concerned some of those from every area evacuated". However, reports from two places in the same area might give utterly different impressions, depending on the commonsense and social understanding of those making them, as well as on the actual condition of the evacuees on arrival.[26]

A confusion of Morality with Manners is common in English middle-class circles. The fact that children from poor homes had never worn pyjamas was taken as a sign of near-criminal negligence on the part of their parents – who often merely could not afford such strictly inessential additions to the wardrobe. Certainly a number of the children, and their habits, would have struck hardened social workers as pretty deplorable. But the social worker would have known about the poverty which had produced them. This was a lesson which the more intelligent and sensitive middle-class billetors, recovering from the shock, began to learn for the first time. H. G. Wells exulted that "Parasites and skin diseases, vicious habits and insanitary practices have been spread, as if in a passion of equalitarian propaganda, from the slums of such centres as Glasgow, London and Liverpool, throughout the length and breadth of the land."[27]

A careful study suggested that about five to ten per cent of the evacuees may have lacked proper toilet training. There was a classic case of a Glasgow mother who expostulated with her six-year-old child – in Scotland, mothers went with the school-children as well as with the infants – "You dirty thing, messing up the lady's carpet. Go and do it in the corner."[28] It throws light on the Glasgow tenements, where one broken-down lavatory might be shared (or ignored) by thirty people, and it was the cleanest families who refused to use the communal closets.

Because evacuation had begun in the school holidays, a routine medical inspection of the children had not been carried out. A very high proportion – up to fifty per cent of those evacuated to some luckless areas – were certainly verminous. The vermin objected to might be fleas, but were usually headlice. Reports of school medical inspections before the war had suggested that about one child in six in London and one in five in Liverpool was lousy, though it was later suggested, with different statistical backing, that this was a very great underestimate. Impetigo and scabies were equally common in the cities; in 1937, Sheffield had treated over a quarter of its school population for skin diseases.[29]

What headlice and scabies pointed to was lack of cleanliness. But in large tracts of the nation's cities, it required an immense effort to keep clean. At this period, nine-tenths of the families in Stepney had no baths; nor had four-tenths of the houses in Hull, half of the people of Glasgow, and one-third of the dwellings of Birmingham.[30]

Billetors were often appalled by the incomprehension with which evacuees confronted knives, forks, hot meals and green vegetables. They learnt to their horror that in the slums mothers would hand their children a slab of bread and margarine for supper, which they would eat standing up, or would send them out for a bag of chips. Such children, it turned out, might never have slept in a bed. Anxious hostesses tiptoeing in to visit their charges on the first night assumed they had fled until they found them sleeping on the floor *under* the bed. ("The country is a funny place," one child remarked. "They never tell you you can't have no more to eat, and under the bed is wasted."[31]) In the worst quarters of the cities, the absence of tap water often made it impossible to cook vegetables; overcrowding meant that children shared beds with their parents and siblings, or did without; bread and margarine was often all that families could afford.

And poverty, of course, was responsible for the appalling clothes in which many children arrived, and for the frequent absence of any change of clothing. The city of Newcastle admitted that of its thirty-one thousand children registered for evacuation, one-eighth were "deficient" in footwear and one-fifth in clothing, and its standards for measuring "deficiency" were likely to be lower than those of the villages which received them. In Manchester, about twenty per cent of the children arrived for rehearsals of evacuation in plimsolls.[32]

The weather in September 1939 was glorious. City children explored the fields, picked berries, climbed trees, and went for long walks with their teachers. Cheap shoes fell to pieces; cheap clothes were torn and worn, and were not worth mending. Foster parents were often bitter at the "neglect" which they attributed to parents who sent children out in such a condition and then refused to pay for new clothes. Some re-equipped their charges according to their own standards, at their own expense. Charitable funds were organized, and the Government secretly distributed thousands of pounds to the education authorities for "necessitous cases".

There were a large number of these. For the families of unemployed men (of whom there were still a million or so), or for those relying on low wages, clothes were a luxury. Many had fallen for the temptations of cheap-skate "clothing clubs" which purveyed such items as shoes with cardboard soles and cheap cotton blankets, or had relied on second-hand garments, often infested, from street markets. Indignant billetors cited stories of parents who said they could not afford clothes, but sent their children generous pocket money; the point was that only one or the other was possible. Later in the war, when full employment and rising earnings had alleviated much of the nation's poverty, the Board of Trade, responsible for rationed clothing, was confronted with an "immense, unsatisfied demand for children's shoes even though production increased".[33]

There was, indeed, a small minority of cases where children had been neglected by their parents, and the latter found evacuation an excellent means of getting rid of unwanted offspring. But the truest measure of the rarity of wanton neglect is found in the miniscule numbers of evacuees who were still unclaimed by their parents, without good reason, when peace returned in 1945.[34] From the point of view of the success of the evacuation scheme, what was worrying was not the occasional case of abandonment, but the extreme rapidity with which, within a few days of the initial evacuation, parents began to snatch their children back from their billets.

V

Cambridge had expected 24,000 evacuees. It received 6,700. By November 11th, 1939, only 3,650 remained. By July 14th, 1940, this had fallen to 1,624. These figures were not exceptional. Evacuation failed. By the beginning of 1940, nearly seven hundred thousand evacuees in England and Wales (four out of every ten

children and approaching nine-tenths of the mothers and
children under five) had gone home. The drift back was even
faster north of the border; by the end of September, three out of
every ten evacuees from Clydeside had returned; by Christmas,
three-quarters.[35]

In spite of all the fuss, there had been many cases of successful
billeting. One rich lady, for instance, rejoiced in her six lads from
the East End who were "making this dreary, lonely war not only
tolerable, but often enjoyable".[36] Committees were set up to
provide clubs and clothing for the children. When Christmas
came along, local officials, teachers and foster parents collaborated in providing parties, outings and presents. (Richmal Crompton, the favourite author of children's stories, imagined her "bad
boy", William, being approached by a deputation of village
children who wanted him to evacuate *them*. One observes bitterly,
"Those 'vacuation kids get everythin' new. An' the way they
swank makes me sick."[37])

The mothers were harder to make happy. They worried about
their husbands' meals or their fidelity. Entertainments were
scarcer than in the towns; maternity and child welfare services
were less well developed. The mothers left for home at twice the
rate of the unaccompanied children. The system of billeting
allowances did not help.

From the beginning, the Government had promised to pay an
allowance to householders who took in evacuees. But it was not
until September 14th that an official pronouncement made it
clear to some of the parents of evacuated children that they would
be expected to contribute towards the allowances. Furthermore,
it was not until October 4th that the Government announced the
terms under which contributions would be made; the delay
undoubtedly encouraged parents to bring their children back.
To cap it all, the scheme for exacting contributions included a
"means test".

The billetor was receiving from the state ten shillings and sixpence for the first child and eight shillings and sixpence per head
if he took in more than one. This was supposed to cover full
board and lodging. It was certainly pretty adequate for a child
billeted with an agricultural labourer, who might bring home no
more than thirty-five shillings a week. But for a middle-class
housewife, accustomed to higher standards, the allowance was
derisory. The flat rate also bore hard on those taking in fast-
growing, husky adolescents with big appetites; this was recognized, in a small way, when the allowance was set, in October, at

ten shillings and sixpence for all children over sixteen, and when this age limit was lowered to fourteen in February. But by this latter date, food prices had risen by fourteen per cent since the outbreak of war.

For mothers and infants, the billetor was expected to provide lodging only, at a cost of five shillings per adult and three shillings per child. So the mother was expected to buy and cook her own food in the billetor's kitchen, or to eat out. The former course produced friction; the latter was not always possible.[38]

The children were having a far better time. Many had never been outside their own city and its dusty streets. There were innumerable comic-pathetic stories about the reactions of city children to nature. Certain evacuees were amazed to discover that apples grew on trees and not in boxes and that cows, which they had seen only in pictures, were bigger than dogs. More tangibly, many evacuees showed startling improvements in health after only a few weeks of fresh air and ample food. A letter in *The Times Educational Supplement* in October claimed that "Some children from a poor area have become almost unrecognizable within a few weeks. One small girl was so chubby that she needed a larger size gas mask."[39]

Evacuees from London billeted in Cambridge were asked to write essays summarizing what they liked about their new environment and what they missed most. The answers were, predictably, very various. A girl of fourteen, who had clearly been lucky in her billet, remarked, "We have very nice food such as venison, pheasant, hare and other luxury which we cannot afford at home." The drift of the children's remarks was portentous for the evacuation scheme. With both boys and girls, parents, relatives and friends who had not been evacuated headed the list of things they missed. One girl of seven wrote poignantly, "I miss dolls Pram and mummy and Daddy and granma and bathing her at night and putting her to bed and put cums down her throat and bits of fish and dressing her in the morning and put her plats in and cloming her hair and nursing her."

The main cause of the trek back to cities was, of course, the fact that no bombs fell. The Cambridge Survey concluded that three subsidiary causes, intimately related to each other, accounted, within the context of this major cause, for the departure of four out of every five children who left the city. Straightforward family solidarity was the chief of these – homesickness among the children, the loneliness and concern of the parents. The second was the dissatisfaction of the parents with the foster home, or the wish to avoid a change of billet. (A significant case was cited where two small children from a poor London home settled down very happily with a professional couple with children of their own. All was well until the first visit of the parents after five weeks. "The two pairs of parents seemed to speak a different language. The London parents felt the Cambridge parents 'too uppish' and removed their youngsters.") The third chief cause of return was financial strain.[40]

Evacuation, in several ways, brought poverty home to the family. One social worker wrote, ". . . I have seen an unemployed father in tears because of a son's letter saying that, while he knew his father could not send the ten shillings demanded by the hostess for clothing, he would rather come home than endure the situation any longer."[41] The Government was far from harsh in its exaction of contributions from parents. The maximum contribution was set at six shillings, but the average amount collected in the early months was only two shillings and three pence. A quarter of parents were asked to pay nothing at all because their earnings were low or they relied on public assistance – from that quarter must have come most of the more "shocking" evacuees.[42]

But contributions were not the whole story, even if the humiliation of the means test was added. There were "extras" involved in evacuation; train fares, clothes which would satisfy the foster parents, postage. Once the retreat from evacuation started, it was sure to become a rout. Parents from the same street or block of flats, travelling down to see their children at the week-ends and travelling back again together, would soon form a common resolution to bring their children back again. Where children had won places at a selective secondary school which had evacuated itself in body and spirit, parents and children submitted longer, as a rule, to evacuation; the child's prospects in this case depended upon his or her extracting the maximum from this educational opportunity. Even so, many of these children also returned.

In February 1940, the Government came up with a new scheme, to evacuate some 670,000 children, without their mothers, after heavy raids had actually started. There would be a complete medical check-up on all children beforehand. Parents would register in advance and guarantee not to bring their children back. Despite a costly publicity campaign, the scheme was a failure from the start. Only one householder in fifty in the reception areas was ready to offer a billet, and many of these were already looking after evacuees. Only one child in five in the evacuation areas had registered by April 20th.[43]

Meanwhile, the nation's education system had reached a consummation of chaos.

VI

The first of September 1939 was to have been the day when the school-leaving age would have been raised from fourteen to fifteen (with an important exception for children given a certificate sanctioning entry into "beneficent employment" which in practice would have restricted the numbers staying on very greatly). This reform, first provided for in an act of 1918, was not now introduced for eight years.

Though the condition and equipment of schools in the cities gave no grounds for complacency, those in the country were very often much inferior. The details of the evacuation plans had been kept secret from education authorities in both the sending and receiving areas. Teachers faced days and weeks of chaos.

The improvisations which were resorted to can be illustrated from the experience of children sent out by the London suburbs of Croydon, which at one stage had over twenty thousand of its scholars scattered in a hundred and ten different towns and villages from Penzance to Newcastle upon Tyne. "For weeks in some cases, teachers and children assembled at some agreed point and walked the country lanes until they could be housed in some suitable hall. And what a variety of buildings was used! A Salvation Army citadel; a Church of England hall; a hall behind a public house; two St. John Ambulance halls and several derelict schools and village halls were taken . . . A family mansion with minstrel gallery above the baronial hall was one of our schools for a time."[44]

During the First World War, shortage of teachers had led to the introduction of "double shifts" – half-time education – in many schools. Teachers made strenuous efforts to avoid such an educational catastrophe this time. They could not always be successful, when buildings were in short supply; the education authority in Blackpool resorted for a time to triple shifts.[45] An evacuated school would commonly take it in turns with its hosts to use existing school buildings and whatever halls, rooms or warehouses could be found near by, so that all children had full-time education.

The experiences of East End schools evacuated to Oxford illustrate the variety of educational results which attended evacuation. One school kept together much as before (with double shifts for a while); another, housed in inadequate premises, almost collapsed. A third flourished magnificently in a country mansion and a fourth did well in a holiday camp, while others more or less merged into village schools.[46] Even those schools which struggled most successfully to preserve their identities were faced with the problems added by the drift back to the cities. A selective "secondary" school, depending on specialist teachers, would face a dilemma when most of its pupils had returned; if teachers went back to look after them, this might deprive those who remained of their chance to learn, say, Latin or biology.

But evacuation, it was often argued at the time, was basically good education, even if it led to bad formal schooling. Town children had their horizons broadened while country children picked up new ideas and new ambitions from their guests. The Board of Education had rubbed its hands enthusiastically over the opportunities which evacuation would offer for fruitful changes in school curricula – local surveys and nature rambles for instance. In some cases, the partial response to evacuation meant that schools arriving in the country had the advantage of far smaller classes than had been the rule before, and the shared experience of evacuation commonly drew teachers and pupils closer together. The good teacher, now very much *in loco parentis*, relished this new intimacy – though as the winter drew in, he found himself escorting small girls home through the dark lanes after school, and racking his brains to find new out-of-hours activities to keep the children away from their much-tried foster parents, yet out of trouble. But smaller classes in some schools must mean larger classes in others, especially as more and more young male teachers were called up.

In the reception areas, most schools were open by mid-September. In the neutral areas, schools were reopening as fast as they could – though the provision of trench shelters to satisfy A.R.P. regulations meant that this was not always very fast. In the cities, over a million children were left to run wild. Children whose education was half complete took jobs. Others turned to hooliganism – so often were public air raid shelters wrecked by children that the authorities were compelled to keep them locked. It was not only teaching which the child lost; he also missed the free milk, and free meals for the very poor, which went with the schools. While the nation buzzed with talk of scabies and headlice, it was not until mid-1941 that medical inspection in schools returned to its peacetime scale and standards.

School buildings had become fair game for any authority wishing to requisition premises for war purposes. Some two thousand state elementary and secondary schools (excluding a number of victims in the reception areas) were wholly or partly taken over, in the great majority of cases by the Civil Defence services. Two-thirds of London's schools were requisitioned; six out of every ten in Manchester.[47] For a while, schemes for Home Tuition were used to plug the gap. Peripatetic teachers, in London and other cities, would visit small groups of children in rooms lent by parents or borrowed from welfare centres and clubs, would give them perhaps one and a half hours' instruction daily, and would leave them with homework.

To reopen the schools would be to admit the failure of evacuation, but even the Chamberlain Government could not hold back for long. On November 1st, it announced that such schools as *could* be reopened in the evacuation areas would be made available "for the education of the children of parents who desire them to attend". But those in the most dangerous areas and those without air raid shelters could *not* be reopened. For months, in many cases, shelter construction was held up by haggling between local authorities and the Government as to who should bear the cost. The Board of Education at first suggested that shelters for schoolchildren need not reach the standard of protection laid down by the "Civil Defence Code". Some authorities protested and were then told that their schools must be closed because their A.R.P. was inadequate.[48]

The young relatives of cabinet ministers continued to enjoy an uninterrupted education at expensive "public" schools. A visitor to Eton College in April 1940 remarked that "the dug-outs were mostly complete a year ago and the principal sign of change is that the boys go into school bare-headed so that they may repair to the said dug-outs without a preliminary fight over their top hats."[49]

Statistics for January 1940 showed that about a quarter of the schoolchildren in the evacuation areas had now resumed full-time education, and nearly as many were getting part-time instruction. But another quarter were receiving only one form or other of Home Tuition, and the final quarter – 430,000 children in all – were still getting no teaching at all.[50]

Meanwhile, there had been many calls for the restoration of compulsory education. In February 1940, the Government at last called on local authorities to prepare to reintroduce it after April 1st. As fast as they could, the authorities complied. To make up for lost time, the London County Council decided to keep its schools open throughout the summer holidays, with staggered leave for teachers, and other authorities followed its example. But before long, the blitz would bring the second long holiday of the war for many children.

ANTI-CLIMAX

Everyone seemed to be feverishly occupied in disencumbering himself of responsibilities . . . Everywhere houses were being closed, furniture stored, children transported, servants dismissed, lawns ploughed, dower houses and shooting lodges crammed to capacity; mothers-in-law and nannies were everywhere gaining control.

They spoke of incidents and crimes in the blackout. So-and-so had lost all her teeth in a taxi. So-and-so had been sandbagged in Hay Hill and robbed of his poker winnings. So-and-so had been knocked down by a Red Cross ambulance and left for dead.

They spoke of various forms of service. Most were in uniform. Everywhere little groups of close friends were arranging to spend the war together. There was a territorial searchlight battery manned entirely by fashionable aesthetes who were called "the monstrous regiment of gentlemen". Stockbrokers and wine salesmen were settling into the offices of London District Headquarters. Regular soldiers were kept at twelve hours' notice for active service. Yachtsmen were in R.N.V.R. uniform growing beards.

Conversation in a London uclb, from Evelyn Waugh's *Men at Arms*[1]

I

During the Munich crisis, over half a million people had enrolled in the A.R.P. services, and others had enlisted as part-time soldiers in the Territorial Army or had joined the R.A.F. Volunteer Reserve. But a lesson which the Chamberlain Government remembered from the First World War was that it was most unwise to let military fervour proceed unchecked. In November 1938, therefore, a Schedule of Reserved Occupations was published. This was followed in January by a handbook sent to every household in the country, which catalogued the various full-time and part-time war jobs. It was designed to check impulsive volunteering by skilled workers and to help others to find the appropriate service. By midsummer, over three hundred thousand had volunteered for the armed forces and there were one and a half million recruits for the Civil Defence services.

At the outbreak of war, the regular army and its reserves numbered about four hundred thousand, and there was a roughly equal number of territorials. The Military Training Act of May 1939, while introducing conscription, applied only to young men aged twenty and twenty-one, who were required to undertake six months' military training, but on the first day of war, parliament passed the National Service (Armed Forces) Act, under which all men between eighteen and forty-one were made liable for conscription.

Thereafter, the actual "call-up" seemed to one sardonic commentator "to progress with the speed of an elephant trying to compete in the Derby'.[2] The registration of all men in each age group in turn began on October 21st with those of twenty to twenty-three. By the following May, registration had extended only as far as men aged twenty-seven, and it did not reach those aged forty until June 1941. When men registered they gave full particulars of their occupations, and stated a preference as between the three fighting services. Those whose occupations appeared on the Schedule were "reserved" from the forces if they exceeded the stated age. (Lighthouse-keepers were reserved at eighteen, physicists at twenty-one, trade union officials at thirty, to cite three examples.) Skilled workers below the age of reservation were called up to serve at their trades, or allied ones, in the armed forces.

From November 1939, employers could ask for the "deferment" of call-up for individual key workers employed in one of the Scheduled occupations, but below reservation age. "Deferment" was soon extended to cover men outside the reserved occupations altogether; by the end of 1940, more than two hundred thousand men had been granted deferment at their employers' request. In addition, there were special schemes for the various professions, under which advisory committees representing expert opinion were set up centrally. A man could himself apply for postponement of his call-up on grounds of severe personal hardship. Over the whole war more than two hundred thousand such applications were accepted, and a sizable proportion of the applicants had their postponement renewed.[3]

Finally, provision was made for conscientious objection to military service – not only on pacifist grounds, which had been accepted in the previous world war, but on political grounds. Twenty-two in every thousand of the first age group called up to register claimed the rights of conscience and went before tribunals, which granted unconditional exemption to a minority who seemed unquestionably sincere, and gave exemption to others on condition that they took up specified work, usually on the land. The tribunals varied greatly in their attitudes from region to region. Up to May 1940, the proportions of "C.O.s" who were exempted unconditionally varied from two per cent in London to twenty-five per cent in south-west Scotland, and the proportions totally rejected ranged from six per cent to forty-one per cent. The percentage stating conscientious objection fell steadily from registration to registration. At the registration on March 9th, 1940, only sixteen in a thousand did so; by the midsummer, fewer than six in a thousand.[4] Clearly, the pacifist attitudes common in the early 'thirties had lost most of their currency.

The youngest registrants were summoned first, single men before married men. A medical examination followed; only those placed in the lowest of the four grades were regarded as unfit for any form of service, though only those in Grades 1 and 2 were in practice taken. Those who so wished could hasten the process by offering themselves and approaching one and a half million volunteers were admitted into the services in the course of the war.

It is perhaps harder, at this distance, to understand why men volunteered than to grasp the motives for conscientious objection. There was little of the jingoism which had disfigured public life in the First World War, and only rarely, this time, did ladies send white feathers to "shirkers". But there was a great deal of moral and social pressure felt by young men out of uniform. Apart from this, some men wanted adventure for its own sake. Others had studied Nazism and wished to help destroy it (some two thousand Britons, it should be remembered, had volunteered to fight Franco in Spain) – but for all the spate of political best-sellers which had preceded the war, these must have made up a small minority. Others calculated that if they got in early, they might find it easier to come by the safe or prestigious types of service they coveted. Others, more prosaically still, sought relief from a boring job, from the boredom of no work at all, or from an unsatisfactory home life. (One candid serviceman no doubt speaks for many others when he admits that he rejoiced that "War service had made separation between husband and wife not only respectable, but positively laudable . . .")[5]

But a truculent spirit soon established itself in service barracks and bases. "I am distressed to hear from many sides," wrote Bishop Hensley Henson in his diary in March 1940, "that the prevailing temper of our troops is a half cynical boredom, as remote as possible from the high crusading fervour which their situation authorizes and requires. They are not pacifists, or disloyal, but "bored stark". Religion makes little appeal, and patriotism no appeal at all. They have neither the enthusiasm of youth, nor the deliberate purpose of age, but just acquiescence in an absurd and unwelcome necessity."[6]

The Bishop was well-informed. The conscripts, and the volunteers, of this new war were healthier, better educated and had higher expectations, on the whole, than their fathers in 1914. Hollywood and the B.B.C. between them had opened up new vistas. And they were determined not to be fooled as their fathers had been. Everyone knew the story; Lloyd George had promised "Homes for Heroes", and when the heroes had come back, there had not even been jobs for them. In 1914, Rupert Brooke had spoken for the first ardent volunteers – "swimmers into cleanness leaping". Herbert Read wrote a very different sort of poem, "To a Conscript of 1940", remembering his own time in the trenches:

> But the old world was restored and we returned
> To the dreary field and workshop, and the immemorial feud
> Of rich and poor. Our victory was our defeat . . .

"To fight without hope is to fight with grace," he added.[7] Not more than a few thousand servicemen can have read his poem, but with remarkable solidarity the services obeyed his instruction "to fight without hope". That way, you could be sure you weren't being fooled. If you died, that was your own affair, not a "heroic sacrifice for freedom". What freedom, pray? The freedom to be unemployed?

The Government did nothing to discourage this attitude by creating a new class of poor from the wives and dependants of servicemen. It paid a private's wife seventeen shillings a week, plus five shillings for the first child, three shillings for the second, two shillings for the third, one shilling for any subsequent child. (The disparity between this scale and the eight shillings and sixpence allowance for evacuated children is worth noting.) Her husband contributed a further seven shillings, leaving himself with roughly one shilling a day.

By December 31st, 1939, over one and a half million men were experiencing military discipline; 1,128,000 in the army, the remainder divided equally between the navy and the R.A.F. In addition, there were 43,000 girls in the Women's Auxiliary Services – "Wrens" (Women's Royal Naval Service), "Ats"

(Auxiliary Territorial Service), "Waafs" (Women's Auxiliary Air Force), and members of various nursing services. At this stage of the war all these girls were volunteers. They tended to come from the better-off sections of society and had put travel or adventure higher on their agendas than the dubious pleasures of marriage in wartime.

Other girls played their part by offering sexual solace to young men in uniform, a custom which inspired a remarkable paragraph from the novelist Henry Green:

> In night-clubs, it has been described, or wherever the young danced, couples passed the last goodbye hours abandoned to each other and, so Richard felt, when these girls were left behind alone as train after train went out loaded with men to fight, the pretty creatures must be hunting for more farewells. As they were driven to create memories to compare, and thus to compensate for the loss each had suffered, he saw them hungrily seeking another man, oh they were sorry for men and they pitied themselves, for yet another man with whom they could spend last hours, to whom they could murmur darling, darling, darling it will be you always; the phrase till death do us part being, for them, the short ride next morning to a railway station; the active death, for them, to be left alone on a platform; the I-have-given-all-before-we-die, their dying breath.[8]

II

But this time, everyone believed, the first "troops" in the front line would be the civilian population of the big cities, where preparations to survive, rather than resist, the attack had been proceeding during the months since Munich. The trenches in the parks were not filled in, and as the crisis tightened in August, more frantic digging was seen. Notices pointing "To the Trenches" made their startling appearance in busy shopping streets. By the outbreak, enough covered trenches were available to shelter half a million people. Besides this nearly one and a half million free "Anderson" shelters, named after Sir John Anderson, who now became Home Secretary and Minister of Home Security, had been distributed to householders with gardens. But the needs of the civilian population were far from fully covered.[9] Meanwhile, responsible citizens fortified rooms in their own homes.

By the end of 1938 the demand for sandbags had been absorbing the entire production of the Scottish jute industry. Millions of yards of sand were now excavated to fill them. They appeared everywhere in the towns, protecting the doorways of important buildings, swaddling the ten by eight feet concrete boxes which were to be used as A.R.P. wardens' posts, and shrouding, symbolically enough, the famous statue of Eros in Piccadilly Circus.

Barrage balloons, more numerous by far now, appeared in a shining galaxy over London, though provincial centres were less well provided; Southampton, one of Britain's chief military ports, had only a single flight of six balloons. Their portly yet strangely serene and beautiful shapes were to stay poised over the cities for longer than anyone, in September 1939, would have dreamt possible. The journalist, J. L. Hodson, describes them, "shining silver in the sun, or turning pink or golden or shades of blue in the varied lights from dawn to evening, their cable singing some kind of tune, maybe, in a high wind, and, just occasionally, the balloon itself, if something has gone wrong, turning over and over like a playful porpoise or, again, lashing about with the fury of a wounded whale". They were wound up and down and controlled by crews from R.A.F. Balloon Command, operating on sites in parks and open spaces. It was harder work than it looked, but later achieved its modest purpose in discouraging dive bombing and low-level attacks. In the first months of war, however, the "blimps" inspired an irrational sense of immunity among civilians. This was encouraged by an early propaganda film *The Lion Has Wings*, which depicted a mass raid by Luftwaffe bombers turning back in fear and confusion at the sight of Britain's terrifying balloon barrage.[10]

More gruesome measures of "passive defence" were in evidence. The tops of Post Office pillar boxes were given a coating of yellowish gas detector paint. Local Gas Identification Squads had been recruited from the ranks of the qualified chemists, and Decontamination Squads had been organized, mostly composed of street cleaners. Adults still had their gas masks, which they were supposed to carry everywhere; children had "Mickey Mouse" masks with red rubber face pieces and bright eye piece rims; and there was now an adequate supply of the macabre gas helmets for babies into which mothers would have to pump air with a bellows. The public had been alerted against the various types of gas which might be expected – lung irritants, tear gases, sneezing gases, blister gases – and there were plenty of false alarms from people who had smelt floor polish, mustard, musty hay, bleaching powder, horseradish, geraniums, peardrops, or any other of the tell-tale odours.

Many of London's taxis were requisitioned, given a coat of grey paint and turned into appliances for the Auxiliary Fire Service. Local authorities ordered large numbers of shrouds and papier-mâché coffins, and took over private cars and tradesmen's vehicles for ambulances. Tents were hired and distributed by the Ministry of Health to provide cover for ten thousand beds for air raid casualties who could not be accommodated inside the emptied hospitals. (By November many of them had blown down, and those still standing were soon removed because their "startling whiteness" caused panic among local inhabitants.) To the manifest sorrow of their keepers, the snakes in London Zoo were put to death.

In Scotland, large stocks of highly inflammable whisky created a headache for the Civil Defence authorities. One local authority after another refused to have them in its area. At length, a shipload worth a million pounds set off for the safety of America. But the vessel carrying it ran ashore in a fog on the island of Barra, where delighted Hebrideans welcomed the wreck as treasure trove and a gift from Providence.[11]

On September 3rd, the B.B.C. at once closed down its regional services and supplied only one "Home Service"; cunning arrangements had been made to ensure that its transmitters could not be used for direction-finding by enemy bombers. For some days it provided the types of programmes which would have suited "blitz" conditions: News broadcasts every hour on the hour from seven a.m. to midnight, a stream of official instructions and advice, gramophone recitals, pre-recorded programmes, and a very few "live" shows – notably the indefatigable Sandy Macpherson's herculanean efforts on the theatre organ in an otherwise deserted London studio. For a few days all sports arenas, cinemas and theatres were closed, for fear of mass slaughter in crowded places.

The good citizen, already preoccupied with gas-proofing one of his rooms with cellulose sheets and tape, or erecting an Anderson in his garden, had to rush to the shops to buy blinds, curtains, blackout paint, cardboard, drawing pins, brown paper or whatever could be used to seal his windows at night. (And, if he was prudent, he had strips of sticky tape over the glass, to minimize the shattering effects of blast.) All these commodities rapidly became dear or unobtainable.

The cities, without neon signs or cinema posters, were utterly transformed after dark – some thought for the better. Even country people, already used to the problems of making their way home without much light, found the nocturnal landscape subtly altered. On the first evening of war, one countryman walked up to the moorland ridge above his house on the Yorkshire coast, commanding a wide panorama. "At night, in clear weather", he wrote, "while the hills and coastline would have been blurred, I could have picked out every individual farm and village in that landscape and, especially in the holiday season, the lights of Whitby and Scarborough would have made a big yellow glow in the sky. Now, although the weather was fine, there was not a pinprick of light anywhere, not even upon the sea."[12]

III

The word "phoney", as applied to the period of the war which ended in April 1940, was an American usage later adopted by the British. At the time, it was the "Bore War", the "funny war" or, in Chamberlain's phrases, used by him in November, "this strange war", "this strangest of wars".

The entire British Commonwealth, with the exception of Eire (which had taken the opportunity of Edward VIII's abdication virtually to break off its relationship with the Crown), was committed in Britain's support by September 6th. King George VI, the modest and devoted younger brother who had succeeded King Edward in 1936, made a broadcast to the Empire at six p.m. on the first evening of war. For sensitive listeners such occasions were something of a trial; the King had a painful speech defect which he had struggled bravely to overcome and was no orator. But no one doubted his sincerity as he concluded:

> There may be dark days ahead, and war can no longer be confined to the battlefield. But we can only do the right as we see the right, and reverently commit our cause to God. If one and all we keep resolutely faithful to it, ready for whatever service or sacrifice it may demand, then, with God's help, we shall prevail.
> May He bless and keep us all.[13]

Britain had assisted the dismemberment of democratic Czechoslovakia, and had then rashly committed herself to the aid of near-Fascist Poland. It was in this cause, to begin with, that the King asked for God's help. Not much else, certainly, could be of assistance to the Poles, at the mercy of powerful neighbours to the east and west,[7] and almost cut off from their tardy allies, Britain and France. Within two days, the Polish Air Force was virtually annihilated; within two weeks the Polish Army had ceased to exist as an organized force. On September 17th, Russian armies crossed Poland's eastern frontier. By the end of the month, Poland had been utterly vanquished and was partitioned between her two enemies.

But even at this stage only the most literal-minded Englishman could have believed that he had gone to war *for* Poland. The nation, at last, was fighting *against* Hitler. There was, by now, some purpose in this for almost everyone. Jews, of course, had a special stake in the struggle; but anti-Semitic right-wing patriots hated Hitler as a reincarnation of Kaiser Wilhelm, if nothing worse, and fought to defend the British Empire from the Huns. Catholics, after the Nazi-Soviet pact, could deceive themselves for a while that they were fighting Russia, and most Christians identified Nazism with paganism. Conservatives fought to conserve Britain's power; Liberals on behalf of liberty; Socialists to preserve the modest gains of trade unionism.

Opposition to the war came from a handful of pacifists; from the dwindled Mosley Fascists; from the small but influential Communist Party; from the tiny, dying Independent Labour Party; from the utterly obscure Trotskyists; and from certain Nationalist quarters in Wales and Scotland. Besides these there were Conservatives in high places who still hankered for an agreement with Hitler. There was also the great leader of the Great War, David Lloyd George, who had pointed to the folly of supporting Poland without an alliance with Russia, and was plausibly accused of defeatism.

The Labour leaders at once made their support for the war clear, and soon reached an agreement with the Government and the Liberal Party whereby candidates for vacancies in the House of Commons should be nominated by the party in possession without opposition from the other two. This was, it should be noted, an "electoral" and not a "political" truce, and it was still open to candidates from the fringe parties, or from no party at all, to contest by-elections. However, the electoral register was "frozen"; no new voters were admitted as they reached the age of twenty-one, and those who moved from one constituency to another (an enormous proportion of the population) had no chance of voting in their new home towns. Un-opposed returns became common. So elections grew increasingly unrepresentative as the war went on. Meanwhile, elections for local government were suspended entirely, and the party caucuses in the town halls nominated new councillors as the old ones died or retired. The results of this immunity from democratic influences were not always happy.

Proud memories of resistance to war twenty-five years before still affected sizable sections of the Labour Party. Only six Labour M.P.s declared their opposition to the war at the outset, but in many local Labour parties, and within individuals, a struggle went on for some time between hatred of war and detestation of Hitler. As the Bore War proceeded, more Labour M.P.s swung over to temporary support for peace negotiations, and in November, twenty-two signed a manifesto calling for a world conference of powers and an armistice as soon as a date could be fixed. (The significant portions of this document did not appear in the newspapers, at the request of the new Ministry of Information.) Over seventy constituency Labour parties supported the call for a truce. But a commentator early in the New Year suggested that "To judge from speeches at small conferences and in the branch rooms, this dilemma of conscience is being resolved in the great majority of cases in favour of a reluctant support for the war; often on the significant ground that Labour would otherwise abdicate its chance to lead the country."[14]

Meanwhile, the quasi-revolutionary left of the party, led by Stafford Cripps and Aneurin Bevan, was engaged in sorting out a different sort of dilemma. For many months (years in some cases), its supporters had worked very closely with the Communist Party. The C.P.G.B. admitted to only eighteen thousand members in July 1939 (its pre-war peak); but its intellectual influence was great, its support in the trade unions included some key leaders, and it influenced, by open and covert means, the policies of many local Labour parties.

The Nazi-Soviet Pact struck a dire blow at this influence. But Harry Pollitt, the C.P.'s figurehead, was the most bellicose anti-Nazi in the country. On September 2nd, the C.P. produced a manifesto in enthusiastic support of the war. Pollitt wrote, in a passionate pamphlet, "To stand aside from this conflict, to contribute only revolutionary-sounding phrases while the Fascist beasts ride roughshod over Europe, would be a betrayal of everything our forbears have fought to achieve in the course of long years of struggle against capitalism." But, within a month of the outbreak, the C.P. Central Committee was handed new tablets from Sinai, or rather Moscow. It announced that it had been guilty of an error; this was an imperialist war, like the last one. It was the duty of Marxists to copy Lenin's tactics and to fight the British ruling class. The defeat of that class by Hitler would give the C.P. its chance to seize power, though naturally, this idea was not made explicit in the party's public pronouncements; it contented itself with whipping up feeling against Chamberlain and the bosses and making cynical comment on the progress of the war. Pollitt publicly recanted, and was banished to the lower echelons of the party for a period of penance.[15]

Cripps and Bevan, in the pages of their journal, *Tribune*, had greeted the war by calling, like Pollitt, for a struggle on two fronts: against Hitler and against Britain's capitalist Government. They adhered to this line, and a period of confusion ensued in which comrade attacked comrade. There was a considerable falling off in Communist support in the course of the next few months, and the party lost its credit with many Socialists and Liberals who had admired its devoted opposition to Fascism. It also lost the services of its leading missionary to the intellectuals, John Strachey, and its influence over the Left Book Club. But the party remained a potentially dangerous force in industry.

The I.L.P. was, however, no trouble to anyone. Its policy theoretically resembled the Communists' (except in its great distaste for Joseph Stalin), and its more ardent spirits hinted darkly at Leninist revolution. But its leader, Maxton, was the gentlest soul alive, at least in the estimate of his innumerable friends inside and outside the House of Commons. In practice, the I.L.P.'s position was pacifist rather than revolutionary, and it had in any case no great resources with which to create disruption. Its three M.P.s were all Scots from Glasgow, the only centre where it retained much significance.

IV

Britain and France did not expect to be able to deploy their full military strength until a couple of years after the outbreak of war. Allied strategy had been concocted on the assumption that Italy would go to war if Germany did. The allies had decided to attack Italy and destroy her flimsy pretensions as soon as possible, and meanwhile to stand on the defensive along the frontier between France and Germany.

But Italy did not declare war. The allies were left with the defensive part of their strategy. The French marched sixteen miles forward into the Saar. Then they marched sixteen miles back. In October, four divisions of the British Expeditionary Force took up their stations on the Franco-Belgian frontier. By March, six more had arrived. Occasional patrols and shots provided the only news from the West Front. Before long, the newspaper sellers were sardonically calling out "Germans in Berlin . . . Evening Paper . . . Scotsmen in Aberdeen."

The war at sea did provide news, mostly grim. Before September 3rd was over a passenger liner outward bound from Britain, the *Athenia*, was torpedoed by a U-boat and sank, with much loss of life. For Britain's merchant navy there was no "phoney war". In that first winter, the menace of the German magnetic mine was confronted and mastered; but this, with the U-boats, took a steady toll of seamen's lives. In December Nazi planes began to bomb and strafe fishermen going about their business in the North Sea.

The Royal Navy, still endowed by the man in the street with a mysterious aura of infallibility, provided the best news of the first months, and its spicy acts of aggression – the rounding up of the German battleship *Graf Spee* just before Christmas, the dramatic rescue of British prisoners from the *Altmark* in February – garnered valuable credit for the First Lord of the Admiralty, Winston Churchill.

On October 14th, the deficiencies of his predecessors were helpfully emphasized when a U-boat sneaked into the great naval base at Scapa Flow, in the Orkneys, and sank the battleship *Royal Oak* as it lay at anchor. Two days later, the Luftwaffe bombed cruisers in the Firth of Forth. For the first time a real air raid (as opposed to rumoured holocausts) had occurred. Shrapnel fell on Edinburgh and Dunfermline, and the Scots were outraged by the fact that no air raid warning had been given. Twenty-five sailors had been killed, but no civilians. For a moment, it appeared that the war had actually started. Instead, there were more false alarms, caused by mechanical defects in the air raid warning system, nervous tension among those in charge of it, or bogus alarms given over the telephone. During November some part of Britain was under alert almost daily, and the public grew less and less prone to retire humbly to its shelters when this happened.[16]

Meanwhile, the R.A.F. had conducted some raids on the enemy. They had dropped, not bombs, but propaganda leaflets.

The Government, basing its hopes on exaggerated versions of the effect of blockade on Germany in the First World War, intended to starve Germany into submission by "economic warfare". To certain articulate spirits, their lack of better ideas for conducting war than a gentlemanly and ineffectual blockade, suggested that Chamberlain, Hoare, Simon and Halifax – the inner ring of appeasers who dominated the War Cabinet – simply did not want to fight Hitler. When Leo Amery suggested to the Secretary for Air, Sir Kingsley Wood, that he should set fire to the Black Forest, the jovial little man was most upset. "Are you aware it is private property? Why, you will be asking me to bomb Essen next."[17]

Yet it is hard to blame Chamberlain for his reluctance to sanction raids on civilian centres which would provoke reprisals against Britain by the much stronger German air force. Even his optimism, which now seems so feckless, was shared by other leaders of both major parties. He wrote to his sister on November 5th, "... I have a 'hunch' that the war will be over before the spring. It won't be by defeat in the field but by German realization that they *can't* win and it isn't worth their while to go on getting thinner and poorer when they might have instant relief and perhaps not have to give up anything they really care about."[18] The public seemed to share this optimism. A Mass Observation survey about the same time indicated that only one person in five expected the war to last three years or more, and an equal number gave it no more than six months to go (two in five didn't know, didn't care or gave facetious answers). Approval for Chamberlain's premiership in the opinion polls, which had been running at an average of sixty per cent before the war, had increased now to an average of nearly seventy per cent. This was "public" opinion; but private opinion was disillusioned, and Mass Observation noted that there was steadily less and less applause for the Prime Minister from cinema audiences when he appeared on the newsreels.[19]

The fact was that the gulf between the leaders, in their ministries and London clubs, and the led, in their back streets and pubs and factories, which it had been possible to tolerate in peacetime, was dangerous in wartime. Immediately after the outbreak two official posters, in vivid red with white lettering, appeared on hoardings, shop fronts and railway platforms all over Britain. One read FREEDOM IS IN PERIL / DEFEND IT WITH ALL YOUR MIGHT, and attracted much unfavourable comment because it seemed hypocritical.

The other proclaimed:

> YOUR COURAGE
> YOUR CHEERFULNESS
> YOUR RESOLUTION
> WILL BRING
> US VICTORY.

Most working-class people thought that "resolution" meant something you made at the New Year. But beyond that, who, people asked, was this mysterious US to whom "your" efforts would bring triumph? Fat men in the city of London, humourless bureaucrats in Whitehall, the bosses, the generals, the party caucus sprang variously to mind. (Mosley's Fascists, succinctly enough, changed US to JEW.)[20]

Kingsley Martin, the editor of the *New Statesman*, spoke for many outside his own especially troubled section of opinion on the left when he wrote, early in 1940, ". . . The most important single fact in the psychology of the public during recent years has been the co-existence of several 'opinions' at the same time in almost everyone; we have all been conscious of having within us a tendency to isolationism and pacifism, as well as to bellicosity, righteous indignation and the urge to set the world right." He added, "In the past it has been true that once war has started, such emotional conflicts are promptly settled." But this time, he pointed out, the absence of focus on war-like action had frustrated this "hardening process".[21]

The spate of patriotic songs that flooded the hit parade in the first months of the war was one sign that people craved the certainty of purpose which only action could bring. By mid-November, "There'll Always Be An England", a vapid yet enduring song by one Ross Parker, was top of the sheet-music selling list. It was succeeded by another notorious ditty:

> We're gonna hang out the washing on the Siegfried Line.
> Have you any dirty washing, Mother dear?
> We're gonna hang out the washing on the Siegfried Line,
> 'Cos the washing day is here.

The Siegfried Line was the system of fortifications along Germany's border with France. When that was smashed the war would soon be over, and every night singers, paid and unpaid, wishfully smashed it.[22]

One minister only could convince the public, for a moment, that it was really at war. Chamberlain sent the House of Commons to sleep with his summaries of what was happening, but Winston Churchill aroused it with oratory. This contrast was felt over the wireless, too; his broadcast early in October caused real excitement. On January 27th, 1940, he confirmed his reputation with the first of those major speeches by which he was to import so many new phrases into common currency. To an audience in Manchester he called:

> Come then: let us to the task, to the battle, to the toil – each to our part, each to our station. Fill the armies, rule the air, pour out the munitions, strangle the U-boats, sweep the mines, plough the land, build the ships, guard the streets, succour the wounded, uplift the downcast, and honour the brave . . . There is not a week, nor a day, nor an hour to lose.[23]

In that case, a cynic might have asked, why had his colleagues contrived to lose so many hours already? And why were there still over a million unemployed?

V

So the first impact of war was felt, not like a hammer blow at the head, to be warded off, but as a mass of itches, to be scratched and pondered. Most of the discomforts and frustrations of the period were very minor foretastes of the years of regulations and austerity which followed. The blackout, however, was an exception. Its impact was comprehensive and immediate. One of the most impassive official historians of the British effort observes, without exaggeration, that it "transformed conditions of life more thoroughly than any other single feature of the war".[24]

In the first place, most people had to spend five minutes or more every evening blacking out their homes. If they left a chink visible from the streets, an impertinent air raid warden or policeman would be knocking at their door, or ringing the bell with its new touch of luminous paint. There was an understandable tendency to neglect skylights and back windows. Having struggled with drawing pins and thick paper, or with heavy black curtains, citizens might contemplate going out after supper – and then reject the idea and settle down for a long read and an early night. "There's no place like home, But we see too much of it now" ran a popular song of the period.[25]

For to make one's way from back street or suburb to the city centre was a prospect fraught with depression and even danger. In September 1939 the total of people killed in road accidents increased by nearly one hundred per cent. This excludes others who walked into canals, fell down steps, plunged through glass roofs and toppled from railway platforms. A Gallup Poll published in January showed that by that stage about one person in five could claim to have sustained some injury as a result of the blackout – not serious, in most cases, but it was painful enough to walk into trees in the dark, fall over a kerb, crash into a pile of sandbags, or merely cannonade off a fat pedestrian.[26]

The casualty figures were worst in September, before petrol rationing began to restrict the number of private cars on the road. Their gravity compelled some relaxation. From mid-October, members of the public, hitherto in peril of prosecution if they struck a match in the street, were allowed to use hand torches, if these were dimmed with a double thickness of white tissue paper and were switched off during alerts. Civilian drivers were permitted masked headlights, like the fighting services. (Early next year a new A.R.P. headlight mask was made compulsory for drivers; the light came through a narrow horizontal slit.) In November, it was agreed that the blackout should begin half an hour after sunset and end half an hour before sunrise. There was further relief before Christmas. Churches, markets and street stalls could be partially illuminated. A small measure of light was allowed in shop windows. Restaurants and cinemas could use illuminated signs, though all lights must still be doused when the sirens sounded. Soon afterwards "glimmer lighting" or "star-lighting" was introduced – a tiny pinprick of illumination might be directed downwards from street lights in city centres and at road junctions, though not all towns were willing to bear the cost or take the risk. In February 1940, "summer time" was brought in early and retained all year round (until 1941, when it was replaced for the summer months with "double summer time"). This gave the citizen extra daylight in the evening, but made the journey to work in the morning still more unattractive.[27]

Vera Brittain describes the trains as they now became – "slow, crowded and devoid of restaurants. Before nightfall the blinds are drawn down, and the railway carriage, if lighted at all, is illumined by a blue pin-point of light not strong enough to enable me to distinguish the features in the pale ovals which are my neighbours' faces."[28] In the buses, where a similar dimness prevailed, conductors could barely distinguish silver coins from copper.

Meanwhile, there had been a wave of absurdly high fines imposed for petty breaches of the regulations. There was said, without much foundation, to have been an increase in robbery after dark, and many women now went outside at night only if they had to. After a while, this fuss subsided and one no longer saw half a dozen people straggling in a formless crocodile behind a person lucky enough to have snapped up a torch while the shops still had them; the blackout was taken, grudgingly, for granted.

Social life survived, and revived somewhat. By December, the dance halls were packed again. Cinemas and theatres outside the cities had been allowed to reopen before a week was out, and from September 14th the rest were permitted to follow suit if they shut at ten p.m., though those in the West End of London were closed at six for a time. League football was soon resumed, though on a much reduced basis, with only small crowds permitted. In November there was welcome news for the hardened addicts among the millions who, before the war, had filled in football pools. The leading promoters patriotically merged themselves, as "Unity Pools", for the duration, and to spare the Post Office printed their coupons in the newspapers. Soon sizable wins – eleven thousand pounds for a penny in one case – were being recorded again, and were evoking indignation among moralists.[29]

Nor was motoring for pleasure destroyed by the introduction of petrol rationing three weeks after the war started, though it was claimed that the month's basic civilian ration could easily be exhausted in a day. The gas companies attempted to exploit the shortage by popularizing gas propulsion as an alternative, and by May 1940 London had a network of supply points. But the idea did not catch on markedly. Meanwhile, the motorists' spokesmen were still showing plenty of fight; when a speed limit of twenty m.p.h. in built-up areas was imposed, to begin in February, they denounced the "Nazi methods" of the authorities and declared they would encourage careless pedestrianism.[30]

For those who still preferred to stay safely at home, the Home Service had rapidly resumed something like a normal balance of radio programmes, and from early in the New Year, listeners were able to tune in to the new Forces Programme, based on light entertainment.

The first new radio personality of the war was not one of the inspirational, patriotic speakers now commonly heard on the B.B.C., but an American-Irish-Briton named William Joyce, a former lieutenant of Oswald Mosley, now nicknamed "Lord Haw Haw". The nickname was first used by a columnist in the *Daily Express* on September 18th. It was based, not on Joyce's nasal tones, but on the "haw hawing" upper-class voice of Norman Baillie Stewart, a former subaltern in the Seaforth Highlanders. It stuck to Joyce, who gradually usurped Stewart's position as the Nazis' chief English language broadcaster. The Haw Haw broadcasts aimed to undermine British confidence in the news supplied by the censored press, as well as making direct propaganda against Winston Churchill (already identified in that quarter as the chief enemy), the Jews and the plutocracy. The scripts, produced by Germans with the idea that phrases like "honest Injun" were current English colloquialisms, were at times ludicrously inept. But Joyce himself was a talented propagandist, and succeeded, as we shall see, rather more than was admitted. Curiosity, and the absence of absorbing war news, gained him an enormous audience. A survey in the first autumn of war suggested that six million adults – a sixth of the listening public – tuned in regularly to Haw Haw, and another eighteen million listened occasionally. At the end of January over a quarter of a representative sample said they had heard the news in English from Germany (Joyce's programme) on the previous day. But a month later, this proportion had dropped to one-sixth and the decline continued. In February, the Germans launched a "black" radio station, purporting to be run by British patriots under cover somewhere in England, but the "New British Broadcasting Station" never achieved Haw Haw's notoriety.[31]

However, the B.B.C. with its comedy series, ITMA (short for "It's That Man Again"), had a most successful novelty of its own. Tommy Handley and his talented team of mimics gave the first wartime broadcast of ITMA on September 19th, and its characters, notably the ineffectual German spy, Funf, were soon universally known. An excerpt from the first broadcast will help to explain its popularity. We meet Mr. Handley, nicely set up as the "Minister of Aggravation", a neat compound of Agriculture and Information, in the "Office of Twerps". He addresses his secretary:

> TOMMY. . . . Take a memo: "To all concerned in the Office of Twerps: Take notice that from today, September the twenty-tooth, I, the Minister of Aggravation, have power to confiscate, complicate and commandeer . . ."
> VERA. How do you spell commandeer, Mr. Hanwell?

TOMMY. Commandeer – let me see. (*Sings*) Comm-om-and-
ear, comm-on-and-eer, Tommy Handley's wag-time band,
comm-on-and-eer, etc.
Er, where were we? "I have the power to seize anything
on sight."
VERA. Oh, Mr. Handpump – and me sitting so close to you.[32]

The ministers and their assistant twerps had begun, in a
gingerly fashion, to throw their weight about. Before the outbreak
of war the Government had distributed four Public Information
leaflets to every householder in Britain; two more followed
shortly afterwards. They covered an exorbitant number of
subjects – blackout, evacuation, food, pensions, telephones, and
so on – and were aimed to show the responsible citizen how he
should behave in an emergency. Mass Observation, however,
found that not more than one-third of the public proved to have
read them with any great care.[33]

Under the Emergency Powers Act, the Government could do
virtually what it liked with the freedom and property of any
citizen simply by issuing the appropriate regulation. Censorship
was imposed on overseas mail, and telephone trunk lines, though
the public did not know this, were tapped. By October, a National
Register of all citizens had been completed. Everyone received a
buff-coloured identity card with a personal number of six or
seven digits.

The press, frustrated by lack of news, filled their pages in the
first autumn of war by attacking the uses which the bureaucracy
made of its new powers. The new Ministry of Information (which
told the papers what they might not say) was a prime target for
criticism, along with the Office of Works. There was a pretty
general feeling that the Government had grossly over-prepared
against air attack. By October, polls suggested that about half
of the working-class population believed that there would be no
raids at all. Only a very small percentage expected raids of any
severity.[34]

Failure to carry gas masks was never a punishable offence
though in many cases factory and office workers were compelled
to bring them to work by the management, and sudden mock
attacks were staged in crowded streets from time to time. Even
in the first week of war, no more than three-quarters of Londoners
seen in the streets were carrying gas masks. By November it was a
minority habit, weaker among men than among women, some of
whom had replaced the official containers with nattier ones sold

by the department stores. By the following spring almost no one bothered.[35] Meanwhile, the Government had instituted a monthly inspection of masks by the air raid wardens; the citizen would be charged for the replacement or repair of a mask which he had allowed to deteriorate, or had mislaid. (The lost property offices of the railways were stacked high with unclaimed containers.) This innovation was one more blow at the popularity of the wardens, by now, significantly, sometimes misnamed "blackout wardens".

On August 23rd, the London Region Headquarters for Civil Defence had begun a twenty-four-hour vigil. On September 1st, the staff for the local control rooms had been called to their posts. All over the country, all the time, from now until almost the end of the war, the machinery of civil defence would remain permanently alert. Even in the countryside, which the Government had to some extent left out of its preparations, many villages had bought their own sirens by public subscription, and wardens had been appointed. Cecil Beaton, the society photographer, volunteered to serve as a control room telephonist in the small town of Wilton, in Wiltshire.

> Our squad [he wrote in his diary] is on duty from eleven at night until eight a.m. . . . We have been only rather vaguely briefed in our duties; at the sign of an alarm I am bound to get hopelessly entangled with all the various wires and plugs at the switchboard. Mr. Lush, the town clerk, is here in case we need help, and Mr. Keating, a retired civil servant, is our rather quavering lead.

There were a couple of gentleman farmers, a lady with her debutante daughter, and Lady Pembroke and her Jeevesian butler.

> Grouped together in this room, reinforced against blast with stanchions of rough wood and sandbags and curtained with the heaviest felt, we gradually settle down to read, the women to sew; each has a turn to lie on a truckle bed for an hour's sleep . . . We are resigned to be together for the duration of the war; a pretty grim prospect.[36]

The control-room staffs (full-timers and volunteers) had the advantage that their activities were hidden from the general public. The wardens, by contrast, were exposed to abuse and ridicule. To working-class men, the wardens often appeared to be no more than lackeys of the police, a traditional enemy. A

proportion of bossy and bad-tempered wardens gave the whole
service a bad name. With other civil defenders they trained on
duty and staged mock "incidents" in the streets. The spectacle of
grown men play-acting in public still further diminished confidence in A.R.P.; citizens were enlisted as air raid victims and
painted for the part. (One sardonic "casualty" in such an exercise
retired, leaving a note, "Ave bled to death and gorn ome.")

The Civil Defence services had reached their full complement
of one and a half million men and women at the outbreak of war.
Only four hundred thousand of these were paid full-timers; the
rest were part-time volunteers, many of whom dropped away as
boredom waxed and prestige waned. The press was soon suggesting that the full-timers were overpaid army-dodgers. No more
than eight days after the start of the war, the Government began
to back-pedal furiously, with heavy cuts in personnel. By
December, over half the full-timers had been fired or had quit
in disgust.[87]

The men of the Auxiliary Fire Service suffered worse still, since
they were attacked on their other flank by the regular peacetime
firemen. There were only about six thousand of the latter, compared with about ten times as many A.F.S. full-timers, and
hundreds of thousands of part-timers. The peacetime fire service
was underpaid – in London its wage rates were not far above the
basic C.D. pay given to the auxiliaries, and outside London some
regulars had their wages increased to bring them up to the C.D.
level. Now, along came throngs of "amateurs" who had agreed
to serve for these low wages, and to work for an unspecified
number of hours without sick leave, without holidays and, in
many cases, without even a uniform.

When the auxiliaries poured into the fire stations on 1st
September, many came straight from their work in offices and
factories, some in grimy dungarees, some in pin-striped suits
and bowler hats. Whatever accents they had they endured acute
discomfort together in their improvised stations, a motley assortment of private houses, schools, disused lecture halls and newly
built huts. "Conditions in some stations were indescribable,"
relates the historian of the Fire Brigades Union (which discovered,
when it formed a separate section for them, that eight out of ten
auxiliaries who joined had not been members of a trade union
before). "At Bradford firemen were in a basement where police
had previously 'put to sleep' stray dogs."[88]

As the months went by, the chief job the A.F.S. had in many
areas was pumping out flooded Anderson shelters.

... So bad did the feeling become in some places [one volunteer recalls] that Auxiliaries never wore their uniform (if they possessed one) in public, if they could avoid it. Not being thin-skinned the candid remarks so often heard about three-pounds-a-week men doing b — all for their money didn't worry me at all, but quite a number of competent firemen gladly got themselves into one of the services, usually the Air Force, in order to get away from the cutting remarks of ignorant members of the public.[39]

Meanwhile, there was patronage and scorn from the regulars – who, in some stations, refused to allow the A.F.S. to use their shower-baths, even when they returned from practice at an authentic fire.

VI

Britain had, of course, been involved in a "total" war within the adult memory of anyone over forty. Elaborate plans had remained in the files of Whitehall, and had been adapted and improved in the 'twenties and 'thirties. The Government knew that if the war was to be a long one – which they preferred to doubt – they must as soon as possible take firm control over the activities of the people both as consumers and as producers. They must direct the economy so that it moved, straight and fast, towards the maximum production of weapons consistent with adequate manpower for the armed forces and with the maintenance of civilized life and a contented populace. They knew this very well, but they havered. They were frightened of interfering with private firms. They were terrified of provoking the trade unions. They were scared of the middle-class reaction to rationing and other "belt-tightening" measures which would help to divert workers, factories, raw materials and shipping space from peacetime amenities to warlike manufactures. The U-boats, the magnetic mines and the introduction of a convoy system slowed down merchant shipping, but the Government confronted the problem of maintaining imports in "a mood of muddled cheerfulness".

Yet broad plans were laid down at once for a three-year-war – the Commonwealth was to raise an army of fifty-five divisions; the rate of ship-building was to be almost doubled; two million more acres were to come under the plough. And new ministries, as we have seen, sprang into existence from the brow of Whitehall armed *cap-à-pie* with immense powers. "The war machine,"

A. J. P. Taylor remarks, "resembled an expensive motor car, beautifully polished, complete in every detail, except that there was no petrol in the tank."[40]

In these early months, the Government became the sole importer of many crucial raw materials, ranging from wool to molasses, from tin to hemp. By May 1940 approaching nine-tenths of the main imported raw materials were state monopolies. Allocations were controlled by bodies set up under the Ministry of Supply and the Ministry of Food. In most cases these "Controls" were run by the trade associations which represented the appropriate sections of private industry, or by individuals selected by the industries' leaders. Thus, a director of the British Aluminium Company was in charge of allocating supplies of aluminium; the chairman of the British Iron and Steel Federation was controller of iron and steel. As one of the many critics of this type of arrangement put it, "The trade associations which had nominated the Controllers were now in the position of being controlled by the Controllers. The happy relation established was plain for all to see."[41] In the summer of 1940, a High Court judge was called in by the Government to report on the impartiality of the Controls, and he found little wrong with the system. But rumblings of criticism persisted throughout the war; as late as 1944 the workings of the Chemicals Control were sharply attacked by the Select Committee on National Expenditure (an all-party committee of M.P.s set up as a watchdog in 1939), which pointed out euphemistically that "on the whole" the Control's operations had "tended to strengthen rather than diminish the preponderance of the strongest interests in the chemical industry". (That is, I.C.I. was now in a more commanding position than ever.) It was very hard to believe that the staff of the Cement and Concrete Association who largely composed the Cement Control, or the staff of the Non-Ferrous Metals Control who were actually paid by the British Metal Corporation, were capable of acting without concern for the long-term private interests of the firms involved.[42]

Allocations to civilian industry were far too generous, and material allocated for exports or "war production" leaked into the shops at home. Failure of the same kind was seen in the control of foreign exchange and of imports. The list of inessential goods which might be imported only under licence was far from comprehensive, and licences were not hard to come by.[43]

So the belts of the well-to-do did not tighten very much. In the spring of 1940 there were still twenty different makes of car, some of them new models, on the home market. Luxury gas mask containers were sold, luxury foods were copiously consumed (indeed, the enjoyment of French delicacies was excused as a mode of supporting the gallant ally across the Channel). The bookings for Christmas banquets in London were almost normal.[44]

The first budget of the war, introduced by the Chancellor, Sir John Simon, near the end of September, was a timid affair. The standard rate of income tax was increased from five shillings and sixpence to seven shillings. The price of a pint of beer was pushed up a penny by extra duty. Tobacco and sugar were taxed more heavily. Such tinkering as this was not likely to sustain a mighty war effort. With a single stroke, the Government succeeded in annoying both private industry and its Socialist critics; an Excess Profits Tax was introduced at sixty per cent. This meant that only part of increased profits brought about by wartime disruption and shortages would be siphoned off by the Government.

The Government was painfully aware that war would inevitably produce inflation and that very stern measures were required to repress it. Import prices would mount steeply and the Government itself was bound to pour out money into private hands if it wanted to mobilize the economy. J. M. Keynes argued powerfully in *The Times* that the only answer was drastic taxation of working-class incomes, with a refund after the war which would amount to "forced saving".[45] But this politically fearsome course was rejected.

Meanwhile, prices rose with appalling speed. The Government did peg the rents of virtually all unfurnished accommodation soon after the outbreak of war. But the official Cost of Living Index, which was an antiquated device based on the pattern of spending of a typical working-class family in 1914, and which certainly underestimated the real increase, showed that food prices had risen by one-seventh by February 1940, and prices of clothing by a quarter. Mass Observation found a housewife noting that "A kettle half the size of one I used to buy in Woolworths for 6d. now costs 10d., candles which used to cost 10d. a packet now cost between 1s. 6d. and 1s. 8d.[46] Rising prices bore especially hard on the wives and dependants of servicemen. They also threatened to provoke demands for wage increases from the unions.

In November, attempting to sweeten the unions, the Government introduced, as a temporary expedient, a device which became a permanent and valuable feature of the war economy. The Ministry of Food reported that a rise was necessary in the prices of the staple foodstuffs which it now controlled. This instantly would have thrust up the cost of living to the point where all-round wage claims would have been inevitable. To prevent this the Government agreed to bear the loss of sixty million pounds a year which would result if prices of staple foods were held steady.

In January, an ineffectual Order was issued which sought to peg profits on a range of cheap consumer goods at their level of August 1939. Almost all it did was to encourage manufacturers to produce the higher price items, which were exempt.[47]

Ration books had been ready since 1938. The public knew very well that rationing had been necessary in the last war and was quite prepared to have it again this time. Bacon, butter and sugar were already in short supply, because of the pressure on shipping space. People minded doing without their usual quantities less than they minded the unfairness which came with the shortages. Rich women descended on shops in working-class districts and bought up sugar by the carload if they could. The shops themselves were forced to ration customers unofficially, and there was always the feeling that wealthier customers were favoured.

But the Government dillied and dallied. Following the compilation of the National Register at the end of September, the ration books were issued. At the beginning of November, the imminent rationing of butter and bacon was announced, and people were told that they must register with their chosen retailers before November 23rd. Public opinion, which was little influenced by the clamour of the right-wing press against rationing, was thoroughly irritated by the delay. A Gallup Poll on November 20th showed that six people out of ten thought rationing was necessary.[48] The Government, at last, proclaimed on the 28th that it would begin on January 8th. Each person would receive four ounces of bacon or ham and four ounces of butter per week, if he wanted them. Just after Christmas, sugar rationing was announced, to begin on the same day at twelve ounces per week. On January 29th, the bacon ration was raised to eight ounces, which was actually greater than the average consumption per head before the war. Meat rationing followed on March 11th, on a value basis; each person over six was entitled to 1s. 10d. worth of meat per week, while the under-sixes had 11d. worth. "Offal" was not rationed and the humble organs covered by this term became the object of intense competition among housewives.

When the Ministry of Supply had been set up in July 1939, the new minister had appointed an Advisory Industrial Panel exclusively composed of businessmen. In October, the General Council of the Trade Union Congress went in a body to see the Prime Minister about this particular grievance, and it was redressed by the setting up of a Central Advisory Committee composed of equal numbers of trade unionists and employers. In the following month, the T.U.C. felt bound to complain about the absence of trade union representation on the local Food Control Committees. Again, this was followed at once by a change of policy on the part of the Ministry of Food.[49] As these incidents showed, it was not the case that the Government was unwilling to placate the trade union leaders. There were harrowing memories in Whitehall of enormous waves of industrial unrest in the First World War. The Government saw the unions not as potential allies, but as potential enemies. The unions reciprocated with a strong mistrust of the Government. Failing to communicate, the Government tried appeasement.

In October, any hopes that wages could be pegged were thrown aside when the Government permitted the colliery owners to give the miners a rise in wages to match that of the cost of living index. Increases in other industries followed. Ministers agreed that they must "educate" the T.U.C. Early in December, at a meeting of the National Joint Advisory Council, which had recently been set up to represent both sides of industry, Sir John Simon set about this missionary task, appealing timidly, but unsuccessfully, for voluntary restraint.[50]

The Government's failure to win the confidence of the unions hampered its not very forceful attempts to come to terms with the "manpower" situation. There were two related problems here. Firstly, labour must flow from the less essential to the more essential industries, and to the expanding "war industries", not only to replace men lost by the call-up, but also to increase the scale and momentum of armament production. Secondly, the shortage of skilled workers which had emerged in the crucial engineering industry during the rearmament period before the war must be combated.

The Ministry of Labour (to which that of National Service was added) was the key department so far as these problems were concerned. But it began the war with relatively minor status. It was chiefly associated in the public mind with its Labour Exchanges, and hence with unemployment. Little was done to revitalize it. It was complacently assumed, meanwhile, that with a million and a quarter unemployed at the outbreak, and others newly thrown out of work in trades like holidays and building, which were instantly affected by war conditions, there was a reservoir from which warlike industries could draw all the men needed; for the moment no compulsion would be necessary.

Yet unemployment actually rose, largely because of an exceptionally bad winter. The total did not begin to decline until March and still stood at over a million in April. By June 1940, the proportion of male workers employed either in munitions manufacture or in the undoubtedly essential industries, serving both forces and civilians, had risen by only five per cent (from fifty-one per cent to fifty-six per cent), as compared with twelve months before.[51]

Failure to redistribute and increase the supply of skilled labour was one factor limiting the expansion of war industry. Apprenticeship training in the engineering and the shipbuilding industries had been one of the casualties of the depression, and the period between the wars had seen a sharp decline in the number of actual and potential skilled workers. Yet, at the end of March, there were only seven thousand men – a pitifully small proportion of the unemployed – in training for skilled work at the Government's training centres.

In the first month of war, the Government introduced a so-called "Control of Employment" Act, without securing the prior agreement of the trade unions. This was designed to govern the movements of skilled men by providing that employers in certain industries could engage specified workers only through the Labour Exchanges, or through an approved trade union. It was too hedged with qualifications and compromises to have any effect.

By the early spring of 1940, competition was such that some engineering firms in Lancashire and the midlands had lifted wages for skilled men to what then seemed the very high level of seven or eight pounds a week, by bonus rates and merit bonuses. A hundred per cent bonus to piece workers was quite usual in firms employed on big Government contracts. In the areas where skilled men were scarcest, employers resorted to "poaching" them from each other. "Labour scouts" were sent round to their homes in the evenings and bribed them with offers of big bonuses to leave their present jobs. The vital machine tools industry was losing men to less skilled but higher paid jobs in aircraft manufacture; yet the aircraft factories depended on the production of more and more machine tools.[52]

The First World War had clearly revealed the need for "dilution" of skilled men by semi-skilled. It had also shown that women could be brought in successfully to perform jobs hitherto done by men. Here, too, the Ministry of Labour dragged its feet. These recipes had proved unpopular in the former war and the ministry was reluctant to accept responsibility for industrial unrest. In August 1939, the Engineering Employers' Federation and the Amalgamated Engineering Union had reached an agreement that when war broke out, the latter would permit the "upgrading" of less skilled workers to skilled work and the use of semi-skilled workers to assist skilled men. But in January, the Federation reported that only four hundred and ten agreements, covering the derisory total of sixteen hundred "dilutees", had been made in the industry since the outbreak of war.[53] The total number of women in civil employment increased by less than five hundred thousand between June 1939 and June 1940, to 5,306,000.

But the "industrial front", as people were already beginning to call it, was not too gloomy for those who were returning to work after long unemployment. J. L. Hodson, the journalist, visiting the shipyards in April, found Clydeside and Tyneside humming with unwonted activity. High earnings on overtime compensated for the rising cost of living, as the navy's demand for new ships was met. Though over a thousand unskilled workers were still unemployed in Jarrow, Hodson reported "men of sixty or seventy years of age now going off to work again . . ." The mayor was a splendid example of fighting spirit. He was a works foreman. After twelve hours on the night shift, he got home at eight thirty a.m. At eleven o'clock Hodson found him on his allotment, "digging for victory" as the Government recommended.[54] Meanwhile, Lancashire's cotton industry was booming again, with the huge demand for uniforms and other supplies for the forces.

But wartime inconveniences had begun to plague many of the country's workers. The blackout bore very hard on those working outside at night – in great marshalling yards only a sixth sense could help railwaymen to remember the order of the waggons they were handling and their destinations. In many factories the only practicable way of achieving blackout was to cover all the windows with paint or some other permanent material and to use artificial light during the day. Ventilation went by the board in too many cases. Alerts were another annoyance. Factory A.R.P. was still very backward. It would have provided small consolation for the ordinary workers in the

factories, shops and offices, which were still mostly without
shelters, to know that the Government was equally behindhand
in implementing its schemes for the safety of its own employees.[55]

VII

1940 provided the coldest January and February for forty-five
years. The Thames froze hard for eight miles of its length. Main
line expresses were sometimes a day late. Huge falls of snow
added new perils to the blackout in the cities and cut off villages
and even towns from the outside world.

What news there was divided the British people rather than
united them. On January 6th, Leslie Hore Belisha, the Minister
of War, was sacked. The breezy Belisha had struck the general
public as, after Churchill, the most war-like member of the
Government. ("Belisha Beacons", the road safety device which
he had introduced before the war, still testify in Britain's streets
to his talent for self-publicity.) He had been at the War Office for
nearly three years, had modernized the pattern of the army, and
was regarded as a good friend of the private soldier. It was said,
not altogether without cause, that his dismissal was due to the
resentment which the "brasshats" and "Colonel Blimps" felt for
his democratizing touch.

Meanwhile, the war which the Russians had launched against
their neighbour, Finland, was creating hysteria in political circles.
The Russians were attempting to improve their frontiers in case
of aggression from Germany, but even the left-wing *Tribune* could
find no excuses for this action. The T.U.C. and the Labour Party
denounced it forthrightly. D. N. Pritt, M.P., who defended
Russia's action with all his considerable gifts as a propagandist,
was eventually expelled from the Labour Party for doing so.
The press found no praise too high for the gallant Finns.

For that matter, Chamberlain's cabinet was far more interested
in helping the Finns against Communism than it had been in
aiding the Poles against Hitler. In January, a bureau for recruiting opened in London and five hundred volunteers enlisted, of
whom three hundred reached the front. Several score of British
aircraft were rashly sent. Apart from the Communists, prominent
voices in the Labour and Liberal Parties opposed what the owner
of the loudest of them, Hugh Dalton, called "Midwinter Madness". And public opinion was strangely unimpressed by anti-
Russian propaganda. A poll taken after the Finnish War had

ended showed that about five people wanted Britain to have closer relations with Russia for every one who thought she should be shunned.[56]

The British and French agreed early in February that they would prepare an expeditionary force for Finland, and some hundred thousand troops were assembled for this purpose. There was a little method in this madness, for all that it would have ranged another powerful enemy against the allies. The idea was that by striking through Narvik, in northern Norway, across Scandinavia, the allies might cut the Germans off from their supplies of Swedish iron ore. The obstinate neutrality of Sweden and Norway frustrated this chivalrous scheme. On March 12th, the Finns accepted Russia's peace terms.

The fierce winter gave way to a spring of peculiar brilliance and loveliness, of hot sun and blue skies. Militant patriotic songs were losing their popularity, and a haunting sentimental number called "We'll Meet Again" was the latest pride of Tin Pan Alley. Easter fell at the end of March. Trippers flocked to the coast for the four days' holiday and seaside resorts did as well as in peacetime.

The allies had long suspected that Hitler would make an offensive in the west when spring came, but Chamberlain remained wilfully and wishfully optimistic. On April 4th, he made a speech which was remembered later as cruelly as his promise of "peace in our time". The Germans, he told the Central Council of the National Union of Conservative and Unionist Associations, had had their chance in September, when "their war preparations had been far more complete than the allies". Now they had lost it. Hitler had "missed the bus". Next day, the *Daily Express* published an interview with the Chief of the Imperial General Staff, General Ironside. His message was the same as Chamberlain's. "Our army has, at last, turned the corner . . . We are ready for anything they may start."[57]

Three days later, the Bore War was over. The allies violated Scandinavian neutrality on April 8th, mining Norwegian waters in the hope of thwarting German shipping, which had made good use of them. Hitler, who had expected the allies to try to catch this particular bus, promptly walked over Denmark and landed troops at several points in Norway. The Norwegians, fighting bravely but hopelessly, appealed for aid. The first troops sailed on the 12th. The expensive education in geography which was to familiarize the British people with such hitherto arcane place-names as Velikiye-Luki, Kharkov, Tobruk, Benghazi,

Bataan, Okinawa, Lubeck and Hiroshima, began with Narvik
and Trondheim. By the time the course was over some thirty
million people, of all nations, relatively few of them British,
would have been killed.

Chapter Three

Spitfire Summer: April to September 1940

It may be a privilege to see history in the making, but we have a feeling that it is being overdone at the present time.

Editorial in Hampstead A.R.P.'s *Warden's Bulletin*, August 1st, 1940

THE MAN WITH THE BIG CIGAR

A. Ah bet tha heard Churchill.
B. Aye – I did.
A. He doesn't half give it to them. I corn't go to sleep when he's on. He's the best talker we have.

Conversation in Bolton, October, 1939[1]

One sniff of the Old Havana – we'd follow him right to Fugi-Yama,
We'd follow him most anywhere, the man with the big cigar,
Tra-la-la-la, tra-la-la-la, tra-la-la-la-la-la.

Victory ITMA, 1945[2]

I

"CHURCHILL", Dr. Goebbels noted in his diary after a discussion with Hitler early in 1942, "has never been a friend of the Tories. He was always an outsider, and before the war was regarded as half crazy. Nobody took him seriously. The Fuehrer recalled that all Englishmen whom he received before the outbreak of the war were in agreement that Churchill was a fool. Even Chamberlain said so to the Fuehrer."[3]

Goebbels, as was his habit, made an overstatement. Churchill, so far from having "always" been an outsider, had been born into a noble family and had mixed from his youth in the highest political circles. Yet Goebbels was not far out in his estimate of Churchill's standing in the 1930s.

Born in 1874, he had entered parliament as a Conservative in 1900, after a brief but glamorous military career, and had at once begun to attack his own leaders. In 1904 he had become a Liberal, and had made anti-Conservative speeches which his opponents, forty years later, loved to quote against him. The Tories had loathed him as a renegade. As President of the Board of Trade from 1908 to 1910, he had sponsored improvements in working conditions in several downtrodden industries, had given the first official recognition to Labour Exchanges and had been hot for reforms, then introduced, which had laid a basis for the Welfare State. But any credit this had won for him among the working classes had been spoilt by his reckless use of troops to break strikes in the docks and railways when he had become Home Secretary in 1910. (He was repeatedly accused in later life of having set troops to fire on striking Welsh miners at Tonypandy in 1910. The story stuck because it was true to his character, though not to historical fact.)

In 1915, as First Lord of the Admiralty, he had borne personal responsibility for the disastrous Dardanelles expedition, which had confirmed his reputation for rash aggression. In 1919, as Secretary of State for War, he had been the chief advocate of British intervention to quell the Russian Revolution. Out of parliament from 1922 to 1924, he had made peace with the Conservatives, and he had reappeared in 1924 as their Chancellor of the Exchequer. At the Treasury, he had been responsible for Britain's foolish return to the Gold Standard in 1925 (and had successfully advocated cuts in spending on armaments). Many who had forgotten these episodes when the war broke out still remembered his role in the General Strike of 1926. With the trade unions solid in support of the coal-miners, Churchill had pursued deliberately provocative tactics and had emerged as the strikers' most bitter enemy.

When the Conservatives lost power in 1929, Churchill entered the most unpopular phase of his controversial career. From the age of fifty-five to the age of sixty-five, normally the prime years of a politician's life, he was out of office. He quarrelled with his leader, Baldwin, over the latter's proposal to grant eventual self-government to India, and, denouncing Gandhi as a "half-naked fakir", emerged as the arch-imperialist. When he made his famous speeches warning that Britain must prepare to resist German aggression, his campaign was readily dismissed as another Churchillian stunt, just Winston baying for blood again. In the House of Commons he was laughed at and heckled from his own Conservative benches. He seemed a spent force, an old and wilful war-horse betraying his youthful promise; above all, he seemed unreliable. His character still fascinated his contemporaries, but the coming of war, while it vindicated his stand against appeasement and brought him new popularity with ordinary people, did not restore to him the confidence of the six hundred-odd members in the House of Commons who had their various reasons to dislike or distrust him.

His new colleagues found him a handful; constantly trying to interfere in provinces far away from his own at the Admiralty, rambling pompously and not always relevantly at cabinet meetings. Chamberlain, philosophically, regarded these foibles as "just the price we have to pay for the asset we have in his personality and popularity".[4] By November, something like friendship was ripening between the two men, who had been colleagues in the 1920s. Churchill recognized that the Prime Minister now hated Hitler, the man who had cheated him, with all the fury of his wounded vanity and he could admire Chamberlain's methodical, industrious ways.

By April 1940, the political opposition to the war had had ample chance to prove itself negligible. The British Union of Fascists had fought three by-elections between February and May 1940; just under thirteen hundred people had voted for its candidates altogether. The Communists had been rejected almost as utterly. Perhaps the most striking result of this phase was at Southwark Central in February 1940. A local Labour councillor resigned from the party to fight its nominee as a "Stop the War" candidate. The Communists poured in to help him. He distributed nearly 130,000 copies of twenty-two different pieces of literature. On one day, he had no less than three thousand helpers. This latter figure proved to be almost twice as great as the number of votes which he managed to poll.[5]

More serious opposition to Chamberlain was emerging on the right. He had made the important mistake, while bringing in Churchill and Eden, of leaving out of his wartime Government a number of the ablest anti-appeasement Conservatives; Amery, Duff Cooper and Harold Macmillan among them. These, together with the small personal followings of Churchill and Eden,[7] formed a nucleus for action designed to dispose of him.

Early in April 1940, there was a minor cabinet reshuffle. Wood gave up the Air Ministry to Hoare and succeeded to Hoare's post as Lord Privy Seal. The luckless Lord Chatfield resigned and his duties as "Minister of Co-ordination of Defence" (the inverted commas are necessary) were taken over by Churchill. One excellent appointment was made; Lord Woolton, a businessman who had been raised to the peerage as Director General of the Ministry of Supply, now moved from this administrative job to take charge of the Ministry of Food.

But the changes altered the complexion of the Government very little. The new budget which Simon introduced on the 23rd showed the now familiar want of resolution. The standard rate of income tax went up to seven shillings and sixpence (but this had been announced in September); the exemption limit was reduced from £125 to £120; there was another penny on beer, and a penny halfpenny more on a packet of ten cigarettes. Postal charges were increased, hitting families scattered by war in a peculiarly mean way.[6]

Meanwhile, it had become painfully clear that in Norway, Britain had been "forestalled, surprised, and . . . outwitted", in Churchill's modest words. Churchill had cut a poor figure in the House of Commons explaining the affair – "vague oratory coupled with tired jibes", wrote Harold Nicolson in his diary; and Nicholson, one of the small band of National Labour M.P.s, and a member of the "Eden Group", was one of Churchill's few unreserved admirers.[7] It was soon clear that the attempt to take Trondheim, one of the two objectives of British action, had failed, and the troops were evacuated. At Narvik, there was stalemate. The reverses which Britain's finest troops, the Scots and Irish Guards, were sustaining at the hands of the well equipped German invaders highlighted the nation's unpreparedness, for which Chamberlain must take the blame.

He was an old man; the question of his successor had long been on men's minds. Chamberlain's was made up; he had written in March, "I would rather have Halifax succeed me than Winston."[8] But for the moment he was very ready to continue to shoulder his burden; and the aura of indispensability which gathers round a national figurehead, especially in time of war, was working in his favour.

On April 4th, Lord Salisbury, a veteran Conservative statesman of great prestige, assembled the dissident Tories as a "Watching Committee". By early May this was pressing for the formation of a coalition Government. Labour, it was presumed,

would not agree to serve under Chamberlain. But what alternatives were there? Anthony Eden was immensely popular with the
electorate, especially with women who were charmed by his
suave good looks. But at forty-two, he was too young to command the necessary authority. Lloyd George, at seventy-seven,
was too old; he was suspected of defeatism and in any case could
not even call the Liberal Party his own. There remained Halifax
and Winston Churchill. The latter was the hero of the popular
press; but the former was taken far more seriously in political
circles.

Halifax, Foreign Secretary since Eden's resignation in 1938,
was the younger man by half a dozen years. Tall, gaunt and
ascetic in appearance, he was a devout Anglo-Catholic, and
admiration for him among Christians cut across party lines. He
had been the least whole-hearted of the inner ring of appeasers
and had an unusually high reputation for moral probity. But he
was a dim speaker, fond of constructions like "I should have
thought that one might say that it could reasonably be held
that . . ." (It is pleasant to imagine him saying, "This, on the
whole, seems to have been their finest hour.") And he was a
member of the House of Lords, which, whatever qualities it had
as a forum for debate, did not represent the nation.

But as for Churchill: the Conservative whips, ancient enemies
of his, were even now putting it about that he, not Chamberlain,
was responsible for the Norwegian fiasco, "another Dardanelles";
the Labour leaders were supposed to distrust him, and some
certainly did; there was the rumour that he was well over the hill,
perhaps even drowning himself in alcohol. The agitation for a
coalition, in so far as it focused itself at all in the first week of
May 1940, focused its hopes around Halifax.

When the House of Commons assembled on May 7th to debate
the Norwegian campaign, fierce speeches and high passions were
expected; but almost no one expected it to bring about a coalition
led by Churchill.

II

The temper of the House of Commons during the "Norway
Debate" was, according to Harold Nicolson, "one of actual fear.
But," his diary added, "it is a very resolute fear . . ."[9]

Chamberlain set the debate going by announcing that the
evacuation of the expedition to Trondheim had now been

completed. He tried to minimize the gravity of the setback and reminded the House, either pointedly or tactlessly, of the Dardanelles – "The withdrawal from southern Norway is not comparable to the withdrawal from Gallipoli." His speech was interrupted more than once with cries of "missed the bus". He crossly defended that phrase and implied that the House was very lucky that it was allowed to debate Norway at all. "Our military advisers have told us in very solemn terms of the dangers of holding such a discussion." Attlee replied with a typically sharp speech which opened up the wider themes of the debate – he reminded the House of Czechoslovakia and Poland. "Everywhere the story is 'Too late'." But neither he, nor the Liberal leader, Sir Archibald Sinclair, could lift the debate out of the rut of party sniping.

This was achieved by the sixth speaker, Admiral of the Fleet Sir Roger Keyes, one of those who had deplored the Munich settlement, who appeared in full uniform, complete with a chest of medals, because, he said, "... I wish to speak for some officers and men of the fighting, sea-going navy who are very unhappy." He told the House he had wanted to lead an attack on Trondheim, but had been informed by the Admiralty that the success of the army made such a desperate venture quite unnecessary. He was a shocking speaker, sometimes inaudible, but the Commons heard him in breathless silence, and gasped audibly at this revelation. His criticism reflected first and foremost upon Churchill, though he stressed his great personal admiration for the First Lord. He sat down to thunderous applause. The dissatisfaction which had been growing among the Government's supporters since September had suddenly found an unanswerable voice, the voice of a brave man without political ambition.

Half an hour later came Leo Amery, an ex-minister of considerable standing. The House was half empty when he spoke; it was dinner time, and he was, in any case, a notorious bore. But on this occasion he, too, surpassed himself. He switched attention from Churchill and Norway to Chamberlain and the entire conduct of the war. As he ended, he opened another breach in the dyke which protected Chamberlain, the dyke of his supposed indispensability. He said he would quote Oliver Cromwell. "I do it with great reluctance, because I am speaking of those who are old friends and associates of mine, but they are words which, I think, are applicable to the present situation. This is what Cromwell said to the Long Parliament when he thought it was no longer fit to conduct the affairs of the nation: 'You have sat too long here for any good you have been doing. Depart, I say, and let us have done with you. In the name of God, go.' "[10]

Yet that night, after further speeches had emphasized the weakness of the Government's defences, the Tory rebels met and decided not to table a motion opposing the Government at this stage. It was left to the Labour Party to force the issue. When its parliamentary executive met next day, Attlee put it to them that they should call for a division – not on any explicit motion of censure, but simply on the motion already before the Commons, merely "That this House do now adjourn". Dalton opposed the idea of forcing a vote; Herbert Morrison was irresolute, but the idea prevailed. That evening, when Morrison opened the second day's debate, he set the House laughing with a quotation from a recent speech by Hoare on Norway. "Today our wings are spread over the Arctic. They are sheathed in ice. Tomorrow the sun of victory will touch them with its golden light . . ." It was an effective, needling attack, and when Morrison concluded by announcing that Labour would force a vote, Chamberlain rose to make a reply which showed how his vanity had been hurt by the debate – especially, no doubt, by Amery's tirade.

"The right hon. Gentleman began his speech by emphasizing the gravity of the occasion. What he has said, the challenge which he has thrown out to the Government in general and the attack which he has made on them, and upon me in particular, make it graver still . . . I do not seek to evade criticism, but I say this to my friends in the House – and I have friends in the House." He gave a "leer of triumph" as he uttered these words, meaning, those present concluded, that he confidently expected the majority which had endorsed his Munich settlement to support him now. He went on to accept the challenge. Chamberlain's complacency lost him the esteem of a good number of his "friends", though David Lloyd George, making an unexpected intervention, drew attention to it rather too savagely. "It is not a question of who are the Prime Minister's friends. It is a far bigger issue." After indicting Chamberlain's record from Munich to Norway, he too called on him to quit.[11]

Further weighty attacks from Duff Cooper and Cripps followed. The pattern of the debate was by now clear. Men of proven ability on both sides of the House shared a sincere disgust with the Government. Five Conservatives had spoken against Chamberlain; only six, apart from ministers, had supported the Government, and they had been mediocre figures making mediocre points. There remained Winston Churchill, who wound up the debate. He could not mend the dyke. Worse, near the end of an eloquent defence of the Government – and of his own part in the Norway campaign – he lost his temper with some Labour members after persistent barracking from the Opposition benches and was involved in an unseemly verbal brawl.

The confirmed Tory rebels had not wanted to make a show of national disunity at this perilous time. But their hands were forced – hitherto loyal and quiescent followers of Chamberlain were saying that they felt they must vote against the Government. Into one lobby with the Opposition parties went Amery, Duff Cooper, Macmillan, Nicolson and their friends – but also a number of serving officers, making forty-one Government supporters in all. "When I went into our lobby," wrote Hugh Dalton, "it seemed to be full of young Conservatives in uniform – khaki, Navy blue and Air Force blue all intermingled." Duff Cooper saw one of them, "who had been for long a fervent admirer of Chamberlain, walking through the Opposition lobby with the tears streaming down his face". The number of rebels would have been far greater had Chamberlain not put it about that he would make changes – perhaps even sack Simon and Hoare – if the House continued to support him. As it was, about sixty Conservatives abstained.[12]

When the voting figures were announced, it was found that the Government, which usually commanded a majority of about two hundred and forty, had won the division by only two hundred and eighty-one votes to two hundred. There were shouts of "Go Go Go!" But the vote left matters in suspense, and Chamberlain for one believed that he might yet remain Prime Minister. Churchill was urging him to carry on. Surely this was not the time to change pilots?

Next day, Chamberlain manoeuvred. Amery and the Tory rebels, some sixty in number, met and sent word to him that they would neither join nor support any Government which did not include Labour and Liberal ministers, but would support anyone, Chamberlain included, who could form such a Government.

In the afternoon there was a famous and crucial meeting between Chamberlain, Churchill, Halifax and the Conservative chief whip Margesson. The question was raised; whom should Chamberlain recommend as his successor if Labour refused to serve under him? It has been suggested that Churchill held the trump card at this interview; by refusing to serve under Halifax –

and he had decided·to remain completely silent if asked – he would destroy the latter's chance of success in forming a coalition. But it is difficult to see what could have halted Halifax, if he had wanted the post; every significant political leader would have accepted him except Churchill, who would therefore have risked a return to the wilderness. Popular ministers had gone before – Belisha was one.

Chamberlain said he would serve under either man. He looked expectantly at Halifax. Halifax had been suffering from stomach-ache since Chamberlain had put it to him, earlier that day, that he thought he should succeed him. There was what felt to Churchill like a "very long pause". If there was bluff involved, Halifax broke first. He suggested that his peerage would make his task impossible. Churchill did not contradict him. In fact, the King, who favoured Halifax, would readily have sanctioned an arrangement by which Halifax could have spoken, or even have sat, in the Commons; the problem, in the context of total war, was a minor one. But so the succession was decided.[13]

It remained for Chamberlain to discover whether Labour would join a new administration headed by himself. Attlee and Greenwood were summoned to Downing Street and refused to commit their party, though they made it clear that there was little hope of its members consenting to serve under Chamberlain. They agreed to put his offer to the other Labour leaders, who were meeting at Bournemouth prior to their party's conference.

Next day, the few men in Britain who were aware that the Prime Ministership trembled in the balance awoke to brilliant sunshine and frightening news. The Germans had invaded Belgium and Holland. When Chamberlain met his cabinet in the morning, he was remarkably cheerful; perhaps because he thought that this catastrophe must keep him in power. It was, of all people, Sir Kingsley Wood, who had deftly switched horses the day before and was now backing Churchill, who told Chamberlain bluntly that he must go, expressing the opinion of other ministers. ("Like being bitten by a gramophone", one Tory has since observed.[14])

But it was not a case of "*Et tu, Brute*". The Labour Party, which had given the "Old Man" the first decisive push by forcing a vote over Norway, now completed its work with a second. In spite of the news, its National Executive at Bournemouth resolved unanimously that Labour would serve under anyone but Chamberlain. Just before Attlee and Greenwood left for London, around five o'clock, to carry on the negotiations arising from this decision, an anxious Chamberlain phoned and learnt the answer to his question. He went to give his resignation to the King.

At six o'clock, Churchill was summoned to Buckingham Palace and was asked to form a new Government. There was, he has recalled, no crowd outside the Palace gates; the evening papers were full of the news from the Continent, and there was nothing about cabinet crises. Even M.P.s were dumbfounded when the voice of Chamberlain, at nine o'clock, came over the radio announcing his resignation.

Although they came so early in the war, these events were its central political crisis. No conspiracy brought down Chamberlain; he fell because of a conjunction of personal decisions by men of left, right and centre. As Paul Addison has suggested,* the cardinal reason for his fall was probably his Government's failure to overcome the distrust of the trade unions, which underlay the disappointing performance of "war industry", which in turn was so obviously allied with the inadequate armaments of the British forces in Norway, which in turn prompted the crucial intervention of Admiral Keyes and the adverse votes of young Conservatives in uniform. To bring the trade unions into enthusiastic co-operation, the Labour Party must enter the Government; this was the mainspring of the quest by Salisbury and his friends for coalition, and this was why Labour's second blow, aimed from Bournemouth, was the fatal one.

From these concatenations and confusions, Winston Churchill, to the amazement of his fellow politicians, emerged to guide the fortunes of the nation. Large sections of the Labour Party, whose leaders had had Halifax, not Churchill, in mind when they had voted on the 10th, retained their mistrust for the new Prime Minister. Loyal "Chamberlainites", still comfortably in the majority in the House of Commons, in some cases carried mistrust as far as loathing.

But one man at least that night had no doubts as to the new Prime Minister's capacity. ". . . As I went to bed at about three a.m.," Churchill has recorded, "I was conscious of a profound sense of relief. At last I had the authority to give directions over the whole scene. I felt as if I were walking with destiny, and that all my past life had been but a preparation for this hour and for this trial."[15]

On the 13th, Churchill addressed the House of Commons for

* I am grateful to Mr. Addison for permitting me to use his arguments in advance of publication.

the first time in his new role. He was cheered from the Labour benches when he appeared, but the Conservatives mostly kept their ovation for Chamberlain, who, with Attlee and Greenwood, sat on the Front Bench beside him. "I have nothing to offer," Churchill told the House, "but blood, toil, tears and sweat." His war aim, he said, was simple – "Victory – victory at all costs, victory in spite of all terror, victory, however long and hard the road may be . . . Come, then, let us go forward together with out united strength."[16]

Meanwhile, the German armies were breaking through on the Continent. That morning, an incredulous King George VI had received a phone call at five a.m. from Queen Wilhelmina of Holland, begging him to send aircraft to her country's aid. He wrote in his diary, "I passed this message on to everyone concerned, & went back to bed. It is not often one is rung up at that hour, and especially by a Queen. But in these days anything may happen, & far worse things too." By the end of the day, the Dutch Royal Family were in England.[17]

III

In building a new Government, Churchill's hands were tied by the weakness of his own position. Even if he had not admired his abilities, he would have had to find a prestigious job for Chamberlain; he gave him, in fact, the Lord Presidency of the Council and a seat in the War Cabinet. Halifax stayed in the War Cabinet, and at the Foreign Office. Hoare was sacked, but Simon was merely translated to the House of Lords, as Lord Chancellor, to occupy himself with legal matters. Sir Kingsley Wood, to the astonishment of the herd, who did not know of his last-minute change of sides, became Chancellor of the Exchequer. Of the thirty-six leading ministerial posts filled by May 15th, twenty-one went to men who had held office under Chamberlain. Anderson kept the Home Office and Woolton stayed at the Ministry of Food. The Tory rebels were badly rewarded. Amery was given only the Secretaryship of State for India; Salisbury's son, Lord Cranborne, became Paymaster General; and poor Duff Cooper went to the hot seat at the Ministry of Information, putting a promising future behind him.

During his first seven weeks as Prime Minister, the overwhelming majority of Conservative backbenchers maintained a sullen silence when Churchill entered the Chamber, and when he rose to speak. His legendary orations of the summer of 1940 were, to begin with, greeted with enthusiastic cheering by Labour M.P.s rising to their feet in front of him, and with still silence from most of the Tories behind him. Paul Einzig, then a lobby correspondent, wrote to Chamberlain to warn him of the ominous conclusions which foreign diplomats and journalists were drawing from the attitude of his supporters. Chamberlain, replying on July 1st, hinted that he would do something about it. Three days later, after Churchill had made an important speech in the House, the usual scene was about to repeat itself. Then, suddenly, after a pause, the chief whip, Margesson, rose to his feet and waved the Tory backbenchers on to theirs. They began to cheer fervently. Churchill wept.[18]

Chamberlain served Churchill loyally and impressed Clement Attlee, for one, with his cunning and efficiency. But his continuance in office was bitterly resented by vocal sections of popular opinion. Early in July, the most famous political tract of the war (and perhaps of the century) appeared in the black and yellow dust-jacket of Victor Gollancz. *Guilty Men*, written in haste by three Beaverbrook journalists using the pseudonym "Cato", established the left-wing myth of the 'thirties in its classic form. Why had Britain's armies been defeated? Because of the "regime of little men", the iniquity of the appeasers who would have preferred not to fight Hitler. Though full of praise for Churchill, this polemic was boycotted by many booksellers and sold in bundles in the street – "like a pornographic classic", one of its authors, Michael Foot, modestly observes. A Gallup poll at this time suggested that three-quarters of the public now wanted Chamberlain removed from office. There was strong feeling against the lesser "Guilty Men", Halifax, Wood and Margesson. Churchill could not remove them; partly because they were able ("If one were dependent on the people who had been right in the last few years," he remarked at this time, "what a tiny handful one would have to depend on"), and still more because the Tory benches might turn on him.[19]

Chamberlain, in any case, was now a very sick man. Towards the end of that summer, an exploratory operation showed that he had cancer. He resigned from the Government on October 3rd, and died on November 9th. The War Cabinet, to whom Anderson, the new Lord President, was now added, acted as his pallbearers. Churchill delivered a noble tribute in the Commons, describing Chamberlain somewhat oddly as "an English Worthy". Meanwhile, on October 9th, he had assumed the leadership of the Conservative Party which the dying man had vacated.

This action was much criticized, then and later (though only about one member of the public in eight was prepared to say that it was a bad thing at the time[20]). But even if Churchill had not been genuinely anxious to lead the party which he had supported, after his fashion, for nearly twenty years, he would have been a child to allow any other man to take over such an excellent base for anti-Churchill intrigue.

The Conservatives, as was their wont, accepted him unanimously. Their natural passion for blind loyalty, already a strength to him as coalition Prime Minister, was redoubled when he mystically united, in his one person, the essences of National Unity and Conservatism; though some of Chamberlain's supporters certainly took their dislike of him to the grave. Armed with this new authority, he was strong enough to despatch Halifax to Washington as ambassador in December, replacing him as Foreign Secretary with Eden.

So much for the Conservative component in the coalition. The terms which Churchill offered the Labour leaders on May 10th were quite generous; two out of five seats in the new, smaller, War Cabinet, in return for swallowing the retention of Chamberlain. With grave news pouring from the Continent, the Labour Conference at Bournemouth, meeting on the 13th, set its seal of approval on them by 2,450,000 votes to a mere 170,000.

Attlee and Greenwood were given the two War Cabinet seats, as Lord Privy Seal and Minister without Portfolio respectively. Albert Alexander, a pillar of the Co-operative movement, succeeded Churchill at the Admiralty. Morrison was given the important seat at the Ministry of Supply; Dalton the Ministry of Economic Warfare, Emanuel Shinwell, another veteran of MacDonald's Government of 1929–31, was offered an under-secretaryship, refused it, and flounced into opposition, where he formed an odd threesome with Hore Belisha and Earl Winterton, two other ex-ministers whose talents had been spurned. Cripps (now an independent figure on the left moving rapidly towards the centre) was shortly sent to Moscow as ambassador.

The Liberals were no trouble, with their handful of M.P.s. Their leader, Sinclair, was given the Air Ministry, but had no place in the War Cabinet. That, bar under-secretaryships, was their whole reward.

As the factions balanced, the Conservatives, with the "National Liberal" and "National Labour" parties, whose leading men were given ministries, and with "non-party" men like Anderson and Woolton, who were Conservative in all but name, had twenty-nine of the thirty-six leading appointments. Since the country had indisputably moved left since 1935, the "great coalition" was certainly not at this stage representative of the nation's politics. Nor was the balance altered by the many changes later. In the normal course of events, there should have been a general election in the autumn of 1940. Instead, parliament voted itself another year of life, and in this way the House of Commons which had supported Chamberlain to Norway and beyond was renewed, year after year, until 1945.

In making two appointments, Churchill struck firmly away from orthodoxy. Ernest Bevin, General Secretary of Britain's largest union, the Transport and General Workers', accepted the Ministry of Labour on May 13th. Churchill had got on well with him during the early months of the war, when they had met over the problems arising from the Admiralty's need for fishing boats. Bevin, with his jealous ally Walter Citrine, was the dominant force in the T.U.C. He was not an M.P., and never had been, though a seat in the Commons was now found for him.

Beaverbrook, whose appointment was announced next day, had been a minister in the First World War, when he had become a crony of Churchill's. Though their relationship since had not always been harmonious, Churchill now created a wholly new Ministry of Aircraft Production for him (by amputating a limb of Sinclair's department), trusting that he would show the same flair for producing Spitfires as he had put into boosting the sales of his newspaper, the *Daily Express*, the nation's best-seller.

This was the only new ministry which Churchill, at this stage, created. He himself writes of May 1940 that "The fundamental changes in the machinery of war direction were more real than apparent."[21] The chief innovation was that he took to himself the title of "Minister of Defence" as well as that of Prime Minister. The "ministry" had no physical existence in the usual sense, but the title signified Churchill's power to direct the Chiefs of Staff Committee and so control the forces in the field. The ministers at the three Service departments became mere organizers under him. (Churchill as First Lord had been a power in the land; Alexander was an amiable and efficient nonentity.) Churchill's work as generalissimo does not concern us here (nor, mostly, do the criticisms made of it during and since the war). But it is of importance for the civil history of the war, that it gave Churchill little time for home affairs.

Formally, home affairs were commanded at this stage by five committees of ministers, with the Lord President's Committee under Chamberlain controlling and coordinating them. So Chamberlain could be seen as "Home Front Prime Minister", and when Anderson succeeded him in October, the latter in fact amassed some of the coordinating power which that title suggests. But Churchill flatly and publicly rejected the popular notion that there should be an office specially created for a man to rule home affairs as Churchill himself ruled defence. The Minister of Defence, he pointed out, was powerful precisely because he was also Prime Minister, and a corresponding figure in the civil field would not have that supreme and ultimate power to back his actions.[22]

So in fact, individual ministries conducted their affairs in competition rather than in accordance with directives issued by a master planner. Churchill himself interfered on the home front whenever the spirit moved him, and ministers had to make at least the motions of jumping when he asked them to jump. Anderson, as we shall see, eventually came to wield a formidable weapon of central planning, the "manpower budget", but this chiefly affected the ministries concerned with industry. The Ministry of Food, its official historian concludes, could in the last resort be forced by the Lord President's Committee to act against its own will, but generally "The logic of events, rather than the activities of a ubiquitous planning intellect, limited the ministry's freedom of choice . . ."[23]

So Churchill was king of the home front, too. Insulated by an obsolete House of Commons from the trends, mostly leftward, of public opinion; dominating the War Cabinet with his monologues; swooping from a height from time to time on quavering ministers outside the cabinet, he became the nearest thing to a dictator which Britain had owned since the days of absolute monarchy. There were, as we shall see, moments when the Commons might have overthrown him, and when sizable elements in it thought he must go. But by 1941, his speeches and bearing had made him appear unchallengeable. Victor Gollancz, on the far left, saw "no one on the horizon" who could "for a moment" compare with him. Geoffrey Dawson, Churchill's bitter opponent in the days of appeasement, expressed what was now almost a truism in his last editorial for *The Times* in September 1941. "So far as any man in the world can be regarded as indispensable, Mr. Churchill has earned that much abused title."[24]

IV

The man who found himself "walking with destiny" on May 10th, 1940, was a man of action and a man of war. "It is the most extraordinary brain, Winston's, to watch functioning that I have ever seen," Halifax wrote in his diary after a cabinet meeting that summer, "a most curious mixture of a child's emotion and a man's reason."[25] The child had assembled a collection of nearly fifteen hundred toy soldiers. The man enjoyed playing with real ones. In time of peace, emotion and reason were at odds; in time of war, man and boy were at one.

His ancestor, Marlborough, was one of his cardinal heroes. As a young cavalry officer, in the disappointingly peaceful 1890s, he had gone out of his way to find danger – in Cuba, on the north-west frontier of India, and in the Sudan. As a reporter in the Boer War, he had embroiled himself in action, had been imprisoned, and had electrified the British press with the daring of his escape. Thrown from office in the First World War, he had gone to France as a major, and had served for a few months in the trenches.

"A jolly life with nice people," he had said of that episode. But he had met with the realities of modern warfare. In *My Early Life* (1930), he complained that "War, which used to be cruel and magnificent, has now become cruel and squalid. In fact it has been completely spoilt. It is all the fault of Democracy and Science ... Instead of a small number of well-trained professionals championing their country's cause with ancient weapons and a beautiful intricacy of archaic manoeuvre ... we now have entire populations, including even women and children, pitted against one another in brutish mutual extermination, and only a set of blear-eyed clerks left to add up the butcher's bill ... To Hell with it!"[26] But if the rules had changed, he was still prepared, in 1940, to abide by them.

Along with his boyish love for the drama of war went a precocious child's view of history. Isaiah Berlin seems to judge this perfectly from Churchill's own historical writings. "The units out of which his world is constructed are simpler and larger than life, the patterns vivid and repetitive like those of an epic poet, or at times like those of a dramatist who sees persons and situations as timeless symbols and embodiments of eternal, shining principles."[27] For the bread-and-margarine of everyday existence, for those obscure lives which make up the large life of history, there was little space in his domineering historical imagination; it was kings he loved, and if no better specimens were available, Victor Emmanuel of Italy and George of Greece would do.

And in the centre of that canvas of history, as brightly coloured as his own uninhibited paintings, there was Winston Churchill himself. "He is always unconsciously playing a part – an heroic part," the great journalist A. G. Gardiner had written before the First World War, when Churchill had found no grander use for soldiers than the breaking of strikes. "And he is himself his most astonished spectator. He sees himself moving through the smoke of battle – triumphant, terrible, his brow clothed with thunder, his legions looking to him for victory and not looking in vain. He thinks of Napoleon; he thinks of his great ancestor. Thus did they bear themselves; thus, in this rugged and awful crisis, will he bear himself."[28]

And yet he could not, like a general of the better days of war, send only picked men to battle in his name. He owed his position, not to his ancestry, but to the processes of parliamentary democracy, and so, ultimately, to the people. All his people, "including even women and children", were his soldiers when the invader threatened, the bombs fell, His imagination easily resolved this contradiction. While he led them, they all must be – implicitly they all were – heroes, "timeless symbols".

To help him clutch reality to his imagination, he had his supreme asset, his domination over words. Churchill had the instinct of a natural writer; what could not be described in first-rate prose did not exist, since it must be forgotten. As soon as he had found wars to fight in he had found a style to describe them and had side-tracked into journalism. And when he became Prime Minister, he insisted that only his written instructions should be heeded, and lavished on his pettiest minute the resources of that prose, processional yet sprightly in its rhythms, sombre yet ironic in its utterance, which he had learnt from Gibbon and Macaulay. His doctor and confidant, Lord Moran, went so far as to judge that "Without that feeling for words he might have made little enough of life. For in judgment, in skill in administration, in knowledge of human nature, he does not at all excel."[29]

There was nothing spontaneous about Churchill's speeches – even his crushing ripostes to unexpected questions in parliament, one of his closer friends has revealed, had sometimes been "previously recruited and drilled ready to go into action should the occasion for them ever arise". In his early days, he had learnt his speeches by heart. Now, he would take six or eight hours to prepare one, while the war went on around him, first dictating it to a secretary, then checking and revising it two or three times, then, finally, breaking paragraphs, sentences and even phrases into the exact periods in which they would be delivered.[30]

Before he rose to deliver it, he would sit hunched up on the front bench, his head sunk on his shoulders, his mouth pulled down at the corners in that characteristic "bulldog" fashion, betraying his nervousness by stooping down, absent-mindedly, to pick up stray sheets of paper from the floor. When he rose, he fell at once into his characteristic gesture, "smoothing his palms down across his frame – beginning by patting his chest, then smoothing his stomach and ending down at the groin". Like so many celebrated orators, he had an impediment in his speech, his famous difficulty with the letter "s" – "we shall fight them in the hillsh". He had, one of his admirers wrote, "no charm of voice, no facility of gesture". It was that extraordinary rhetoric, half laboured half instinctive, which held his hearers–and in the 1930s, that had seemed stagey enough, to his friends and enemies alike.[31]

As the speech moved to the expected mighty peroration, Churchill's method was to take his listeners up and down an emotional switchback. One of the speeches which he made in secret session of the House of Commons (an occasion when grave matters were discussed of which the public must not hear) was delivered, most unusually, from skeleton notes. These have survived. He was talking, on June 20th, 1940, about the danger of night bombing, and at one point the notes read as follows:

> We have had a couple of nights of bombing,
>   evidently much worse than that.
> Folly underrate gravity attack impending.
> But if 100 to 150 bombers employed
>   entitled to remark:
>   Not very cleverly employed.
> Hardly paid expenses.
> Learn to get used to it.
>   Eels get used to skinning.
> Steady continuous bombing,
>   probably rising to great intensity
>   occasionally,
>   must be regular condition of our life . . .

Without the fatty flesh of Gibbonian language, the method is clearly seen in this skeleton. First, the warning, the stress that the danger must not be underrated. Then the joke that the raids up to now had hardly paid the Germans' expenses. Then the note of courage – "learn to get used to it" – then the swoop "into the intimate and the conversational" which Harold Nicolson thought so typical of him, the deliberate exploitation of bathos, "eels get used to skinning". Then the warning again, stronger this time; the audience of M.P.s, made bold by the sound of its own laughter, was ready to be told, accurately as things turned out, that bombing would be "a regular condition of our life". The bracing note of bulldog determination was sounded a little later. "This supreme battle depends upon/the courage of the ordinary man and woman./Whatever happens, keep a stiff upper lip."[32] The method had two main features. Churchill would descend from lofty rhetoric to irony or even low humour, never devaluing his favourite mighty words by over-using them. And he mingled warnings with buoyancy ("learn to get used to it"), so that listeners thought, here is a man who has foreseen the very worst that may befall, and yet remains confident.

"I always hesitate to say anything of an optimistic nature, because our people do not mind being told the worst," he explained to the House of Commons in October, when the worst might well have seemed to be happening. Later, he reminded the House of Commons rather too persistently that he had never promised anybody anything but "blood, sweat, toil and tears". Goebbels complained, at Churchill's darkest hour in February 1942, that this slogan made him "totally immune from attack. He is like a doctor who prophesies that his patient will die and every time the patient's condition worsens, smugly explains that, after all, he prophesied it."[33]

The mythical figure, "Churchill in 1940", the embodiment of Britain and her past, the embodiment of freedom, the embodiment above all of courage, has long since obliterated the reality of his position. The story of those summer days has been written from hindsight by the very people who were most wholly under Churchill's spell; by political colleagues, fascinated by the spectacle of his complex personality expanding to completeness as he enjoyed supreme power, and by writers, biased by their own sensitivity to words and by his own evident mastery of their craft. Churchill meant one thing to those closest to him, another to the lesser leaders of public opinion who watched him and, if they were lucky, had some slight communion with him, something different again to his middle-class subjects, and different things still to various sections of the working class.

Even in private, those old acquaintances like Beaverbrook who were familiar with his weaknesses and could play on them, saw a different Churchill from politicians, military men and civil servants who came to know him at first hand only after he had become Prime Minister, and was armouring himself in legend.

"His appearance was always a surprise," recalls one civil servant in the Cabinet Office, George Mallaby. It was not just the gaudy dressing gowns which he sometimes wore in company, or the famous siren suits ("rompers", he called them), made to his own design by a famous London firm; he usually dressed conventionally, in "a short black coat, striped trousers, a blue bow tie with white spots and impeccably clean linen". It was, rather, that one expected someone "rough and rugged like Cromwell or proud and remote like the younger Pitt". Mallaby continues:

> He was nothing of the kind. He was short, delicate looking, pink and white, round-faced, had wispy hair, frail artistic hands. He stumped along rather than walked, but when he sat, he sat heavily, broodingly, like a man six feet tall and twenty stone, monolithic in his chair. Then when the discussions began that child-like face became the reflection of the man – the set bulldog look ... the sulky look of a pouting child, the angry violent look of an animal at bay, the tearful look of a compassionate woman and the sudden spontaneous smiling look of a boy. The moods changed rapidly.

As a boss, Mallaby adds, confirming other accounts, Churchill was tyrannical and abusive, yet "Anybody who served anywhere near him was devoted to him."[34]

His extraordinary habits increased the strain on those around him, however devoted they might be. He always went to bed "at least for one hour as early as possible in the afternoon". He explains, "By this means, I was able to press a day and a half's work into one." So refreshed, he could drag yawning colleagues into discussion at ten o'clock at night, and run rings round their heavy heads until two a.m. or later. At eight or nine, he would be back at work. According to his bodyguard, he worked a "regular 120-hour week" from 1940 to the end of the war.[35]

Just as his afternoon sleep, when first met with, created the impression of an aged, weary man near his grave, so his steady

consumption of alcohol throughout the day was open to interpretation as habitual drunkenness. In fact, Churchill drank
continuously, but slowly, and rarely if ever indulged himself
beyond his own, clearly considerable, capacity.[36]

Not all those who met this utterly egregious man were captiva-
ted. He could charm into a feeling of intimacy those tense and
overawed mortals who were privileged to meet him. "Churchill
radiates friendliness," one American journalist exclaimed. "It is
awfully difficult not to start calling him 'Winston' after knowing
him for two hours."[37]

Yet perhaps this friendliness, and the boyish sense of fun which
he could communicate to large assemblies as well as to small
groups of friends, were less spontaneous than they appeared; he
was still Gardiner's Churchill "playing an heroic part", and this
time perhaps it was Henry V before Agincourt offering "a little
touch of Harry in the night". Certainly, his old and close
acquaintance Harold Nicolson observed him differently. At
lunch at Number 10 Downing Street one day, not a grand affair
of state but a sociable gathering, he watched Churchill's eyes.

> They are glaucous and look dead ... There is a faint ex-
> pression of surprise, as if he were asking, "What the hell is
> this man doing here?" There is a faint expression of angered
> indignation, as if he were saying, "What damned cheek com-
> ing to luncheon here!" There is a mask of boredom and
> another mask or film of obstinacy, as if he were saying,
> "These people bore me and I refuse to be polite." And with
> it all, there are films of stubbornness, perhaps even a film of
> deep inner thought. It is very disconcerting. Then suddenly
> he will cease thinking of something else, and the film will
> part and the sun comes out. His eyes then pucker with
> amusement or flash with anger. At moments they have a
> tragic look. Yet these passing moods and phases do not
> flash across each other; they move slowly and opaquely like
> newts in a rather dim glass tank.[38]

Others were equally disconcerted by the moments when
Churchill retreated into his own thoughts when in company,
abstracted for a moment into his own sense of destiny, perhaps
anticipating the successful conclusion of the business before him
and saying over to himself phrases from the memoirs he would
write. On the first occasion when John Winant, the American
ambassador in London from 1941, saw Churchill at work in
committee, something suddenly angered him; he left his chair

and paced the room, muttering to himself, "this stocky figure, with a slight stoop, striding up and down, suddenly completely unconscious of any presence beyond his own thoughts . . ."[39]

"Winston", remarks Lord Chandos (Oliver Lyttelton), "regarded committees as an opportunity for ventilating his own views, or even for giving his speeches a trial run: he was frequently irrelevant and often impatient."[40] When he chaired the War Cabinet, its members had to accept that, as some writers "think on paper", Churchill thought by talking, and they were present primarily to assist the progress of his thoughts.

By contrast, Churchill at first, when he had to, wooed the Commons like a youthful gigolo questing for the fortune of an ageing widow. He became essential to their self-esteem. In the secret sessions, one independent left-wing M.P. relates, Churchill was "at his greatest . . . He would share with us facts and figures which seemed, on any basis of logic, to add up to inevitable and imminent disaster. But his own stubborn courage made nonsense of logic, and we would troop out of the House at the end of the debate feeling that Britain was invincible."[41]

'. . . I am first of all a parliamentarian and House of Commons man," he assured M.P.s, not insincerely. "If I have any say in matters at the present time, it is due mainly to this House . . ." His task, he suggested on another occasion, would be "superhuman" without, of all things, their "guidance". This obsequiousness grew less marked as his state of "indispensability" dawned more fully upon him, and by 1942 his attitude was, like Neville Chamberlain's only more so, "My friends, leave it to me." The House, he chided it in July 1942 when it seemed to have some cause to dispose of him, "must be a steady, stabilizing factor." It must leave him a free hand "to act and dare". When at last, more or less by accident, it defeated his coalition in a vote, over such a small question as whether women teachers should receive equal pay with men or not, Churchill was petulant. He had maintained his ingratiating habit of dropping into the smoking room of the Commons and holding court there over a small, slow glass, which made every M.P. feel that the Great Man was his personal crony. There, at this time, Harold Nicolson found him rounding on a hapless member who had suggested that Churchill was perhaps making too much of this small issue. " 'No,' said Winston. 'Not at all. I am not going to tumble round my cage like a wounded canary. You knocked me off my perch. You have now got to put me back on my perch. Otherwise I won't sing.' "[42]

Not every M.P., in Lyttleton's phrase, "swallowed it whole". Besides the anti-war members, who were given a hearing but not taken seriously, there was an all-party band of malcontents, Shinwell included, who raised awkward questions and sometimes voted against Churchill, and there was a small group of Labour members, including Aneurin Bevan, who came to provide a consistent Socialist ginger-group-cum-opposition. Bevan also read history, and cast himself as Fox to Churchill's Pitt. As early as August 1940, while admitting Churchill's "unchallenged" leadership, he was pointing out that "in a democracy, idolatry is the first sin." Later, he ventured impolite comparisons between the House of Commons and Hitler's Reichstag. He was Churchill's only peer in debate now that Lloyd George was almost silenced by age. He had overcome his own impediment, a stutter, and, speaking fluently without many notes, his silvery Welsh accent and his savage turn of phrase made him a formidable adversary. To the loyal mob he seemed diabolically sinister. It was Eleanor Rathbone, a woman M.P. normally Independent in fact as well as in name, who declared, after one of Bevan's on-slaughts, "It is with disgust and almost loathing we watch this kind of temperament, these cattish displays of feline malice."[43]

Mrs. Churchill once said to her husband's doctor, "You prob-ably don't realize, Charles, that he knows nothing of the life of ordinary people. He's never been in a bus and only once on the Underground." When Churchill remarked to him, absurdly, "I don't know about oratory, but I do know what is in people's minds and how to speak to them," Moran mused, "Though he may have learnt by long experience the feel of an audience, he knows nothing of their lives, their hopes and aspirations. When he speaks it is to express his ideas; he says a piece." But Moran went on to enunciate what soon became the received opinion on Churchill's relationship with the British people in 1940. "His countrymen [Moran wrote] have come to feel that he is saying what they would like to say for themselves if they knew how."[44]

This view can neither be contradicted nor accepted on the basis of any factual evidence. But it does seem true, almost a truism, that Churchill's famous phrases – "blood, sweat, toil and tears", "their finest hour", "we shall never surrender" – did express something inarticulate, perhaps dormant but perhaps not, in the hearts and minds of his countrymen, of most classes. They achieved their effort by a heroic yet very simple expression of the will to resist ("we shall fight them in the hills"), and by invoking the naïve sense of nationhood and history which most of his literate subjects shared with him. Undoubtedly, the middle classes at least, hearing his perorations, felt that they stood with Churchill on the heroic landscape of his imagination, and that the spirits of Alfred the Great and Nelson were with them. No other politician had the literary equipment and physical presence to give that kind of lead. One may ask, however, whether this was the only kind of leadership which could have rallied the nation, or if, indeed, the nation was much in need of rallying.

For, although Churchill had made a large impact in the "Bore War" period, he appeared in May 1940 as the new man, thrown up by the very situation which he called on all classes to defy. He was part of that situation, he did not transcend it, he expressed defiance, he did not create it, and as those particular circumstances receded, so his magic dwindled. In 1940, he had the nation behind him but not yet, completely, the House of Commons; after 1941 he had the House of Commons for his footstool, while the nation increasingly saw him as another politician, "the best talker we've got".

The public opinion polls show that between July 1940 and May 1945, never less than seventy-eight per cent of those questioned said they approved of Churchill's Prime Ministership, and never more than one in six, on any individual poll, disapproved of it.[45] Allowance must be made for the constant official warnings against "defeatist" talk – how were those polled to be sure that their questioner was not an *agent provocateur*? But Churchill clearly achieved and retained a popularity far greater than – because different in kind from – that of any peacetime leader. For he was seen as essentially a war leader, and his rejection by the electorate in 1945 was the result of this longstanding image of him, not of any sudden access of ingratitude.

Meanwhile, in the summer of 1940, how did the public know him? Primarily, through the microphone. Baldwin, the first British leader to master the radio, had achieved his effect by talking plainly and warmly, as if he were part of each of the cosy groups gathered round the fire to hear him. Churchill, however, never tried to adapt his technique to radio. He orated into the microphone; and perhaps, in the summer of 1940, this helped to make listeners feel that they were putting domesticity behind them for the time being. He radiated his courage over the microphone as successfully as he pumped blood into the sclerotic arteries of the House of Commons. He made only five broadcasts between May 13th, 1940 and September 11th, and one of these was merely a re-reading of a speech previously given in the

Commons; but when he spoke nearly seven out of ten people heard him.[46]

There were also photographs, and glimpses. In these, Churchill appeared well out of the usual rut of politicians. There were, of course, the famous cigars. In private, Churchill chewed the ends and often let them go out while he was working; they would last him up to a couple of hours. In public, he was studious never to be without one. Admirers begged the stubs from those around him, or swooped to pick them up where they fell. There were his endless variations on the theme of sartorial unconventionality; his "rompers", his sailor suits, his peaked naval cap, his sea boots in the snow. The crowds who lined the street saw an old man, surprisingly short, stumping along with a stick, turning to thrust his forefingers at them in the famous V salute, a reversed and bowdlerized variant of a gesture known to schoolboys as "the figs".

And whatever their private opinions, all classes were clear that there nowhere was, nor ever had been, anyone quite like this man they were cheering. Such singularity, in such a high position, could only amount to greatness, and it was profoundly reassuring to suppose that Britain was led at this moment by a great man.

V

The war aims of the new administration had been defined for it by Churchill, in one word: Victory. At which many worried souls on the left, and some on the right, murmured, yes, but for what? Since September 1939, there had been a clamour of Liberals and Socialists calling for "positive war aims". From May 1940 the same voices called insistently for the Labour leaders to force Churchill to answer the question. And Attlee himself, Harold Nicolson gathered in July, was anxious that "we should put before the country a definite pronouncement on Government policy for the future . . . a positive and revolutionary aim admitting that the old order has collapsed and asking people to fight for the new order."

Nicolson, now Parliamentary Secretary to the Ministry of Information, found that Duff Cooper, his chief, was inclined to agree that "nothing will prove an alternative to Hitler's total programme except a pledge of federalism abroad and socialism at home." Cooper, like other thoughtful Conservatives, was badly rattled by the events of 1940. But when Nicolson himself had joined Lord Halifax in drafting a statement of war aims along these lines, Churchill, in January 1941, turned it down flat, giving the reason in cabinet that "precise aims would be compromising, whereas vague principles would disappoint." In practice, Churchill violently deprecated any mention of war aims by his ministers.[47]

What this meant was, not that the coalition had no war aims, but that willy-nilly its aims were Churchill's. And his aim was simply to defend Britain's power. In a celebrated speech in November 1942, he declared, "We mean to hold our own. I have not become the King's First Minister in order to preside over the liquidation of the British Empire."[48]

Imperialism was part of the very texture of his personality. He had written, "I was a child of the Victorian era, when the structure of our country seemed firmly set, when its position in trade and on the seas was unrivalled, and when the realization of the greatness of our Empire and of our duty to preserve it was ever growing stronger."[49] Which was true of his leading colleagues as well. Of those who at various times served in the War Cabinet, Beaverbrook (born 1879); Greenwood (1880); Halifax, Wood and Bevin (1881); Anderson (1882); Attlee and Woolton (1883) had all been in their thirties before the First World War had clouded the skies of the Empire on which the sun never set. Morrison (1888) and Cripps (1889) had been only slightly younger, and the babies, Lyttelton (1893) and Eden (1897), had been old enough to hear the Elgarian themes of national greatness at their loudest before the din of guns had drowned them. While the Conservative Party was emotionally committed to Empire for its own sake, Labour was intellectually committed to its mutation, through self-government, into something less brazenly British. But both viewed the overseas possessions, together with the Dominions, as actually or potentially an immense power for good in the world.

Conversely, Churchill retained a vestigial liberalism which led some commentators to diagnose his politics as Whig rather than Tory. His youthful role of the Fearless Reformer had long since been discarded, but he was not merely making propaganda late in 1940 when he cried out in a broadcast to the French, "Long live . . . the forward march of the common people in all the lands towards their just and true inheritance, and towards the broader and fuller age." Much later in the war he explained that the principle on which the coalition had always been based was

"Everything for the war, whether controversial or not, and nothing controversial that is not *bona fide* needed for the war."[50] Nationalization of coal, which he was talking about, was not a "*bona fide*" need in his estimation. But as a practical political technician committed to victory, he could not and did not strive to resist the inexorable pressures pushing the nation towards what his generation called "socialism". Like the Labour leaders he thought of socialism as consisting essentially in the central organization of national resources – it might be, by the present ruling class. Socialism was a marriage of planning and the old sort of liberal-capitalist democracy; there was no thought of a new democracy.

"I can remember no case where differences arose between Conservatives, Labour and Liberals along party lines. Certainly not in the War Cabinet. Certainly not in the big things," Attlee has said. ". . . When one came to work out solutions they were often socialist ones, because one had to have organization, and planning, and disregard vested interests. But there was no opposition from Conservative ministers. They accepted the practical solution whatever it was." Lord Woolton implicitly supports this. ". . . We arrived at a position", he writes, "in which, in time of war, the practices that would be normal under a socialist state seemed to be the only safeguards of the country."[51] Attlee and Morrison would seek to preserve some, but not all, of these "practices", Churchill and Woolton hoped to dismantle them, but for the moment all were in agreement, except when it came to large-scale nationalization.

Churchill saw nothing controversial about "plans" of a less odious kind which would sustain "the forward march" in the transition from war to peace. Arthur Greenwood was made Minister with Portfolio at the end of 1940 and was entrusted with setting such plans in motion in what Churchill called "four or five great spheres of action" in which "practical and immediate advance" might be made if national unity were maintained into the hypothetical peace.[52] Pensions, homes, jobs; the sorts of questions which Churchill had once tackled boldly as a Liberal minister.

In a famous cartoon of May 1940, David Low showed Churchill and the Labour leaders marching together at the head of the coalition ministers, rolling up their sleeves. To depict reality, he should have shown Churchill walking apart and ahead with a small group of confidants, Ernest Bevin striding away by himself not far behind them, and the rest following in double file.

Churchill's intimates exercised much more influence than the War Cabinet members did, collectively or individually, though Brendan Bracken, a witty and enigmatic financier, distinguished by a flaming crop of untidy red hair, held no ministerial post until he became Minister of Information in the summer of 1941, and Frederick Lindemann, who became Lord Cherwell in 1941, had no ministry until 1942, when he became merely Paymaster General.

Lindemann had long been a crony of Churchill's. A reserved, eccentric and reactionary bachelor, he had been a distinguished physicist, Professor of Experimental Philosophy at Oxford. Churchill called him "the Prof". When he went to the Admiralty in 1939, he took Lindemann with him to run a statistical branch. After May 1940, this remained his personal statistical staff. Churchill did not have a truly "scientific" cast of mind, but he loved gadgets and could rapidly grasp the potential of new weapons. This was initially his common ground with Lindemann. But Lindemann's influence went far beyond technical matters. One of his assistants in the statistical section has remarked, ". . . from my own observation I would say that he devoted more time to economic questions than to those of science."[53] One of Lindemann's favourite subjects was food. This valetudinarian, who munched egg-white sandwiches at official banquets, confirmed his friend Churchill in his vigorous resistance to any premature introduction of "austerity" measures.

Lord Beaverbrook was the most spectacular of the cronies. He had been born in Canada, in a Presbyterian manse, and throughout his career he showed an unusually acute sense of good and evil, generally choosing the latter. In the First World War, he had been at the centre of the intrigues which had replaced Asquith with Lloyd George, and he had never lost his taste for plotting. He was, more even than most public figures, a man of contradictions. When his friend was under fire for his activities at the Ministry of Aircraft Production (which had involved him in noisy rows with the Air Ministry, the Ministry of Labour, the Ministry of Supply and even, so provocative he was, with the Ministry of Agriculture), Churchill told the House of Commons that Beaverbrook was "a man of altogether exceptional force and genius, who is at his very best when things are at their worst". Yet, in eleven months at this post, Beaverbrook attempted to resign no less than four times before he finally departed on grounds of "ill-health". At this juncture, he told Churchill, "you are the only guardian of Mankind."[54] One is often pleased to

discover odd hints of whimsy and irony lurking beneath the
ultra-laconic, ultra-businesslike surface of Beaverbrook's staccato
prose, but there is no doubt that he admired Churchill to the
verge of hero worship. On the other hand, if there was one
minister whose actions during the war suggested that he hoped
to replace Churchill, that man was Beaverbrook. He was obsessed with power, yet terrified of failure if he exercised it;
plagued with an asthma symptomatic of a divided soul. Cartoon-
ists always portrayed him with a huge impish grin splitting the
large head which dominated his small body; yet his colleagues
knew him as a man commonly grey and grim.

The *Daily Express*, under his ownership, had become Britain's
most widely read, but perhaps least influential, national newspaper. In recent years, it had supported Chamberlain. It had
insisted in 1939 that there would be no war; once war had started,
it had ineffectually but loudly attempted to whip up popular
feeling against rationing and other necessary extensions of
bureaucracy. Beaverbrook certainly directed his paper's policies,
but to see him as an orthodox man of the far right, on the strength
of this and his besotted devotion to the Empire, would be wide of
the mark. The *Express* (like its evening stablemate, the *Standard*,
which employed Low) hired many of the best left-wing journalists.
In the 1930s, to increase its circulation in Scotland, Beaverbrook
had ostentatiously flirted with Scottish Nationalism. In the
winter of 1939, for whatever dark reasons, Beaverbrook had
invited the three I.L.P. M.P.s to meet him at his London mansion
and had offered to give at least five hundred pounds for every
candidate they put up, and all the resources of publicity at his
command, if these pacifists would fight every parliamentary
vacancy. They had declined. Beaverbrook was capable of
turning up, twinkling mischievously, in any corner of the field of
politics. ". . . No man in any party trusts Max," Lloyd George
had remarked in 1918; it was still true.[55]

Yet Churchill not only tolerated his stream of resignations and
the bad tempers which he caused in cabinet, he relied heavily on
Beaverbrook's friendship – Attlee remarked later that he "took
him as a kind of stimulant or drug".[56] In August 1940, he brought
him into the War Cabinet, several weeks before Beaverbrook's
enemy of enemies, Bevin, was given the same honour.

Bevin, by contrast, was a man of clear, great, yet limited ambitions, and intense undeviating loyalties. Born the son of a
landless Somerset farm labourer, he had begun work as a farm
boy at eleven; at eighteen, the age when most of his new colleagues

had been contemplating the transition from public school to university, Bevin had been a drayman in Bristol. He had not joined a trade union until he was nearly thirty, but between the wars he had engrossed nearly two score lesser unions into his own massive Transport and General Workers'. Its bloc vote had made him the biggest man at Labour Party conferences; he had wielded it heavily and consistently in support of armed resistance to Hitler.

He hated "intellectuals" and applied the term indiscriminately to anyone on the left who disagreed with him. "He had a majority mind," one of his biographers remarks.[57] He enjoyed power blatantly, and ruled his union despotically. He was addicted to the first person singular. Yet he gave Clement Attlee, an intellectual in fact, his absolute loyalty. He gave similar loyalty to Churchill, though of all War Cabinet members he was the one who could, and would, argue with the Great Man.

His favourite joke in the summer of 1940 was, "They say Gladstone was at the Treasury from 1860 to 1930. I'm going to be Minister of Labour from 1940 to 1990."[58] Some T.U.C. colleagues were surprised that he should accept the hitherto minor post of Minister of Labour. But Bevin saw a chance to fulfil his work as a union organizer, which had lain largely amongst sweated or ill-organized trades, and those who worked in peculiarly bad conditions. Having acquired what seemed to him sufficient power over the fortunes of the working class, he clung jealously to it, as Beaverbrook found. He built his ministry into a great office of state; more important, at the time, than the Exchequer itself.

Towards the organized working classes, whom he called, biblically enough, "my people", his attitude was that of an elder brother left to rear an enormous family. As Churchill conceived a race of Drakes and Nelsons, so Bevin embodied and spoke for and to a working class of, well, Bevins – sober, thick-sinewed men who had overcome their early abhorrence of their employers, had educated themselves, and would now show the bosses how to do the job properly. After the failure of the General Strike in 1926, Bevin had led the retreat from industrial action towards "Mondism", a doctrine which sought to win for the trade unions a confirmed place in the councils of their industries, neither as serfs or masters, but as partners. No one was less of a red revolutionary than Bevin, an early convert to the ideas of J. M. Keynes. Yet he remained aggressively proletarian, strewing his aitches down the corridors of power, refusing to broadcast on the "prestige spot" after the nine o'clock news on Sunday which was fancied by other ministers, and choosing instead to go out after the one o'clock news, when he could speak to "his" people, "sitting down nice and comfortable to their Sunday dinner".[59]

To the middle classes, on the left as well as on the right, he was a somewhat disgusting phenomenon, though those who expected a raucous Cockney bellow were surprised by his voice, which was still the rich, slightly husky Somerset burr of his youth. His speeches read badly; they were studded with the mutilated torsos of powerful thoughts. Yet to those who heard him give them, the impression of power and of startling, wide-ranging intelligence overrode his verbal limitations.

Like Beaverbrook, he inspired love or loathing, never indifference. The Archbishop of Canterbury noted nervously in his diary in July 1940 that in Bevin he seemed to see "a possible Labour dictator of the future". To J. B. Priestley, in a famous broadcast given at about the same time, when he described looking down from the House of Commons gallery on Bevin's powerful, fleshy body with its squashed looking, square, bespectacled face, as it slumped beside Churchill's on the Government front bench, he seemed to represent "the other half of the English people".[60]

Sir John Anderson, on the other hand, represented no section of the human race whatsoever, unless he can be seen as the epitome of the Civil Service where he had made his career. Before the computer was perfected, Anderson was a tolerable substitute. Early in 1940, Mass Observation had noted that "Probably no cabinet minister has a lower public appeal ... His rather formal and uncompromising manner has never infused into the machinery for which he is responsible any warmth, humour or general sympathy likely to appeal to the many."[61] Even among civil servants where he was most at home, he was nicknamed "Pompous John" or "Jehovah". He was alleged, by one or two admirers, to have a streak of dour humour in him; if so, his wit was as dry as a fine, invisible dust. The Bishop of Winchester was present on one occasion when Anderson was talking to King George on the subject of air raid shelters. At one point, Anderson absentmindedly responded to the King's remarks with "But my dear man!!" The King roared with laughter. Anderson remained impassive.[62]

The son of a petty Edinburgh fancy stationer, he had entered the Civil Service with the second highest mark ever recorded in its examination; had his paper on political science not been poor, he would have been second to no one. He had then followed a distinguished course of repression. He had controlled the Black and Tans in Ireland; he had invented the regional machinery now used in Civil Defence for the purpose of repressing the General Strike; he had left the Home Office to go to India, as Governor of Bengal, to repress the natives, then restless. Returning in 1938 and entering parliament, his unique talent for repression had been recognized by Chamberlain, who had made him Lord Privy Seal to perfect the mechanisms whereby a panicking population might be repressed in the event of air raids; in three letters, A.R.P. "Don't talk to us as though we were a lot of niggers," an exasperated Labour M.P. once shouted across the Commons during one of Anderson's uniquely tedious speeches.[63]

Yet after Bevin, Anderson was probably the most essential of Churchill's ministers. Who else, with centralized planning in a rudimentary state, could so calmly have confronted the enormous statistics of the war economy and coped with them? When, in October 1940, Anderson was removed from the delicate position of Home Secretary to succeed Chamberlain as Lord President, the press, hooting after him, thought he had been "kicked upstairs". In fact, the Lord President's Committee became, in Churchill's words, "almost a parallel cabinet concerned with home affairs". Had the mocking Gods chosen, they might easily have made Anderson, whom Churchill once referred to as his "automatic pilot", the Prime Minister of Britain. When both Churchill and Eden flew to Yalta near the end of the war, Churchill advised the King that Anderson should succeed him if both died in a crash.[64]

Attlee was, therefore, Churchill's deputy but not his heir-apparent. Legend has it that Churchill once called him "a modest little man with plenty to be modest about". With his slight build, his neat dress, his bald pate and his unflamboyant moustache, Attlee looked like a town clerk or a public school housemaster. He had become leader of his party almost by default. When George Lansbury, after a ruthless attack by Bevin, had resigned shortly before the 1935 General Election, Attlee was one of the very few men actually sitting with the tiny Parliamentary Labour Party who had had any administrative experience. (This was not so accidental, however, as it seemed; Attlee had given his devotion to the East End, and sat for a Stepney seat which had proved unconquerable in 1931 when other Labour strongholds had been smashed.) When Morrison and Dalton, more notable men than Attlee, had duly found themselves seats again in the election, Attlee was already entrenched. Dalton took this in good part, Morrison not so well.

Morrison, the brisk and bouncy one-eyed son of a policeman, had risen to prominence in London's local government, and in 1934 had become "Prime Minister" of Labour's majority on the London County Council. He was usually called "a typical Cockney" by commentators who knew no Cockneys. He had no look or sound of the East End about him; in his origins and early life, he belonged to the world of H. G. Wells's Kipps and Mr. Polly, the shabby-genteel outer suburbs. Ernest Bevin, perhaps partly for this reason, abhorred him, and it was on the rock of Bevin's opposition that attempts before, during and after the war to replace Attlee with Morrison were shattered.

In fact, Attlee remained leader of his squally party for twenty years, an all-comers' record in British politics. Even to his own supporters, he seemed colourless, almost transparent. Yet his speeches were concise and effective; his laconic humour was real, and often memorable, and his chairmanship belied the legend of insignificance. Attlee spoke to ministers as sharply as Churchill spoke to civil servants; if he chaired a committee in Churchill's absence, far more work was done, though far less fun was had by all. Attlee now seems an oddly inspiring figure, almost unique as a politician in his lack of corruption. His modesty, not a negative quality, but an exact knowledge of his own limitations, was his most remarkable strength.

The other future Prime Minister who sat in the War Cabinet was Anthony Eden. Almost throughout the war, he was the minister most popular with the general public, primarily because of a youthful face which would have commanded good money in Hollywood. As Dominions Secretary, Secretary for War and Foreign Secretary, he could do little which affected the man in the street, who could therefore lay no grievance at his door. It was not until he finally reached the highest office that it was found that he had a great deal more to be modest about than Attlee.

Eden's one important intervention in the lives of the British people at war was an immensely popular one – nobody realized that the idea which his pleasant voice announced over the radio on the evening of May 14th, 1940 had been launched under his predecessor at the War Office.

The German success in Belgium and Holland, Eden explained, had shown how dangerous parachute attack might be to Britain itself.

Since the war began [he went on], the Government has received countless inquiries from all over the kingdom, from men of all ages who are for one reason or another not at present engaged in military service and who wish to do something for the defence of the country.

Now is your opportunity. We want large numbers of such men in Great Britain who are British subjects, between the ages of fifteen and sixty-five, to come forward now and offer their services in order to make assurance doubly sure. The name of the new force which is now to be raised will be the Local Defence Volunteers.[65]

Enrolment was to take place at the local police stations. Within twenty-four hours, long before most people had much notion who the members of their new Government were, over a quarter of a million men had offered their services.

DUNKIRK

I said, "Any ideas about *how* we shall win?"

"Oh, the usual formula," said Carter. "Mastery of the air with American help. Bomb their factories to blazes. Stir up trouble in the occupied countries, and there you are."

"Time factor for this process – ?" I said.

"Oh, God knows," said Carter with a grin. "We leave that bit out."

I said, "Oh well, we always do win things."

"Yes," said Carter. "Between ourselves I think that's really the best argument at the moment."

Conversation in the autumn of 1940, from Nigel Balchin's
Darkness Falls from The Air[1]

I

The weather in the early summer of 1940 was glorious. Day after day was warm, dry and sunny; in June the temperature reached ninety degrees. A mood was built out of the contrast which was felt so strongly between the familiar smells of mown grass and sticky grease, and the news from the Continent.

At first, optimism was possible, as French and British soldiers moved into the Low Countries to counter the German attack. ". . . B.E.F. SWEEPS ON" was a *Times* headline on the 13th. But next day Rotterdam was bombed (by mistake). Though only a thousand civilians were in fact killed, it was thought at the time that thirty thousand had died, in a foretaste of the Armageddon which the British had ceased to expect. On the 15th, the Dutch army capitulated. Churchill had been woken that morning by a call from Reynaud, the French Prime Minister. "We are beaten," Reynaud said. "We have lost the battle."[2] The Germans had broken the French front near Sedan, and were pouring their tanks and armoured cars through the breach. They, not the allies, had absorbed the new tactics which the British experts on armoured warfare, Fuller and Liddell Hart, had been teaching, and they moved at a pace never known in warfare before.

On the 17th, Brussels fell. That day, the American Embassy advised the four thousand or so U.S. citizens in Britain to return home as quickly as possible. (But some stayed, and in spite of a still more urgent warning early next month, an American squadron of the Local Defence Volunteers was formed in London.) A mood of panic was gripping upper-class circles. "My own private courage was badly bruised," writes Cecil Beaton, "and each person one spoke to was more depressing than the last." He decided, after some hesitation, to fulfil a contract in the U.S.A., and travelled to Liverpool with a trainload of "dark and depressed refugees" – mostly German-speaking. "A huge businessman, slumped opposite me, was in a ghastly state of apprehension. He groaned, sighed, raised his eyes to heaven and tried to command sleep, but his tortured imagination prevented that, and he came to in a renewed frenzy."[3]

For this was "Blitzkrieg", lightning war. It was novel enough; but, stunned by the collapse of their expectations of a repetition of the First War, people in Britain exaggerated the novelty of the German tactics. Anything seemed possible, to judge by exaggerated accounts of what had happened in Norway, Holland and Belgium. There might – there would – be massive airborne landings in Britain. There would be parachutists disguised in British uniforms or dressed as nuns. Fifth columnists – Fascists, aliens, and also previously blameless pillars of the community – would assist the Germans. And there would be the all-destroying air raids to which the name "blitz" eventually attached itself.

By nightfall on the 20th, the Germans had reached the Channel coast. Feeble French generalship had left most of the British Expeditionary Force, the Belgian troops, and many Frenchmen, surrounded in a small pocket inland from Dunkirk.

On the 22nd, the House of Commons passed, in exactly three hours, an extension of the original Emergency Powers Act of the previous August. Introducing this, Attlee explained, "... It is necessary that the Government should be given complete control over persons and property, not just some persons of some particular class of the community, but of all persons, rich and poor, employer and workman, man or woman, and all property."[4] Ernest Bevin, as Minister of Labour, was empowered to direct any person to perform any service he thought fit, and set the wages, the hours and conditions of the job. Excess Profits Tax was raised to a hundred per cent. On the same day, parliament passed a Treachery Act providing for the use of the death penalty in grave cases of espionage and sabotage. The bark of the new measures proved to be far worse than their bite. But their psychological impact was considerable.

By the 24th, it was clear that the B.E.F. was cut off. In a London children's hospital, "The out-patients' department was unusually quiet. The mothers talked to each other in low voices ... Even the children had no heart for the rocking horse."[5]

As the Belgian defence crumbled, Lord Gort, the commander of the B.E.F., decided to evacuate his men through Dunkirk. Unwashed, unshaven and exhausted British soldiers moved in a steady stream into the port, which was smoking from the enemy's bombs. It seemed at first that only about one-fifth of the 250,000 British troops could possibly escape. But the German armour, with Hitler's acquiescence, was halted south of Dunkirk on the 24th and did not roll again until the 27th. This was a crucial error by the Germans. The Luftwaffe alone, harassed by fighters operating from bases in England, could not prevent the evacuation. Fighter Command, however, had to use its planes thriftily; for periods of forty to ninety minutes, there would be no air cover over the port, and the R.A.F. was roundly cursed by the soldiers and sailors below.

On the 27th came the expected news that the Belgians had given in. The destruction of Belgian resistance was especially sickening to those who remembered the heroism of these allies in the First World War. King Leopold, unlike the Queen of Holland, stayed with his defeated people, and was much execrated as a traitor to the cause of freedom.

But meanwhile, on the 26th, the evacuation from Dunkirk had begun. Each day brought miraculous, unhoped for signs, in advance of official confirmation, that more, and more, and more troops had been brought out; eight thousand on the 27th, eighteen thousand on the 28th, forty-seven thousand on the 29th, fifty-four thousand on the 30th, a peak of sixty-eight thousand on the 31st, sixty-four thousand next day. There was relief for anxious relatives; a calming of fears that Britain might be left defenceless; and a steadily growing wonderment at what seemed to be a triumph of improvisation. From the humiliation of defeat, the British clutched symbols of defiance – a brightly painted paddle steamer, a tiny pleasure yacht, a trawler, a shrimper, a crabber, a tug, braving the Stukas and the mines of the Channel to bring the boys home.

Over the one o'clock news, the fishermen of Leo Walmsley's Yorkshire village heard the appeal for small boats of any kind to help in the evacuation. In the harbour, men worked furiously that afternoon to launch two keelers "neaped" on the beach for repainting. Efforts to dig them away were failing when somebody brought in a fire engine and two A.F.S. motor pumps to deepen the channels with their jets. Then came disappointment – the men whose wives had worked to provide the three days' rations the Government had ordered for the trip, learnt, late in the afternoon, that they were not needed.[6]

But other boats had gone. After daylight evacuation had become impossible, the dark Channel was full of craft large and small, travelling without lights through wrecks and minefields. The navy, of course, brought most of the men out. The next greatest part was played by Southern Railways' Channel steamers, familiar as buses to peacetime holiday-makers abroad, *The Maid of Kent, The Isle of Guernsey, The Maid of Orleans* and their stablemates. Hundreds of small boats of all kinds made a contribution small in statistics, but huge in its moral effect.

"We've known them and laughed at them, these fussy little steamers, all our lives," said the comfortable Yorkshire voice of J. B. Priestley in a broadcast, on June 5th, which made him a rival to Churchill as a master of morale. "We have called them 'the shilling sicks'. We have watched them load and unload their crowds of holiday passengers – the gents full of high spirits and bottled beer, the ladies eating pork pies, the children sticky with peppermint rock." He mourned the loss of the *Gracie Fields*, pride of the Isle of Wight ferry service, sunk in the Channel. "But now – look – this little steamer, like all her brave and battered sisters, is immortal. She'll go sailing proudly down the years in the epic of Dunkirk. And our great grandchildren, when they learn how we began this war by snatching glory out of defeat, and then swept on to victory, may also learn how the little holiday steamers made an excursion to hell and came back glorious.'"[7]

In the ports and towns of the south coast, large sections of the population were swept up into the feverish activity which surrounded the troops' return. The hitherto obscure railway station at Headcorn, in Kent, with a staff of one master and two porters, suddenly arrived at celebrity by feeding 145,000 troops. Forty or fifty ladies of the neighbourhood worked eight-hour shifts for nine days and nights to prepare the food which the army had provided.[8]

Elsewhere, the Women's Volunatary Service, formed two years before primarily to assist in A.R.P., performed prodigies of foot washing, sock darning and food serving.

But the mood of the troops was not one of pious gratitude for a great deliverance. Many of them had not even fired a shot in anger. They had left their tanks and cars and artillery behind them. ENSA (the Entertainments National Service Association) was asked to lay on non-stop film shows for the men who had returned. Its director, Basil Dean, went down to Bridport in Dorset to further this scheme.

> The town [he writes] was crammed to suffocation. In a small pub . . . we exchanged impressions and made further plans, listening to the seething soldiery (yes, that is the only adjective to use) expressing blasphemous resentment at what had happened to them. There was a typical "Sergeant Troy" in the bar whose loud-mouthed criticism of the junior officers of his Ack Ack unit in seizing the only available transport and making for the French coast, leaving their N.C.O.s and men to fend for themselves, was gaining angry corroboration among his listeners. These dismayed men, savagely wounded in their pride, were seeking relief in bitter criticism of those set over them. We promised each other that whilst the war lasted we would never speak of what we had seen and heard that night, and we never did.[9]

But though civilians were bound to be struck and infected by this very general attitude, their own first reaction was usually one of relief, of pride, of triumph. The *Daily Mirror* headlined an editorial on Dunkirk:

BLOODY
MARVELLOUS

On June 4th, the British rearguard was withdrawn from the port; two days later, after a great many French had followed them, the approach of the Germans at last halted the evacuation. Altogether, 338,226 troops had been brought off, of whom 225,000 were British.

Churchill, addressing the Commons that evening, reminded his audience that "Wars are not won by evacuations." Dunkirk, he said, represented a "colossal military disaster". He dwelt on the dangers of invasion, and prophesied that much would depend on the Air Force. He ended with a peroration aimed at American as well as British opinion:

> ... We shall not flag or fail. We shall go on to the end, we shall fight in France, we shall fight on the seas and oceans, we shall fight with growing confidence and growing strength in the air, we shall defend our island, whatever the cost may be, we shall fight on the beaches, we shall fight on the landing grounds, we shall fight in the fields and in the streets, we shall fight in the hills; we shall never surrender, and even if, which I do not for a moment believe, this island or a large part of it were subjugated and starving, then our Empire beyond the seas, armed and guarded by the British fleet, would carry on the struggle, until, in God's good time, the new world, with all its power and might, steps forth to the rescue and the liberation of the old.

Of the many apocryphal anecdotes about Churchill, perhaps the best of all is the one that has him muttering, at a pause in that famous peroration, "and beat the b——s about the head with bottles: that's all we've got."[10]

Instead of coming straight across the Channel after the B.E.F. as many people in Britain expected, the Germans turned southward, to strike at the heart of France. The evacuated French troops passed out again through English ports to resume the battle and with them went Britain's only two formed divisions, to join the 51st Highland Division, which was still fighting; when the latter was forced to surrender on the 12th, eight thousand Scotsmen passed into prisoner of war camps. Further small "Dunkirks" took place later to bring the rest away, 136,000 in all.

On June 10th, Mussolini, who had hovered like a vulture over France's struggles, declared war on the allies. On the 14th, the Germans entered Paris. On the 16th, Reynaud resigned and was succeeded by Marshal Pétain. On June 22nd, an armistice between France and Germany was signed at Compiègne.

On the 18th, when it was clear that Britain "stood alone", Churchill again appealed, implicitly, to the U.S.A., but what he said provided two new stock quotations for the British:

What General Weygand called the Battle of France is over.
I expect that the Battle of Britain is about to begin . . . Let us
therefore brace ourselves to our duties, and so bear ourselves
that, if the British Empire and its Commonwealth last for a
thousand years, men will still say, "This was their finest
hour."[11]

II

Returning to London after handing out tea and chocolate to
two long trainloads of French *poilus* at Guildford station,
Mrs. Robert Henrey observed that, "all along the line young
men in flannels were playing cricket in the sunshine on beautifully
tended fields shaded by stalwart oaks and poplar trees."[12]

From such sights, the myth of the *sang froid habituel* of the
perfidious English drew great strength. When General de Gaulle,
then relatively obscure, arrived in London on June 9th, he found
that it had "a look of tranquillity, almost indifference. The
streets and parks full of people peacefully out for a walk, the long
queues at the entrances to the cinemas, the many cars, the impressive porters outside the clubs and hotels, belonged to another
world than the one at war." During that summer, it is recorded,
the efforts of some three hundred bird-lovers to maintain a day
and night guard against egg collectors over the half a dozen
nesting places of the rare kite in the Welsh hills were crowned
with success. The American journalist, Drew Middleton, writes,
of the conversation in a Kentish pub in July, "This was a period
when the English habit of considering war as a series of small
personal affronts tried the nerves of foreigners in their midst.
Tea rationing had begun on July 9th and a good part of the
conversation was devoted to what 'my old woman' had said
about the Government as a result. There were also some highly
disrespectful remarks about the appointment of the Duke of
Windsor to be Governor of the Bahamas. Of the prospects for
survival and victory, nothing."[13]

But if Middleton had wished to present a different picture, he
would have found plenty ready for his pen. To the *Radio Times*,
a Mr. Wilkins wrote from Buckinghamshire, "I beseech you to
cease broadcasting racing and sports news at such a time . . .
shame, shame, shame." George Orwell wrote in his diary on
June 6th, "Everything is disintegrating. It makes me writhe to be
writing book reviews etc. at such a time, and even angers me that

such time wasting should be permitted." On May 26th, perhaps as a symptom of precisely such trouble in the souls of many, the churches had been unwontedly full for a National Day of Prayer, "miraculously" rewarded in the week which ensued. In Southampton, "Even the Guildhall was not big enough to accommodate more than half the congregation that flooded to the united service," and two thousand stood in the forecourt to hear it relayed through loudspeakers.[14]

Donald Johnson, then medical officer at a regimental headquarters, recalls of the Dunkirk period:

> From the moment when you woke up and thought, "Oh, my God" as you realized the position afresh, every morning was nightmarish. It was only after two or three beers at lunch that the situation did not seem quite so bad. But by three thirty in the afternoon it was desperate again – and it was time to get back to the Mess for another drink. Then in the evening the outlook depended entirely on the amount of alcohol you managed to consume. I use the plural "you" because everyone was in the same boat. That is everyone with the exception of the quartermaster, a British Israelite, whose readings of the Pyramids left him no room for doubt that, despite all appearances of disaster, Britain would be victorious. Serene, bespectacled, the quartermaster alone kept steadily, never varying, to his single pint of beer, morning and evening.[15]

Some people, especially young people, found the sense of danger exhilarating. "... There was this strange soaring of spirits," one woman has recalled. "Even the very colours of the summer seemed heightened, the sky bluer, the clouds whiter, and the darkness darker." For the cynical young leftists of the 'thirties, who had preoccupied themselves with the decline of British capitalism, the combination of violence with a cause to fight for might well be a relief. One of them, the poet Roy Fuller, wrote:

> At last the push of time has reached it; realer
> Today than for centuries England is on the map
> As a place where something occurs, as a springboard or trap.[16]

And, inevitably, people grew used to the sense of imminent peril. By June, the carrying of gas masks by civilians had risen again, from virtually nil to thirty per cent of those seen in the streets. By August, it had dropped back to ten per cent. People had been asked officially to make a habit of wearing them for a quarter of an hour each week. But, rightly as it turned out, most people now thought that gas would never be used.[17]

There had been real air raids, of no great significance outside the circles of those few who were killed or maimed, inoculating jabs before the "real" blitz. On April 30th, when a German mine-laying bomber with its mines on board had been shot down over Clacton in Essex, two people had been killed and a hundred and sixty-two injured; this had been the first test for Britain's Civil Defences. May 10th had seen the first deliberate attack on the mainland of Britain (though a raid on Scapa Flow had produced the first casualty, an Orkneyman, on March 16th). Bombs fell, without killing anyone, near Canterbury. During May and June, there was some light bombing of military targets. The first industrial town to suffer a raid was Middlesbrough, on May 24th. From June 18th, there were light raids every night, on the midlands, East Anglia and elsewhere. On June 19th, a bomb fell on the fringe of London.

There was a revival of the old shelter controversy, now that there was something to shelter from, and a first-rate scandal over the shortage of cement which had developed, and which was attributed by Communists and others to the manufacturers' "Cement Ring". On June 12th, the ineffable Anderson announced in parliament the completion of the shelter programme which he had launched some nineteen months before. Twenty million people, over half the civilian population, could now find shelter space simultaneously.[18]

When France fell, a great many people were worried by the thought that the Luftwaffe could now turn its attention wholly to Britain. But it is a superficially curious fact, attested from many sources, that a great sense of relief was a common emotion. "Now we know where we are! No more bloody allies!" a tug skipper shouted across the Thames to A. P. Herbert. George VI, that not untypical member of the English upper classes, wrote to his mother, "Personally I feel happier now that we have no allies to be polite to & to pamper."[19]

The alliance with France had meant little enough to most Britons. A war fought by the British alone had the merit of being a simple nationalist matter, like "international" football. The better side would win, and on 1914–18 form, that should be Britain. Those who knew their history could cheerfully follow form back for many centuries. "We're in the biggest mess since the Battle of Hastings," said one Welsh M.P. to Vera Brittain, on

June 18th.[20] People grew addicted to quoting Shakespeare's *King John*: "This England never did, nor never shall, Lie at the proud foot of a conqueror . . . Come the three corners of the world in arms, And we shall shock them."

III

The coalition brought a new attitude to the war but not, at first, many radically new measures to control the war economy.

The shift of attitude was, however, crucial. In May 1940, "Britain at last threw economic prudence to the winds." Spendings on the war rose from a weekly average of thirty-three million pounds in April to fifty-five million pounds in June. Chamberlain had been greatly interested in financial policy and had been identified with orthodoxy. Churchill was not greatly interested in finance and was prepared to tolerate unorthodoxy. While his Government maintained the anti-inflationary policy of its predecessor, it shifted the emphasis on to physical resources, away from the mysteries of money. If Britain was conquered, dollars would be no use to her; very well, let her commit herself to buying whatever munitions the U.S.A. could produce.[21]

The new Chancellor, Kingsley Wood, paid his own tribute to unorthodoxy by bringing the notorious John Maynard Keynes into the Treasury, as an adviser. But the budget which Wood introduced in July, to catch up with the new rate of expenditure, was sadly orthodox – *The Times* complained of "a few more turns of the old familiar screws". The standard rate of income tax was raised to eight shillings and sixpence in the pound. Surtax rates were raised and adjusted, so that those earning twenty thousand pounds or more were paying a peak rate of eighteen shillings in the pound, income tax and surtax combined. But there was also an increased burden on wage earners and small salary earners. The major innovation had already been forecast by Simon in April; this was the introduction of a totally new Purchase Tax, which was bitterly attacked by Labour M.P.s as regressive. Food and drink were exempt, as were children's clothing and boots. The basic rate would be thirty-three and a third per cent for luxuries and sixteen and two-thirds per cent for more necessary items, and a long list of consumer goods was affected. All this, coupled with further increases in the price of beer and cigarettes, led to cries in the House of Commons that this was an anti-working-class budget.[22] For an adequate adjustment to the rapid acceleration of the war effort the nation had to wait for the crucial budget of the following spring, in which Keynes's influence was very apparent.

The Nazi conquest of Europe, and the entry of Italy into the war, had made the import situation immensely graver. Major sources of such things as timber, iron, phosphates, flax, hemp and pit props for industry, and bacon, butter, milk, onions and tomatoes for the table, were now denied to Britain. The Mediterranean was now closed, which meant that ships from Asia and Australia must journey round the Cape of Good Hope. Yet as late as June, copper was still being used in sizable amounts for jewellery, curtain rails and other inessentials. Luxury foodstuffs were still being imported. The summer and autumn of 1940 saw only tentative measures to adjust the consumption of the British people to their siege position; 1941, again, was the year of reckoning.

In the summer of 1940 a committee of nutritional experts was appointed to advise the War Cabinet on food policy. They worked out a "Basal Diet" which, if the worst came to the worst, would be sufficient to maintain the health and the basic metabolic processes of the British people. Each citizen could survive, it was suggested, on twelve ounces of bread, a pound of potatoes, two ounces of oatmeal, an ounce of fat, six ounces of vegetables and six-tenths of a pint of milk per day, supplemented either by more of the same foods or by small amounts of cheese, pulses, meat, fish, sugar, eggs and dried fruit. Churchill, backed by Lindemann, reacted violently against this proposal, and the Ministry of Food, which also opposed it, was glad to put it harmlessly away for the rest of the war.[23] The sugar ration came down to eight ounces in May; the bacon ration to four ounces in June. Tea (two ounces) and margarine and cooking fats (jointly with butter) were rationed in July. But Dame Austerity had hardly begun her long reign.

Indeed, the most striking development of food policy that summer was the Government's decision, in July, to give free or cheap milk to mothers and small children. When the Ministry of Health had suggested in the previous December that a subsidy might be necessary to prevent the inevitable rise in the price of milk hitting those who needed it most, the Treasury had found the idea "objectionable". But, with the new economic approach, "A social reform of the first magnitude, that at one time looked like languishing for months, if not years, was put into effect almost within days."[24]

In June, the Government made a first large-scale attempt to restrict the supplies of consumer goods to the home market. The Limitation of Supplies Order cut the production of seventeen classes of goods – ranging from cutlery and pottery to toys and jewellery – to two-thirds of the 1939 level. Restrictions of supplies of textiles for civilians, first imposed in April, were tightened in September.

The intention was to divert, not only raw materials, but workers, to war industry. Ernest Bevin now had vast powers to hasten this process, though he had not asked for them, or wanted them. In a memorandum which he had drafted and circulated within three and a half days of his arrival in office, he had advocated several innovations in the control of war industry which the cabinet later adopted; but he had made clear his own faith in a free labour market. So far as was possible, workers should move only of their own free will. It had been Neville Chamberlain who had insisted that the Minister of Labour must have comprehensive powers of direction, and had had his way in the War Cabinet.

Bevin's first few days in office were dramatic enough. While the new Emergency Powers were being passed through parliament on May 22nd, he was meeting the National Joint Advisory Council of employers and unionists and securing its co-operation. On the same day, an agreement was reached between the engineering employers and the relevant unions which provided for a temporary relaxation of customs which might check expansion. Three days later, Bevin met the executive committees of all the trade unions, who pledged him their full support.

On June 4th, as the Dunkirk evacuation ended, the Joint Consultative Committee, a smaller body which Bevin had asked the Joint Advisory Council to set up, exceeded his own hopes by spontaneously arriving at a most important agreement. Seven representatives from the British Employers' Federation, and seven from the T.U.C., concluded that there should be no interference with the joint negotiating machinery by which wage claims were settled. If disputes proved irreconcilable, they would be referred for arbitration to an independent body, and its decision would be binding on all parties. In July, this agreement was given effect in Order 1305, which made strikes and lockouts illegal wherever collective bargaining between unions and employers existed. Either side might appeal to a new National Arbitration Tribunal.

Nothing could have been more to Bevin's taste. The agreement strengthened collective bargaining, the cause to which he had given his life, and it accorded due recognition to the power and importance of trade unionism. It made any "wage freeze" or "wages policy", as he hoped with justification, quite unnecessary. But it could not, and did not, stop strikes, though the months after Dunkirk saw very few of these and unheard of co-operation was briefly achieved between unions and employers.

Another job in the centre of Bevin's desk was that of preventing employers from bidding against each other for the scanty supplies of skilled labour in building and engineering. But the Restriction of Engagement Order which Bevin introduced in June was quite insufficient to ensure that skilled men stayed where they were needed; a workman who wanted to move could still get himself sacked. More effective in tackling the problem were Bevin's decision to expand the Government Training Centres and to throw them open to others besides the un-employed, and the registration of skilled engineers in August. All men who were working in certain specified engineering trades, but not on Government contracts, and all others under sixty-five who had had twelve months' experience in these trades within the previous ten years, were asked to come forward to register, and fifty thousand engineers were located who had drifted into other jobs. In Plymouth, for instance, registration disclosed engineers working as greengrocer, as milk roundsman, and as mace bearer to the Lord Mayor, all of whom now returned to industry.[25]

But in general, people were still working that summer where they wanted to work. It was a voluntary labour force that the new Minister of Supply, Herbert Morrison, called upon with a famous slogan, to GO TO IT.

At the outbreak of war, the British army had had equipment for five more or less adequately provided divisions; the Germans for a hundred and six. In the period up to the fall of Chamberlain, British efforts had served merely to keep the gap stable, not to catch up with Hitler. At the end of May 1940, the fifteen British infantry divisions still at home had only about one-sixth of the field guns and anti-tank guns to which they were entitled. There were only a hundred and sixty light tanks in the hands of effective fighting units. The vital sector of the coast between Sheppey and Rye was manned by one division with "twenty-three field guns towards an establishment of seventy-two, no anti-tank guns, no armoured cars, no armoured fighting vehicles, no medium machine guns, and about a sixth of the anti-tank rifles to which

it was entitled".[26] Dunkirk and the further evacuations which
followed redressed the sheer shortage of men. But the British
Expeditionary Force had had the pick of what weapons had been
going. It left behind it virtually all its heavy equipment, including
six hundred tanks. Britain found herself in June 1940 "standing
not only alone but also unarmed".[27]

American industry was not yet ready to make weapons on the
scale required – though half a million rifles for the Local Defence
Volunteers crossed the Atlantic that summer and were gratefully
received. So Britain's factories were psychologically very
much in the front line, and from the upsurge of effort in those
days, the phrase "Dunkirk Spirit" has entered the English language.

Like many such phrases, its current use cloaks rather than
evokes the reality on which it was based. With all the will in the
world, arms on the scale required could be provided only as the
factories planned months or years before came slowly into full
production. As one of the official historians puts it, "the summer's effort was not so much a sudden spurt as a steady uphill
slog." The rate of deliveries of tanks and field guns increased
only slowly. Output of wheeled vehicles remained almost
stationary during the summer.[28] The really dramatic leap was in
aircraft production, and was achieved at the cost of holding back
the re-equipment of the army.

And, while many concerns outside "war production" were
beginning to feel the strain of trying to maintain output while
young men were called up, not everyone could work flat out. In
the coalfields of Durham and South Wales, which had largely
depended on the French export market, there was renewed
unemployment.

But to the men (and the slowly increasing number of women)
in the offices and shop floors of engineering factories, the spurt
was real enough; self-destructively real, as it turned out. Inspired
by urgent calls from Morrison and Beaverbrook, factories worked
twenty-four hours a day, seven days a week. The Whitsun and
August Bank holidays were cancelled, along with the "wakes"
held locally in various parts of the north. Normal concern for
finish and polish, and for the maintenance of machinery, went
by the board. A small factory in Birmingham which made all the
carburettors used in the Spitfire and Hurricane fighters doubled
its weekly output in less than a fortnight. "Normal" working
hours were set from eight a.m. to seven p.m., seven days a week –
but almost every worker exceeded them, and many kept going

till midnight, nodding over their machines, then slept on couches in the office or on sacks in a corner of the toolroom.[29]

The same sort of story could be told of small-arms factories and of the state-owned Royal Ordnance Factories, where men and women worked ten- to twelve-hour shifts seven days a week. Perhaps the most dramatic work of all was done by the workers employed on producing radar equipment, still top secret. The spurt began as Germany invaded the Low Countries; all the workmen and supervision staff involved in radar at the Metropolitan Vickers factory in Manchester worked for forty-eight hours without a break to dispatch eight special transmitters. The historian of Metrovic's war effort writes: "Men and women sacrificed hours, leisure, health, everything to radar. At the time of Dunkirk men whose sons were known to be involved in that dark episode, worked four days and nights without ever going home, so that urgently needed sets could be got out." But an experienced industrial correspondent observed that "To meet men and women who had worked on special rush jobs continuously for thirty-six hours was a commonplace experience."[30]

This heroic effort did not impress the experts on industrial health and the proponents of "scientific" personnel management. Such critics had already been worried by the increase in overtime in munitions work during the "phoney war" period. Their prophecies came true; the new effort negated itself. Production rose by a quarter in the first week after Dunkirk; but by the fifth week it was practically the same as before, although sixty to seventy hours a week were still commonly worked. This confirmed the lesson of the First World War, when it had been shown that a twelve-hour day produced no greater output in the long run than a ten-hour one. Excessive hours produced fatigue and poor health, and so increased both voluntary and involuntary absence from work. Dog-tired men would take a day off in the middle of the week, losing an ordinary day's pay – then turn up on Sunday to earn double pay.[31] A vested interest in Sunday work and in overlong hours was created, and stood against Ernest Bevin's well-conceived attempts to revive sanity.

Bevin had great sympathy for modern ideas of management. In June 1940 an order was made limiting women to a sixty-hour week, and next month Bevin advised industry to restrict men to the same figure, and to provide regular rest days. This was one of his quarrels with the manic Lord Beaverbrook, who ignored this appeal and continued to insist that Ministry of Aircraft Production contractors worked on Sundays.

IV

In the 1930s the new peril of aerial bombardment had largely
driven traditional fears of invasion from memory. By 1937, it
had seemed so slight a risk that entries bearing on the evacuation
of civilians from threatened areas had been deleted from the
Government "War Book". Even Liddell Hart, the *avant garde*
military expert, had announced in a book published in July 1939
that there was "sound cause for discounting the danger".[32]

The danger, as it materialized in May 1940, was all the more
morbidly and frantically conceived for having been ignored for so
long. Ministers, as we now know, greatly exaggerated the chances
of airborne landings. The Germans at this stage had no more
than six or seven thousand trained parachutists, and very few
gliders; they never planned the independent employment of
airborne forces against Britain. But, as Peter Fleming has
observed, "This delusion, though it led to some diversion of
effort, was salutary; for, since there was no telling where the
attacks might fall, it had the effect of putting the whole country
in the front line, of giving everybody a more or less equal sense of
urgency and purpose."[33]

Equally misleading, but in some ways equally salutary, was the
illusion that Germany had a superbly organized, smoothly
expanding war industry which was geared to a master plan for
the conquest of Europe, including Britain. The British at this time
not only greatly overestimated the number of planes which the
Luftwaffe possessed, but failed to understand the economic
implication of "Blitzkrieg", lightning war. German war industry
was geared to short wars, to "short but intensive bursts of economic effort. Given a situation in which only a certain unchanging
sector of the economy was consecrated to war production purposes it would be necessary to change the composition of the
output of this sector according to the war to be fought." The
army, navy and S.S. competed for the services of a restricted
section of industry.[34]

When the Germans reached the Channel that May, only their
navy had drawn up plans for the subsequent conquest of Britain –
and the German navy, much inferior to its British counterpart,
was far from keen on the idea. Amphibious operations on the
necessary scale were a novel notion in warfare. The Germans,
superficially cocksure, were in fact at a loss, including Hitler

himself. Not till July 16th did the Fuehrer issue his celebrated *Directive No. 16* – "As England, in spite of the hopelessness of her military position, has so far shown herself unwilling to come to any compromise, I have decided to begin to prepare for, and if necessary to carry out, an invasion of England." This was not, it has been pointed out, a very crisp or decisive pronouncement.[35]

The most obvious of all defensive preparations for Britain was to increase the number of trained men in the army as fast as possible. 1940 was the peak year for recruitment into the forces. In the first quarter of the year, 310,000 men had gone into uniform; in the second quarter, 425,000 followed; in the third, a wartime peak of 460,000; in the fourth, 340,000. By July 1st, the services had absorbed more than half of British males aged between twenty and twenty-five, and more than one-fifth of the entire male population between sixteen and forty. In June and July, the registration of age groups was taken up to thirty-four, and the rate of compulsory enlistment under previous registrations was trebled.[36]

One of the new "rookies" has recalled:

> We drilled at first with broomsticks owing to the dearth of rifles, then an actual rifle appeared and was handed round the square, though our platoon hadn't much time to learn its mechanism before a runner came to attention in front of our sergeant saying: "Please sar'nt our sar'nt in No. 8 says could we have the rifle for a dekko over there 'cause none of our blokes so much as seen one yet."

Even in September, about half the twenty-seven infantry divisions in Home Forces had had little collective training.[37]

Meanwhile, from May onwards, hurried preparations were made which affected the sights and sounds of Britain for years to come. By the third week in June, some one hundred and fifty thousand civilians, quite apart from the army and the part-time enthusiasts of the L.D.V., were engaged on defensive works of various kinds.[38]

To prevent gliders landing, fields, downland, golf courses and recreation grounds near the south and east coasts were scattered with timber baulks, or with an extraordinary variety of improvised hazards. A traveller in Kent noted, in one field alone, a car, a hayrake, an old kitchen range, a bedstead and a harrow. Iron hoops, with a somewhat surreal elegance, were set to span broad stretches of arterial road. The havoc wrought on sports pitches perhaps explains a curious report on the German radio, early in July, that a "revolt against plutocratic cricketers" had taken place in England; "the people tried to destroy the playing grounds at night, and this led to a state of war between the population and the English sports clubs."[39]

A similar lust for improvisation was shown in the erection of "tank traps" on the roads. Curious barricades appeared in every country lane as the Local Defence Volunteers got into their stride – derelict carts, broken down motor cars, old tyres. The idea was to shift these barriers into the enemy's way; on either side, there would be ditches dug and barbed wire strewn. But in a great many cases, the enemy would have found little problem in circumnavigating these obstacles and proceeding on his way. This applied even to many of the superior roadblocks which replaced the first flurry of junk – concrete abutments with five hundred pound cylindrical blocks piled beside them ready to be hauled on to the highway. Inexperienced civilian contractors committed many blunders, even siting pill-boxes so that they would face in the wrong direction.[40]

Miniature forts made their appearance on the approaches to London, not only beside the highways, but on street corners in towns. Policemen were armed to cope with parachutists. Twelve armoured trains were made, to patrol the railway systems. Precautions were introduced to prevent the enemy from augmenting his resources with British transport, as he had with French. Special wheel-locking devices were fitted on buses to immobilize them while they were unattended. Armed guards protected the garages at night. Under a new order, motorists were compelled to immobilize their own cars when they parked them – the usual method was to remove the rotor arm of the distributor. If this was not done, the police would deflate the tyres or pull out the ignition leads. Prosecutions were common, and fines of up to fifty pounds were imposed. The number of petrol pumps at garages in the eastern and southern coastal areas was reduced, and detailed plans were issued for destroying the rest if the invader came.[41]

On May 30th, it was ordered that "no person shall display or cause or permit to be displayed any sign which furnishes any indication of the name of, or the situation or the direction of, or the distance to any place." Signposts and street names were removed. (They did not reappear in urban areas until the autumn of 1942, and in rural areas until mid-1943.) Milestones and war memorials were assiduously mutilated. The armed forces themselves soon requested a partial restoration of signs, and boards were erected with vague slogans like "To the South-west", but drivers were still subjected to bafflement and nervous exhaustion if they ventured into unfamiliar territory. Users of public transport suffered further annoyance by the removal of destination boards from buses and trams, and by the restrictions on the naming of railway stations. Within twenty miles of the south and east coasts, the latter might not be named at all. Elsewhere, only miniature names (in letters not more than three inches high) were permitted on the platforms.[42]

To frustrate any plans Hitler might have for capturing the B.B.C. and issuing false information, from July 13th, the B.B.C. newsreaders, hitherto known only by nicknames, announced their identities – "Here is the one o'clock news, and this is Frank Phillips reading it." Meanwhile, on June 13th, an order had banned the ringing of church bells. Henceforth, they would be sounded only by the military, or by the police, to give warning of airborne attack. It was arranged that if invasion seemed imminent, or had started, the code word "Cromwell" would be passed to the military commanders. Troops would go to battle stations and the army would take over essential telegraph lines. The civilian population would then dispose itself, either actively or passively, to await the paratroops, the dive bombers, the tanks and the licentious soldiery. The main active part would be taken, of course, by the Local Defence Volunteers, who, at the end of July, were renamed the Home Guard.

V

It was easy to find precedents for the raising of bands of civilians to resist invasion, as far back as the Muster of 1545. Churchill in October 1939 had concerned himself with the fact that middle-aged volunteers for war service were being cold-shouldered, and had suggested to Anderson that a "Home Guard" of half a million men over forty should be formed. Similar ideas had occurred spontaneously to more than one imaginative civilian – as early as March, Lady Helena Gleichen in Herefordshire had organized her staff and tenantry, to the number of eighty , as the "Much Marcle Watchers" and had unsuccessfully asked the military for arms.[43]

So Eden's appeal on May 14th had surprised few and had delighted many. The first Volunteers arrived at local police stations even before the broadcast finished. Before the end of

June, the L.D.V. had nearly one and a half million members. One veteran of 1914–18 called it "the complete answer to the 'old sweat's' prayer".[44] There was no medical exam; the upper age limit of sixty-five was limply enforced; and the only other limitation was that recruits were "vetted" in case the L.D.V. turned out to be the complete answer to the Fifth Columnist's prayer as well.

More than a thousand L.D.V.s were on duty in Kent by ten thirty p.m. on the 17th, keeping vigil over the white cliffs and adjacent areas. Many of them, it seems, had disregarded Eden's remark that Volunteers should be able to fire a rifle or shotgun. Outside the vulnerable eastern and southern coastal belt, progress was slower, but by peacetime standards the recruiting went on at good speed. In the remote Welsh township of Llandudno, for instance, two hundred men had volunteered by four o'clock on the 15th – in little more than a month there were over seven hundred.[45]

It would not be quite true to say that the L.D.V.s' organization grew up spontaneously; on May 30th, a major-general from the War Office was given the task of reducing them to order, with the help of the counties' Territorial Associations (which had organized part-time soldiers in peacetime). Operational control was given to the Commander in Chief, Home Forces, now General Ironside. But in the prevailing urgency, by the time adequate organization had emerged at the top, it had often been matched or outstripped by improvisation at the bottom. The chief commanders – over areas, zones and groups – were appointed by the military, who found selection simplest in areas whither plenty of retired army officers had been lured by adequate facilities for huntin', shootin' and fishin'. Before the war, David Low had invented Colonel Blimp as a symbol for exactly this class of devoted but somewhat blinkered patriots. In less favoured areas, "Blimps" were perforce diluted with other "men of substance". Successful businessmen were chosen where nothing more feudal was available. These men selected the company commanders, platoon commanders, and section leaders – or accepted those chosen by the Volunteers themselves.

In the Sussex village of Wilmington, for instance, one of the men moved to join at once by Eden's broadcast was asked to help recruit a platoon by a former major who lived locally. He commandeered a car and, with the village publican, went round persuading the farmers and cottagers to join. A meeting was arranged, naturally enough, at the pub:

There were shepherds, farm hands, gardeners, village shop-keepers, a retired civil servant from India, a retired school-master, and one or two folk who worked in London and had cottages in downland. We held a subsidiary meeting at another village over the hill. Men came in from their work in the fields, and we stood round a farm waggon in a farm-yard and discussed things and elected a local section leader, calling him corporal. Communications were the difficulty, so we went to the big house of a local colonel to get him to agree to let us use his telephone. The corporal's wife (a domestic there) could answer if need be . . .

Then came the "election of officers", which was a serious and difficult matter. The local section leader must obviously be a chap always there in the village, so the choice fell on Roy, mine host at the pub.

"He's the best rabbit shot in the neighbourhood," said one of his backers.[46]

They should not have called the man a "corporal". At this stage, the L.D.V.s were not intended to have officers and N.C.O.s in the usual sense; some privates, so to speak, would be more private than others and would be appointed to lead at various levels. This raised doubts as to whether the L.D.V. qualified as an irregular force under the Geneva Convention, but the Germans swiftly settled the question in the negative by denouncing them as "murder bands" of *francs tireurs* and declaring that they would be shot if captured.

L.D.V.s were not paid, though some could claim a tiny sub-sistence allowance for long hours of duty. Even the zone com-manders worked voluntarily; and commanders at every level down to the section leaders found themselves dipping deeply into their own pockets in the scramble to get the Volunteers established. Group commanders were given only a derisory allowance for organizational expenses (swiftly raised, but not to a very high level). This meant that few lower middle-class or working-class Volunteers could have afforded to become officers, even if they had been asked. Commanders with full-time civilian jobs found life very hectic. The battalion commanders in Middles-brough, for instance, "perspired under a cascade of denim suits, shot-guns, belts and boxes – dodging in from work to give an hour, and back to work . . ."[47]

Ex-soldiers did not always make the best recruits. Though Colonel Blimp gave generously of his time and money, he

irritated his comrades by turning out in a uniform gorgeous
with medals at a time when most Volunteers thought themselves
lucky if they had sets of thin overalls which fitted them. The
Old Sweat of the First World War was known to refuse to drill,
to refuse to accept responsibility, or to get hoity-toity when he
found he had to share a rifle with two (or perhaps ten) other
Volunteers. One zone swore irreverently that its zone commander
had been tended personally by Florence Nightingale in the Crimean War; but the press concluded that the oldest L.D.V. was
probably a former regimental sergeant major from Crieff, in
Perthshire, who had first seen action in the Egyptian Campaign
of 1884–85.[48]

Veterans, of later vintages, did make up a large part of the
first great influx of Volunteers. Churchill told the House of
Commons in November that nearly half of those then serving had
fought in the previous war. One Berkshire Volunteer wrote:

> I think that none of us will forget our first L.D.V. route
> march. On it a quarter of a century slipped away in a flash.
> There came memories of the Menin Road, of loose, shifting,
> exasperating cobbles, of the smell of cordite and the scream
> of shrapnel, of the mud and stench and misery of Flanders,
> of hopes and fears in battles long ago . . . There were few
> youngsters in that first platoon of ours . . .[49]

Later, a great many veterans would be retired on ground of age,
and the hierarchy would be purged of military dodos. But the
Home Guard would always retain something of the flavour which
an early and enthusiastic recruit, George Orwell, ascribed to it,
that of "A People's Army officered by Blimps".[50]

A "People's Army" it was, not just a regrouping of the British
Legion. In the villages, poachers and gamekeepers, farmers and
farm hands, marched together. In the mining districts, the colliery
L.D.V.s would parade "in their dirt" soon after coming off a
shift. Southern Railways set a lead for the public utility companies
by organizing its own L.D.V.; by the end of June, Volunteer
railwaymen were patrolling at nearly five hundred vulnerable
points in its system – four times as many as the army were
guarding.[51] The Post Office, the B.B.C. and the Fleet Street
newspapers established their own forces.

Factories also had their own troops, which tended too often to
take on the character of independent "private armies", and which
were not fully integrated into the Home Guard until 1942. Along
with that of the south and east coasts, the defence of arms

factories was given priority over all other local defence in the summer of 1940. Aircraft factories were divided into three categories. About two hundred and fifty Priority A factories were given specially produced armoured cars named "Beaverettes", "Beavereels" or "Beaverbugs" in honour of the minister, and their L.D.V.s were also relatively well armed. Well over a thousand Priority B factories had what was left; Priority C factories had to content themselves with "good advice".[52]

"Volunteers", Eden had said, "will be provided with uniforms and will be armed." In about one year's time, that would be generally true. It was certainly not true on July 23rd when Churchill referred to the L.D.V. as the "Home Guard" in a speech, following which the name was officially changed; the replacement of armbands ("brassards") marked "LDV" with armbands marked "HG" was for many volunteers a comprehensive transformation of their uniform. The Volunteers who had turned out in Kent during the second half of May had had about one rifle between ten men, and they were far better equipped than L.D.V.s in other parts of the island.

The public were invited to give their shotguns and pistols to the L.D.V. and about twenty thousand weapons were handed in. Many rural L.D.V.s, of course, had their own guns already. But, quite apart from the priority which must be given to the regular army, the authorities were not altogether intoxicated with the idea of arming the lower classes. The War Office left it to local commanders to decide whether individuals kept their own rifles or not; and it was reported that in some cases the commanders, having wheedled their shotguns away from the local yeomanry, promptly locked the weapons up at the police station.[53]

At first, a lucky few in the L.D.V. were given Short Lee Enfield rifles, which had been standard in the First War. But even in Berkshire, a vulnerable enough area, one battalion received, as its first issue of arms, four rifles per one hundred men and ten rounds per rifle. In any case, after Dunkirk, these were surrendered to the army. A fowling piece was a pretty superior item of equipment in the L.D.V. Picks, pickaxes, crowbars, niblicks, choppers, or even dummy rifles which might bluff paratroopers into submission, were taken out on the first all-night patrols. One Lancashire battalion borrowed a quantity of rifles which had been used in the Crimean War and the Indian Mutiny; another provided each man with a six-foot spear and a heavily weighted truncheon. Engineering workers turned out coshes and sticking knives after finishing the day's shift; in one Derbyshire colliery, the miners invented their own bizarre but serviceable anti-tank gun.[54] But the Molotov cocktail, which had proved itself in Finland, was the method of tank disposal commonly envisaged. The Volunteer (or his wife) filled a bottle with a mixture of resin, petrol and tar, gave it a fuse, and hoped that it would flood a Nazi tank with burning spirits.

A huge consignment of ·300 rifles arrived from the U.S.A., but the rapture felt when they appeared in the battalions in July was somewhat diminished when they were found to be glutinous with the preserving oil in which they had been stored since their manufacture in 1917 and 1918. In Cambridge, it took two hundred and fifty volunteer ladies a fortnight to clean a batch of eight thousand. The first "uniforms" would arrive as an issue of, say, ten "brassards" to fifty men. There followed, at a variable interval, the celebrated khaki denim overalls. Each suit required a buckle and eleven buttons and rings; these were issued mixed, in apparently random proportions. The shortage of denims for men with well-filled waistlines was such that unfortunates would be seen drilling abjectly in "civvies" even when the rest of the platoon had been equipped. The field service caps which were issued were usually far too small, and in some places took a very long time coming. In March 1941, one company commander wrote to his superior to ask for guidance as to which civilian headgear should be approved for men without them:

A list is given [he added] of the different local varieties worn here by the Home Guard in the order, so far as it is possible to estimate, of their respective popularity:
(a) Homburg or Trilby
(b) Porkpie
(c) Cloth cap
(d) Bowler
(e) Various – such as moleskin caps with earflaps, straw boaters, berets and early Victorian deerstalkers.

By the autumn, however, some lucky battalions were getting khaki serge battledress, and such luxuries as greatcoats, waterproof capes and steel helmets were soon in limited circulation.[55]

The L.D.V.s, drilling with stakes on village greens and city parks, looked ridiculous enough; and the proud title "Home Guard" now summons up an image of overgrown schoolboys playing at soldiers. Hindsight, as always, makes fools of us. Even before Churchill's speech, the Volunteers expected to fight in the

fields and in the streets and never to surrender. How effectively
they might have fought in these early days, one may doubt. One
afternoon that summer, a parachute landing was reported in
Croydon; a local platoon commander had only one Volunteer
available, as the rest of his men were at their work in London,
and when he was able to assemble fifteen of them, their armament consisted of one rifle, ten cartridges, a revolver and a shotgun.[56]

But the L.D.V. settled down to fulfil a very useful function.
The army, as we have seen, was short of training. If a great proportion of its members had had to spend their time guarding the
five thousand miles of the island's coastline, defending aerodromes, keeping watch over vital factories and public utilities
and manning roadblocks, training would have been impeded.
The vigil, the routine precaution against surprise attack and
sabotage, could be handed over to the L.D.V. But it was clear
from the outset that no modest role as observers would content
the L.D.V. when the time came. Volunteers intended to defend
their villages and streets, and to blow up a few tanks in the
process. As equipment, very slowly, became available, Britain
acquired a network of amateur garrisons which would have
harassed and held up a determined invader. Out of a two-way
flow of ideas between amateur strategists at the bottom and
military men at the top, the role of the Home Guard developed
over its first year or so of existence.

Training in the L.D.V. began on a free-lance basis. Individual
commanders made their own arrangements. Schools were set up
on private initiative; of these, the most famous was created at
Osterley Park in Middlesex, by the generosity of wealthy backers,
for Tom Wintringham. Wintringham, an ex-Communist, who
had commanded the British contingent in the International
Brigade during the Spanish Civil War, emerged in that summer as
the best known "popularizer" of war, with articles in newspapers
and magazines inculcating a "do it yourself" offensive spirit.

Other lecturers at Osterley had also served in Spain; notably
three Spanish miners who had specialized in destroying tanks
and who "immediately became the idols of the L.D.V." Osterley
taught Volunteers how to decapitate motor cyclists with trip
wires, to camouflage themselves, to conduct guerilla warfare in
occupied territory, and to follow the best techniques in street
fighting. Between July and October, five thousand Home Guard
passed through the school. In October, it was taken over by the
Government as "War Office No. 1 School" for the Home Guard;

its authority had been deferred to previously, when various
Guards regiments had sent detachments to train at it.[57]

During the summer, a guerilla role had already been assigned
secretly to certain selected Volunteers. Twenty-odd "Auxiliary
Units" were set up, including army officers and "cells" of Home
Guard, who were trained in sabotage and the use of high explosive, and became responsible for dumps and hideouts stocked with
guerilla necessities.[58]

But for the moment it was the British civilian who suffered
from the Volunteers' offensive aspirations. The L.D.V. were
empowered to demand a show of identity cards from motorists
at the roadblocks. Some travellers did not hear the challenge, or
preferred not to obey it. The Volunteers took a nightly toll of
casualties as they fired wildly at passing vehicles. Courting
couples were sadly harried.

But the routines of the night watch were rarely dramatic. From
the village or town in the valley, the L.D.V. made their way in
the summer dusk, after a day's work, to keep vigil on the hillsides.
At first, men went out compulsively night after night, resting in a
shepherd's hut or a borrowed caravan. In Berkshire, one Volunteer records, ". . . We considered ourselves fortunate if we had
one night's sleep in four or five." Apart from the occasional
chance of capturing German airmen whose planes had crashed, it
was a life of false alarms. In a quiet village street, an unfamiliar
footstep provoked wild suspicions. The munching of horses was
mistaken for marching feet. Puffs from A.A. shell-bursts were
often identified as parachutists – as were a bewildering variety of
other sights, from a swan descending in a lake to a mere cow.
The stalking of boulders on the moors might provide a few
breathtaking minutes; but in the remote hills of Shropshire, it
was admitted, "the sudden appearance of a cat on a gate post
was regarded as an interesting piece of excitement."[59]

VI

Large tracts of the east and south coasts, at a time when they
would normally have been entertaining holiday-makers, became
"Defence Areas", to visit which a citizen required a permit. At
London's termini, hundreds of stations on the coast were listed
which might not now be visited for "holiday, recreation or
pleasure". Sea-front hotels were requisitioned, machine guns
sprouted from piers, bathing was prohibited on many beaches,

barbed wire straggled everywhere, curfews were imposed. When
J. B. Priestley visited Margate in July, "The few signs of life only
made the whole place seem more unreal and spectral."[60]

In May, a second major movement of evacuation had begun.
Children who had been sent to areas within ten miles of the coast
in East Anglia, Kent or Sussex were transferred to South Wales.
Then all state schools were closed in the vulnerable areas and
parents of local children were invited to send them westwards.

As the French front fell to pieces, the Government reversed its
decision that no further evacuation from the cities should take
place before raids started. Between June 13th and 18th, nearly a
hundred thousand children were evacuated from the London
area, many of them for the second time. More followed under
what was called the "trickle scheme", and there was further
movement from other cities on the south and east coasts.
Altogether, about 213,000 unaccompanied children were evacuated during May, June and July. The Government also introduced
a scheme for "assisted private evacuation" to help those "non-
essential" adults and small children in the coastal belt who wished
to leave. By mid-July, nearly half the population of the East
Anglian coast towns, and roughly two-fifths of the inhabitants of
Kentish coast towns, had left for safer parts.[61]

Yet once again, there was a drift back. The total of 519,000
evacuees officially billeted in England and Wales on August 1st
was smaller than in January. In September, when blitz came to
London, there were over 520,000 children of school age in the
metropolitan area. In Cambridge, the news of Dunkirk actually
speeded up a rate of departure for London which had been
falling. Families, it seems, preferred to die together if die they
must.[62]

The response to another new scheme launched at this time
might seem to contradict this. At the end of May, offers to take
British children began to pour in from the U.S.A. and the
Dominions. The Government established a Children's Overseas
Reception Board ("CORB") which, by July 4th, had received
211,000 applications for billets overseas for children of school
age, and had then to announce that no further requests could be
entertained. However, it is probable that most of the enthusiasm
for the scheme came from middle-class parents who were less
likely to be deterred by the incidental expenses which would be
involved even after the Government had met the cost of the
voyage. (Contributions were taken from parents on a sliding
scale, involving a means test.)

Shortage of shipping meant that the scheme had barely begun to operate by September 17th, when the *City of Benares* went down in the Atlantic with the loss of seventy-three "seavacuees". With this horrifying, if predictable news, the official scheme was at once wound up, after "CORB" had sent 2,664 children overseas, mostly to Canada. In addition, up to fourteen thousand children went by private arrangement, and over five thousand of these found homes in the U.S.A.[63]

Meanwhile, Britain had to billet more than thirty thousand refugees from the Continent, amongst whom Poles and Belgians were most numerous. (Whole communities of French and Belgian fishermen arrived in the south-west with their boats.) In addition, some ten thousand, five hundred Gibraltarians appeared in Britain after a compulsory evacuation. The saddest welcome was given to twenty-nine thousand people from the Channel Islands, about one third of their population, who were brought off on June 21st–24th and were billeted chiefly in Lancashire and Cheshire. The holiday islands, loyal to the Crown but as much French as British in some respects, were clearly doomed to occupation after the fall of France. Everyone who wanted to go went; mothers and children to safety, young men to join the forces. The Germans took over Guernsey on June 30th, and Jersey next day.[64]

The hordes of refugees who had impeded allied troop movements in France as the German columns advanced must not, it was wisely decided, be imitated in Britain. When those who wanted to go had left the coastal areas, the rest of the population must remain where they were. "Stay Put" was the slogan propagated by streams of leaflets and advertisements, offering detailed instructions which were often vague and sometimes self-contradictory. An official advertisement in *The Times* on July 11th was typical:

> What do I do?
> I remember that this is the moment to act like a soldier.
> I do *not* get panicky. I *stay put*. I do *not* say: "I must get out of here." I remember that fighting men must have clear roads. I do *not* go on to the road on bicycle, in a car or on foot. Whether I am at work or at home I just *stay put*.[65]

But Churchill's broadcast on July 14th conjured up a different picture. "We shall defend every village, every town, and every city," he said – could this imply a population placidly standing by? General Ironside had told a meeting of L.D.V. commanders early in June that the German columns, if they came, would act "with the utmost brutality". He had proceeded: ". . . I think it is up to us to tell the people and everybody else [*sic*], if we also do not act in the same way that they will take us and finish us off." As for parachutists, ". . . When they come down you can shoot them, shoot them, shoot them without any reference to taking any kind of care of their future." While the L.D.V. applied their minds to the best ways of slaughtering Germans *en masse*, others evolved their private schemes for "taking one of them with me when I go". According to their trade union leader, the miners of South Wales had plans to blow up the pits if the Germans reached them, to take to the hills "and to fight against Nazi tanks with picks and shovels". More modestly, the Women's Voluntary Services in Sussex started to organize a service of messengers with bicycles to maintain communications if roads were blocked and telegraph lines cut.[66]

And no one of any prominence could neglect to consider what he would do if the Nazis reached him. ("They'll kill *me*, but they'll torture *you*, Prof," said Beaverbrook waggishly to Lindemann.) Harold Nicolson and his wife decided to commit suicide and supplied themselves with lethal pills. Another M.P., Vernon Bartlett, persuaded his wife to make him a small chamois leather bag in which he carried fifty pounds in notes strapped round his waist, "so that I should not be entirely without funds when I took to the hills."[67]

But it is certain that Britain would not have flouted the laws of human behaviour, and that, besides a no doubt tiny number of active Fifth Columnists, many reputable people, great and small, would have collaborated with the Nazis when the time came. Trying to decide in advance who these were induced an unedifying hysteria amongst the authorities and the public at large.

The most obvious targets for hatred were German nationals living in Britain. The small German community of fifteen to twenty thousand had been augmented before the war by refugees, mainly Jewish or left-wing, from Nazi persecution. At the outbreak of war, there were over sixty thousand German and Austrian refugees and some eight thousand Czech refugees in Britain. In September 1939, a large number of Nazi sympathizers, together with some left-wing refugees and even some Jews, were rounded up by the police; after internment in various improvised camps, they found a home on a racecourse in Surrey. Almost all other "enemy aliens" went before tribunals which classified them. "A" class aliens were interned; "B" class were restricted in their movements, and "C" class, which included the vast majority of the refugees, were allowed to go free. In spite of a campaign by Beaverbrook's *Sunday Express* early in 1940, it seemed that public opinion more or less accepted their presence.

On May 12th, 1940, Anderson, at the urging of the military authorities, interned some two thousand male "enemy aliens" living in the vulnerable coastal areas. From the 16th and 17th, all "B" class aliens, men and women, were rounded up, in great haste and secrecy. Men were given no time to put their affairs in order or to tell their relatives what was happening. A number of refugees committed suicide at the mere idea of internment.

By now, the press was baying indiscriminately against all aliens. INTERN THE LOT was a slogan of the times. It was suggested, possibly with justice, that it was a guilty conscience which prompted the *Daily Mail* (which had once backed Mosley's Fascists) to shout most stridently of all. The effect, in any case, was to create something unpleasantly close to "pogrom-minded-ness" among sections of the population. Some employers began to sack all foreigners, or even British of foreign ancestry; some local authorities turned aliens out of council houses. Men of alien parentage or origin, including one V.C. of the First World War, were turned down by the L.D.V.

The entry of Italy into the war provoked attacks on Italian restaurants and ice-cream parlours in London and elsewhere. (The *Hotel Review* smugly rejoiced that "the excessive Italianiza-tion of our hotels" might now be checked.) Four thousand Italians with less than twenty years' residence in Britain (includ-ing some more anti-Fascist refugees) were immediately interned. By June 20th, Anderson authorized the chief constables to round up any "C" class Germans or Austrians about whom they felt "doubt", and after the 25th, all "C" class men under seventy were brought in, with the exceptions, in theory, but not always in fact, of invalids, key workers and certain other special cases. By mid-July, some two-thirds of all the German and Austrian men in the country were interned, and the round-up continued until very few were left.

The authorities intended to shift internees to the Isle of Man, and then deport them to the Dominions in a steady flow. Mean-while they passed through transit camps run by the military until August 5th, when the Home Office took them over. These varied greatly, but in some conditions were appalling. At Sutton Cold-field, aliens, including some invalids, were put up in tents, without mattresses, on damp ground. At Wharf Mills in Lancashire, others were detained in a derelict cotton factory infested by rats. Few blankets, scanty food, minimal medical equipment, absurd postal censorship, newspapers, radio and even books forbidden, men and wives interned separately, families left with no idea of the whereabouts and condition of ailing fathers and grandfathers – these were among the complaints which reached the ears of members of parliament. The climax of outrage arrived on July 2nd, when the *Arandora Star*, carrying fifteen hundred German and Italian internees to Canada, was torpedoed and sunk off the west coast of Ireland. It became clear, in spite of Government prevarications, that not all those drowned had been Nazis or Fascists, and some had been refugees and notable opponents of Hitler.[68]

Meanwhile, class "C" aliens still at large were subjected to curfew and restrictions on their travel, and were not allowed to own cars, bicycles or maps without permission. Among the men in this position were a high proportion of the scientists working in Britain, under the utmost secrecy, towards the creation of an atomic bomb. There was no alternative to using them, since most native physicists of high calibre had been absorbed into other vital work. While this perfectly ironic situation was known to only a very few people, it was clear to many more that a great deal of talent was now idle on the Isle of Man. (But it should also be noted that a Gallup Poll in July showed that forty-three per cent of the public wanted all aliens interned, as compared with only forty-eight per cent who wanted friendly and harmless ones to be spared.[69])

The Government had been in a difficult position. While the haste of the detentions had been a political decision, the bungling and hardship which had followed had been caused by the normal insensitivity of military and civil bureaucracy. When the House of Commons debated the issue on August 22nd, Anderson was bitterly criticized, notably by one of the younger Conservative M.P.s, Major Cazalet, who spoke of "horrible tragedies" and said, "Frankly, I shall not feel happy, either as an Englishman or as a supporter of this Government, until this bespattered page of our history has been cleaned up and rewritten." The Government promised that releases would be made where possible, and a tribunal would be set up to adjudicate.[70] Sure enough, over a thousand aliens were soon released for work in agriculture or industry.

Other releases followed. By 1943 nine out of ten employable aliens (including many Belgian, Czech, Dutch and Polish refugees)

were at work, many of them in skilled jobs. It is pleasant to
record that the lot of those who remained temporarily on the
Isle of Man was far from arduous. Eugen Spier, a devout Jew
with many years' residence in Britain before the war, and a most
active supporter of Churchill's in the 'thirties, was amongst those
unluckily interned at the outbreak and in the summer of 1940
was deported to Canada. Allowed to rejoin his wife on the Isle
of Man in 1941, he found that the atmosphere was that of the
peacetime holiday resort which the island had been. The internees
had set up their own university and had a rich cultural life. Three
members of the now famous Amadeus Quartet met for the first
time on the Isle of Man – one of them has remarked that internment gave him a chance to practice properly, and another has
called it "a fabulous time".[71]

There was less concern over the internment, without trial, of a
variety of political elements. On May 22nd, an extension to
Defence Regulation 18B gave the Home Secretary the right to
imprison anybody he believed likely to endanger the safety of the
realm, while a Treachery Act passed by parliament curtailed and
simplified the provisions for the trial of suspected traitors. Only
four British subjects were prosecuted under the Treachery Act
during the war, but a good number were imprisoned under "18B".

On May 23rd, Sir Oswald Mosley was arrested in his home. On
the 30th, his British Union of Fascists was dissolved and its
publications were banned. Virtually all the Fascists who remained from Mosley's cohorts of the 'thirties were rounded up
and imprisoned. Amongst others arrested were Captain Ramsay,
M.P., a member of the anti-Semitic Right Club, and Admiral Sir
Barry Domville, a former chief of Naval Intelligence, who had
been chairman of an Anglo-German friendship organization
called "The Link". Ramsay was allowed to continue to table
parliamentary questions, but was not released until mid-1944.
Certain people were arrested who were not really German
sympathizers; among them, H. St. John Philby, the Arabian
explorer, and father of "Kim" Philby who was even then
covertly demonstrating the inadequacy of any system of
"security".

In August, a peak number of sixteen hundred of His Majesty's
subjects were under detention without trial. The leading male
detainees were held in Brixton prison, where, during that hot
summer, they amused themselves by playing cricket in the court-
yard under Ramsay's tuition. By mid-1941, only four hundred
were still detained – most of them people of non-British descent

who had escaped imprisonment as enemy agents by technicalities. Mosley remained; he and his wife were eventually given a flat in Holloway Prison, with the right to employ other prisoners as servants.[72]

Many members of the Irish Republican Army, which had committed several notable bomb outrages in Britain during the "phoney war" period, were rounded up and interned in Ulster. But members of the I.L.P., the Trotskyite factions, and the Communist Party were not held. The authorities no doubt reasoned, correctly, that the C.P. would have taken pains to prepare an underground organization against the contingency of suppression, and that this might well be more dangerous than open activity.

At "Speakers' Corner" in Hyde Park that summer it was still possible to hear members of the Peace Pledge Union and the Anti-Fifth Column League performing on adjacent platforms. But as "Fifth Column fever" spread, citizens with strong political views, especially those to the left, often found themselves subjected to the attentions of the police. One of those who suffered was the editor of the Co-operative movement's paper, the *Citizen*. On July 18th, five plain clothes policemen entered his home, produced a search warrant, kept his wife and daughter in one room and himself in another, and ransacked the house for an hour and a half. They found nothing. It emerged that information had been given which in the eyes of the authorities "necessitated an immediate search". But the citizen in such a position was not allowed to know who had given the information.[73]

The existence of a strong Fifth Column was taken for granted, it would seem, in the highest circles. In May, the Vice Admiral in charge of the port of Dover reported to the Admiralty that "numerous acts of sabotage and Fifth Column activity" had occurred there. In his speech on Dunkirk, Churchill spoke of "this malignancy in our midst" as though it were a well known fact of important dimensions. The irrepressible General Ironside, shortly before he was replaced by the more sober General Brooke, announced that the military had "got examples of where there have been people quite definitely preparing aerodromes in this country"; and added, "My experience is that the gentlemen who are the best behaved and the most sleek are those who are doing the mischief. We cannot be too sure of anybody." The climax of mania was perhaps reached when Edinburgh Corporation forbade anglers to fish in its reservoirs, on the grounds that agents seeking to poison them might adopt this disguise.[74]

But the Fifth Column offences for which people were actually prosecuted were minor enough. Amongst others: a woman on the Isle of Wight was sentenced to death for cutting military telephone wires, but her punishment was later reduced to fourteen years' imprisonment. A man was sentenced to seven years' for smashing telephone booths. A schoolmaster was jailed for advancing "defeatist" theories to his pupils.[75] These offences were perhaps quite serious in their context, but would hardly have hammered the nation to its knees.

Since the previous September, press censorship had encouraged wild rumours. In the early weeks of war, every city of any size had been bombed to extinction by wagging tongues. After May 10th, 1940, the habit had more to feed on.

> Do not believe the tale the milkman tells;
> No troops have mutinied at Potters Bar.
> Nor are there submarines at Tunbridge Wells.
> The B.B.C. will warn us when there are.

So A. P. Herbert advised his readers in that month. An Emergency Regulation in June made it an offence to circulate "any report or statement' about the war which was "likely to cause alarm or despondency'. Fines up to fifty pounds could be imposed.[76]

Spies and parachutists were favourite subjects for rumour. Those spies who actually reached Britain from the Continent that summer appear to have been poorly trained and specious to a degree. One pair who landed on the Morayshire coast were at once rounded up when they failed to understand the request of a booking clerk at a railway station for "one-eight-six". Another, who waded in from the sea with a Homburg hat, a trench coat and a green suitcase, was observed by two farm-workers, who phlegmatically refrained from mentioning his arrival for several hours.[77]

But during May and June, there were so many reports of parachute landings that an official denial was deemed necessary, on July 10th, that any enemy had as yet descended. How the logic of hysteria worked itself out may be seen from Peter Fleming's quotation from the War Diary of 45 Division, which guarded the south-east at the time of Dunkirk. On May 21st, there was a note: "A number of unaccountable lights continue to be observed. It is for consideration whether some of the lights reported are caused by enemy parachutists burning their parachutes. The fact that there is no record of a parachute being found lends colour to this theory." An official pamphlet in mid-

June stressed the fear of disguise. "Most of you know your
policemen and your A.R.P. wardens by sight. If you keep your
heads you can also tell whether a military officer is really British
or is only pretending to be so." (This was bad luck for the Polish,
French, Czech and other foreign officers now wearing British
uniform.) The German "underground" New British Broadcasting Station was delighted to make matters worse by announcing that Germans would descend dressed as miners.[78]

The regular German broadcasts and the N.B.B.S. were augmented during the summer by three other pretended "underground" stations, which would broadcast for only a few minutes
each day. On July 8th, a "Worker's Challenge" was inaugurated
which incited violence against the bosses and denounced "that
bloated rat Bevin" in the supposed accents of a working-class
anti-Fascist revolutionary. Ten days later, "Radio Caledonia"
was launched to encourage Scottish separatism, and early in
August broadcasts from a fictitious "Christian Peace Movement"
began to counsel pacifism. The voices were partly provided by
British prisoners of war in Germany enlisted as traitors by
William Joyce.

But what Joyce and his colleagues said was far less important
than what people believed they had said. In many different parts
of the country, a quaint little legend gained currency: Haw Haw
could virtually read the time on the public clock. It was said in
Wolverhampton, for instance, that a clock stopped one night at
8.55 p.m. and at 9.15 p.m. Bremen radio broadcast the fact.
A resident of Banstead had a story that he had heard Haw Haw
say, "We know all about Banstead, even that the clock is a
quarter of an hour slow today" – and sure enough, it had been.
Why spies might devote themselves to relaying the intimate
details of life in the suburban lanes of Banstead was a question
which credulous people did not ask themselves. More serious
was the same type of rumour concerning munitions factories.
A big factory in the midlands was said to have suffered a drop in
production after it was rumoured that Haw Haw had threatened
that it would be bombed shortly and had proved his local
knowledge by adding, "Don't trouble to finish the new paint
shed."

A few people were prosecuted for inventing such rumours. In
fact, German intelligence about Britain was notably poor.
Joyce never made specific threats, but contented himself with
general remarks about coming air raids; though his remarks were
on occasion unpleasantly close to the truth, as when he said of

Dunkirk, "What the politicians regarded, or professed to regard, as a triumph, the soldiers regarded as a bloody defeat . . ."[79]

Early in July, Churchill announced that he had sent a telegram to civil servants and military commanders, urging them to "check and rebuke expressions of loose and ill-digested opinion in their circle, or by their subordinates" and to report or remove without hesitation any of the latter who were found "to be consciously exercising a disturbing or depressing influence . . ."[80] There were two related worries prompting official concern about wagging tongues. One was the danger to security – it was at this time that the famous slogan CARELESS TALK COSTS LIVES was coined; a poster showed Hitler and Goering sitting smugly behind two gossiping housewives in a bus, and perhaps tended to confirm the impression that the Germans were omniscient, ubiquitous and so omnipotent. The other worry was morale.

So the luckless notion of a "Silent Column" was launched. Advertisements showed photographs of typical but dangerous citizens. There was "Mr. Secrecy Hush Hush" pretending to divulge top secret information; Mr. Knowall; Miss Leaky Mouth; Miss Teacup Whisper; Mr. Pride in Prophecy ("*Give him a look* that tells him what you think of him"); and Mr. Glumpot. Such characters should be rebuked and told to "JOIN BRITAIN'S SILENT COLUMN – the great body of sensible men and women who have pledged themselves not to talk rumour and gossip and to stop others doing it". A few people took the hint and informed on their neighbours. There was a spate of ridiculous prosecutions for "defeatist" remarks. The Ministry of Information was still unpopular with the press, and there was an outcry at this time about its recently established Wartime Social Survey whose investigators were denounced as "Cooper's Snoopers". The ministry began to back-pedal – "Talk, grumble," it advised the public, "but give nothing away" – and on July 23rd Churchill himself informed parliament that the "Silent Column" had "passed into innocuous desuetude".[81]

VII

The fantasy of the Fifth Column was one of the waves of a profound tremor which shook political discussion in Britain in 1940. Its effects were seen much later in the fact that people who were young in the 1940s were of all age groups most prone to vote Labour in the 1960s. "If we can survive this war," wrote an

over-optimistic George Orwell, "the defeat in Flanders will turn
out to have been one of the great turning points in English history.
In that spectacular disaster the working class, the middle class
and even a section of the business community could see the utter
rottenness of private capitalism. For the first time in their lives,
the comfortable were uncomfortable, the professional optimists
had to admit that there was something wrong."[82]

What *had* gone wrong? The soldiers from Dunkirk had an
incoherent answer. John Lehmann wrote of them in his diary,
on June 11th, "A more effective army of revolutionary agitators,
penetrating to the furthest villages, could not be imagined –
could not have been organized by the cleverest political party."
Guilty Men tried to give their message coherence, with its lurid
vignettes from the evacuation – "One Bren gun and one hero
against eight Heinkels . . . Three bayonets and three heroes
against machine guns . . . Relays of Nazi bombers against
non-existent British fighters."[83]

The "old gang", the old system, the "Old World" (as men
came to call it) had failed. At a time of mass unemployment, the
system had not produced the arms to defeat Hitler. The fact that
the Labour Party had for a long time opposed rearmament – on
the grounds that only collective security would work – was now
overlooked or excused. Hatred focused on Chamberlain,
Hoare, Simon, and beyond them the Conservative party, and
beyond them the businessmen whom they represented in parliament.

And for the moment, the "old gang" themselves lost their self-
confidence. The conclusions drawn from the crisis by those mild
and sensitive old gangsters, Duff Cooper and Harold Nicolson,
have already been noted. More remarkable was the leader which
appeared in *The Times* on July 1st – a favourite text thereafter
for the prophets of the New World:

> If we speak of democracy, we do not mean a democracy
> which maintains the right to vote but forgets the right to
> work and the right to live. If we speak of freedom, we do not
> mean a rugged individualism which excludes social organiza-
> tion and economic planning. If we speak of equality, we do
> not mean a political equality nullified by social and economic
> privilege. If we speak of economic reconstruction, we think
> less of maximum production (though this too will be
> required) than of equitable distribution . . . The European
> house cannot be put in order unless we put our own house

in order first. The new order cannot be based on the preservation of privilege, whether the privilege be that of a country, of a class, or of an individual.[84]

The Liberal and Socialist left had long been urging that this war could not be seen as a territorial conflict of the old type, where one nation opposed another. Rather, one class opposed another, or decent men everywhere opposed the vileness of Fascism. The Fifth Column scare gave imaginative weight to their arguments in lay minds. If there were elements in Britain which would collaborate with Hitler, and large elements in Germany who had opposed him and (wishfully it was thought) were still opposing him, the first were enemies, the latter natural allies. The internationalist, ecumenical Bishop of Chichester suggested, echoing many others, that this was "a war of faiths in which the nations themselves are divided". Tom Wintringham, inspirer of the Home Guard, called it "a People's War", and whoever originated it, this was a phrase which stuck.[85]

The concept of course was never universally accepted. But its influence over the press, the films and the radio was enormous; it shaped the rhetoric of five years of official and unofficial propaganda. The extent to which the phrase became a cliché can be seen in the remark of a Lancashire justice of the peace, in 1942, that "There is a war on and it is a people's war as well as ours."[86] "Us" in this context meant the "Old Gang" – businessmen who now feared revolution so much that they accepted planning as the lesser evil, aristocrats whose country houses were now war nurseries or battle schools and who sadly concluded that the gracious world of croquet lawns, pink gins and tweedy, reactionary culture had gone for ever. But "us" for the "people" meant several different things. For the miners, it meant miners; for the working class, it meant the working class; for those sections of the middle class who now deserted the "Old Gang", it meant managers and workers, bosses and clerks, rowing together towards the Happy Island, lending each other a hand to build the New Jerusalem. And for these last, a prophet arose in 1940, a plump prophet with a cosy Bradford accent and a big pipe.

In March, the B.B.C. had launched, as an answer to Haw Haw, a series of "Postscripts" broadcast after the news on Sunday night. They began innocuously enough, but in the summer of 1940, they provided a regular spot for J. B. Priestley, already, of course, extremely well known as a novelist. Over thirty per cent of the population, it was estimated, were tuned in for any one "Postscript". Adding his regular broadcasts at this time to the U.S.A., the B.B.C. credited Priestley with "the biggest regular listening audience in the world".[87]

After his notable broadcast on Dunkirk, Priestley's message began to emerge. At first, it was simple enough. If Churchill evoked Henry V and Thomas Babington Macaulay, Priestley's heroes were Falstaff and Sam Weller. He depicted the "little man", who preserved the spirit of English comedy within himself, embattled against Nazis whom he variously described as "robot men", "warrior ants", and "overgrown tormenting, cruel schoolboys – middle-aged 'dead end kids' . . . Let the Nazis in," he warned vividly, "and you will find that the laziest loudmouth in the workshop has suddenly been given power to kick you up and down the street . . ."

But a note which his Conservative listeners thought uncomfortably "political" had soon crept in. On July 21st, he launched an attack on, of all sacred things, property. Property, he said, was an "old-fashioned" idea, which should be replaced by "community".

> And I'll give you an instance of how this change should be working. Near where I live is a house with a large garden, that's not being used at all because the owner of it has gone to America. Now, according to the property view, this is all right, and we, who haven't gone to America, must fight to protect this absentee owner's property. But on the community view, this is all wrong. There are hundreds of working men not far from here who urgently need ground for allotments so that they can produce a bit more food. Also, we may soon need more houses for billeting. Therefore, I say, that house and garden ought to be used whether the owner, who's gone to America, likes it or not.[88]

And, as he went on to observe, the change of values was already occurring.

By November, Mass Observation was reporting a quickening movement of opinion in politics, especially amongst the better-off classes. ". . . In the last few months it has been hard to find, even among women, many who do not unconsciously regard this war as in some way revolutionary, or radical." It was not a matter of a conventional swing towards Labour, but "a trend towards uncertainty and questioning of the *status quo*", with a great increase in political talk.[89]

Whatever produced this critical mood, it was not Winston Churchill's speeches; nor could Priestley have done it single handed. But it is hard to resist the conclusion that Priestley expressed the popular mood in 1940 more fully than Churchill. The battle in the skies above Britain, which reached a climax in August and September, was presented by both men as a supreme symbol of courage. Churchill had already compared the young pilots of Fighter Command with the Knights of the Round Table and the Crusaders. Priestley had spoken in very different terms, in a broadcast on July 28th, when he had evoked the life of a bomber pilot and all its arduousness and danger, and had suggested that if the pattern of the last peace were repeated, such young men would be wearing shabby suits after the war and would be lucky to have jobs as vacuum cleaner salesmen.[90] Neither exactly spoke for the men in the R.A.F., but of the two, Priestley came closer.

THE BATTLE OF BRITAIN

It was no picnic despite what anyone might say later . . . Most of us were pretty scared all the bloody time; you only felt happy when the battle was over and you were on your way home, then you were safe for a bit, anyway.

Colin Gray, fighter pilot[1]

I

Everyone agrees that there was a Battle of Britain in 1940 – the first battle fought over British soil since Culloden; and most concur with the American authority who describes it as "the pivotal event of the war".[2] But some writers regard the night bombing of British cities which began on a large scale on September 7th as part of it, while others include only the daylight air battles. Even amongst the latter there is disagreement as to whether the battle began in July, with the first systematic inroads of German fighters from France, and ended as late as November, or whether only the struggle in August and September deserves the name.

The British official account places the opening of the battle on July 10th, but even this delimitation is somewhat arbitrary. The first phase involved attacks by the Luftwaffe on convoys passing through the Straits of Dover, and was, from their point of view, unprofitable. The Luftwaffe lost twice as many aircraft of all types as the R.A.F. lost fighters, and not much merchant shipping was sunk. However, the tip of Kent around Dover earned the name of "Hellfire Corner", and it was there, on July 10th, that raiders arrived when a B.B.C. reporter, Charles Gardner, was reading from a prepared script. Gardner seized this opportunity enthusiastically and established one attitude to the Battle of Britain by treating the dogfights which developed in the skies as if they were a combination of boxing match and motor race. "There's one coming down in flames – there somebody's hit a German – and he's coming down – there's a long streak – he's coming down completely out of control – a long streak of smoke – ah, the man's baled out by parachute – the pilot's baled out by parachute – he's a Junkers 87 and he's going slap into the sea and there he goes – sma-a-sh . . . Oh boy, I've never seen anything so good as this – the R.A.F. fighters have really got these boys taped."[3]

Meanwhile, Hitler continued to hope that Britain would surrender without an invasion, encouraged by the fact that the Churchill Government still kept open unofficial channels whereby peace might be negotiated. Dithering, he gave the R.A.F. and the ground defences of Britain a precious month of grace. On July 16th, he issued his direction for the invasion. But on the 19th, addressing his Reichstag, he called for peace. . . . "A great Empire will be destroyed," he warned, " – an Empire which it was never my intention to destroy or even to harm . . . I consider myself in a position to make this appeal since I am not the vanquished begging favours, but the victor speaking in the name of reason."[4] Within an hour, to the amazement and disappointment of the Germans, the B.B.C., on its own initiative, had broadcast a blunt rejection of this offer, confirmed by Halifax on the 22nd.

On the night of August 1st, German bombers scattered green and yellow leaflets over Hampshire and Somerset, entitled, "The Last Appeal to Reason", and giving the text of Hitler's speech. These were gleefully collected and were auctioned successfully for the Red Cross. On the next day, Goering ordered the Luf-waffe to destroy the R.A.F. If Britain was to be invaded, it was essential that Fighter Command should be knocked out of the air. August 13th was set as *Adlertag* – Eagle Day – when the hitherto invincible German air force would commence its destruction.

It was believed at the time that, if the battle was a sporting contest, Fighter Command was the "underdog". This was not exactly the case; while the British planes were outnumbered, they had many advantages, and it was a most equal match.

The three Luftflötten attacking Britain had, on August 10th, seven hundred and two single-seater fighters and two hundred and sixty-one heavy fighters; just under a thousand serviceable long-range bombers, and about three hundred serviceable dive-bombers. Fighter Command shortly before this date had a tactical strength of six hundred and sixty-six aircraft, with nearly seven hundred and fifty either grounded temporarily or in reserve.[5] Because of its very high standards of training, it was seriously short of pilots, but British aircraft production was expanding on a growing base, while German production was restricted by the limitations of "Blitzkrieg" economy. British fighters shot down over British territory could be salvaged, and their pilots might be saved. German fighters, conversely, must be written off, and their pilots became prisoners of war. The Germans were trying to run up a downward-moving escalator. In spite of heavy losses, Fighter Command was growing stronger in relation to the Luftwaffe during both the earliest and final phases of the battle; only in the crucial period between August 24th and September 6th was the Luftwaffe gaining ground; and then the R.A.F.'s greater weakness was a shortage, not of planes, but of pilots.

The German single-seater Me 109 was as good a plane as the Spitfire (which accounted for only one-third of the R.A.F.'s modern single-seater fighters). It was certainly superior to the Hurricane, which made up the remaining two-thirds. But it had a cardinal weakness; its operational endurance was only one and a half hours, and this meant that it could fight for only a few minutes over Britain before it had to head for home. Its stable-mate, the twin-engined Me 110, was so unwieldy in combat that it was a liability. The dreaded Stuka dive-bombers had been effective enough against frightened men on the ground, but the R.A.F. found them excellent target practice; they were slow and weakly armed. The Heinkels, Dorniers and Junkers of the German bombing force had also been designed for co-operation with the army rather than the "knockout blow" which opinion in Britain had expected before the war. They were relatively fast, but as the winter of 1940–41 showed, they did not carry the scale of bomb-load required to knock out a major industrial country. It was the British, not the Germans, who had planned giant four-engined bombers for such a purpose. The pilots of the Me 109s had the frustration that they were tied to protecting these rather blunt instruments and could not chase the British fighters freely.

But the defence had its problems too. The Luftwaffe had the advantage of choosing its targets; the R.A.F. could not commit its whole strength against any one wave of bombers, and so its pilots were usually greatly outnumbered. It was for this reason that a struggle developed behind the scenes in Fighter Command. Air Vice Marshal Park, commanding No. 11 Fighter Group which guarded London (and so figured most frequently and heavily in the battle), stood by a policy of harrying the enemy piecemeal wherever he appeared; Leigh Mallory, commanding No. 12 group in the midlands, espoused the theory that the fighters should be assembled in "Big Wings" to attack the Germans in strength, even if the time taken meant that London (for instance) was bombed. Until the battle was almost over, Park's more strictly defensive view prevailed.

The R.A.F. was the youngest of the three services. Formed out of the Royal Flying Corps in 1918, it had established in the First World War its traditions of informality, heavy drinking, collective and individual modesty, and habitual understatement. J. L. Hodson noted in his diary in February 1940, "They're so fed up with such phrases as 'dicing with death' that they'll apply it to a game of darts just to show what they think of it." Pilots who bragged were fined by their comrades for "shooting a line", the North Sea was known irreverently as "the drink", and sophisticated modern aeroplanes were called "kites" or "crates".[6]

The reputation of the R.A.F. in July 1940 was not very high. The survivors of Dunkirk were bitter about the lack of air cover. The head of Fighter Command, Air Chief Marshal Dowding, was a remote, unattractive figure known to his men as "Stuffy". It was he who, in the middle of May, had persuaded the War Cabinet that no more British fighters should be wasted in defending the lost cause of France. While further fighters were subsequently sent, and the R.A.F. could not but intervene in the Dunkirk evacuation, there is no doubt that Dowding's insistence was crucial in preserving sufficient forces for the defence of Britain.

The peacetime R.A.F. had been greatly augmented, initially by absorbing its reserves. The Volunteer Reserve of week-end fliers had been over sixty thousand strong when war broke out. These reinforcements had confirmed the service's reputation for individualism, gaiety and unconventionality. One group captain noted of an auxiliary squadron which arrived at his station that they were "the motleyest collection of unmilitary young men I had seen for a very long time". The most famous of the newcomers, thanks to Richard Hillary's book *The Last Enemy*, have been the "long-haired boys" from Oxford University. Hillary explained the attraction which Fighter Command had for himself and his friends: "In a Spitfire we're back to war as it ought to be – if you can talk about war as it ought to be. Back to individual combat, to self-reliance, total responsibility for one's own fate." Substantially more than half the men in the R.A.F. were volunteers, which reflected its special appeal for the technically minded, the vain and the brave.[7]

Of the aircraft which saved Britain from invasion, the Hurricane was the more orthodox. Though one German air ace called it "a nice aeroplane to shoot down", it destroyed more enemy aircraft than any other Second World War fighter during a long career in which it was adapted to almost every climate and to almost every conceivable military purpose. Designed on strong, simple lines by Sidney Camm of Hawker Siddeley, it had a wing span of 40 feet, was 31 feet 5 inches long, and could travel at 340 miles per hour (but rarely, of course, did so). Cold calculation compels the judgment that the Spitfire was superior. The latter was some three inches shorter in the wings. It could reach 370 miles per hour before the battle ended; its manoeuvrability was legendary, and compelled far from grudging respect from the Germans who faced it.

The pilot of one of these planes could train on an enemy the concentrated fire of eight machine guns. His life depended on split-second anticipation and constant watchfulness. Yet the notion that these were independent knights errant, honour bound to "individual combat", is more attractive than appropriate. They were the most vital part of an intricate and extensive system of defence, and depended on others as fully as those others depended on them.

Most importantly, they depended on the radar system, based on a chain of coastal stations, which provided warning of the approach of the German bombers before they reached the coast. More will be said about the invention and development of radar later; meanwhile, it is sufficient to note that the public were not made officially aware of its existence until 1941, when it was referred to as "radio-location", that the American term "radar" was not adopted until 1943, and that the Germans, who had known for some time that Britain's assemblage of radio masts on the coasts was of importance in the defence system (and who had their own radio devices, backward in some respects, advanced in others), failed to grasp how crucial it was. Had the radar chain not existed, Fighter Command would have wasted its strength ineffectually in standing patrols; as it was, the British planes could rise relatively late to anticipate the intruders.

II

August 8th was the bloodiest day so far. The R.A.F. shot down thirty-one German planes – and claimed to have destroyed sixty. The Luftwaffe, who had accounted for twenty opponents, claimed forty-nine. Such exaggerations were typical of the days which followed. They were caused, primarily, by the confusion of pilots in the heat of battle; and if the Germans were regularly more inaccurate than the British, it should be remembered that they were fighting over foreign soil and had no chance to count the wrecks on the ground.

On the 10th, Richard Hillary and his friends were moved from Edinburgh to take part in the great struggle which was now expected. "Twenty-four of us flew south," he wrote, ". . . of those twenty-four eight were to fly back."[8] Fighter Command had already been under severe strain, but it was now that the life of its pilots became a hectic blur of fear, fatigue and fear again, and that the ordinary citizens of southern England began to realize how much depended on this struggle which they glimpsed overhead.

On the 12th, the Luftwaffe unleashed a major attack on the airfields and radar masts of the south-east. The radar station at Ventnor, in the Isle of Wight, was knocked out, and for ten days there was a gap in the protective shield. But Goering now made the first of his important blunders. Believing that assaults on the radar masts were, for technical reasons, likely to be fruitless, he shortly called them off.

On the 13th, the systematic destruction of Fighter Command in the air and on the ground was to begin with Eagle Day. This would precede the invasion, Operation Sea Lion, by one month; in four days, the Luftwaffe should have thrust Dowding's "boys" out of its way. But Eagle Day went off at half-cock. Bad intelligence (so much far Haw Haw's clocks) meant that bombs were wasted on the wrong airfields. The Luftwaffe, flying nearly fifteen hundred sorties, lost forty-five aircraft to the R.A.F.'s thirteen – but they claimed to. have destroyed ninety-eight British fighters, and believed that they had now knocked out eight major bases.

That night, German bombers scattered a large number of empty parachutes at various points in the midlands and in the lowlands of Scotland, along with radio transmitters, maps and other items. The feint was discredited by the fact that no human tracks could be observed leaving the fields where they had fallen. But the "New British Broadcasting Station" for several days propagated the legend that parachutists had descended, and were now being harboured by Fifth Columnists; some of them, it was announced, were equipped with an "electro-magnetic death ray".[9]

August 15th saw the maximum German effort of the battle; more than the 13th it deserved the name *"Adlertag."* The Luftwaffe supposed that the R.A.F. was now reduced to some three hundred fighters (whereas, in fact, it had double that number). For the first and only time, all three German air fleets in the west, including Luftflötte 5 operating from Norway, were committed in simultaneous daylight attacks. The Luftwaffe flew nearly eighteen hundred sorties; more than it would ever be able to mount again.

It was a fine, warm day. The bombers of Luftflötte 5, attacking the north of England without cover from Me 109s, were ignominiously routed and forced out of the battle; not a single British fighter was lost in repelling them. The R.A.F., by the end of the day, was ready to claim the destruction of no less than one hundred and eighty-two German aircraft, and had in fact brought down seventy-five, for the loss of thirty-four of its own fighters. Though the Germans claimed over a hundred scalps, they were bewildered by the ubiquitousness of Fighter Command, still assisted by virtually complete radar coverage. They managed, however, to do a good deal of damage, notably at Croydon airport. The houses and factories around the airfield also suffered, and this was the first time that Greater London had been seriously bombed. About two hundred houses were affected by bombs or blast; sixty-two people were killed, and three times that number made homeless.[10] It was a small foretaste of what was to follow.

Next day, the southern suburbs of London suffered again; but so did the Luftwaffe. On August 18th, a cloudy Sunday, another huge attack was combatted successfully. Several days of relative calm followed, when the weather was unsuitable for massed German assaults. On the 20th, Churchill sang the valour of

Fighter Command in the House of Commons. "Never in the field of human conflict", he said, "was so much owed by so many to so few." At which one fighter pilot is alleged to have remarked, "That must refer to mess bills."[11]

III

Conversely, never had so few warriors owed so much to so many. The Crusader had depended on his steed, his armourer and his squire; to produce fighter planes and keep them in the air involved thousands, eventually millions, of people. It is significant that Dowding, who controlled the British air defence, has not joined Nelson and Wellington in the Pantheon of British heroes, well though he worked. To assign credit for the successful outcome of the battle is a complex and eventually impossible task. It is sometimes most helpful to see it, not as a struggle between men, but as a contest between rival technologies, of which the British proved superior. Had the superb planes and the excellent (though far from infallible) radar system not been in existence that summer, no commander, however sagacious, and no daring brotherhood of pilots, however well trained, could have resisted the Luftwaffe. Even so, had the latter been better equipped for the job in hand, the outcome would probably have been very different.

Besides the pilots, many unpraised heroes exhausted themselves in maintaining the brittle and intricate structure of defence. Most immediately of all, there were the mechanics, technicians and engineers of the ground crews, working round the clock to keep the planes fuelled, armed and in repair, and the women of the W.A.A.F. who, often under bombing, drove vehicles, cooked food and maintained the vital switchboards.

There was the Royal Observer Corps, founded in the 1920s, who watched the German planes from their posts after they had passed the radar chain, and so helped to guide the fighters to their mark. The great majority of the thirty thousand or so observers were part-timers, exposing themselves to weather and to danger in crudely protected posts, without uniforms, and with steel helmets only if they were lucky. They were, however, remarkably efficient.

There were the civilians of the Post Office War Group who throughout the battle managed to maintain communications between radar stations, observer posts, and the R.A.F.'s operations rooms and airfields. There was the Civilian Repair Organization which by mid-July was returning a hundred and sixty aircraft per week to operational usefulness. This work involved garages, warehouses, car dealers and many hundreds of small contractors directly in the battle. At the No. 1 Civilian Repair Unit at Oxford, the official working day was fourteen hours, and a seven-day week was the rule. Men would travel in from distant villages on milk lorries, hours before they were due at work, because there were no buses and their absence would immobilize whole gangs of fifteen to twenty workers. Pilots sometimes flew damaged fighters straight to Oxford for "first aid", and machines were known to come back there two or even three times a week.[12]

And there was the aircraft industry, which in the summer of 1940 was presented with a new master, Lord Beaverbrook, and ordered to work as it had never worked before. ". . . The work you do this week fortifies and strengthens the front of battle next week," Beaverbrook told its hundreds of thousands of men and women. "The production which you pour out of your factories this week will be hurled into the desperate struggle next week."[13]

In April, the monthly output of fighters had been 256. In May, 261 were expected; 325 were delivered. In June, 446 were delivered; at a peak in July 496; twenty fewer in August and 467 in September. Altogether, over that period, some 650 more fighters were produced than had been planned for before Beaverbrook's arrival. The R.A.F. never had less than 127 Spitfires and Hurricanes in reserve at any time during the battle.[14]

Beaverbrook's achievement, however, remains controversial. As we have seen, the long hours which he asked for, and got, rapidly achieved more harm than good. His results were largely achieved at the expense of tank production; had the Germans fought the battle more wisely, they might have invaded in September, and then a very different light would have been cast on Beaverbrook's finest hour. His insistence that his ministry's contractors should have anything they wanted in the way of skilled workers made it quite impossible for Bevin to bring order to that dangerous situation. The unfortunate side effects of Beaverbrook's activities were felt, directly in the aircraft industry and indirectly elsewhere, for several years. But Churchill's reliance on the R.A.F. was right, and history has justified his friend.

Beaverbrook's hagiographers (or flattering demonologists)

have sometimes written as if "M.A.P.", as the new ministry was called, had sprung from his brow fully armed in May 1940. In fact, he took over a thriving department of the Air Ministry, together with its leading men, Air Marshal Sir Wilfred Freeman (the individual most responsible for the current quality · of British fighters) and Sir Charles Craven, seconded from his post as boss of Vickers Armstrong.

Before its offices were ready, M.A.P. began life at Beaverbrook's own London home. A hectic atmosphere was readily established, with typewriters in the bathrooms, papers on the beds, and never silent telephones. An eighteen-hour day became the rule, with Beaverbrook himself setting an example. Into his ministry he brought industrialists and journalists to form the crew of what soon earned the reputation of a pirate bark. Trevor Westbrook of Supermarine (the firm which made the Spitfire) and Patrick Hennessy of Fords joined Craven to provide Beaverbrook with a high-powered team of industrialists at the very summit of his organization. Established civil servants wrung their hands at the resultant structure – if, indeed, M.A.P. had any structure. "Titles and designations," remarks an official historian, ". . . meant very little to Lord Beaverbrook; he was inclined to distrust them, believing that the definition of functions limited activity and tended to destroy initiative." Or, as Beaverbrook himself put it in two slogans which he pinned up on the wall of his own room at the ministry – "Committees take the punch out of war" and "Organization is the enemy of improvisation".[15]

Beaverbrook and Craven agreed at once that the situation was so urgent that priority must be given to five different types of plane; the Spitfire, the Hurricane, and three bombers. Among these, the fighters had priority at a pinch. The pinch was felt.

Bevin pressed when he arrived in office for the creation of a "Production Council" at ministerial level to act as the "pivot of the production machine". This was set up, under the chairmanship of Arthur Greenwood, who proved ineffectual. The council met rarely and was never able to override the independent ministries. Beaverbrook sabotaged it by staying away altogether after its first meeting. The council established a system of "priorities" to guide those officials responsible for providing such scarce things as machine tools, skilled labour and steel. Aircraft, along with A.A. equipment and small arms, were an obvious choice for "Priority 1A". Other service needs were classified 1B or (in effect) 2, but these included items like tanks and machine guns which would soon be equally vital if indeed they were not already. In practice, the "priority" system gave Beaverbrook and his ministry a licence to beg, poach, borrow or commandeer what they liked. By the autumn, it was clear that this crude tool of planning might lead to disaster, and the War Cabinet ruled that henceforward scarce resources must be allocated between the three supply departments according to the scale of their existing programmes; but Beaverbrook pursued a vigorous rearguard action even then.[16]

More than any other minister, Beaverbrook cultivated the "Dunkirk Spirit". He gave orders that every manager of every plant should report in full at the end of each day on whatever shortages of materials and components were holding up production. When a factory did well, a telegram signed "Beaverbrook" would appear on the works notice board to spur on further effort. "Week-ends were often crisis time," one of his aides has written. One Friday afternoon it emerged that there was a shortage of the fabric used for making barrage balloons. "The managers of the factories concerned were summoned, most of them from the north of England. The minister met them at M.A.P. early on Saturday morning. By the afternoon they were on their way back with orders to get their works busy on the job that very day. And in the local cinemas that evening there was flashed on to the screens a message from Beaverbrook addressed to all the workers at the factories concerned. 'The Minister of Aircraft Production asks you to return to work at once where an urgent job awaits you.'"[17]

Beaverbrook's enthusiasm extended to salvage. The arduous work of the R.A.F.'s No. 50 M.U. (Maintenance Unit) should not pass unrecorded. Its personnel were mostly civilians, employees of the Morris motor works at Oxford. During the battle it provided a twenty-four-hour service, clearing away crashed aircraft from bombed aerodromes. One gang spent eighteen days at a badly hit fighter base, as new wrecks were beaten down around them, under persistent bombing and strafing from the Luftwaffe. ". . . From the time we left our lodgings in the morning until our return in the evening," records the gang leader, "we were lucky if we had a piece of bread and cheese."

A vast "Metal and Produce Recovery Depot" extended over a hundred acres of farmland near Oxford. It had eight miles of highways, nicknamed "Hurricane Road", "Spitfire Road" and so on, and "it looked not so much like a cemetery as a wartime mushroom town; a City of Wreckage where the oblong piles of debris were the fantastic houses, and the wing tips poking their way out from the irregular rooftops were the crazy, smokeless chimneys." Here, at the height of the battle, a man from the Spitfire factory near Southampton might be found searching the wrecks for precious parts urgently needed for new machines.[18] This valuable technique was known as "cannibalization".

With "stunts" of the sort which he had used to sell his newspapers, Beaverbrook helped to engage the general public in the battle. His first "stunt" misfired. In May, he broadcast an appeal for garage mechanics to leave their jobs and bestow their skills on the aircraft industry. The response was immediate. But many of the volunteers were car washers or pump attendants, and even the skilled men could be employed, without further training, only as fitters, the type of skilled labour least in demand. The result was that in August nearly three thousand of those who had answered the call were still unemployed.[19]

There was a similar element of farce in the Great Aluminium Scare which followed. On July 10th, the very day when the battle was beginning to intensify over the Channel, Beaverbrook issued a manifesto through the newspapers. "We will turn your pots and pans into Spitfires and Hurricanes, Blenheims and Wellingtons," he promised. He asked that "everyone who has pots and pans, kettles, vacuum cleaners, hat pegs, coat hangers, shoe trees, bathroom fittings and household ornaments, cigarette boxes, or any other articles made wholly or in part of aluminium, should hand them over at once to the local headquarters of the Women's Voluntary Services. . . . The need is instant. The call is urgent. Our expectations are high." The public, not excluding the Royal Family, loyally stripped its kitchens. The War Office gave up five hundred tons of saucepans. The Secretary of the Fly Fishers' Club wrote to *The Times* urging fishermen and golfers to part with their cherished gear. Vigilant housewives soon noted, however, that the hardware stores were still offering aluminium goods for sale. Beaverbrook's explanation came oddly from the bold, bad pirate; he had, he said, no power to pilfer from the shops. In fact, all the knick-knacks in the country, as he knew very well, would not yield much high-grade aluminium; and meanwhile, the scrap merchants were protesting that they still had large stocks.[20]

The Spitfire Funds, however, were a largely spontaneous outflow of public opinion, which Beaverbrook's propagandist flair turned to striking effect. The idea was that the people paid for their own Spitfires. In sober truth, money was now quite irrelevant to the production of fighters; but the pennies and pounds which contributed had a useful anti-inflationary effect.

The idea was born after a leading Jamaican newspaper had phoned M.A.P. to ask how much a bomber cost. A round figure of twenty thousand pounds was improvised; within a week, a cheque arrived for that amount. This, and further unexpected gifts, were publicized, the idea caught on, and hundreds of funds sprang up all over Britain and the Commonwealth. As the money rolled in, a Spitfire was "priced" at five thousand pounds, and an individual, city or group contributing that amount could "buy" a new aeroplane. Soon, the B.B.C. was giving lists of the latest donations at the end of the news bulletins. The average takings were over a million pounds per month and a total of over thirteen million pounds was reached by April 1941.

In the end, almost every big town in Britain had its name on a Spitfire. (Only a few donors chose to "buy" Hurricanes.) The hat was passed round in A.A. batteries and even in aircraft factories. Though unemployment was rife amongst them, the miners of Durham "contributed" two Spitfires. For those who wanted to know exactly where their money was going, a "price list" of components was issued; this idea originated in August, when a schoolboy sent Beaverbrook a guinea for a Spitfire's thermometer. Sixpence "bought" a rivet, two thousand pounds a wing. Only fifteen shillings was demanded for the blast tube of a machine gun, which was surely a bargain at the price, and for those who already dreamt of vengeance, twenty-two pounds would pay for a small bomb.[21]

IV

In any case, the public was clear by the middle of August that this was the biggest international fixture of all. Not everyone, even at this time, was overflowing with enthusiasm for the R.A.F.; inhabitants of the great ports of Hampshire, who were often bombed in Fighter Command's absence, and who saw bombers screeching about their housetops with apparent impunity, were far from impressed. But most people accepted the "scores" which news-vendors (deprived by paper shortage of their printed posters) chalked up on their placards – "BIGGEST RAID EVER – SCORE 78 TO 26 – ENGLAND STILL BATTING." A couple of reasons seemed obvious enough – the British planes were superior and the British pilots were braver. Sophisticated minds which were not quite satisfied with these explanations wishfully found others. British economic warfare had deprived the Germans of petrol, so they did not give their pilots sufficient training. British political warfare had deprived them of the will to fight. German planes, it was sagely said, had been found to have no instruments when they were wrecked – clearly, the Huns were short of raw materials or skill. (The origin of this interesting fallacy perhaps lay in the activities of defence scientists, who were naturally anxious to remove novel gadgets from the planes before small boys could do so). To add to the wonderment and gratitude of all, the R.A.F. were believed to be more thoroughly outnumbered than they were – figures of a hundred to one were loosely given. But it should be remembered, in case all this seems mere smugness, that the Head of the United States Military Mission which was in Britain during the battle announced that he thought the R.A.F.'s estimates of German losses to be "on the conservative side".[22]

Very few British civilians could distinguish a Hurricane from a Messerschmitt, even at fairly close quarters. Most had little chance of seeing either engaged in actual combat. Far away from the battle in the midlands, one might count the fighters roaring away from their bases in the early morning, and count them back, sadly, in the evening, when several would not return. In the north, except on August 15th, there was very little to see; in the west, where Plymouth was guarded by doughty but obsolete Gladiator biplanes, not much. Those who lived in the home counties had the best view of the match, but even they could not read the numbers on the players' backs. The most thrilling sight of all was also the most menacing – a perfect "Valhalla" formation of scores of German planes: When the fight was high, spectators might see no more than vapour trails, converging, circling and forming calm patterns in the depths of the sky, from which a blazing plane might, suddenly and almost incongruously, plummet. If the fight raged lower, the sunlight would pick out the planes in the blue above, and watchers would see them twisting and turning and hear their guns rattling "like someone a long distance away drawing a stick across railings". A parachute would gleam in the sun, a hurtling fighter would crash in the near distance. If someone who sounded sure of himself shouted "Messerschmitt!", who were the rest to contradict him? There were less flattering sights to be seen; the random destruction of bombs among cottages and fields, the grotesque downward smear of a withered barrage balloon after a raider, as was common, had found himself with nothing more urgent on hand than to shoot it into flames. But when the sirens sounded and battle was joined, it was easy to resist the lure of shelter to glory in what was usually adjudged another British victory. A few refrained from showing their interest. Early in September, strollers in Hyde Park had a splendid view of dogfighters chasing through the A.A. barrage over London; a group of men with their coats off and their sleeves rolled up continued to move to the slow rhythms of bowls, no doubt a little conscious of themselves as repositories of the spirit of Sir Francis Drake.[23]

Where the planes, German or British, had fallen, a rustic comedy might ensue as the village policeman cycled furiously across the fields to anticipate the local children, enjoying their summer holiday more than ever. A Home Guard would sternly mount guard over the wreck to prevent pillaging before the military and the salvagemen had had their way with it. Gawpers would stare avidly at bomb craters trying to imagine, or preferring not to imagine, the force of the blast which had made them, but if a town or village were carelessly struck by a Heinkel jettisoning his bombs to gain speed, bystanders might learn more graphically what blast and splinters did with the human body.

The parachutist descended from peril into peril. The Home Guard were armed and looking for trouble. One platoon in Kent was credited, quite preposterously, with bringing down a Dornier by controlled rifle fire. When the only fighter pilot to win a V.C. during the battle baled out over Hampshire, badly burnt, after a dogfight, he was shot at by a trigger-happy Home Guard. Late in the battle, when an R.A.F. pilot made a forced landing on a small field covered with anti-invasion obstacles, he had no time to congratulate himself before "a fairly elderly V.A.D. nurse . . . complete with toy pistol (belonging to her small son)" leapt through the hedge and pointed her weapon at him "in a most terrifying manner". On September 5th, the Air Ministry issued a notice reminding the public that not all parachutists were enemies. But for many, to confront a real German at last, on one's home ground, inspired not martial sentiment but swift, unexpected compassion. A. G. Street, a keen Home Guard, joined in a chase through Wiltshire after a German airman who had baled out. On capture, he proved to be "a very ordinary, decent-looking lad". He observes, "As I was driving home I realized that I, a civilian, had just experienced my first taste of war, and that I disliked it intensely. I was dead keen to hunt that fellow, felt the same exhilaration as I did when hounds were running, and would have shot him on the instant if need be. But, somehow, when he was caught I had no further quarrel with him."[24]

But these ordinary young men were doing plenty of damage. By day, work in offices and factories was interrupted as everyone filed to the shelter. Railway travellers in the south sat in halted trains with the blinds down, by order, listening to vague thumps and bangs; and bombs on the line meant lengthy diversions. At night when Fighter Command could not stop the Luftwaffe roaming freely, the siren jolted people from their sleep. "Every time I fly," one German navigator calculated "a million people take to their shelters." The warning system in use was somewhat inflexible, and the authorities had a serious problem. If they gave ample warning to all the areas which might be reached by a particular handful of "nuisance raiders", it might create disproportionate disruption. On the night of June 24th, for instance, "the whole of the country south of a line from Hull to Liverpool was under 'red' warning" – that is, sirens had been sounded – "though only Bristol was threatened by more than one or two aircraft". On the other hand, when Aberdeen was attacked on the night of July 12th, and more than fifty people were killed or seriously injured, the public warning had not been given.[25]

As August proceeded, the attacks intensified. In a more recent parlance, the war "escalated".

V

When the end of the spell of cloudy weather permitted the Luftwaffe to resume heavy attacks, on August 24th, it adopted new tactics. By constant patrols over the Channel and by feint attacks to baffle the radar system, it confused and wore down the defences, and was able to punish very severely No. 11 Group's vital ring of seven sector stations, the keys to the defence of London. In the next fortnight, Britain came very near to losing the battle.

Over that period, British losses of fighters, not only in the air, but bombed on the ground, far outstripped the rate of new production from the factories. Throughout the battle (this is too often forgotten) the R.A.F. had regularly lost more fighters than the Luftwaffe; it was bombers which swelled the big scores, and to break even, the R.A.F. had to shoot down a great many of them. In the critical fortnight, they could no longer manage to do this. In the week which ended on September 6th, Fighter Command lost a hundred and sixty-one planes in air battles alone for only a hundred and eighty-nine German planes of all types brought down, and this exchange rate was too low. What was worst was the loss of pilots. During the fortnight, a hundred and three British pilots were killed and a hundred and twenty-eight wounded, a weekly wastage rate of over ten per cent of Fighter Command's combat strength. The experienced pilots were now either dead or exhausted. The new men coming from the training units were insufficient in numbers to make up the loss, and few of them were, as yet, really battle-worthy.[26]

Squadrons which went into battle full of excitement and confidence were withdrawn ten days or a fortnight later battered and decimated. "We were dead," one pilot has written. "We were too tired even to get drunk. You simply never saw a pilot drunk."[27] Young men, often very young indeed, bombed on their airfields as they tried to take off or land, swept aside in the air by the Me 109s, flying as many as half a dozen sorties a day, might parachute wounded from their planes, hitch-hike back to base, and take the air again next morning. The strain, of course, told. Inhabitants of the suburbs, who saw and heard the destruction of the sector stations, the planes screaming in low to attack, were aware of a crisis. Six of the seven sector stations were bombed to the point where the whole system of defence might soon have collapsed.

Perhaps we should hail as the cardinal saviours of Britain that summer, certain German pilots who lost their way on the night of August 24th. Directed to attack aircraft factories and an oil refinery in the home counties, they bombed the central London area by mistake, contravening Hitler's direct and emphatic orders to his pilots. Considerable fires were started in the City; the East End suburbs had their first scattering of bombs since 1918. Churchill ordered a reprisal. Next night, eighty R.A.F. planes were sent to bomb Berlin. Again, there was a mistake; those who reached the German capital damaged "civilian" as well as "legitimate" military targets. There were further raids on Berlin, night by night, and, ineffectual though they were, the first civilians were killed there on August 28th. Hitler had promised his people that this would never happen; the disillusionment of the Berliners was obvious, and dangerous.

After smallish attacks aimed at factories in the midlands on the nights of the 25th and 26th, Goering ordered what the Luftwaffe intended to be its first major attack on a British city.

On the 28th, 29th, 30th and 31st, a nightly average of over a
hundred and fifty bombers were sent to punish Merseyside.
In effect, these were "nuisance" raids on the familiar pattern,
keeping people awake but doing little damage, for the Luftwaffe
wandered so widely that other towns in the south, north and
west received bombs designed for Liverpool. But on the 31st,
over a hundred and sixty fires were kindled in the city's commercial centre.[28]

The day before, Hitler had given permission for reprisal
attacks, with strong forces, on London. On the 31st, over the
same week-end when Biggin Hill sector station in Kent endured
six punishing raids in three days, wheels were set in motion for a
fatal change of German tactics. On September 4th, Hitler made a
surprise appearance at a rally of woman nurses and social workers
in Berlin. He promised invasion. "In England they're filled with
curiosity and keep asking, 'Why doesn't he come?' Be calm.
Be calm. He's coming! He's coming!" Then he brought the
women to their feet with hysterical applause as he swore, "When
the British Air Force drops two or three or four thousand
kilograms of bombs, then we will in one night drop 150, 250,
300 or 400 thousand kilograms. When they declare that they will
increase their attacks on our cities, then we will *raze* their cities
to the ground. We will stop the handiwork of these night air
pirates, so help us God!"[29]

It was not only the need for reprisals to sustain German morale
which provoked the switch of tactics. The calm of Dowding, the
stubbornness of Park, the sleepwalking courage of their pilots,
by postponing the Luftwaffe's success, had left the Germans with
very little time in which to invade before the winter. Goering was
impatient. On Park's orders, the R.A.F. were shunning combat;
the bait was not working. A huge raid on London would lure
them out. There were, according to Goering's information,
relatively few of them left anyway. September 7th would see the
final blow. By that day, British reconnaissance had shown a
striking concentration of barges in north-west France and
Belgium, waiting for the invasion.

VI

Even in that splendid summer, Saturday, September 7th, stood
out as a beautiful day. In spite of everything, tea cups clinked in
suburban gardens and tired workers dozed in the sun.

The Luftwaffe's change of tactics took Fighter Command by surprise. A force of hundreds of bombers broke through the defences, arranged to protect the sector stations, and streamed with its fighter escort towards London. Arriving about five o'clock, the first bombers set the docks alight with their incendiaries. Guided by those flames, others followed in a shuttle service until four thirty next morning, pouring high explosive into the blazing East End.

From one of the inner suburbs, Barbara Nixon, an air raid warden, watched "the miniature silver planes circling round and round the target area in such perfect formation that they looked like a children's toy model of flying boats or chair-o-planes at a fair."[30] Streets all over the sprawling city soon clanged furiously with the bells of fire engines heading north, south or east to the towering, apocalyptic white cloud of smoke which blackened round the edges and turned an angry red as the evening drew in. Riding in their grey appliances which had been improvised out of requisitioned saloon cars, the men of the A.F.S. went into action. Most of them had never before faced a serious fire.

A group of silent men stood high on the colonnade of St. Paul's Cathedral, part of the devoted body of volunteer watchers who had long been preparing to save Wren's masterpiece if possible in the event of just such a catastrophe as this. "At last someone spoke, 'It is like the end of the world,' and someone else replied, 'It is the end of *a* world.' "[31]

A Polish Hurricane pilot, returning after chasing some bombers back to the coast, wrote in his combat report that his heart was heavy, in spite of his victories, "for the whole eastern suburb of London seemed to be burning. It was a very sorrowful sight, reminding me of a flight a year ago over Poland, near Lublin; it was the same spectacle." Air Vice Marshal Park, his superior, also passed over London that evening. The flames, he has recalled, made him "very angry". But, as he goes on, ". . . I said 'Thank God', because I realized that the methodical Germans had at last switched their attacks from my vital aerodromes on to cities."[32]

The Chiefs of Staff were meeting Churchill at Downing Street, very much within earshot of the bombs, which seemed, as one Londoner recalls, to come down "with a tearing sound as well as a whistle; they did not fall, they rushed at enormous velocity, as though dragged down towards the earth by some supernaturally gigantic magnet." In his East End parish, Father H. A. Wilson heard doors slamming and windows rattling round him as the bombs made the floor beneath his feet tremble, and "had no hope of living through that night . . . I do not think that I ever said a prayer [he wrote later]; beyond an occasional 'Oh God!' if that may be accounted a prayer. I was frightened as I had never been before." Not far away, in Stepney's Jewish quarter, people remembered Haw Haw's threats and believed that the beacon was designed to light the bombers specifically towards the destruction of their race. Bernard Kops, then a boy of fourteen, recalls that day "like a flaming wound in my memory. Imagine a ground floor flat, crowded with hysterical women, crying babies and great crashes in the sky and the whole earth shaking . . . The men started to play cards and the women tried a little singsong, singing, 'I saw the old homestead and faces I loved' or 'Don't go down in the mines, dad, dreams very often come true' or 'Yiddle mit his fiddle'. But every so often twenty women's fists shook at the ceiling, cursing the explosions, Germany, Hitler."[33]

Just after eight o'clock, the Chiefs of Staff, no doubt mustering all the calm they could, issued the code word CROMWELL. Over the hours that followed, it passed down, officially, to the army's commanders, and unofficially, to the Home Guard.

At Llandudno, on the North Wales coast, the usual parades had been held, the usual guards posted, but long after the bar at the British Legion club where the Home Guard had their headquarters had been closed for the night, a Signals corporal was still teaching drill to a few enthusiasts. An officer answered a call from one of his Home Guard superiors, a colonel. "The zone commander's been ringing," the latter announced. ". . . I'm damned if I can make him out. All he'd say was 'Cromwell' " The corporal had stopped his demonstration and caught the word. With an exclamation, he ran off. Suddenly, the light dawned on the others. This meant invasion. Within a short time, the Llandudno Home Guard had been called out in their denim uniforms, and had been ordered to their battle stations – the town hall, the sea front, the golf links.[34]

Similar scenes occurred in the army and Home Guard headquarters in more vulnerable areas. Many commanders forgot that "Cromwell" did not necessarily mean that an invasion was in progress. The Home Guard rang the church bells. The army, in some places, blew up bridges. Throughout that night, amateur and regular troops kept a tense vigil.

From the Chilterns, from the Downs, thirty miles from London, they saw the glow in the sky and tried to imagine what was happening. They could not. The deputy chief warden of the East End borough of Poplar, who worked that night in the thick of the raids, wrote years later: "They could not see stick after stick of bombs dropping into the flames and hurling burning wood, embers and showers of sparks hundreds of feet into the air; they could not see gangs of A.R.P. workers clearing earth from buried Anderson shelters and bringing the occupants, dazed and half suffocated, out into the revivifying air which was, none the less, heavy with smoke and redolent of charred timber; they could not visualize wardens picking their way through debris and, since phones had gone, making their way hurriedly to Control to report fresh incidents; . . . they could not see the Control staffs, perspiring, exhausted, foodless, endlessly ordering out fresh parties, nor could they hear the gasp of the telephone girl taking the air raid message dealing with her own home."[35]

While the Battle of Britain was still very much in progress, what is sometimes called the Battle of London had begun. It was the battle of an unarmed civilian population against incendiaries and high explosive; the battle of firemen, wardens, policemen, nurses and rescue workers against an enemy they could not hurt. The front line troops were doctors, parsons, telephonists, and people who in peacetime life had been clerks, builders' labourers and housewives. Where the bombs fell, heroes would spring up by accident; a sixteen-year-old messenger boy riding through cratered streets on his bicycle, an elderly hospital porter flinging himself over a trapped nurse to save her at the cost of his own life as yet more masonry fell.

On that first night it was above all the firemen who had to rise to the occasion. A. P. Herbert has described what he modestly calls "my most fantastic journey through London". As a petty officer in the Royal Navy's Thames Auxiliary Patrol, he commanded his own small motor boat, and that night he set off down river from Hammersmith towards the glow he had seen in the sky to the east. "As far as Vauxhall", he writes, "there was the light of early dusk, and after Lambeth it was nearly the light of day . . . The Temple and its lawns were brilliant and beautiful . . . The Pool, below London Bridge, was a lake of light." He reported for duty and was sent on a mission down to Woolwich. Rounding Limehouse corner, he saw "a stupendous spectacle. Half a mile or more of the Surrey shore was burning . . . The wind was westerly, and the accumulated smoke and sparks of all the fires swept in a high wall across the river." Herbert, mindful of his mission, pressed on with a wet towel over his face into "the incandescent cloud". Inside, "the scene was like a lake in Hell. Burning barges were drifting everywhere . . . We could hear the hiss and roar of the conflagration, a formidable noise, but we could not see it, so dense was the smoke. Nor could we see the eastern shore."[36]

In peacetime, a fire which had engaged thirty pumps had been a very big one indeed. Shortly after midnight on September 8th, there were 9 huge conflagrations rated at "100 pumps" each. Besides these, when the raiders left that morning, there were 19 fires rating 30 pumps or more, 40 10-pump fires, and nearly a thousand lesser blazes.

In the Surrey Docks, which Herbert had passed, the raiders had fired two hundred and fifty acres of timber. The fire officer in charge of the resulting inferno sent an exasperated message to his superiors, "Send all the bloody pumps you've got; the whole bloody world's on fire". Elsewhere, that night, "There were pepper fires, loading the surrounding air heavily with stinging particles so that when the firemen took a deep breath it felt like breathing fire itself. There were rum fires, with torrents of blazing liquid pouring from the warehouse doors (nor any drop to drink) and barrels exploding like bombs themselves. There was a paint fire, another cascade of white hot flame, coating the pumps with varnish that could not be cleaned for weeks. A rubber fire gave forth black clouds of smoke so asphyxiating that it could only be fought from a distance, and was always threatening to choke the attackers."[37]

Firemen were cut off and perished in the acres of flame; men bent their faces to the nozzles of their hoses, craving the draught of pure cold air which dwelt round the water jet. Yet for others, it was the cold which was unbearable, coupled with thirst and hunger. One pump at least was continuously in action for forty hours, with A.F.S. men taking turns on the heavy branch. Their arms and shoulders ached, for the force of the water made the hose difficult to hold, and the back pressure made it difficult to keep the branch up foward to the fire. "Gradually", one of them recalls, "we got wet; the film of mist blown by the wind off our jet settled on everything, till in a very little while we were just covered in a cold, sticky mixture of oil, petrol and water . . ."[38]

It was days before these fires were extinguished, and meanwhile others were created; in those days, the flames fused the A.F.S. and the regular firemen together in unity, to form a new class of never resting sleepwalkers.

Many East Enders lived virtually on islands, connected only by bridges with London's mainland. In the Surrey Docks, fires threatened the two bridges across which the 'local inhabitants could escape. By heroic action, a thousand people, old and young, mothers and children, were evacuated. One of the heroines was the local W.V.S. organizer, who collected a convoy of cars and, when these proved insufficient, appealed for anything on wheels; " 'even the dust-carts.' she added, and the dust-carts came." In the following days, two other dock areas in a similar plight were evacuated; on the 9th, the town clerk of Stepney, entirely on his own initiative, arranged for a thousand people to be taken to safety in river steamers.[39]

The Sunday which followed the first night of blitz had, some time before, been designated a National Day of Prayer. There was little time for prayer in the East End. Churchill, accompanied by the Chief Administrative Officer of the London Civil Defence Region, Harold Scott, went to see the damage for himself. In the early afternoon, he passed pitiful groups of shelterers, already taking their bedding and belongings to the hiding places they had marked down for the night. They dropped what they were carrying and cheered when they saw Churchill. "Putting his hat on the end of his stick, he twirled it round and roared, 'Are we downhearted?' and they shouted back, 'No!' with astonishing gusto." The Prime Minister went on towards the dock area of Silvertown, one of those in danger of isolation. He passed down roads covered with debris and broken glass and great coils of firehose. At one point, tallow from a burnt candle factory made the road slippery; at another, the air was thick with odours from a scent factory. Elsewhere, there was the choking smell of burning wood. Red-eyed, weary, filthy firemen were still struggling with the many fires which yet raged. On the way back, a shop just in front of Churchill's car was blown to smithereens. But Scott noticed that the Prime Minister was enjoying himself: "his spirits obviously rose with the excitement of action."[40]

Four hundred and thirty civilians had died on the first night, and sixteen hundred had been seriously injured, while thousands more were now homeless. On the evening of the 8th, Bernard Kops found himself in a huge crush of people who were trying to get into the Liverpool Street tube station, the East Enders' gateway to the underground railway system. At first the authorities would not let them in, but "The people would not give up and would not disperse, would not take no for an answer. A great yell went up and the gates were opened and my mother threw her hands together and clutched them towards the sky. 'Thank God. He heard me.' "[41]

Just after eight o'clock, the bombers came back. By next morning, over four hundred more Londoners had been killed. Three main line termini had been put out of action on the first night. After the second, every main line to the south was blocked. On Monday night, the raiders came back again and the death roll was three hundred and seventy. For seventy-six consecutive nights, excepting November 2nd when weather conditions ruled it out, London was raided, and almost always the attack was heavy.

VII

The code word CROMWELL remained in force for twelve days, during which the army stood ready for invasion. Rumour, whose tongues flickered more busily than ever in the home counties, held that an invasion had been attempted and had failed with many deaths, and although this was quite untrue, it was pleasant to think of. Hitler had sounded so sure of himself – "He is coming. He is coming."

In fact, Hitler was far from sure of himself. He hoped more than ever now that this difficult and perhaps dangerous invasion would be unnecessary, and the assault on London was wishfully seen in Berlin as a substitute. Morale in London was said to be cracking; surely the British must sue for peace now? Sealion had been postponed from September 15th to the 21st; the German navy would need ten days to make its own final preparations. But on the 11th, Hitler made no decision; he left matters to ride until the 14th. On the 14th, he postponed his decision again, till the 17th. Meanwhile, R.A.F.'s Bomber Command was coming into its own, playing havoc with the invasion barges.[42]

In London, morale rallied after the first shock. On the 11th, Churchill broadcast to his people. He described the effort of the Luftwaffe to obtain mastery of the air as "the crux of the whole war"; he announced that barges for the invasion had congregated across the Channel; he said that the next week ranked in British history "with the days when the Spanish Armada was approaching the Channel, and Drake was finishing his game of bowls; or when Nelson stood between us and Napoleon's Grand Army at Boulogne" – indeed, this crisis was of graver consequence than those had been. "Every man and woman will therefore prepare himself [*sic*] to do his duty, whatever it may be, with special pride and care . . ."[43]

The weather, after September 7th, again helped Dowding and his men. Only light activity was possible on four days of the next week, though there were big daylight raids aimed at London on the 9th, 11th and 14th. The fearsome wounds of the sector stations began to heal as they received no further maulings. However, Fighter Command put up a resistance which seemed to the Luftwaffe merely desultory. Its losses in repelling the raid of the 11th were twenty-nine to the Germans' twenty-four, and the Me 109 was still very much king. To Goering, it seemed that one more effort by his men would suffice.

So sure were the Germans on September 15th that they did not bother to execute their now habitual diversionary flights. This was another important error.

The sky that morning was cloudless, but after midday, thin veils of cloud began to develop, and it was on a delicately luminous afternoon that people in southern England glimpsed the Luftwaffe's humiliation. At about eleven thirty, the leaders of a great horde of bombers crossed the coast heading for London. The first battles developed over Canterbury. Park, with more time than usual, called for help from Leigh Mallory in the north. Mallory's pet "Big Wing" was assembled and hit the Germans as they reached London. The formations were broken and fled in confusion to the coast. In the afternoon, the Germans came back in strength. Fighter Command put every plane it could into the air, with happy results. While considerable damage was caused in London, nothing like the ruthless precision of the September 7th attack was possible. A final attack came at six o'clock, a minor one on the Supermarine Spitfire factory near Southampton, and this too was repelled.

The largely inexperienced British pilots were more optimistic than usual in their claims. The B.B.C. announced that night that 185 German planes had been destroyed. The actual total remains in dispute (as do most of the statistics of the battle already quoted here) but it was probably 52. Even so, the victory was striking, for Fighter Command had lost only 26 planes and 13 pilots. The German losses were serious enough, after the Luftwaffe's weeks of attrition, and the dismay of the pilots, who had seen the ghosts of Spitfires and Hurricanes believed dead rise up before them, was matched by a sober reaction from their commanders.[44]

The battle had now turned decisively in Britain's favour; over the next ten days or so, the Luftwaffe's losses outnumbered

Fighter Command's by more than two to one. Sealion, in Telford Taylor's phrase, was "pinched to death" – the invasion could not be launched because Fighter Command remained very palpably unvanquished, and the ships assembled could not be held indefinitely at the ready in the face of Bomber Command's attacks. On the 17th, Hitler in effect postponed Sealion indefinitely. On the 28th, the Fuehrer directed that the economy should be mobilized towards the invasion of Russia. When that stroke came, he would still have an enemy to the west of him, hard pressed but not finished, and the failure of the Luftwaffe had sealed his fate.

Throughout the second half of September, daylight raids on London continued whenever the weather was favourable. On the 16th, a German communiqué gave exceptional delight to the British by announcing solemnly that Goering himself had flown over London in one of the small attacks on that day. (He was, in fact, far too large to get through the door of a German bomber.) On the 27th, a grand attack on London almost comparable to that of the 15th was mounted. It was broken up over Kent; only 20 out of 300 raiders reached central London and the Germans lost 55 planes to 28. The ratio in the last major daylight battle on September 30th was even more favourable to Fighter Command.[45]

Meanwhile, belatedly, the Luftwaffe had begun to devote systematic attention to British aircraft factories. During the crucial phase of the battle it had delivered punishing attacks on factories in Kent, Surrey and Hampshire, crippling production for a time and killing many workers. Now that the battle was virtually over, it extended this policy with much success. On the 25th, the Bristol Aeroplane Company's works at Filton was bombed, with over two hundred and fifty casualties, and this blow was followed up on the 27th. Supermarine at Southampton, already subjected to much attention, was completely devastated on the 26th. But Short's at Rochester, bombed on August 15th, had already shown the way by dispersing its production over other sites. The makers of the Spitfire followed suit and established production in thirty-five improvised workplaces.[46]

Beaverbrook had embraced the idea of dispersing not only factories but stores, with great zest. By the end of October, M.A.P. had begged, borrowed or stolen over three hundred premises for dispersal factories. The last method was especially useful. M.A.P., as a new ministry, had been late in the queue for requisitioning property. Beaverbrook told his lieutenants to grab anything they could find, whether another department had earmarked it or not, while all over Britain, single aircraft were stored in sheds, garages and barns. Through a storm of protests, Beaverbrook could be heard threatening to put them in Winchester Cathedral if nothing else came to hand. He also pursued the idea of building factories underground. The largest of these was set up in caves a hundred feet underground near Bath, and gun barrels for fighters and Bristol aero-engines were eventually made there. This Wellsian creation was complete with lifts, moving staircases, laboratory, canteens and offices. Construction cost nearly twelve million pounds and involved a force of about eight thousand men before it finally went into production in the summer of 1942. Understandably, in view of the cost, there were only three other major underground schemes.[47]

On October 8th, Churchill warned the House of Commons that invasion was still possible; but by now most people felt, rightly, that Fighter Command had saved them until the next summer at least, and that Britain would grow relatively stronger as the days proceeded. In October, the Luftwaffe resorted to sending over mostly fighters by day, while its bombers hammered London, and other centres, by night. Its losses remained relatively very high in the daytime, but Fighter Command had, as yet, no adequate techniques or even planes for night operations.

The Germans continued their heavy bombing of civilian centres partly to persist with the policy of "reprisals"; partly, no doubt, because Hitler and Goering were sadists; and partly because the raids were clearly effective, in disrupting communications, ruining sleep, and watering whatever small shoots of defeatism existed in Britain. There was nothing to be done in London but to aim to survive and, more constructively, to help others to survive.

Chapter Four

Blitz: September 1940 to May 1941

It so happens that this war, whether those at present in authority like it or not, has to be fought as a citizen's war. There is no way out of that because in order to defend and protect this island, not only against possible invasion but also against all the disasters of aerial bombardment, it has been found necessary to bring into existence a new network of voluntary associations such as the Home Guard, the Observer Corps, all the A.R.P. and fire-fighting services, and the like . . . They are a new type, what might be called the organized militant citizen. And the whole circumstances of their wartime life favour a sharply democratic outlook. Men and women with a gift for leadership now turn up in unexpected places. The new ordeals blast away the old shams. Britain, which in the years immediately before this war was rapidly losing such democratic virtues as it possessed, is now being bombed and burned into democracy.

J. B. Priestley, *Out of the People*

THE EVEN TENOR OF THE BLITZ

"Medals? We don't want no — medals. The whole — borough deserves a — medal."

Heavy rescue workers of Bermondsey, asked to nominate some of their number for decorations, May 1941[1]

1

A GREAT provincial city like Sheffield could erect a dummy town in the neighbouring hills to attract and deceive the Luftwaffe, but the sprawling size of London made it impossible to disguise, and the U-shaped bend of the Thames round the Isle of Dogs, in the heart of Dockland, was unmistakable from the air.

Ten or a dozen miles from the centre of the capital, to north, south, west and east, lay the outer suburbs, from which office workers surged towards the centre in the morning, and to which they swarmed out again in the evenings. Harrow and Hornsey, Ealing and Richmond, Woodford, Wimbledon, Croydon and Bromley were the heartland of the English middle class, zones of tidy gardens, extensive green playing fields, quiet and propriety. Now tired commuters struggled home somehow on slow trains (when there were any) and went straight to their Andersons for the night, perhaps to read Trollope, whose pictures of the croquet lawns and country houses of the mid-Victorian age of equipoise were enjoying a marked but easily explained boom. Few footsteps, after darkness, echoed in the avenues. The warden's post was the liveliest social centre which the blacked-out, owner-occupied acres could afford. Within this outer ring of pebble dash, red brick and ornamental trees lay intermediate suburbs, shabbier genteel; then, to the north and west, older suburbs which gave flats and mansions to the well-to-do. Some, like Chelsea, were battered remorselessly. Others, like Hampstead, came off relatively lightly. Incendiaries would lodge in the rafters of mansions deserted by their owners, and burn them out. At the hub of the wheel lay the twin cities of London and Westminster. With Whitehall, Bloomsbury, Fleet Street, St. Paul's, the Bank of England, the central area still concentrated within its few square miles Britain's cultural past, its commercial present and its legislative future. The raider could be sure that whatever he struck there was of objective or sentimental importance, and later this would become the most heavily blitzed area of all.

But on September 7th and the days which followed the bombs poured chiefly on Stepney, with its inimitable mixture of races, where nearly two hundred thousand people lived at an average of twelve per dwelling; on the tailors of Whitechapel; the factories, warehouses and gasworks of Poplar; the woodworking firms of Shoreditch; the docks of West Ham and Bermondsey. They poured on the sweated clothing trade, on the casual labour of the docks, on petty businesses Jewish and Gentile, on jerry-built Victorian slums, on marshy land which had made it hard to provide decent shelters. They poured on Cockneys who often knew little of the world beyond their immediate neighbourhood, who found their shops, their entertainments and their marriages near at home, who often spent their lives in the streets in which they had grown up, where two or three generations of the same family would commonly be found living in adjacent houses, where poverty and community flourished on the same stalk.

Here communism had found its best base in Britain outside a few mining districts. Here, in the mid-'thirties, Mosley had sought a foundation for his British Union of Fascists. The monotonous sequence of small bankruptcies in the tailoring and furnishing trades had given him his chance. Jews whose fathers had fled from the pogroms of eastern Europe had had their shop windows smashed and their lives threatened. When Mosley had limped through the narrow streets, thickets of arms had shot up on each side, though strong socialist feeling had thwarted the break-through he had needed.

"Everybody is worried about the feeling in the East End," wrote Harold Nicolson in his diary on September 17th. ". . . There is much bitterness. It is said that even the King and Queen were booed the other day when they visited the destroyed areas."[2] Had the East End lost all heart, the chain reaction might have crippled London's morale. This nearly happened, but not quite, and after a few days the attack shifted noticeably westwards. But dockland witnessed frightful scenes, not all by any means of the Luftwaffe's making.

The authorities, drawing up and implementing the plans for civil defence, had based them on the expectation of a swift, gigantic assault, probably by daylight. So the blitz caught A.R.P. on the wrong foot when it came. The elaborate precautions against gas and the proposals for mass burial in quicklime were mercifully redundant. But the attacks took place at night, thanks to Fighter Command, and they might last for twelve or fourteen hours. This at once exposed the inconvenience of the private and public shelters; that people would have to sleep, eat and excrete in them night after night had not been allowed for.

Because the casualties were relatively light, and because the squalid dwellings of the East End were easily ravaged by blast, people who should, according to plan, have been dead, were flooding the rest centres. While there were too many stretcher parties for carrying off casualties, the men of the Heavy Rescue Service – the Demolition Squads as they were loosely called – were on duty for twenty-four-hour shifts, extricating the living and the dead, shifting and loading debris, shoring up buildings and salvaging personal belongings. Troops soon had to be called in to assist with demolition.

Aggravating every difficulty, there was another unexpected factor, the unexploded bomb, or "U.X.B.". Perhaps one in ten of the bombs dropped on London were duds; but others were equipped with delayed action fuses and all "U.X.B.s" had to be treated as if they were "D.A." At first, all premises were evacuated and all roads closed within a six hundred yard radius of each bomb. Only a handful of troops, Royal Engineers, were present to deal with them, and by the end of October, though a special organization had been created, there were three thousand U.X.B.s waiting for treatment. Hundreds, even thousands, of people might be made homeless by one dud bomb. The cold courage of the bomb disposal squads was one of the marvels of the period. It was spectacularly in evidence when the most famous U.X.B. of all entered the ground at an angle, very close to St. Paul's, on September 12th, and began to creep towards the foundations of the cathedral. With great bravery, it was finally extricated on the 15th, was driven in a lorry at headlong speed through the East End, and exploded in Hackney Marshes, where it made a crater one hundred feet in diameter.[3]

Fairly or unfairly, the reaction of the East Enders to the failure of the authorities to plan for the real nature of the blitz was first bewilderment, then anger. Yet they did not revolt nor, truly speaking, panic. Explaining this phenomenon, some journalists of the period created a myth of the Cockney wisecracking over the ruins of his world, which is as famous as the myth of the Few soaring into battle with laughter on their lips, and equally misleading. Other journalists, running the risk of censorship and suppression, did visit the battlefronts of Stepney and West Ham to report what they saw in cold, angry terms, and to spearhead the storm of protest which swept westwards to Whitehall.

The reasons, so far as they can be analysed, why morale in the East End did not collapse, may help to explain, *mutatis mutandis*, why morale in Berlin was not shattered by its still more destructive raids later in the war.

In the first place, those who wanted to, or thought they had to, fled. From the East End, the homeless and the fearful trekked out in the mornings, pushing their chattels in prams or hand carts. Such towns to the west as Reading, Windsor and Oxford coped with a sizable influx of helpless refugees. Vera Brittain, who visited Oxford in the early days of the blitz, found babies' nappies drying in the august Tom Quad of Christ Church; the colleges acted for a while as clearing houses while the authorities found billets for the refugees. Five hundred to a thousand people were put up for nearly two months in the Majestic cinema on the city's outskirts:

> Covering the floor beneath the upturned velveteen seats of the cinema chairs [wrote Miss Brittain], disorderly piles of mattresses, pillows, rugs and cushions indicate the "pitches" staked out by each evacuated family. Many of the women, too dispirited to move, still lie wearily on the floor with their children beside them in the foetid air, though the hour is eleven a.m. and a warm sun is shining cheerfully on the city streets. Between the mattresses and cushions, the customary collection of soiled newspapers and ancient applecores is contributing noticeably to the odoriferous atmosphere.[4]

Other frightened or homeless people trekked out to the open spaces in or near London. Several thousand, as Richard Titmuss puts it, "trudged off to Epping and sat down in the forest", where camps were set up for them. It was in this area of suburban Essex that an influential local dignitary, confronted with the idea that the homeless should be compulsorily billeted there, said flatly, "I will not have these people billeted on our people".[5] Even now, when the need for evacuation was obvious enough, some of the well-to-do people of the suburbs and countryside still revealed the bleak class hatred which had underlain the first response to evacuation a year before.

It follows that those who remained in the blitzed areas, night by night, were those who preferred to stay, or felt they had to stay. Their work or their business lay in the East End. They were, perhaps, wardens or Home Guard, who felt the call of duty (though in London and elsewhere, there were wardens amongst those who fled). In this case, they had to adapt themselves to danger. As they did so, they set an example of calm and courage which others, in their turn, felt constrained to follow. Local leaders – parsons, doctors, social workers – stuck to their posts and tried to bring order to the hideous chaos. Others, fearful at first, found themselves drawn to assist in various more or less spontaneous activities designed to alleviate conditions.

Political agitation was bound to fail. Anti-semitism persisted, and was inflamed to some extent when better-off Jews (like better-off Gentiles) bought their way out of London. Fascists still scrawled "This is a Jewish War" on some of the walls which still stood, and anti-semitic feeling in the shelters was always a problem. But what could have been more ludicrous than to smash up Jewish homes when the Luftwaffe was smashing up

Jewish homes? What rescue worker asked himself, as he burrowed into a shattered building, whether the girl trapped inside was Gentile, Jewish, or, as was likely enough in Stepney, Indian or Chinese?

For the Communists, also, the immediate physical enemy was bound to distract attention from the theoretical class enemy. Communists remained faithful to their long-standing interest in A.R.P. as a potential revolutionary flashpoint. They agitated more than ever now for deep shelters, while the public simply equipped itself with deep shelters – the tubes. Fearful Communists, clearly, did not wish to agitate during air raids. Fearless ones were conspicuous enough; one would see girls standing in the raids selling the *Daily Worker* from their familiar pitches. The story is told of a young cripple who was so distressed when the breakdown of public transport meant that he did not get his big parcel of *Workers* regularly, that he would cycle with his one leg each night to the office (which was in one of the hardest hit quarters), take three heavy rucksacks of papers, and make his way back as best he could along the blazing Thames waterfront.[6] Such courage did not spread defeatism, it set an example of defiance.

There seems to have been only one significant left-wing demonstration. Detailed descriptions, with photographs, of the revelling which continued in the West End had appeared in the newspapers. The Savoy Hotel had equipped its underground banqueting hall as a restaurant-dormitory. On September 15th, about a hundred East Enders, under Communist leadership, rushed on the hotel when the alert sounded in the evening and insisted on occupying the restaurant. The demonstration was frustrated by a freak; the siren, exceptionally, sounded the all clear soon afterwards. The invaders retreated. According to one somewhat unlikely version, they passed a hat round and poured a pile of coppers into the hand of the head porter on the way out. It was, in any case, a polite enough occasion on both sides.[7]

Even if the Luftwaffe had realized that raids concentrated solely on the East End might have been their most effective tactic, the bombers were not accurate enough to ensure such a concentration. From the first, other areas of inner and outer London suffered considerable damage. In a less intense way, morale was endangered throughout the metropolis. The feeling that the bombers were allowed to roam the skies unimpeded was not a happy one from the Government's point of view. The British night fighters remained ineffective until near the end of the blitz, but they complicated life for the anti-aircraft gunners. The A.A. barrage was in any case far from formidable. Thanks to an ineffectual system of sound locators, firing was sporadic, almost inaudible, and almost useless. On September 11th, the night fighters were withdrawn. London's "Ack Ack" had been reinforced from the provinces and the redoubtable General Pile ordered his troops to blaze away with every ounce of energy they could muster. The resulting, hideous noise kept most Londoners awake for most of the night, but they loved it. Shelterers laughed for joy, "even at three a.m.", reports Barbara Nixon. The barrage, in strictly military terms, remained quite ineffectual, though it forced the raiders to fly higher. Falling shell fragments added to the perils of the streets, and Pile's men killed far more British civilians than German pilots. One borough asked Ack Ack to remove itself on the grounds that its thunders were cracking the lavatory pans in council houses. But few people took up the Government's offer of ear plugs, and many were ready to stand free drinks to the soldiers of the Royal Artillery – who thoroughly deserved them, for they lived in crude dugouts and for the first eight days got almost no sleep themselves.[8]

Another boost for morale came somewhat paradoxically on the morning of September 13th. A lone German raider was foolish enough to attack Buckingham Palace. Nothing was more calculated to arouse a feeling of solidarity across the classes. The Queen remarked, "I'm glad we've been bombed. It makes me feel I can look the East End in the face." The palace was hit twice more, once in November and once in March.[9]

After the first wave of terror, workers began to return to their daily jobs, from the rest centres and the forest, and from billets as far away as Bishop's Stortford, thirty miles to the north. The attack was extended to the central and western boroughs, and remained general for the rest of the long first phase of the blitz. Up to November 13th, an average of 160 bombers dropped an average of 200 tons of high explosive and 182 canisters of incendiaries nightly. The average was much exceeded on nights of full moon, "Bombers' Moon", and Londoners came to expect a particularly heavy attack in the middle of the month. On October 15th, there were 410 raiders over London, and they dropped 538 tons of high explosive – sufficient, by pre-war estimates, to cause more than 25,000 casualties. As it was, more than 400 civilians were killed, nearly 900 seriously injured, over 900 fires were started and nearly all rail travel in and out of London was shut off.[10] But the Port of London was never knocked out completely. Chaos never became ungovernable. The effect of two months of continuous blitz was to spread the habit of adaptation from those who were brave and active to those who were not, so that increasing proportions of the population became brave and active. In the immensity of Greater London, with its peacetime population of nearly nine million, three or four hundred bombers would waste their efforts.

On October 8th, Churchill exercised his wit in parliament at the Luftwaffe's expense. Announcing that casualties were less than one-tenth, on a typical night, of those expected, he proceeded, "Statisticians may amuse themselves by calculating that after making allowance for the working of the law of diminishing returns, through the same house being struck twice or three times over, it would take ten years at the present rate, for half the houses of London to be demolished. After that, of course, progress would be much slower."[11]

Even after the R.A.F. had consolidated its control of the daylight skies, minor day raids continued to be frequent. Churchill records that at the approach of half a dozen aeroplanes, or only one, or even at the sounding of a false alarm, "all the occupants of a score of ministries were promptly collected and led down to the basements, for what these were worth. Pride, even, was being taken in the efficiency and thoroughness with which this evolution was performed." Factory workers were spending more time in the shelters than at their benches; where only damp crowded trenches were available, men might be found calmly playing cards on the deserted shop floor rather than using them, but in any case, no work was done. Churchill, whose vagrant intelligence fastened on this problem, called, on September 17th, for the training of workers as "Jim Crows or lookout men", who would watch from the roofs of factories and office buildings and would give an alarm when danger was truly imminent. As this system was slowly adopted, the problem was solved. The important Ford's factory, in east London, lost nearly 380 hours of work through alerts in September. In October, when the spotters were at work, only 145 hours were lost, though the area had been under alert for 350.[12]

Those caught in the streets while raids were in progress rapidly adjusted to what seemed a minor enough danger when they compared the random carnage of the day with the wholesale slaughter of the nights. At first, buses had drawn up and disgorged their passengers into the nearest shelter, post offices and shops had shut, tradesmen had unharnessed their horses and tied them to the rear of their carts. But soon such behaviour ceased, and Londoners began to continue casually with their business. A visiting American journalist was shocked by their calm. In a police station, registering as an alien, he did not hear the siren.

> A policeman from the street simply stuck his head in the door and blew loudly on a police whistle. I jumped a mile. The room was suddenly still. The sergeant in the middle of the counter chanted in a monotonous voice without looking up:
> "An air raid alarm has been sounded. There is a shelter underneath this building. The man at the door will show you the way to it. If you do not choose to go to the shelter we will carry on."
> Nobody went. The buzz of conversation resumed.[13]

But at night, no pretence of normality was possible. Except in the depths of the tube, no one escaped the noises of the blitz, and even there those with their bodies against the walls felt its vibrations.

First, there was the alert, a wail rising and falling for two minutes, "warbling" as the official handbook somewhat inexactly put it. There was not one siren but a series, as the note was taken up by borough after borough. Then, there was the heavy, uneven throb of the bombers. "Where are you? Where are you?" Graham Greene imagined them saying. Then there were many noises. The howling of dogs; the sound of a high explosive bomb falling, like a tearing sheet; the clatter of little incendiaries on roofs and pavements; the dull thud of walls collapsing; the burglar alarms which destruction had set ringing; the crackle of flames, a relishing, licking noise, and the bells of the fire engines. Each individual A.A. gun, to the increasingly sensitive ears of Londoners, had its own voice. One set near John Strachey's warden's post in Chelsea was called "the tennis racket" because it made "a staccato, and yet plangent, wang, wang; wang, wang." The shells shrieked and their splinters pattered on the pavements. A bomb falling half a mile away gave you ten seconds' warning by its swish and rush through the air, but the one "with your number on it", the one which killed you or buried you alive, was heard only when it was almost upon you, because the sound waves caught up with themselves.[14]

Outside, if bravado or duty sent the citizen outside, there was a world of beauty; Charlotte Haldane has said that for her, the "aesthetic pleasure" which the fires provoked "banished all sense of fear". "The sky over London," as Evelyn Waugh saw it, "was glorious, ochre and madder, as though a dozen tropic suns were simultaneously setting round the horizon . . . Everywhere the shells sparkled like Christmas baubles." Searchlights crossed and recrossed in stiff and awkward arcs, plunging thousands of feet into the sky, each terminating in a "mist area" which reminded Harold Nicolson of "a swab of cotton wool". The raiders, to begin with, would drop parachute flares, magnificent fireworks which drifted slowly down in a constellation, illuminating earth and sky with an amber or greenish light and casting exotic shadows over grubby and familiar townscapes. Suddenly, a street would be carpeted with brilliant incendiaries, hissing and sparkling with a whitish green glare. A high explosive bomb, by comparison, was disappointing; its upward streaks of yellow or red were as crude as a little boy's painting of Guy Fawkes' Night (a fixture which few citizens found it hard to forgo on November 5th). Once, in October, a bomb struck a gasholder in the south. Five thousand cubic feet of gas burnt in a couple of seconds, and "an enormous uprush of white light, like a gigantic mushroom with a huge black cap" suddenly towered over London.[15]

But there were other colours, those of the injured in bombed buildings, white with plaster dust and streaked with black blood. J. L. Hodson wrote, after the office of his own newspaper had been hit, "What strikes me so forcibly is the tawdry look, the cheap and nasty look this sort of thing wears after the explosion . . . So often it exposes, or seems to, that everything is jerrybuilt – makes it seem so even if it wasn't. One is humiliated by it."[16]

And the smells were evil. On September 10th, the Luftwaffe breached the northern outfall sewer, which discharged its contents into the River Lea. Early in October, London's main sewage outfall was destroyed. The Thames stank first of excrement, then of the chemicals poured into it. Blitzed or burning warehouses filled the air with disconcerting odours, the familiar suddenly made strange, the devil's Christmas dinner. The sickly, bitter-sweet smell of a blitzed chemist's shop might make a warden reach hurriedly for his gas-mask.

Above all, there was what John Strachey called the "harsh, rank, raw smell" of an "incident", of a bombed street.

Its basis certainly came from the torn, wounded, dis-membered houses; from the gritty dust of dissolved brick-work, masonry and joinery. But there was more to it than that. For several hours there was an acrid overtone from the high explosive which the bomb itself had contained; a fiery constituent of the smell. Almost invariably, too, there was the mean little stink of domestic gas, seeping up from broken pipes and leads. But the whole of the smell was greater than the sum of its parts. It was the smell of violent death itself.[17]

There were comic, or superficially comic "incidents". A lady hurled out into a Mayfair street in her bath; a man blown clean out of his bedroom who risked his life to go back for a clothes-brush. Some people were caught on the lavatory when the bomb dropped. But if people were not trapped in the debris or torn apart so that no trace was found of them, they were likely to be stabbed by splinters of flying glass. Graham Greene, then a warden in Bloomsbury, looking back on a major "incident", remembered chiefly, "the squalor of the night, the purgatorial throng of men and women in dirty torn pyjamas with little blood splashes standing in doorways . . ." When Barbara Nixon saw her first casualty, she was "not let down lightly. In the middle of the street lay the remains of a baby. It had been blown clean through the window and had burst on striking the roadway. To my intense relief, pitiful and horrible as it was, I was not nauseated, and found a torn piece of curtain in which to wrap it."[18]

Most of the high explosive bombs which fell on Britain up to May 1941 were relatively light – fifty or two hundred and fifty kilograms – though later in the war the proportion of heavier bombs, up to two thousand, five hundred kilograms, increased greatly. The blast from any bomb could tear a man to shreds, or it could kill him without an obvious wound. Houses well away from the explosion would pitch like ships and appear to shift on their foundations, and their windows would shatter. Within ten days of the start of the blitz, the Luftwaffe began to drop sea mines by parachute, and these were known as land mines; huge cylinders, eight feet long and two feet in diameter, which swung silently down at about forty miles per hour, but seemed to float like sycamore seeds. They did not penetrate the earth and their blast, which was not muffled by the soil, could blow a man a quarter of a mile and throw thirty-five ton train cars into the air like shoe-boxes, or, such were its freaks, tweak the slippers from a man's feet several streets away.

The thermite incendiaries, by contrast, weighed only a couple of pounds. They were eighteen inches long and were shaped like hock bottles. They were dropped in containers of various sizes –

seventy-two incendiaries was an average "breadbasket". A man could easily smother one with a sandbag, and if that were lacking could cope with tongs or heavy gloves. But unless they were dealt with swiftly and thoroughly incendiaries were the most destructive of all bombs. In December, the sport of "I.B." hunting which was popular with London's doughtier citizens was spoilt when the Germans began to drop a proportion of incendiaries with explosive charges; thereafter, far great caution had to be used.

The all clear was a steady two-minute blast on the siren. At night, the noise and fires made it seem that large areas must be completely devastated. Next morning, the damage was surprisingly small. "Ow! Don't it look as if the mice 'ad been at it," one Cockney girl exclaimed as she stood in a small crowd staring at the B.B.C.'s headquarters the morning after the news had been interrupted by a crash and listeners had heard a voice whisper to the announcer that it was "all right".[19] In the suburbs, one saw housewives busy with their brooms each morning, making neat little piles of debris for the borough workmen, and heard the broken glass grating on the pavements. Boys searched the ruins, still occasional enough, for shrapnel, prizing pieces of German bomb more highly than the splinters of A.A. shells.

There would be many streets barred where the police had set up a yellow board marking Diversion. Behind these, the grim mingled with the normal. John Lehmann recorded the scene when a U.X.B. drove him from his Bloomsbury home:

> Mecklenburgh Square was a pretty sight when I left it. Broken glass everywhere, half the garden scorched with incendiary bombs, and two houses of Byron Court on the east side nothing but a pile of rubble. Clouds of steam were pouring out of one side, firemen still clambering over it and ambulances and blood transfusion units standing by with A.R.P. workers and police. The road was filled with a mass of rubble muddied by the firemen's hoses, but the light grey powder that had covered the bushes at dawn had been washed off by the drizzle. The time bomb in the Square garden sat in its earth crater, coyly waiting. The tabby Persian cat from No. 40 picked her way daintily and dishevelledly among the splinters of glass on her favourite porch.[20]

At first, such vistas seemed marvellous, bizarre, but the eye grew accustomed to their like. Freaks would still catch it – two beautiful porcelain vases standing undamaged behind the shattered plate glass windows of an elegant furniture shop, "corpses" from Madame Tussaud's waxworks scattered beside the road. Walking through a park, Inez Holden saw "the highest branches of a tree draped with bits of marabout, with some sort of silk, with two or three odd stockings and, wrapped round the top of the tree, like a cloak quick-thrown over the shoulder of some high-born hidalgo, some purple damask. Below it, balanced on a twig as if twirled round a finger, was a brand new bowler hat."[21] What never palled, above all, was the sudden, curious insight which a bomb might give into the lives of "those people across the way", the Londoners' usually unknown neighbours. Their taste in wallpaper and bedlinen was mercilessly exposed to the autumn sunshine.

In that sunshine, the day became, in the words of Elizabeth Bowen, "a pure and curious holiday from fear". It appeared to her that "The very soil of the city at this time seemed to generate more strength; in parks the outsize dahlias, velvet and wine, and trees on which each vein in each yellow leaf stretched out perfect against the sun blazoned out the idea of the finest hour." But she adds that people were soon "disembodied" by tiredness. "The night behind and the night to come met across every noon in an arch of strain. To work or think was to ache."[22]

The manufacturers of Horlicks found a new focus for the invocation in their advertisements of "deep, healing sleep". After a time, nervous people grew used to the noise and slept somehow through the raids, but even then the swish of a bomb falling especially near would shake them awake. John Strachey remarks that for the air raid warden, whose work kept him awake and about night after night in those early days, "Sleep replaced food as the simplest, most everyday, object of desire. Whenever he had anything over half an hour to spare during the day, he had not the slightest doubt as to what to do with the time. He slept."[23]

In the same way, people adapted themselves to the fear which returned night after night. "The individual's reaction to the sound of falling bombs", Ed Murrow told his American audience, "cannot be described. The moan of stark terror and suspense cannot be encompassed by words, no more can the sense of relief when you realize that you weren't where that one fell." The luckiest, as well as the bravest, were those whose jobs took them out into the raids, where danger was visible and visibly limited. A writer in the Hampstead *Warden's Bulletin* noted laconically early in December, "Not all, of course, were able to stand firm against the new conditions, but it is noteworthy that our resignations have been offset by new enrolments . . ."[24] To many, Civil Defence work acquired a new attraction, if only because it quenched curiosities both sensational and sociological.

Others found less prestigious techniques of adaptation. We learn of one woman who had laid in a remarkable stock of brandy and "simply drank herself stupid every night . . . One night she fell down the whole flight of stairs when a heavy bomb fell, but she simply lay at the bottom dead to the world and quite unharmed."[25]

Fear found its antidote both in relief and fatigue. ". . . Every morning one is pleased to see one's friends appearing again," wrote Harold Nicolson in his diary twelve days after the start of the blitz. "I am nerveless, and yet I am conscious that when I hear a motor in the empty streets I tauten myself lest it be a bomb screaming towards me." ". . . As time goes on," wrote the film director Paul Rotha, early in November, "you get experienced. A plane overhead, a scream, you count one-two-three-four, they either get closer or get distant. If closer, you seek handy shelter – a doorway usually. If distant, you go on doing what you are doing. . . . It's remarkable how sensitive your ears get."[26]

A man from Hampshire who visited London on the third weekend of the blitz went to the cinema with friends. "The performance began nightly at about eight o'clock, with the first bomb five minutes later, I was told, and so it was." He found among those he stayed with "an indefinable lightheartedness, springing perhaps from the feeling, 'why take care for tomorrow, for tomorrow may never come?' "[27] The prosperous classes settled down to "the even tenor of the blitz", as one lady called it.[28] Danger became boring rather than harrowing. London, in the slogan of the day, was "taking it", and self-respecting citizens resolved to "take it".

Shops became a favourite symbol of defiance. Big and small, they had their windows blown out. The West End stores would erect painted wooden fronts with only tiny panes of glass to replace them; the little fruiterers and grocers would often do without any glass at all. The impromptu signs became favourite blitz jokes. "MORE OPEN THAN USUAL" was a common one. "BLAST!" was the most laconic. One pub advertised, "OUR WINDOWS ARE GONE BUT OUR SPIRITS ARE EXCELLENT. COME IN AND TRY THEM."

But the machinery set up by the Government to cope with the new calls for evacuation was never swamped, and demand grew less as the weeks went by. The Government meditated compulsory evacuation of schoolchildren, but quite soon realized that there was no possible method of compelling parents to send them away. "Assisted private evacuation", whereby the Government gave free travel vouchers and billeting certificates to those who found their own accommodation in the countryside, was offered to many groups – mothers with small children, pregnant women, old, blind or sick people, and those made homeless by bombs. But, as Richard Titmuss points out, "fewer people left London during the first nine months of air attack than the number who went away either just before or just after the declaration of war."[29]

By the end of November, the population of central London had dropped by a quarter, but most of the workers remained at their posts. Very few firms or organizations removed their headquarters from London unless they were bombed out. Mark Benney, who was working in an aircraft factory, has recorded that

> There was very little absenteeism caused by the raids; in part because we all felt that the raids gave an added importance to our work, but much more because we knew that if we didn't turn up our mates would be worrying. You would see men staggering at their work from lack of sleep, snatching a ten minutes' doze in the canteen over their food, and still, when knocking off time came, going off with a cheerful, "See yer in the morning, boys!"
>
> It became a sort of war cry, a common affirmation of faith pregnant with unstated defiances and resolutions, that phrase. We threw it at each other gaily, but always with the implication very near the surface, "If I don't see yer, it means they'll be digging me out."[30]

There were perhaps half a million munitions workers living within a fifteen-mile radius of London. Nothing showed the stubbornness which set in better than the dogged fashion in which these, and the workers in important offices, strove to get to work on time.

Several train services out of London were blocked for months at a time, though railway employees would work valiantly to try to clear a line before the first of the morning's trains was due. By October 17th, so many buses were "blitzed" that London

Transport had to appeal for reinforcements from the provinces, and black, white, brown, green and blue buses from places as far away as Exeter and Inverness joined the familiar red double-deckers in the streets. Trolleybuses, with their overhead electric wires, were especially vulnerable to cut lines and craters in their path, and "linesmen" sometimes struggled with repairs standing on their tower wagons while the blitz proceeded around them. A special boat service on the Thames was laid on for a period of six weeks after most of central and southern London had been deprived of trams and trolleybuses by U.X.B.s.

Queues stretching back a hundred yards from the bus stops were a common sight. What buses ran were forced to take uncouth, circuitous routes. Letters from one London postal district to another might take a week or more to arrive. Telegrams, unless they were official, were subject to unlimited delay. Telephone lines were cut with monotonous frequency, and it was a matter for congratulation if someone with an urgent call found that the exchange which he was phoning was actually in business that day.

Every time a bomb pierced a road it tore through the mass of pipes, cables and conduits which lay like a nervous system under the city. Repair went on as the bombs still fell. Where a gas main had been broken, a man from the gas company had to plug its end, working in scorching, poisoned air, or force his way through blazing debris to cut off the supply. Men were properly given decorations for repairing flaming splinter holes sixty feet up on the crowns of gasholders. When a telephone cable was severed, as many as two thousand, eight hundred wires might be broken, each requiring reconnection. Men did this finicky work night after night; thanks to them, and their counterparts working with water conduits, electricity cables and sewage pipes, the trappings of civilization, somewhat erratically, persisted.

Food remained relatively plentiful. The meat ration, during the last quarter of 1940, was at its highest level of the war, because of a glut of slaughtering. But when gas and electricity were cut off, it was not always easy to cook it, and after-raid feeding was a major problem for the authorities. Women would improvise field-kitchens in the gardens or the roads, and burn shattered woodwork or furniture to give their husbands something hot to eat. Water spurted one day from the gas stoves of Pimlico, and all the cooking at the Ritz Hotel was done, for several days, on two up-ended electric radiators.

Eating out in expensive West End restaurants continued;

besides the Savoy, several other well-known establishments offered all-night shelter as part of the service. There was only one serious incident in a West End resort. In March 1941 the fashionable Café de Paris, crowded with young officers on leave, was blitzed as the clients danced to the music of "Snakehips" Johnson. The macabre scenes which followed were among the most indelibly horrifying of the period. One woman had her broken leg washed in champagne, while looters plundered rings from the fingers of the dead and wounded.[31]

Theatres rapidly shut their doors; after ten days of blitz, only the Windmill kept open with its blend, now doubly defiant, of bare flesh and comedy. Many London cinemas "took it" in their stride, though sixty were totally destroyed by bombing over the period of the war. Of those of the small Granada chain, based on London, one was destroyed, and nine others closed for longer or shorter periods; but "the remaining ten cinemas never missed a day nor curtailed a performance".

The absence of panic in the many incidents which occurred in cinemas was one of the most remarkable features of the blitz. Granada offered shelter and entertainment throughout the night for their clients, and those who stayed might enjoy five feature films in succession, together with impromptu sing-songs and amateur variety. People took to bringing their blankets to the last house. Though the strain on the staffs soon ended this experiment, the historian of the chain is surely right to suggest that the cinemas in this phase were confirming themselves as the new centres of communal life.

One morning when a score of fire engines were still busy in Leicester Square, the usual long queue was seen to form outside the cinema which was showing *Gone With the Wind*. Granada's figures suggest that total attendances fell by about five-sixths in some hard hit boroughs in September, but they soon picked up and were actually above normal in Christmas week.[32] By the beginning of 1941, most other places of entertainment had reopened, and the pubs had recovered their appeal.

Certain younger cinema patrons preferred to take their girl-friends to the empty, because perilous, dress circles. Individual public shelters were monopolized by courting couples, to the concern of moralists. Barbara Nixon was standing outside a surface shelter one night when a couple emerged. "The gunfire was getting heavy, and the girl was anxious – 'I can't stop now. Tom, really. I must get down the shelter. Mum will be worrying, But I'll meet you tomorrow, same time, same sandbag.' "[33]

A sensible fatalism made risks in pursuit of pleasure acceptable. "If your number's on it, the bomb'll get you" was the philosophy of the poor; and the rich accepted it too. "When my time is due it will come," said Winston Churchill to his "shadow", exposing himself to danger, as was his joy and his habit, on the roof of the bomb-proof "annexe" to No. 10 Downing Street which he had been persuaded, with some difficulty, to occupy at nights.[84]

Superstitions, taboos and rituals flourished. One Nigerian air raid warden in an inner suburb was regarded as a lucky omen by shelterers; when they saw his dark face they felt safe for the night.[35] It was clearly religion, not reason, which now prompted an enthusiastic, and sometimes violent, defence of the rituals of blackout, It was absurdly, but very widely believed that a German bomber a couple of miles up would see the light from a cigarette in the street, or from the dim torches which A.R.P. workers used at incidents, and would aim deliberately at it. A belief which was quite as illogical but equally current was that "they" never hit the same building twice, so you were safe enough in a bombed house. There was also a prevalent rumour that "they" had developed a bomb which could chase you round corners.

But Miss Leaky Mouth and Mr. Glumpot, those staunch adherents of Rumour in the Silent Column days, could now content themselves with facts. The crowds of sightseers, often well dressed for the day out, who would inquire at railway stations where the worst damage might be found, naturally infuriated rescue workers. But it was probably good for those who were apprehensive that they should stare at destruction rather than imagine it; this, too, was a method of adaptation.

So was the freedom with which people now conversed with total strangers. By the time a shaken citizen had told a dozen people in buses or pubs about "his" bomb or "his" near-miss, it didn't seem so bad after all. It was, rather, a matter for pride. Little boys fought over whose bomb had been worst. In self-defence, some people took to wearing badges, "I'VE GOT A BOMB STORY TOO". One of the best was Willie Gallacher's. One lovely day, he was walking down a main London thoroughfare just after lunch. The all clear had sounded, but a bomb hit the side of the road a few yards from him, dug in and hit a water main. "The bursting of the water main synchronized with the exploding of the bomb, and the force of the water was so strong [he relates] that it sent everything, blast and rubble, straight up into the air, like a great oil gusher. Although it was just outside, not a pane of

glass was broken in Unity House."[36] Fortunately, no doubt, for
his reputation for veracity, Gallacher was a total abstainer.

War had already weakened the famous English reserve; the
blitz swept it away. The shift of values which Priestley had
exhorted was implicit in shared disaster and danger. A grocer
excavating the ruins of his store, handing tins of soup and milk
to those who wanted them, and saying quite solemnly, "Put it on
the account"; a pub standing drinks out of hours to the local
raid victims; a manager staying on late at the factory so as to
give a lift in his car to weary workmen – such things were
unknown before September 1940; and after June 1945. Neighbours forgot their censorious rivalries and joined together in
impromptu parties to fight fires, to repair each other's houses, to
look after children, to cook meals. Life, briefly, seemed more
important than money. Ed Murrow observed that no one talked
about the cash value of the damage, even when their own homes
and offices had gone. ". . . It's much more important that the
bomb missed you; that there's still plenty of food to eat – and
there is."[37]

This new attitude should be considered in relation to the looting which undoubtedly occurred in many places. Some of it
seems to have been organized by gangs, and was callous and
inexcusable. But what of the A.F.S. men – "selfless heroes" one
moment, "criminals" the next – who were quite often convicted
of looting? As Murrow pointed out, most of those citizens who
came before the courts for this offence were not "criminal" types.
Trivial things like books and ribbons and coal were carried away
or pocketed. "One has a strange feeling, or at least I have," said
Murrow, "in looking at the contents of a bombed house or shop,
that the things scattered about don't belong to anyone . . .
Picking up a book or a pipe that's been blown into the street is
almost like picking an apple in a deserted and overgrown orchard
far from any road or house."[38]

But there were many people in London who had never had
much property to speak of, anyway. These could not refresh
themselves with week-ends away from "town", nor retreat to
their country cottages or the houses of well provided friends
when bombs blasted their streets; nor could they eat out in
comfortable restaurants when the gas failed. In the public
shelters, another American journalist, Negley Farson, recorded
the comments of the poor:

"We didn't ask for the blinking war, *did* we?"

"No wonder Germany's not fed up – they've *got* some blinking air raid shelters!"

"My man's in the Army. At Dunkirk, he was. And I'm *here*!"

"We're prisoners of war: that's what we are."

"The official attitude is horrible!"

"No use looking to Labour. They let us in for this war, they did."

"Bloody L.C.C. red tape!"

As Farson saw it, "these people were beginning to lose faith – faith in all degrees of people higher up."[39]

III

To pre-war Governments, it had seemed that the knockout blow from the air would mean huge "incidents" in great numbers if the public was assembled in large public shelters – unless, of course, these were so deep underground that they were impregnable, in which case the craven populace invented by the official imagination would contract out of the war effort and immerse itself more or less permanently in the womb-like security they would provide.

So the Chamberlain Government, intent on dispersing the population as widely and evenly as possible, had made the Anderson shelter the spearhead of its policy, and had otherwise recommended that householders should strengthen basements and ground-floor rooms for use as shelters. Not until a few days before the outbreak of war had the local authorities been asked to build structures specifically designed as public shelters. The Anderson had first been planned as a shelter for erection inside a small working-class home, but technical objections had ensured that it became an outdoor shelter. Unfortunately, under a quarter of the public, Mass Observation pointed out, had gardens.[40]

The Anderson was a masterpiece of cheap and simple engineering, and the two and a quarter million Andersons which the Government had given away free by the start of the blitz represented a formidable investment for the security of the more fortunate sections of the working class. Two curved walls of corrugated steel met in a ridge at the top and were bolted to stout rails. The Anderson was sunk three feet into the ground, and covered with eighteen inches of earth (in which many proud owners grew flowers or vegetables). The entrance was protected by a steel shield and an earthen blast wall. The Anderson would protect up to six people against practically anything but a direct hit, and many were grateful for it when the blitz came. There is no doubt that it was well worth the £6 14s. to £10 18s. which was charged for it when, in October 1939, it was put on sale to those earning over two hundred and fifty pounds a year, who did not qualify for the free issue. However, less than a thousand were sold.

The Anderson at once revealed snags which might well deter a prospective buyer. Many flooded as soon as they were installed and continued to flood in spite of repeated balings out. Most of those delivered after the start of the war were, for reasons of economy, somewhat too small to sleep in. There was a further, pre-eminent disadvantage which ensured that many never used their free Andersons after the raids started; they did not shut out the din.

As the steel shortage led to the falling off and then to the cessation of the production of Andersons, the Government turned in March 1940 to a new type of brick and concrete surface shelter – a "communal" rather than "public" shelter designed to protect some fifty residents from a single street or block of dwellings. This policy in turn ran headlong into another shortage, that of cement. An unfortunate ambiguity in a Ministry of Home Security circular of the spring of 1940 persuaded some borough engineers and local builders that these shelters might be constructed without any cement in the mortar at all. (In fact, so the official account goes, the Government was only suggesting dilution with lime.) In London region alone, well over five thousand shelters were built without cement; besides this, unscrupulous contractors were quite often guilty of faulty workmanship.[41]

These squat erections were the common type of shelter in many working-class districts. Their ventilation was limited; they were cold, dark and damp; even where chemical closets were provided, they stank and sometimes overflowed. Not surprisingly, the surface shelters were generally unpopular, especially when they showed a disconcerting propensity to collapse, through poor construction, when bombs fell near by.

There were also many trench shelters in public gardens and parks. Authorities had been told to make permanent those dug during the Munich crisis, by lining and covering them with concrete or steel. But trenches had fallen out of official favour well before the blitz began; the supplies of lining materials were erratic, and they were often impossible to keep waterproof. A typical trench, also, would hold some fifty people, who were liable to find themselves sitting out an all-night raid with stinking water lapping over their shoes. But they were more popular than surface shelters; people felt safer even a few feet underground.

This did not by any means exhaust the variety of shelters. Strong buildings of any sort lent themselves to this function, and many public or communal shelters were improvised in basements by the local authorities. The case of the London borough of Paddington, socially a very mixed area, will provide an example, not necessarily representative, of the balance of various types. Some 76,000 people could take shelter within the borough on any one night; 21,000 of these could go to Andersons; 39,000 to other types of domestic or communal shelter. Forty public shelters had been adapted from existing buildings; eleven were surface shelters specially constructed, and there were four trenches.[42]

The public and communal shelters rapidly developed individual characters. There were quiet, genteel ones; noisy ones, where people brought beer in after the pubs closed; shelters on main roads which served drunks and casual passers by; shelters favoured by taxi-drivers or prostitutes. Specialized shelters developed where people had to work late or be on call all night; hospitals turned their underground vaults into nurses' sleeping quarters and casualty wards. Dignity and privacy went by the board. In one block of flats in a well-to-do suburb, where there was no shelter but the corridors might be slept in quite safely because the building was steel framed, "it was really extraordinary", one resident relates, "to see all these people who had spent so much time avoiding each other in the past now giving each other cups of tea or handing over chocolate, which was then unrationed and very scarce. It was the first – and last – time that big block of flats ever came near to having a soul and individuality of its own."[43]

Indeed, by November most Londoners were not using specially created shelters. The first "Shelter Census", early that month, suggested that in the central area only 9 per cent slept in public shelters; 4 per cent in the underground railway system (though some accounts of the blitz make it sound as if almost everyone took to the tubes); and 27 per cent in domestic shelters. In the outer suburbs, these proportions were even lower.[44] The rest were in most cases either on duty or sleeping in their own homes; if not in their bedrooms, at least in ground floor rooms, under the stairs or in cupboards. Though these figures are for only one

night, at a stage when adaptation to the blitz had reached its
peak, they should put the somewhat lurid stories which follow
into perspective. However, London's population was so vast that
a smallish proportion of it was sufficient to produce some
impressive social phenomena.

Early in the blitz, some enterprising Londoners discovered the
existence of a fine set of caves in the sandy hills at Chislehurst in
Kent. These were ancient workings, pleasant, airy and equable in
temperature. Families took over individual caves and set up
homes – sometimes with double beds, armchairs and tables.
Special trains were run from London every night, and the caves
eventually came to have their own barber's shop, concerts and
church services. Several thousand people might dwell there in
great safety.[45]

There was, among some, an urge to congregate in familiar
centres. Father Wilson of Haggerston found that his church hall,
though it was far from safe, was regularly used by between
seventy and two hundred people. "I continued to impress on all
and sundry", he wrote, "that the hall was not an official shelter;
but the few such things in the neighbourhood were filled to
capacity; the hall was warm, airy and well lit; it gave its temporary
inhabitants both a sense of security and the companionship of
their friends and neighbours. They liked to be there. I had not the
heart to turn them away." The mayor of the borough gave a
radio; the local wardens provided impromptu concerts; refreshment was purchased at the pub; there were card games and
dances, and the East Enders had a good time. When the wireless
packed up as the raiders approached, somebody would thump
away at the piano, louder and louder as the bombs crashed
nearer and nearer. The assistant curate sat among the shelterers
reading the letters of Madame de Sévigné.[46]

Railway arches were chosen by many for shelter. They looked
secure enough, but the authorities knew that they could be death
traps. The most famous, or notorious, of all London's shelters
was found under the Tilbury railway arches in Stepney. Part of a
complex of cellars and vaults had been taken over by the borough
council as a public shelter for three thousand people. The other
part was the loading yard of a huge warehouse. The shelter was
famous as a popular refuge in the raids of the First World War,
and people flocked to it from a wide area. Communists encouraged the shelterers to overflow into the "unofficial" part of
the arches, where massive steel girders maintained an illusion of
safety. This became the largest, and perhaps the most unspeakable

of all London's shelters; as many as fourteen or sixteen thousand were estimated to use it on certain nights.

Great stocks of margarine were stored in the "unofficial" section. There was sanitation only for the handful of workmen usually employed there. Children slept among trodden faeces and soiled margarine; so did Indians, Lascars, Negroes, spivs, prostitutes and Jewish refugees. Parties of sightseers from the West End would make the Tilbury Arches the highlight of their tour of black spots. American journalists were taken there to shudder; though Negley Farson found its "vital, impulsive life" oddly "inspiring", and when Harold Scott visited it, "A girl in a scarlet cloak danced wildly to the cheers of an enthusiastic audience; a party of Negro sailors sang spirituals while someone played the accordion . . ." "Tilbury" became the spearhead of the agitation for a general improvement in public shelters which journalists and social workers began to conduct as soon as the blitz settled in.[47]

Another big shelter in Stepney, "Mickey's Shelter", rivalled the "Tilbury"; indeed the Minister of Health referred to it as the worst in London. Mickey Davis, who soon gave his name to it, was an East End optician, three feet, three inches tall and hunchbacked. On the first night of blitz he found himself in a cellar, designated a shelter but not yet made safe, which had accommodation for five thousand people; more than twice that number had crowded their way into it. "The heat of that cellar", Davis wrote, "became literally hardly bearable. A steady stream of semi-conscious or unconscious people was passed towards the doorway . . ." One Red Cross nurse, with one man helping her, was trying to cope with the sick.

Davis inspired his fellow shelterers to create their own order out of something which it seems polite to call chaos. A shelter committee was democratically elected; and when Davis was replaced as leader by a "shelter marshal" officially appointed from outside, the committee insisted on his reinstatement. As the state of the shelter became known, voluntary help came from outside. A gleaming canteen was installed by Marks and Spencer's chain stores. From its profits, free milk was given each day to the children. When Wendell Willkie, Roosevelt's Republican rival, visited London that autumn, he was taken to "Mickey's Shelter" as a showplace of British democracy.[48]

Official policy had rejected the use of the Tubes as shelters. Apart from the fear that "deep shelter mentality" would develop there, the railways should be kept clear for troop movements.

The public overruled the authorities very simply, and without much disorder. People bought platform tickets for a penny half-penny, quite legally, and camped on the platforms.

Mercifully, one danger had been thoroughly provided against. If the tunnels under the Thames had been breached without due precaution having been taken, a very large area of the Tube would have been flooded. Such a breach did occur, very early in the blitz, but well before then a system of floodgates had been constructed, at huge cost. Even so, many Tube platforms seemed much safer than they really were. The deepest were more or less invulnerable, but a high explosive bomb could penetrate up to fifty feet through solid ground. When a small bomb scored a direct hit on the Marble Arch subway, filled with shelterers, on September 17th, its blast ripped the white tiles off the walls as it burst and made them deadly projectiles. Twenty people died. In October, four Tube stations were hit in three nights. The most terrible incident, at Balham, involved six hundred shelterers. A bomb tore through the road above the platform, smashing through mains, cables and conduits so that water, sand and rubble cascaded down on the platforms. A similar incident at Bank station in January 1941 killed a hundred and eleven shelterers and travellers.[49]

Yet confidence in the Tubes survived these horrors. They were dry, they were warm, they were well lit and the raids were inaudible. The authorities beat a retreat. A short branch line to Aldwych station was closed and largely given over to shelterers. ("Pray let me have more information about this, and what has happened to supersede the former decisive arguments," Churchill, who favoured this development, minuted huffily; his colleagues had recently insisted when he had raised the matter at the cabinet that the use of the Tubes as shelters was "most undesirable".) Three disused stations were specially opened to the public. An uncompleted extension running from Liverpool Street under the East End became one vast shelter holding about ten thousand people, where a visiting American walked for half a mile "literally after each step having to find a place to put the next foot down without stepping on something human". Some seventy-nine stations in Greater London became *de facto* shelters, and at a peak near the end of September, 177,000 people were sleeping in the Underground system.[50]

Sefton Delmer calls it "the panic slum on the Underground"; the sight of it filled this hardened war correspondent with "shame". "For the first time in many hundreds of years," Mass

Observation pointed out, "civilized families conducted the whole of their leisure and domestic lives in full view of each other . . . Most of these people were not merely sheltering in the Tubes; they were living there." Queues began to form outside the stations as early as six in the morning. Children or servicemen on leave would be sent to establish priority for their families – "The constant worry", writes Bernard Kops, "was whether we would find a space for that night. We lived only for four o'clock when they let us down . . ." Spivs joined in, to reserve places on the platform for which they would charge half a crown or more when the raid "hotted up". Rain, wind, and even daylight bombing did not shift the queues.[51] Two white lines had been painted on the platforms. Until seven thirty in the evening, shelterers must keep within the one drawn eight feet from the edge, leaving the rest for passengers. From eight until ten thirty, they might encroach as far as the second line four feet from the edge. Then the Tubes stopped running; the light was dimmed; the current was cut off in the rail. People would sling hammocks over the rails, and would walk a little way down the dark tunnel to relieve themselves. In the early days, the platforms were packed tight, and people slept on the escalators or even on the bannisters between them. The snoring rose and fell like a loud wind.

In the Liverpool Street extension, where there was no compulsion to leave, some people stayed down for weeks on end; this, and the queues, did justify to some extent the fears of a "deep shelter mentality", but those who acquired it were a minority within a small minority, no more significant to the life of the city as a whole than the rich, idle women who had fled to luxury hotels in the Lake District. And many of the Tube dwellers were homeless; looking at the rows of unrepaired houses, the squalid rest centres, the chaos of billeting arrangements, which characterized some parts of London, could anyone blame them? Bernard Kops, with other children, adapted gaily to life in the dusty stations. ". . . I got bars and bars of chocolate out of the chocolate machines and weighed myself incessantly. Here was a new life, a whole network, a whole city under the world. We rode up and down the escalators . . . and I used to ride backwards and forwards in the trains to see the other stations of underground people."[52]

But where the Tubes lay below the level of the sewage mains, there were no sanitation or washing facilities on the platforms. Winds, now hot, now cold, howled through the tunnels. Mosquitoes flourished in the fug; lice crawled from head to head.

In the mornings, people shook the dust and germs from their blankets over the line. One witness remarks that "The stench was frightful, urine and excrement mixed with strong carbolic, sweat, and dirty, unwashed humanity."[53]

Ignoring the East End, the progress of a Tube shelter can be charted from the *Swiss Cottager*, organ of the self-appointed "shelterers' committee" at Swiss Cottage station in the wealthy and cosmopolitan suburb of Hampstead, where a motley gathering of thirteen to eighteen hundred English, Austrians, Czechs, Poles, Hungarians, French, Dutch, Belgians, Swiss and Spaniards, many of them refugees, assembled every night.

The Committee began as a somewhat matronly group of "busybodies" who tried to ensure hygiene, order and co-operation with the London Transport staff – organizing voluntary collections to pay for first aid equipment and to give something to the transport workers who had to clean up each morning; laying on a nightly cup of tea for the shelterers; spraying (or at least proposing to spray) the throat of each shelterer with disinfectant. In the second issue of their magazine, they warn against agitators who "have endeavoured to instil dissatisfaction where none existed".

But the committee members themselves turned agitators. The fourth issue, published in November, reveals that they took part in an "Inter Station Conference of Tube Shelterers" – though they later withdrew protesting about Communist interference. The bulletin inveighs "against shameful apathy, indifference amounting almost to callousness, neglect, soulless contempt for elementary human decencies, against red tape, authority, and officialdom, and against practised experts in the time-honoured game of 'passed-to-you-please'." The Ministry of Health had promised that the first aid post, which was in any case inadequately equipped, would at least be open from the moment the shelterers were admitted each afternoon, and this promise had not been fulfilled. Two cases of infectious disease had been found, not by the medical staff sent in by the local council, but by the committee, and a child had died of meningitis. The buck appeared to have been passed between the ministry, the local authority and London Transport, and meanwhile the nurse worked in a space "little larger than a telephone booth".[54]

It was the anger and concern of sensible, moderate people like these which brought immediate improvement in the shelter situation, always anticipating action by the authorities. Clearly, such action had to be taken. The steel-framed buildings in the West End notoriously provided much better protection than the nineteenth-century slums to the east. The contrast between the arches and the Tubes and the shelter provided for the occupants of the Dorchester Hotel in Park Lane was one which might well make the most myopic bureaucrat feel uncomfortable. The Dorchester had converted its Turkish baths, and there was "a neat row of cots, spaced about two feet apart, each one covered with a lovely fluffy eiderdown. Its silks billowed and shone in the dim light in pale pinks and blues. Behind each cot hung the negligee, the dressing gown ... The pillows on which the heads lay were large and full and white ... There was a little sign pinned to one of the Turkish-bath curtains. It said, 'Reserved for Lord Halifax'."[55] There was, furthermore, the factor which had prompted social reforms in the nineteenth century; the health of Whitehall itself was endangered if epidemics broke out in Whitechapel.

A week after the blitz began, the government set up an expert committee under Lord Horder to investigate conditions in the shelters. It reported, verbally, within four days, and formally before the end of September. It stressed the dangers to health from overcrowding and urged the importance of proper medical facilities and supervision. Its recommendations were followed, but not always rapidly, and some areas did not feel the full force of the improvements till after the blitz had ended in May 1941.

Between early in December and the end of April six hundred thousand bunks were provided in the shelters. (This improvement was not always welcomed; it meant that fewer people could use a favourite shelter, and restricted the space available for card games and dancing.) Small coal stoves or electric fires had been introduced. Food was usually available in the larger shelters, provided by private caterers, local authorities or voluntary bodies like the Salvation Army and the W.V.S. In some big shelters, full-time "shelter wardens" had been installed, with power to expel undesirables. The social life of the shelters was developed, with official support; gramophones, concerts, play readings, discussions on current affairs, religious services, film shows, libraries, even play centres for the children, were provided by outside bodies or improvised by the shelterers themselves. One close observer notes that, as quiet nights became more frequent towards the end of 1940, "The shelter crawl became almost as popular a pastime as the old-time pub crawl. The advantages of this and that shelter were compared, and thus there set in a remarkable redistribution of the shelter population."[56]

Thanks partly to the installation of first aid posts, and partly to sheer good fortune, there were no epidemics. Hospitals observed a serious increase in scabies, impetigo and lice. The Anglican Pacifist Fellowship set up the famous "Hungerford club" in arches near Charing Cross station, and segregated some four thousand, five hundred down-and-outs from the rest of London's shelterers. Through the club's agency, a good number of pathetic vagrants were resuscitated.[57]

The Government also rethought the question of deep shelters. The outward motives for its change of policy were technical – the Germans were using heavier bombs, and the fact that people were spending all night in the shelters ruled out the objection that deep caverns would have to be so widely spaced that most citizens could not reach them in time. But it is likely that the invasion of the Tubes really carried more weight. Eight enormous shelters, eighty to a hundred and five feet underground, each of them to hold eight thousand people, were constructed; work on the first of them started in November. Had they ever been fully used, the cost would have amounted to thirty-five pounds per shelterer. None were ready until long after the blitz had ended, but Londoners found shelter of unsurpassed comfort and safety there during the flying bomb attacks, and they provided General Eisenhower with his D Day invasion offices.[58]

Meanwhile, the authorities embarked on the structural improvement of existing shelters and the provision of more. (In February it was announced that public shelters were available for 1,400,000 people in the London region, and domestic shelters for 4,500,000; this still left about one Londoner in five "unprotected", but since so many people insisted on sleeping in their beds, the deficiency was purely theoretical.) In March 1941 it was decided that all the brick surface shelters made without cement should be demolished at Government expense. By the autumn of that year, most of the dampness in the remaining shelters had been countered. A further improvement was the invention and introduction of the "Morrison", named after the new Minister of Home Security. This, like the Anderson, was a family shelter, free for most people, but it could be erected indoors. It had a steel plate on top which could be used as a table in the daytime, and sides of wire mesh, two feet nine inches high. Though few were in use by the end of the blitz, over half a million had been distributed by November 1941, and they gave good service in later attacks.[59]

IV

To judge from certain versions of the blitz, it was a mean and pusillanimous Londoner indeed who did not emerge from the debris with a wisecrack on his lips. It was true that old women would be pulled out calling loudly for bottles of Guinness or asking after their canaries, and that most casualties were too stunned to make much noise. But it was something close to hysteria which produced many of the gay remarks, and those who made them might be found, a few hours later, sobbing uncontrollably in the rest centres. A true, and chilling, anecdote illustrates the condition. One elderly woman refused to leave her stewpot and stayed on in her blasted house in a huge area of devastation. A stretcher-bearer, to humour her, asked to taste her cooking, and found the pot was full of plaster and bricks.[60]

Formidable provision had been made for the physical casualties. A multitude of first aid posts shielded the hospitals from the minor casualties. One doctor has recorded, however, that the early days of the blitz were "hectic times" in his hospital, "when it often seemed that the whole of the elaborately arranged casualty services of the London region must break down, that flesh and blood in the form of nurses and doctors could not possibly survive nights and days of continuous work, when the bare sight of an operating theatre began to fill me, at least, with a sense of distaste so strong as to become almost nausea".[61]

The typical blitz victim arrived covered with grit and dust, and pierced or torn more or less badly by glass splinters. Many of the hospitals were themselves hit, and all were affected by the damage to public utilities. One nurse reports of the casualty department she worked in that "for more than two weeks there was no running water at all, and we had to make do with a single basin of cold water for the whole day's work. After each dressing we washed our hands in this, and by the end of the day, when the same water had been used more than fifty times, it was like thick soup."[62]

But the needs of the injured had been foreseen; other types of distress had not. The authorities were faced "abruptly" (as one of the official historians puts it) "with such cases as – John, aged one year, six months; mother killed in air raid. John crawled out of the wreckage next morning. Father in a pitiable state of distress, too unhinged to work. Terry, aged two years. Both parents burnt to death. Terry pulled out of blazing house with sight of one eye gone."[63] The Ministry of Health turned to various voluntary bodies, notably the W.V.S., to cope with the evacuation and care of unaccompanied or orphaned children.

For reasons already given, the authorities were unprepared for the immense problem of homelessness which the blitz created. One million, four hundred thousand people, or one Londoner in every six, had been made homeless at some period before the main blitz ended in May. The mean houses of the East End were peculiarly easy to damage and peculiarly hard to repair. In Stepney, four out of ten houses had been destroyed or damaged by November 11th.[64]

The most fortunate, those of the class from which the civil service was drawn, suffered the inconvenience of paying for the removal of any surviving furniture and renting a flat in London or a cottage in the home counties. The less fortunate must needs rely upon the poor law, for at the outbreak of war, the poor law authorities, the local public assistance committees, the men of the means test, had been asked by the Government "to organize 'feeding stations' and temporary shelters of some kind for homeless people". Readers of *Oliver Twist* will recollect the English poor law. Its execution had softened over a hundred years, and it was already superseded by new social services in various fields, but the attitude which had shaped its early days remained. The poor law made the localities responsible for those destitute within their boundaries; it kept them alive, but they must not "ask for more". Richard Titmuss comments with deserved rigour, "A philosophy of life, cool, detached and secure, which failed to contemplate the possibility that such things as clothing, rough shelter, soup and margarine might have to be provided by the community for others besides the deserving poor was almost bound to call upon the agency of the poor law. It was inconceivable, according to this philosophy, that the accident of war, even with the bomber thrown in, would alter the fact that the poor would still be poor and the fortunate still fortunate."[65]

It was hoped that the better-off sections of the working class would make their own arrangements like their social superiors; and in fact, only one in seven of London's homeless went through the rest centres. But one in seven was two hundred thousand people. The centres were designed to provide for ten thousand on any one night – but twenty-five thousand were staying in them nineteen days after the first attack.[66]

The typical rest centre was a school building hastily taken over for the purpose and manned by teachers and volunteers. It had few blankets and no first aid equipment. When the homeless arrived at it, weary and encrusted with filth, they found minimal washing facilities, little bedding, and often very few chairs. To eat, they were offered for days on end the dietary of the poor law and its institutions – "bread, margarine, potted meat and corned beef, jam, biscuits and tea, varied only by soup". In one school in Stepney, two or three hundred homeless people had the use of ten pails and coal scuttles as lavatories, which overflowed on to the floor where they slept; there were seven basins, no soap and no towels.[67] It had been assumed that people would "rest" in such an environment for a few hours and then go away. In fact, many lived in the centres for weeks, while chaos reigned outside over the arrangements for rehousing them.

Into the breach, as in the shelters, flocked the volunteers. From the sober pages of Richard Titmuss's official history surges the memorable figure of "Mrs. B", a beetroot-seller in the hard-pressed borough of Islington.

> Her weather-beaten face and good loud voice were the result of years of market selling. When the raids started she left the first aid post where she was a part-time volunteer, walked into Ritchie Street rest centre and took charge. She found a supply of milk for the babies, bedded them down early with their mothers, and administered powders. What was in them no one knew, but sleep was not long in coming. Then she put the oldest and feeblest on the remaining beds and benches and had the whole household, one hundred to three hundred in all, asleep or quiet as the bombs came whining down. In the morning she organized the washing, bathed the babies, swept the floors, supervised breakfast, and went home about eleven o'clock to sleep (or sell beetroots?). In the evening she was back again. She made one rest centre a place of security, order and decency for hundreds of homeless people.[68]

Organized charity strove valiantly to distribute blankets and clothing provided by the Canadian Red Cross. Social workers commandeered cutlery from the schools. Within a few days, the Minister of Health intervened. The poor law was thrown out of the rest centres, which became a national burden. The London

County Council was given a free hand to expand and improve them.[69]

Meanwhile, the volunteers went on working. Bathrooms were constructed out of salvaged materials; armchairs, wireless sets and even flowers appeared. By the end of the blitz the rest centres had been transformed; it was said that everything the homeless needed "from a kind word to a safety pin" could be found in them.[70]

The same lack of foresight and the same swift voluntary response were seen in the provision of communal feeding – not only for the homeless, but for those who had lost their supply of gas or electricity, and whose local shops had been bombed out or evacuated. In Stepney,

> Father John Groser, one of the historic figures of the "blitz", took the law into his own hands. He smashed open a local food depot. He lit a bonfire outside his church and fed the hungry. There wasn't a cabinet minister or an official who would have dared to stand in his way or to challenge this "illicit" act. Similarly, in another London borough a local official of the Ministry of Food found a crowd of homeless uncared for. He broke open a block of flats. He put them in. He got hold of furniture by hook or by crook, he got the electricity, gas and water supply turned on, and he brought them food.[71]

According to the general secretary of their union, there were "fewer than six" mobile canteens serving firemen at the start of the blitz, and "men sometimes drank Thames water for refreshment". Wardens and rescue workers were equally ill served. This was quite apart from the more general needs of the homeless. The Y.M.C.A., the Salvation Army and the W.V.S. provided a few vans. Mrs. Flora Solomon, who had already been running a highly successful communal feeding centre on her own initiative, stepped in to organize more vans. Within three weeks of the start of the blitz, Woolton gave the L.C.C. powers to launch a huge experiment in communal feeding. By May, there were a hundred and seventy "Londoners' Meal Service Centres", most of them in school buildings. There were twenty-seven "community kitchens" maintained by voluntary organizations, and over a hundred and ninety mobile canteens. Meanwhile, there had been the enormous improvement of feeding facilities in the shelters and rest centres, of which the most remarkable tokens were the special canteen trains running between the Tube stations.[72]

But the rehousing of the homeless was more intractable. Before the blitz began, the L.C.C. and the borough councils had been given power to provide billets and to take over empty houses, but little preparation had been made.

After six weeks of bombing, when some 250,000 had been made homeless, 25,000 were still in the rest centres, and only 7,000 had been rehoused by official action. Ample property had been requisitioned by this stage, but the problem was not just one of fitting people into houses; as with evacuation, the right people must be fitted into the right houses. Attempts to billet East Enders in deserted West End mansions created unhappiness; even within West Ham itself, homeless people from the poorest part of the borough found it hard to adjust to life in the better-off quarter.[73]

And even when the homeless knew about the various services that might provide them with money from emergency funds, with storage for their furniture, with new identity cards and ration books, with billets and with clothing, to make use of them often involved traipsing all over a large borough. Children under five were being evacuated by the W.V.S., those of school age by the L.C.C.; in Stepney, "there were different offices for children going alone or with their mothers; there were other offices for persons who knew of billets to which they could go, and others for people who wanted billets for them. A mother with several children could spend days going round from one office to another trying to get all of them sent away . . ." One reporter saw women "stranded in the Commercial Road, crying with fatigue and despair".[74]

H. U. Willink, a Conservative M.P., was appointed Special Regional Commissioner for the Homeless, and began to introduce logic into their treatment. Welfare inspectors were appointed to deal with difficult cases of rehousing. The various offices with which raid victims might have to deal were concentrated in one centre in each borough. Advice was given in rest centres. Leaflets, pamphlets and posters were distributed in great numbers. Money was given generously from public and private funds. By the time the blitz ended, the post-raid services were working smoothly and compassionately.

Meanwhile, the repair of damaged houses had been given increased priority by the Government. There was a dire shortage of builders and materials. The Government set up a special organization to assist local authorities. Mobile squads were created, including men specially released from the army, and these could be switched to any heavily attacked area. (During April 1941, the Directorate of Emergency Works put sixteen thousand repairers into London in little more than a week.) By August 1941, over 1,100,000 houses had been made wind-and-weather-proof, and so just habitable, and only 50,000 still required similar treatment.[75] With boarded windows and tarpaulins on the roof, home might not be sweet, but at least it was home.

It will already be clear that London borough councils emerged discreditably from the blitz. An inordinate number of examples of squalor and neglect can be culled from the annals of Stepney and West Ham. Stepney was relieved of some of its powers by the Ministries of Health and Home Security in November. West Ham's council, like Stepney's, was overwhelmingly Labour in its composition. It had a decent pre-war record on public assistance, education and health, subjects on which the Labour Party laid special emphasis. But something more than traditional competence was now required.

One terrible story illustrates the failure of local government in West Ham. The council had taken over a school as a rest centre. There were no shelters there. After three nights of bombing, it was crammed with homeless, who were waiting for coaches which local officials had promised to take them out of the area and which were long overdue. It was bombed itself. Next day the coaches arrived, after hundreds of homeless had needlessly lost their lives. The borough was later involved in an intricate wrangle with the regional commissioners (the heads of London's Civil Defence), who wanted to appoint the town clerk as A.R.P. controller. The council refused, fearing that it would be by-passed by this arrangement, and suggested the mayor-elect instead, who was quite unsuitable, if only on grounds of age. Finally, the deputy town clerk was appointed. During a heavy raid in the following March, the new controller was absent from the borough. The regional commissioners threatened to take over West Ham completely. At last, a Presbyterian minister who had worked magnificently to alleviate the horrors of the blitz, was put in as controller and improved matters.[76]

It was the considered opinion of a journalist who had witnessed numerous boroughs in battle that their administrators and officials "with certain exceptions for whom no praise is adequate", were everywhere "futile and incompetent" at coping with the crisis.[77] Two exceptions were certainly found on other Labour councils. The East End borough of Poplar, under the brave and resolute leadership of Alderman Charlie Key, had a most effective

service of elected wardens with a superb *esprit de corps*; it was
typical of Key that when he was appointed regional commissioner
with special responsibility for shelters early in 1941, he stayed on
the Poplar A.R.P. committee. Mayor Henley of Bermondsey went
without sleep night after night during the raids, ate his Christmas
dinner in the A.R.P. control room, and was killed "on duty" in
the last and worst night of blitz in May.

But in general nothing emerges more forcibly from the blitz
than the contrast between laggard councillors, obsessed with
their own prestige, and the self-sacrifice of the volunteers who
strove indefatigably to remedy the position which bumbledom
had created. Most of the 200,000 or 250,000 people who served
their fellows in the various post-raid services or in the shelters
were volunteers. Most of the men and women of the Civil Defence
services were volunteer part-timers. These were the "militant
citizens" of whom J. B. Priestley wrote. He saw in them the seeds
of a new democracy.

Over the nation as a whole, the organized "militant citizens"
formed a very large and important section of the population.
There were one and a half million men in the Home Guard, whose
duties took them into the raids, who were often called in to assist
the police, and who frequently joined in rescue work. The Civil
Defence (General) services included the wardens, the rescue and
stretcher parties, the staffs of the control centres, and the messenger boys. The casualty services embraced the emergency ambulance workers and the staffs of the first aid posts. The Fire
Service included full-time and part-time regular firemen and full-
time and part-time auxiliaries. Altogether, these numbered over a
million and a half people in December 1940. To these should be
added just over a quarter of a million full-time and part-time
policemen, who did all sorts of A.R.P. work in addition to their
much complicated peacetime duties of maintaining order and
controlling traffic. Outside London (where the special complexities of local government made this impossible), the Chief Con-
stable of a borough was usually its Chief Warden as well, and the
whole Civil Defence service was built round the police force. The
peacetime forces had been strengthened by a full-time police war
reserve, and a very large number of part-time "specials" – special
constables.

Even this impressive roll-call omits the members of the
Women's Voluntary Service, never really countable, but certainly
running into hundreds of thousands. The frequency with which
the initials W.V.S. have already appeared in this book should

have suggested the character of the service; in raids, as in many
other spheres of wartime effort, its members were maids, or more
normally matrons, of all work.

V

In 1938, the Home Office had asked the redoubtable Stella,
Marchioness of Reading, to start an organization which would
draw women into the A.R.P. services and bring home to the
whole sex what raids would mean to it. The W.V.S. is often hailed
as one of the triumphs of the British genius for voluntary
organization. Only about seven hundred members received a
monetary grant from the Home Office, and only about two
hundred key workers, excluding paid typists, were given more
than their out of pocket expenses. Many well-to-do women gave
their whole-time services freely. Local councils provided free
premises and furniture. The local centres had their own organizers, and responsibility was devolved to village representatives and street leaders; but all appointments were made from
above.[78]

An unimpressed American who watched W.V.S. loading up a
food trailer during the blitz remarked that they reminded him "of
the housewives of a small village preparing a light refreshment
for a charity bazaar".[79] In fact, the W.V.S. throughout the
country was built round the sorts of ladies who provide light
refreshments for charity bazaars. Not so many working-class
women had time for such activities, so the familiar English voluntary lady tended to pronounce her aitches with an air of effortless
superiority which provoked laughter in sophisticated circles and
dark resentment in the lower orders.

Members had to pay to acquire the W.V.S. uniform – a green
tweed suit with grey woven into it, a beetroot red jumper and a
schoolgirl felt hat – and later on they had to give clothing
coupons for it. Yet, such was the onslaught of the People's War
that the W.V.S., in certain times and places, transcended its
apparently basic middle classness. A post-war observer has
remarked that before 1939 it "would have been almost inconceivable that in a philanthropic organization the relations of e.g.
committee members and clients could be interchangeable or that
members of particular trades or industries or even residents in a
"poor" locality could take part in social services . . ."[80] But war
disrupted the lives of middle-class and working-class women

indiscriminately. The former, when their homes were bombed, might find themselves leaning, however temporarily, on "charity" or calling for help from voluntary organizations. The latter were drawn in to "man" the enormous new range of social safety nets which had to be erected and for which there were simply not enough upper-middle-class ladies to go round. Whether "Mrs B" was technically a W.V.S. member or not, she was a symbol in her rest centre.

In the blitz, the W.V.S. plugged scores of gaps. In the last six months of 1940 it received and distributed a million and a half pounds' worth of clothing (much of it from America and the Commonwealth). In its national system of stores, depots and dumps it held the major part of the country's gift clothing for emergency issue. It organized a "Housewives' Service" for women who could help A.R.P. workers without necessarily leaving their own streets – for instance, by giving cups of tea to shocked casualties from nearby incidents; by keeping the census of residents which wardens relied on; or by going on "mercy" errands to blitzed homes.[81] It is quite impossible to tell where W.V.S. membership and W.V.S. activities began and ended.

The other Civil Defence services, by contrast, had an important stiffening of paid full-timers, and trained men and women as specialists. By the summer of 1940, they had lost so many of their personnel through the competition of the Home Guard and the services, that there was undermanning in key centres, notably in London, and this had led to an infringement of the voluntary principle. In June, police and firemen had been "frozen" in their jobs, and it had been announced that men between thirty and fifty might opt for them as alternative to military service. Next month, the rescue and stretcher parties had also been frozen and had been "reserved" at thirty from military service. (This had soon been raised to thirty-five.) Before the blitz had begun, full-time London wardens, who had been quitting at an alarming rate, had been given temporary deferments. In October they too were "frozen".

When the blitz began, full-time A.R.P. workers and A.F.S. men were drawing pay of £3 5s. a week for men and £2 3s. 6d. for women. Part-timers who were losing money through their service might be recompensed with a few shillings per day. There was no overtime; though A.R.P. workers were theoretically limited to seventy-two hours per week, this was normally much exceeded when the blitz began. There was twelve days' annual leave, but only three weeks' sick pay. Uniforms were slow in coming and inadequate when they finally arrived. Wardens, for instance, had initially received blue cotton overalls, but no rank badges. In the summer of 1940, the Government had more or less simultaneously announced a standard badge and tried to withdraw all uniforms. "Presumably," wrote one warden bitterly, "the new badges were to be sewn on our pyjamas." A spate of orders and counter orders had created rage and confusion, but in the end the wardens had kept their "uniforms". They were surpassing thin and capes and waterproofs were not issued until well after the blitz had started. Not until May 1941 did the full-timers and regular part-timers get "real" uniforms of blue serge, with overcoats, berets and boots.[82]

"The general idea of an air raid warden", an official circular had announced in March 1937, "is that he should be a responsible member of the public, chosen to be a leader and adviser of his neighbours in a small area, a street or a small group of streets, in which he is known and respected."[83] In practice, the warden's service was rarely democratic in the manner implied here; but if one thing was true of it everywhere in Britain, it was that its nature was essentially local. The coverage varied from city to city and borough to borough; in London, ten warden's posts to the square mile was the standard. The vast majority of wardens – about nine-tenths – were part-timers. The full-timers, however, were essential, since they could oversee the area during the day, when most of the others would be at work. The part-timers sometimes knew little or nothing about their duties when the blitz started, and those who joined in London after September were trained on the job.

A London borough would have a chief warden, commonly a retired military man. It would be partitioned into districts, under district wardens; each post would have a post warden; its area would be divided into half a dozen or more sectors, each covered by, say, three or six wardens under a senior warden. Sectors often had "sub-posts" of their own. Wardens assembled at the posts when going on and off duty, and patrolled their own sectors during the warning periods. The post was connected directly to the borough control centre by telephone.

The good warden knew where everyone in his sector slept at night, so that if an incident occurred he could direct the rescue men to the appropriate quarter of the debris. When a bomb fell, he rushed to the incident and reported it quickly, concisely and accurately to Control. (The standard of reporting varied, especially at first, and a fanciful warden could bring numerous civil defenders hot-foot on a wild goose chase.) Before, during and after the bombing, the good warden calmed the general public and gave them information about the A.R.P. and post-raid services. He made a point of popping his head into the public shelters and telling the denizens how the raid was proceeding.

At a minor incident, the good warden and his comrades might put the fire out, rescue the inhabitants, administer first aid and direct the homeless to the rest centre without troubling the other arms of Civil Defence at all. On him fell the dangerous (but oddly attractive, and certainly prestigious) duty of investigating reports of U.X.B.s. Before the "Fire Guard" came into being in mid-1941, the warden trained street fire-fighting parties. He was the eyes and ears of the whole Civil Defence machine. His indispensability was duly acknowledged when the time came for cuts in the C.D. services in the summer of 1941; London region was ready to deplete the other services to keep its wardens.

Who were the wardens? Almost the only generalization which seems possible is that in London in the autumn of 1940, and in Plymouth and Liverpool the following spring, they were hollow-eyed, had a craving for sleep, and were suffering from indigestion. About one in six were women. Most wardens had come on duty from their jobs or their housework. They were predominantly middle-aged, and many were elderly. In London, three months after the blitz had finished, only about one-third of the seventeen thousand paid male wardens were under forty-one.

It was hard for a key war-worker or a heavy labourer to find time and energy for wardens' duties. An overwhelmingly working-class area like West Ham found it harder to recruit wardens than a prosperous one like Hampstead. But a Mass Observation survey of volunteers in one west London borough in the summer of 1939 had suggested that about two-thirds were working-class. The wardens would reflect, in their occupations and accents, the character of their neighbourhood. Barbara Nixon served in two posts at opposite ends of her borough. In Post 2 "we had a variety of trades, from railway workers, post office sorters, lawyers, newspapermen, garage hands, to a few of no very definable profession." At Post 13, there was a small-time burglar and three men who had joined because the race tracks from which they had earned a dubious livelihood were now closed, and they had thought A.R.P. would be easy money. (She suggests, plausibly, that the C.D. services generally were a natural haven for those in fringe jobs – bookies' touts, "intellectuals", opera singers, street traders, chorus girls – whose occupations had been swept away by the war.) However, Post 13 was certainly not out of touch with the local community. All the wardens except herself "had been to the same local school, though at different times, and they knew the family history of nearly everyone in the neighbourhood".[84]

At a post in north London which included a Mass Observer among its volunteers, it became clear in the first weeks of blitz that a large proportion of the wardens were virtually useless. One ebullient full-timer is reported as saying, "They started off this service with the idea that it was a kind of muck-heap for anyone they didn't want in the army. Can you tell me of four wardens at our post, bar you and me, who can run fifty yards without conking out? Or climb over six feet of clay like we've just done? Of course they can't . . . Here's old G. is stone deaf; he's no use. Old R. can't hardly walk, don't talk about running. The general's nearly eighty, his daughter was telling me; and H. can't walk without a stick. Talk to me about the lame, the halt and the blind! Cor!"[85]

Real or apparent incompetence by wardens, allied to the resentment which the self-importance of a minority in the service had already wakened, meant that relations with the public were not always happy even after the blitz had started. But the good warden might walk through his home streets like the squire of a village; in the shelters, the sight of his "tin helmet" (in fact made out of steel) inspired immense, if spurious, confidence. When the notorious "Tilbury" shelter suffered a direct hit and was plunged into gloom, "A single warden, standing at the top of a narrow passage, was able to control about three thousand people, who calmly and coolly groped their way through the darkness exactly as he ordered."[86]

If the good warden was indeed the "leader and adviser" of his neighbours, he was so by virtue of being much the same kind of person as they were. The rescue teams, by contrast, were gods from the Civil Defence machine, descending on an incident in a lorry laden with equipment and tools. The "heavy rescue" men, so distinguished from the stretcher parties who came with them, and eventually merged with them into one rescue service, were mainly peacetime building workers – skilled bricklayers, plumbers and carpenters as well as labourers – who now applied their techniques in reverse. Their understanding of buildings was confronted with as many different problems as there were types of house – "a big city office with perhaps one caretaker or fire-watcher pinned (who knows where?) under huge chunks of masonry; an old-fashioned block of nineteenth-century brick-built flats, dissolved with the peculiarity of that type of building into a compact pile of something strangely like earth, with bricks, paper, pipes, clothing and fragments of furniture embedded as in a giant plum pudding, and underneath it an uncertain number of tenants, alive or dead; a domestic dwelling of which all the floors have collapsed into the basement in layers, and trapped between them an old man or old woman, crushed and burning beside the remnants of a kitchen fire".[87]

One heavy rescue man is said to have replied to the King, "It's all in the day's work, sir, we all get the same pay," when complimented for getting a twelve-year-old girl out of a wrecked house through a twenty- or thirty-foot tunnel after she had been buried for four and a half days.[88] This remark, as it happens, was more generous than true, since skilled men on rescue work were paid above the basic Civil Defence rate. But it expresses a type of selfless courage which was common enough in the blitz. In September 1940, the King instituted the George Cross, an award for great heroism on the home front comparable to the Victoria Cross given for extreme bravery in the fighting forces. But most George Crosses went to soldiers, notably to men of the bomb disposal squads.[89] It is hard in any case to see how decorations for civilians could be anything but invidious, in a situation where so many people, confronted suddenly with danger or emergency, acted at once and effectively with a courage which surprised their neighbours and themselves.

VI

A mine exploded. The nearest warden raced towards the sound, assessed the extent and character of the damage, and ran to his post to report to the control centre, a bomb-proof fastness in the borough town hall. From there, messages went to the police, to the public utilities, and to the fire, rescue and casualty services in their various depots. If the borough was especially hard pressed, a call for help might go to the group control centre which served several boroughs. Word would go also to the regional headquarters. This was located, oddly enough, in a museum in South Kensington, with walls mainly of glass, barely a pane of which was shattered during the war.

There were twelve regions in all. Everywhere except London, they were presided over by one regional commissioner, a man of national rather than local standing who was expected to coordinate, and if necessary overrule, the squabbling county

councils and borough councils and to assume quasi-dictatorial
control if and when circumstances seemed to him to warrant
it.

London was unique. Its area embraced an unusual number of
authorities. The L.C.C. was almost a state within the state, and
besides the metropolitan boroughs which existed subordinately
but autonomously, there were the county boroughs of West Ham
and Croydon, with major powers of their own. London region
had a senior Regional Commissioner, who was, when the blitz
began, a Conservative M.P. (Captain Euan Wallace). Beneath
him, it was not clear who overruled whom among the two lesser
commissioners and Harold Scott, the region's Chief Administrative Officer. But these three men were all imaginative appointments, and they worked together effectively. Scott was an
unusually warm civil servant, whose own theory was that he had
been chosen "because they suspected that I was a bit slapdash and
unorthodox". One of the commissioners was Sir Ernest Gowers, a
distinguished civil servant who was known as a deadly opponent
of Whitehall jargon. The other was the cheerful Admiral Evans,
"Evans of the Broke", a veteran of Scott's Antarctic expedition
and a hero of the First World War, who had been told that his job
was to keep up the Londoners' spirits. To this end, he "literally
visited thousands of incidents" and made himself a familiar
figure in the shelters, where his immaculate naval uniform, complete with white kid gloves, raised laughter and cheers.[90]

At the top of the whole structure was the Minister of Home
Security. The replacement of Anderson with Herbert Morrison in
October 1940 was hailed as a victory for the multifarious protests
against conditions in the shelters and rest centres, and was duly
followed by the improvements already mentioned; but cause and
effect in this episode were more complex than the public supposed. Psychologically, however, it was important that the
energetic Morrison, with his democratic manner and his rubbery
London voice, was now in charge. His junior minister was Ellen
Wilkinson, M.P. for Jarrow, a tiny, passionate woman who had
once led her constituents on a celebrated "hunger march" from
Durham to Whitehall. Even more than Morrison, "Red Ellen",
with her unsparing energy, convinced hard-pressed social workers
and civil defenders that the Government was on their side.

The communications upon which the whole system depended
were bombed, of course, as haphazardly as everything else. The
girls who manned the telephones in the control rooms, and the

messenger boys who took over when the lines were knocked out, had plenty of hair-raising stories of their own to tell. But the purpose for which the machine was run was the saving of life; the "incidents" were the front line.

At the incident, the wardens would be alone for perhaps half an hour with the cries of casualties, the debris and the noise of the raid. They would begin the tasks of fire fighting and rescue, assisted by those residents who were still able to help, and perhaps by passing Home Guards and even casual pedestrians. When the first and least serious casualties, shaken but cheerful, were led from the ruins, W.V.S. housewives would provide cups of tea, sofas and blankets in their houses near by while they waited for the ambulance to arrive.

Let us say this was a big incident. Several houses had been destroyed and more than a score of people had been killed. When one warden shouted to another, dust would seem to fill his mouth and muffle the sound. Because of the blackout, only screened hand torches could be used to penetrate the murk, though the fire which had broken out among the ruins gave some assistance. Drivers searching for the spot would find the whole geography of a familiar area transformed.

The firemen and the rescue team would quite soon appear, and the heavy rescue men would begin at once to negotiate the wreckage with care and yet with amazing speed. The stretcher party, according to the pre-war scheme, was supposed to stand by until the casualties were brought out or the ruins were safe to enter, but its members were normally disinclined to remain idle and would help their more expert colleagues.

If the police appeared, there would be an unedifying argument between the officer of the law and the senior warden over who had the right to control the incident. The policeman would say that the ultimate responsibility was his; the warden would argue that the police knew nothing of Civil Defence; while the effective leader of the operation might well be the chief man of the rescue team. (Still less edifying demarcation disputes would occur when bombs fell on the boundaries between post areas or boroughs, and two teams of wardens disputed jealously over whose they were.) The policeman would probably have his way. It was over two years before this problem was settled.

Every so often, the clatter of activity would stop, and the leader of the rescue team would call for silence as his men listened for the faint moaning or the muffled cry which would lead them to a trapped casualty. A grey auxiliary ambulance, a high-powered saloon car with a square van back, would have arrived; and its woman driver might well be smoking to calm her nerves after a tortuous trip through craters and explosions. There would also be a mobile first aid post, a car with three nurses and a doctor.

At this point, we may let one such nurse bring us back from typicality to actuality. What follows is a report written by a fully trained nurse who, with two untrained assistants, helped at such an incident. She calls the rescue men, "demolition men".

"On arrival we were told that there were a number of trapped people and several dead. Four of these we saw, but they had been certified by a private doctor as dead before arrival. We stood by and then found a man who was suffering very severely from shock. A. helped to put him into a bed in a basement nearby; he was given hot tea, hot water bottles, and generally treated for shock. Dr S. saw and ordered 1 gr Phenobarbitone. I gave this and was able to obtain particulars. MPC 46 given. We also found slight cuts over several parts of his body, and Dr S. queried embedded glass. The casualty was told to see his own doctor in the morning (later sent for treatment to Post 'C' first aid post). Demolition Squad asked doctor and me to stand by as they were trying to reach a woman (trapped by legs) in a lavatory. She was quite cheerful, and kept up a conversation with the men and also spoke to me. I did not see her, and she had not been rescued when I left at 0700 hours. Screams were also coming from debris nearby; men were working to release trapped people. These also were still trapped at 0700 hours. We were then called to a heap of debris (No. 16 was on the gatepost) where a girl was trapped. While taking a short cut with A. and S., S. tripped over a body; this was a female who was decapitated and disembowelled. We helped to put her on a stretcher and then went on to the trapped girl – who was too ill to give her name. Dr S. ordered $\frac{1}{2}$ gr morphine (we checked this and I gave it. Given at 5.43 a.m.). Hot tea was also given her. The demolition men got debris away as far as her feet and I was able to give her hot water bottles (provided by neighbours). At 0634 hours, Dr S. ordered another quarter of a grain of morphine (checked by Dr S. and given by me). The girl remained conscious, but was in pain and was very brave. As I came out of the hole I noticed the back part of a body in a green skirt under the above girl's trapped legs and told demolition men. The demolition men then unearthed a girl's hand (not the girl in the green skirt). The men made a hole and the girl made noises – I gave them a rubber tube which the girl was able to put into her mouth to help her to breathe. Fires started to break out under this debris and the firemen were ordered to keep it down with a gentle flow of water. We stood by until 0700 hours when I was relieved by Sister S. . . . Both A. and S. were excellent in helping us and looking after me. A. pulled aside a man when a beam fell and S. shouted to me and I was able to fall over backwards out of its way. Thanks to them, a nasty accident was avoided."[91]

As morning cast a pale light through the dust, the rescue workers could at last see what they were doing. Sightseers would stand vacantly about in clusters; tearful relatives would tug at the rescuers' sleeves and beg for information; a yellow diversion sign would advertise another blocked thoroughfare. In exceptional cases, the work would carry on into the following night's raid, even for several days. At some stage, the leader of the rescue team must decide that he could no longer risk several lives, and keep his men back from other incidents, for the sake of just possibly saving one life. It was not a decision which could be taken lightly. Later in the blitz, one girl on Merseyside was buried for a hundred and six hours, with a dead child in her arms, and brought out alive.[92]

But in some cases, even the remains of the dead would not be found. They might come to light in the final work of demolition, perhaps a year later. They might perhaps figure in the basket of "unidentified flesh" which wardens were expected to collect. If enough remained recognizable, a body would be taken to the mortuary, where attendants and volunteers would work on it. One volunteer, useful because she was an artist trained in anatomy, has written: "We had somehow to form a body for burial so that the relatives (without seeing it) could imagine that their loved one was more or less intact for that purpose. But it was a very difficult task – there were so many pieces missing and, as one of the mortuary attendants said, 'Proper jigsaw puzzle, ain't it, Miss?' The stench was the worst thing about it . . ." She adds, "It became a grim and ghastly satisfaction when a body was fairly constructed – but if one was too lavish in making one body almost whole, then another would have sad gaps . . . I think that this task dispelled for me the idea that human life is valuable . . ."[93]

COVENTRATION

"Where's the gents?"
"Everywhere's the gents now."

Repartee in a Plymouth pub, May 1941[1]

I

During October, the weight of the Luftwaffe's attack shifted somewhat from London to the provinces. A hundred and seventy people died in Birmingham on the night of the 25th.

But in most parts of the country, the tendency was to pooh-pooh the stories of what was happening in London. If a town had been attacked, however lightly, the locals wanted to know why London had all the publicity. If not, a stiff silence was maintained on the subject of raids; people perhaps felt, superstitiously, that it would bring the Germans to their street if they discussed them.[2] Almost everywhere, the defects of preparation which the bombs had exposed in London were regarded with complacency. From Glasgow to Plymouth, there were grim brick surface shelters and few good ideas about how to cope with the homeless.

The fate which befell Coventry on November 14th marked the beginning of a new phase. From November 18th to January 19th, London experienced only six major raids and two lighter ones. In that much needed respite, there was time to put its own house in order. Its worst raids were still to come, but it was now only one target among many.

The Germans had developed, long before they raided Britain heavily, a radio device named the *Knickebein*. Beams from two radio stations on the Continent could be arranged to intersect over any target in the midlands or southern England, and would, it was hoped, guide bombers "blind" to it. In June, the British had learnt of this device, and had countered it effectively by deflecting or jamming the beams. Churchill relates the experience of an officer's wife, evacuated to the country with her children, who watched in astonishment while over a hundred heavy bombs dropped on fields miles from any town. The Germans revised their methods. The famous Kampfgruppe 100 was used as a "pathfinder" force, employing a different radio guide to set a target area on fire with incendiaries so that the rest of the bombers could steer for the flames. The British could also have jammed the "*X*" *Gerät*, as the Kampfgruppe's apparatus was called, if one British scientist had not made an error of calculation; so great events now depended on obscure men working with pens and figures in "the back room".[3]

Coventry was the first city attacked with the new method. The raiders first fired the medieval centre, crowned by its beautiful cathedral, which was gutted. They then poured hundreds of tons of bombs into the city, in an attack which lasted for ten hours. Approaching one-third of the city's houses were made uninhabitable, over half its buses were damaged or wrecked, and six out of seven telephone lines were put out of action. All the main railway lines passing through the city were blocked. A hundred acres of the city centre were destroyed. Five hundred and fifty-four people were killed, eight hundred and sixty-five seriously wounded.[4]

Next morning, Hilde Marchant drove into the town; as a journalist she was allowed through the cordon which the authorities had wisely flung round it. As she neared it, she saw the refugees straggling towards her, in lorries and cars; pushing handcarts or prams; carrying their bedding. "Five miles outside the town we had picked up the first thin smell of smoke, but as we went nearer the air thickened and carried charred bits of wood in through the car window. It was a heavy, stifling smell that bit into your throat and lungs. Then suddenly, as we came to the edge of the city, the air became as warm as a spring day. Though it was noon, the city was darkened by the black fog that clouded the sky and the thick banks of soot that were suspended over the streets. The people who walked the streets had grimy faces and their eyes were reddened with the heat and the smoke." They dithered, they reacted slowly to the car's horn.[5]

For those who had lived through it, this had been something bigger than the London blitz. Coventry was a relatively small and compact town (213,000 people in 1938).* Nearly everyone had heard the fall of nearly every bomb; nearly everyone knew someone who was dead, or missing, or homeless. Mass Observation sent in three observers. (M-O's reports on blitzed towns are of particular value, because they were not designed for publication, and so avoided the platitudes imposed by patriotic self-censorship.) They concluded that "the small size of the place makes

* This, and other figures quoted for different towns later, are found in M. P. Fogarty's *Prospects of the Industrial Areas of Great Britain* (1945) pp. 26–30. All refer to 1938 and are given purely for comparison. Coventry itself had swollen considerably by 1940.

236   THE PEOPLE'S WAR

people feel that the only thing they can do *is get out of it alto-gether* . . . 'Coventry is finished', and 'Coventry is dead' were the key phrases in Friday's talk."

They went on: "There were more open signs of hysteria, terror, neurosis, observed in one evening than during the whole of the past two months together in all areas. Women were seen to cry, to scream, to tremble all over, to faint in the street, to attack a fireman, and so on . . . There were several signs of suppressed panic as darkness approached. In two cases people were seen fighting to get on to cars, which they thought would take them out into the country, though in fact, as the drivers insisted, the cars were going just up the road to garage."[6]

Four or five hundred retail shops had been put out of action, and many people had lost their ration books. The tradesmen who survived, according to a local official, were "stunned for a couple of days and dazed for some days afterwards". Rationing was suspended. A hundred thousand loaves were rushed from neighbouring cities in a single day. The W.V.S. brought in their mobile canteens and cooked stew in the ruined streets. For some time, all drinking water had to be boiled.[7]

The Germans, foolishly, did not repeat the attack. On the night of the 15th, the bombers returned to London, where the tradesmen were no longer stunned by such occurrences, and only a handful visited Coventry, which was one of the keys to the British war effort. Much damage had been done to production. Twenty-one important factories, twelve of them directly concerned with aircraft manufacture, had been severely affected by fire or direct hits. Work at nine more stopped completely because of the disruption of utilities. But the limitations of terror bombing were exposed. The buildings were destroyed, but not the machines inside them; the streets were obliterated, but economic life continued. Six hundred thousand square feet of roof had been blasted off the Morris Motor Engines Works. Even in the first week after the raid, five-sixths of the employees turned up for work. They went on with their jobs under the open sky, through snow, wind and rain, in greatcoats, sou'westers and gumboots, and sometimes with tin hats to ward off chunks of falling masonry. Within six weeks, Morris's production of tank engines, airscrews and other vital components was back to normal.[8]

Nazi propaganda now coined the verb "*Coventrieren*", to "Coventrate". The word embodied the idea of the physical and psychological destruction of an entire city. "Coventation", as it was applied to other British cities, never involved the loss of very great numbers of lives. But the raid on Coventry was a precedent for Dresden and Hiroshima.

It was certainly the prototype for the provincial blitz, as this affected small and medium-sized cities, rather than the great conurbations of Birmingham (1,041,000) and Glasgow (1,127,825). The centre would be levelled by fire and high explosive. People would flee in great numbers to the fields and villages around. Organized evacuation would get under way slowly and inadequately. The rest centres, usually as bad as London's had been at the start of the blitz. would be overwhelmed. Feeding arrangements would break down. Local government would be as helpless as a boy with a feather duster attacking a tiger. Cities formerly puffed with local pride would become nerve-wracked ghost towns.

This was not because people in the provinces were any less brave than those in London, though it should be stressed that, throughout the period of heavy raiding which followed Coventry, the capital remained the prime target. Over the eight months from September to May, London had about nineteen thousand tons of bombs aimed at it, and five thousand fell after November 14th, in fourteen raids. In the latter period, no other city had more than two thousand tons of bombs or eight major raids.[9] When the bombs came, there were many acres of suburb, many miles of Tube, in wh ch people from the worst hit areas could take shelter. If the clothes shops in the borough's High Street were hit, there were other clothes shops within walking distance. So London could absorb the strain of continuous bombing, not without large-scale disruption, but without collapse.

In a smaller, isolated city, the quality of life for the survivors would be far more seriously reduced. When the centre was razed, the symbols of local pride and the centres of local pleasure perished with it. Small raids were interspersed unpredictably with periods of lull and fierce blitzes, and no "even tenor" could be established.

Bristol (415,000), for instance, had had small raids by day and by night; but its "Coventration" on November 24th was something quite new. A quotation from the diary of a Bristol woman for that night will suggest the more intimate scale of the provincial blitz.

Jerry is here early tonight. Siren went five minutes ago. Yes, he's here all right. Some bombs are being dropped and a fire has started already to the east of us. I've got a nasty feeling

in my tummy too at this moment. God grant it is going to be
all right for us. 11.5 p.m. same night: We've been through
hell. Never have I experienced anything like it. Tummy still
wobbly. Fires and bombs everywhere. Went to the cellar at
first, but couldn't settle down, so went to the sitting-room.
We didn't need any light for the room was lit up with the
glare of the fires. Wine Street looks as if it is no more. Fires
all seem centred in that direction, though up the hill at the
back of our place there are fires also. One looks like the
Princes' Theatre. Our sitting-room window woodwork is so
hot you can hardly bear your hand on it. The house rocks
as the bombs drop. It is like a "Wellsonian drama" come
true. I must pay my tribute to the firemen. All the time the
dreadful bombing was at its height one of them swayed about
on a water tower playing on the fire at Budgett's wholesale
warehouse. Sometimes he was completely obliterated by
great clouds of smoke, but always when it cleared he was
still there, though Jerry kept bombing time after time.[10]

Before the end of November, Birmingham and Southampton had
received attention on a similar scale. On fifteen nights in December, weather conditions forced the Luftwaffe to leave Britain
almost undisturbed, but there were eleven major attacks, and five
moderately heavy ones, on British cities. London had three big
raids, and smaller ones on twelve other nights. Merseyside,
Manchester, Birmingham, Sheffield, Portsmouth and Leicester
also suffered.

On December 29th came the "second Fire of London", of the
City proper, some two hundred and fifty years after the first one
which had destroyed old St Paul's and had given Christopher
Wren his opportunity. This time, his masterpiece provided the
classic photographic image of the blitz, as its dome rode the sea
of flames and smoke which surrounded it, miraculously unscathed.

It was a Sunday evening, when the offices and warehouses of
the City were locked up. Many had no fire watchers; from those
which had, men watched helplessly as the flames gained control.
In a two-hour attack, the raiders started almost fifteen hundred
fires in a relatively small area, over fourteen hundred in the City
itself. Only bad weather conditions prevented them from returning to cause unimaginable havoc. As it was, with the Thames at
its lowest ebb, the Fire Service was all but overwhelmed. Air
Marshal "Bomber" Harris, the Deputy Chief of the Air Staff,

was watching. He writes, "Although I have often been accused of being vengeful during our subsequent destruction of German cities, this was the one occasion and the only one when I did feel vengeful, and then it was only for the moment. Having in mind what was being done at that time to produce heavy bombers in Britain I said out loud as we turned away from the scene: 'Well, they are sowing the wind'." The citizens of Hamburg and Dresden would reap it. As many as 135,000 people may have died in the Dresden firestorm of 1945; 163 perished in the City, which was not a residential area.[11]

II

The danger from incendiary bombs had been recognized long before the war. But the authorities' approach to the problem of fire prevention had been slow and halting. By June 1940, only some sixty-eight thousand stirrup pumps had been distributed to local authorities, and while Anderson had exhorted all citizens to supply themselves with them (at a pound apiece), they had remained in short supply. Wardens, police and Home Guards, along with the supplementary fire parties organized from local residents in some areas, cornered most of what was going. When the blitz came, most people had some idea what they should do with I.B.s, and had provided themselves with sandbags and pails of water in readiness, but only a minority were ready to sit up and wait for them to fall, though some street fire parties were spontaneously formed, as two or three neighbours would agree to share the vigil. In one suburb of London at least, a "chain of little notice boards, generally home-made, announced from front gardens the duty rota for the week."[12]

But even if street fire parties had been universal, they would not have solved the problem of unoccupied buildings, which at night included many small commercial and industrial premises. The first Fire Watchers Order, issued in September 1940, applied somewhat ludicrously only to large factories, warehouses and yards, where a vigil was made compulsory. The Fire of London rubbed home a lesson which should have been learnt at Coventry. On New Year's Eve, Herbert Morrison announced the beginning of compulsory fire watching, and he soon produced regulations which could compel all men between sixteen and sixty to register for that purpose. The emergency water supplies of London and other cities were reinforced and improved.

Men could now be compelled to fire watch for a maximum of forty-eight hours per month. But at first, most effort remained voluntary. Wardens and firemen trained new supplementary fire parties; some local authorities gave them steel helmets and armbands marked S.F.P. But no attractive voluntary tradition had been established, and the S.F.P.s came too late to capture the imagination of a public already much occupied with the Home Guard and Civil Defence. It was especially hard to find people ready to keep watch over private business premises, which was uncomfortable, lonely and often dangerous. The fire watching regulations were notoriously hard to understand and notoriously easy to evade. Just how large the loopholes were was shown when the House of Commons burnt down in May 1941. M.P.s and members of staff had not provided sufficient volunteers to protect it, and it had not been clear which authority was responsible for ensuring adequate precautions.[13]

The result was that the Fire Service took the brunt. Before the war, there had been only eighteen hundred and fifty pumps protecting the whole of Britain; on December 29th, in the City of London alone, there were two thousand pumps from London region at work, and three hundred more sent as reinforcements from outside. To the many great blazes of that winter, the firemen had to drive their appliances somehow round diversion signs, over craters and debris, past dangling telephone and trolley bus wires, over the carpet of splintered glass, through cordons of people who begged them to stop and save their homes. Then, in the smoke and heat, they had to manhandle their heavy brass nozzles and hard canvas hosepipes, sometimes climb a hundred foot watertower to fight the flames. (One watcher who saw them working from their ladders in a frustrated effort to save London's Guildhall on December 29th said that "it just looked like little boys peeing on an enormous bonfire".) Either there was the fierce kick of the water, or, worse, there was not, and the man on the branch swore helplessly as the pressure dwindled and the supply ran out. As many as a hundred million gallons of water might be used in London during a twenty-four-hour period, and much of it was merely wasted when mains were hit and punctured.[14]

At times, fires raging close together so raised the general temperature that everything was ready to ignite. The updraught "would cause flying brands of burning material to whirl in the air like autumn leaves in a storm, and, as the windows would by then have been shattered by the heat or blast, fire might travel down a street as fast as a man could walk". This was the force which swept through Dresden; in Britain it never gathered all-destructive strength. During the war, 793 firemen and 25 firewomen lost their lives, while 7,000 were more or less seriously injured. Many were temporarily or permanently blinded by heat or sparks. All were liable to suffer in their health from the extremes of heat and cold, from exorbitant hours, from the lack of regular meals and the constant physical and nervous strain. During Merseyside's "May Week" in 1941, Sir Aylmer Firebrace, the Regional Fire Officer for London, "actually saw one Liverpool fire officer collapse in the main control room. Without any warning he gave a stifled cry, and immediately lost consciousness – sheer exhaustion of mind and body."[15]

Firemen's hours, standardized at forty-eight hours on, twenty-four hours off, far exceeded those of other civil defenders. Unlike wardens and rescue men, they had some discipline other than the threat of the sack; they could incur heavy fines. If full-time A.F.S. men were ill they received only three weeks' full pay and three weeks' half pay; when they were injured, they had thirteen weeks' full pay and were then dismissed if they were still not fit. Accommodation, bad in many London stations, was even worse in some provincial cities; Manchester achieved special notoriety.[16]

The full-timers were joined at nights by part-time auxiliaries, who over the country as a whole, serving one night on duty, one night on call, one free, outnumbered them by roughly two to one. Their efforts were not assisted by official complacency and incompetence.

There had been 1,666 local authorities organizing fire brigades in Britain before the outbreak of war. Very few indeed had had more than twenty full-time firemen; and, of course, peacetime conditions did not warrant immense organization. But even after the war had started, many provincial brigades remained poorly equipped. (London, under Firebrace, was a model.) One city provided no towing vehicles in its dock area, so pumps had to be pushed to the fires by hand. The Birmingham service performed so badly in its first blitz that its Chief Officer resigned. It was inevitable that individual city brigades would be overwhelmed, and that help, on nights of "Coventration", must come from outside. There were cases of generous assistance – nothing, surely, illustrates better the way in which bombs overrode traditional fissures than the fact that brigades from neutral Eire arrived to help when Belfast was blitzed. But provincial brigades usually sent inexperienced auxiliaries rather than their best men. Some brigades charged for their help, or even refused to attend because no prior arrangement over costs had been made. Local fire chiefs sometimes let houses burn down rather than call in help, lest the council should criticize them for unnecessary expenditure. When outside help did arrive, chaos often resulted because ranks, words of command and messages were not standardized. Nor was equipment. As Plymouth and Portsmouth burned, reinforcements who had travelled great distances had to stand by helplessly because their apparatus did not fit the local hydrants.[17]

Morrison had to take action. On May 13th ,when the blitz was all but over, the creation of a National Fire Service was announced in the House of Commons. Firebrace became "Chief of Fire Staff" – a suitably militant title. The myriad local brigades were replaced by less than fifty "fire forces", operating under one unified control. Many A.F.S. men were preferred to former "regulars" for high posts. The reorganization was completed before the autumn; with remarkable speed, but none too soon, an efficient organization was shaped from a chaos of petty interests.[18] Such things were possible in total war.

III

During January, bad weather continued to limit the German attack. London had only two major raids (and three other sizable attacks). Bristol had a surreal raid on January 3rd, when it was bitterly cold and icicles hung in the wrecked houses after the firemen had left them. Portsmouth, Cardiff and Manchester also suffered.

In February, there were no really massed attacks, though Swansea endured three successive nights of moderate bombing. But the second and third weeks of March saw twelve major blows against ports and industrial cities. London had three major raids. On the 13th and 14th, the small burgh of Clydebank, by Glasgow, had a two-night blitz of classic ferocity.

There had been disturbing signs of poor morale in Clydeside just before the blitz. Class warfare in the shipyards and factories continued much on peacetime lines. There was still, in March 1941, much grumbling about war-time inconveniences which in the south were now taken for granted. Mass Observation found that only one Glasgow resident in eight expected heavy raids in the near future; like the inhabitants of Dresden four years later, Clydesiders had developed all kinds of wishful theories, political or "scientific", as to why the Luftwaffe would never bomb them.

"The blitz? What's that, lass? . . ." asked one Dumbarton woman at this time. The shelters on Clydeside were either of the infamous brick surface type, or "strutted closes", often no more than the roughly protected entrance passage to a block of crowded, murky tenement dwellings into which the occupants could throng together when the time came.[19]

Now all but seven of Clydebank's 12,000 houses were damaged, and 35,000 of its 47,000 inhabitants were made homeless. Its night population dropped to two thousand, as the overwhelmingly working-class population took to the moors. In absolute numbers, Glasgow lost many more houses in the same raids, but its small neighbour had the honour of suffering the most nearly universal damage of any British town.[20]

Immediately before this, John Brown's important shipyard in Clydebank had been the scene of a well-publicized dispute in the bitter Glasgow tradition; in spite of the patent inadequacy of local transport, the management had locked out men who arrived late for work. Yet, on the morning after the blitz, a "good proportion" of John Brown's employees turned up. Although the yard provided no hot meals at midday, and some men were billeted up to thirty miles away, "the vast majority were back at work after an average absence of about eleven to fourteen days."[21]

In this phase, Bristol suffered again; Cardiff and Portsmouth had three and five big nights respectively. On March 19th, London had its worst so far, in which seven hundred and fifty civilians died. Plymouth followed with a two-night blitz on the 20th and 21st which levelled the whole area within a six-hundred-yard radius of its Guildhall.

By now the new pattern was clear. In the twelve weeks from February 19th to May 12th, of 61 raids involving more than 50 aircraft, 39 were directed against the western ports, at the ends of Britain's supply lines from the sea, and only 7 against London. Yet a catalogue of major raids oversimplifies the range of the blitz. While the worst hit cities contended with frequent minor attacks, a multiplicity of smaller centres suffered by accident or design. In the period of slacker attack which followed the first "Coventration" of Plymouth, the Luftwaffe visited Shanklin, Ipswich, Gloucester, Hull, Yeovil, Bristol, Hythe, Poole, Folkestone, Norwich and Eastbourne. (Even Fair Isle, north of the Orkneys, had a tiny share of bombs).

When the Germans resumed major effort in the middle of April, the raids had a new purpose. Besides causing economic damage, they were intended to distract attention from German preparations to invade the U.S.S.R. Clydeside and Coventry suffered again, the latter very severely. On Good Friday, Bristol had yet another punishing raid. On Easter Tuesday, the 15th, Belfast was "Coventrated". On the 16th and the 19th, London received two poundings still remembered as "The Wednesday" and "The Saturday"; well over a thousand people died on each night. The unprecedented scale of these attacks may be judged from the fact that 148,000 houses were damaged or destroyed in two raids, whereas in September and October, damage to houses had been running at the rate of only about forty thousand per week. Yet the much improved rest centres and the other post-raid services took the crisis in their stride.[22]

But Plymouth (220,270), despite its severe experience, had not learnt "the lesson of London". In its two-night blitz in March, more than eighteen thousand houses had been destroyed or damaged. The municipal offices and the A.R.P. control room had been destroyed; the two largest hospitals had been damaged. On the first night, people had sworn that they had heard Drake's Drum beating, for this as for other momentous occasions.[23] Newbolt's jingoistic verses came readily to mind:

> If the Dons sight Devon,
> I'll quit the port o' Heaven,
> An' drum them up the Channel as He drumm'd them
>   long ago.

Tawdry or not, the myth of the shattered Armada and the seadogs who had fought it was probably of more help to Plymouth than the post-raid services provided by the city council, when the time came for a second hammering.

On April 21st, and again on the 22nd, and on the 23rd, and on the 28th, and on the 29th, the raiders came back in force. The housing "casualty figures" for Plymouth came to exceed the total number of houses, as many were hit more than once. Several well-known hotels and about a hundred and fifty pubs were hit. The main shopping streets were gutted.[24] As in other stricken cities, soldiers and sailors joined officials and voluntary workers in the overwhelming task of restoring something faintly corresponding to normality. Thirty thousand people were homeless. As many as fifty thousand may have spilled out to sleep in the rural and sparsely populated hinterland of the town: in kind homes, in barns, in churches, in quarry tunnels, even in ditches and under hedges. One observer came across forty people on the edge of Dartmoor. "They were walking about, and I asked them what they were going to do for sleep. 'Oh, we will be all right. The moor soon dries off, then we will roll ourselves up and keep warm . . .' I found that these people do not talk much to strangers. All the time I heard only one complaint, why were the people not ready to get us away after the first big raid . . . Some began to cuddle their children up in rugs, others still walked about and quite a few started back to town. As it began to get bitter cold about eleven p.m., and by that time it had dried off, I sat down with a few men and women who were smoking. The children had been rolled in the bedding. This group was bombed out and were getting their children away in the morning, but it was hard work getting them to talk, they just sat and smoked. I tried to snatch a sleep when the men lay down but was too cold so went walking. After a time others got up and by daylight there was a general walk back. I am sure the children had some sleep, but not many of the grown-ups did. Most of them on the way back said they would not come again after the children had gone. I don't know how they kept cheerful because it was frosty and I was dirty, tired and frozen."[25]

Plymouth, along with Bristol, was a "neutral" area for evacuation, which meant that it was hard to "get the children out" unless the parents had money. Fifty thousand "trekkers" must be seen in a context of peculiarly widespread destruction. "The civil and domestic devastation in Plymouth", wrote Mass Observation's now experienced team of investigators, "exceeds anything we have seen elsewhere, both as regards concentration throughout the heart of the town, and as regards the random shattering of homes all over the town." "One begins to wonder how much longer the mental and physical strain can last? Surely we have reached the limit," wrote a local journalist in his diary at the end of the week of blitz.[26]

After the March blitz, Mass Observation had found morale relatively high. Even at the end of April its team reported that Plymouth made "an impressive show of courage and cheerfulness . . . Strong local pride and a tradition of toughness connected with the sea, make people determined to show that they can take it just as well and better than anywhere else!" But under the brave surface, there were, not surprisingly, tokens of "deep and lasting shock". There was little attempt to pretend that morale was perfect. The local papers carried highly critical reports of the post-raid services, and those in a position to know freely admitted that morale had suffered.[27]

Then came Merseyside's "May Week". For eight successive

nights, at the beginning of the month, the raiders wreaked havoc
in the grimy streets of Liverpool and the neighbouring boroughs
of Bootle, Birkenhead and Wallasey. Bootle Borough Council
had jealously resisted the idea that its fire brigade should amal-
gamate with Liverpool's. The results were all too apparent over
its shattered acres. In Bootle, only about one house in ten escaped
damage, and all but one of the rest centres were put out of action.
Once again, "trekking" took place on a huge scale. The surrounding suburbs and villages took the strain. Maghull, for instance,
with a normal population of eight thousand, had made preparations to take seventeen hundred and fifty refugees under such
circumstances. One evening, there were six thousand and every
church and school and hall, together with an important hospital,
had to be opened.[28]

Meanwhile, lurid rumours flourished as far afield as London.
A working-class Mass Observer in Leek, Staffordshire, reported
on May 17th: "*General Morale:* Very unsteady. This has been a
week of gruesome rumours which were briefly as follows –
(1) Train loads of unidentified corpses have been sent from
Merseyside for mass cremation. (2) Martial law has had to be put
in operation in several heavily raided industrial areas. (3) Homeless and hungry people have marched around in bombed areas,
carrying white flags and howling protests. (4) Food riots are
taking place." The rumour that Liverpool was under martial law,
fostered no doubt by the cordon which was placed around
Merseyside and the difficulty of getting letters out, was credited in
London, an observer noted, by an M.P., by a B.B.C. official, by
the editor of an important newspaper, and by a senior officer in
the services. Many of the most responsible Liverpool citizens
believed that a demonstration for peace had been staged, and the
story was still current years later. There was, indeed, more anger
on Merseyside than had been seen elsewhere; its main ingredient
was fury at the ineptitude of the city council and the Government,
which was "heard from working men and business men, Conservative and Labour, officials and anti-officials, parsons, service
personnel, fire watchers, wardens, an R.A.F. pilot". This was
municipal trauma on a bigger scale than Stepney's.[29]

It was a feature of the dangerous state of morale that rumours
of fifty thousand deaths were current. (Though "add a nought to
it" was a common enough reaction in blitzed cities when the
official casualty lists, always unexpectedly small, were made
public.) The casualties were some nineteen hundred killed and
some fourteen hundred and fifty seriously hurt. The homeless

may have numbered seventy thousand. The docks for a time worked at only a quarter of their previous level of tonnage.[30]

Meanwhile, Belfast had its fourth raid. Then Hull and Nottingham were badly hit, the latter for the first and only time – raiders mistook it for Derby, thanks to the activity of the British scientists still successfully fighting what Churchill called "the Wizard War".

On May 10th came the last and worst night of the London blitz; the night, it might be said, when London itself was "Coventrated". It was a night of "Bomber's Moon", and, as on December 29th, the river was at a very low ebb, and water was especially short. Fires raged over an unprecedented area, from Hammersmith in the west nearly as far as Romford in the east. A British record was set with 1,436 people killed in a single raid; 1,792 Londoners were seriously injured. Westminster Abbey, the Law Courts, the War Office, the Mint and the Tower were hit. A quarter of a million books were burnt in the British Museum and one hundred thousand pounds' worth of gin in the City Road. There were altogether two thousand, two hundred fires, including a huge conflagration at the Elephant and Castle.

Next morning, a drifting cloud of brown smoke blotted out the sun. Charred paper danced in the woods thirty miles from the City. Churchill wept over the ruins of the House of Commons. A third of the streets of Greater London were impassable; 155,000 families were without gas, water or electricity. Every main railway station but one was blocked for weeks. Not for eleven days were the last pumps withdrawn from the fires, while exhausted civil defenders and a badly shaken population waited for the blow which must surely finish off the capital; the blow which never came.[31]

The Luftwaffe shifted across Europe, to be ready to attack Russia. Small (but damaging) raids on London and provincial targets were experienced in June and July, and Hull, an easy target on the east coast, suffered very severely while the rest of Britain's blitzed cities were licking their wounds. But the Luftwaffe could not work in strength in two places at once; it slowly became clear that the breathing space must last for some time.

IV

John G. Winant, the American Ambassador to London, told Roosevelt in April 1941 that "The Prime Minister's method of conducting a campaign on what one might call a morale front is unique. He arrives at a town unannounced, is taken to the most seriously bombed area, leaves his automobile and starts walking through the streets without guards. The news of his presence spreads rapidly by word of mouth and before he has gone far crowds flock about him and people call out to him, 'Hello, Winnie', 'Good old Winnie', 'You will never let us down', 'That's a man'." Winant was able to send glowing reports of British morale to his President. Churchill himself proclaimed in a world broadcast on April 27th that it was where "the ordeal of the men, women and children" had been "most severe" that he had found their morale "most high and splendid". He continued: "Indeed, I felt encompassed by an exaltation of spirit in the people which seemed to lift mankind and its troubles above the level of material facts into that joyous serenity we think belongs to a better world than this."[32]

This exotic passage was no doubt uttered sincerely on the strength of Churchill's own somewhat specialized first-hand experience. Yet he must also have seen the reports on morale which were reaching Herbert Morrison (from Mass Observation as well as from other sources), and very different conclusions could be drawn from these. Harold Nicolson, a member of the Civil Defence Committee of the War Cabinet, noted in his diary on May 7th, "Herbert Morrison is worried about the effect of the provincial raids on morale. He keeps on underlining the fact that the people cannot stand this intensive bombing indefinitely and that sooner or later the morale of other towns will go, even as Plymouth's has gone."[33] The existence of these grave doubts at the highest level may help to explain the strange case of Rudolf Hess.

On the evening of May 10th, when the Luftwaffe was doing its worst over London. Hess, who was to Hitler what Eden was to Churchill, the young crown prince, took off alone in a Messerschmitt fighter, flew to Scotland, and landed accurately within twelve miles of the home of the Duke of Hamilton, the Lord Steward, whose support he was confident of enlisting in his proposal of a peace settlement. The 3rd Renfrewshire Battalion Home Guard, who proudly picked him up, had no idea of his identity. Churchill, amazed by his arrival, gave orders that he should be treated as a prisoner of war and confined in a house near London where he might be "studied" (though it was not until June 10th that the cabinet sent a minister to interview him). The press was prohibited from mentioning his arrival until the

German radio announced, on May 12th, that he had had a "progressive illness" and was the victim of "obsessions" which explained his flight. Even then, the British censorship was ordered to suppress any reports that he had brought proposals for peace. While the papers were allowed to say that he was "talking freely", they might give no inkling as to what he was talking about.[34]

This reticence infuriated intelligent members of the public. The most obvious motive for it was the value of keeping the Germans themselves guessing, once it was known for sure that Hitler himself had not sanctioned the flight. But it seems likely also that Churchill's colleagues may have feared that the merest hint of a German "peace-feeler" at this juncture would be altogether too tempting for the people of the battered cities – and perhaps for the rest of the population, who were currently taking a spate of dire war news, a reduction in their diet, and new restrictions on their liberties.

In any case, when Churchill's oratory took to the air in the manner of the extract quoted, he left large sections of the British public on the glass-strewn streets beneath him; he no longer spoke what seemed simple truth to his hearers. Swansea, as it happened, fitted the clichés better than most, during and after its relatively moderate three-night blitz. The Welsh, after all, had been hardened by the constant imminence of disaster in the coal valleys. The homeless, it seems, were readily absorbed into the houses of family and friends. A Mass Observer was told, by a butcher who had sent his own family to relatives outside Swansea, "There was my house standing empty, but do you think anyone would take it? No. I've offered it to three customers who were bombed out – oh, they were staying up here somewhere, in someone's house."

But the comment of one Swansea man sums up the reaction of clearsighted people to the B.B.C's effusions. He said, "The people were marvellous, especially the women – they can take it all right. But not like that bloke said on the wireless on Thursday night – they don't go about smiling about it – the people who have lost friends and relatives, they don't go about grinning."[35]

Nowhere in the provinces did the civil defenders have more than eight successive days of heavy raiding; but the conditions which they endured along with their fellow citizens made their efforts very brave. The response was usually as fine as in London. Plymouth could rely on a ninety per cent turn-out of its wardens in a raid. When Sheffield had two nights of "Coventration" in December which left thirty-seven thousand people homeless,

threequarters of the rest centres were put out of action in the
first raid. Prodigies of improvisation followed. "In the midst of
the most frantic appeals for help (relates a local account), a young
clerical assistant, aged sixteen, rang up, said he had commandeered a picture house and a couple of schoolrooms, formed a
pool of food and clothing from the wrecked homes of the people
he was caring for single-handed: but he had had to spend a few
shillings without permission and he hoped it would be all right."[36]

Another symptom of resurgence which was remarked on everywhere was the jealousy with which the inhabitants of each blitzed
city insisted on regarding it as the worst hit of all. People whose
communal pride had centred on fine churches or on big department stores now focused it upon their ruins. Three days after
Bristol's Good Friday raid, the same Bristol woman whose diary
was quoted earlier noted ". . . the city is full of morbid sightseers . . . All the big papers on Sunday have given us a good
write-up; they say we have had the worst raids outside of London
so far, and Bristol is the worst blitzed city of the lot."[37]

There were many plausible claimants. Coventry could claim the
first shock and the most beautiful cathedral damaged; Sheffield
the most dramatic ruins. Herbert Morrison himself gave the palm
to Hull.

Statistics suggest that Plymouth, Birmingham and Liverpool
were top of the league with eight major raids over the blitz period,
followed by Bristol with six. But statistics take no account of
nerves strained by "minor" raids, and local totems smashed.

The great southern port of Southampton (180,100) was, by the
weight of bombs dropped on it, a minor challenger. But, like
other tempting targets on the coast, it had frequent alerts and
minor raids long before the main blitz and long after it. From
mid-June 1940 to the end of 1944, it had sixteen hundred and
sixty-seven attacks.[38]*

The city had its first general raid, as opposed to attacks on its
docks and factories, on November 23rd, 1940; seventy-seven
people were killed and several thousands made homeless. A week
later, the city centre was "Coventrated". "Every second or two,"
writes a local man, "the town was shaken to its foundations. The
air was a whirling frenzy; hot blasts swept the streets . . ." To one
who watched from high ground in a suburb, it looked as if "the
town had become a blazing furnace in which every living thing
seemed doomed to perish."[39]

* London had 354 attacks by piloted aircraft alone; Yarmouth, on the
east coast, had 97; Birmingham, by contrast, only 50.

(Such remarks almost always sprang to the lips and pens of those who saw their home cities on nights of heavy blitz. "A veritable volcanic cataclysm," wrote the Lord Mayor of Bristol. A Plymouth observer wondered "whether anything would be left standing when the dawn came . . ."[40])

On that November 30th, 1940, Southampton's main telephone exchange was demolished and its water mains were wrecked. Next night, when only the supplementary water supply remained, when many firemen were injured or sick from the previous raids and the rest exhausted, the bombers came back. Firefighters arrived from seventy-five other districts, from as far afield as Nottingham, but many suburban houses had to be left to burn so as to save water for the more crowded districts where the fires were fiercest.

On the morning of December 2nd, apart from the ancient Bargate, "the central portion of the town had largely vanished . . . Nothing remained that was not wilting, wasted or warped . . . Such walls as remained standing were wet and dripping: it looked impossible to touch them without leaving the fingers bloody." Dr Garbett, the Bishop of Winchester, motored into the city that morning. He found "the people broken in spirit after the sleepless and awful nights. Everyone who can do so is leaving the town . . . Everywhere I saw men and women carrying suitcases or bundles, the children clutching some precious doll or toy, struggling to get anywhere out of Southampton. For the time, morale has collapsed. I went from parish to parish and everywhere there was fear."[41]

A hundred and thirty-seven people had lost their lives and nearly two hundred and fifty had been seriously injured in the two successive raids. All the large drapers' and outfitters' stores had been burnt, along with their stocks. Homeless people went without bedding or clothes in bitter winter weather, until a Board of Trade official came down to cut red tape. Nearly three weeks after the attack, only a hundred essential telephone lines had been connected, with immense effort, to the switchboard. Water and gas had still not been restored in some quarters by Christmas week.

Ten days after the blitz, only a fraction of the population was sleeping in the city. There were far too few mobile canteens in the streets. (The Queen's Messenger Convoys, eighteen fleets each of twelve vehicles, almost all provided by American generosity, which later stood ready to rush hot meals into any smitten town, were not yet in action. Later, staffed by the W.V.S., they did good

work at Liverpool and Plymouth.) Cigarettes were virtually
unobtainable. Cinemas and pubs had almost all closed.

Even at the end of February, when the town had enjoyed
several weeks of comparative quiet, Mass Observation's team
found Southampton depressing to revisit. Most facilities were
now back to normal, but public transport stopped at seven p.m.,
and most cinemas, cafés and restaurants which had not been
bombed also closed early. The better-off people had either left the
town altogether, or spent their nights out in the country. The
attitude of those who stayed on was summed up by one working-
class woman who said, "I don't think they will come back, there's
nothing to bomb now, is there?"[42]

But Southampton was less chilling than Portsmouth, which had
suffered repeatedly from moderate to severe raiding. At night, the
Mass Observers reported, Portsmouth was "a tomb of darkness".
Morale had worsened, it was found, over the months; people who
had said they would stay put whatever happened and had poured
scorn on those who had left, had quitted it themselves after further
attacks. A third of those who remained, in mid-March, said they
would evacuate if they could; only financial and other difficulties,
or vital jobs, restrained them. It was estimated that not more than
a quarter of the population was now living in the city.

But the local authorities refused to evacuate mothers and
children unless they arranged their own billets, and this roused
great resentment. One woman, not untypical, said, "My God.
I wish I could get away. Look, I've got four children, all under
four ... I don't know anybody to go to and I can't find anybody.
I feel as if I'm going mad. They ought to help you." There were
still "few signs of open defeatism", but Mass Observation's view,
confirmed by social workers, local officials, even a town councillor, was that pacifist feeling was latent.[43]

The worst feature of morale, as the Mass Observers saw it, was
the feeling of helplessness which emerged as the weight of remembered and anticipated fear, and of present inconvenience, sank
down on the shoulders of populations which did not, like
London's, have the stimulus to adaptation provided by nightly
raids. The phenomenon of "trekking" reflected this feeling in
those who left and reinforced it in those who remained. Essentially, trekking reflected the same, not irrational, instinct of self-
preservation which had prompted the capture of the London
Tubes for the people. But those who slept in the Tubes remained
under London, part of London; trekking was a fissure in the body
of a provincial city. (In some places, however, shelter life on the

London scale did develop. In a giant shelter at Liverpool, the conditions of the Stepney railway arches were reproduced months after those horrors themselves had been cleaned up. In Bristol, a deep underground tunnel on the outskirts was appropriated by about a thousand people; half of it was flooded, and there were only two water closets.)[44]

Yet to suggest that Goering's bombing had succeeded in instilling terror and breaking the will to fight; or that it would have done so even if the ferocity of the last raids had been continued, would be to fly in the face of three kinds of evidence. In the first place, there was a degree of adaptation, coupled with the feeling that if London could take it, then Bristol or Plymouth should. Both emerge in the superficially depressed, but in fact courageous, attitude of a working-class woman in Portsmouth: "Sometimes I say if we could stand Monday, we could stand anything. But sometimes I feels I can't stand it any more. But it don't do to say so. If I says anything my girls say to me, 'Stop it, Ma! It's no good saying you can't stand it. You've got to!' My girls is ever so good."[45]

Secondly, the Luftwaffe failed to retard British war production so greatly that it made much difference. The most obvious point should not be overlooked; despite their various maulings, London remained an administrative and economic capital, Portsmouth and Plymouth continued to serve the Royal Navy, the Liverpool docks remained open, and Coventry, as will emerge from frequent references to it later, was still a booming and vital centre of British war production. There were serious, but not disastrous, losses of food stocks in the docks, there were trifling losses of oil, and there was a slight but eventually unimportant check to the expansion of aircraft production, but the official history of British war production accords the blitz only nine scattered mentions.[46]

The attacks on docks and railways, the side effects on public utilities and transport, nervous tension, casualties and sleepless nights, had results which could not be measured, though they were clearly significant. But in spite of eight months of almost continuous blitz, during which a typical worker would spend fifteen hours a day in labour and travel, the Ford factory in east London could claim that absenteeism barely existed. At one Royal Ordnance Factory, every single worker reported for duty on Christmas Day. Even where a whole town suffered, the only factor making for absenteeism which had any significance was the amount of house damage. Ministry of Home Security figures showed that a worker whose home was rendered permanently uninhabitable lost, on average, six days from his job, during which he had to find a fresh home and gather his family. Trekkers, what is more, lost no more time at work, on average, than "stay-putters". Workers came into Southampton, for instance, from as far afield as Salisbury, twenty-two miles away. No trekker could lightly add the loss of wages to his other worries.[47]

Thirdly, and most overwhelmingly, there is the evidence from Germany that heavy bombing could not, by itself, destroy a nation's will to work and fight. A "major raid" on Britain meant a hundred tons of bombs. A. J. P. Taylor points out. "Three years later the British were dropping sixteen hundred tons a night on Germany – and even then not with decisive effect." Churchill himself, in his memoirs, stops a moment to compare the Londoners' ordeal with that of the Germans. "Of course," he writes, "if the bombs of 1943 had been applied to the London of 1940 we should have passed into conditions which might have pulverized all human organization." The Germans, he admits, had far better shelters.[48] But even so, judging from the experience of Hamburg and Berlin, one may presume that, as improvements in the shelters and post-raid services were introduced, Britain would have "taken it".

In any case, the extreme experiences of the blitz were mostly confined to the cities; and not all of these suffered very greatly. Manchester had only three really major raids. Birmingham, though frequently visited, was let off lightly for its size and importance. Leeds, Bradford and Newcastle had few scars to show.

But the effect on popular attitudes of even a single sharp raid should not be underestimated. Leicester was bombed, relatively lightly, for eight hours on November 19th. A hundred and eight people were killed, two hundred and three injured and five thousand made homeless. Rumour, and perhaps local pride also, exaggerated the matter. "Many fantastic tales swept through the city about the damage," writes a local resident, "the hundreds, some said, even thousands that had been killed, the number of aircraft brought down and in fact, anything that people would listen to, was bandied from mouth to mouth." Then, for several months, no more bombs dropped. "There was nothing but the incessant drone of enemy planes – and the constant vigil. Many people devised a system of comfort. They waited anxiously for the first twenty minutes following the sounding of the 'Alert' and then if nothing was heard except the planes, they breathed a sigh of relief ,and said quite complacently, 'Well, they are not coming for us, this time.' "[49] "They" never came back in strength again.

Over most of the country, it was hard to avoid the sights and sounds of blitz entirely; even on the Welsh hills, one saw the searchlights groping over the midlands and heard the throb of the bombers looking for Liverpool or Crewe. If they missed their target and scurried for home, the bombs would fall on peaceful hill farms, thatched villages. (Early in 1943, "tip and run" raiders attacked a picturesque little village in Devon. "There was hardly a house which was not damaged . . . one-third of the village was rendered uninhabitable. The beautiful thirteenth-century church was destroyed."[50]) The eastern and southern coastlines, during the main blitz and for a long time afterwards, were constantly harried by small groups of bombers or single raiders. Trains were very often strafed or bombed. Fishing villages and holiday resorts became regular targets. By November 1941, Yarmouth, in East Anglia, had had seventy-two raids, had lost a hundred and ten people, and had had eleven thousand five hundred of its homes damaged. Coastal towns from Fraserburgh in north Scotland (eighteen raids) to Falmouth in Cornwall (thirty-three raids) had suffered, sometimes relatively as badly as London itself.[51]

One of the most unlikely heroes of the blitz, who made his way into the Ministry of Information's pamphlet on the subject, was a shepherd in Somerset, who found himself in the centre of a seven-hour raid involving thousands of incendiaries. Except for his flock, he was quite alone; even his dog ran away. His lambing pens were destroyed, but he led his charges through the flames while high explosive poured down around him.[52] If the homeless had always been so well cared for, the question mark over morale which has been raised and dismissed here might never have appeared.

V

West Ham, towards the middle of the war, was a borough of ghosts. Part of it had been so completely devastated that the infantry used it as a training ground for street fighting. Only four of West Ham's thirty-five cinemas were open. The pubs had suffered badly. In the poorer parts of the borough, a great majority of shops had faded out of existence; their owners could not afford to repair them. Social conventions had often broken down. "Neighbours of either sex frequently throw in their lot together," an investigator reported. "A woman will live with her neighbour who is a small shopkeeper, looking after his domestic affairs; a man and a woman who work together during the day will also share their home arrangements and their shelter; those who are the sole remaining members of evacuated families pool their domestic resources."[53]

Nor was it only the East End which harboured spectres. When Verily Anderson moved to the formerly handsome and wealthy suburb of St John's Wood, towards the end of the war, "Only one other house in the road was inhabited. Behind us a long crescent of over a hundred huge empty villas was slowly disintegrating, with the aid of the weather and former bombing. It was an eerie street to go along, with some of its ornate houses lying flat in their own gardens. Rotting laths and powdered plaster mingled with the mud along the untended roadway."[54]

In fine weather, there were compensations. St Paul's stood in solitary, blackened grandeur on the verge of the greatest single area of devastation in Britain, a surreal waste of tangled girders and occasional jagged walls. Pink rosebay willow herb ("fireweed"), and yellow Oxford ragwort flourished on the bomb sites. London had a new breeding bird, the black redstart; pairs flew in to nest in the ruins. Mallards swam in the emergency tanks of static water which were made from the basements of destroyed buildings, and which reflected the delicate pastel shades of wallpaper washed pale by the rain.

In the provinces, local inhabitants compared the blitzed centres of their cities with the ruins of the Colosseum and Pompeii. Moonlight poured through the tattered frames of giant department stores, shining on crumbled concrete and twisted iron. Not for years after the war would the tokens of blitz be replaced by square modern buildings.

A leading architectural writer, J. M. Richards, pleaded for the preservation of at least a few of the ruins. He wrote of the sheer beauty of "the scarified surfaces of blasted walls, the chalky substance of calcined masonry, the surprising sagging contours of once rigid girders and the clear sienna colouring of burnt-out brick buildings, their rugged cross walls receding plane by plane, on sunny mornings in the City."[55] Such special pleading, naturally enough, was not heeded, though many years after the end of the war visitors to the headquarters of the political parties in Smith Square, Westminster, could still admire the heroic shell of Archer's church of St John the Evangelist, perhaps the most dramatic and forceful piece of baroque architecture in Britain, consummated by the bombs which had wrecked its interior.

Architects and others were concerned about the unnecessary demolitions of bombed national monuments which took place early in the blitz. A National Buildings Record was set up late in 1940, and panels of architects advised local A.R.P. controllers. The Government took responsibility for making necessary repairs at once to culturally important ruins, to prevent the climate from completing their destruction before it could be decided whether they should be restored or demolished.[56] But much of the loss was permanent. Fifteen Wren churches in the City of London were gutted or destroyed. There was havoc in the Inns of Court and among the historic halls of the City Companies. There was further slaughter of fine churches in the provinces, at Bristol and Plymouth in particular; Coventry, and later Canterbury, Norwich and Exeter, lost greater or lesser portions of their rich medieval heritage.

But Oxford, Cambridge and Edinburgh, the three cities which most people would have chosen to preserve at a pinch, were virtually unscathed. It would be idle for any observer of modern Britain to pretend that the Luftwaffe added much to the ignoble efforts of peacetime demolition firms. Private enterprise, over the centuries, had accounted for nineteen of Wren's City churches, irreparably.

By June 19th, 1941, over two million houses had been damaged or destroyed, sixty per cent of them in London. Over the remaining years of war, this increased to an estimated three and three-quarter million, or two houses out of every seven, of which a quarter of a million were beyond repair. In the central London area, only one house out of ten would have escaped damage of some kind.[57]

This was not sheer loss. Even before the war, the slums of the city centres, including the East End's, had been losing population as local councils completed housing estates on the verges of the conurbations. The Luftwaffe effected a much overdue programme of slum clearance; after the war, Stepney and Poplar were replanned on the basis of four people living where ten had lived before. Even so, old ladies who knew only these ugly streets dwelt on in their ruins, resisting the attempts of parsons and local officials to evacuate them.

Before the war, psychologists had speculated gloomily that bombing would cause an enormous increase in mental disturbances and illnesses; it was even suggested that mental cases might outnumber physical casualties by two or three to one. (So if the expected casualty figures had obtained, everyone in London would very soon have been either mad or dead.) But the war led to no great increase in neurotic illness in Britain, none, at least, which could be measured in the usual ways. There was no indication of any increase in insanity, and the number of suicides fell, while drunkenness statistics dropped by more than a half between 1939 and 1942.

Very few "psychiatric air raid casualties" were reported, in Britain or in Germany. Those people who had experienced a "near miss", who had been buried alive or who had suffered directly from blast commonly showed marked neurotic symptoms, and many others seem to have suffered from apathy, lethargy and general despondency as a side effect of the raids and the weariness they brought with them. But certain types of mentally sick people actually felt better.[58]

Evacuation, of course, had been designed to remove from the cities those most prone to panic. Its failure was shown most dramatically at Clydebank. The burgh had 7,640 schoolchildren in June 1939. Of these 2,652 were evacuated in September. Just before the two-night blitz in March 1941, only 164 children were still in the reception areas. As one provincial city after another was hit, the new arrangements made in London – evacuation on the old terms for schoolchildren, "assisted private evacuation" for others – came to apply to them as well. Cities which had not previously been "evacuable" were given assistance (sometimes very belatedly) in sending mothers and children away. Altogether, it is estimated, some 1,250,000 people were helped by the Government to leave the bombed cities, in the period between September 1940 and the end of 1941. By February 1941, the number of evacuees officially billeted in the reception areas stood at 1,370,000 – only about a hundred thousand short of the first exodus. In September, after confused cross-currents in which some people drifted back to the cities again and others were driven out by further bombing, there were still 1,205,000.[59]

Meanwhile, the bombs had helped to produce what can only be called a change of heart in the authorities. The need to adapt and augment existing social services in the reception areas if evacuation was to succeed, had been clear from the outset. But while volunteers in many areas had done their best, local authorities had tended to drag their feet, encouraged by the numerous opportunities for buck-passing afforded by the British system of local government, and by the niggardliness of the Treasury. Late in 1940, the Government began to remove many of its restrictions on the spending of money for welfare purposes. "There were to be more hostels, group homes, social clubs and welfare centres; more money was to be spent on them and more staff with experience of social work were to be employed on evacuation duties in the reception areas." While the normal peacetime health and welfare services, which had wilted at the outbreak of war, remained inadequate, a wide range of emergency services was encouraged. The character of the evacuation scheme, as the authorities saw it, began to change. "Its original role as a means of transferring children to safety diminished in significance," Richard Titmuss has written. "Instead, it operated as a receiver of social casualties . . . "[60]

It provided, for instance, for the children of sick mothers with husbands in the services, for those whose mothers had to work or responded to official incitements that they should work, for those from broken homes, and for those who were out of control. By mid-1941, there were six hundred and sixty hostels in England and Wales, accommodating some ten thousand children – largely "difficult cases" sent on by foster parents or local authorities. Hundreds of clubs and canteens had been opened to provide meals, occupations and interests for evacuated mothers. Ninety emergency maternity homes had been opened, and two hundred and thirty residential nurseries for children under five – notably, of course, for the orphans of the blitz. Such services depended heavily on the work of W.V.S. and other volunteers; it was hard to equip and staff them in the context of shortages of manpower and materials. But the emergency schemes represented something of a revolution in the state's attitude to the welfare of its less fortunate citizens.[61]

The revolution came about because the need was so pitifully obvious. The effects of the blitz on the children who lived through it, direct or indirect, are incalculable. One psychiatrist claimed from teachers' reports on eight thousand children evacuated from Bristol that there were about eight times as many cases of psychological disturbance among those who had remained in the city each night as among those who had gone to the tunnels on the outskirts. A nurse in a London children's hospital has described the behaviour of patients whose nerves had cracked. "When they heard distant gunfire, they would sit up in bed and whimper like puppies. One little girl had gone completely dumb through terror, and another small child I knew went as stiff as a ramrod every time she heard the sirens. Her face turned scarlet, and she opened her mouth to scream, but no sound came."[62]

About one in five of the nation's schools were damaged by bombing. Others became rest centres. Pupils either did without teaching or packed into larger classes elsewhere. West Ham had sixty council schools. At one time, because of bomb damage, only sixteen of these could be used. Towards the end of 1941, when there were still only thirty-nine schools open, it was found that in one large elementary school, not a single child of seven could read.[63]

The effects of the first disruption in 1939–40 were amplified. The post-war intake of National Servicemen contained a dismaying proportion of illiterate or educationally retarded youths. Charles Segal, who had studied children in a poor suburb of London before the war, found that over half the children in one junior school were backward readers after the war, as compared with about one in five in a previous survey. " . . . All the children in the school [he wrote in 1949] were under school age at the beginning of the war. Apart from two who attended nursery schools, they were not caught up by the evacuation scheme . . . What schooling there was in North Kensington was erratic. There could not be steady routine work – the interruptions were too frequent. There were air raid warnings. Teachers were changed about from school to school. They went to and from evacuation centres . . . It can truly be said that boys and girls now leaving the primary schools have lost up to five years of formal education."[64]

A sharp increase in convictions for juvenile delinquency attended the disruption of the schools. The number of young people under seventeen found guilty of breaking the law in England and Wales rose by over one-third between 1939 and 1941; the figures for malicious damage and petty stealing rose by seventy and two hundred per cent respectively. Whether these figures meant that more children were breaking the law, in circumstances of chaos which encouraged them to do so, or merely that more adults made it their business to catch them and punish them for doing it, this was an important by-product of war. It was a reflection of the nervous strain of the magistrates themselves that six times as many small boys were birched on their orders in 1941 as in peacetime, when this dubious corrective had been justly falling out of favour. Children, left to their own devices in a hostile, and later terrifying, environment, might well develop anti-social attitudes.

There were other sinister statistics which showed that the nervous and physical strain on the adult population meant less care taken of babies and children. More infants than usual were suffocated in their cots, or choked over their food; more fatal accidents befell children in their homes; though there were fewer cars on the roads, those that remained killed more children than in peacetime; more children drowned, notably in the emergency water tanks. Working on war jobs, or faced with domestic crises which were impossible to handle now that Father was in the army and the neighbourhood community had disintegrated, mothers turned to their older children to assume domestic responsibilities; this was reflected in the serious rise in school absenteeism noticed in many industrial areas, even in 1943 when the schools had settled down into a show of normality.[65]

Yet the transformation in official attitudes to social policy did bring some progress for "normal" children. More children, in the later years of the war, were taking cheap or free milk in their schools. While the incidence of scabies, lice and impetigo increased, nearly seven million children, in 1940–45, were vaccinated free of charge against diphtheria. This was a direct product of official fears of epidemics during the blitz. The result was a startling decline in the number of deaths from the disease.[66] The physical condition of Britain's children improved during the war. Their psychological and intellectual development was another matter.

In 1940 and 1941, approximately 43,000 civilians in Britain were killed by bombs, and some 17,000 died in the remaining years of war. About half of all deaths (nearly 30,000) were in London. The total number of people injured more or less seriously is impossible to state exactly. If it is said that about 86,000 were seriously injured and went to hospital, and about 151,000 people were slightly injured, this is probably an underestimate. Over the war, 264,000 members of the armed forces lost their lives; but "Not until over three years had passed was it possible to say that the enemy had killed more soldiers than women and children."[67]

Statistics, however, are more than usually inadequate. London and Coventry take their places in a grim litany of names – Guernica, Dresden, Hiroshima, Hanoi – which have become symbols, obscuring rather than representing the facts of life and death which underlie the arguments of strategists and the systematically muffled cries of protest. One elderly air raid warden in Hull speaks for many men in many countries.[68]

One night, as he related, he had gone down to the post, and when he came back, his street "was as flat as this 'ere wharfside – there was just my 'ouse like – well, part of my 'ouse. My missus

were just making me a cup of tea for when I come 'ome. She
were in the passage between the kitchen and the wash'ouse, where
it blowed 'er. She were burnt right up to 'er waist. 'Er legs were
just two cinders. And 'er face – The only thing I could recognize
'er by was one of 'er boots – I'd 'ave lost fifteen 'omes if I could
'ave kept my missus. We used to read together. I can't read
mesen. She used to read to me like. We'd 'ave our armchairs on
either side o' the fire, and she read me bits out o' the paper. We
'ad a paper every evening. Every evening."

Chapter Five

Through the Tunnel:
October 1940 to December 1942

The first generation of ruins, cleaned up, shored up, began to weather –
in daylight they took their places as the norm of the scene; the danger-
less nights of September two years later blotted them out. It was from
this new insidious echoless propriety of ruins that you breathed in all
that was most malarial. Reverses, losses, deadlocks now almost un-
noticed bred one another; every day the news hammered one more nail
into a consciousness which no longer resounded. Everywhere hung the
heaviness of the even worse you could not be told and could not desire
to hear. This was the lightless middle of the tunnel.

Elisabeth Bowen, *The Heat of the Day*

FROM BROWN TO RED

Now what I always think of as the Brown Period began. Browned-off
was the phrase one heard most often in X Company, the other recruits
owing to difficulty in finding any skirt started jocosely to talk of having
Bits of Brown (buggery), the R.A.F. blokes stationed next door called
us Brown Jobs, it was autumn and the leaves were brown, and everything was uniquely brown.

Julian Maclaren-Ross[1]

I

"AFTER shooting Niagara we had now to struggle in the rapids."
So Churchill sums up the phase of the war which followed the
Battle of Britain.[2] In the blitzed cities, it was a hectic period of
courage and improvisation; but even as the blitz proceeded, what

might be called the "amateur" war was coming to an end. 1941 was the year in which the war economy emerged in something close to its final vigour; the year when shortages of food and consumer goods began to become oppressive; when the recruitment of women for the war effort was taken in hand; when the workers in the factories and in Civil Defence were subjected to compulsion; when political sourness re-entered the organs of public opinion. 1940 had been the year of individual efforts coalescing in desperate activities; 1941 was the year in which the Central Statistical Office was formed as part of the War Cabinet secretariat, the year in which Government departments began in earnest to redress their lack of knowledge of Britain's economic units of production, sale and consumption, and to reduce such activities to neat tables of numbers.

How on earth could this war be won? This was a question which few people liked to ponder. Churchill even hinted at a ten-year struggle. Surely, some sections of the left argued hopefully, conquered Europe must rise? The German people themselves would hurl off their chains? But meanwhile, the prospects for immediate offence were limited.

"The bombers alone provide the means of victory," Churchill told his colleagues on September 3rd, 1940. After all, the strategic bombing of Germany was what the R.A.F. had been built for; even now the production of giant four-engined bombers was getting under way in British factories. Churchill, very soon after the blitz had started, began to press for retaliation in kind. On October 30th, the War Cabinet agreed that "the civilian population around the target areas must be made to feel the weight of the war." Six weeks later, it sanctioned an experimental "terror raid" on Mannheim, by a hundred and thirty-four British bombers. "Thus British and Germans alike", writes Basil Collier, one of the official historians, "were soon engaged in destroying cathedrals and hospitals and killing non-combatants of all ages and both sexes, either in the course of impracticable attempts to bomb strictly military objectives, or in accordance with the theory that built-up areas were themselves military objectives and that any course of action which promised to shorten the war was both legitimate and sound."[3]

Churchill heard people calling out as he toured the blitzed areas, "Give it 'em back, Winnie." But if the raids on Germany were seen as reprisals, it was those who had suffered most in Britain who, by and large, approved of them least. The inhabitants of London, Southampton and Plymouth heard, after all, that the Germans described their own raids as "reprisals". Apart from a natural reluctance to imagine other people suffering as they had suffered, they might calculate prudently that the result of terror raids on Berlin would be further terror raids on London, Southampton and Plymouth. There were, as Mass Observation found, few spontaneous calls for "reprisals" in the bombed cities. A Gallup Poll published early in May 1941 showed that the most determined demand for them came from Cumberland, Westmorland and the North Riding of Yorkshire, rural areas barely touched by bombing, where some three-quarters of the population wanted them. In central London, conversely, the proportion was only forty-five per cent.[4]

In August 1941, a member of the War Cabinet secretariat made an independent survey, based largely on the study of reconnaisance photographs, of the real effect of British bombing. Its conclusions (which were not, of course, made public at the time) were that one-third of the planes despatched did not attack the target. Of those which did, only one-third got within five miles of it. We now know that more R.A.F. personnel than German civilians were killed in the raids of 1940–41.[5] The conclusion drawn in Britain was not that strategic bombing was an *ignis fatuus*, but that its techniques must be improved. The air offensive, broken off in November 1941, was resumed in 1942. Meanwhile, those British civilians who liked the idea could content themselves with imaginary vistas of shattered German towns, and even those few who protested based their protests on the notion that the raids were effective.

More cheering than the illusion of reprisals to the harried people of London was the news from the Mediterranean. In October, an Italian invasion of Greece was repelled; in November, half the Italian fleet was put out of action by the Fleet Air Arm at Taranto. Meanwhile, Marshal Graziani had marched a large army into Egypt, threatening the Suez Canal, but had halted because of bad transport and communications. In December, British forces, commanded by General Wavell, mounted an assault. Its success was exhilarating. In two months, British and Dominion troops advanced five hundred miles, totally destroyed an army which outnumbered them by about five to one, and captured a hundred and thirty thousand prisoners while losing fewer than two thousand of their own comrades.

As this episode illustrated, Britain had never truly "stood alone". Goebbels jeered that in North Africa, the British pushed men from the Dominions in to do their fighting for them. But, while the Dominions were of great assistance, somewhat under-valued in Britain at the time, their support could not be decisive. Hopefully, public men in Britain looked towards America.

The news of Roosevelt's re-election in November 1940 had an "immensely cheering effect". Mass Observation quoted the case of a seventy-year-old labourer in a west country village, who before then had shown "the absolute minimum of interest in any-thing outside the two-mile radius", but "registered delight" at this news and "commented on it spontaneously".[6] The news was taken as a firm reassurance that America was on Britain's side. More positive signs still were the manifest sympathy of many of the American journalists covering the blitz in Britain (Quentin Reynolds became one of Priestley's most renowned successors in the Sunday evening "Postscript" series) and the great quantities of clothing and other immediate succour sent from the U.S.A.

During the Battle of Britain, the U.S.A. had been granted ninety-nine-year leases of bases in the Caribbean and the western Atlantic in return, ostensibly, for fifty old destroyers (a fact which caused Lord Haw Haw much amusement). But the implication of this odd bargain was that the U.S.A. would provide the economic and financial support which would make continued resistance possible; all Britain's dollars were now pledged to the payment for existing contracts with American industry, an area where Beaverbrook had shown much useful energy. When Roosevelt's Lend-Lease Bill passed into law in March 1941, it empowered him to give Britain virtually anything she needed, on terms to be decided at his own discretion. "Give us the tools and we will finish the job," Churchill had called to America in a broadcast in February; here was an assurance that the tools would be forth-coming. For the moment, Lend-lease in arms was of little direct importance – since the arrangement was not retrospective, most of the weapons which crossed the Atlantic in 1941 were still paid for in dollars. But Lend-lease meant that the British Government could "mobilize and concentrate, much more confidently and ruthlessly than would otherwise have been possible, their own war-making power". And Lend-lease shipments of dried eggs, evaporated milk, bacon, beans, cheese, lard and canned meat, which began in the summer of 1941, were crucial in the battle to maintain the quality of the nation's diet. The first consignment reached Britain on May 31st, and Lend-lease contributed one-fifteenth of all food arriving in the country in 1941. Such blessings were so much appreciated that Mass Observation, in August, found that more people wanted America to stay out of the war

than wished she would come in; chiefly because it was presumed
that there would be less aid for Britain in the latter eventuality.[7]

The diet available in the early months of 1941 was the poorest
of the war. Food imports were running at only two-thirds of their
pre-war level. British farmers continued to make a remarkable
response to the calls for more homegrown food – but these could
be met only by reducing livestock. The meat ration had temporarily soared to two shillings and twopence a week in the
autumn of 1940, but by the New Year, the Ministry of Food was
casting around desperately for any supplies which might prevent
too drastic a fall. In January, the ration came down to one
shilling and twopence and stayed there.

Whitehall anticipated that Britain would receive thirty-five
million tons of imports in 1941; this estimate was revised to
thirty-one million in the spring, and in fact only 30·5 million were
brought in successfully. Early in February, Hitler ordered the
intensification of attacks on seaborne traffic bound for Britain,
and also on the ports by which its cargoes would enter the
country. The U-boats achieved spectacular results, augmented by
the Luftwaffe's heavy blows at Bristol, the Mersey and the
Clyde, which now deputized for London and other eastern ports,
as well as handling their own normal traffic. The convoy system
and the obstruction of the Mediterranean meant that merchant
ships took longer over their voyages.

The first peak of the Battle of the Atlantic came with the three
months ending in May, when U-boats alone sank a hundred and
forty-two merchant ships (British, allied and neutral), and air
attack accounted for a hundred and seventy-nine. Up to December 1940, the monthly average of tonnage lost had been just under
three hundred thousand. In February over four hundred thousand
tons of shipping were sunk, in March over five hundred thousand,
and in April, nearly seven hundred thousand. On April 14th,
Churchill ordered the Ministry of Information to discontinue the
weekly publication of figures for shipping losses, a practice useful
to the Germans, and increasingly dismaying for the public at
home.[8]

II

Two new ministries emerged from this phase of the war. In
October 1940, the Office of Works became the Ministry of Works
and Buildings. The depleted building industry had been greatly

overtaxed by contracts for a variety of competing Government departments. The chief inspirer of the new ministry was Ernest Bevin; its job was to centralize the control of contracts for such various tasks of construction as airfields, camps, coastal defences, factories and the repair of bomb damage, and also to deal with the post-war reconstruction of buildings. The new post was given to Lord Reith, most famous as the B.B.C.'s first Director General, who had been brought into the Chamberlain Government as Minister of Information.

The other new ministry was prompted by a second winter of crisis on the railways and the new chaos in the ports. The agreement reached between the Chamberlain Government and the railways in February 1940 had achieved, and merited, notoriety. In 1938, only one of the four main-line railway companies had paid a dividend to its ordinary shareholders, and that had been of only one half per cent. The Government had guaranteed this markedly unprofitable industry a minimum annual revenue of forty million pounds, six million pounds more than it had earned in the last pre-war year. It could keep the whole of any revenue up to forty-three and a half million pounds, and half of any further excess up to fifty-six million pounds. Railway shares had risen by nearly two hundred million pounds in the three weeks following the announcement of these terms. In return for this, the Government asked little; the managers of the four companies settled things as they liked. The lack of co-operation and co-ordination which resulted from this continued independence was one element in the transport crisis of 1940–41. Another was the blitz; there were thousands of individual cases of damage on the railways. A third was petrol rationing, which meant extra passengers for public transport. A fourth was the deliberate diversion of imports to the west-coast ports. At this point, the railways problem merged with the problem of the docks.[9]

In the solution of this problem, also, Bevin's initiative was important. As early as June 1940, he had produced an order requiring all dockers to register, and had prepared a scheme for transferring dock labour to the west when need arose. The need had arisen in the autumn of 1940, and with the switch had come confusion, aggravated by bombing. Imports were being needlessly reduced because the rate of "turning round" ships was slow. Traditionally bad labour relations did not help. In December 1940, a cabinet committee was set up to improve matters. On Bevin's recommendations, regional port directors were appointed for the Clyde and the Mersey, and were made responsible for the employment of dock labour. It was typical of Bevin's creative spirit that he made this necessary improvisation an instrument of rough social justice. He saw a chance of ending the evils of the casual system of employment against which he had fought, as a trade unionist, for thirty years. The dockers in these ports were registered as a permanent labour force and guaranteed a minimum wage, a reasonably good one, in return for their agreement to work when and where they were required. The scheme, which came into operation in March 1941, was successful; after that spring, congestion in the ports was never a major problem.[10]

Meanwhile, the Government's agreement with the railways had been revised. They would receive a fixed annual payment of forty-three million pounds, and would be much more tightly controlled. On May 8th, 1941, the Ministries of Shipping and Transport were merged into a new Ministry of War Transport. Churchill went right outside conventionally "political" circles to find his minister. The new post went to Frederick Leathers, given a peerage as Lord Leathers, who had been boss of the P. & O. shipping line when Churchill had sat for several years on its board.

In spite of so much constructive work, Bevin was far from being the hero of the hour. Political controversy was coming sharply to the fore again in the winter of blitz. Those who attacked the Government could rely on an almost inexhaustible stream of damaging quotations from reports of the Select Committee on National Expenditure, a group of thirty-two members of parliament, on which all parties were represented but Conservatives preponderated, which had been given powers early in the war to investigate the many uses to which public money was now being put. Just before Christmas, the committee made a popular point when it complained that the staff of Bevin's ministry were "only using their compulsory powers to a very minor extent". Others who supported this criticism ranged from the influential, liberal-radical businessman's weekly, the *Economist*, to the somewhat unholy trinity of Winterton, Shinwell and Hore Belisha.[11] It was to be characteristic of the criticism of the Government which became very noisy in the press and in parliament in 1941 that its spokesmen held diverse and incompatible views on every subject under the sun; all that they concurred in was that the coalition's policy for war production was going badly wrong. If they tended to agree on any one remedy, it was the establishment of a Ministry of Production with powers to co-ordinate the three supply departments.

In January, Churchill replaced the unwieldy and ineffectual

Production Council presided over by Greenwood with a smaller Production Executive, consisting of the three supply ministers meeting under Bevin's chairmanship. This convened far more frequently than its predecessor, and took a far better- grip of the situation, but it dealt only with peripheral problems and still had no more power than the sum of its parts. If the four ministers disagreed it could do nothing. To prevent Beaverbrook's snubbing the executive as he had snubbed the council, it assembled in his office at M.A.P. Though he continued to work at his desk during its proceedings, he was inevitably drawn into its discussions. But the new arrangement failed to satisfy those who wanted a "Home Front Dictator".[12]

However, on the issue of compulsion of labour, events had moved in a way to suit the critics. In December, Sir William Beveridge unveiled (in secret) the report which the Production Council had asked him to make on the manpower situation. This was as much a turning point in the economic history of the war as its author's much more famous report on social security was later to be in its political history.

The Manpower Requirements Committee which Beveridge had headed had been prompted by a call from the army, in August 1940, for 357,000 recruits the following March and 100,000 a month thereafter. Beveridge had cross-examined each government department on its programme, and had totalled up the results in terms of the manpower each would require. Though the figures so provided were far from exact, this was the first successful attempt to engross the new wartime demands on the nation's manpower in a statistical framework. The results were horrifying.

The three services and Civil Defence together would need, it seemed, an extra 1,750,000 men and 84,000 women between September 1940 and the end of 1941. This would entail the withdrawal of about half a million men from the munitions industries. Yet the munitions industries had to expand by approaching one and a half million above the three and a half million already employed in order to equip the armed forces recruited on this scale. The answer to this conundrum was that women would have to provide over half these extra workers. Altogether, one and a half million women would have to leave their kitchens, their hearths, or work in such relatively unimportant fields as catering and domestic service. But this posed a new puzzle. Such numbers of inexperienced workers could only be absorbed if the Ministry of Labour could find enough highly skilled men to set their tools, direct their work and so on. Training would provide a solution only in the long term. Meanwhile, "dilution" must be introduced to the point where three skilled men could do the work of four.

Bevin could only accept such arguments, though they meant the beginning of the end of his policy for voluntaryism. On January 20th, the War Cabinet agreed to his proposals for a three-pronged attack on the problem, which were presented to parliament on the following day.

Firstly, the basis of reservation was altered. The block reservations of whole occupations meant that a skilled engineer servicing machinery which made toys was, if over the specified age, as immune as an aircraft worker. Bevin now proposed to create a category of "protected establishments". Workers in factories and undertakings engaged on important jobs would be reserved at a lower age than those in inessential work. Meanwhile, the scheduled ages for a considerable number of occupations were revised upwards in three stages – on April 10th, July 1st and October 1st. By the end of 1941, about a hundred thousand firms were on the Ministry of Labour's Register of Protected Establishments.

Secondly, Bevin proposed to make much more use of his power to direct people to essential work and to register them so that direction would be possible. The Registration of Employment Order was published in March, and a start was soon made with the registration of men over forty-one and of women of twenty and twenty-one.[13]

The latter was the more dramatic innovation. Bevin used his powers over women only with reluctance, though by the end of the year, registration had been extended upwards to those aged thirty. (Eventually, women between eighteen and fifty were registered.) In March, and even later, Bevin was still appealing for women to volunteer. His bashful attitude is indicated by a joke he made in a speech delivered in June, "I saw one headline the other day which said: 'Bevin wants a hundred thousand women, the State to keep the children.'"

Men up to forty-six had also been registered by the end of 1941. Those who registered were invited for interview at the local labour exchange if they were not already doing essential work, and were asked to consider one or two more important jobs which needed filling. Most workers were open to suggestion, and direction was used only against stubborn cases. Between July 1941 and June 1942, only thirty-two thousand compulsory directions were made (but this was ten times the number previously issued since Bevin's arrival in office). In the later years of war, direction became a common instrument for coercing men to work on big construction jobs in isolated areas and over three-quarters of the one million directions issued in 1941–45 applied to workers in building and civil engineering. Only eighty-eight thousand directions were issued for women.[14]

Bevin's third prong was the Essential Work Order, which became law on March 5th. He took power to declare work done in any establishment to be "essential". Thereafter, the employer could not sack any worker without the consent of a Ministry of Labour National Service Officer. Nor, conversely, might the worker leave his job without permission. Both sides had the right to appeal to local boards. Serious absenteeism by a worker could be reported to the National Service Officer, who would have power to order the man to work stated hours.

This was the negative side of the order, the answer to "poaching". Its positive side, however, made the order an instrument for progress as well as a warrant for bondage. Following his application of the Restriction on Engagements Order to engineering, coal-mining and agriculture in the previous summer, Bevin had received appeals from other industries which had been losing key men – brick-making, iron-mining, baking. He had made application of that order conditional upon negotiated rates of pay and acceptable conditions. Now the E.W.O., as the new order was soon called for short, contained the same types of condition, backed by greater power, and gave Bevin the opportunity to push through reforms. Yet these were prudential as well as idealistic. To force people to work for low wages in primitive factories would be to sow the seeds of discord and bad morale.

E.W.O.s were applied very soon to engineering and aircraft work, shipbuilding, the railways, the mines and the building industry. The Dock Labour Order of the autumn of 1941 followed the lines of the schemes already introduced in Merseyside and Clydeside, but the responsibility for labour in the other main ports was placed on a new independent body, the National Dock Labour Corporation. The Merchant Navy Order was another variant. It is estimated that more than a quarter of the men who began the war in the Merchant Marine had been killed or disabled before it ended. Yet at the outbreak, able-bodied merchant seamen had been earning under ten pounds a month, including danger money. The order did something for the heroes of the Battle of the Atlantic; while they might not leave the service, they were given more adequate leave and a guaranteed wage between voyages.

By the end of 1941, thirty thousand undertakings had been scheduled under the orders, and approaching six million workers came under their provisons.[15]

Also in March 1941, the Board of Trade published the gist of a new "concentration" policy for the civil section of industry. These had already been squeezed by restrictions imposed on their supply of raw materials. Work within each industry would now be concentrated in "nucleus" factories, releasing labour and finding space for war industry. Nucleus firms, once they had been so designated, would have their labour protected. The scheme produced, directly, only a fraction of the war workers which had been hoped for. One reason was that so many firms in the civil sector had already gone over to meeting service needs on war contracts, and this was, in fact, the most common method whereby workers were transferred to essential production in 1940–41. But "concentration" did mark the new thoroughness of the Government's approach.

Bevin had months before challenged the assumption that any man acquired by the army was necessarily doing an essential job; conscripts, he argued, were being wasted in headquarters work, air defence, training depots and other sidelines. On March 6th, Churchill issued an important directive which showed that not even the forces' demands were sacrosanct; he set a ceiling for the army at "about two million British". In April, the women's services became part of the Armed Forces of the Crown, and so subject to military discipline for the first time. This was to check the drifting out of young women who had volunteered and then had thought better of it. Registration and call-up still proceeded fast. By the middle of the year, all men up to the then final age limit of forty-one had been registered, and the Ministry of National Service soon began to call up boys of nineteen.[16]

The voluntary character of A.R.P. was a significant victim of the pressure of manpower shortage. While Morrison called the success of the voluntary basis "one of the greatest things in history", he successfully proposed to parliament that the A.F.S., the Police War Reserve, and a new Civil Defence Reserve should become Civil Defence "forces", and an act of April 1941 made it possible to compel men to join them. Nearly twenty-five thousand men were eventually drafted into the A.F.S. in this way, though the Civil Defence Reserve was allotted only two hundred and sixty recruits, so stringent had manpower shortage become.[17]

By June, thirty-seven per cent of the working population were in the forces or the munitions industries, as compared with thirty per cent a year before. Beveridge had predicted the imminent shortage, not only of skilled labour, but of all kinds of labour. By the summer, this was developing, and the day of the "man-power budget" was at hand.

III

Meanwhile, Sir Kingsley Wood's more familiar kind of budget was presented to the house of Commons on April 7th. Combined with the new manpower regulations, this marked the watershed of the economic history of the war. "After that date", the official historian of financial policy observes, "the remaining wartime budgets were primarily designed to consolidate ground already won, and to trim the rough edges from the new measures of the earlier days."[18]

The credit belonged less to Wood than to his advisers, most notably to John Maynard Keynes. The new budget, following Keynes's suggestion, abandoned the narrow conception of Government income and expenditure in favour of a general survey of "national income". Wood made no attempt to "balance" it in the familiar way.

Wood openly announced the Government's intention to stabilize the official cost of living index at between twenty-five and thirty per cent above pre-war, by means of subsidies and price control. To close the "inflationary gap" between Government expenditure and taxation, which Keynes estimated at five hundred million pounds, Wood still relied in great part on voluntary saving. But the standard rate of income tax went up to ten shillings in the pound, the reduced rate to six shillings and sixpence, and the exemption limit was lowered to a hundred and ten pounds per annum. With one stroke, Wood created four million new tax-payers, making the deep bite into working-class incomes which Keynes had long advocated. Another Keynesian idea mitigated the severity of this; a portion of the increased taxation would be paid back after the war as "post-war credits". Certain allowances which had previously protected many working-class earners from income tax were now cut, but the tax paid in these cases would be offset after the war by a "credit" which might be claimed from the Post Office Savings Bank.

An important stimulus to the Government's acceptance of these superficially unpalatable developments had been given by an independent survey conducted by Charles Madge, formerly one of the organizers of Mass Observation. Madge had announced that working-class people were far more worried about the immediate physical problems of blitz and food shortage than a few bob a week more or less on taxation, and his findings had convinced the Treasury that Keynes's theories were acceptable in practice. Most people, Madge discovered, would have preferred restriction of consumption by comprehensive rationing. But there was much support for the idea of "forced savings" and nobody wanted rising prices, which was the other alternative.

Churchill had objected violently to the idea of increasing income tax, which would amount "to almost complete confiscation of the higher rates of income". Wood rejected an idea prepared by Simon long before that the surtax level should be dropped to fifteen hundred pounds, and set about mitigating the severity of Excess Profits Tax. While for the moment this would still be raised at one hundred per cent, twenty per cent would now be repayable after the war, so that some incentive to acquisitiveness was restored.[19]

Bevin saw to it that the idea of a wage freeze, popular with the Government's critics, did not become part of the new battery of anti-inflationary devices. There is evidence that even this might have been accepted by public opinion; later in the year, Mass Observation found majority support in one sample for the idea of a "standard wage" for all civilians. But Bevin was adamant and bullied the Treasury out of the idea. Wages, he insisted, must be left to collective bargaining between management and unions. A wage freeze, he pointed out when the idea reared its head again later, would entail, initially, adjustment upwards of the wages of the lowest paid workers, involving subsidies to entire industries. If it was imposed, he threatened, labour would demand the nationalization of all industry. So the Government's wages policy rested, in the words of one of the official historians, on "a combination of faith and works – faith in the moderating influence of the trade unions, and action to control the cost of living".[20]

Such action was now very urgent. The annual average of wholesale prices of all goods rose by almost exactly fifty per cent between 1939 and 1941. Shortages of popular foods and consumer goods meant not only ever lengthening queues outside shops which had them, but sky-rocketing prices, conspicuous black market activities, and profiteering. If prices of scarce goods were fixed without some form of rationing, they tended to sell out at once or disappear "under the counter". When Maximum Price Orders were applied to onions, rabbits and turkeys in the autumn and winter of 1940, without any concomitant attempt to allocate supplies fairly, these items merely "vanished" from the sight of the ordinary consumer. Yet the Ministry of Food proceeded to announce a "price freeze", in December 1940, covering a large range of standard groceries, from poultry to nuts.[21] Meanwhile, the price of clothing rocketed from an average 137 per cent of pre-war levels in June 1940 to 175 per cent in May 1941.

Apart from the continuation of food subsidies – now admitted to be a long-term fixture – and attempts to enforce price control more effectively, the logic of the Government's policy of stabilizing the cost of living pointed to two more measures – the extension of rationing and increasing control over the actual production of consumer goods. Only by such means could it mask the deceit of the cost of living index with a bold, if hypocritical, face.

In March, preserves – jam, margarine, syrup and treacle – were rationed on a new basis, whereby everyone was entitled to a "minimum share" of eight ounces per month. But in July this was dropped in favour of a "straight" ration, which soon afterwards rose to one pound. In May, cheese was rationed for the first time, initially at the pitiful level of one ounce per week. In June, shell eggs came under a scheme, not quite of rationing, but of controlled distribution, which ensured adequate supplies for "priority consumers".

Clothes rationing was another logical step. Churchill, who had consistently fought to retard the development of "austerity", predictably opposed the idea. Oliver Lyttleton, another businessman recruited for the Government, who had become President of the Board of Trade in October, has recorded that Churchill's veto was finally overcome only when two senior members of the cabinet buttonholed him while he was busy following the sinking of the *Bismarck*. "Do what you like," the Prime Minister rasped, "but please don't worry me now."[22]

To prevent a run on the shops, extreme secrecy was preserved until rationing was actually introduced early in June. It involved the first application in Britain of the idea of "points rationing", already developed in Germany. Instead of giving the consumer a fixed amount of one common article, points (or in this case coupons) permitted him to choose between a range of goods, each with a different points price. The German example was also followed in a rash of special schemes to meet valid claims for extra clothing from different sections of the community, over and above what could be bought with the basic rate of sixty-six coupons per person per year.

Consumption of coal in the home had been restricted, loosely and erratically, since the outbreak of war. Local shortages in the first two winters had been caused by the cutting off of coastwise shipping and the confusion of the railway system. But by 1941, the overall shortage of coal itself was becoming more important. On July 1st, domestic users were cut down to one ton per month, but no real rationing scheme was introduced, and consumers with electric and gas fires were at an unfair advantage.

The policy of stabilizing the cost of living index was never wholly successful. Shortages and queues, the physical symptoms of inflation, persisted and, in fact, grew worse. Violent price increases for uncontrolled goods continued, and price control was never very effective, even over those goods which it covered. After a brief check, wage rates resumed their rise. The stability of the cost of living index was only maintained by disingenuous and tortuous manoeuvres. Since the cost of clothing continued to rise, that of sugar had to be reduced by subsidies paid for by wage earners out of taxation. Conversely, when the prices of common garments were brought down in 1942 by increasing Government intervention in their manufacture, food prices, at the behest of the Treasury, rose. As the official historian of food policy puts it, "The picture of officials gravely pondering whether a halfpenny on the price of hake would not have a 'trigger effect' on the index is hardly edifying . . . ' The most efficiently controlled prices moved up and down with "apparent aimlessness". But the index was held steady until 1944, when it was allowed to rise to fluctuate between 130 per cent and 135 per cent of pre-war. And Wood's policy succeeded, in so far as inflation never became unbearable.[23]

IV

In spite of all these measures, the Government continued to rely on voluntary appeals; sometimes in conjunction with compulsion, sometimes in areas where compulsion seemed doomed to failure, sometimes (it would appear), chiefly for the sake of appealing. In one issue of the *Farmer's Weekly*, two different pronouncements appealed to farmers to make better use of their straw. One exhorted them to pulp it for cattle food, the other to sell it for paper. "Taking a short walk from the office where this report is being written," Mass Observation commented at this time, "you will see forty-eight official posters as you go, on hoardings, shelters, buildings, including ones telling you:

to eat National Wholemeal Bread
not to waste food
to keep your children in the country
to know where your Rest Centre is
how to behave in an air raid shelter
to look out in the blackout
to look out for poison gas
to carry your mask gas always
to join the A.F.S.
to fall in with the fire bomb fighters
to register for Civil Defence duties
to help build a plane
to recruit for the Air Training Corps
to save for Victory."[24]

A typical advertisement told a story in pictures, entitled "Marion finds a fighting job, too – "

When Matron's boy friend was called up, *she* wanted to be in it too.
So she asked the employment exchange about war work . . .
In next to no time they had fixed her up at a Government Training Centre, learning to make munitions . . .
And before long she was in an important war job. At last she felt she was really "doing her bit" . . .
Jim *was* proud of her when he came home on leave! He knows how much equipment counts in modern warfare!

Such infantile appeals supported "War Worker Campaigns" all over the country. It transpired that the nation's Marions disliked the stories they had heard of long hours and dirty, monotonous work, and also the idea that once they were in a war factory, they would be unable to get out; they felt it would be a come-down from genteel occupations like typing and serving in shops. The results fell far short of what had been hoped.[25]

So many appeals were bound to cancel each other out, and to develop a healthy resistance in the human mind. In spite of an intensive Government campaign in the winter of 1940–41, only a very small minority, it seems, bothered at any time to carry or wear something white in the blackout. The Government begged the public not to travel from home on August Bank Holiday; all those who wanted to simply ignored the appeal and went away as they would have done in peacetime.[26]

Along with this venial apathy went a growing lack of interest, or profession of lack of interest, in the war news. In May 1940, only one person in eleven had told Mass Observation that he or she was not following the news, or was uninterested in it. By the autumn, this proportion had more than doubled; in May 1941, no less than four out of ten returned such answers, though perhaps they meant that the respondents had some idea what was happening, but had no stomach for hearing or reading about it.[27]

In the middle of February, Lieutenant General Rommel had arrived in North Africa. From then until October 1942, the British public was not to hear of one victory on land (in the Middle East or anywhere else) which seemed at all meaningful. There was a monotonous procession of evacuations, seiges and defeats. During this phase, Rommel walked out of real life into myth. As one British general after another failed against him in the desert, British soldiers and public began to treat him, with odd masochism, as their own hero. "... May I say across the havoc of war, a great general"; Churchill himself paid public homage before long.[28] In March 1941 Rommel, with his force of Italians and Germans, began a brilliant attack which drove the British back to the Egyptian frontier, leaving them a garrison holding the port of Tobruk, a town mentioned often in the next fifteen months, and usually with trepidation.

For the British, the Middle East remained the greatest theatre of war; for Hitler, it was a sideshow. In April, he mounted a serious campaign in the Balkans. The Germans tore through Yugoslavia, to confront a British force hastily and foolishly assembled to assist the defence of Greece. Churchill, characteristically, hoped that this hapless contingent would make a stand at Thermopylae. "The intervening ages fell away. Why not one more undying feat of arms?"[29] Because it would have been silly. The British retreated from Greece without having fought a major battle.

Worse followed. There was good news in May; the Italians capitulated in Abyssinia, and the *Bismarck* was sunk. But everyone knew that the Italians were no match for anyone, and that the Royal Navy was invincible. What came as a shock was the apparently triumphant success of a German airborne assault on the island of Crete, which Wavell's men now defended. At the end of May, eighteen thousand British and Dominion troops were pulled out of Crete, leaving five thousand behind them. The navy had been very seriously weakened, and five thousand, five hundred soldiers and sailors had been killed or wounded.

In mid-June, Wavell mounted an offensive against Rommel. It

was called off on the third day. The German anti-tank weapons, reinforced with a number of eighty-eight millimetre A.A. guns which could smash British tanks at a mile or more, had crippled so many that by this stage Wavell had only forty still fit to fight. The British two-pounder guns were proved almost useless.

This spell of miserable war news coincided with the last and grimmest phase of the blitz and the worst of the Battle of the Atlantic. "As each week passed", writes Jane Gordon, the wife of a gossip columnist now making his living by writing patriotic books, "the news from the war fronts got worse and worse. People were beginning to talk quite seriously about the possibilities of a negotiated peace. Even the most optimistic characters had given up all hope of America coming into the war, and no one even pretended to believe that England could hold out indefinitely." During the Germans' Balkan offensive, the carrying of gas masks in the streets became quite common again.[30]

Yet as A. P. Herbert wrote, "Bold is the citizen who makes a public utterance in the present war. If we say 'It is a fine day' we are 'complacent'; if we say 'It is raining' we are 'defeatist'; and if we say 'It looks like rain' we are Fifth Columnists." The *Time-Life* correspondent, Walter Graebner, remarked, "very few will criticize Churchill openly except in the House of Commons. It is so much in vogue to say that Churchill is a great man and a great leader that criticism by the masses is almost unknown. However, if one hints that perhaps Churchill isn't all that he's supposed to be, a great many people respond immediately and will begin to tell all kinds of things that they dislike about him."[31] The doublethink extorted by patriotism on the one side and stern facts on the other combined with the despondency which saw signs of inefficiency and corruption everywhere to produce a hysterical, almost suffocated, climate of political debate in 1941 and 1942.

V

By-elections, normally an early-warning system for discontent, were unimportant at this stage of the war. The only results which might, at other times, have caused some interest, had been at Argyll, where a Scottish Nationalist had won some forty per cent of the poll immediately after Hitler's invasion of the Low Countries, and Newcastle North, a month later, where an independent Conservative had defeated the official nominee. Polls were extremely low – at North Croydon in June 1940, only one voter in six bothered to exercise his democratic rights.[32] Most contests merely proved that pacifism appealed only to a small minority; there was nothing to worry the authorities. The non-electoral activities of the Communist Party were much more serious.

The logic of the C.P.'s Leninist practice had driven it, during the phoney war period, into a position which was so anti-Chamberlain as to be virtually pro-Hitler. Events in the summer of 1940 led to an apparent shift in its policy. Its candidate in an East End by-election in June emphasized her own militant anti-fascism and said almost nothing to suggest that the C.P. wished to "stop the war", and the party began to call instead for the exorcism of the "Men of Munich" from the cabinet and for the creation of a "People's Government".[33]

The chosen instrument of C.P. policy was now an organization called the People's Convention. Its figurehead, an attractive one, was D. N. Pritt, M.P., a brilliant and charming barrister of deceptively Pickwickian appearance who had recently been expelled from the Labour Party. Pritt was not a member of the C.P., but his unswerving devotion to the Soviet Union was among the wonders of the epoch.

On July 7th, 1940, as France was falling, a national "People's Vigilance Committee" was set up, which proceeded to call for "friendship with the U.S.S.R.", for the re-establishment of "democratic rights", for the defence of the people's standard of living and an end to profiteering, and for a new Government, "truly representative" of the people of Britain, which could pave the way for an enduring "people's peace". It followed this manifesto with an appeal to members of the Labour Party to dissociate themselves from their leaders in the Government.[34]

It has so long been obligatory to pour moral scorn on the activities of the C.P. at this period that it should be pointed out emphatically that its stand was not only principled, in its own terms, but decidedly non-opportunistic. Had the C.P. supported the war and attacked the Government, it might indeed have snatched the leadership of large sections of the Labour movement from Attlee and Morrison. As it was, the most the C.P. could manage was the equivocating Convention; and even this tactic was ominously successful. Intelligent and well-meaning people, some left-wing socialists, some pacifists, were attracted by the call for a "People's Government". When, in September 1940, the People's Vigilance Committee issued a summons announcing a great convention in support of its aims, the signatories included, besides well-known Communists and fellow-travellers, such non-Leninist personalities as the Reverend Mervyn Stockwood (later Bishop of Southwark), the authors Olaf Stapeldon and Rosamund Lehmann, and the actor Michael Redgrave. Another signatory, Doctor Hewlett Johnson, the "Red Dean" of Canterbury, assured Victor Gollancz that he was "convinced" that Hitler "must be resisted with all our might" and that he regarded Churchill as "irreplaceable" so long as there was a danger of Nazi victory. But he insisted that only a "People's Government" could enlist against Hitler "the whole-hearted and creative energies of the people".[35]

The notion of a "people's peace" grew more attractive as the blitz proceeded. The C.P. line on the blitz, as advertised in the *Daily Worker*, was to emphasize the horror of it all and to insist that people were suffering in an imperialist cause. "1,000 CASUALTIES IN 'REPRISAL' RAID ON COVENTRY", ran one *Worker* headline. A leading article on the same day said, "The people are dumb and horror-stricken. Which town will be the next victim?" "COVENTRY A SHAMBLES" was the disturbing, if accurate, headline two days later. Pollitt demanded that "all valuable labour and materials" should be used to "build deep bomb-proof shelters throughout the East End of London". The disruptive intentions behind all this were amply illustrated by the *Worker*'s line on the appointment of "roof spotters" in factories. Having advocated such a system on August 31st, it attacked it, under the headline "WHO'D BE A SPOTTER?", after Churchill had made it official policy.[36]

In the munitions factories, the Convention attracted considerable interest. In one London engineering works, a prominent ex-Communist, J. T. Murphy, heard the Convention being advanced as a means of dealing with Hitlerism more effectively. "Suddenly we saw a goodly number of men wearing the People's Convention button on their coats or overalls." There were over three hundred supporters in this factory alone. It was, Murphy said, "an unquestionable fact" that the Convention retarded the war effort. Many of its supporters refused to work overtime; its influence fomented discontent and lowered morale.[37]

But how could a People's Government come to power? Pritt hinted, somewhat obscurely, that a general election would install it, but the mechanisms whereby even this might be achieved under conditions of total war were left shrouded in impenetrable vagueness and the Convention refrained from testing its strength in by-elections. It was difficult to resist the conclusion that the

C.P. still hoped that the defeat of Britain would create chaos in which a Communist coup would be possible, and meanwhile the Convention, which was never explicitly defeatist, would maintain and extend Communist influence. The C.P.'s opponents on the left drew this conclusion and exposed it angrily.[38]

However, there is little reason to doubt the sincerity of Arthur Horner, the pugnacious Communist leader of the South Wales miners. when he told J. L. Hodson, "If Hitler won, that would be the death of me. At the best, it would be a change of masters, at the worst . . ." (Though when Hodson asked him how far he was prepared to go in actually fighting Hitler, Horner, after some hesitation, said, "I stop short at defence.") It was an unhappy and confusing a time for all but the most hard-boiled C.P. loyalists. Claud Cockburn, the *Daily Worker* journalist who acted as the Convention's P.R.O., has since suggested that the whole time-consuming manoeuvre was "totally futile".[39]

But the organizers seem to have been quite genuinely surprised by the success of the Convention itself, when it finally assembled on January 12th, 1941. An overflow meeting was necessary. The organizers' claim that the 2,234 delegates "represented" some 1,200,000 people was disingenuous. The "delegates" in many cases were simply members of the bodies concerned – trade union branches, shop stewards' committees, tenants' associations, shelter committees and other well-trodden alleyways of C.P. activity – who made it their own business to attend. But there were plenty of people present who were not habitual fellow-travellers. Mass Observers who mingled with them found that many disagreed with parts of the Convention's programme, and some even remarked that it was a pity it was so left-wing. The delegates were mainly working-class and preponderantly in their 'twenties and 'thirties. Enthusiasm was high, and in the hall and in the lobbies it was enthusiasm for peace. "Perhaps the best way of summing-up feeling on this subject," Mass Observation concluded, "is that people were 'looking for a way out of the present mess'."[40]

The most applauded speeches came from the Communist leaders, Pollitt and Dutt, and the future Indian Foreign Minister, Krishna Menon, who denounced British imperialism with wit and venom. In spite of close C.P. management, the affair had life and spontaneity; one by one apparently "typical" soldiers, house-waves and trade unionists appeared on the rostrum to make brief and widely acceptable statements. The charade disarmed some of the journalists present, and the Convention surfaced into newspaper publicity of a quite favourable kind – except, notably, from the left-wing press.[41]

At this point, Herbert Morrison lost his patience. Using his powers under Defence Regulation 2D, which had been granted in the previous summer for employment in the event of invasion, he suppressed the *Daily Worker* on January 21st. The ban remained in force for some eighteen months, and probably helped to weaken the Convention's influence; directly, by robbing it of the outlet for its arguments and directives, and indirectly by side-tracking the C.P. into agitation against the ban itself.[42]

But as Aneurin Bevan pointed out, Morrison's action suggested that the Government lacked faith in Britain's morale, and was afraid of sharp criticism. This was neither the first, nor by a long way the last, case of Government interference with the press. During the campaign against Sir John Anderson in the autumn of 1940, a deputation of press proprietors had been told that if such "vicious and malignant" criticism (in Churchill's phrase) continued, the Government would introduce legislation which would extend censorship from the news itself to the views expressed about it.[43]

That not everyone found such interference acceptable was shown in March when the B.B.C. asked a number of well-known broadcasters, including Michael Redgrave, to withdraw their support from the Convention or submit to suspension. Vaughan Williams declared that the B.B.C. might no longer play his music if that of the Communist composer, Alan Bush, was banned. E. M. Forster and Rose Macaulay protested by withdrawing their services. The B.B.C. climbed down. More sinister, because more covert, was the manner in which Priestley was ousted from his regular Sunday evening spot. His first series of "Postscripts" had ended at his own request. Public clamour had brought him back for a second. This time, his talks were still more "political", and he was taken off the air. The Ministry of Information told him that the decision was the B.B.C.'s. The B.B.C. explained that a directive had come from the Ministry of Information.[44]

But scandals of many kinds still found their place in the newspapers, and the tabloid *Daily Mirror* was exceptional only in the gusto with which it presented them.

VI

Badgering Colonel Blimp was a favourite occupation with the *Mirror* as well as with the *Worker*. Memories of the Belisha episode had faded; Gort and Ironside, that worthy pair who had seemed blood-brothers of Blimp, had been banished from their lofty positions, but Blimp was believed to have many surviving allies in the officers' messes.

On January 15th, 1941, one of them exposed himself rashly to fire. Lieutenant Colonel Bingham, who was in charge of an Officer Cadet Training Unit (OCTU), published a letter in *The Times*. He noted with sadness that the "middle, lower middle and working classes are now receiving the King's commission. These classes, unlike the old aristocratic and feudal (almost) classes who led the old army have never had 'their people' to consider . . . This aspect of life is completely new to them, and they have very largely fallen down on it in their capacity as army officers . . . Man management is not a subject which can be 'taught'; it is an attitude of mind, and with the old school tie men this was instinctive and part of the philosophy of life."

Margesson, who had succeeded Eden at the War Office, quickly removed Colonel Bingham from his post, and told parliament that he regretted that the letter had been published. Hardly had the howls of derisive protest died away when Margesson announced in the House of Commons, in March, that an analysis of the commissions given from a selection of infantry OCTUS showed that over a three-month period at the end of 1940, twenty-six per cent had gone to public schoolboys; seventy-four per cent to men educated in the state system. Cassandra of the *Mirror* was swift to deduce that, taking into account the tiny proportion of public schoolboys among the nation's children, this meant that they had fourteen times as good a chance of becoming officers.[45]

What inspired and goaded critics of the military hierarchy was that this was so clearly not the kind of war in which "leadership" of the old "feudal" type was appropriate. A booklet of tips for officers, published in the momentous year, 1940, included such gems of advice as "Don't, because the soldier happens to be your father or brother, drink with him in a public bar. Find somewhere private. He is sufficiently proud of you not to want to behave in a manner unbecoming to your rank." But it was hard for an officer to "find somewhere private" in a tank moving into battle; his authority stood or fell on courage and intelligence, not etiquette. It was in the R.A.F. that the old ideas of leadership were most patently outmoded. Of the seven men in the crew of a big bomber, only one or two might be commissioned, and another rank was often in command, since the rule was that the pilot was always captain, even if the navigator and tail gunner were officers. But J. L. Hodson was outraged to discover that if a Pilot Officer and a Sergeant Pilot, both flying Spitfires, distinguished themselves equally in combat, the former received the Distinguished Flying Cross, the latter the Distinguished Flying Medal. The commissioned officer was accorded free first-class railway travel; the sergeant must go third-class.[46]

In fact, from the outbreak of war the army had made all prospective officers serve in the ranks before going on to OCTUs. But the boards of regimental officers who considered aspirants for commissions were notorious (fairly or unfairly) for asking such questions as "What does your father do?", "Do you hunt?" or even "Which pack do you hunt with?" Dismayed by the high failure rate in the OCTUs, the army, with a portentous recognition that science, as Churchill had put it, had spoiled war, introduced psychological methods of testing in 1941, and put psychiatrists on the selection boards.

But institutionalized class resentments remained one element in the mood of soldiers at home in 1940–41. "It's odd, the mixture there is in the army," wrote the poet Alun Lewis about this time. "Centralized and socialized in distribution and production of goods, monastic in its celibacy and its veto on private property, communal as hell: and yet absolutely crucified by repression, regimentation, precedence and the taboos of hierarchy." He had, he added, been attempting to "humanize" his unit by organizing a debating society, a weekly magazine and a scheme of lectures on world affairs; "and all I have earned is suspicion, resentment, a petty charge and reduction to the ranks".[47]

The mood of the soldiers is summed up by three of their favourite slang expressions. "Bullshit" or "bull" referred primarily to "spit and polish", to the irritations of useless routine, though in practice, as the lexicographer Eric Partridge observes, "anything that one didn't want to do was so named." It also signified "nonsense!" (or "balls!"), the stock reaction to official exhortation and propaganda. Two other universal terms were "He's had it" (or "You've had it") and "browned off". The former originally indicated that "he" had "had" his issue of clothing, food, cigarettes or comforts, and so was entitled to no more. It came to mean either that "he" was dead, or that he could *not* have it "whatever 'it' may happen to be". "Browned off" had probably originated in Kipling's India. It meant "bored" and "fed up".[48] While the term was general, it belonged especially to the army, the members of which were aptly nick-named "brown jobs" from the displeasing khaki of their uniforms. In a period which spawned ominous clusters of initials (M.A.P., E.P.T., E.W.O., A.F.S.) the soldiers revived an unofficial one of their own: "P.B.I.", poor bloody infantry.

The army was by far the most populous of the fighting services. In June 1941, it numbered two and a quarter million men, of whom an impressive proportion were "browned off" in camps in Britain. The navy (395,000) and the R.A.F. (662,000) were, by contrast, always fighting. The navy, Mass Observation found, was the least criticized of the services, regarded with some awe. The R.A.F. was the most admired by the general public "as a brilliant set of individuals", though its members ("Brylcreem Boys" to the P.B.I.) were widely regarded as somewhat conceited. Men in blue uniforms, it was said, could get lifts from cars and free cups of tea much more easily than "brown jobs". Members of the women's services (just over a hundred thousand in June 1941) were said to grade escorts in an order of eligibility by which "R.A.F. officers rated tops, being classified in turn by rank and number of decorations; naval officers came second and brown jobs a long way behind."[49]

Even within the army, some forms of life were much lower than others; A.A. Command, before the Battle of Britain, suffered from a plague of dimwits, and at rock bottom, the Pioneer Corps absorbed pacifists and aliens. Another staple criticism of the army in 1940–41 was that it wasted much of the best material that reached it. In particular, it was said to demand far more skilled tradesmen than it could really use. So clamant did these rumours become that in May 1941, the inevitable Sir William Beveridge was appointed to head a committee to investigate them. It reported in the autumn, confirming the worst, and disclosing such individual cases as "Lance-corporal, twenty-eight, formerly electrician at a university, studied for three years at a college of technology. Now cooks for a section of military police." As a result, the Government banned any further intake of many types of engineering tradesmen into the services until August 1942. There was a belated recognition of the existence of the wider problem; from 1942, all recruits were given six weeks' basic training and put through aptitude tests to decide which branch of service would suit them best.[50]

Though the blitz tended to reduce the serviceman's resentment of the fact that men of his own age in reserved occupations were now making big money on overtime, this feeling was latent, and essentially demoralizing. The allowances for privates' wives were increased in 1942 (so that a woman with two children received forty-three rather than thirty-eight shillings per week) and there was a direct increase in pay for other ranks. But neither wives nor other ranks, observing the continued rise in the cost of living, felt any better off.

An anecdote related by a civilian lecturer suggests how far soldiers in the forces at home, many of whom were scattered over isolated A.A. sites, might dissociate themselves from the war. He recalls "making his way with some difficulty to a site placed equidistant between the villages of Great Snoring on the one hand and of Little Snoring on the other. Pleasant places enough no doubt, but as the names suggest, scarcely teeming with bustle and activity. The inn door in the former bore the legend, 'Sorry, sold out', that in the latter the less apologetic but more definite announcement, 'No beer'." This unfortunate situation meant that no one had bothered to leave the site for some time. The ration lorry had not made its usual call and the wireless set was out of order. "The result was that the lecturer was able to bring them news of the sinking of the *Bismarck*, an event which Mr A. V. Alexander had made known four days previously." In case it is thought that such readily accepted isolation was rare, it should be noted that as late as 1943, long after the important developments which must now be described, a sample investigation showed that at least fifty per cent of the troops *in Great Britain* did not see a daily paper, nor were able to listen to radio news.[51]

Education had played a minor role in the peacetime services. After the outbreak of war, the small Army Education Corps had been mostly assigned to other duties. Universities, the Workers' Educational Association and other interested bodies had come together in the first winter of war to establish a "Central Advisory Council for Adult Education in H.M. Forces", through which lectures and short courses had been organized for the troops. But up to Dunkirk, such activity had taken place only on a very small scale.

The summer of 1940 transformed the situation. It was clear that the greater part of the army would be based at home for months, if not years, to come, and the military authorities were seriously worried about the combined effects of defeat, inactivity and bullshit on the morale of the troops. A special committee reported in September 1940 that education, in a broad sense, was indispensable to morale and advocated that every unit should have its own education officer. The Army Education Corps was greatly expanded. The demand for civilian lecturers boomed and continued to grow, until in a peak period from April to September 1943, 3,750 short courses and 62,123 single lectures were given by thousands of part-time lecturers with every variety of specialized knowledge – silversmiths and town clerks as well as professors – who might, if they wished, claim a guinea per lecture. In addition, the army launched a very wide range of correspondence courses for soldiers, at home or abroad, who wished to prepare for professional or technical examinations.[52]

The response to this flurry of activity reflected the immense variety within the army. In some units, the throwing together of men of all classes under a sympathetic commanding officer might produce eager do-it-yourself education through discussion groups and brains trusts led by soldiers and officer without any outside help. It was cases like this which prompted the Master of Balliol, A. D. Lindsay, to exclaim that "there had not been an Army in England which discussed like this one since that famous Puritan Army which produced the Putney Debates and laid the foundation of modern democracy." But in other cases, there was the "suspicion" and "resentment" of which Alun Lewis wrote, and it was estimated in the summer of 1941 that eight soldiers out of ten were still untouched by any direct educational influence.[53]

It was in this situation that the un-Blimpish new Adjutant-General, General Sir Ronald Adam, prompted the creation of ABCA, the Army Bureau of Current Affairs. Adam believed that it was not only the soldier's right, in a modern democracy, but also his duty, "to reason why". Only men who knew what they were fighting for, and something of the facts which underlay the crude news from the battle-fronts, could maintain morale through such a lengthy war. ABCA was created in August 1941 with a prominent educationalist, W. E. Williams, as its director. Its basic idea was revolutionary; compulsory adult education for the P.B.I., for at least one hour a week, to be taken out of training time. The platoon commanders themselves were expected simultaneously to improve the knowledge of their men, and their knowledge of their men, by leading the ABCA sessions, using factual briefs supplied by the bureau to introduce, of all things, political discussion.

Indifferent or hostile commanding officers could still see to it that this notion was not carried out within their purlieus, but six months after its initiation, about six units out of ten had organized ABCA discussion groups. The scheme eventually extended itself to all theatres of war, and involved exhibitions, wall newspapers, educational films, special plays about current affairs, and "Information Rooms" in many of the largest units which provided a livelier sort of reference library for those who had curiosity to satisfy. Under the "Winter Scheme" of 1942–43, no less than three hours were commandeered from training and working periods for education, and a course in "citizenship" entitled emphatically "British Ways and Purpose" was introduced to acquaint the P.B.I. with the perfections of the society they lived in. How far this worthy obsession with education went is revealed by the experience of an officer, taking shelter in a barn from German mortaring in north-west Europe after D Day, who found "a corporal and twelve men earnestly discussing 'What shall we do with the Germans after the war?' "[54]

It was not until after the 1945 general election that the Conservatives concluded that Army Education had been a monstrous left-wing plot. "Most of us, at the time, took little notice of it," relates Lord Woolton; "I only became suspicious of it when one night Sir Stafford Cripps gave me what was tantamount to a lecture on the work that it was doing." But left-wing opinion had, very often, dismissed ABCA as so much political bromide. "All army education, lectures and discussions are based on the alleged eternity and sacredness of our present social system," complained one "Serving Soldier" anonymously in *Tribune*.[55] While Williams himself was radical enough, the bulletins which ABCA issued were generally uncontroversial.

However, where ABCA was taken at all seriously the discussion was bound to range on to controversial points which could not be cleared up by reference to the bulletins, and where the officer in charge was not always competent to intervene. If he did intervene, ABCA would be dismissed by those present as yet more "bullshit". If he did not, an opinionated Marxist private could sweep all before him. In addition, many of the civilian lecturers were left-wing, and some of them were sacked for letting this show. But ABCA did not create the ready hearing which was given to left-wing views in the army, nor the left-wing opinions of many of the younger officers themselves. Woolton should have complained, rather, about the fact of war itself, and the spirit of the age.

VII

The army was never, of course, universally inactive. Even over-seas, a good number of men were settling down to untaxing, if boring, wars, in such roles as the making of underground forti-fications in Gibraltar, or the training of native troops in West Africa. But in the first seven months of 1941, 144,000 servicemen were sent to Egypt, on the long route round the Cape. Although deaths in action were lower in 1941 than in any year of the war, over fifty thousand servicemen were killed. Bomber Command's losses were of the rate of one aircraft for every ten tons of bombs dropped. J. L. Hodson cited the case of a woman returning from the death-bed of her eldest son, who had crashed after bombing Brest, only to hear over the radio that the *Bismarck*, in the course of its penultimate encounter, had sunk the British battlecruiser *Hood*, on which was her youngest boy.[56] There was consolation for the bereaved if their loved ones had died in a successful action. There was no such consolation for those who lost sons or fiancés in the battle of Crete. The pangs of sorrow sharpened the con-troversy over the munitions industries on which the services relied.

In this controversy, the old arguments of the political parties were heard again in muted, sometimes in transmuted, form. Members of the Labour Party, and in particular of its left wing, believed that the root of the problem of war production was the continued private ownership of industry. They shrank from advocating action, such as unofficial Labour intervention in by-elections, which would split the coalition; they feared, perhaps rightly, that the war would be lost if party bickering divided the nation. But they knew that public opinion had moved in their direction to a quite startling degree, and they assumed that the pressure of events was on their side. Kingsley Martin, editor of the *New Statesman*, wrote in the summer of 1941, "if you press for a constructive programme of the highest production you will automatically expose the waste and inefficiency of capitalism, and this Government, which is completely committed to this war, may be prevailed upon to make great changes which will be dis-tasteful to many employers, but which are absolutely necessary for winning the war."[57] The titles of a few of the great spate of left-wing books and pamphlets which appeared in the first two years of war will indicate clearly enough what socialists were pressing for – "Start Planning Britain Now", "What Are We Waiting For", "Democratize the Empire", "Privilege Must Go", "End Poverty and Insecurity", "Forward March". Such tracts were avidly bought and read.

The right, on the other hand, were currently demoralized, and were left with little but reflex counter-cries. Bevin was bidding for dictatorship; E.P.T. was an iniquity (since everyone knew that unless the rich retained the incentive of profits which would make them yet richer, they would be hard put to lift a finger to help their country); wages, on the other hand, were far too high; and all this interference by the Civil Service in industry was destroying the liberty of capitalism, for which, it had been understood, Britain was fighting. However, the more intelligent younger Conservatives, notably Harold Macmillan and R. A. Butler, had long seen which way the tide was flowing. The shrewder captains of industry likewise prepared to *reculer pour mieux sauter*. "If industry doesn't plan for revolution, there'll be revolution," the managing director of a large munitions firm insisted to a Mass Observer about this time. " . . . And we can only avoid it by anticipating it, by meeting the needs of the people and the times, by taking the great changes that are going to be forced on us anyway if we don't do it ourselves."[58] Meanwhile, the Conservative majority in the Commons dared not frustrate measures which it was bound to concede were necessary.

Liberal opinion, with a small "l", found an interesting manifestation in the "1941 Committee", the bias of which is summed up in the title of one of its publications – "Planning and Freedom". The committee was a fairly informal pressure group of left-wing publicists who met at the house of Edward Hulton, the Liberal publisher of *Picture Post*. Its chairman was J. B. Priestley, a socialist who was not a member of the Labour Party. On its far left was Sir Richard Acland, a Liberal M.P. who had, since the outbreak of war, announced his conversion to the outright "common ownership" of virtually all industry, but who wished to convert industrialists themselves to this view. On its right, the economist, Thomas Balogh, argued simultaneously in favour of some degree of nationalization, and the lowering of E.P.T. to restore incentive. Other members were socialists, Kingsley Martin for instance, or unaligned radicals like Vernon Bartlett, M.P., and J. L. Hodson.[59]

"I grow weary of listening to stories of waste and bungling," wrote Hodson in his diary on March 13th, 1941, at a period when he was travelling widely up and down the home front. "Hotel life in Torquay is grotesque," he noted at the time when near-by Plymouth was undergoing its ordeal, " – evening clothes and dancing every night. The breakfast menu gives you fish and an egg or brisket of beef, together with toast, porridge, and jam. Dinner is seven shillings and sixpence – soup (or cocktail), entrée of ham, poultry, sweet, coffee. Officers I know had a lunch the other day which included eggs, fish and meat."

Industrial resources, so the stories went, were being wasted everywhere. A trade union official in south Wales told Hodson of a railway waggon which was sent from London to Liverpool, carrying nothing but two small spare parts for a gun, which could have gone by post. In Sheffield it struck many people as "inexplicable" that "after seventeen months of war, Sheffield's light trades – silver and electro-plate industries – are not making all the munitions they would like to be". Hodson received the impression that highly skilled firms were clamouring for work which the Government would not give them.

Then, there were the tales of profiteering. A friend in Lancashire told Hodson that he had been auditing the accounts of a builders' merchant who had earned a thousand pounds a year from his business before the war, but in the last year had drawn over fifteen thousand pounds in director's fees – this for a small firm employing half a dozen people. The same accountant spoke of two war factories where the auditors had insisted on paying out the wages themselves, and had found that hundreds of pounds were reaching the firms in respect of non-existent workers.[60]

These tales were not the carefully selected ammunition of a lonely red revolutionary. The buses, and even the newspapers, were noisy with such anecdotes. In the spring of 1941, the chairman of the North Midland Region Food Price Investigation Committee, Sir Douglas McCraith, announced that cans of soup, sold by manufacturers at six shillings and sixpence a dozen, were reaching the public at fourteen shillings and sixpence a dozen, having passed through the hands of six middlemen, one of whom had bought the goods twice. "Speculation is rampant; goods are changing ownership many times like stocks and shares without even leaving the warehouse . . ." The trivial fines imposed by some magistrates for proven cases of profiteering were, he added, a matter for ridicule. Other notable abuses included the canning by smart operators of dried beans, prunes and peas, for sale at large profits; and the peddling of worthless "substitutes" for common foods now rare. Mixtures of flour, salt and baking powder were sold as "milk substitutes" at five shillings a pound; "onion substitutes" might be no more than "water and a smell". The existence of a "black market" was little disputed. Mass Observation found, indeed, that a surprising number of people were willing to admit quite freely that they had bought scarce goods through it.[61]

From the right, Henderson Stewart, M.P., claimed in mid-June that "The flower of our manhood has been mown down at two shillings a day in Crete and elsewhere through lack of arms to defend itself. Factories at home which could make these arms are frequently the scenes of deliberate slacking, deliberate idleness and shameless agitations for higher wages." A couple of days later, the president of the Amalgamated Engineering Union alleged, contrariwise, that the troops in Crete had been "let down by men who believe that patriotism is another name for profits and that democracy means dividends", and went on to attack profiteering by firms on Government contracts of the "cost plus" type.[62]

"Cost plus" was a reaction by the Government departments which dealt with industry to the fact that in wartime it was difficult or impossible to follow the normal peacetime practice of getting a job done at a prearranged price. Effective competition ceased to exist, both the scale and the urgency of the demand increased, and the hasty introduction of new types of weapon and the arrival of quite unprecedented sorts of work prohibited the accurate cost estimation upon which a "fixed price" contract could be based. Ministries therefore resorted to a variety of more elastic types of contract, of which the agreement to pay cost plus a fixed *percentage* was the one most open to abuse. Otherwise, they could pay cost plus a fixed *profit*, a somewhat different matter, or could set a maximum price or a target cost. Cost plus percentage was, however, the quickest way of reaching agreement with a contractor if the job was urgent, and it was really the only basis on which firms could be asked to manufacture a wholly new product.

The system had been exposed to the public gaze during and after the blitz, when "cost plus percentage" was the standard method of contracting for urgent repair and demolition of bomb damaged buildings. From the East End, in the aftermath of the raids, Doreen Idle reported that "During one day the following numbers were noted at sites under demolition in West Ham: out of two gangs of ten men each, four men in one case, and three in the other, were actually working; in a gang of twelve men, five were working, and in a gang of twenty men, ten were working. In nearly all cases, those who were working were doing so in a very desultory way, chucking one brick on to a lorry and then resting before repeating the process, and so on."[63]

Confronted with such a spectacle, the right winger denounced the working classes; the left winger pointed out that on "cost plus" the employer stood to make more money if he permitted idleness and inefficiency which would push up his costs. There was also, for an engineering firm, an incentive to hoard skilled labour of which it could not make much, or any, use. The allegations of 1941 which implied that virtually the whole munitions industry was grafting along in this fashion were certainly wild. But there were plenty of flagrant instances.

Excess Profits Tax should theoretically have siphoned off ill-gotten gains. But in practice, quite apart from the twenty per cent rebate which the Government now promised, evasion of E.P.T. was no harder (and, probably, no less widespread) than evasion of super tax in peacetime. A business man M.P., Austin Hopkinson, was kind enough to explain to his colleagues in the House of Commons how it might be done. "One simply employs one's poor relations at exorbitant salaries, and adds more and more to the salaries of the staff and to expenses, and buys more Rolls-Royces on the firm, and generally runs up the standing charges until they absorb all the excess profits there are." The big engineering firms may well have been more honest than most; it was harder to enforce E.P.T. effectively on small private companies, farmers, traders and independent workers.[64]

Yet was not Whitehall the nation's watchdog? The left, on the contrary, suspected that the recruitment of businessmen to fill key positions in Government departments meant that Whitehall was now prejudiced in favour of private interests. A popular novelist, Nigel Balchin, sourly imagined one temporary civil servant saying to another, "After all, what d'you expect? If you try to run a thing like this with just civil servants it just gets wrapped round with redtape. If you run it with businessmen it's a racket. So they mix them up." "And get," the other replied, "a racket tied up with redtape."[65]

It had been quite well understood before the war that industry was run for profit; yet in wartime, the discovery that this might still be the case was considered worthy of moral outrage. In a survey of war production published early in 1942, Mass Observation shrewdly remarked, of the innumerable "shocking" anecdotes then current, that "an appreciable proportion of the many

inefficiencies and hold-ups described were not necessarily *proved*
inefficiencies . . . but were incidents which looked like inefficiencies from the particular point of view of the people seeing them.
In the industrial field at present there is a marked readiness for
anyone seeing anything which seems to him wrong, *immediately*
to assume that it is very wrong, shocking."[66]

The Select Committee on National Expenditure listed several
reasons why hold-ups in production and idle time might occur.
Some were indeed avoidable – faulty work by sub-contractors,
bad management within the works. But others could not be
helped; when air raids damaged vital factories and shipping or rail
transport was interrupted, this was bound to have repercussions
over wide areas of industry. Another factor was changes in
design.[67] If M.A.P. insisted on a modification which would make
the Spitfire (say) a better plane, the flow of work in the factory
would be affected. Yet, in fighting terms, this was "efficiency".

In the aircraft industry, production had been quite badly disrupted by the dispersal of the factories, though this had been
accomplished in some cases with remarkable speed. When the
Birmingham Small Arms factory had been hit on November 19th,
1940, the vital programme of Browning machine guns for fighter
planes had been threatened; but by the end of the month six new
factories in the midlands had been found in which to make them.
The first to start was at Bromsgrove in Worcestershire, where two
adjacent factories were requisitioned. "The first lorry-load of
machine tools arrived on the afternoon of Tuesday, November
26th," relates the historian of B.S.A., "and from that minute it
was a case of the Browning gun equipment being moved in at the
front as the glove, shoe and woodworking machinery went out at
the back. Permission had been given for a glove order to be
completed and at one time millwrights were standing round three
machines on which the girls were working. As each finished her
job, her machine was disconnected and trundled out." All the
leather workers were employed by B.S.A., to work alongside
experienced craftsmen brought out from Birmingham, and the
new production was in full swing within five weeks. It is easy to
see how disruptive dispersal was in the short run; but, as this
anecdote suggests, in the long run it strengthened the industry,
by bringing in new floor space and new workers, which, as
production moved back into the parent factories after the raids
ceased, remained as net gain.[68]

Aircraft production, more than doubled in the second and third quarters of 1940, fell back somewhat in the fourth quarter. It resumed its upward rise in 1941; but not at the rate which Beaverbrook laid down.

Beaverbrook's personality was a subsidiary cause of the malaise of war industry in "the middle of the tunnel". At M.A.P., he had made himself, in Mass Observation's phrase, "the psychological leader of industry." He provoked "few lukewarm feelings", but "exceptionally violent partisanship, for or against". The stories which gathered around him were as double-edged as his reputation, like the one told of him by the head of a northern engineering firm:

> Beaverbrook was inspecting a big aircraft factory, when he saw a new type of plane. He asked when the plane would be ready, and was told "two months". He said he must have this new type at once. It must be up in the air and bombing Berlin within two days.
> The whole factory was organized into getting the plane ready in two days. The whole production schedule was disorganized, the assembly lines stripped, everything concentrated on to the plane. By a stupendous effort of organization the plane was ready in two days, flown to the aerodrome, and handed over to the R.A.F. The job Beaverbrook asked for had been done, though the production of the factory would be interfered with for weeks after.
> That night, within forty-eight hours of Beaverbrook's visit, the plane went over to bomb Berlin.
> When the bomb aimer pulled the stick out fell two members of the night shift.[69]

A characteristic product of the Beaverbrook regime at M.A.P. was the so-called "Carrot Programme", or, more formally, "Target Programme". The idea was simple; the aircraft industry would be set impossible targets and would follow them like a donkey lured on faster and faster by a carrot suspended just in front of his snapping jaws. The fallacy was also simple; people were not donkeys.

The first carrot was dangled out in October 1940. Beaverbrook set the industry to make 2,782 aircraft of all types per month by December 1941. Current production was around fifteen hundred per month. It was assumed that in its race to reach the carrot, the industry would burst through the bottlenecks in the way of further expansion. There was the more immediate advantage that such a programme would entitle M.A.P. to demand more labour, tools and material than it really needed in which case it might be allowed enough to supply authentic necessities.[70]

In June 1941, when the target was more than 2,500 aircraft, only 1,628 were produced. There were two likely reactions from the factories which repeatedly failed to achieve their monthly targets. One was to deduce that the target was in fact unreasonable and to pay no attention to such things in future. The other was mutual recrimination between labour, management and M.A.P. Meanwhile, the chief men in Beaverbrook's own ministry assumed that the targets were illusory and merely invented their own. So that, in the case of one of the new four-engined heavy bombers, "there were (one M.A.P. official reveals) as many different Stirling aircraft programmes being used for planning component production as there were production directors." The men responsible for engines and the men responsible for propellers went their separate ways, and the result might well be aircraft standing idle for want of vital parts – yet another "shocking" sign of "lagging" production.[71]

In May 1941, Beaverbrook finally succeeded in resigning from the hot seat at M.A.P. After a few months during which Churchill accorded him the vague and unprecedented title of Minister of State, Beaverbrook reappeared at the Ministry of Supply, where he was expected to do for tanks what he had done for Spitfires. He was the third Minister of Supply to serve in the "great coalition"; Morrison had been succeeded by Sir Andrew Duncan, yet another man brought into the Government from business, an affable monopolist, formerly chairman of the Iron and Steel Federation.

The fact that the story of British tank production had been a sorry one had little to do with the shortcomings of ministers or the malpractices of industry. In fact, although tanks were not given top priority status until July 1941, production was then running at more than four times the rate of the spring of 1940. The trouble with British tanks, as Rommel had had little difficulty in showing, was technical rather than numerical, and this reflected the lack of interest which the army had shown in tanks between the wars; under fifteen hundred had been produced in the four years 1936–39. The engines were not strong enough to carry the armour, and until well into 1942, the guns were too light. The historian of one famous car firm (Vauxhall) which had been enlisted to produce tanks reveals that, because the Government insisted that production must be pushed forward at all costs, machines were sent out to the Middle East which the manufacturers knew to be faulty.[72]

The indubitably bad feeling which existed in industry in 1941 was only parfly reflected in an increase in strikes. In 1940, thanks to Dunkirk, only 941,000 man-days had been lost to industry through strikes, as compared with 1,354,000 in 1939. In 1941 the figure was back to 1,077,000, though it was not until 1942 that the pre-war total was actually exceeded. It would be quite wrong to suppose that, confronted with a common enemy, management and workers had buried their hatchets. A Mass Observation report from a group of war factories in the north stressed that "The most striking feature of the industrial situation here is the survival of strictly peacetime procedure in the conflict between employers and men, which is still today the predominant conflict here."[73]

The First World War had been followed by a slump; almost everyone, in spite of J. M. Keynes, believed that the Second must end in a repetition. Mass Observation found that about two-thirds of all workers, middle and working class alike, were worried about the prospects for post-war employment in their own district. Both trade unionists and management feared that concessions made now would leave them at a disadvantage in the post-war depression. Workers who resisted dilution or refused to scrap restrictive practices were certainly contributing to the inefficiency of war industry, but the 'twenties and 'thirties had made such attitudes very hard to break down. In 1942, Bevin pushed through an Act which guaranteed the return of pre-war "trade practices", but this was just a promise; there had been many promises in 1918.

Meanwhile, when the inefficiency of war industry was raised, the various sections of industry fell back on recrimination. Large employers blamed the Government, especially the Ministry of Supply. Smaller employers, who found it hard to get the labour they wanted, blamed the Ministry of Labour, the trade unions, the big firms. Lower grade managerial personnel added the incompetence and self-interest of managing directors to the list of culprits, and accused the workers of lack of spirit. Skilled workers, who would lose overtime pay when production halted awhile, blamed Cost Plus, the capitalist system, the management, and even the Labour leaders in the Government. Mass Observation found that half the male population of Britain seemed to think war industry was "inefficient". A sizeable minority felt that workers' wages were too high, but far more people thought that the employers were taking excessive profits. Many people hankered for a "standard wage" policy, but an equally strong tide of opinion favoured the nationalization of war industry.[74]

VIII

At four o'clock on the morning of June 22nd, the Germans attacked Russia. Hitler's armies swept towards Leningrad, towards Moscow, and towards the third industrial centre of Russia in the Donetz basin. In twenty-four hours, they took ten thousand prisoners, destroyed perhaps twelve hundred Russian aircraft, and advanced up to fifty miles. Most of the War Office experts gave Russia no more than two weeks or ten days. Churchill himself had drawn most forcibly of all British spokesmen what had seemed the obvious moral from the Finnish war of 1939–40. The Finns, he had said at the time, had "exposed, for all the world to see, the military incapacity of the Red Army and of the Red Air Force . . . Everyone can see how communism rots the soul of a nation . . ."[75]

But Churchill had remarked, only the day before the German attack, "If Hitler invaded Hell I would make at least a favourable reference to the Devil in the House of Commons." As soon as he heard the news, he decided to broadcast that night, and spent the whole day preparing his speech. It was a brave performance. "The Nazi regime", he told the world at nine o'clock, "is indistinguishable from the worst features of communism . . . No one has been a more consistent opponent of communism than I have for the last twenty-five years. I will unsay no word that I have spoken about it." But now he summoned his unsurpassed capacity for nebulous generalization to his aid. "The past with its crimes, its follies and its tragedies, flashes away . . . I see the ten thousand villages of Russia, where the means of existence was wrung so hardly from the soil, but where there are still primordial human joys, where maidens laugh and children play . . . The cause of any Russian fighting for his hearth and home is the cause of free men and free peoples in every quarter of the globe."[76]

This went down a good deal better than some of Churchill's recent broadcasts had done. A naïve admiration for Russia as a workers' state had persisted in spite of everything among the British working class. But public opinion in Britain was thoroughly surprised by the attack, and the first reaction was somewhat divided. Approaching half of a Mass Observation sample were glad that the attack had taken place, giving such obvious reasons as the rest it would give to Britain, the losses it was sure to cause the Germans, the adherence (at last) of a powerful ally, and the sheer relief from the monotonous series of petty defeats. A few people liked the idea that the two dictatorships would destroy each other. But there was commonly strong sadness, especially among women, at the idea that more people would now be bombed and blitzed – "They'll be fighting in heaven presently," someone said, unaware, of course, of Churchill's very different expression. Only a small minority expected Russia to win.[77]

The Germans at first continued to make spectacular progress. But it soon became clear that the Russians were fighting back with a hitherto unknown savagery. On July 3rd, Stalin broke an ominous silence and broadcast to the Russian masses, announcing the "scorched earth" policy which appalled yet captured the British imagination, and calling for the formation of partisan groups behind the German lines.

Interest in war news quickened. As often happens, the recoil of public opinion from its belief that the Russians were poor fighters, took it swiftly to the opposite extreme, so that every sign of resistance was greeted like a major offensive. And people began to feel shamefaced that Russia was pouring out her life blood while Britain, except on her east coast, enjoyed a respite from bombing. Guilt mingled with relief and with something more like optimism than any sentiment since the time of Dunkirk. It was at this time that the B.B.C.'s celebrated "V for Victory" campaign, designed to encourage resistance to Hitler in Europe, was taken up spontaneously by the British public. In many parts of the country, one could not go a hundred yards without seeing a defiant "V" sign chalked or painted on a wall. Mass Observation called it "the biggest citizen war reaction since 'Pots to Planes' and the L.D.V. recruiting".[78]

The Communist Party, driven underground to some extent by the suppression of the *Worker*, had set up a "front" news agency, which had busily supplied the press with "inefficiency" stories of the sort which the *Worker* would have carried. This had achieved a notable "scoop" when the undergraduate daughter of Margesson, the War Minister, emerged in public as a supporter of the People's Convention. The Convention had continued to burrow, and in mid-June, ironically, achieved a great success when the National Committee of the A.E.U., in spite of the denunciations of the union's executive, passed a motion adopting the call for a "people's peace" and a "people's government"[79]

Then, literally overnight, everything changed. The C.P. switched its line at once to full-blooded support for the war. The Convention followed suit and soon began to clamour for a "Second Front" in Europe. In this, it was shortly joined by Beaverbrook's *Daily Express*. By mid-August, *The Times* itself was declaring, "Russia has astonished the world, and particularly the enemy, by her resistance . . . We cannot afford to neglect anything which may help Russia . . ." "The favourite quip now", wrote George Orwell about the same time, "is that we are giving Russia all aid short of war."[80]

Stalin was calling for all possible help – especially aluminium, planes, tanks and a second front. Beaverbrook, who had long been suspicious of American intentions with regard to the British Empire, embraced this alternative ally with importunate fervour, and made himself the spokesman for Russian demands in the War Cabinet. By the end of September, four hundred and fifty aircraft, twenty-two thousand tons of rubber, three million pairs of boots and large stocks of raw materials had been sent east, and British ships were sailing the dangerous Arctic supply route to Archangel.[81]

On September 22nd, "Tanks for Russia" week began in British factories. Workers were told that everything they produced until the 29th would go to the eastern front. Beaverbrook launched an appeal – "Come then, in the foundries and forges of Britain, in the engine works and the assembly lines, to the task and duty of helping Russia to repel the savage invaders, who bring torment and torture to mankind." There was also a personal appeal from M. Maisky, the long-serving Russian ambassador, an Anglophile who had maintained the friendship and respect of many British politicians even through the period of the Finnish war and who had once been accorded a warm ovation on an unannounced visit to a big shelter in Stepney. At a midlands factory on the 22nd, Maisky's wife named the first tank for Russia to leave the assembly line, "Stalin". On other tanks around, the workers had chalked such unofficial titles as "Marx", "Lenin" and "Another for Joe".[82]

It was reported that in one factory where labour relations were unusually bad, a big order from the Soviet Union transformed them overnight; the job cards were stamped "GOODS FOR RUSSIA" and the trick was done. A railways works in Kent finished an order of a thousand freight waggons for Russia in less than ten weeks, in spite of seventy-six air raid warnings. Russian flags and slogans decorated the shop, and, as a far from left-wing journalist records, "If for a single moment a single man seemed to be taking life easily he was urged on by his fellows with 'Come on! old Joe wants that one.' All worked double shifts night and day, and produced double the usual output in each shift."[83]

But where work continued on British orders, the effect of the "Russian glory" was to exacerbate rather than to soften friction in industry; which now seemed to be letting down Uncle Joe as well as the boys in the Middle East. The Communist-controlled Shop Stewards' National Council held a mass meeting in London in October where delegates recounted case after case of "inefficiency"; this triggered off a new spate of such stories in the press. Further credence was lent to such stories in the New Year, when the leader of a delegation of Russian trade unionists which had visited British war factories accused "certain factories" of deliberately restricting production.[84]

Sir Walter Citrine, who had so loudly denounced Russian aggression in Finland, and now found himself establishing friendly relations with the "trade unions" of Russia, was only one of innumerable dignitaries who ate their words. General Sir Hubert Gough had written during the phoney war period that he was sure that Britain must sooner or later fight Russia, perhaps even in alliance with Germany. Some twenty-six months later, he was on his feet asking a packed meeting, "Where do you think we should have been today had it not been for the Russian Army?" In that first winter of Russian fever, the august Athenaeum elected Maisky to its membership. Ladies who had knitted comforts for the Gallant Finns now made them for the Gallant Russians. Mrs Churchill issued an appeal for Aid to Russia, and eight million pounds were eventually subscribed to her fund.[85]

There was, however, a notably ludicrous occasion where, at a football match in aid of Mrs Churchill's fund, at which Russian representatives were present, every national anthem of the allied nations was played except the *Internationale*. The B.B.C. had, from the first, refused to play the *Internationale* alongside the anthems of the Czechs, Dutch and so on which preceded the nine o'clock news on Sunday evening. After much angry comment, it compromised with a Soviet military march; until the Ministry of Information had declared there were too many anthems now anyway and had stopped the practice altogether.[86]

And some "premature anti-Communists" refrained from joining the general cries of admiration. One Conservative M.P. publicly remarked, late in July, "It is best for us that our two chief

enemies should seek to destroy one another." The new Minister
of Aircraft Production, Moore Brabazon, was foolish enough to
say such things at a private meeting when trade unionists were
present, and was angrily denounced by the president of the
A.E.U. at the Trades Union Congress in September.[87] There was
renewed talk of "Men of Munich" in high places.

Meanwhile, such unlikely Russian place-names as Velikiye
Luki were haltingly pronounced in buses and pubs as the Ger-
mans continued to advance towards Moscow. The onset of the
Russian winter held them up. On December 2nd, one German
division reached the outer ring of the Soviet capital's last ditch
defences. But their supply lines were stretched to the limit, the
Russians were fighting back strongly, and when the year ended
Moscow was intact and it was already tempting to compare
Hitler's rash venture with Napoleon's.

There were no glorious feats of British arms to match the
starry-eyed accounts of what was happening in Russia, but in the
second half of 1941, the Battle of the Atlantic was going Britain's
way, not least because the U.S.A., ostensibly in self-defence, was
increasingly drawn into it. On August 12th, Churchill met Roosevelt for the first time at Placentia Bay off Newfoundland. Together, they agreed on the so-called Atlantic Charter – technically
nothing more than a press release, but providing at last a joint
statement of war aims. The Charter's eight points were replete
with high principles. Britain and the U.S. had no aims of territorial aggrandizement for themselves; all peoples had the right
to choose their own form of government, and the Anglo-Saxon
nations wanted others to have access on equal terms to trade and
raw materials. (Though an added phrase tacitly entitled Britain
to maintain its Ottawa agreement with the Commonwealth
countries.) Churchill and Roosevelt wanted all nations to collaborate in the economic field, "with the object of securing for all
improved labour standards, economic advancement, and social
security". Peace should bring "freedom from fear and want", and
disarmament of the aggressors, pending "the establishment of a
wider and more permanent system of general security . . ."[88]

The charter at first somewhat disarmed those in Britain who
had called for "positive war aims". But its impact on public
opinion was little greater than its effect on the course of world
events, which was negligible. The two leaders had omitted any
mention of the two areas of social reform which most keenly
interested the British working class; homes and jobs. Even the
reference to social security only appeared at the insistence of the

British War Cabinet, prompted by Ernest Bevin, and Bevin's suggestion that full employment should become a war aim was ignored.[89]

On Sunday, December 7th, the Japanese air force struck at the U.S. Navy where it lay at anchor in Pearl Harbour, Hawaii. American power in the Pacific was gravely weakened. Japanese forces moved against the Americans in the Philippines and against the British possessions of Hong Kong, Malaya and Burma. Though Japanese aggression had long been expected, the initial surprise was more perfect than any which Hitler had achieved. Britain at once declared war on Japan. Germany and Italy, on December 11th, declared war on the United States in support of their Japanese ally.

For Churchill, this was a moment of vindication and exhilaration. "So we had won after all! . . . England would live; Britain would live; the Commonwealth of Nations and the Empire would live . . . We might not even have to die as individuals. Hitler's fate was sealed. Mussolini's fate was sealed. As for the Japanese, they would be ground to powder. All the rest was merely the proper application of overwhelming force."[90]

Yet the months which followed this windfall were, for Churchill and his subjects, the most dismal of the war.

THE END OF THE BEGINNING

My diary for 1942 has the same backcloth to every scene: Winston's conviction that his life as Prime Minister could be saved only by a victory in the field.

Lord Moran, Churchill's physician[1]

I

Two of the biggest and best ships of the Royal Navy, the *Prince of Wales* and the *Repulse*, under the command of Admiral Tom Phillips, had been sent east to deter Japanese aggression. On the 10th came the news that Japanese aircraft, in little more than two hours, had sunk both ships off Malaya. Phillips, with six hundred men, had been drowned.

Robert Bruce Lockhart, the Director General of Political Warfare, has described the scene in the club where he went to lunch that day. "There were drinks on the tables, but gloom on every face. Officers spoke in low tones. The atmosphere was heavy with the dead weight of tradition. Military defeats are the initial fate of the English in almost every war and can be borne with stoical courage. A disaster to the navy is unthinkable and unbearable." With his statement to the Commons next day, Churchill did nothing to dissolve the gloom. "In my whole experience", he said, "I do not remember any naval blow so heavy or so painful . . ."[2]

The loss helped to ensure that the entry of the U.S.A. into the war left the British public more or less cold. Rational calculation assured them that it was a good thing. But there was much scorn expressed that America should have let herself be caught napping by the Japanese, and it was common to hear people say that it "served the Yanks right" for not coming fully into the war long before. "We simply can't be beaten with America in," Harold Nicolson wrote to his wife. "But how strange it is that this great event should be recorded and welcomed here without any jubilation . . . Not an American flag flying in the whole of London."[3]

And Pearl Harbour opened a new cycle of disasters. The U-boats could now take advantage of American waters and shipping losses were soon worse than ever. In 1942, imports fell to under twenty-five million tons. While MacArthur conducted a dogged American rearguard action in the Philippines, the British retreated less gloriously in Malaya, which had been invaded on December 8th. Hong Kong was besieged, and, on Christmas Day, the British garrison surrendered. Churchill now sent reinforcements to the Far East, under pressure from a truculent Australian Government. It was believed that, come what might, Singapore could be held.

The diversion of troops and aircraft to South-east Asia, coupled with serious naval losses in the Mediterranean, weakened Auchinleck's position in North Africa. In mid-November, he had commenced an offensive which had driven Rommel's Axis troops from the whole of Cyrenaica, with the loss of roughly one-third of their strength. But in January, the resourceful Rommel struck back, and recaptured Benghazi. That keen student of the British press, Dr Goebebels, noted with amusement that "By way of providing a good excuse" Rommel was "praised beyond measure".[4]

On December 12th, Churchill had left for America, where he remained for five weeks. In the long run, the war had been taken out of his hands. The U.S.A., with its enormous resources in men, factories and materials, was bound to be the dominant partner. The end of 1941 was the moment of truth for Britain; she could no longer imagine herself the supreme world power, and the empire on which her pretensions had been based was now, in the Far East, visibly on the road to ruin. But neither a German nor a Russian victory in Europe would commend itself to the U.S.A. It was agreed that victory in Europe should have priority, and the Americans found themselves committed to Churchill's somewhat personal war in the Mediterranean.

Churchill, having got more or less what he wanted, returned to confront a political storm at home. The latest reverses had brought his critics to the fore. How, it was asked, could one man combine the duties of Prime Minister and Minister of Defence? The War Cabinet, which had long since swollen to nine, was correctly regarded as something of a sham; surely, it was argued, what was needed was a smaller body of men without heavy administrative duties, such as Lloyd George had had in the First World War. There were also new demands for a Ministry of Production. On January 1st and 2nd, Sir William Beveridge had contributed two powerfully argued anonymous articles to *The Times* putting the case for "a supreme informed body to plan and control production". Such a ministry would also rob Churchill of power. His critics usually spoke as if no central authority was co-ordinating the work of the three supply departments. In fact there was such an authority, in the supply meetings of the Defence Committee of the War Cabinet. Churchill, as Minister of Defence, presided over and dominated its proceedings, while Ernest Bevin, the chairman of the Production Executive, was not even present. Churchill derived his economic ideas chiefly from Lindemann and his Statistical Section. It was the "Defence Committee (Supply)" or, more exactly, Churchill and the "Prof", who in effect settled the distribution of resources by directives which went straight to the supply ministers, by-passing the Production Executive.[5]

Churchill had previously challenged the Government's critics in the House of Commons in May 1941 and had been given a vote of confidence by 477 to 3. He now determined to crush opposition again in like manner. The debate took place on January 27th–29th. Churchill insisted that parliament must make it clear, to Roosevelt, to Stalin and the whole world, that he spoke for opinion in Britain. Since returning from the U.S.A., he reported, he had "had anxious inquiries from a dozen countries, and reports of enemy propaganda in a score of countries, all turning upon the point whether His Majesty's present Government is to be dismissed from power or not."

The tone of the debate was, in Churchill's words, "unexpectedly friendly". Winding it up, he deliberately taunted his opponents in order that a division might be forced and the scale of his support numerically demonstrated. But he also conceded that there should be a Minister of Production, advancing as a reason, not the arguments usually proffered, but the consideration that Donald Nelson, of the U.S. War Production Board, must have a counterpart empowered to discuss with him on behalf of the whole of British war industry. ". . . I offer no apologies, I offer no excuses, I make no promises," he concluded. The three I.L.P. members forced a division; since two of them had to act as tellers, the majority was 464 to 1. Roosevelt sent warm congratulations. For the moment, the Great Man's position seemed as secure as ever.[6]

II

By July 1941, the shortage of manpower was clearly becoming general. In that month, the War Cabinet asked the Ministry of Labour to furnish a fresh survey of manpower resources and of the demands upon it. This was completed in October. It showed that no less than two million men and women were required for the forces and the munitions industries by the following June. When the manpower budget was added up, there was a deficit of over three hundred thousand. Even before the report went up to the War Cabinet, the situation had been made still tighter by Churchill's decision in September that the bomber programme must be increased to an extent which would eventually imply eight hundred and fifty thousand extra workers.

It fell to Anderson's Lord President's Committee to find ways of squaring the vicious circle. Anderson and Bevin agreed on draconian new measures. Call-up should be extended downwards to eighteen-year-olds and upwards to men aged fifty-one. All "block reservations" for the reserved occupations were scrapped. Instead, individual deferments would be introduced for key workers and each case would be judged on its own merits. All people, of both sexes, from girls of eighteen to old men and women of sixty, would be obliged to undertake some form of "national service", so freeing able-bodied men from Civil Defence and other essential tasks. Most momentously of all, women were to be conscripted, for the first time in any civilized nation.[7]

This last stroke was accepted by the War Cabinet only after much heart-searching and over the resistance of Churchill himself. But there was no alternative. As Churchill himself has put it, faced with the competing demands of the various arms of the services, not to speak of those of industry, he "was like a keeper in the zoo distributing half-rations among magnificent animals". Bevin, that other great egoist, still defended his faith in voluntaryism, while preparing the public for the news. In a speech at Stoke in October, he said, "Now things are getting tight. I have to take some more steps in order effectively to distribute this population . . . It was no good doing it before. What was the good of my going to this length when the factories were not built, when I had no place to put the people? . . . Now the time has come when we have to have national service on a more intense scale. I still want to do as much as I can by leadership, but the compulsion will become stricter."[8]

When the conscription of women was announced, along with the other new measures, on December 2nd, 1941, the cry in the press and parliament was chiefly, why had it not come before, rather than why had it come at all. Voluntary appeals to women had clearly failed, most grievously in the case of the women's services, which had a bad reputation for impropriety. But they had failed because women themselves were reluctant, hesitant, or, in their own opinions, busy enough already. One typist wrote, "I can lay my hand on my heart and say truthfully that I have not yet met a woman in the twenties who is not in *an awful state* about conscription . . ."[9]

However, the form which conscription of women took in the National Service (No. 2) Act which became law on December 18th banished the idea of grandmothers firing machine guns which the phrase conjured up. Only unmarried women between the ages of twenty and thirty were to be called up. (The nineteen-year-olds were brought in early next year.) They would all have a choice between the auxiliary services and important jobs in industry. Those who opted for the former would not be posted to "combatant duties" unless they volunteered for them. In any case, the tasks of A.T.S. and W.A.A.F.s were clerical and culinary rather than Amazonian, though the use of women at A.A. batteries was becoming a commonplace.

With this formula, the Act gained general acceptance. Ninety-seven per cent of women, so the Wartime Social Survey found, agreed "emphatically" that women should undertake war work. Some men were privately, or even publicly, very glad of the extra money which women pushed into industry now brought into the home. J. T. Murphy reported from his London factory, "Many times have I heard older men say: 'I wish to hell my old woman wasn't above the age limit.'"[10]

The compulsion now thoroughly introduced into Civil Defence and Home Guard duties caused great resentment among the gallant volunteers of 1940. Bevin was empowered to direct men and women to take up part-time duties in the police, the Fire Guard or Civil Defence, and all part-timers, old and new, were to be "frozen", though those who had volunteered were given the right to resign if they did so within a fortnight. (This could only be a gesture as those who quit would be liable to direction into the same, or other, part-time work.) This seemed ungracious treatment to some of the heroes of the blitz.[11]

Home Guards were also permitted to leave if they disliked the new compulsion, and many did so, though the forty-eight hours' duty per month which was the maximum they could be compelled to put in fell far short of what the keen man had been accustomed to perform freely. Colonel Josiah Wedgwood who, in his late sixties, had been the first M.P. to volunteer, claimed that through compulsion "The spirit that was intended to defend England would be destroyed." But no amount of idealism could halt its advance, and in February 1942 ,every Home Guard, volunteer or directee, became a "private".[12]

There was, at this time, a resurgence of a notorious folly of the First World War. There was some pressure in the newspapers for the indiscriminate transfer of young men into the armed forces, and an epidemic of "white feathers" caused at least two suicides and forced the Government to develop a badge to identify men exempted from service on medical grounds. In the atmosphere of 1941–42, few mourned the passing of the schedule of reserved occupations, except managers who had already had enough trouble coping with the encroachments of dereservation in 1941.[13]

As the ages for reservation in all jobs were pushed up a year at a time at monthly intervals, District Manpower Boards were set up to consider applications for deferment. The onus for applying for it rested on the employers, though workers had the right to appeal at the time when they were medically examined for the forces. Men in munitions work, or with valuable skills, would in practice be transferred to more important work if their present jobs did not rate deferment. Deferment might be temporary or indefinite, and a man's chances of getting it depended on age. They declined as the war went on. Altogether, in 1942–45, the manpower boards dealt with over five million applications, of which 915,000 were rejected.[14]

The development of the manpower budget did, for the first time, give the Government a really powerful weapon for planning the use of all the nation's resources. In A. J. P. Taylor's words, it showed "conscious recognition for the first time of the socialist doctrine that labour lay at the root of all wealth". Such recognition came only as the bottom of the barrel was being feverishly scraped; at this time, the labour manager at a vital factory was complaining, "Men over sixty and even over seventy. Men taken from non-essential work. Women and girls from all sorts of jobs and from no job at all. Cripples, weak hearts, discharged servicemen, half wits, criminals, all sorts of people so long as they can stand or even sit and turn a handle. These are our material." The sheer shortage of able bodies compelled rethinking and reaction in industry. Bevin wrote to Churchill in April 1942 pointing out that "Further demands for the forces must in the main be met from production . . . Our main reliance must be upon increased efficiency in management to secure the best use of the resources which we have."[15]

The situation was made for Bevin, the man who had swung the T.U.C. over to "Mondism" and co-operation with the bosses. He could force firms to improve wages and conditions, to install canteens and employ personnel managers, by the simple device of threatening to withhold labour. He could favour his friends, the good managers, against his enemies, the bad ones, and make the latter copy the former.

The situation was made, also, for Anderson, who kept the manpower budget under his wing even after he moved on to become Chancellor of the Exchequer at the death of Kingsley Wood in 1943. For by the end of the war, as the official historians put it, "the manpower budgets were the main force in determining every part of the war effort from the numbers of R.A.F. heavy bombers raiding Germany to the size of the clothing ration."[16]

III

However, the man who suddenly emerged as a possible alternative to Churchill in January 1942 was neither Bevin, nor Anderson, but Sir Stafford Cripps.

Cripps was an enigmatic figure. In one aspect, he was the last of the great Victorians, a devout Anglican, the scion of a noble family, wedded to the rigours of service to his fellow men. Yet in another aspect, no British politician of the first rank was so clearly as Cripps the harbinger of a new age. He had followed the course, doubly unusual among men in his class, of passing from public school, not to Oxford or Cambridge, but to London University, and not to read classics or history, but to study science. As a young man in the First World War he had become assistant superintendent of the largest explosives factory in Britain. He had moved on to the law and had become one of the greatest advocates of the age, incomparable in his ability to master and expound a complicated brief. At the age of forty, he had been persuaded, by Herbert Morrison, to join the Labour Party, for the somewhat opportunistic reason that Ramsay Macdonald's Government needed a Solicitor General. When that Government had fallen, Cripps had embraced revolutionary socialism with the fervour of a sixteen-year-old convert.

One may surmise that Churchill had seen a chance of killing two birds with one stone when he had sent Cripps as ambassador to Moscow in May 1940. On the one hand, this had removed an able but extreme politician of the left from the national scene, where he might have caused trouble. On the other, it had been assumed that someone who had got on well with Harry Pollitt might well be the best man to talk to Stalin. The first intention was now more than fulfilled. Cripps had moved sharply rightwards after the outbreak of war and by the time he returned from Moscow, after pleading for some time that he should be relieved, Sir Stafford, while still excommunicated from membership of the Labour Party, was in his opinions more or less on its right-centre.

When he reappeared, on January 23rd, 1942, most of the public had forgotten his calls for revolution and his attacks on the Royal Family. In his drawn, ascetic features, they descried, as they thought, the man who had cemented the Anglo-Soviet alliance, a confidant of Stalin himself. They were wholly deceived. Cripps had had an unhappy time in Moscow, and it had been Lord Beaverbrook who had found a kindred spirit in Uncle Joe. The left had a sudden, wishful glimpse of a revolutionary with sufficient prestige to oppose, and even to replace, Churchill, and banged the drums busily on his return. For everyone, Cripps glittered as a major political figure, the only one, who was not tainted with the hardships and mistakes of the last two years.[17]

Though Churchill was not, on the whole, very sensitive to the personalities of those around him, preferring to find in the human race radiant heroes and jet-black villains rather than men with something of his own complexity, it is clear that Cripps got on his nerves. Cripps was in the most direct antithesis to himself. While he inspired devotion in his assistants, who found him warm and gay, Cripps in public radiated austerity – to such a degree, indeed, that the two had become almost synonymous by the end of that austere decade. (A joke, possibly near the truth, which was current later in the war, had Churchill remarking on his return from the Libyan desert, "There are miles and miles of nothing but arid austerity. How Cripps would like it.") Cripps was a teetotaller and a vegetarian, and somehow it showed. "You can just see the home-made lemonade boiling in his veins," an irreverent observer once remarked when Cripps was in full oratorical flow.[18]

But if Churchill found his sanctimoniousness irritating, he was in no danger, early in 1942, of underestimating either Cripps's talent or his ambition. "The trouble is, his chest is a cage in which two squirrels are at war, his conscience and his career," Churchill once remarked to Stalin.[19] He now strove, eventually with success, to play one squirrel off against the other until conscience triumphed.

As Cripps stood expectantly, vestured in the Russian glory, the press, which was already clamouring for changes in the Government, demanded that he should be given high office. Churchill, on the defensive, put in a low bid and offered him the Ministry of Supply, from which Lord Beaverbrook had been busily attempting to resign. This was on January 25th. A few days later, Cripps replied that the ministry, as organized at present, was not sufficiently powerful, and he must decline. Having thus raised the stake, he "bore himself", in Churchill's words, "as though he had a message to deliver".[20]

It was under "external pressure", as Churchill has admitted, that he now began to rearrange his Government. The fact that America was now in the war, since it made victory probable, had immediately robbed him of the status of "the indispensable man"; this no doubt explains the new vociferousness of his critics. From one angle, such captiousness was unfair; from another, all Churchill's mistakes might now be quite justifiably drawn out of the pack for use against him. "Upon the broad and powerful shoulders of Mr Churchill rests the entire burden of the criticism of the war effort," wrote one of his least deferential subjects, "Cassandra" of the *Daily Mirror*. "Who put it there? None other than Mr Churchill himself." Churchill still had higher support in the opinion polls than Chamberlain had ever had, but in the eight

months from February to October, the proportion who were prepared to express disapproval of him, though only some eight to
fifteen per cent, was at its highest, and Churchill himself was
under no illusion that he had maintained his popularity. In February, when the Gallup pollsters asked people whether they were
satisfied or dissatisfied with the present personnel of the cabinet,
four were dissatisfied for every three who were pleased, and only
one-third actually expressed satisfaction.[21] Churchill could find
scapegoats to discard; but he had, after all, chosen these ministers
and maintained them in office.

On January 14th, Harold Nicolson had attended a small meeting of National Labour M.P.s – an amorphous but significant
band of centrist politicians, some very able. Except for himself,
all had felt that Churchill "must be brought down . . ., yet they
all agree", he had noted in his diary, "(a) that there is no apparent
successor, and (b) that his fall would give an immense moral
shock to the country." A month later, when worse news had intervened, Cecil Beaton, a friend of several Conservative politicians,
wrote ". . . People talk of his faults and ask, 'Who else is there?'
From having had to admit there was nobody they now answer,
'Stafford Cripps.' "[22] Cripps, in fact, had the trumps.

It was soon known that Cripps had refused office. The left
hoped, and others supposed, that this meant that he intended to
take a stand against Churchill. Interest increased. On February
8th, he delivered his message. Speaking at Bristol, he summed up
the burden of many discontents. "There seems to be a lack of
urgency in the atmosphere of this country," he said, comparing
Britain with Russia. "It is almost as if we were spectators rather
than participants. Perhaps I might compare it to the difference
between a keen and enthusiastic supporter of a football team and
one of the members of the team." On the same night, he delivered
a "Postscript" over the radio. "Had our efforts in production
been greater," he said sternly if perhaps inaccurately, "we should
not now be retreating in North Africa." According to Mass
Observation, which went on to make an exhaustive survey of
Cripps's appeal, the effect of the broadcast was "sensational".
Cripps had a higher favourable response – ninety-three per cent –
than Churchill or Priestley at their highest.[23]

The very fact that Cripps's sober delivery contrasted so greatly
with what one respondent called "Churchill's flamboyant
rhetoric", helped to commend him. His voice seemed full of
human sympathy. "The austere lawyer of public imagination
became, after quarter of an hour on the radio, the friendly coun-

sellor of millions of listeners up and down the country." His appeal was strongest of all in the belt of society which included clerks and skilled workers, but it was marked enough among the better-off. Lacking much knowledge of him, except that he had been in Russia, people created an ideal Cripps to suit themselves. He was incorruptible. He was independent of the increasingly discredited political parties. He was immensely intelligent. Each discontented saloon-bar politician could see Cripps doing the great, vague things which he himself thought needed doing. Above all, it seemed there was now a positive lust for self-sacrifice and austerity surging through society. Cripps brought this feeling into the open and expressed it. He was the "new man" of 1942, as Churchill had been of 1940.[24]

Meanwhile, the decision to create a Ministry of Production gave Churchill an opportunity to rearrange his cabinet. When Beaverbrook's appointment to the new ministry was announced on February 4th, it was accorded a very mixed reception. Frictions between Beaverbrook and Bevin had recently reached a pitch where the former had refused to attend cabinet meetings at which Bevin was due to be present. When a White Paper describing the functions of the new ministry was presented to parliament on the 10th, after a week of heated argument in the War Cabinet, Hore Belisha and Shinwell at once leapt to their feet to ask why manpower had been excluded from its province. Beaverbrook himself defined it pretty accurately, as a "foreign office of supply". It inherited the effects, such as they were, of the old Production Executive. The three supply ministers retained the right to appeal over the Minister of Production's head to Churchill and the War Cabinet. Bevin, now the "indispensable man" in his own field, was to have equal status with the new minister.[25]

On the 12th came a new naval disaster. Hitler had ordered that the battleships, *Scharnhorst* and *Gneisenau*, should leave their hideout at Brest and re-enter the North Sea in case the British decided to land forces in Norway. In a cunning and daring operation, they slipped through the British defences and steamed up the Channel with a powerful escort. The navy and the R.A.F. were taken by surprise and in a vain attempt to sink the German ships, some two score aircraft were lost. For many in Britain this humiliation, which reawakened fears of invasion, exceeded even the sickening blow which followed.

Churchill had promised, as the Japanese continued their advance in Malaya, that Singapore would be defended "to the last inch". But after the remaining British and Dominion troops had fallen back on the island, it proved impossible to hold. On February 15th General Percival surrendered, and eight thousand troops went into captivity, in what Churchill himself calls "the worst disaster and largest capitulation in British history".[26]

He had ostentatiously shouldered responsibility for the decisions which had led to this disaster, yet he was so ill-informed that, two months later, he was still unable to explain it to the House of Commons. The blow seemed enough to undermine all faith in the British Empire itself. Churchill, and others, unconvinced that lack of air support and shortage of supplies could by themselves have produced this abject surrender, concluded that the present British soldiery could not be the men their fathers had been. They had lost Malaya without fighting a major battle, in disturbing contrast to MacArthur's Americans in the Philippines. Months afterwards, Lord Moran was present when Churchill suddenly stopped drying himself after a bath, gloomily surveyed the floor, and remarked sadly, "I cannot get over Singapore."[27]

On the night of that Sunday, February 15th, he broadcast to the people. This, he suggested, was "one of those moments" when "the British race and nation" could "draw from the heart of misfortune the vital impulses of victory". But the rhetoric of Dunkirk was impotent now. Bishop Henson, no coward soul, confided to his diary that he had found the speech "both in tone and in substance depressing . . . Beyond stating that Singapore had fallen, he told us nothing of that immense failure, and, throughout his speech, his voice and manner suggested a depression and even dismay, very unlike his accustomed buoyancy of carriage".[28]

When the Commons assembled on the 17th, Churchill was involved in angry exchanges and accused its members of being "in a mood of panic". But he assured them that he did not wish to stifle criticism, and a debate was arranged for a week later.[29]

Meanwhile, he finalized the cabinet changes which had so long been demanded. Cripps was offered, and accepted, the offices of Leader of the House of Commons and Lord Privy Seal (the latter an honorific post of which, it was said, the only thing certainly known was that its holder was neither a Lord, nor a Privy, nor a Seal). With them went a seat in the War Cabinet, for which Cripps sacrificed the more dubious glories of opposition. The War Cabinet was reduced from nine to seven by the removal of Sir Kingsley Wood, who remained Chancellor, and of Greenwood, who now left the Government altogether to become acting leader of the Labour Party in the Commons (a position hitherto filled by ageing nonentities). But this abbreviation was more apparent than real, and in any case did not create the cabinet of three or four overlords which some critics, including Beaverbrook, had wanted.

Meanwhile, Beaverbrook himself was suffering an obscure personal crisis. This has been variously ascribed to trepidation that he would fail as Minister of Production, which is held on the medical authority of Lord Moran to explain the asthma from which he suffered greatly at this time; to a conviction that Churchill must fall and that he, Max Aitken, might replace him (a fantasy which the Prime Minister, in a moment of sentimental gloom, seems to have encouraged); and, by Churchill himself, his patient friend, to a "nervous breakdown". Possibly all three combined when on February 19th, the day on which Churchill made the changes public, Beaverbrook, after a renewed wrangle about his powers, protested that his views were being ignored, flounced out of a meeting and resigned. Oliver Lyttleton, who had gone to Cairo as Minister of State, was hastily recalled to replace him as Minister of Production.[30]

So the new War Cabinet consisted, besides Churchill, of Attlee, Cripps and Bevin to the left, and Anderson, Lyttelton and Eden to the right. Only the first and last of these were orthodox party men, a fact which perhaps enhanced the almost unanimous delight with which the public greeted the arrival of Cripps in high office. The last surviving "Man of Munich", Kingsley Wood, had superficially been demoted, and when lesser changes were announced on the 22nd, there was added joy in the dismissal of Margesson, who had been branded in *Guilty Men* as one of the arch villains of appeasement, and Moore Brabazon, most unpopular since his indiscretion over Russia.[31] The former was replaced at the War Office, in yet another unorthodox appointment, by his Permanent Under Secretary, Sir James Grigg, a right-wing civil servant who soon made a forceful, if mixed, impression by his truculence in the House of Commons. Among four other important changes Hugh Dalton went from Economic Warfare to the Board of Trade.

So the promised debate on the fall of Singapore on February 24th took place in an atmosphere of relief and anti-climax. Cripps made his first speech as cabinet minister in the House of Commons on the 25th. He condemned "personal extravagances" and prepared the way for new measures of austerity – there would be no petrol for "pleasure motoring", the clothes ration would be cut, sporting events would be curtailed. Odd though it seems now, this was given exceptional acclaim by the press and the general public. It appeared that people craved such stern leadership. Appeals for voluntary restraint were bound to fail; if people saw others still taking trains to go on holiday or wasting their petrol ration on a long drive to a race-meeting, they would follow suit themselves. One observer summed up the popular attitude as being "Tell us to cut our throats, for goodness' sake, and we'll cut them; but not until you tell us to." Thus, Mass Observation found, seven people had favoured clothes rationing when it was introduced for every one who had voiced the slightest objection. Even when the new National Service Act had been introduced in December, the ratio had been three to one in favour. When a minor matter like sweet rationing was in question, the ratio was nineteen to one. As for large-scale property, which few possessed, the ratio was ten to one in favour of Government ownership of "essential" industries, seven to one in favour of the nationalization of coal.[32]

IV

In 1942, austerity, after further steep climbing, reached a plateau. Food imports were running at less than half their pre-war level, and the Japanese conquests in the Far East cut off Britain's normal sources for large proportions of her rice, sugar, tea and so on, quite apart from rubber, tin and other important raw materials.

The points rationing principle had been extended, in November 1941, to cover a group of canned foods – meat, fish and vegetables. Each consumer was given sixteen points for four weeks. This was a long overdue measure, prompted by much public criticism of the unfair distribution of unrationed foods, and it was at once extremely popular. People knew that the well-to-do could no longer corner all the tinned salmon, for instance, by paying fancy prices. In January, dried fruit, rice, sago, tapioca and pulses were added; in February, canned fruit, tomatoes and peas; in April, condensed milk and breakfast cereals; in July, syrup and treacle; in August, biscuits and finally, in December, oatflakes and rolled oats.

There were two further extensions of rationing in 1942, the last of the war. In the grimness of February, soap was brought on ration at sixteen ounces for every four weeks. In July, a "personal points" scheme for chocolate and sweets began, at eight ounces per four weeks, raised to twelve in October. Meanwhile, the basic civilian petrol ration was extinguished in March, though supplementary rations still went to those who needed cars for their work. The fate of the private motorists can be judged from the total quantities of petrol which they were allowed to consume; in 1940, 823,000 tons; in 1942, 473,000 tons; in 1943, 301,000.

The Government never rationed beer or tobacco, the other major male self-indulgences, though both were often in short or non-existent supply. Beer was copiously diluted, so that while the consumption of pints and half pints rose, the alcohol taken in from them actually fell. It had also soared in price, thanks to the attentions of Kingsley Wood and his predecessor. In 1939, the excise duty on a barrel of beer had been twenty-four shillings; in the second half of the war it stood around seven pounds.[33]

Nor was bread rationed, until after the war, though the Government toyed with the idea in August 1942. The extraction rate of wheat had been raised from its pre-war figure of seventy per cent to seventy-six per cent, but until mid-1942 bread which was more or less white could still be bought, although about a seventh of the nation's flour milling capacity had been destroyed in the blitz. The Ministry of Food had made unsuccessful attempts to popularize a "National Wheatmeal Loaf" made from flour of eighty-five per cent extraction, but this accounted for only one-twentieth of consumption. In March 1942, the shipping situation made white bread an impossible luxury. Eighty-five per cent became the extraction rate for all flour, and within a few months the War Cabinet was considering raising this to ninety or even ninety-five per cent. Oliver Lyttleton records that when the matter was discussed, at a meeting when Attlee was in the chair, Ernest Bevin interjected, " 'I say, Deputy Prime Minister, that the loaf is indigestible. I can't digest this stuff in the middle. I throw it away: it's just waste.' At this point he belched undisguisedly. 'There you are, you see. What did I tell you?' "[34]

The public, by and large, shared his distaste; only about one person in seven actually preferred National Wheatmeal to white bread. The Ministry of Food was deluged with protests. A report on trends in letters which was circulated within the ministry noted, "For a few weeks people indignantly ascribed every minor ailment or malaise from which they suffered to 'this nasty, dirty, dark, coarse, indigestible bread'. The more ingenious found out how to sieve it – through old silk stockings – and one lady wrote triumphantly, but anonymously, 'I got all your vitamins out and gave them to the pigs.' "[35]

But such initiative was sternly discouraged by the ministry's anti-waste campaigns, which produced such items in the newspapers as this:

Bread Wasted

Miss Mary Bridget O'Sullivan, Normandy Avenue, Barnet, Herts, was fined a total of ten pounds, with two guineas costs, at Barnet today for permitting bread to be wasted. Her servant, Miss Domenica Rosa Persi, was fined five shillings for wasting the bread.

It was stated that the servant was twice seen throwing bread to birds in the garden, and when Miss O'Sullivan was interviewed she admitted that bread was put out every day. "I cannot see the birds starve," she said.[36]

By now, the diet had reached a dreary equilibrium. There was plenty of food; at least, there was plenty of bulk. The potato – "that puckish vegetable", Sir William Beveridge had called it – was, like the universal grey loaf, unrationed. "Potatoes are available for everyone", enthused the *Manchester Guardian*'s cooking correspondent, "and what unsuspected uses they have! . . . Baked or fried or steamed, they accompany our exiguous scraps of meat." Her examples, alas, were all too predictable. "A dish of leeks and potatoes, covered with cheese sauce, pleased a rather fastidious luncheon party last week . . . Tea, a more important meal when lunch is so slight an affair, is enlivened by potato scones."[37]

Manufactured foods were poorer in quality and restricted in variety. For instance, the number of types of biscuit which any one manufacturer could produce was reduced from as many as three hundred and fifty to only twenty. (*my* PEACE TERMS, sighed the smiling woman in the advertisement, "A new type of Government for Germany . . . A fresh set of chair covers . . . and back to fresh butter, cream cheese and Crawford's Cream Crackers.") Technical palm oil was found to be edible and was used instead of whale oil in the standardized national margarine. The use of milk in the manufacture of chocolate and ice cream was prohibited.[38]

Shortages of any and every type of article were now commonplace. In spite of their increased usefulness now that petrol was non-existent, the number of new bicycles available was only a third of pre-war production. Railwaymen and other workers who had to be up early suffered from the virtual disappearance of alarm clocks; it was now almost impossible to get old clocks repaired, since men skilled in such work would probably now be employing their talents in the aircraft industry.

As early as March 1941, the following notice had been seen on the door of a chemist's shop in Southampton:

WE REGRET WE ARE UNABLE TO SUPPLY

Vacuum flasks
Saccharines
Lipsticks
Rouges
All tubes of vanishing cream
All barley sugar sweets
Rolls razors
     ”   ” blades
Gillette ”   ”
7 o'clock razor blades
Brushless shaving cream
Nivea cream

UNTIL NOTICE REMOVED

The shortage of razor blades was a common complaint; the forces' insistence on a high standard of shaving was one of its causes. In August 1942, A. P. Herbert, in his capacity of *Punch* humorist, indited,

> I see a day, before we win this war,
> When razors – and cosmetics – are no more;
> When whiskered bishops will unite in joy
> The paintless maiden and the bearded boy.

The Board of Trade, however, was fighting stoutly to maintain a supply of cosmetics, which it deemed essential to the preservation of female morale.[39]

The bishops, though not yet whiskered, had special problems of their own. In June 1942, the new Archbishop of Canterbury, William Temple, wrote to the new President of the Board of Trade, Hugh Dalton, to complain that a small firm which supplied "nearly all the church furnishing houses" had had their quota of textiles cut from half to one-third of pre-war supplies. A grave shortage of hassocks was likely. "... Kneelers", he warned, "will be almost unobtainable to the great inconvenience of men in the forces in whose temporary chapels or churches

these are almost the only supply of comfort." Dalton was helpful;
perhaps expecting a *quid pro quo*, he wrote to Temple a couple of
months later to ask if the Archbishop would announce that
women, without impropriety, might come hatless and stocking-
less to church. Temple obliged. After all, he observed, St Paul had
specified "veils".[40]

The jovial, booming-voiced Dalton (who looked much like a
bishop himself) lacked Cripps's personal frugality, but his actions
at the Board of Trade identified him almost as completely with
Austerity, and with that gloomy dame's brisker brother, Utility.

The clothing industry had suffered from drastic over-applica-
tion of the "concentration" policy in 1941. With a dwindling force
of ageing workers, its resources were insufficient to meet the
clothing ration at its original level. So this was cut, in the spring
of 1942, to a rate of sixty coupons per fifteen months – effectively,
forty-eight coupons per year. At this rate, a man with only the
basic ration could buy one pair of socks every four months, one
pair of shoes every eight months, one shirt every twenty months,
one vest and one pair of pants every two years, one pair of
trousers and one jacket every two years, one waistcoat every five
years, one pullover every five years, and an overcoat every seven
years, leaving about three coupons a year for such odd items as
handkerchiefs. If he were less prudent, he could blue the lot at
once; or employ it to appease his wife, or to seduce his girl.[41]

Meanwhile, quotas imposed on manufacturers under the Limitations of Supplies Orders had never been successful, except in
accelerating the upward rise in prices. Restricted in the quantity
of any one broadly defined type of item which they might produce, manufacturers had tended to devote themselves to the less
essential but higher priced brands. It was to meet this danger that
the Board of Trade, soon after the introduction of clothes rationing, had begun to plan its Utility scheme, which came into force in
1942. Briefly, the object of Utility was to ensure, through stan-
dardization, that the depleted industry could provide enough
clothing at the prices which working-class families could afford.

So-called "Utility clothes" were garments with specified uses
made out to stated Utility cloths. Before the war, there had been
thousands of different cotton cloths. The Board of Trade's
experts selected some hundred of these as Utility cloths, covering
a wide range of uses and qualities. The result was not to lower
standards, but to raise them, since desirable but rare qualities like
crease resistance were generally included for the first time. With

wool cloths, where close specification was harder for technical reasons, the Utility goods were not always so satisfactory.

Colour and design of Utility garments were not specified. Top fashion designers were invited to help popularize the scheme by devising women's clothes suitable for Utility production. All Utility clothes were rigorously controlled in price; and Utility coats for children (for instance) were put on sale beside non-Utility garments of very similar quality, at only three-fifths of the cost. Not surprisingly, such newcomers were warmly welcomed by the public. From May 1942, the Board was empowered to tell manufacturers exactly what to make, and Utility clothing eventually accounted for about four-fifths of all production, though except in a few uncontroversial cases like overalls and sheets, it was never universal.[42]

But Dalton's notorious "Austerity Regulations" of the early summer of 1942 did circumscribe design. Some forbade such trimmings as embroidery and appliqué work; others limited the use of scarce raw materials. Manufacturers were prohibited from producing more than a set number of basic designs for the same type of clothing – six shapes, in the case of female underwear – the object being to encourage long and economical runs in production. The number of pleats, seams and buttonholes in women's outerwear were fixed, and so were the widths of sleeves, hems and collars. For men, trouser turn-ups and double cuffs were prohibited, shirts were shorn of two inches of tail, pockets were limited, and socks must not exceed nine and a half inches.

These apparently petty expedients saved enormous quantities of textiles. But widespread evasion was a clear sign of their unpopularity. Dressmakers used metal studs instead of sequins, or stencilled designs instead of embroidery. It is easier to understand the preference for long socks (which were not permitted again until after the war) than the howls of dismay from men deprived of their turn-ups. It was not hard to persuade a bespoke tailor to make trousers too long, and then turn them up at home. When the obnoxious restrictions on men's outerwear were removed in February 1944, Dalton remarked memorably, "On the whole we have done something to lift the morale of the country – particularly the morale of the men. The morale of women has always been high, but that of the men has been depressed by not having enough pockets."[43]

There was no question of rationing the wide range of other essential consumer goods. When the Government contemplated the introduction of a points system for household linen, bedding and utensils, it was calculated that "After allowing for the special claims of new households, the general ration might be about a penny three farthings a head a week."[44] Rationing was not just a restriction, it was a promise that a fair and useful share would be available for all; if that could not be guaranteed, the devil must still take the hindmost.

But from the autumn of 1941, the Board of Trade licensed all production of "hollow-ware" – kettles, pans, buckets and so on, and gave licences only to those who were prepared to work to Utility specifications. Eventually, production of a very great variety of articles was brought under one form or another of the Utility principle; besides boots and shoes (which were part of the clothing ration), one might instance domestic electrical appliances, carpets, sports gear, lighters, pens, umbrellas and musical instruments. The principle was seen at its simplest in the case of pencils, where from May 1942 only those of a certain size and type might be produced. More pencils were duly made by fewer workers.

Two more famous schemes were those for pottery and furniture. In June 1942, when it was estimated that current supplies might be falling short of minimum needs by at least a hundred million pieces of crockery per year, the production of any domestic pottery outside a narrow range of simple types was prohibited, except for transatlantic export. So plain white cups only were produced, and for a long time, many of these were without handles. Time-consuming floral designs on plates were outlawed.[45]

For those who had always found such designs mainly distasteful, this development had a certain attraction. This was still more true in the case of furniture, where public taste was notoriously poor. From July 1940, the supply of timber for domestic furniture had been cut off, though small quantities had been produced to meet the needs of bombed-out families. (Local authorities lent furniture to the homeless for three months, after which they might either buy or return it.) By 1942, the extreme shortage and the increasing need had encouraged the production of much shoddy furniture made from poor substitutes. Newly weds might buy such stuff, or bid for second-hand furniture at high prices. The trials of those who attempted to set up house in mid-war can be judged from the shifts to which one couple were reduced in London. They converted a broken lawn sprinkler blown over the fence during the blitz into a standard lamp, they purloined a nursery fireguard from a bomb site, and they collected curtain rods, rings and coat hooks, which were now quite unobtainable, by looking, and even digging, in the gardens of empty houses.[46]

From August 1942, the Government prohibited the manufacture of all furniture except for twenty-two articles, each with a prescribed timber content. Two qualities, and usually three designs, were specified for each article. The designs were established by a committee under the chairmanship of an eminent industrial designer; they were simple and serviceable, and although hardboard was used instead of plywood and a matt finish instead of the usual polishes, the Utility pieces at their best made an aesthetic virtue out of austerity. "Priority classes" – newly marrieds, people setting up house because they were about to have children, and bomb victims – were issued with "dockets", which were permits to buy furniture up to the value of a certain number of "units", and each Utility piece was given a units price. The scheme was later extended to cover curtain materials, linoleum, sheets, blankets and mattresses.[47]

In circumstances where such essential household goods were in pitifully short supply, it was inevitable that the summer of 1942 should also see prohibition imposed on the manufacture of "a long list of fripperies", to use the curt expression of the official historians. There were few who regretted the purge of grape scissors and asparagus eaters, which figured somewhat surprisingly in the rogue's gallery of condemned cutlery, along with soup spoons and butter knives. There were more to mourn the proscription of gold, silverware and jewellery, both real and imitation. Also included were practically all leather goods and all glassware except for simple jugs, mugs, tumblers and small mirrors. While billiard tables and fruit machines were good Crippsian targets, there was something wantonly savage in the persecution of toys; all those which included rubber, cork, hemp, kapok, celluloid or plastics derived from cellulose, casein or synthetic resin were summarily outlawed.

The wartime upsurge in the birth rate had been a surprise for the Government (and for many of the mothers). There was a sad and even dangerous shortage of prams, baby baths, teats and fireguards. Babies growing up in wartime might well regard Ministry of Food orange juice as the highest treat to which infancy could aspire, but to older children, the deprivation was more evident – for a birthday party, there were no crackers, no balloons, no paper hats, and perhaps not even an iced cake. The Government relaxed the bans on toys for a period before Christ-

mas in 1942 and 1943, but meanwhile opportunists were making
tawdry ones out of scrap and charging fantastic prices.[48]

Yet of what significance were plastic cars, ornamental glassware, and even white bread, when they were compared to the loss
of life among merchant seamen, thirty thousand, at a low estimate, over the whole war? Only the pettier features of austerity
earned much resentment; the largest of all, rationing, was almost
universally accepted, because it was believed to be fair, and Lord
Woolton remained perhaps the most popular of all Churchill's
ministers. Many people felt that the Britain in which no one
except those who needed it most could buy new furniture was a
more decent and just one than the pre-war nation in which
Jarrow at the bottom, and the Dorchester Hotel at the top, had
been poles apart in every respect.

Yet such social justice as existed depended on the vigorous use
of compulsory powers by the Government, and the virtual
nationalization, inter alia, of food distribution and the textiles
industry. Opinion in the Conservative Party and in industry was
increasingly torn in two opposite directions, by the realization
that "controls" were necessary and that "planning" had probably
come to stay, and by the instinctive reaction that "planning" must
not stay. In the controversy over Dalton's attempt to extend
rationing to fuel, it was reaction which came uppermost.

V

Cripps's return from Russia and the political crisis coincided, it
is well worth noting, with a cold spell of unprecedented length
and bitterness – there were forty-six degrees of frost on January
15th. In the third bad winter of war, the transport of coal, by rail
and road, broke down yet again. In her "tiny north-facing study"
in London, Vera Brittain "struggled to write", she recalls, "wearing a thick woollen shelter suit with long trousers and a Pixie
hood".[49]

But transport was not the only problem. The situation as it
now presented itself was, briefly, that the number of coal-miners
had fallen, that those who remained were ageing, and that their
productivity was, not unnaturally, declining. There had been
766,000 men in the pits in 1939. By the spring of 1941, there were
only 690,000, and those who had gone were mostly young men.
The shortage of skilled and powerful face-workers was especially
serious. After the application of the Essential Work Order to the

mines, Bevin had appealed, in June 1941, for fifty thousand men to return voluntarily to the pits. This had failed. In July, he had ordered the registration of all men with experience in the mines who were now employed elsewhere. Thirty thousand had been brought back, to bondage as they felt. For a brief period, productivity and production had risen, and the crisis was postponed. But in the first half of 1942, both sagged again. Since industry was calling for more and more coal, the public must take the brunt of the shortage. Dalton was asked to make plans to ration all fuel.

It was an exceedingly difficult task, and Dalton turned to the ubiquitous Beveridge who, amongst his other qualities, had an expert knowledge of rationing dating back to the First World War. He devised a variation of points rationing, whereby rations could be taken as coal, gas or electricity, or as a mixture of all three. Rations for the household would depend on the number of rooms. Dalton thought the plan "beautifully simple", and precipitately announced his intentions long before Beveridge's report was published.[50]

In the atmosphere of that March, both the public and the House of Commons accepted the case for rationing; a Mass Observation poll showed seventy per cent in favour of the scheme and only ten per cent against. But the weeks which intervened between Dalton's announcement and the publication of the scheme at the end of April saw a bitter campaign against the notion by Conservative backbenchers and the right-wing press.[51]

The motives were partly self-interested. But besides the resentment which the coal, gas and electricity interests felt against any outside interference with their money-making, there were confused political motives. Dalton was not only a socialist (of a rather right-wing cast) but an anti-appeaser whose stand had been justified. To consummate this combination of odious qualities, he was an Old Etonian who had betrayed his class by joining Labour. The Secretary for Mines, the junior minister who served under him at the Board of Trade, was also a Labour man; he was David Grenfell, an ex-miner himself. Beveridge was a known radical, who was even then occupying himself with a suspicious-looking report on social security which yet another Labour man, Arthur Greenwood, had commissioned. The Parliamentary Labour Party had shown clear signs of restiveness. In the debate on manpower on December 4th, 1941, forty-two Labour members had voted against the Government on an amendment which had demanded that, as a corollary to the conscription of men and women, property should be conscripted and "transport, coal-mining and the manufacture of munitions should be brought under public ownership . . ." A third of the party, furthermore, had abstained.[52]

It was crystal clear. Fuel rationing was a Labour plot designed to hasten the nationalization of the coal-mines – the Labour Party had only recently joined the Miners' Federation in publishing a scheme for complete state control of the mines during the war. This had, in fact, been introduced in the First World War and it was one clear answer to the present crisis. But in 1914–18, coal had still been a buoyant industry, able to defend itself. It was now a decrepit and demonstrably inefficient one; if it were nationalized now, it would stay nationalized. So, as W. H. B. Court puts it in his shrewd official history, "The rationing plan became a sort of unacknowledged test of the relative strength of parties and interests within the coalition Government and in parliament . . ."[53]

Superficially, the cabinet reshuffle had altered the balance; this also enraged the backbenchers, who had seen the one loyal (Chamberlainite) Conservative, Kingsley Wood, displaced from the War Cabinet by Stafford Cripps. In fact, as the 1922 Committee (which represented the Tories not in office) now proceeded very forcibly to demonstrate, the ghost of Neville Chamberlain was still master of the Commons. The committee threatened, publicly, that it would revolt if the Government forced the issue.[54]

When the issue was debated on May 7th, Dalton pointed out that during the winter the public utilities' stocks of coal had run so low that enemy action would have meant a stoppage of gas and electricity over "large and important areas". He argued, as Beveridge had done, that rationing was the only way to safeguard the weaker consumer; the Conservative press had enjoyed themselves discovering anomalies and injustices in the scheme, for which special provision might now be made, but, he stressed, ". . . unless you have a rationing system, people whose houses are damaged by bombs, others who use their houses as business premises and people who are sick will get no special attention at all."[55]

Only one of the critical M.P.s had any alternative scheme to offer. The rest blamed the miners, a richly traditional scapegoat. But Dalton was receiving only lukewarm support from his colleagues, Labour as well as Conservative. In the face of the threatened revolt, the scheme was dropped, pending a complete plan which would cover all sides of the problem.[56]

The result was a system of "dual control" of the mines by

owners and Government, an inept compromise which was introduced in a White Paper early in June. Rationing passed out of Dalton's hands into the province of a new Ministry of Fuel and Power; and soon vanished from view. The public had been convinced by the press that Beveridge's scheme was a bad one, and even the poorest classes were now strongly against it. Apart from this, there was the overwhelming objection that transport conditions remained so bad that the ration could not have been guaranteed.[57]

The miners had their own attitude to all this; the summer saw a wave of strikes. Meanwhile, appeals for voluntary restraint were the best course open to the Government. The urbane and wheedling voice of Freddie Grisewood over the radio spearheaded a publicity campaign. The public were exhorted to restrict their baths to five inches. A mild winter, fortunately, followed, and the public responded so well that they saved half a million tons more than had been required of them by the coal budget, another innovation which signified, like the manpower budget, that such concrete physical phenomena as miners with bad lungs working to extract a filthy mineral from two-foot seams mattered, or should have mattered, a great deal more than money.[58]

VI

Towards the end of April, Churchill confirmed, in secret session, that his spell over the Commons had not been broken, when he detailed a long catalogue of recent reverses and was given a splendid ovation.[59] There had been new calamities since Singapore. On March 8th, the allied forces in the Netherland East Indies had surrendered. On the same day, the Japanese had entered Rangoon. Early in April, Ceylon was raided, which forced the British Eastern Fleet to retreat to Kenya. The capture of Madagascar from the Vichy French, which was undertaken as a precaution early in May, was sheer bathos, yet this was the first "victory" for many months.

Meanwhile, the war at sea went badly. In the first half of 1942, the tonnage of merchant shipping sunk by the Germans in the North Atlantic was nearly a million tons greater than in the first half of 1941, and there were heavy losses also in other oceans.

One answer to the U-boat was the use of long-range aircraft over the sea. But the British air staff countered all suggestions that the bomber force should be reduced or disbanded in order to free such planes for maritime co-operation, with the argument that they could do more damage by bombing Germany. In fact, the effect of bombing on U-boat production in 1942 was minimal. In 1942, German industrial output, given co-ordination for the first time by the redoubtable Speer, actually rose by eighty per cent in spite of repeated attacks.[60]

On February 23rd, Sir Arthur "Bomber" Harris became Commander in Chief of Bomber Command. Harris has been unfairly blamed as a bloodthirsty ogre. His own retort that he did only what the War Cabinet (that is, Churchill) told him to do may seem too close to Adolf Eichmann's for comfort, but it is justified; Churchill was easily persuaded by Lindemann that attacks on working-class houses were the way to stop Germany. When Harris took over, "The general idea," he records, ". . . on what civil servants always call 'a high level', was that the main and almost the only purpose of bombing was to attack the morale of the industrial workers." Harris himself was impressed with the possibilities of fire raids towards these ends, and he ordered an experimental attack on the Baltic port of Lubeck, a historic town of much beauty. "It was not a vital target," he has written, "but it seemed to me better to destroy an industrial town of moderate importance than to fail to destroy a large industrial city." On the night of March 28th–29th, at least half the town was destroyed, mainly by concentrated incendiary attack.[61] The German response came swiftly; on April 14th, Hitler ordered the so-called "Baedeker raids".

Since the summer of 1941, when Hull had suffered five sizable raids after the main blitz had ended, air attack had been unimportant in Britain's life, though occasional raids had touched many parts of the country; in September 1941, for instance, a mere twenty-eight bombers over Newcastle had killed fifty-seven people, made a thousand homeless and started several major fires, including one which destroyed no less than eight-five million cigarettes. "Tip and run" raids, by fighter bombers flying in fast and low, harassed the remaining inhabitants of the eastern and southern coastal areas.[62]

In the Baedeker series, however, the Germans set out quite deliberately to destroy British towns of which the chief claim to attention was the beauty of their medieval or Georgian architecture. The towns chosen were weakly defended and, at first, had no reason to expect a blitz. The post-raid services and fire precautions still suffered from defects which now had been remedied in the major cities.

On April 24th, 1942, about twenty-five bombers conducted a low-level raid on Exeter, involving bombs of exceptional weight and cascades of incendiaries. Bath was then attacked on two successive nights, when four hundred people were killed. On the 27th, it was the turn of Norwich, which suffered again two nights later. Meanwhile, York had been raided and had lost its fifteenth-century Guildhall. On May 3rd, ninety aircraft resumed the attack on Exeter, this time with really vicious effect. The fire services were overwhelmed, the shopping centre was largely destroyed, the cathedral was hit and the many historic buildings wrecked included nine churches.

Another attempt against Norwich later in May was frustrated, either by a hastily assembled balloon barrage, or by the presence of a decoy site near the town. But on May 31st, eighty bombers raided Canterbury. Though the cathedral seemed to be a target, it escaped serious damage. The attack was repeated on June 2nd, and again on the 6th. The last Baedeker raid, on Norwich, fell near the end of that month.[63]

These were not very big attacks by London or Coventry standards. They were big enough to reproduce the conditions of blitz in these small, peaceful centres. Canterbury will serve as an example. There were less than a hundred casualties in the city's three raids, but voluntary workers toiled for months to help the homeless and eight hundred men were still at work repairing damaged houses in September. "Trekking" took place again; shelter sleeping became a habit; and a neurotic atmosphere persisted well into the autumn, when two small, sharp attacks confirmed it.[64]

Meanwhile, Harris was impatient to test his techniques on a major city. On May 30th, he assembled every man and plane he could – including half-trained crews and obsolete bombers – and launched the R.A.F.'s first thousand-bomber attack, against Cologne. Reconnaissance reported that six hundred acres of the city were devastated, But those who thought that such operations would help to achieve swift victory were slowly undeceived.

VII

As the portentous discussion "at high level" over the question of diverting bombers to the U-boat war developed in March 1942, the War Cabinet, it would seem, vented some of its own perplexity and frustration on the *Daily Mirror*.

The *Mirror*, a paper with a long right-wing history, had been converted in the mid 'thirties, under the inspiration of a new editorial director, H. G. Bartholomew, into a tabloid of revolutionary format and democratic pretensions. Sledgehammer headlines in black type one inch deep – MARRIAGE AT 9 SHOCKS US WOMEN – and such beguiling stunts as an attempt to hatch out some eggs under a bedridden girl, had attracted to the paper a new type of following. While the Labour- and T.U.C.-dominated *Daily Herald* continued to appeal to traditional proletarian sympathies, the *Mirror* was outstripping it as the leading organ of the left, going over its head to a new working class which had grown up in relative affluence.

The *Mirror* continued to attract new readers during the war by its galaxy of strip cartoons, in which the nubile, scantily clad but virtuous "Jane" was the brightest star. "Jane" was a prime pin-up in the forces, for Spitfire pilots as well as their mechanics. The *Mirror* increased its appeal with columns which gave sound legal and practical advice to servicemen; and also by a sustained campaign against Blimp and his bullshit. At one time "a daily leader appeared for two consecutive weeks criticizing the Government or army leaders in some way or other," as the house historian of the *Mirror* proudly points out. The most explosive constituent of the *Mirror*'s formula was William Connor, the columnist "Cassandra," a former copy-writer who used his typewriter like a verbal machine gun. Cassandra led a crusade against polished buttons, church parades and recruiting drill, besides conducting his own "Gutskrieg" against lavish eaters out in restaurants, and describing Herbert Morrison, in connection with Regulation 18B, as "the well-known chief censor and public turnkey".[65]

The *Mirror* had been warned more than once that such "irresponsible" criticism would get it into trouble. In January 1941, Churchill himself had told Cecil King, the director responsible for the *Mirror*'s political policy, that he regarded its tactics as "much the most effective way in which to conduct a Fifth Column movement at the present time". The *Mirror*'s criticisms, he complained, awakened class and party dissensions and spread the idea that the Government was incompetent, thus creating a spirit of "despondency and resentment, of bitterness and scorn", which "at the proper moment" might be "suddenly switched over into naked defeatism . . ." The *Mirror*, thus rebuked, did tone down its criticism.[66]

But on March 6th, 1942, it published a cartoon by Philip Zec which for some reason reduced cabinet ministers to fury. A powerful realistic drawing depicted a torpedoed sailor adrift on a raft in the sea, over a caption suggested by Cassandra: " 'THE PRICE OF PETROL HAS BEEN INCREASED BY ONE PENNY' – Official". While many readers seem to have accepted this at its face value as an injunction that they should not complain about shortages and rising prices at such a time as this, Morrison took it to mean that seamen were risking their lives for profiteers at home. Ernest Bevin agreed with him, and Churchill wanted instant suppression of the paper.

On March 19th, Bartholomew and his editor were summoned to see Morrison. He told them that the warning which he had to give was the unanimous decision of the War Cabinet. He reminded them of the fate of the *Daily Worker* and told them that if their paper were closed, it would stay closed for a long time. Within a few days, Cassandra joined the army.[67]

In the House of Commons, Morrison made it clear that complaints from the War Office about the *Mirror*'s supposed effects on the morale of the troops had played a major part in the cabinet's decision. He quoted an editorial where the occupants of the War Office had been referred to as "brass-buttoned boneheads". But Fleet Street, which had shed no tears over the *Worker*, now rose against the threat to its privileges. Only a few very right-wing newspapers supported Morrison. The rest criticized him sharply, notably *The Times* which warned him that "yesterday's reminder to one newspaper will in no way deter the rest from the discharge of their duty." But no doubt it did, especially as another critical journalist, Frank Owen of the *Evening Standard*, was suddenly dereserved in his late thirties, and joined Cassandra in uniform.[68]

However, not even Churchill could blame the press for printing the news when the electorate began to overthrow Conservative nominees in by-elections.

There had been straws in the wind for some time. The I.L.P.'s policy was to press for a socialist Government which would offer "a socialist peace" to the world and fight solely to defend Britain and the Soviet Union; this complex formula boiled down to virtual pacifism. Nevertheless, its candidates in 1941 had polled a steady twenty to thirty per cent of the vote in various constituencies, presumably because Labour supporters saw this as a way of identifying themselves. In September 1941, one W. R. Hipwell, who edited a cheesecake magazine called *Reveille* which had a modest circulation, chiefly in the forces, had stood at Scarborough as an independent. Supporting most policies which might prove attractive, he had secured four-tenths of the poll. In March 1942, this same Hipwell went to Grantham in Lincolnshire, to act as agent for Denis Kendall.

Kendall was well-known locally as a welfare-minded employer, and nationally as an expert critic of the Government's production policy. He was managing director of a large arms factory, an energetic man of thirty-eight who was described in *Picture Post* as being "like something out of the highest-speed Hollywood film". He had offered himself to the local Conservative Party as candidate for the division; having been rebuffed, he stood as an independent, with a programme which promised something for everyone.

"Denis Kendall is another Stafford Cripps – Independent yet Churchillian", he announced in one leaflet. He promised "Support for the Prime Minister" yet called for "The Right Men" (presumably including Kendall) in the "Right Jobs" (that is, the big ones). "Speed up Production", he exhorted, demanding the abolition of cost plus (it was no doubt a result of some oversight that his own firm was shortly pilloried by the Public Accounts Committee for taking excessive profits). To complete the attractions of his platform, he proposed that there should be a comprehensive system of social security covering "everything from the cradle to the grave", with pensions for all, agreeably enough, at forty. He now claimed to be a Labour Party supporter and the local Labour candidate helped him.

His opponent, Air Chief Marshal Longmore, had commanded the air force in the Middle East during Wavell's period there. His election address was succinct enough for anyone at this time of paper shortage; it confined itself to support for Churchill and the invocation of national unity. It was sufficient to secure him the energetic support of the Communist Party, which now made a practice of backing all coalition candidates.[69]

The register was out of date; young voters and those in the forces were disfranchised; the whole tone of public life weighed in favour of national unity and support for Longmore. It was therefore a great shock on March 25th when Kendall won, by 11,758 votes to 11,391. A good deal of attention now went to Rugby, where W. J. Brown was standing as an independent in Margesson's former seat, against a pillar of the local Conservative association.

Brown was a leading civil service trade unionist and a well-known broadcaster, a former Labour M.P. who had left the party in 1931. His political attitudes, as distinct from his somewhat incoherent views, boiled down to a manic hatred of the party whips and perhaps in their essence to a profound belief in the inalienable right of W. J. Brown to say what he liked, where he liked, when he liked, and for as long as he liked. But he won considerable support from within the Rugby Labour Party. Amongst the other vague things, he called for aid to Russia "directly *now*". At the end of April, he was elected by a narrow majority.[70]

More extraordinary, though it attracted less attention, was the result in Brabazon's former seat of Wallasey, which was announced on the same day. A well-known local journalist named George Reakes, a former Labour mayor of the borough who had been excommunicated by the party for supporting Chamberlain over Munich, won with a sensational majority of six thousand votes, while his Conservative opponent received less than one-third of the poll.

Brabazon, it seems, had not been universally popular with the local Conservative association. Local Conservatives had approached Reakes and asked him to stand. Wallasey had hitherto been a staunchly Conservative dormitory suburb, but the air raids (which probably had their effect on the result) had sent many better-off citizens scurrying to safer parts. The population had dropped to under half its pre-war level. Reakes, shrewdly enough, fought his campaign chiefly on housing, and the need to control prices.

This convivial little man attracted the support of Sir Richard Acland's Forward March movement, which had been worried by the Grantham result into contemplating electoral intervention. In return, he professed to support its programme. Reakes and the dedicated, earnest and lanky Acland made an odd Quixote and Panza combination as they toured the pubs together, the one exuding bibulous bonhomie, the other preaching the socialization of all property. The Conservative, a local alderman, had vigorous support from both the Labour Party and the Communist Party. Perhaps to slay memories of Brabazon's premature anti-Stalinism, he flew the red flag over his committee rooms, while the C.P. decorated their premises with red, white and blue posters. "Red Ellen" Wilkinson herself spoke from his platform. Meanwhile, Stafford Cripps's brother Leonard, an ultra-right-wing Liverpool shipowner, stood as an independent, and was supported by a local Conservative M.P., and by the protean Denis Kendall. In spite of his surname, he lost his deposit.[71]

It was clear to everyone that something extremely odd had

happened to British politics, and very few orthodox politicians liked it, whatever it was. At very best, individualism was now running riot, as if in tacit protest against identity cards, austerity and utility. At worst, some gloomy spirits on the left saw Brown and Kendall as portents of a new British Fascism. These two now formed a parliamentary team with a couple of relapsed Conservative supporters, and promoted a short-lived "People's Movement", with virtually no programme except for the abolition of political parties. Acland, Priestley and other independent left-wingers issued a socialistic "Nine Point Manifesto" for use in further by-elections. There were now two competing teams of independents, and it seemed that anything might happen.

The swing in 1942 against Conservative candidates was the biggest of the war years, and, meanwhile, Labour held its seats without trouble. But the radical press expatiated in the spring of 1942 on what it called "the movement away from party", meaning by "party", all parties, and suggesting that the public hankered for more independents, like Cripps.[72]

In April, Cripps became the first minister seriously to challenge Eden at the top of the opinion polls when people were asked who they thought should succeed Churchill. The Great Man, however, was very much alive, and produced a notion eminently well calculated to disillusion Cripps's left-wing following and to disperse his aura of infallibility. On March 22nd, Cripps left for India. His mission was to pacify the Congress leaders, who had refused to support the war unless India was given independence; it was transparently a mere manoeuvre, prompted by the new danger to the sub-continent from the Japanese. Cripps offered the cabinet's promise of full independence after the war. Mahatma Gandhi, with justice, refused to accept what he called a "post-dated cheque". The talks broke down in early April. Within a few months, Gandhi and Nehru were imprisoned, and a rising of their supporters was put down with great violence. The left, naturally, lost much of its faith in Cripps, but he now won added popularity on the right, and public enthusiasm for him remained very high indeed.[73]

There were many more signs to support the theory of a "movement away from party". The ageing House of Commons was now discredited.[74] Apart from the leading members of a Government which remained unpopular, the best-known M.P.s were the rebels, who came from all parties and none. The shifting coalitions of the inter-war years had long since produced a confusing number of splinter groups – National Liberal, National Labour,

Churchillian Conservatives. Now there were Bevanites too.

It seemed that the two, or three, party system had long been breaking down, and that the war had administered the *coup de grace*. "Where, anywhere in the country," asked the *Economist* in April 1942, "can there be found any body of men or women who sincerely and passionately believe that salvation lies through the Conservative, Labour or Liberal Parties – except, of course, among those who have some vested interest in the various machines?" Mass Observation returned an answer. In December 1941, it found that one person in six in a sample said the war had changed his or her political views. Eight months later, in August 1942, the proportion was one in three. At this time it was also found that only one-third of the voters expected any of the existing parties to get things done as they personally wanted them after the war. This minority was mostly Labour or Communist. The entire Conservative front had caved in, yet Labour, in coalition, could not take advantage of this, and remained in its own trenches. In no-man's land, Brown and Kendall found their place.[75]

The retreat of Conservatism was evident in the press, both popular and serious; indeed, one of its symptoms was that the popular papers now aped the serious ones. The *Mirror*, for all its alliteration, was earnest enough now in calling for social change. The Beaverbrook papers, now that their proprietor had less time on his hands and was not (officially) allowed to interfere with them, indulged more openly the radicalism which many reporters had previously professed covertly. "All of them", George Orwell had explained to his American public in 1941, "print articles which would have been considered hopelessly above their readers' heads a couple of years ago." He added, "to find any straightforward expression of reactionary opinion . . . you now have to go to obscure weekly and monthly papers, mostly Catholic papers."[76]

The most significant shift of all came in the columns of *The Times*. In 1941, Robert Barrington Ward had succeeded Geoffrey Dawson as editor. As the historian of the newspaper puts it, he was a "Radical Tory", who was "inclined by temperament to welcome social change in advance, prepare for it, and so control it". *The Times* leaders on home affairs were handed over to the distinguished, but leftish, historian E. H. Carr, and consistently expounded the idea that the Government must promise now to create social justice as soon as possible after the war. In September 1942, diehard *Times* readers must have shuddered on perusing a leader which advocated, as a post-war policy, Government control of all monopolies, and of all industries where trade associations eliminated competition, "either through a public utility corporation", or by other means. Indeed, one right-wing M.P. was later moved to describe *The Times* as "the threepenny edition of the *Daily Worker*".[77]

Post-war reconstruction was now coming to the fore as a topic for public discussion. This was not the result of any sudden rush of optimism to the head. Very early in the war both Government departments and private institutions had seen clearly that nothing was ever going to be quite the same again. The blitz had been "the end of *a* world". Work had been set in motion, in 1940 and 1941, on many official and unofficial reports. Arthur Greenwood, as minister responsible for post-war planning, had been given a small staff and set to co-ordinate the work of a number of committees set up at ministerial and departmental level. In February 1942, Churchill had sacked Greenwood without replacing him, but had added "Planning" to the title of the Minister of Works. Meanwhile, R. A. Butler, chairman of the new Conservative Post-war Problems Committee, had been given the Presidency of the Board of Education and had soon begun to excite teachers and educationalists with the prospects of reform.

But for the moment reconstruction was all talk. And the issue of the ownership of industry and its relationship to the state, with the related question of full employment, could not, it seemed, be settled by a coalition Government. Why, people asked increasingly, did this Government not commit itself to positive proposals? It was above all as a potential post-war Prime Minister that Cripps appealed to a very sizable proportion of the population; let Churchill win the war quickly, and then let Cripps win the peace.[78]

Meanwhile, the more intelligent businessmen had made plans, not so much for winning the peace, as for ensuring that they did not lose it. According to the *Economist*, the "old controversy" round "the question of whether the state should make itself responsible for the economic environment" was "as dead as a doorknocker – that is, useful for making a noise but nothing else". The textiles baron Samuel Courtauld (who was, it should be noted, R. A. Butler's father-in-law) stated the situation as a few *avant garde* capitalists saw it. "Government control has come to stay," he wrote in a famous article printed in April 1942. The growth of monopoly made it inevitable. ". . . No Government can tolerate the existence within its borders of an organized and completely independent power with a radius of action as wide as its own. The same overriding principle should apply to trade unions as developed today . . . Unless the men in possession are prepared to adapt themselves and compromise, there is no alternative to a complete socialist revolution." The railways, he said, should be nationalized. On the boards of all companies over a certain size, directors appointed by the Government should sit. Agreements between employers and trade unionists should be legally enforceable.[79]

But at the same time, a report produced for the President of the Board of Trade by the powerful Federation of British Industries was unanimously adopted by the F.B.I.'s Grand Council. This foresaw that "a measure of Government control over industry" would be necessary during the immediate post-war period. But any more permanent control should be introduced only with the consent and collaboration of the firms. In their opinion, "the future organization of industry should be decided by the industrialists, always subject to the overriding principle that it must be in the national interest." (As defined, no doubt, by the industrialists.) Each industry, the F.B.I. argued, should be governed by its own trade association. Later in the year, a group of a hundred and twenty prominent industrialists, including Lord McGowan, the chief of Imperial Chemical Industries, signed a somewhat more imaginative document. "Properly administered amalgamations", they argued, provided "a more effective spur to efficiency than unchecked competition." The authority of the trade unions should be strengthened and increasingly close collaboration introduced between them and the various managements. Each industry should supply pensions schemes and proper housing for its employees, and in fact conduct itself as a miniature welfare state.[80]

Such arguments, as we have seen, had been widely accepted between the wars, when the steel industry had become a prototype of rationalized, self-governing, competition-free autonomy. But they were advanced now in a context where the demands of war on industry were in fact tending to produce many of the changes demanded. The big firms waxed bigger as "concentration" and other wartime controls threatened the "small man". Both directly, by intention, and indirectly, by provoking defensive reactions from industry, Government intervention stimulated increasing centralization.

The Liberal Party had once been the spokesman both for free enterprise and for social progress. As the two had become increasingly incompatible in the course of the twentieth century, the party had been torn apart. The Liberal family of Benns illustrated the process to perfection. Wedgwood Benn, in the 1920s, had joined the Labour Party, which both he and his son were to serve in high office. His brother Sir Ernest, a well-known publisher, had gravitated towards Conservatism, but had kept the spirit of Cobden fairly clean within him. In the middle of 1941, he had begun to organize regular lunch parties for a group of self-styled "individualists". Authors, intellectuals and financiers had attended, but so had Lord Perry, the chairman of Ford's, and Lord Leverhulme of Lever Brothers. Benn was soon complaining in his diary, "The group contains one or two energetic people . . . who would be glad to come out boldly and campaign against the control of everything. The rest, being milder and perhaps more responsible people, hesitate to indulge in too much criticism while the war lasts. The group altogether is a fine example of the way in which the moneyed, managerial and responsible class is prepared to suffer anything rather than endanger the national unity."[81]

In August 1942, the individualists intrepidly issued a "Manifesto on British Liberty". They insisted that "state interference" with the liberty of the subject should be "reduced to a minimum" and protested against "the swamping of self-help by state-help". Three months later, Benn formed his supporters into a Society of Individualists, with himself as President and Leverhulme as chairman of the National Council. It soon claimed to have more than ten thousand names in its card index. But Benn began to have doubts. Towards the end of 1943, when he lunched with the chairman of Metropolitan Vickers and another businessman, he noted that, "These people, like Perry of Ford's, or Leverhulme of great combine fame, are all a little wobbly as Individualists . . ." Before the end of the war, he himself had more or less capitulated. His small society was ineffectual and he merged it with a National League for Freedom which included some forty Conservative backbench M.P.s, led by a noted monopolist. Many loyal Individualists protested that these people were reactionaries, monopolists, protectionists, mercantilists. "A cohort of Cobdenite and Georgeist members was in arms." But the amalgamation went through and Benn's libertarianism became a front for big business.[82]

The Liberal Party itself, remote from power, had become, in Asa Briggs's phrase, "pre-eminently a party of ideas". In August 1941, Seebohm Rowntree, the veteran sociologist and businessman, had agreed to direct for it a large-scale investigation into the problems of reconstruction. Rowntree himself was in something of a dilemma over the direction which economic change was taking. The numerous sub-committees set up to consider individual topics included, not only Liberals and independent experts, but Labour men and Conservatives, and were deeply split over basic political issues. Little of note came from them. Meanwhile, a number of younger Liberals, with Sinclair's blessing, had set up a Liberal Action Group in November 1941. It passed a resolution calling for a "complete restatement of Liberal economic policy", in the light of changes since the outbreak of war. Its own formula, expressed in April 1942, was that "both community-owned industry and private enterprise" should "play their part in harmony for the common good".[83]

The left wing of the Labour Party, and indeed a large proportion of its rank and file, were more restive, but no nearer power. The plans of the F.B.I. added to their unease. Aneurin Bevan found a typically vivid phrase to sum up their suspicion of the type of compromise which they feared might be evolving. "When the state extends its control over big business, big business moves in to control the state . . . The state ceases to be the umpire. *It becomes the prize.*"[84]

The local Labour parties had in some cases been bombed out of their premises. Call-up, evacuation and dispersal had taken loyalists away; war work had left no time for political meetings. Individual membership of the party had fallen by nearly half between 1939 and 1942, from 400,000 to 220,000. Now, independents had started to pilfer seats which Labour could and should have won. Labour's cabinet ministers seemed to have been duped; surely Churchill was protecting his Tories by giving them unpleasant jobs such as suppressing newspapers and abolishing trouser turn-ups?

But the Labour leadership, throughout the political crisis of 1942, remained utterly loyal to Churchill. It must be remembered that in 1940, Labour had had only a quarter of the seats in the House of Commons, and Attlee and Dalton and Morrison had had no certainty of ever holding office again. They were now enjoying power and, they thought, making good use of it. The party, in the middle of the war, published a booklet called "Labour In The War Government – A Record of Things Done". The Atlantic Charter, the Beveridge inquiry into the social services, immediate improvements in those same social services, the increase in wages, the strengthening of collective bargaining, the control of profits, high incomes and property – all these were

attributed, to some degree at least, to their tenure of office
Indeed, they amounted to a better Labour record than those of
both MacDonald's minority Governments added together.

Bevin owed office to Churchill, and relished his opportunity.
Another Labour man who made good use of his chance was Tom
Johnston, the Secretary of State for Scotland since 1941. With
humour and determination, he had done his best for his native
land, so much depressed before the war. In 1942, he set up a
broadly based Scottish Council of Industry which attracted so
many contracts to Scotland, that in six months the total of
Government production there increased by over two hundred and
fifty per cent. He created a really bold and imaginative health
scheme for the Clyde Basin, which set out to prevent disease as
well as to cure it. He even introduced a measure of nationalization, with the help of leading ministers in all parties. In 1943, both
Commons and Lords, without a single division, passed his bill
setting up a public corporation to exploit the hydro-electric power
of the Highlands.[85]

But such relatively minor advances were not enough to satisfy
the more ardent members of the party rank and file. An extraordinarily vague "interim" policy statement issued in 1942
informed them that Labour was not, in coalition, "entitled" to
press for any measures "on party grounds". Hopes of "revolution
by consent", to use Professor Laski's term, were fading. Resentment mounted against the electoral truce. Churchill asked the
Labour leaders to propose an extension to the terms of the truce
when their annual conference met at Whitsun. Instead of the
merely negative condition that Labour would not oppose Conservative candidates, he now, following Grantham and Rugby,
demanded positive co-operation in their return. Morrison, introducing this proposal to the delegates, assured them that this
charity would not be extended to really obnoxious Conservative
nominees. But only a tiny majority, based largely on the bloc vote
of Bevin's union, was recorded in favour of the idea, and it was
widely assumed inside and outside the party that the truce was
virtually dead.[86] In fact, it survived, with growing inefficiency, for
three years more; and, since there had been a majority, Attlee
was perfectly within his rights to add his name to a joint message
of support signed also by Sinclair and Churchill, which from now
on went to all coalition nominees.

However, any hopes that the demoted Greenwood might control the unruly Parliamentary Labour Party, were shattered on
July 29th, when sixty-three M.P.s voted against what they con-

sidered to be an inadequate rise in old age pensions. As political feeling rose again, a revival of the constituency Labour parties slowly got under way. The rest of the war, in fact, saw a steady "movement back to party".

Early in 1942, Sir Douglas Hacking, who had commanded the Conservative Party machine as its chairman, resigned, saying that he had found his duty of urging "patience and forbearance" on the local Conservative associations "somewhat invidious". His successor was soon busy calling on them to be "prepared for a contest at any time, undesirable and trivial as by-elections appeared against the background of the war" – no seat, he said, was now immune from the dreaded independents. Meanwhile, at a meeting of the party's Central Council in March, the most significant figure, R. A. Butler, remarked, during a lengthy discussion of organizational problems, "This is a critical moment for our party . . . I would like to see all our supporters out on patrol in forward positions, with forward advancing ideas, and not simply defending vested interests."[87] If these injunctions failed, it was partly because lack of confidence in capitalism now afflicted the very fabric of the Conservative Party in the constituencies, and partly because so many of the remaining loyalists were wedded to the defence of vested interests before all else.

VIII

Churchill, in January 1942, had publicly rebuked those who were chalking SECOND FRONT NOW on the walls, indicating that Britain's resources were so fully stretched already that such action was out of the question. He still saw North Africa as the key to victory. But most of the American leaders, including General Marshall the chief of army staff, wanted a direct onslaught in western Europe as soon as possible. Churchill had for the moment to defer to American strength; in mid-April, the British and American staffs agreed to plan for a large-scale second front in 1943 and for a smaller landing to capture Cherbourg in 1942.

Meanwhile, a great majority of the public had come to favour such landings in the near future. The press was now almost unanimous in calling for swift action; when Maisky said acidly, "There is no time to wait until the last button is sewn to the uniforms of the last soldier," the Conservative *Daily Mail* praised his "sound sense". Lord Beaverbrook, of course, owned the biggest newspaper of all. After his resignation, he had travelled to America on a semi-official mission, with Churchill's blessing. On April 23rd, in New York, he made an extraordinary speech demanding a second front. "The war can be settled in 1942. Communism under Stalin has produced the most valiant fighting army in Europe . . . Communism under Stalin has produced the best generals in this war."[88]

In private, Churchill was dismayed by his friend's remarks; in public he maintained his good humour. In a broadcast on May 10th, he welcomed the second front agitation as a sign of "the militant, aggressive spirit of the British nation". The *Daily Express* organized mass meetings up and down the country, and Beaverbrook himself took the platform, as well as Shinwell and other socialists.[89] The spectacle of Beaverbrook cycling tandem with the Communists seemed to be yet another bizarre manifestation of the "movement away from party".

The C.P. had launched a recruiting drive in January, with a target of fifteen thousand new members. In three months, it had obtained twenty-five thousand. By the end of the year, its membership had risen from just over twenty thousand to the record figure of fifty-six thousand. (Indeed, the leadership found that sheer size was militating against the tight discipline they favoured; many recruits were appalled by the heavy demands made on their time by the party they had joined too casually, and numbers quite soon began to fall again.[90])

In May, an estimated fifty thousand people attended a second-front demonstration in Trafalgar Square. Molotov arrived secretly in London. A "Twenty Year Pact" of alliance between Britain and Russia was signed, and the Foreign Office statement which followed Eden's announcement of the pact in June suggested that full agreement had been reached "with regard to the urgent tasks of creating a second front in Europe in 1942". At a huge rally in London that month to celebrate the anniversary of the invasion of Russia the audience applauded "like baying wolves", one speaker noted, "at every mention of the second front".[91]

But before this Churchill had gone to Washington to demand that North Africa, not France, should be the target for allied invasion in 1942. Shortly after his arrival came news that Tobruk had fallen on June 21st and its long siege had ended with the passage into captivity of thirty-three thousand survivors of its garrison. "Defeat is one thing," Churchill has written of this shock; "disgrace is another."

The reaction of the *Manchester Guardian*, a great Liberal newspaper which Churchill himself had recently praised for its "splendid but instructed independence", shows how deeply this new blow bit. "Norway", an editorial suggested, "could be forgiven as a scratch affair; Dunkirk followed the defection [sic] of our allies; the first Libyan failure was due to a human error of judgment and to the diversion of forces to help the forlorn hope in Greece; Hong Kong, Singapore, Java were an almost inevitable sequence after our gamble of Eastern unpreparedness had failed. But Libya as the ordinary man sees it is another matter. Here at least we were supposed to be strong ... The Government will have to put itself in the place of the workers who find that after they have worked so hard and so long their production is thrown away in the field, battered by superior weight, or left as booty to the enemy."[92]

Tom Driberg, a socialist who wrote for the *Daily Express*, was standing at Maldon, in Essex, as an independent candidate. In the four days remaining before the poll, he produced and circulated a leaflet on the disaster. "Our sons and brothers fighting in far lands hang on desperately for munitions that don't turn up, while profiteers haggle with the Government at home." After scenes of great enthusiasm, he transformed a Conservative majority of eight thousand into an independent one of six thousand. "ANGER IN ENGLAND", "TOBRUK FALL MAY BRING CHANGE OF GOVERNMENT", ran headlines in the New York press as Churchill persuaded Roosevelt to send three hundred tanks to Auchinleck, who was meanwhile preparing to evacuate Cairo in the face of Rommel's advance. By the end of June, Auchinleck had fallen back to a strong natural defensive position at El Alamein, while Churchill was in England to confront a motion of censure in the House of Commons.[93]

On the day of Tobruk's fall, Lord Beaverbrook in a broadcast had made the intriguing charge that "people in high places" had opposed helping Russia in 1941 and were opposing the second front now. In the week which followed, he called Ernest Bevin, of all people, to see him and, it seems, implied to him that they might now displace Churchill together. Bevin had a good head for heights and angrily interrupted Beaverbrook's hint of "all the kingdoms of the world in a moment of time". He preferred to follow his master and in a public oration a few days later exclaimed, "This wicked filthy business of trying to break up national unity by playing Winston Churchill off against his colleagues by certain newspaper millionaires is the most diabolical thing I have ever known. He came, in 1940, when the country was under the weather – and I am prepared as a trade unionist to go on under the banner of Winston Churchill working with him as a colleague, fighting for him to the end."[94]

So Churchill's colleagues all stood ready to defend him. But over the previous weeks, there had been calls, inside and outside parliament, for a change in the organization of the war at the top, and these had perceptibly shifted towards the hitherto almost unthinkable, but now almost inevitable, open expression of loss of confidence in Churchill himself. Amongst those who had tended this way was Sir John Wardlaw Milne, a Conservative backbencher, once a solid Chamberlain man, who now had much prestige and influence as the chairman of the all-party Select Committee on National Expenditure. The motion of censure stood in his name: "That this House, while paying tribute to the heroism of the Armed Forces of the Crown in circumstances of exceptional difficulty, has no confidence in the central direction of the war." The seconder was none other than the hero of the Norway debate, Admiral Sir Roger Keyes; and many minds strayed back now to that unexpected occasion.

As battle had continued in North Africa, Wardlaw Milne had developed cold feet. He had asked for permission to withdraw the motion. Churchill insisted on a trial of strength; he could not afford to let the world have the impression that he was hanging on in office solely by slippery manoeuvre. So Milne rose to open the debate on July 1st; an imposing, self-important, but inwardly confused man. He began sensibly, urging an end to Churchill's dual role as Prime Minister and Minister of Defence. Then, he suddenly made a halting digression; "It would be a very desirable move – if His Majesty the King and His Royal Highness would agree – if His Royal Highness the Duke of Gloucester were to be appointed Commander in Chief of the British Army – without, of course, administrative duties." The duke, a military but obscure personage, was the King's younger brother. The House of Commons, torn in twain between a panic of embarrassment and the urgent calls of hilarity, produced an extraordinary gasping, groaning, guffawing wave of noises. Churchill's face lit up with relief and pleasure. The motion, at this point, collapsed. Keyes made its rout still more certain; while Milne had argued that Churchill was interfering too much with the day to day conduct of the war, Keyes, who had been hurt when Churchill had relieved him of his post as Director of Combined Operations, was incapacitated from attack by old loyalties. When a Labour man intervened to point out that if the motion was carried, the Prime

Minister would have to go, Keyes protested that this would be "a deplorable disaster".

Yet feeling against the Government ran high. Lyttleton had a rough time when he tried to deal with the complaints made against British tanks. The second morning of the debate was opened by Aneurin Bevan, with what the loyal Harold Nicolson admitted was a "brilliant offensive, pointing his finger in accusation, twisting and bowing". He told the House that the country was beginning to say of Churchill "that he fights debates like a war and the war like a debate". He concluded by expressing the widespread feeling that the Government was deceiving the Russians over the second front. "Do not in these high matters speak with a twisted tongue; do not use words with double meanings; do not use sentences with hidden purposes. On these high matters, speak truthfully and simply, so that the people can understand and trust . . ."

But eloquence was insufficient. Churchill clearly enjoyed winding up the fiasco. His speech showed all his characteristic devices to perfection. There was devastating candour in his recital of the facts; fifty thousand men had been lost in the Middle East in the last fortnight; Rommel had advanced nearly four hundred miles; the fall of Tobruk had been a total surprise for himself. There was hauteur; he complained that he had been "barracked from his homeland in his absence". There was anti-climatic humour, when he recalled that the Government had ordered a new tank in 1940, off the drawing board, to be ready for 1942. "As might be expected, it had many defects and teething troubles, and when these became apparent the tank was appropriately rechristened the 'Churchill'." There was invective, when he accused his critics of "nagging and snarling". And there was defiance – "the duty of the House of Commons is to sustain the Government or to change the Government. If it cannot change it, it should sustain it. There is no working middle course in wartime."[95]

Daring the Commons thus, he got his victory. Four hundred and seventy-six M.P.s opposed Milne's motion, and only twenty-five supported it (including a handful of Conservatives). There were, however, some forty deliberate abstentions. It was notable that some habitual rebels, including Shinwell and Acland, voted for Churchill or abstained. What, after all, was the alternative? Probably Eden, an amiable but still somehow unconvincing youngster; there was no question that the King would call for Cripps, or for a maverick like Belisha, Shinwell or Bevan. In May

1940, Chamberlain's critics had included most of the greatly talented men in the House of Commons. In July 1942, Churchill's opponents were ex-ministers, who might readily be accused of vindictiveness, or men of such obscurity that no one could easily envisage them in high office. The one exception, Bevan, was an extremist. The whips of all the parties were in Churchill's pocket. Parliamentary democracy had in effect ceased to exist, since the House did not, and could not, represent the divisions of the country. It was a right-wing weekly, the *Spectator*, which complained after the no confidence debate that "the private member who decides to vote against the Government is made to realize that he takes his political life in his hands." "I want to vote against the Government," the Chamberlainite Conservative Sir Henry Channon had mused in his diary on June 24th, ". . . yet caution (or is it cowardice wedded to self-interest?) warns me not to."[96]

Churchill soon had his own way over the second front. Early in July, the British chiefs of staff ruled out any landing in France in 1942. Roosevelt, who wanted a quick victory for electoral purposes of his own, agreed on July 25th to the operation called Torch; a plan to land over a hundred thousand British and American troops in French North Africa.

IX

The turning point in North Africa came, although no one noticed it at the time, with Auchinleck's defensive victory in the first Battle of El Alamein, which was in progress when Wardlaw Milne's motion was debated. But early in August, Churchill descended on Cairo to dismiss Auchinleck and put General Alexander in his place. As the new commander of the Eighth Army, he chose General "Straffer" Gott, a tough desert fighter. But Gott was killed in a plane crash and Lieutenant General Bernard Montgomery, who had experienced no fighting since 1940, but gave an accurate impression of inexhaustible self-confidence, found himself, much like Churchill in 1940, "walking with destiny".

From Cairo, Churchill flew to Moscow, where he had to break the news to Stalin that there would be no second front this year. At this first confrontation, things went surprisingly well. Meanwhile, on August 19th, an ill-conceived raid on Dieppe, prepared as an experiment in the organization of large-scale landings, took some of the enthusiasm out of the cries in Britain for Second Front. Six thousand troops, mostly Canadian, landed on the French coast and were severely butchered about.

The Germans had now reached the city of Stalingrad, on the River Don, the hinge which would open the door to the Caucasus and the Middle East. The Russian garrison conducted a street-by-street defence of the ruins. The British public was aware of the importance of this grim struggle, but its eyes turned back compulsively to North Africa, on which Churchill's had always been fixed.

Churchill later remembered the September and October of 1942 as his "most anxious months of the war". If the eventual outcome of the global conflict was certain, his own power still hung in the balance. His confidant, Brendan Bracken, told Lord Moran one day, "The Prime Minister must win his battle in the desert or get out . . . I'm afraid of that fellow Cripps. I think he means business." But Cripps's appeal had now waned markedly. As Leader of the House, his job had been to defend Churchill by explaining a succession of defeats. He had, as Churchill puts it, "discharged this task with skill and loyalty"; hence the public increasingly saw him as merely another faithful stooge for Churchill. Meanwhile, he annoyed the House of Commons by his lordly and sanctimonious behaviour, and resentment came to the boil early in September, when he enraged M.P.s by publicly rebuking them for preferring their lunch to their duties.[97]

However, the speaker who had provoked the walk-out in question was Churchill himself, giving an unusually empty commentary on the state of the war, and Cripps was still no mere stooge. When Churchill came home from his travels, he found that Sir Stafford had "developed serious doubts about the state of the national morale . . ." He now demanded, in private, an independent War Planning Directorate to take over some of Churchill's power vis-à-vis the chiefs of staff. When Churchill would not agree with him, he threatened to resign. Churchill and other ministers begged him to stay on until the coming battle in North Africa had been decided. He agreed.[98]

Meanwhile, General Montgomery was preparing to elevate himself to legendary status. He had been put in by Churchill to win a big battle as soon as possible, but he insisted on doing things at his own speed. So far, no British commander had managed to capture the public imagination, as Kitchener, Haig, Beatty and Jellicoe had done in the First World War. The most successful, Dowding, had accomplished his task with very little fuss, and had then been sacked; it was the pilots who had won popular acclaim. The right-wing *National Review* was moved to complain, early in 1943, ". . . this is an anonymous war. Only the People – with a big P – are great and, of course", the writer added loyally, "Mr Churchill." But it could now make an exception for "Monty".[99]

And Monty himself was by way of being the People's General of the People's War. His mystique was based on his novel concept of leadership, which conformed well to the new and swift type of war which was fought in tanks and Spitfires. ". . . Battles are won primarily in the hearts of men," he has written, pointing out that the modern wars are fought, not by military professions, but by civilians in uniform. "Such men are educated, they can think, they can appreciate. They want to know what is going on, and what the general wants them to do, and why, and when; they want to see and decide in their own minds what sort of person he is. I have never believed in dealing with soldiers by a process of 'remote control'; they are human beings and their lives are precious."[100]

It was this attitude, rather than any superhuman military skill, which marked him out from his predecessors. The desert war, with its unprecedented extremes of temperature and speed of movement, had banished the uniformity of "uniform", if only because it gave the British so many opportunities to loot superior apparel and accessories left behind by their enemies. Monty accepted the irrelevance of bullshit and dressed unconventionally like his men; his beret became as famous as Churchill's cigar. His enthusiasm for putting his men "in the picture" with familiar and colloquial "personal messages" showed that he understood the reasons why ABCA had been created. In the centre of "the picture", Monty, of course, placed himself; his excellent opinion of General Montgomery was part of the legend, though many people in and out of the forces disliked him for it. But like him or not, Monty was a competent professional. As he prepared for his big battle, the image of the army surrendered to the accumulated force of some forty years of rapid social change, and Colonel Blimp was pushed almost out of the "picture".

Towards the end of October, Mrs Roosevelt arrived as a guest at Buckingham Palace, where she found Dame Austerity installed, as it were, as a bigamous and morganatic consort. She was lodged in the Queen's own bedroom, a vast one; but bombing had robbed it of its window panes, and casements mainly of wood and isinglass had been installed in their place. "I do not see how they keep the dampness out," she wrote. "The rooms were cold except for the smaller sitting-room with an open fire. In every room there was a little electric heater." There was a clear black line in her bathtub above which she was not supposed to run the hot water. When she sat down to a meal which Lord Woolton assured her "might have been served in any home in England", it struck her as somewhat incongruous that it should be eaten off gold and silver plates. Churchill joined the company for dinner. He was notably distant, then and afterwards, when the patriotic film *In Which We Serve* was shown to the guests. Finally, he excused himself and went to telephone Downing Street. He returned singing 'Roll out the barrel' with gusto."[101]

Monty was in action at El Alamein. He had waited until he was confident of victory. When battle was joined on October 23rd, he had complete ascendancy in the air. With two hundred thousand men, his forces outnumbered Rommel's by about two to one, and he had the same superiority in tanks. But in spite of his caution, or because of it, the British lost more tanks than the Germans and the casualties were fearful. The first attack went badly. With a second attempt, which began on November 2nd, the sheer weight of numbers overwhelmed Rommel at last.

The British public was now thoroughly familiar with the symptoms of approaching defeat. First, a reverse. Then much optimistic news in the press and on the radio, indicating that matters were now in hand and would soon go well. Then, another reverse. They suspected the worst even now.

But when a B.B.C. announcer interrupted the programme on the night of November 4th to warn listeners not to switch off as the best news for years would be given at midnight, his voice was shaking with authentic excitement. Alexander's communiqué from Cairo revealed that the Germans were now in full retreat in Egypt.[102]

There was more to come. On November 8th, the allies landed their Torch troops in Morocco and Algeria, and prepared to move towards Tunis. There was opposition from the Vichy French, however, and public satisfaction in Britain was somewhat vitiated when General Eisenhower, commanding the operation, turned to Admiral Darlan to rally their sympathies in favour of the allies. Darlan, after Pétain and Laval, was perhaps the most notorious Vichy collaborationist of all.

While Churchill was at his most buoyant when he addressed a meeting in the City of London on the 10th he warned against undue optimism. "Now this is not the end. It is not even the beginning of the end. But it is, perhaps, the end of the beginning."[103] His subjects, however, could not but see Alamein as the harbinger of peace. The turning point was marked by a gesture of immense symbolic significance. On November 15th, the church bells all over Britain rang out, not to announce invasion, but to mark Monty's victory. There was light visible at the end of the tunnel.

Chapter Six

The India-Rubber Island:
Britain in 1943-44

As one Controller-General put it, the dream of the Factory Control was "an india-rubber Britain with india-rubber buildings which can be stretched vertically and horizontally and still carry a minimum of five cwt. per square foot."

Hargreaves and Gowing, *Civil Industry and Trade*

WREATHS AND CROSSES – NO TOMATOES

Sign outside a Yorkshire shop, *c.* 1942

STRETCHED

She's the girl that makes the thing that drills the hole that holds the
    spring
That drives the rod that turns the knob that works the thingumebob.
She's the girl that makes the thing that holds the oil that oils the ring
That makes the shank that moves the crank that works the
    thingumbebob.
It's a ticklish sort of job,
Making a thingumebob,
Especially when you don't know what it's for!
But it's the girl that makes the thing that drills the hole that holds
    the spring
That works the thingumebob that makes the engines roar.
And it's the girl that makes the thing that holds the oil that oils
    the ring
That works the thingumebob THAT'S GOING TO WIN THE WAR.

Topical song, *c.* 1942[1]

I

THE victory of El Alamein made Churchill's position as Prime
Minister utterly secure for as long as the war lasted. Complaints
about inefficiency in industry died down at once. The controversy
over production policy ceased; meanwhile, Lyttelton's ministry
was growing in influence and power and playing a valuable, if not
an overweening role. The challenge of Cripps disappeared. He
left the War Cabinet, as he had threatened, but this was now a
matter for relief; and he consented to remain in office as Minister
of Aircraft Production. Herbert Morrison, an orthodox Labour
man, replaced him in the War Cabinet.

From now on, Churchill had only victories to report, and the
public honoured him for performing this service. But controversy
did not perish; it shifted on to new bases. Above all, there was
much bolder argument about the shape of post-war society. The
publication of the much anticipated Beveridge Report on
December 1st came aptly very soon after Alamein and gave the
public a new hero to replace Cripps.

Another vein of controversy was opened up by the anger over
Admiral Darlan. As the allies moved forward to victory, such
cases would often arise, and with them renewed suspicion that
Churchill wanted, not a New Order in Europe, based on the
Resistance movements, but a return to the Old Order presided
over by monarchs, industrialists and military men, whether or not
they had collaborated. Even on the right, many were sickened by
the respect now shown for a man who had associated so closely
with Pétain and Laval.

On December 10th, Churchill surpassed himself with a brilliant
speech in secret session, which pulled the House of Commons
round. Darlan's help, he pointed out, had been enlisted by the
Americans; Eisenhower commanded Torch. "Since 1776 we have
not been in the position of being able to decide the policy of the
United States," he pointed out. "Neither militarily nor politically" was Britain "directly controlling the course of events."[2]

This was plain talk. Though Churchill himself could not fully
admit that 1942 had seen the end of Britain's status as a supreme
world power (had he not told his City audience a month before
that he did not intend to "preside over the liquidation of the
British Empire"?) his subjects were currently digesting the
lesson, delivered in person by a multitude of G.I.s.

II

British civilians had long been used to the presence of small contingents of exotic soldiery in their midst. In the streets of London after the blitz, a motley variety of distinctive uniforms stood out against the increasing drabness of civilian clothing, William Sansom evokes them. "French sailors with their red pompoms and striped shirts, Dutch police in black uniforms and grey-silver braid, the dragoon-like mortarboards of Polish officers, the smart grey of nursing units from Canada, the cerise berets and sky-blue trimmings of the new parachute regiments, all the other gaily coloured field caps of all the other regiments, the scarlet linings of our own nurses' cloaks, the vivid electric blues of Dominion air forces, sandy bush hats and lion-coloured turbans, the prevalent Royal Air Force blue, a few greenish-tinted Russian uniforms and the suave black and gold of the Chinese navy."[3]

The forces from the white Dominions were more like cousins than total strangers. Of the rest, it was the Poles, sailors, airmen and soldiers, who made the greatest impact – especially in Scotland as, years after the war, surprisingly numerous entries under "Z" in Highland telephone directories would testify. The Poles, dressy and romantic, turned the heads of a great many lasses, though their popularity with women was in inverse ratio to the liking felt for them by British servicemen.

The Poles, however, were nothing to compare, in promise or in numbers, with the U.S. troops, called G.I.s after the words "Government Issue" which appeared on their equipment. The G.I.s formed the vast majority of the 1,421,000 allied, Dominion and Colonial troops who were somehow accommodated in the United Kingdom by the late spring of 1944. Two large transports debouched two thousand, nine hundred men at Belfast on January 26th, 1942. The broadly grinning private who had been chosen to appear in the newspapers as the "first" G.I. to land was, in fact, about the five hundred and first because of a hitch in the arrangements.[4] But as further contingents arrived in Ulster and Scotland and fanned out eastwards and southwards towards London and the Channel ports, one of the things which struck the British most forcibly was that their "guests" themselves were supremely efficient.

One Hampshire resident has said, "What impressed me most, I think, was the size of everything. We used to stand in the window positively spellbound by the unending procession of American military equipment . . ." The G.I.s were so smartly dressed, a Devon man wrote, that "unless one was familiar with the markings, it was difficult to distinguish officers from men . . ."[5] American military policemen, with their dazzling white helmets, white gloves and white gaiters, were an eye-catching feature on urban street corners, and so were the truncheons which they carried to prevent unruly behaviour.

Wherever they went, they brought closer the dreaded prospect, not infrequently realized, of alcohol famine. They packed the pubs, appalling the locals by a strange custom of pouring whisky in their beer. Even if the beer was sufficient to meet this invasion, the supply of glasses might not be, and small boys, who had swiftly learnt that to call out "Got any gum, chum?" was one way to beat sweet rationing, could do a roaring trade in jam jars for frustrated drinkers.

But liquor was the only commodity which the G.I.s did not have in superfluity in their own camps; they had their own newspapers, their own films, and their own radio, to which British aficionados, long kept on short rations by the B.B.C., tuned in eagerly for the latest from Duke Ellington or the New Orleans Revival. Maurice Gorham, who was in charge of the B.B.C.'s North American Service, points out that the G.I.s, coming from a "scrupulously American" environment, had nothing in common with the people they met in the pubs; even the news, as they heard or read it, was different. "This seemed to me," he says, "to be one reason why they so often seemed to treat Britain as an occupied country rather than as an ally."[6]

They even imported their own colour problem. There were separate hostels for white and coloured G.I.s. Negro troops were encouraged to spend their off-duty hours in one village or public house, whites in another. There was at least one violent flare-up between white and coloured troops, and reports of lesser incidents found their way into the British newspapers. The British, not yet themselves versed in the ways of Jim Crow, adapted to the pattern they found; when the W.V.S. in Bristol opened two canteens for the G.I.s, one was for whites and one was for Negroes. Yet a poll taken in 1943 suggested that the British people were overwhelmingly opposed to racial discrimination.[7]

But even the Negro troops were far better paid, at the standard rate of fifteen pounds per month, than British soldiers. From the P.X. came in profusion things which, in Britain, were scarce, ersatz, rationed or unobtainable. There were razor blades. There were Lucky Strike cigarettes at threepence for twenty. There were such choice sweets (or candies, as the occupying force insisted on calling them) as Life Savers and Hershey bars. There was soap of peacetime standard. There were fascinating items known as nylons, which soon drove out memories of the silk stockings which had been banned in Britain at the end of 1940. What was more, those last were given away, either in pure friendship or at a price which, to certain British girls, seemed no more than just. One former G.I. has recalled the morning when his sergeant announced to the men at reveille, "I'm told that we've got thirty thousand rubbers in the supply room. I want you people to do something about this."[8] A litter of used contraceptives in shop doorways was a common testimony to the American presence.

The W.V.S., of course, did its best to save the G.I.s from what its leading members would have called "good-time girls". It set up over two hundred British Welcome Clubs to supplement the American Red Cross Clubs, and it encouraged private hospitality – one W.V.S. representative in Somerset distinguished herself by arranging to entertain twenty Americans to tea on four successive Sundays. But British hostesses were somewhat inhibited in following such examples by the feeling that they could not give the G.I.s the quantities of food they were accustomed to. (Eventually, the "guests" were encouraged by General Eisenhower to carry their own rations with them when they visited British homes.) And well-meant hospitality often exasperated the G.I.s themselves. One "land girl" who was dating a G.I. recalls that "half the local camp" used to descend on a Y.M.C.A. club in the evenings. When the World Series was on, they packed the place out and switched the wireless on full blast. Then a pianist turned up to "entertain" them and they had to sit and suffer.[9]

In 1943, when Mass Observation studied the attitude of the British to their allies, it found that the Czechs and the Dutch were the most popular. Little was known about them, except that they were conducting a heroic resistance to Germany. The Free French were well regarded by about half the sample. The Poles, always rather controversial, had lost further popularity by the friction between their Government-in-exile and the Russians. The Americans were only slightly more popular; one-third of those questioned expressed a favourable opinion. After Mussolini's fall in the summer of that year, they were actually less well spoken of than the Italians.[10]

There were other reasons for this besides the fact that the G.I.s were, in the phrase of the time, "over-paid, over-sexed and over

here". The U.S.A., it was well remembered, had intervened at a
late stage in the last war also, had presumed to tell the Europeans
what to do, and had then withdrawn, leaving them to their fate.
"I pray to God they keep out of the end of *this* war anyhow," one
Englishman had said to H. G. Wells in 1939. "We shall never
hear the last of it if they don't . . ."[11] There were political objections not only from the right, who disliked Roosevelt and saw the
U.S.A. as Britain's rival for world power, but from the left also.
While Bevanites as well as Liberals admired the New Deal spirit
and found much inspiration in the Tennessee Valley Authority,
there could be no doubt that the U.S.A. was still the centre of
militant capitalism.

That spokesmen for British opinion might somehow retain a
patronizing attitude towards the U.S.A. is illustrated in an article
about the G.I.s which appeared in a Bristol newspaper early in
1944. "In fairness to our guests," said its well-known author
(S. P. B. Mais), "we should remember these few but fundamental
facts":

1. That they are foreigners. Only a small percentage have
any British forbears.
2. That the similarity between our languages is misleading.
Try out the word "homely" on any American, and you will
see what I mean.
3. That they are all young in spirit as well as in body, and
that the mistakes that they make are likely to spring from too
quick enthusiasm and too little background.
4. That though we may be spiritually far more civilized,
materially they have the advantage. They know the value of
comfort, we don't.
5. That they are no more superior to us than we are to
them . . .
6. That like all children they are very sensitive. They mistake
our British reticence and reserve for the cold shoulder and
positive dislike. They come from a land where everybody
knows everybody, and everybody entertains everybody at
sight. The contrast makes us seem unfriendly.

To which a correspondent rejoined hopefully a few days later that
there were already cricket grounds in America, "and more
Americans may join these clubs after the war".[12]

But it should have been clear to any thinking person that the
cultural traffic was now predominantly one way. In the 'twenties
and 'thirties, mid-Atlantic accents had become almost obligatory

for popular singers, encroaching more and more on the raucous Cockney and fruity Lancashire of the old music hall. The waltz had given way to the foxtrot, and even, in advanced circles, to the jive, as British bandleaders had developed their own imitations of the music of Glenn Miller and Benny Goodman. And above all, there had been the cinema.

When, about the summer of 1945, a British film magazine conducted a survey among its readers, the replies it received from young addicts were most illuminating in this respect. ". . . I always talk to myself in an American accent, and often think that way too," wrote an eighteen-year-old girl. The fourteen-year-old son of a welder went further. "I cannot say that flims [sic] have ever made me dissatisfied with life but I can safely say flims do make me dissatisfied with my neighbourhood and towns. From what I have seen they are not modern for instance there are no drug stors on the corner of the stree where you can take your girl friend and have some ice creem or a milk shake. In our town there are no sky scrappers or really high buildings and there are not half as many buildings which are lit up as those on the flims are such as Broadway."[13] The political influence of the cinema is one of the great undiscussed topics of twentieth-century history; all that can safely be said is that it must have been quite enormous. Tokens were everywhere in the dress, hairstyles, language and manners of young people, especially the girls who strove so earnestly to look like Joan Crawford or Veronica Lake.

It was of some of this generation that a Home Office survey observed, ". . . the sudden influx of Americans, speaking like the films, who actually lived in the magic country, and who had plenty of money, at once went to the girls' heads. The American attitude to women, their proneness to spoil a girl, to build up, exaggerate, talk big, and to act with generosity and flamboyance, helped to make them the most attractive boy-friends. In addition, they 'picked up' easily, and even a comparatively plain and unattractive girl stood a chance."[14]

III

The 1930s had seen much gloomy discussion on the subject of Britain's birth rate. From the 1870s onwards it had fallen "steadily, remorselessly, through war and peace, boom and slump". England and Wales, at the start of the war, had a population of just over forty-one million, which was roughly four and a half million more than in 1914. But there were over two million fewer children under fourteen, and two and a half million more old people over sixty-six. Richard Titmuss calculated that the birth rate in 1940 had been twenty-five per cent below replacement level. "This means, assuming the continuance of present trends, that our population will ultimately diminish by one quarter in each generation." War had made matters worse; in 1941, when those conceived after Dunkirk and during the blitz were born, the birth rate fell to the lowest point recorded in the history of registration, 13·9 per thousand of the population.[15]

A widespread assumption, popularized by Titmuss and others, was that a decadent capitalism, promoting wars and social distress, had deprived married couples of any confidence in the future and had produced a "parents' revolt". But 1942, the year of gloom and austerity, saw a sudden and remarkable change. The birth rate, at 15·6 per thousand, was higher than in any year since 1931. The upward trend continued; 16·2 in 1943, 17·5 in 1944, a check in 1945, then a new peak of 20·6 in 1947. This outburst did not, it seems, indicate any great increase in fertility; it reflected, rather, the delayed effects of a boom in the birth rate immediately after the First World War, and the boom in marriages in 1939–40.

This had produced a record marriage rate of 22·5 per thousand. The rate fell by over one-third, to 14 per thousand in 1943, then rose to 18·7 in 1945. Altogether, more people got married in six years of war than would have done so had the pre-war rates continued, but this was a continuation of the peacetime trend; marriage, perhaps because of increasing prosperity, had become more popular. Another peacetime trend, towards younger marriages, was also enhanced; nearly three war-brides out of ten were under twenty-one. Perhaps more than a hundred thousand girls altogether married servicemen from allied or Dominion countries, and after the war, some eighty thousand "G.I. brides" sailed to the U.S.A.[16]

But the rate of births among married women actually fell, while the number of illegitimate births per thousand single or widowed women very nearly tripled to 16·1 in 1945. There were about 102,000 illegitimate births out of a total of 255,000 between 1940 and 1945, which would not have occurred had the pre-war rate obtained.

The moralists were, naturally, concerned. But the figures did not, in themselves, imply any increase in feminine laxness. In 1938–39, when approaching three mothers out of ten who had conceived their first child out of wedlock, seventy per cent of these children had been legitimized by marriage. In 1945, the proportion was under forty per cent. There was actually a fall in the number of "irregularly conceived maternities" among unmarried women, during the war years. The trouble was that marriage for the mothers was less likely. "Irregularly conceived maternities" among mothers under twenty-five were actually rarer than they had been in peacetime, but amongst women of twenty-five to thirty they increased by a quarter; in the next age group, thirty to thirty-five, by no less than forty-one per cent; and by one-fifth amongst unmarried women aged thirty-five to forty-five. Such statistics pose more puzzles than they answer questions, yet it does seem that it was spinsters kicking over the traces as they neared middle age, rather than young girls obsessed with film stars and crooners, who swelled the sad statistics.[17]

However, conceptions out of wedlock were far from the whole story. The early years of war saw a shocking increase in the number of new cases of syphilis coming forward for treatment – in 1941, figures for male civilians and servicemen showed a hundred and thirteen per cent increase, and figures for women sixty-three per cent. The statistics for 1942 were even worse; and since notification of the disease was not compulsory, many cases may not have been discovered. There was also a very great increase in gonorrhea. The Government had to act. As a result of similar shocks in the First World War, centres had been set up to which sufferers could resort for treatment; their number was now increased. A new Defence Regulation, 33B, provided that any person suspected of having infected two or more patients might be compelled to undergo treatment. The taboo which had hitherto prevented any sane discussion of the subject was lifted. In the autumn of 1942, the Ministry of Health launched a spectacular campaign to make the facts about venereal disease and its treatment more widely known. The ministry's Chief Medical Officer went so far as to raise the matter in a broadcast. There were debates in parliament and, still more remarkable, an intensive press advertising campaign for the rest of the war. New cases of V.D. among men seem to have decreased thereafter; among women, the number reported continued to rise, but this may have reflected merely a greater readiness to come forward.[18]

It is likely that the increasing enlightenment of women in sexual matters (which was surely reflected in a greatly increased demand for sanitary towels) meant that there was more "sin", but that relatively fewer girls suffered for it. One side effect of taking women out of their ruts – their homes, their isolated work in small shops and offices and in domestic service – was greatly to increase their curiosity about, and knowledge of, the world they lived in. Shirley Joseph, a teenage recruit for the Women's Land Army, wrote of her experience, "I defy anyone who has lived in a hostel for any length of time to be narrow minded on any subject . . . My companions just said what they thought, and if I didn't like it, I could just lump it." Worldly and "emancipated" women – and this went for service camps and factories as well – educated their more sheltered compeers. Miss Joseph gives an apt example. The gallantry of G.I. drivers encouraged a few girls to imitate servicemen and hitch-hike. This behaviour at first attracted shocked comment. Then it was generally realized in the hostel that this was the quickest and cheapest way of travelling in wartime, and convention went by the board.[19]

Contraception was a likely topic for emancipating discussion, in this and other hostels. Here again, a taboo makes generalization difficult, and it no doubt explains why the Ministry of Health tried to shrug off any responsibility for maintaining the supply of contraceptives after the Japanese had cut off the major source of Britain's rubber. Complaints from the birth control clinics forced the ministry to intervene.

But those who were silly or unlucky were still made to feel the weight of their "sin" and more. The social services available to unmarried mothers had been bad enough before the war; most had been thrust into poor law institutions. The stress on them was now still worse, since many were away from home on war work or in the services. Service women were discharged as soon as their condition was known and war workers in billets might well be kicked out. It was almost impossible to find billets after confinement. The position of those many women married to servicemen who bore children by other fathers was better in some respects – by the lights of society, any baby brought to birth by Mrs Smith was inherently more acceptable than one born to Miss Smith – but sadder in others. Few statistics were kept of such cases, but in Birmingham, where note was taken, the percentage of irregularly conceived children born to married women tripled between 1940 and 1945. Over half such mothers, in 1945, had husbands in the services.[20]

A married woman had to have her husband's consent before she could offer a child for adoption, so such cases could not be kept secret. One recourse was illegal abortion, which might be necessary even where the husband was the father, because allowances for service wives were so low. (A young woman schoolteacher, working in a Yorkshire factory during her holidays in 1942, was "profoundly shocked" when she heard from one of the men that a woman "back-street" abortionist had just been prosecuted locally for performing such operations. "What shocked me", she wrote in her diary, "was his remark, 'Course, it's awk'ard for 'em, they're mostly soldiers' wives.' ")[21]

Some husbands received the cuckoos into their nests; at least one case is on record of a man who accepted two children whom he had not fathered. But many deserted their wives, or sued for divorce. The divorce rate soared during and after the war. In 1938, there were just under ten thousand divorce petitions filed, forty-six per cent by the husbands. In 1945, there were twenty-five thousand, fifty-eight per cent by the husbands, and seventy per cent on grounds of adultery. The rise in earnings, of course, must have stimulated civilians to start divorce proceedings who could not have afforded them before; while this did not affect the services, the authorities, recognizing the problem, took steps to make divorces quicker, and cheaper, for men in the forces.[22]

In the atmosphere of the war years, very intense moral odium attached to service wives who went out with G.I.s, or, still more "contemptibly", succumbed to Italian prisoners of war. Yet it is hard to feel indignant now. It was tacitly accepted by society that husbands serving abroad had a right to girl-friends or prostitutes. A London probation officer reported sadly that, "Many excellent young mothers have been unable to stand the loneliness at home, particularly when their husbands are abroad, with not even spasmodic leave to break the monotony ... Hasty war marriages, on embarkation leave, sometimes between comparative strangers, with a few days or weeks of married life, have left both parties with little sense of responsibility or obligation towards each other."[23]

Those couples, old and new, who remained loyal in spite of everything were certainly doing much to justify the institution of marriage, but they were not necessarily happier than those who abandoned restraint. In a war factory in Wiltshire, one observer came across a pretty young mother of two who had come to work, as she said, "To occupy my time, I was getting so miserable sitting home and worrying about Bill." Bill, it seemed, was with the R.A.F. somewhere out East. But she had now decided to quit her job. The children were being looked after by her sister. 'I know she does everything for them, but I never seem to see my babies now. I miss it, dressing them and feeding them, and

I sort of feel they'll forget I'm their Mummy – you know what I mean. Starting at six in the morning and getting back at nine, all I see of them is when they're asleep.'[24]

This situation, though typical enough, exemplifies only one of the many ways in which war disrupted married life. Migration and overcrowding, taken together, provided another fertile source of strain.

IV

From the outbreak of war to the end of 1945, some sixty million changes of address took place among a civilian population of about thirty-eight million. Nearly thirty-five million of these changes involved people moving from one local government area to another, and of these fourteen and a half million took place in 1940 or 1941. Some people, of course, changed address more than once, and there were probably millions of people who in peacetime would have moved to a house in a new district, or to work in a new town, and who, because of the war, did not move. But when the men and women in the services are added, it is clear that this was "a war of movement" in other senses besides the military one.[25]

An eagle's-eye view showed that the pre-war distribution of the population broadly persisted, and so did the pre-war drift away from the depressed areas. By the end of 1943, some fifty-five or sixty-five thousand workers had transferred from the north-east coast, a figure equivalent to seven and a half per cent of the pre-war insured population. But within this prevailing pattern, there was a huge drift away from some of the blitzed cities, and a smaller one from the east and south coast areas threatened by invasion. East Anglia as a whole increased its civilian population during the war, while that of its seaside centre at Southend fell by over half. The population of the East End, also, fell by more than half and in June 1943, London as a whole had only seventy-six per cent of its pre-war population, Liverpool stood at eighty per cent, and Southampton at sixty-seven per cent. But new workers continued to arrive in Coventry and Manchester, and the area of light industry north and west of London waxed while the metropolis waned.[26]

These currents ebbed and flowed over a housing situation which had been bad, though improving, before the war, and was now worse, and steadily worsening. House building had virtually ceased. The building industry, as the great initial programme of camp and factory construction had neared completion, had been seized on by the War Cabinet as a likely source of men for the services and war industry. By the end of 1941, the force of builders and civil engineers had fallen by a quarter, but it still stood at 920,000, of whom well over half were fulfilling Government contracts. Churchill had ordered a further reduction, to six hundred thousand by the end of 1942. Then Pearl Harbour had made it necessary to build more camps for the G.I.s. The rundown of building labour was checked, and in the summer of 1942 Bevin dereserved all building workers, then suspended their call-up on condition they agreed to transfer to priority work on Government contracts.[27]

By the end of 1942, some hundred thousand families were living in houses which had been officially condemned as unfit before the war, and a further two hundred thousand in houses which would have been so condemned had the war not broken out. These figures represented a million or more people. In addition, two and a-half million families occupied bombed houses which had received only first-aid repairs. Early in 1943, the War Cabinet agreed that repairs should begin on some of the hundred thousand houses made totally uninhabitable by bombs and that three thousand new cottages should be built in agricultural areas. But these gestures only chipped at the corners of the problem.[28]

The social ulcer of overcrowding spread from the industrial conurbations to smaller country towns which now entertained war industry. Between mid-1938 and October 1942, the population of Reading, for instance, increased by one-seventh. An official investigation then showed that more than a quarter of its "occupied dwelling units" were accommodating more than one person per room; a seventh had more than two people per room. By the standards of Bombay, this was excellent; by the standards of modern Britain, not so good. The notoriously gracious spa of Cheltenham, the seaside resort of Blackpool, now returned similar figures for overcrowding. Conditions had grown so intolerable in certain meccas of war industry that the Government, as early as 1941, had begun to ban the placing of any further contracts with firms there, if they involved more than a handful of workers. Coventry and Luton came under the ban; so did Chelmsford, in Essex, formerly regarded as a peaceful market town.[29]

But Chelmsford's reputation was not so sleepy as that of Chippenham in Wiltshire. When Donald Johnson stood there as an independent candidate in 1943, he found "a town in the throes

of the managerial revolution, a town inhabited by a pallid population working long exhausting hours at armament manufacture
at the large Westinghouse works". Mass Observation described
"a tiny country town of ancient cottages and winding streets", in
the same area of rural Wessex, which had billeted soldiers, civil
servants and evacuees and had been presented with a new war
factory employing a thousand people. The peaceful streets now
resembled "a London railway terminus, with its endless comings
and goings of strangers from all parts of the country; with its
atmosphere of irritable bustle, impersonal pushing and hurry-
ing". The newcomers had arrived "without warning" and, so it
seemed, "without reasons, to eat up the already scarce food
supplies; to buy up all the favourite brands of soap and patent
medicines; to consume all the fish in the fish and chip shops . . . ;
to cram the local cinema at weekends . . ."[30]

And very often they were not made to feel welcome. Householders could be compelled to take in war workers, but they could
not be compelled to feed them and make them comfortable. In
1942, the Telecommunications Research Establishment, which
was responsible for the further development of radar, took its one
thousand personnel to the small Worcestershire town of Malvern,
famous for its spa water and its public school, but already
swollen so that five lived where four had stayed before. The
superintendent of T.R.E. reports that "The average citizen of
Malvern clearly did not want us . . . Potential billetors fell ill with
alarming regularity and the number of destitute aunts who were
being given permanent homes in a few days' time passed all
bounds of reason. Some gave shelter on the understanding that
billetees were in by ten o'clock at night, while others gave it on
the understanding that they stayed out, somewhere, until the same
hour."[31]

The young evacuees were part of the general overcrowding.
Between the autumn of 1941 and the autumn of 1943, the number
of evacuees officially billeted in the country had fallen by over
two-thirds, to 355,000. But while the proportion of children
remaining in the reception areas for long periods was relatively
small, many went through four or more changes of billet. The
headmistress of one girls' secondary school from London which
spent the last five years of war in South Wales, calculated that
"less than fifty out of a stable school population of about three
hundred remained in the same billet all through our stay in
Llanelly."[32] Hostels were built or requisitioned for infants,
difficult children, war workers, old people, soldiers and G.I.s, but

not in such numbers that the weight of the billeting problem was lifted from the shoulders of the ordinary housewife.

V

Yet housing was not the problem which people felt most keenly, for the present, though it exercised their minds a great deal when they thought about the future. Every December since the war had started, Mass Observation had asked its "National Panel" – socially aware volunteers from many walks of life, though chiefly from the better-off strata – what wartime problems most inconvenienced them personally. In 1943, as in previous Decembers, it was blackout and transport which topped the poll.[33]

Nothing could be done about the blackout, that dismal and ubiquitous comrade of Fear and Austerity. But the transport problem affected the war economy in so many ways that the Government was always making new attempts to mitigate it. From industry's point of view, these had some success. From the public's, nothing was of much avail.

In 1939, there had been over two million cars and over four hundred thousand motor-cycles licensed for private use in Great Britain. In 1943, the totals were 718,000 and 124,000. Now that petrol was only issued on proof of need, most motorists had given in and stored their cars for the duration. Expenditure on petrol for private motoring was running at a mere six per cent of pre-war.

Meanwhile, the railways had suffered quite badly from bombing. Locomotives and carriages had grown older, but the railway workshops were now playing an important part in munitions production. By the end of 1943, one of the four main line companies was running nearly five hundred locomotives which in peacetime would have been on the scrap-heap. In the winter of 1942–43 trains were being cancelled at the rate of a thousand and fifteen hundred per week because of the shortage of locomotives. Meanwhile, goods traffic had risen by fifty per cent and passenger travel by nearly seventy per cent. It was not that many more journeys were made – the increase was small. But people were making longer journeys; either to visit scattered members of the family, or because they were now further from their work.

Often, it was a choice of one nuisance or the other. The shortage of "married quarters" for transferred war workers was one of the saddest features of the home front. If a man was told to work in Coventry, his wife would very likely have to stay behind in London. While surprisingly few factories had "dispersed" themselves from such target towns as London, Southampton, Sheffield and Birmingham, homeless or fearful workers had removed themselves relatively much more.[34]

But to accommodate the increased demand, there were approaching ten per cent fewer carriages. Train travel was three times as expensive as before the war, yet it was probably three times as uncomfortable. Reservations were no longer permitted. There were usually no restaurant cars. If trains were not cancelled, they were likely to be late. Sometimes it was literally quite impossible for a grown man to force his way into corridors already jammed with weary war workers and servicemen on leave.

Shortages of staff, spare parts, rubber and petrol had hit the bus services. In the autumn of 1942 the off-peak services had been drastically cut, and a nine o'clock curfew had been imposed, except in the large cities where buses still left up to ten o'clock. London Transport introduced wooden slatted seats into its vehicles to save moquette and rubber. Worn rubber bulbs for drivers' hooters were replaced by a contrivance made of leather and string, and all bus tickets were reduced in size and thickness to save paper. To save petrol, the Goverment encouraged the conversion of buses and goods vehicles to run on producer gas, trailing their generators behind them. By the end of 1942, some thousand private cars had been fitted with gas bags, to use low pressure coal gas from town gas works.[35]

The Post Office had reduced its deliveries and collections by half or more because of loss of staff. Laundries in many places found it impossible to accept new customers, and their slower and lower service was particularly resented now that linen cupboards were running low. More seriously, many doctors and dentists had been called up for the forces; by the end of the war, over one-third of the country's practitioners had gone, and one in ten of those who remained was over seventy.

Then, in some areas, there was a shortage, not only of the things they sold, but of shops themselves. Surveys in seven widely scattered towns early in 1942 suggested that about one shop in ten, over the nation as a whole, must have closed down. The position in individual cities was certainly worse; it seemed that Glasgow and Leeds had lost approaching one-fifth of their shops. While the multiples had closed many branches, it was the small trader, that hero of capitalist ideology, who was most affected.[36]

Much concern was voiced over his difficulties, notably by the Liberal Party.

Certainly, many of the nation's seven hundred thousand or so independent shopkeepers had been badly hit by wartime conditions. Numbers had been called up, and had had to close their businesses if their wives or friends could not carry on. A Liberal Party inquiry committee was partly justified in suggesting that the plight of shopkeepers in these cases was "disproportionate", compared with the position of men in industry who now had statutory assurance (however much that was worth) that their jobs would be given back to them when they were demobilized.[37] From 1942 onwards, the Government was at pains to discriminate in favour of the "small man", prodded by gloomy reports from the Retail Trade Committee which it had set up to investigate the position.

But it should have been clear enough that those "small men" who kept going were in a very good position, at least as compared with their pretty general plight before the war. Then, the small trader had been simultaneously attacked by the Co-operative stores, chain stores and department stores, which by 1941 had engrossed more than half of the market, and by the growing numbers of other small traders. Men who had found it hard to hold a job in the depression had often turned, where they could, to shopkeeping, but many had helped to swell the alarming figures for small bankruptcies among traders.

The war ossified, or even worsened, the small man's long-term position vis-à-vis the multiple (for instance, the Co-operative stores, with only six and a half per cent of the food outlets, had at the end of the war secured a quarter of all registrations for rationed sugar, while the independents, with eighty-five per cent of outlets, handled only fifty-three per cent of registrations). But for the moment, competition had ceased to exist; while the Liberal Party conference was extolling him for maintaining it, the shopkeeper himself was quietly gloating over the loss of it. Some of those bombed out must have revelled, like Mr Polly, in the fires which consumed their burdens and debts. When the Government gave non-food retailers who had been forced to close down since the outbreak the chance to register their names so as to be ensured of an opportunity to set up again after the war, few did so, in spite of widespread publicity. Once bitten, twice shy.[38]

Bank of England figures showed that even in 1943, the worst year in this respect, the total value of sales in shops (as distinct from their volume) was only seven per cent down on pre-war.[39]

The trade in rationed food was absolutely safe. Shortages of practically everything else meant that the small man cleared his shelves as fast as goods came in, and dead stock was a thing of the past. In the pre-war depressed areas, where shopkeepers had often had to ruin themselves by extending credit if they were to sell anything at all, there was now plenty of money to buy whatever could be bought. Even the shortage of labour, while it meant more work for the shopkeeper, also meant economies; those who suffered were the housewives who had to stand in queues because there were too few people behind the counter, and who then had to endure, in many cases, the rudeness and off-handedness of traders who no longer had to flatter their customers to keep them.

Indeed, the queue was a characteristic social institution of the island which the G.I.s invaded. Tired, angry war workers queued in the blackout for buses which when they came, if they came, would be crammed. Men queued forty deep outside Lyons tea shops in the early morning for the sake of one rasher of bacon and one egg off the ration. The housewife, above all, queued, patiently, clutching the family's ration books, for tomatoes, for fish, for offal. In Hull, in the autumn of 1941, an observer had found, at one shop, a queue of about seventy people. This particular shop, he had noticed, nearly always had a queue outside it. Curiously, he had asked a young bystander what the attraction was. "I don't suppose they know what they are queuing for," the Yorkshireman had replied. "It's a hysteria with some people – whenever they see a queue they just join on the end. I expect they end up with two bunches of roses and a stick of rhubarb."[40]

Certainly, those housewives who could not queue, because they had not now got the time, were the unlucky ones. And not many people in Britain in 1943 had very much time.

VI

Britain now depended on American help, not only for food, but for weapons. Lend-lease had increased eightfold, but the proportion sent as munitions had risen from thirty to seventy per cent. Britain's imports, if weapons and oil were excluded, were under half what they had been before the war, and non-military exports had declined by over two-thirds. Britain, to quote an official report, was "living beyond its income".[41]

In America, consumer purchases per head had actually increased between 1941 and 1943. In Britain, they had fallen by approaching one-fifth since the start of the war. On one side of the Atlantic, war meant bereavement and prosperity; on the other, bereavement and austerity. It was not only that Britain's resources were smaller; she devoted a greater proportion of them to the war effort than any of her western allies (and also more than Germany, which in 1943 was still taking in slack). In June 1944, twenty-two per cent of Britain's labour force was in the services, thirty-three per cent engaged in civilian war work. This total of fifty-five per cent compares with forty per cent for the U.S.A. at the same juncture. About the same proportion of Britain's national income was being spent on the war – the only allied nation to come near to equalling this was, rather oddly, New Zealand.

Including all men between fourteen and sixty-four, and all women up to fifty-nine, Britain in 1939 had had a total working population of nineteen and three-quarter million. In June 1944, this had risen to just over twenty-two million, out of a population of 47,700,000. This figure, which of course includes the services, understates considerably the number of people at work. It counts two part-time workers as one unit, and there were some nine hundred thousand of these, mostly women. At least a million older men and women (including Winston Churchill) were at work, but are omitted. Nearly ten million women were occupied on essential household work, and there were nine million children under fourteen and some six million old people to be looked after. At least a million women of all ages were giving voluntary service, inside or outside the W.V.S. There were still hundreds of thousands of volunteer Civil Defence workers. All men who worked less than sixty hours a week, and women who worked less than fifty-five hours, had to undertake compulsory fire-watching for roughly one whole night a week, unless they were already civil defenders or Home Guards.[42]

In June 1944, four and a half million men, about thirty per cent of the working male population, were in the forces. So were over four hundred and fifty thousand of the younger women. The total number of people in civilian employment had fallen, to under seventeen million, and two hundred and eighty thousand of these were whole-time workers in Civil Defence, the fire service or the police. The expansion of the war industries – metal, engineering, chemicals, explosives, oils – from about three million men and women in 1939 to over five million in mid-1943, and the maintenance of the necessary number of coal-miners, agricultural workers and transport workers, had been achieved at the expense of the industries which made or distributed food, goods or services for civilians. (The numbers employed in the textiles industry had fallen from a million in 1939 to six hundred and seventy thousand in 1943.) Some half a million workers were directly or indirectly engaged in providing goods and services for the G.I.s – not munitions workers mostly, but transport workers, builders and others whose labour might otherwise have helped sustain the civilian standard of living.[43]

There was one compensation, however, so simply inherent in the situation that one might almost overlook it. Britain had achieved full employment. Those who wanted work could have it in plenty; those who did not were forced to undertake it; those who could not, it had seemed, hope for it – the blind, the crippled and the invalid – were trained for it.

By 1943, unemployment had virtually ceased to exist. From two hundred thousand in the summer of 1941, the number of unemployed had sunk to sixty thousand two years later. These were mostly in transit from one job to another. Only about twenty thousand were totally unemployable, for physical or psychological reasons. This last figure surprised those who had brooded compassionately over the condition of men in the depressed areas who had known years out of work, and had adjusted so far to worklessness that it had been feared that they could never be employed again. In certain areas unemployment had lingered well into the war. The rate in Dundee had remained at six per cent in the autumn of 1941 when the national rate had fallen to about one and a half per cent.[44] But even the hard cores of unemployment in the depressed areas had since been chewed up by military necessity.

In fact, Bevin had had to turn overseas for more labour. There were already many Irishmen in Britain, familiar figures both in the cities and on the land. Though Eire was neutral, Britain was able to recruit there approaching forty thousand workers for her munition industries. The coloured inhabitants of the West Indies were still a faraway people of whom the British, except in the dock areas, knew next to nothing. Even so, the racial problem was timorously anticipated by the Ministry of Labour officials responsible for handling three parties of young West Indian trainees – a hundred and fifty-five in all – who had come over in 1942 to take courses at Government Training Centres and to ease the manpower situation in north-west England. Learie Constantine, the most electrifying of all West Indian cricketers, was made a welfare officer to deal with their problems. Later more men, unskilled, were brought over for training in Government centres. With a different purpose in view, some seven hundred Indians were trained, who were then sent back to their own country to boost the already very considerable production of munitions there. Italians, already quite familiar, were another race who would be better known after the war. By the time it finished, a hundred and thirty thousand Italian prisoners of war and over ninety thousand captured Germans were contributing to the British effort.[45]

Meanwhile, numerous British citizens did more than one job. Besides the unprecedented development of part-time work for women, tens of thousands of volunteers from every walk of life helped to make munitions in their spare time. The Houses of Parliament had their own volunteer squad; M.P.s put on overalls and glumly discovered that there was more to industrial work than they had supposed.

The Manpower Survey in the autumn of 1942 prompted cuts amounting to over one million in the demands for able bodies made by the forces, war industry and Civil Defence. In mid-1943, the aircraft industry – that is, the bombing industry – was given overweening priority over what was left. Following the 1943 Manpower Survey, Bevin announced that extra demands simply could not be met. "The standards and amenities of the civil population cannot be further reduced," he said, and Churchill, of course, agreed with him.[46] From then on, there was a gradual and judicious running down of the munitions industries, and a slow return of life-blood to the numb civil industries. But June 1944 saw the peak of national activity in all fields combined.

VII

There was never a central plan in Whitehall which laid down exactly what every worker in every factory should be doing, nor could there have been. There was, rather, a gradually assembled collection of controls, over raw materials, factory space, labour, prices, retail outlets. Taken together, they were enough to prevent employers and workers from making goods which the Government deemed inessential. If an entrepreneur saw the chance of a kill in toys and could lay his hands on a few non-directable women and old men, he would still have the trouble of finding materials, and would have to steer his way carefully through a maze of regulations. It could be done, but it was very hard. By

1943, the net of controls had drawn so tight that one could say, with only a little exaggeration, that every seamstress, every railway guard, every pram manufacturer, was as crucial a part of the national effort as the aircraft fitters on assembly work, the soldiers in Tunisia and Burma, the miners hewing the coal on which the whole gigantic enterprise depended, the land girls pulling potatoes from soil won back for the plough. But the spearhead, for which the rest was the stave, was war industry.

The munitions industries had grown from very small beginnings. In the early 'thirties, three Royal Ordnance Factories, the Admiralty shipyards, and a cluster of smallish aircraft firms, together with the large Vickers Armstrong combine and the historic Birmingham Small Arms Company had completed the roll call.

From 1936 onwards, the Government had intervened in several ways to promote expansion. It had built and equipped factories; it had paid for extensions and new equipment for existing arms firms and other likely engineering firms, it had commandeered premises and put them under the management of armament makers; it had placed orders with big firms which would otherwise never have dreamt of making munitions.

Between 1937 and the end of 1939, one great firm alone, I.C.I., had undertaken the construction and management of no less than eighteen "shadow" factories, and these had increased later to twenty-five. By the end of the war, there were a hundred and fifty-nine shadow, or "agency" factories under the Ministry of Supply, eighty-seven under M.A.P., and nineteen under the Admiralty. The Government owned the factories, and had paid for them entirely out of public funds. It met running costs, wages and salaries. The "agent" firm was paid a fee for managing the factory and employed workers under its own usual conditions and rates of pay.[47]

This blend of state ownership and private management was not generally used, however, for the production of small arms, shells, ammunition and explosives – a field in which the state itself had traditionally been the chief specialist. Forty Royal Ordnance Factories had been built from 1936 onwards, to supplement the three historic ones at Woolwich, Enfield and Waltham. At their peak, in 1942, these factories employed over three hundred thousand men and women, and formed together "the largest munitions undertaking in industrial history". Their director general, at the Ministry of Supply, was "managing director", as it were, of over forty factories. The superintendents of individual

R.O.F.s were paid at civil service rates, less than their counter-parts in private industry. There were ten "filling" R.O.F.s devoted to putting explosives into shells; nine which made explosives, and twenty-four engineering factories. Between them, the R.O.F.s accounted for ninety-five per cent of all filling, half the production of propellants and explosives, and more than fifty per cent of the army's small arms. They also made large guns, bombs, mines and tanks.[48]

Out of twenty-three new R.O.F.s approved by 1939, only eleven had been in existence at the time of Dunkirk. In the next three months, the R.O.F.s had taken on eighty thousand new workers, who in some cases had worked under tarpaulin while the factory roof had been built over their heads. Recruitment had continued at a furious level. Rapid growth had accentuated the R.O.F.s' problems. Because they had been located, in most cases, in pre-war depressed areas, they employed an exceptional propor-tion of people whose physique had been damaged by years of unemployment. For safety reasons, they had required huge and isolated sites.

But after gargantuan teething troubles, the R.O.F.s had settled down to give a lead to the rest of war industry. Unlike all but a handful of private firms, they had been able to introduce three-shift working, and they had been far ahead of most in their use of incentives, motion studies and statistical controls of quality. So efficient had most of them become that the Government had suddenly found itself over-provided with capacity for ammuni-tion, and nineteen projected R.O.F.s had been cancelled.[49]

Yet at the climax of their success, the Select Committee on National Expenditure made them the subject for angry, but some-times contradictory, attacks. Having first called on the Govern-ment to provide more hostels for R.O.F. workers, the committee later arraigned it because the new hostels were only just over half full – the workers, it turned out, preferred long hours of travel to the regimented rigours of life in institutions built under the reign of Dame Austerity. The R.O.F.s achieved some of the more spectacular rates of dilution, yet were criticized for not pressing it home harder.[50] There were, of course, political implications in the success of state-run factories, and these helped to obscure the R.O.F.s' achievements.

The most famous (or notorious) of all R.O.F.s was a filling factory which stood two miles outside the Lancashire town of Chorley, in an area which had suffered from the decline of the cotton industry. But by the time it had got going, other war industries had absorbed the expected reserves of labour. So Chorley had recruited workers from population centres many miles away – Blackpool, Manchester, even Liverpool. Daily travelling times of two, three, even four hours had been common. When the worker reached the factory, before the internal transport system became effective, he might have a three-quarter hour walk before he arrived at his shop.

For R.O.F. Chorley was huge, with fifteen hundred separate buildings scattered over more than a thousand acres. At peak, it employed thirty-five thousand people. While this was not extraordinary by American standards, it was so in Britain. There were only about a dozen factories in Britain at this time employing more than nineteen thousand people, and seven of these were R.O.F.s. The ten R.O.F. filling factories averaged fifteen thousand. The explosives factories employed far fewer workers, but because of the special dangers, could cover even larger areas. Even at Chorley there were elaborate safety precautions, though "green" workers were all too prone to employ a hammer on components filled with explosives, or to use a stick of T.N.T. as chalk.[51]

Under the circumstances, it was remarkable that there were only a hundred and thirty-four deaths caused by accidents in R.O.F.s during the war. With certain highly sensitive chemicals, the slightest spark, friction or vibration could cause an explosion. If one fuse or shell went, the shaking might set off others. What could happen was demonstrated at R.O.F. Hereford in May 1944, when a series of explosions occurred, and no less than thirty-two awards for gallantry were made to fire fighters and rescue workers.[52]

Yet by 1943, when the shell programme, too large anyway, had been overfulfilled to the extent that endless dumps of the sinister objects had made their appearance along the nation's roadsides, and when the filling factories were beginning to release labour, the R.O.F.s were popular with those who worked there. After a very bad start, welfare provision had reached a high standard. These new buildings were far smarter and brighter than the pits or dingy old cotton mills which surrounded them. The superintendent at Chorley complained that it was harder to get rid of workers than it had been to recruit them.[53]

Even in the production of ammunition, outside firms had been brought in to supplement the R.O.F.s (One was the famous Bournville chocolate works, for which the filling of A.A. rockets was, on its own estimate, "just the packing of a new kind of

Assortment Box".) Self-contained shell-forging units were installed at Government expense in some two score factories. The Sten gun was developed deliberately as a crude, though effective, weapon, which could not only make use of captured Italian bullets, but could be turned over to inexperienced manufacturers – makers of cheap jewellery, ironmongery, children's scooters. For many workers, the transition to war production simply meant making the same kind of thing as in peacetime, with major or minor variations – armoured cars, for instance, instead of family saloons. It was calculated that in December 1942, out of a total labour force on Ministry of Supply work of eleven million, about a third were still making commercial or near-commercial items. But among the thirty thousand or so firms which were working for the three supply departments, there were some striking cases of adaptation. One car firm, for instance, made army helmets and trainer aircraft in the phoney war period, and switched during the Battle of Britain to producing them for civilians. It made trailer pumps for the fire services and ski clamps for the Norwegian campaign. At one stage later in the war, it was simultaneously engaged on seventy-six different Government contracts, each employing more than fifty workers.[54]

The voluntary diversion to war production of many firms which produced consumer goods, as they found their supplies of raw materials or their export markets disappearing, had helped to explain the somewhat ludicrous saga of the "concentration" policy which the Board of Trade had launched in 1941.

The idea had been that the Board (and the Ministry of Food, for those manufactures which came under its province) would inform each non-essential industry of the degree of concentration required, and would leave it to the firms themselves to work out which stayed open and which closed. Trade associations had also been left to make their own arrangements about compensation. Sometimes the "nucleus" firms had absorbed the closed ones completely, sometimes the latter had rented part of the remaining factory space or had taken a proportion of the profits, sometimes there was a levy on the whole industry to pay for the maintenance of machinery and other assets of the closed firms.

But concentration had naturally been much resisted, especially by small firms which must now hand their trade secrets over to bigger rivals. Progress had been so slow that the Board of Trade had soon had to nominate the "nuclei" itself. For instance, only fourteen carpet factories out of seventy-five were scheduled to go on, and well over half the pottery works were to close down. But

in certain industries (such as cutlery) officially "closed" firms
went on working quite comfortably for a while until the network
of controls caught them. In others there had turned out to be
little or no surplus capacity – such a promising subject as the lace
industry had proved to be mainly engaged on the manufacture of
sandfly netting for the troops in North Africa.

The Board of Trade had met its Waterloo in 1942; a storm of
local protests had forced it to withdraw in confusion when it had
proposed to rob Luton of its famous hat industry. The Ministry
of Food, however, was meanwhile providing the text-book
example of concentration. From 1942 to 1944, the soft-drinks
industry was so thoroughly dealt with that brand names were
abolished, prices were standardized, and lemonade bottles were
distinguished only by numbers. These draconian measures had
been estimated to yield four thousand workers for war production. In fact, far fewer were released, and many of these were
unsuitable for war work anyway. There were, not surprisingly,
some gallant cases of last-ditch resistance to such pettifogging
frenzies of bureaucracy. A soap company in the midlands took on
no less than three Government departments – Labour, Food and
Air – and won by simply refusing to budge. The results of concentration were unimportant compared with those of the Factory
Control, which had been inaugurated about the same time, and
which altogether requisitioned some twenty thousand separate
premises for various Government departments and contractors.[55]

Concentration did, however, contribute to the tragi-comic fate
of the cotton industry, which had remained Britain's largest
manufacturing and export industry before the war, even though a
quarter of its workers had been unemployed as late as 1938. The
export drive and the rush of service contracts at the start of the
war had brought the industry full order books for the first time
for many years. But by 1941, the shortage of cotton caused by
loss of imports, and the great demands for labour from R.O.F.
Chorley and other wartime Molochs in Lancashire, had prompted a severe programme of compulsory concentration. In the
spring and summer of that year, spinning mills had been closing
at the rate of about ten a week. Altogether a third of the nation's
mills, in all sections of the industry, had been closed.

But concentration, so far from ensuring a fuller use of capacity,
accomplished the reverse. Before, the industry had been running
at less than eighty per cent of capacity; after, the remaining mills
had still been using only eight-tenths of their plant. The cotton
workers, who even before concentration had been drifting into

war industry in search of higher pay, had turned the drift into an avalanche as soon as they had heard about the new scheme. In 1941, the industry had lost nearly thirty per cent of its workers, and even thereafter losses had exceeded new intakes. When it had been announced that the Essential Work Order would be applied to the industry, still more workers had escaped. Those who stayed were generally stiffer, older and less efficient.[56]

The same withering and senescence affected other great industries, with the same deterioration of the machines and the environment now that proper maintenance was impossible. The boot and shoe industry provides a sad example. Tuberculosis was the traditional bane of its workers. Before the war, it had seemed vanquished at last. Now that the older male operatives and women were left to cope with more work per head, longer hours and equipment which showed the strain but could not be replaced, T.B. had rapidly increased again.[57]

Indeed, much was happening to the health of industrial workers at this time which could never be measured, nor in some cases certainly attributed to wartime conditions. In February 1965, the City Coroner at Stoke on Trent reported "that blackout regulations during the war had led to the deaths during the past year of six wartime factory workers". The cause was cadmium poisoning. All the men had been employed in non-ferrous metal casting. Blackout had stifled the normal channels of ventilation and the men had inhaled the poison.[58]

VIII

Large factories on vital work were camouflaged, and uniformed factory policemen stood at their gates round the clock to ward off spies and saboteurs. Spotters kept watch on the roof; at night fire-watchers and factory Home Guards lurked in the deserted buildings or mingled with the night shift in the canteen. J. B. Priestley evokes one of the better factories of the period, a "front line" where aircraft were put together, the welfare arrangements were good and the workers were relatively young. "There are no windows. The roofs are darkened. The factory inside is like a colossal low bright cave, lit with innumerable mercury-vapour lamps that produce a queer greenish-white mistiness of light. In there, three in the morning and three in the afternoon look just the same. Nothing tells you except the rhythm of work whether it is noon or midnight ... For this is a cave life." Priestley called the novel in which this description appeared, *Daylight on Satur-day*.[59]

Even before Dunkirk and the follies which had succeeded it, a vicious circle had set in which still kept hours high. Less overtime would mean lower earnings. The abolition of Sunday work, which Bevin and a few allies repeatedly urged, would deprive workers of the high Sunday rates. In one south-western town, towards the middle of the war, more than a thousand war workers had demonstrated against three factories which had proposed to restrict work at week-ends. In this field, some R.O.F.s set a bad example; as late as the summer of 1942, three R.O.F.s were employing men for a seventy or seventy-one hour week. The air-craft industry, always short of workers, continued to demand injurious hours well into 1943, though even the sixty-hour week once proposed as a maximum for women was now regarded as grossly excessive in official circles. By this stage the supply minis-tries had been convinced that long hours were self-defeating, and had joined Bevin in attacking a mentality in industry which belonged to the Stone Age of management. As peace drew pal-pably nearer, employers grew more reluctant to hand out over-time pay, and the Government's pressure at last did something to bring hours down.[60]

Into the hectic and tiring world of war industry a multitude of unlikely new recruits had been swept. In late 1941, one of the Nuffield factories in Oxford had been converted to build Crusader tanks; it had had to make do with oddments and oddities – men who had been college servants, farm hands, butchers, bakers, salesmen, convicts; an ex-miner from Wales who had once led a hunger march on London; a gaggle of Irishmen; a Jew who had worked for fifteen years as a West End night club receptionist; and a university professor who had become a most skilful fitter.[61]

By the middle of 1942, one and a quarter million people in the engineering industry alone were drawing skilled rates of pay, which compared with about half that number in the "engineering and allied industries" at the time of Dunkirk.[62] This had been achieved by transfers from other industries, by up-grading of semi-skilled workers, and also by training, in the factories them-selves and in the Government Training Centres.

The G.T.C.s had originated in the 1920s, and until Dunkirk had existed to help unemployed men. Bevin had increased their number – from sixteen to thirty-eight – and had thrown them open to all men who were above military age or unfit for service, and also to boys of sixteen and over. From early 1941, women were admitted. After complaints from employers that the courses were too general and theoretical, they had provided a basic course of only four to eight weeks, followed by specialized training for promising pupils. Most trainees received little more than a preliminary grounding which suited them for simple repetitive work. Altogether, some three hundred and fifty thousand civilians were admitted to G.T.C.s or technical colleges for the basic course, besides seventeen thousand who received higher grade training. Only two hundred and seventy thousand actually passed and were placed in employment. The drop-outs, significantly, were largely caused by bad health. Besides women, the trainees were mostly made up of ageing and formerly unemployed men, often pathetic flotsam from the depression. There was a leavening of patriotic middle-class people who greatly appealed to the propagandists of the Ministry of Information, which reported a fifty-six-year-old colonel with an estate in Yorkshire who became a storekeeper at an aircraft factory; an opera singer who emerged as an inspector; a soldier who became a draughtsman, and a missionary who graduated as a toolmaker. Refugees from all walks of life humbled themselves to help meet the requirements of the British war economy. As the war had gone on, the supply of potential trainees had dwindled, and only twenty G.T.C.s were still working in 1943.[63]

In due course, the trainees had become dilutees, who worked beside highly skilled tradesmen or took over machines which such men had formerly operated. Even before the war, technical advances in machine tools and metallurgy had made for extensive sub-division and specialization in engineering. While the war produced no fundamental changes in machines or methods, it pushed this sub-division forward at breakneck speed. The trainee who could do only one skilled job replaced the versatile skilled engineer who had served a six-year apprenticeship. Dilution came as a blow to the pride, and, as they thought, to the future prospects of highly skilled craftsmen in war industries. Though there were fewer strikes against dilutees in the Second World War than in the First, craft consciousness still ran high – in the sheet metal shops, for instance, the attitude of the skilled men effectively prevented dilution. Partly because of the different degrees of stubbornness in different sections of engineering, the extent to which dilution was introduced varied enormously, from the big new aero-engine factory in Glasgow where fully skilled men accounted for less than five per cent of the workers, to a number of machine-tool factories where the proportion was "only slightly below the pre-1939 average".[64]

IX

In conscripting women, Britain went further than any other nation – further than Stalin's Russia and far further than Hitler's Germany, where the idea that the role of the feminine sex was to breed and succour the master race helped to restrict the use which was made of it.

Yet, as so often with features of wartime life which evoked cries of horror or admiration from contemporaries, what had happened, above all, was the exaggeration of peacetime trends. Certain of the lighter industries – the northern textile mills were the best known example – had long relied on women for half or more of their labour force. Nearly five and a half million women had been in employment before the First World War, which had raised the figure to seven and a half million. Afterwards, a great proportion had left the factories as swiftly as they had invaded them, but a slow rise had been resumed in the 'twenties and 'thirties.

In mid-1943, the proportion of the nation's women between fifteen and sixty who were in the forces, munitions work and essential industries was about double that in 1918, at the corresponding stage in the previous war. Nearly three million married women and widows were employed, as compared with a million and a quarter before the war. It was calculated that, among those between eighteen and forty, nine single women out of ten and eight married women out of ten were in the forces or in industry. Those women left over were mostly looking after the nation's young children, but hundreds of thousands of women were in part-time employment, many of them in improvised offices and workshops in village halls and even in drawing-rooms, which took the work to those who could not leave their own homes for long. ("Out-workers" reached a high standard in such formidable sounding tasks as the construction of bulkheads for aircraft.)[65]

It was estimated, however, that if peacetime trends had continued without any assistance from Hitler, about six and three-quarter million women would have had jobs outside the home in 1943. Since the official estimate of those employed stood at around seven and a half millions, the number of extra women who were working was no more than about three-quarters of a million – a considerable, but hardly an overwhelming figure. Nor does it follow that those who now worked and who would not have done so without the war necessarily accepted this in a spirit of grim dutifulness. In 1939, there had been thirty-nine insured female workers aged fourteen to sixty-four for every hundred men and boys. (This excludes domestic service.) But in South Wales, there had been only sixteen for every hundred. On the north-east coast, only twenty. Many women in the depressed areas had certainly wanted work and welcomed it now that it was available.

Woman aircraft workers confirmed a peacetime trend, rather than started something wildly new. In 1935, only one engineering worker in eight had been female, but in the expanding, lighter branches the proportion had been much higher – one in three in the case of electrical engineering. A Government survey in 1943 found that nearly half a sample of working women had had experience in the same job before the war. Housewives who had worked before marriage had come back. In the engineering and metal group, the war industries, a quarter of the women employed had done this sort of work before the war, half had come from a different job, and only a quarter from school, or from looking after a home.[66]

A peacetime pattern where women had worked before marriage, and had settled down to household tasks until the children had grown up, had been replaced by a wartime pattern where these same women were persuaded (or, in a minority of cases, directed) to take up work again. Young girls who would have been typists or shop assistants were now in the A.T.S. or the Land Army or munitions factories. Older women took their places in shops, cotton mills and offices. Young married women left their homes for the factories, and, if they were servicemen's wives, were very glad indeed to get the money.

By 1943, it was almost impossible for a woman under forty to avoid war work unless she had heavy family responsibilities or was looking after a war worker billeted on her. Further measures of control had followed conscription. In January 1942, a Control of Engagement Order had blocked the loophole whereby women directed to important work, such as hospital cleaning, which did not come under the E.W.O., had been slipping out into inessential jobs. By 1943, this covered most women up to forty. In the middle of 1942, it had become clear that only about a quarter of conscripted girls would opt for the services, so all those born in 1920 and 1921 had been withdrawn from their jobs and put into uniform, unless their work was vital. In April 1943, part-time workers became subject to direction. In July that year, Bevin announced in parliament that as part of the Government's plans to release younger women for work in aircraft factories, all women up to fifty-one would be registered. There was an outcry, chiefly from Conservatives, against the "direction of grand-mothers", but the project was carried out.

For those in their late teens and early twenties who had actually been called up, the choice at first had been between the auxiliary services, on the one hand, and work in R.O.F.s, Civil Defence, agriculture or domestic service in hospitals or institutions on the other. But in 1943, recruitment for the services was deliberately restricted in favour of Churchill's pet, the aircraft industry.[67]

For other women, registration was the prelude to a summons for interview at the local labour exchange. Special female officers were employed by the Ministry of Labour to conduct the inter-views, on the grounds that women would find other women reassuring. The arrangement certainly removed men from the temptation to abuse their authority. However, it was not always successful. Zelma Katin, a Sheffield housewife with one son over fourteen, asked at the exchange whether she might work a short week, so as to leave her time to look after him. "Now it was a young lady of the superior self-confident type to whom I addressed my petition. She spoke with a Girton accent – Girton and Oxford may be tolerable in the south, but in a northern provincial city they stink – and she proceeded to lecture me. The country was at war, she said, it was my duty to accept the job that was offered me, and my boy was old enough to look after himself. As she spoke I reflected that here was an unmarried youngster fit enough to do a full week's work on a tramcar or in a munition works, yet enjoying a soft job which gave her the right to lecture women old enough to have been unlucky enough to bear her. I called her a 'whippersnapper' . . . and asked her why she didn't give up her job to an older woman and go into the forces if she were so patriotic. It was all very uncouth of me, and she didn't reply . . ."[68]

Those women whose domestic responsibilities were so heavy that they must, if they worked at all, be found jobs near at hand, or even in their own homes, were classified, somewhat ungallant-ly, as "immobile women". They included the wives of men in the forces and the merchant navy, whose husbands, it was thought, would object if their wives were sent away to fill shells and their homes were jeopardized. It was upon young unmarried women that the full weight of the regulations fell. In 1943, things came to

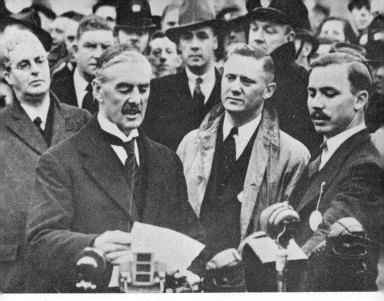

Neville Chamberlain returns to London from Munich in 1938
to proclaim: 'Peace for our time'

Within six months hospital nurses were required to practise
gas drill with tiny babies

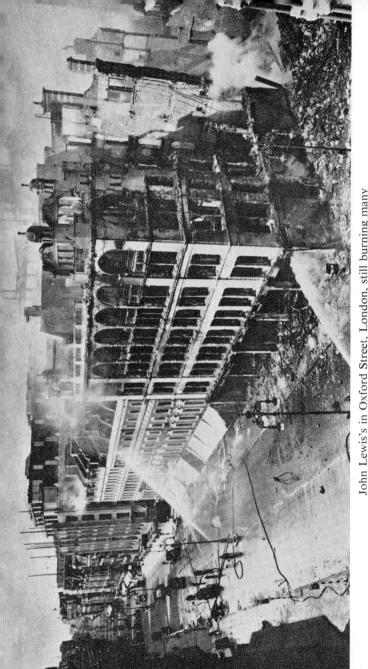

John Lewis's in Oxford Street, London, still burning many hours after a night incendiary raid in September 1940

Evacuation of young children from London and other large cities began just before the outbreak of war.

Some of the 3,000 priceless old masters were removed from the National Gallery for safe-keeping shortly after the outbreak of war, to be stored in disused mines

During the day rescue work wen

... while at night many Londoners took shelter from new air raids in Underground stations and specially constructed shelters

Householders emerging from an Anderson shelter. The flimsy-looking device could take enormous stresses

With the young men directly involved in the fighting, women took over many of the heavy tasks at home, and older men trained for Home Guard and A.R.P. duties

WANTED

FOR SABOTAGE

THE SQUANDERBUG *ALIAS* HITLER'S PAL

KNOWN TO BE AT LARGE IN CERTAIN PARTS OF THE KINGDOM

USUALLY FOUND IN THE COMPANY OF USELESS ARTICLES, HAS A TEMPTING LEER AND A FLATTERING MANNER

WANTED

ALSO FOR THE CRIME OF 'SHOPPERS DISEASE'

INFORMATION CONCERNING THIS PEST SHOULD BE REPORTED TO

A Second Front meeting in Trafalgar Square in 1942. 'Cassandra'
of the *Daily Mirror* stands under a large picture of Pandit Nehru

Despite the most intensive cultivation of private and public
land Britain had ever known, food rationing began in January
1940. It continued into the 1950s

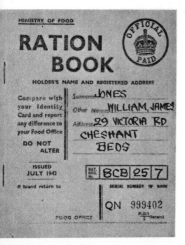

Vera Lynn, the Forces' sweetheart

The B.B.C. Brains Trust in session: *left to right*, Commander Campbell, Professor Joad, Donald McCullough (*back to camera*), A. G. Street, Father Ronald Knox and Julian Huxley

Tommy Handley (*fourth from right*) and the B.B.C. 'ITMA' cast

A German band plays in the Royal Parade, St. Helier, on the Channel Island of Jersey

English women and children serve coffee and exchange conversation with American troops awaiting dispatch to the front line in France

"Never mind about it not being 'arf wot we're giving them –
let's git 'ome." *Sunday Express*, Feb. 27th, 1944

A 'flying bomb' crashing into a side road off Drury Lane in
Central London in May 1944

Sir William Beveridge, author of the Beveridge Report, published in 1942, which was to become the foundation of the modern Welfare State

Sir Stafford Cripps at his home in Gloucestershire: Britain's ambassador in Moscow 1940–42, successor to Beaverbrook at the Ministry of Aircraft Production, and Attlee's chief apostle of austerity in the post-war administration

VE-day: at the fountains in Trafalgar Square, and in Stepney, where children celebrated victory round a bonfire fed with timbers from surrounding bomb-wrecked buildings

Front page of the *Daily Mirror* announcing Labour's election victory in the 1945 polls

Ernest Bevin and the new Labour Prime Minister at 10 Downing Street at midnight on August 14th, 1945, as Mr. Attlee broadcast to the nation news of the Japanese surrender

such a pass that "mobile" women were withdrawn from important work in the less congested areas, transferred to the midlands and replaced with "immobile women". There was nothing more pleasing in the sight of the Ministry of Labour than a pocket of "surplus unskilled mobile woman labour" [sic]. Scotland, Wales and the north and north-east of England were the main "exporting areas". Feeling in Scotland ran very high when it was learnt that Bevin was proposing to send girls south of the border, but the only concession was that no girl under twenty was taken.

Convoys of girls came from Scotland in specially reserved compartments, under the charge of a woman guide, philosopher, friend (and warden). They were received at Birmingham by reception officers whose job was to see them comfortably settled. Many liked the midlands, stayed there and eventually married there. But some were homesick, and if a lassie from Dundee soon fled back to her native hills, it was in practice impossible to compel her to return. As one harassed personnel manager ruminated, ". . . Short of a military escort who can make a woman do what she doesn't want to?" Imprisonment would have defeated itself by ensuring that she played a negative part in the war effort.[69]

It was not only working-class girls who were "mobilized". Well-groomed young ladies whose idea of Hell was a factory, but who liked the alternatives even less, worked machines beside girls from Rhondda whose physique was an eloquent indictment of the years of depression. The young teacher already mentioned, who helped make anti-tank mines in her summer holidays, noted in her diary, "Chief topic of conversation the Dizzy Blonde. She arrived last Monday & has caused quite a sensation, partly by her appearance – wonderful peroxide curls, exquisite make-up etc. – but much more by her conversation. Has told everyone that she has never worked before as she has an allowance & is going to frame the first pound note she gets. Another tale runs that she lost a wallet with £100 in, but 'just didn't bother'; she's saving up for a fur coat, a really good one; 'I had 5 but I've given 3 away.' Mrs Barratt's comment, 'Now we know what she did before the war.' "[70]

At many jobs which they had rarely or never done before, women proved to be quicker and defter than men, with their small fingers used to knitting and sewing. Women were easily trained for welding, which gained much ground in British engineering during the war. But even the jobs which required sheer physical strength were not always beyond middle-aged housewives who had been used to struggling with shopping baskets and small children up several flights of tenement stairs. No woman went down the coal-mines, but in most jobs beneath that level of sheer strength and stamina, a few could always find a place.

By the summer of 1943, more than a hundred thousand railwaymen, mostly under the formal reservation age of twenty-five, had joined the forces. A roughly equal number of women had joined the railways. Men alighting from trains were embarrassed sometimes to find hefty woman porters ready to take their cases. In one railway works a teacher of music became a blacksmith, and two of her colleagues had worked in a greengrocery store and a wine shop respectively.[71]

Even the shipyards experienced an incursion of woman welders. In lighter engineering, dilution with women might reach eighty per cent or higher. Remarkable cases were reported of shops employing women alone, or almost alone, which turned out work previously done only by skilled men.[72] There were three hundred thousand women in the explosives and chemicals industry at peak, over half their total labour force; there were more than a million and a half women in the engineering and metal industries; and over a hundred thousand had passed through the G.T.C.s.

Though the G.T.C. uniforms had undeniable femininity, traditional notions of what it was proper for women to wear inevitably retreated in the face of the requirements of their new jobs. A writer who visited industrial England in 1942 after a long absence was impressed by the transformation. "Before the war," he wrote, "slacks and shorts were worn by girls – mostly of the leisure class – for holidays or sports wear. Now they are wearing trousers to do their work. Milk girls, window cleaners, drivers, railway workers, bus conductors – all are dressed for the job. If the war goes on much longer it may be a sign of eccentricity for a young woman to wear skirts." On the contrary, old women continued to regard with distaste the spectacle of bus conductresses, "clippies", in their trousers. Mrs Katin who, in spite of her unfortunate interview, took a job on the Sheffield trams, reported that to many people the sight of a girl in any kind of uniform "at once suggests immorality . . . Numbers of passengers believe that the last act of a conductress and her driver or motorman each night before going home is the exercise of sexual intercourse."[73]

Indeed, sex could not be kept out of dilution. Mark Benney describes the intrusion of the first woman into the installations section of an aircraft factory in 1941. "We looked at her, nine of us, for days, as though we had never seen a woman before. We watched the dainty way she picked up a file, with red-enamelled fingertip extended as though she were holding a cup of tea. We watched the way she brushed the filings off her overalls after every few strokes, the awkward way she opened and closed her vise, her concern for the cleanliness of her hands, her delicate, unhandy way with a hammer . . . Behind her back we had great fun mimicking her; to her face we treated her with an almost desperate punctilio."[74]

This woman turned out to be a highly competent worker. But many managements were reluctant to use their skilled workers and floor space for training women in whose capacities they had no confidence, and whom they expected to flit back to their parlours at the end of the war. Yet, simultaneously, many workmen expected the bosses to use women to replace them when peacetime anarchy returned. As the A.E.U. president remarked in 1943, "The system which allows women to be brought into industry as 'cheap labour' and uses them with the double object of exploiting them and undermining the men's rates has left its scars on us all." In J. T. Murphy's London factory, "Here and there a man would willingly show a woman how to do the job, but generally the men were reluctant to 'give anything away'." But, he adds more cheerfully, ". . . the sex factor tended to break down the prejudice. It was not easy for men to maintain a hard attitude of unhelpfulness to good-looking and well-built girls and women."[75]

X

"Don't you know there's a war on?" was a familiar catchphrase on the india-rubber island. The tobacconist retorted with it when customers complained about the shortage of cigarettes. "Doesn't she know there's a war on?" asked the clippie when a well-dressed woman fussed about the lack of seats in the bus. "Don't they know there's a war on?" asked the irate Churchillian householder when an independent candidate appeared to solicit his vote.

Many people were excessively aware that there was a war on. Towards the end of 1944, J. L. Hodson lunched at a Sheffield steelworks with, amongst others, a metallurgist. During the meal, the man looked ill. Within half an hour or so he died. "He was a member of ninety-two committees," one of his friends said.[76]

But Emma Smith, who with two girl friends worked on canal

boats as her contribution to the war effort, writes, "Had it not been for the war, we should never have known what it was to travel on a canal. Yet war was little more than a distant noise in our ears. We had no wireless; we never read a newspaper; except from time to time, we met only people to whom 'Europe' was a word casually heard, signifying nothing. The boaters, travelling through the heart of England as their fathers and grandfathers and great-grandfathers had done, were a race apart, little known and knowing little beyond their ancient lore. The life was absorbing, and we were absorbed by it, by the daily problems of advancing as far and fast as possible, and the nightly achievement of tying up."[77]

The war had, no doubt, seemed almost equally distant to some of the ten thousand bookmakers who, it was credibly estimated, were "conscientiously engaged on transferring and retransferring" items of expenditure charged by local authorities against other local authorities as a result of the evacuation scheme.[78] National and local government were, fairly or unfairly, supposed to be the resort of buck-passing, tea-drinking idlers. In fact, the manpower shortage was felt even in the corridors of power. While the numbers employed in Government departments had increased from 388,000 in April 1939 to a peak (as it turned out) of 719,000 in July 1943, this influx merely kept pace, if that, with the onward march of controls and regulations. However, certain bright young men were able, by making themselves indispensable in Whitehall, to avoid army service, a fact which attracted some scandalized attention. Whether they would have "known there was a war on" more, or indeed so much, had they entered that rival and still larger bureaucratic institution, one may doubt. There were a multitude of clerkly and administrative outposts of the army where the more ardent spirits struggled vainly to find useful work to do. There were many new varieties of specialist officers – scientific officers, officers who produced newspapers for the troops or operated radio stations or organized libraries, "antiquities" officers, "locust control" officers. Or a quiet war could be found in the Education Corps, touring isolated A.A. sites in Britain itself.

Boredom and frustration were among the factors which, in 1943, impelled some sixteen thousand men to go A.W.O.L., absent without leave, from the army. In the People's War this was a matter for the psychiatrist, not for the firing squad. Between September 1939 and June 1944, out of a total of some 335,000 men and women discharged from the services as medically unfit,

118,000 were released on psychiatric grounds. Apart from those who were genuinely too neurotic to be useful, there were those who, as it were, came to an arrangement with the military authorities that a relationship disagreeable to both parties should now be honourably terminated. So perfectly healthy young men reverted to civilian life, rejoicing in the knowledge that they had "had" their war. In Soho, a remarkably lively public-house society of Bohemian writers and artists rubbed shoulders with a still more vigorous criminal community, enriched by deserters, who had managed to evade capture. Some eighty thousand men had gone A.W.O.L. from the army alone by October 1944 (in 1941, the peak year, the rate had been about one in a hundred of the entire force). It was estimated after the war that some twenty thousand unpardoned deserters were at large. Without a ration book, there was not much alternative to crime.[79]

In 1939 there had been just over three hundred thousand indictable offences known to the police in England and Wales. (The following figures, to avoid complexity, omit Scotland, where the definitions of crimes were different but the trends were much the same.) In 1943, the total had risen to 373,000, and it continued to rise to 478,000 in 1945. Only 105,000 people were found guilty in 1943 for such offences. The vast majority had committed larceny, or were tried for breaking and entering. Violence against the person had risen, so far as convictions showed, by very little. There were twenty-nine convicted murderers, a fact with little resonance, in a year when Auschwitz and Belsen were well into their stride.

As for non-indictable offences, the number of people found guilty of them in 1943 was at 280,000 almost exactly half the figure for 1939. This was not because citizens had grown basically more law-abiding; it was chiefly attributable to the petrol shortage. In 1939, there had been 360,000 traffic offences punished; in 1943, there were only 100,000, though this was at the rate of about one for every fifteen licensed vehicles.

The war had created a new class of offences, those against Defence Regulations, of which 187,000 people were found guilty in 1943. There were 110,000 cases involving lighting offences. Although 925,000 people – a rate of something like one person in fifty, though many no doubt offended more than once – were judged culpable for infringing the blackout regulations during the war. The peak year had been 1940, with no less than 300,000 successful prosecutions. In 1943, 30,000 people were found guilty under the regulations affecting the control of industry, and 12,500 under the Control of Employment Orders – and for such offences, this was the peak year.

So this was not a homogeneous nation of heroes and Stakhano-vites. Many people remember the war chiefly for its boredom. Amongst those who had cause to yawn in 1943 were the civil defenders, who since the end of the main blitz had heard the old charge of Army dodging levelled at them once again.

XI

Even in 1943, which was the quietest year of all, there was hardly one period of twenty-four hours without at least one air raid incident somewhere in Britain. Tip and run raids on the coast continued. In January, there were two quite heavy attacks on London which killed a hundred and seven people, and other battered cities, also, were not left in peace. In August, for instance, there were a hundred and thirty casualties in Plymouth when German bombers sneaked over among a much larger force of R.A.F. planes returning from the Continent. The tactic was repeated, with seventy-eight casualties, in November.[80]

Such almost random raids would, for a time, encourage local people to go to their shelters at night. A small minority of the population always did so anyway. In 1943, there were still thousands of Londoners spending the night in the Tubes. These had shared to the full in the general improvement of the shelters; there were bunks, libraries, drinking fountains, lavatories and places to store bedding. But they were usually empty, except for this residue of confirmed Tube dwellers. Why did they still come? Mass Observation suggested a convincing explanation. "There were some who went for shelter and found there not only shelter but a whole new life in a new society – a society where they could start from scratch and for the first time in their lives make a name for themselves and shine in their social group. Others came from solitary bed-sitting rooms with a gas ring, and found they could spend evenings in light and gaiety, surrounded by company." And busy mothers had found it handy that the family spent its leisure time away from home. Some shelters had maintained an esprit de corps, a family atmosphere in which a new baby would be a source of pride to everyone, though in others the spirit of community had disintegrated, and isolation and apathy had reasserted themselves.[81]

One incident in 1943 illustrated, by contrast, the remarkable absence of panic in the main London blitz. Bethnal Green station, in the East End, had sheltered as many as seven thousand people during that phase; thereafter the number of regular users had dropped to two or three hundred. But early in 1943, the raids mentioned earlier and a threat of reprisals from Germany for the bombing of Berlin had increased the tension in the area, and by the beginning of March eight hundred and fifty people were using the shelter, and many had begun to hang around it in case of attack. On the evening of March 8th, the warning went, and fifteen hundred people were admitted, without haste or panic, in some ten minutes.

Rockets had now been introduced into A.A. defence. They would add to the colour of the night scene, bursting high in the air into innumerable bright balls of light. They also added, in Bethnal Green that night, a shattering and unfamiliar new noise. A woman with a child or bundle in her arms tripped on the stairs inside the station, and when the panic-stricken crowd continued to push in behind her, people fell on top of each other, five or six deep; a hundred and seventy-three people were killed in the appalling crush of bodies.[82]

However, it had long seemed to most British citizens that the lull in the bombing was there to stay. From 1942, the Government increasingly winkled out full-time civil defenders and sent them to work in war industry. "Interchangeability", once a spontaneous feature of many incidents, had now been institutionalized. The heavy rescue men and the stretcher-bearers had been amalgamated, and various arms of Civil Defence were now expected to be conversant with each other's training. The number of whole-time C.D. workers, 127,000 at the height of the blitz, had fallen to seventy thousand by the end of 1943. Women had come in increasingly as part-timers.

Full-time civil defenders were now a class of "Cinderellas", with neither the prestige and privileges of the armed forces, nor the chance of earning high wages in industry. Without raids, the time dragged, though those who enjoyed knitting or some equally portable and adaptable hobby would have plenty of chance to pursue it. "Well, I think Civil Defence is a marvellous racket," said one warden in his mid-thirties, "It's given me the spare time I've been wanting for years – I've done more solid reading, for instance, than I've done since I was twenty-one . . ."[83]

The poet Stephen Spender, who joined the new National Fire Service in the middle of the war, writes that "The B.B.C. Light Programme and the clicking of snooker balls were the warp and

woof upon which for forty-eight hours out of every seventy-two
... the patterns of my fire brigade experiences were woven." The
number of full-time male firemen had fallen; the numbers of part-
timers had increased, to about a quarter of a million, of whom
approaching one-fifth were now women. There were now some
thirty thousand full-timers as well, following a precedent set in
1914–18. They generally fulfilled similar roles to those performed
by the auxiliary services for the armed forces. When the firewomen of Glasgow had clamoured to form their own pump
crews, and had been given their chance as an experiment, they
had come to agree themselves that they lacked the necessary
strength and stamina.[84]

To relieve the monotony, there was a certain amount of ABCA-
like activity in the C.D. and Fire services. The firemen themselves
had insisted on taking on spare-time war work. By the spring of
1943 there were two hundred stations in London alone where
firemen were engaged in productive work, and others worked on
allotments and farms. Many wardens found similar tasks to
occupy them – making toys for orphaned children, collecting
money for war savings, and a range of other activities which
would have done credit to the W.V.S. itself.

In August 1941, Herbert Morrison, vainly attempting to introduce into the task of compulsory fire-watching some order and
some excitement, had announced that from now on all who performed this duty would be known as Fire Guards. By 1943 the
Fire Guard was, on paper, the greatest of all the bodies of
"militant citizens" with nearly six million members. But it had no
uniform and no esprit de corps; it was simply a weight of wasted
time – forty-eight hours a month – which was hung round the
necks of men and women who tried to slip it off if possible.

The Fire Guard had originally been organized as an adjunct to
the warden's service, from which its "officers" had been drawn.
Its members, however, had their own armlets and their own
depots, where they kept equipment, arranged their rotas, and
perhaps slept and fed when on duty. The fire-watching orders had
been redrafted yet again, soon afterwards, but they had still
provided for the exemption of people engaged "in vital war work
for exceptionally long hours". It was said, even in Whitehall, that
"anyone not a congenital idiot could easily evade fire guard duty,
and in any case a congenital idiot was entitled to exemption." In
its first real test, the Baedeker raids, the Fire Guard had proved
to be undermanned, badly equipped and ill-led. At this period,
women between twenty and forty-five had been made liable for

fire-watching, and training had been made compulsory for the first time.

There was further administrative fidgeting in 1943, when (except in Scotland) the Fire Guard was removed from the province of the wardens and reorganized so that its members in effect acted as scouts for the N.F.S. A new Fire Guard Plan, which, true to the tradition in these matters, ran to no less than seventy-two pages in booklet form, came into operation in September. The public remained unstirred; no one was ever going to boast very loudly about his service as a "Fire Guard Sector Captain".[85]

XII

The Home Guard, however, had maintained much of its old appeal. Though the danger of invasion had receded, there was always the fear (or the hope, for the keener men) that the Germans might make a desperate bid, or at least attempt commando raids.

In 1941, when the danger had still seemed very real, Invasion Committees had been set up in all town and country districts, to take charge if the Germans came and to mobilize such useful things as cars and megaphones in the emergency. These remained in existence until 1944. But after the onslaught on Russia, whatever hysteria about parachutists and Fifth Columnists had still remained had been rapidly eroded. Tom Driberg reported with delight in November 1942 that some boroughs had recently been asking their citizens what public services they would undertake in the event of an invasion, and that two answers from the West End of London had been:

> I could drive a car any day except Thursday, as I go down to Kent on Thursdays to see my husband.
> My maid and I would be glad to help in any way from five to seven any evening except at the week-ends, when we are always in the country.[86]

The Home Guard had been increasingly regularized and disciplined from August 1940 onwards. In that month, Home Guard units had been affiliated to the county regiments, and promised regimental badges. In October 1940, recruiting had been temporarily suspended. In February 1941 ranks, as in the regular army, with commissions for the officers, had been intro-

duced. All officers had been reviewed and many had been purged.
So the Home Guard had become, as it were, part-time regular
soldiers. When the Government had lifted its ban on recruiting, it
had begun to use the Home Guard as a training ground for boys
of seventeen and eighteen prior to their call-up.

Bureaucracy had always been latent in the Home Guard, but
with regularization it had run riot. Commanders were inflicted
with swarms of trivial circulars and had to spend precious
evenings worrying about such minutiae as the total numbers of
buttons in store. The climax of Home Guard red tape had probably been reached in April 1942, when full instructions had been
issued on the burial of Mohammedan Home Guards.

However, equipment had greatly improved, both in quantity
and quality. Whenever boredom and frustration had seemed
likely to overwhelm the Home Guard, a new toy had usually been
found to raise interest again. Thompson machine guns had made
a brief appearance, and had been replaced by crude-looking but
efficacious Sten guns. The Northover Projector was an equally
graceless anti-tank weapon, but fun to use. There was much joy
with new types of grenade. In the autumn of 1941, however, the
War Office had lost its touch in these matters and had produced
the notorious issue of steel pikes, which remains one of the best
remembered gaffes of the war. "Lord Croft's Pikes", so-called
from the junior minister who had issued them, had made the
Home Guard feel that they were back in the primeval days of
1940. The War Office had insisted that they were excellent
weapons for street fighting, but most of the pikes had never left
the battalion stores.[87]

Compulsion early in 1942 brought in some keen soldiers, as
well as many reluctant ones. Though courts martial might have
been used against defaulters, in practice, absenteeism and dis-
obedience were punished in the civil courts, where a month's
imprisonment or a sizable fine might be imposed. Compulsion
produced a good deal of malicious tale-bearing; some self-
righteous Home Guards took to forwarding to the battalion
H.Q. the names of "lazy" or "cowardly" neighbours who had not
joined up.

In the summer of 1943 there were one and three-quarter million
Home Guards, in eleven hundred battalions. The average age,
brought down by many youngsters in their teens, was now under
thirty, and only seven per cent were ex-servicemen.[88] The role of
the Home Guard had developed along two lines, by no means
parallel. On the one hand, it had increasingly sophisticated its

notions of defence; while the older men were expected to garrison the home area, it was proposed that the younger and fitter ones should be almost as mobile as the regular troops. From the winter of 1940, there had been an expanding provision of official training; there were now four War Office schools which sent "travelling wings" to teach units all over the country. Home Guards often engaged the regular army in exercises.

On the other hand, their role in the blitzed cities had made the Home Guards seem a valuable adjunct to the C.D. services, and from 1942 they came within the scope of "interchangeability". All Home Guards were trained in basic Civil Defence techniques, and individuals took courses in rescue work and incident control. Combined exercises with Civil Defence and local Invasion Committees had been a lively feature of the urban scene from 1941 onwards, though the "combination" was not always apparent. (In one such "combined" affair in the streets of a small Buckinghamshire town, as the Home Guards were striving to repel the "invader", a witness noticed that the Fire Service, with a trailer pump, "unconcernedly proceeded to a house marked on the programme as being in flames at a certain time, and brought the pump into action, despite the fact that they were butting into the thick of a battle".[89])

The Home Guard never quite managed to resemble the regular army, though dress and weapons were now almost identical. On a ceremonial occasion, "Rank after rank," as John Brophy describes it, "would march by, heads high, legs and arms swinging in easy rhythm, rifles correctly sloped, indistinguishable from a regular battalion . . . But sooner or later the eye would be caught by a pair of sloping shoulders, or a distended waistline, an arm or a leg which, half pathetically, half absurdly, could never for long merge into the corporate rhythm."[90]

Home Guard officers still had no financial or other privileges over more lowly volunteers. When commissions had come in, the War Office had insisted that all promotion would be on merit, and would take no account of class. Subsequently, it had protested rather too much that this was what had happened. However, there is no doubt that in this "People's Army" there were some remarkable hierarchical transpositions. Wilfred Pickles, who joined the B.B.C.'s Home Guard, remarks "How odd it seemed to see some of the higher officials of the Corporation being ordered about and instructed in the use of the rifle by the commissionaires who had earlier on addressed them with 'Good morning, sir!' when they walked in, umbrellas folded neatly, to start a day's administration." For the commissionaires were former regular soldiers.[91]

Any observer of pre-war British society would have been staggered to learn that one day his bus ticket might be clipped by a commissioned major. Yet such novelties were bound to occur with a specialized Home Guard battalion like the London Transport one which covered scattered bus, tram and repair depots south of the Thames. At Camberwell bus garage, the platoon was naturally commanded by a bus conductor, at Clapham tram depot, by a tram driver, and the majors of the battalion were drawn from a cross-section of the workers.[92]

The variety which had characterized the Home Guard in its L.D.V. phase still survived. There were Home Guard cavalry on the western hills, Home Guard marines on Lake Windermere, and river patrols on the major waterways. Many Home Guards in the Scottish Highlands had been given the role of mountain maquis, and Scottish exercises seem to have had an intensity peculiarly their own, perhaps as a legacy from Wallace and Montrose.

The distinction between the urban and rural Home Guard was basic. In the more remote districts, the Home Guard might be very scattered indeed, hours of agricultural work were almost unlimited, petrol was short, and men might have to walk four miles each way to and from drill after a day's ploughing. Farmers in such areas might well try to keep their men out.

Activity was less restricted in the more benign rural areas, where the village pub would provide a centre, and all rustic Home Guards had the advantage of plenty of open space (and seclusion) to train in. Urban Home Guards, much thicker on the ground, had to expose themselves to ridicule in parks, and establish themselves in Territorial Army halls, or in whatever schools Civil Defence had left them. Their field exercises were noisy short-range encounters on bomb sites. The town units were said to be much more formal – officers might establish messes and even carry swagger sticks, while other ranks stuck to their own canteen. Brass bands or pipe bands were formed, and there was much more parading in public.

A. G. Street describes the scene towards the middle of the war at the headquarters of one west London company, which had taken over the top floor of a school. "In one room a Home Guard armourer was busy overhauling rifles and machine guns. In another an unarmed combat expert was teaching the novices how to make others fall and also how to fall themselves . . . In the largest classroom fifty or sixty men in uniform were doing arms drill, and doing it with a click; in a small one a machine-gun team were stripping and assembling their weapon; while around a full-size billiard-table in another, a squad of recruits in civvies were learning their first lessons under a patient but strict N.C.O."[93]

Boring and exhausting enough for some, after a hard day's work. But for many, the Home Guard had become a wartime substitute for cricket, golf or amateur dramatics, and, like those peacetime hobbies, a subject for jealousy with wives. For men whose families had been evacuated, it provided company in the evenings, and it subdued the guilty consciences of those with brothers or cousins in the forces.

There was schoolboyish pleasure in practising street fighting – lurking in alleyways, leaping up from areas, and occasionally, perhaps, crawling through sewers. There was keen competition for prize cups awarded for bombing, bayonet fighting and musket drill. ("Golf bombing", with "courses" arranged round blitzed buildings, was actually introduced in some places.) Men discussed the tactics of defence as they had once argued about those of the soccer field. And then came the big match – an exercise against the army or another Home Guard company. Though the regulars would usually have the best of it, a combination of local knowledge and low cunning might sometimes outwit them. As for internecine conflict with other Home Guards, it sometimes provoked actual bloodshed, when passers-by would stare at grown men fighting like urchins in the street. An officer umpiring such an exercise in the London dock area found that one of the "defenders" had provided himself with a box full of large rotten potagoes, each pitted with scraps of old razor blades. These, he proposed to employ as grenades. The following exchange, according to the officer, ensued:

> "But, dash it, man, are you mad? You might have killed some of the attackers with these."
> "Not them, mister, you don't know 'em. It 'ud just bounce off most of those b——s."[94]

And on top of this there would, in a city battalion, be a plethora of more conventionally "social" activities. One Home Guard in Edinburgh had complained in March 1941 that "If Hitler were privileged to see our magazine he might be forgiven for thinking that Home Guard activities are confined to suppers, concerts, and whist drives." Far from it – the Fuehrer should also have noted a large dance, battalion darts and football leagues, billiard matches, and a non-military film show.[95]

From 1942, Home Guards were recruited to serve in A.A. batteries so as to release regulars for the front lines. But advertising for volunteers provoked insufficient response and in some cases mass transfers of Home Guards to A.A. batteries took place. In Sheffield, and this was probably typical, the men deeply resented that their Home Guard units should be broken up in this way.[96] By September 1944, there were a hundred and forty thousand or so Home Guard in A.A. batteries, a far cry from the veterans with pitchforks who had mounted their vigil on the hills fifty-two months before.

XIII

Even boy-power was mobilized. The war had seen the disintegration of many youth clubs, though the Scouts and Guides had still been on hand to play a variety of useful roles in the blitz. In January 1941, the Air Ministry had launched an Air Training Corps for boys between sixteen and eighteen. This was the first ever state-directed, regimented national youth movement. Volunteers were given R.A.F. uniform, and with this attraction the A.T.C.'s success was sensational. Within six months it had grown to two hundred thousand. Members came from great distances after their day's work to do what H. C. Dent described as "the dullest and driest academic study in the dingiest surroundings", and "to pore earnestly over the mathematics they had so loathed at school". Sea Cadets and Army Cadets had followed, and a proliferation of competing organizations tapped the same kind of enthusiasm among girls.

Registration of young people had been instituted at the end of 1941. Sixteen- to eighteen-year-olds had been asked what their jobs were and whether they belonged to any youth organization or junior service. Those who belonged to neither had been interviewed, and attempts had been made to persuade them to show willing. (There was no compulsion.) The registration had revealed the extraordinary extent to which some employers were exploiting cheap juvenile labour. A Government White Paper in 1943 divulged that of 611,000 boys and girls interviewed, more than a quarter had such long or inconvenient hours of work and travel that no extra effort could be asked of them. Attempts were made to reduce these disquieting figures.[97]

Meanwhile, the schools had tended to orientate their curricula and hobby clubs towards practical things – pig keeping, vegetable growing, clothes mending and cobbling, for instance. Some schools even made components for aircraft. Harvest camps for town children had grown from small beginnings until by 1943, there were over a thousand camps housing sixty-three thousand children during the summer holidays.[98]

Children joined enthusiastically in the national campaign for salvage. Hundreds of thousands were enrolled in corps of "Cogs" – junior salvage collectors whose official "Cog battle song" began with the fervent cry, "There'll always be a dustbin . . ." Salvage drives were now ubiquitous, and continuous, with the W.V.S. and the wardens, as ever, well to the fore. Salvage shops were opened up and down the land where people might leave or report their scrap materials. Small street depots were set up under the supervision of street salvage stewards. But petrol shortage raised problems of collection in villages, where large dumps had to be accumulated in order to ensure an economic lorry load. As many local authorities were sluggish in dealing with them, unsightly and putrescent heaps lingered on village greens for months and years. Which was doubly a waste, since salvage could be lucrative for those who disposed of it.

Kitchen waste was collected in uncanny quantities, sterilized, processed and fed to pigs. Even the grass in public parks was mown to provide animal feeding stuffs. Tins, bones, gramophone records, films, rags, jars, bottles were obvious items to salvage. So was paper; touring lorries carted tons of it away from business premises. It was a sign of patriotism, not of bad manners, to type a formal letter on the back of correspondence already received and noted. As the War Economy Standard paper grew thinner and poorer, longing eyes were cast on the reserves of high-grade material which lurked in old books, and in 1943, the Ministry of Supply promoted special book drives all over the country. Since many libraries had lost books through bombing, and the forces were calling for reading material of any kind, scrutiny committees were set up to ensure that valuable items were not pulped. But of fifty-six million books collected by October, only six million were spared.[99]

The most famous of all salvage campaigns was the compulsory one which steadily, from 1940 onwards, had deprived parks and gardens of their ornamental iron railings. There is something both inspirational and macabre in the following report from a small west country town in February 1943.

"SMACK IN THE EYE FOR HITLER"
Burnham-on-Sea Railings for Scrap

"I can see Mr Hitler getting a nasty smack in the eye before long," remarked Mr W. H. Hatcher at a special meeting of Burnham-on-Sea Urban Council when proposals of the Ministry of Works for appropriation of iron railings and gates were discussed.

Mr W. E. Pring inquired the position of gates of historic value or erected as memorials, and the surveyor replied that it had been arranged for the memorial gates at the seaward end of St Andrew's churchyard to remain. Mr Cox said they should protest against taking the church gates, and also those at the entrances to the Manor Gardens, because of the possibility of cattle straying, but Mr Pring declared, "People would rather see them take these gates than go in the cemetery robbing graves."

The Chairman: "We must not look at it like that. Someone else would rob them if we didn't."

The clerk reported that it was intended to take cemetery railings and also chains and railings round graves. Altogether eighteen graves would be affected.

He also stated that people who wished to appeal could obtain the necessary forms at his office.[100]

And so even the ghosts, as one might say, were mobilized.

The railings became a symbol. In handsome Georgian squares, in London and other cities, they had maintained the privacy and amenity of shady lawns and bright flower beds for those householders whose property had entitled them to a key. To the privileged, their removal was another tormenting sign that the days of gracious living were over. But for those who preached human equality, it was not only prudent but delightful. The gardens belonged to everyone now, even if they were used for vegetable growing. This was one token of what A. J. P. Taylor has called "the brief period when the English people felt that they were a truly democratic community".[101]

LET THE PEOPLE SING

Supposing the death rate obtaining just before the war among people living in the most prosperous areas of the country – such counties as Surrey, Sussex, Kent, Buckinghamshire and Oxford – applied also to

people living in economically depressed and socially depressing areas
such as Durham, Lancashire, South Wales and so on, what would be
the result? The answer is that every year we should save fifty-four
thousand lives and in ten years some five hundred thousand. These
were the casualties of peace. No medals. No honours. No prayers. Just
premature death. They would have been useful *now*.

Richard and Kathleen Titmuss, 1942[1]

I

"The Seatonian Prize is awarded annually at Cambridge University for a poem on a sacred subject," noted the *Manchester Guardian* drily in February 1943. "This year's subject is 'Holy
Russia'."[2]

Hitler had ordered General Paulus to stand fast in Stalingrad.
The Russians encircling the city slowly closed their jaws. At the
end of January 1943, after much futile heroism, Paulus, with
ninety thousand survivors of his army, surrendered. This has
more claim than El Alamein to be considered the turning-point of
the war. "And now the sons of Stalingrad / Enact another
Iliad . . .",[3] A. P. Herbert had written, grotesquely but no doubt
sincerely, in September. The Red Army's Homeric attributes
stood out more plainly than ever when, on February 20th, cities
throughout Britain celebrated, with long parades and fulsome
speeches, the twenty-fifth anniversary of its foundation.

At Bristol "blood-red floodlights tinted the flags of the United
Nations" at the city's biggest hall, as "a packed, fervent audience
of services and civilians rose to sing the 'Internationale' . . ." The
Lord Mayor, speaking for an array of dignitaries, church leaders,
officials and civil servants from all over the region, announced
that the Red Army had saved mankind. "Together with their
great leader, Stalin – (loud applause) – whose masterly mind has
planned this marvellous war, they have worked miracles." A
dramatic poem by Louis MacNeice, "Salute to the Red Army",
formed, the local paper reported, a "moving finale".[4]

MacNeice's verse was featured again at the Royal Albert Hall
next day, when an invited audience consisting solely of bigwigs
assembled for a national demonstration. The affair was grander
in scale than any the hall had ever entertained. A formalized
perspective of Stalingrad, over a hundred and twenty feet wide
and sixty feet high, gave a backcloth to the pageant, which
included detachments from the Navy, the Marines, the Guards,

Civil Defence, the Home Guard and the nursing services, and
representative groups of coal-miners, transport drivers, firemen,
munitions workers and railway workers. The arts gave of their
best. Special fanfares had been composed by William Walton and
Arnold Bax. The London Philharmonic Orchestra, sections of the
B.B.C. Symphony Orchestra, bands of the Brigade of Guards and
the R.A.F., and buglers from the Royal Marines, were present to
give homage to Calliope, and also to Marshal Stalin. Lieutenant
Laurence Olivier R.N.V.R. and Lieutenant Commander Ralph
Richardson R.N.V.R., were among the famous actors who took
part, and John Gielgud's silken tones were used, most quaintly,
as "the Voice of Moscow Radio".[5]

Red Army Day was merely the greatest expression of an Anglo-
Soviet solidarity already fostered by Aid to Russia Weeks, Stalingrad Festivals and other junketings up and down the country.
The Communist Party, taking advantage of the fact that its
members controlled most of the British supplies of films, photographs and even information about the Soviet Union, was able to
take a lead in organizing them under the auspices of local
authorities. In return for much hard work, and much moral con-
tortionism (as when they found themselves carrying banners with
Churchill's photograph in Anglo-Soviet parades) C.P. members
had the pleasure of hearing Conservative M.P.s praising Stalin
before enthusiastic crowds. It is recorded that the printed programme for one such Anglo-Soviet Week filled its centre pages
with the portraits of Churchill and Stalin over the caption,
"What God hath joined let no man tear asunder."[6]

Yet the C.P. was once again missing its real opportunity to
capture the leadership of the Labour movement. Apart from calls
for a second front and for freedom for India, its current policy
boiled down to unflinching support for Churchill's coalition –
indeed, its major surviving grievance seemed to be that it had not
been asked to join it. C.P. shop stewards embarrassed their comrades by appearing in the King's honours lists for their services to
war production. (Yet the public was sharply reminded in 1943
that the C.P. recognized no monarch west of the Kremlin. In
July, the party's national organizer, D. F. Springhall, was sentenced to seven years' imprisonment at the Old Bailey for inveig-
ling munitions secrets from a girl clerk at the Air Ministry, for
dispatch to Moscow.) The *Daily Worker*, revived when the ban
had been lifted in September 1942 with a printing of a hundred
and twenty thousand, was probably seen by half a million people
daily.

But the enthusiasm for Russia swept over and past the British Communist Party. In the summer, as the Russian armies began to drive the Germans back, and back, and back, nine out of ten people were willing to give the polls a favourable opinion of Russia. That autumn, the Sword of Stalingrad began a triumphal tour of Britain. The King had commanded that this beautiful weapon of the finest steel should be made as his personal gift to the people of the city. In London, where it was exhibited in Westminster Abbey, in Edinburgh, Glasgow, Birmingham and Coventry, people queued for hours to pass before the gorgeous two-edged blade.[7]

Amongst those who puzzled over the purport of all this Anglo-Soviet mania was M. Maisky, the Russian ambassador. ". . . Britain's reaction to the Red Army's successes is complex and contradictory," he wrote in his diary on February 5th, 1943. While "among the masses" the feeling of admiration was "infinite and unquestionable", the better-off classes had many reservations. The intellectuals, it seemed to Maisky, were bewildered by the discovery that "Communist dictatorship" could produce such heroism. The reaction of the ruling classes struck him as "even more complex". While they were glad that the Russians were beating the Germans for them, they feared already that the Red Army would reach Berlin before the troops of the western allies.[8]

Maisky's observation seems accurate enough. Anti-communism, on the left as well as on the right, had been bemused but not destroyed. When, about this time, the Board of Education issued a memorandum designed to encourage the study of Russian affairs in schools, the ultra-right *National Review* acidly observed, ". . . Russian valour has so shaken the wits of many of our public men that they appear to be ready to alter our political system and to rush into Bolshevism at all costs." Here was a ministry led by the Conservative R. A. Butler explicitly recommending the perusal of the works of the Webbs, Lenin and Stalin, the "heady stuff of propaganda". Could the House of Commons, asked the writer, be aware that this was going on? ". . . These must be some Conservatives in it," he apostrophized plaintively.[9]

Indeed, there were, and besides those who openly continued to express sentiments after the *National Review*'s own heart, there were those, like Harold Nicolson, who swam hopelessly with the tide and confined their real opinions to the privacy of club smoking rooms. David Low, in one of his cartoons, depicted Blimpish rats digging busily under the "Foundations of Victory" and uttering such rat-like remarks as "Undoubtedly Stalin aims at world conquest", "Gad sir, Goebbels is right about the red menace", "My husband says Russia will attack *US* next" and "Question is – will it pay us to see Stalin defeat Hitler?" As the issue of Poland's future began to agitate opinion in Britain, such remarks gradually became more acceptable. Mass enthusiasm for Russia had waned significantly by 1944, though it was still enormous.[10]

While this enthusiasm was naive, it was certainly not wholly unpolitical. Right-wingers, nervously noting this, tried to justify it on the grounds that patriotism was noble in any nation, and that the Russians, of course, had every right to their own political system. These arguments were identical to those which had been advanced to excuse the appeasement of Hitler some five years before. "Forgive and forget" was the keynote of the right's reaction, as it had been of Churchill's. ". . . May I remind you", wrote one newspaper columnist, "that not so very long ago many of us thought our own Liberals a ghastly crowd".[11]

But ordinary people seem to have accepted the left-wing picture of Russia largely composed from materials provided by Sidney and Beatrice Webb, whose massive and illusion-ridden study *Soviet Communism – A New Civilization* had been published in the late 1930s and was still regarded as the last word. According to this version, Russia was organized by ordinary people on behalf of ordinary people, and was utterly free of Blimps. The prevailing feeling was summed up in a ditty which was sung by soldiers in North Africa to the tune of the "Lincolnshire Poacher":

> That Hitler's armies can't be beat is just a lot of cock,
> For Marshal Timoshenko's boys are pissing through
>   von Bock,
> The Fuehrer makes the bloomers and his marshals take
>   the rap;
> Meanwhile Joe smokes a pipe and wears a taxi-driver's
>   cap.[12]

If Russians were patriotic, it was because they owned their own country. If Russia was beating Germany, it was because its people knew what they were fighting for. As Arthur Koestler pointed out, this kind of argument implied that Tsarism, which had once defeated Napoleon, had been a pretty fine system. But the false connection was widely accepted.

Women had the same rights as men, in the land of the Red

Dawn; in 1942, ocular proof had arrived in Britain in the form of Lieutenant Ludmilla Pavlichenko, a well-built but good-looking "maiden", as Churchill would have called her, who was said to have three hundred and nine dead Germans to her credit, and certainly wore the Order of Lenin. Over there, it was confidently asserted, the workers ran the factories. And Stalin, enigmatic but unmistakably proletarian, wore his famous cap. Ironically enough, many thinking Britons now saw Uncle Joe Stalin's Animal Farm as the "truly democratic society".

II

If democracy implied equality and a just distribution of wealth, Britain herself in 1943 was still manifestly undemocratic. However, the war had produced much levelling down at the top, at least in theory, and much levelling up from the bottom. "In general," Sidney Pollard has concluded, "it would be broadly true to state that personal consumption was stabilized at the pre-war skilled artisan level, and that of other classes cut down to approach it."[13]

National Income statistics show that between 1938 and 1944, the total of all wages earned (if the pay and allowances of the armed forces are included) increased by more than a hundred per cent. Over the same period, the total paid in salaries increased by little more than one-third, and personal income from rents, dividends and interest by about one-ninth. Wages as a proportion of all personal income rose from under forty per cent to nearly fifty per cent. This was not an equal share, but it was a juster share.

Meanwhile, the cost of living had risen steeply. In 1943, average weekly wage rates stood at around thirty-five per cent above their 1938 level. Retail prices, according to the authoritative London and Cambridge Economic Service, had risen, at a general estimate, by forty-two per cent. Actual earnings, however, had increased on average by about three-quarters over pre-war. What these three statistics together implied was that many people were earning more, in real terms, not because their rates were relatively better, but because they were putting in longer hours. Average hours worked weekly by men over twenty-one had been 47·7 in 1938 and were 52·9 in 1943.[14]

Averages, notoriously, conceal as much as they make manifest. While engineering workers were a good deal better off in real terms, the rise in earnings for transport and storage workers (again, merely an average) had only just outpaced the rise in retail prices. While it was generally true that the highest price rises had occurred with luxury goods – and rents, that basic drain on working-class incomes, had been stabilized – a heavy smoker would pay out his extra earnings in increased prices for tobacco.

By 1944, some ninety-five per cent of all household expenditure went on price-controlled goods. But in spite of the greater severity with which the Government punished offences against price control orders – nine hundred people were found guilty of over-charging for non-food consumer goods alone in 1944 – maximum prices were hard to set and still harder to enforce. More positively, food subsidies, so casually undertaken by Chamberlain's cabinet, had swollen to huge proportions. (In June 1945 it was officially stated that consumers were paying a penny a pound less for bread, threepence three farthings a pound less for meat, and considerably lower prices for other essential foods, than would have been possible without them.) But this was a conjurer's trick. The working class paid out, in extra taxes on beer and tobacco, what was needed to provide subsidies to stabilize the mendacious cost of living index in order to persuade their unions to restrain demands for higher wage rates. There were few beneficiaries except for non-smokers with large families.[15]

If the armed forces are taken into consideration, inequality within the working class itself had increased. On the one hand, a minority of highly skilled men working very long hours in muni-tions production were drawing pay which, while it still fell short of the salaries of professional men and women, was high by the standards of clerical workers. Their prosperity was highly pre-carious. Until 1944, the basic rates for engineers remained lower than they had been in 1921, before a famous lockout in which the employers had triumphed and forced wages down. On this humble foundation rested a complex and fragile structure of overtime pay, piece rates and bonuses which swelled the few big pay packets. The quite exceptional earnings in some sections of the aircraft industry will be mentioned later. Meanwhile, to stress their egregiousness it should be pointed out that when Mass Observation, in 1942, had obtained from the managing director of a provincial war factory the figures for the twenty highest earners among his two thousand employees, these were, with only three exceptions, men working more than sixty hours per week. The highest pay of all was £12 0s. 5d. earned by a man working no less than ninety-five and a quarter hours; after deductions, including income tax, he drew £10 12s. 3d.[16] By comparison, the salary of a girl reporter on Fleet Street, which did not depend on fluctuating and temporary overtime, might be six hundred pounds per year.

While the average weekly earnings for men rose from about £4 10s. a week in July 1940 to £6 4s. 4d. a week in July 1944 (and then fell back slightly as war industry contracted and overtime decreased), average earnings in the metal, engineering and shipbuilding industries had reached a peak of around seven pounds a week in January 1944; this was thirty shillings to two pounds higher than in other manufacturing industries.

But when all this is said, there is no doubt that large sections of the working class were better off as a result of the war, and that there was levelling up, as well as levelling down, towards the skilled artisan's standards. The most important advance, of course, had been the abolition of unemployment, and the earnings of wives and daughters now supplemented the man's in more cases than before. Beyond this, the disparity between skilled and unskilled rates of pay was generally narrowed during the course of the war. In engineering, the time rate of unskilled men was on average seventy-five per cent of that of skilled men in 1939, but eighty-two per cent in 1945; in the railways, there was a bigger leap, from sixty-one per cent to seventy-six per cent. The wholesale shift of men and women into engineering from other industries was a shift towards the highest pay. Leaving engineering on one side, the greatest increases in earnings, by both men and women, had occurred, generally speaking, in the industries where pay had been worst before the war, and the smallest in such fields as food and clothing manufacture and public utility services which had been relatively prosperous.[17]

The cardinal reason for this levelling up was full employment, which made it essential to pay better wages in vital but underprivileged industries, but it was, of course, Ernest Bevin's deliberate policy to advance the pay of the worst-off workers and to extend collective bargaining to poorly organized trades. Trades Boards, an idea originated under Winston Churchill before the First World War, had, by the outbreak of the Second, extended protection to over a million workers in such industries; these were bodies, on which both employers and workers were represented, which had power to set minimum standards. Bevin pressed further along this course, notably in the case of agricultural workers, and in 1943 he had a showdown with the Conservative Party over the issue.

The catering industry, covering employees scattered in hotels, boarding houses, cafés, bars and canteens, remained the largest of those in which wages, hours and conditions of work were still uncontrolled by collective agreement or statutory regulation. Bevin had refused to impose an E.W.O. on an industry where hours were so often very long and wages so often very poor. But, with the striking development of industrial canteens, catering was becoming more and more vital to the war economy. In the summer of 1942, Bevin had decided to attack the problem, with proposals which had at once run into strong and concerted opposition from the catering employers. A Parliamentary Committee on Catering had been set up under the leadership of Sir Douglas Hacking (whom we last heard of as retiring chairman of the Conservative Party organization) and by November, this had the support of more than two hundred M.P.s.

Bevin was undeterred by the committee's widely publicized allegation that he intended to make himself "dictator" of the catering trades, and produced his Catering Wages Bill at the end of January 1943. This proposed a Catering Wages Commission, consisting of two employers, two workers from the industry, and three independent persons. Where collective bargaining already existed in the industry, the commission need not interfere. Where it did not exist, the commission could recommend the Ministry of Labour to appoint a wages board with statutory power to fix pay, hours and holidays. Bevin, unlike Hugh Dalton a few months before, managed to maintain the support of both Conservative and Labour colleagues, and in the debate on February 9th, defeated his critics by 285 votes to 118. Those who voted against the Bill were almost all Conservatives, but a greater number of Conservatives actually voted for it. It became law in April.[18]

Bevin's Wages Council Act of 1945 renamed the Trades Boards and further increased their powers and scope. Under this Act, most areas of retail distribution came under regulation, with a million and a quarter employees. By 1950, some four and a half million workers were protected by statutory wage regulation, a fourfold increase over 1939.[19]

The lower-paid salary earners had rises, in many cases, which were comparable to those enjoyed by wage-earners; this was associated with their increasing tendency to identify themselves with the unionized manual workers. The National Foremen's Union, in 1942, changed its name to ASSET to mark its new appeal for higher supervisory grades, and by January 1943 had quintupled its membership, to ten thousand, since the start of the war. But the upper rungs of the salariat did not increase their pay sufficiently to keep pace with the rising costs of living and it seems certain that many white-collared workers were worse off, absolutely as well as relatively, than before the war.[20]

Levelling down, indeed, was more conspicuous than levelling up, granted the reduction in the numbers and quality of things which money could buy. Increased and extended income tax was one of the major social novelties of the period. Before the war, less than one million manual workers had been liable to income tax, and their payments had averaged little more than three pounds per year. By 1943–44, this number had increased to seven million, averaging over twenty-eight pounds per head.[21] This expansion created another novelty, P.A.Y.E.

From 1931 onwards, employers had been permitted to collect income tax from their employees by monthly deductions, but very few had bothered. Wood's first budget of July 1940, to simplify collection of the greater number of larger tax payments, had made deduction by employers compulsory. Since employers collected taxes weeks or months in arrears, the tax on high earnings during a spate of overtime might be called for when the worker's pay had fallen. The insecurity and even hardship which had resulted from this had contributed notably to the malaise of war industry. But there was no change until 1943, when the Government contemplated with horror the prospect of trying to collect tax when incomes declined, as they were expected to do, at the outbreak of peace. So the Government now introduced a Pay As You Earn scheme. The idea was so welcome when it was announced in September 1943 that salary earners pleaded for admission to the scheme and were included when it began to operate in April 1944, initially covering about twelve million people.[22]

Manual workers, when they paid it, hardly saw income tax as an instrument of social advance. Yet the *Economist* hailed the generally progressive tax structure which held sway after the crucial 1941 budget as "not the least of the social triumphs of the war". The later wartime budgets produced few major changes. Bad habits were swinged even more harshly; the duty on an average packet of twenty cigarettes rose from elevenpence farthing in 1941 to one shilling and fivepence in 1942 and one shilling and ninepence in 1943. Excess Profits Tax was notably mitigated; the 1944 budget effactually exempted some ten thousand smaller firms from E.P.T. and gave relief to twenty thousand more. There were one or two income tax concessions directed at removing inequities.[23] But the broad principle established under Keynes's tuition in the early war years was maintained; the working class must be soaked, but they could not be expected to accept this treatment unless the rich were soaked still more thoroughly.

So the higher a man's income had been at the start of the war, the smaller, in general, had its increase been, and the greater the proportion taken as tax. This levelling should not be exaggerated. In 1938, it is estimated, the top one per cent of earners took fourteen per cent of all private income after tax. In 1947, they still took eleven per cent. The share of the top ten per cent in after-tax income fell from thirty-eight per cent to a not exactly egalitarian thirty per cent. The top fifty per cent still took seventy per cent in 1947, as compared with seventy-three per cent in 1938. Nor should the manifold opportunities for tax evasion open to the better-off be overlooked. E.P.T., as noted earlier, encouraged firms to give payment in kind, in the form of expense allowances, and by the end of the decade the upper middle class had grown used to shaking one fist angrily at the "socialists" and their "crippling" taxes and clutching undeclared riches in the other. (Hence, education in public schools, despite huge increases in their fees, was more in demand than ever after the war.)[24]

However, the sheer shortage of all kinds of luxury, from petrol upwards, made it hard to spend ill-gotten, or, for that matter, hard-earned hoards of money so long as the war lasted. Between 1939 and 1944, the proportion of personal income spent on consumer goods and services fell from over eighty-five per cent to under seventy per cent. Over the same period, net saving from personal income increased from two hundred and twenty-two million to one thousand and seventy-five million.[25]

Indeed, saving was by 1943 an even more obvious national obsession than salvage. The National Savings campaign spent greater sums on advertising than the Ministry of Food itself, and it was National Savings posters which appeared on the sand-bagged pyramid masking the statue of Eros in Piccadilly Circus and on the plinth of Nelson's Column in Trafalgar Square. After the six o'clock news every Sunday, the B.B.C. broadcast "weekly savings news". Special "drives" had already produced a series of local occasions in every big city, with parades, speechifying and exhibitions on the same scale as those in honour of the Red Army – War Weapons Weeks in 1941, Warship Weeks in 1941–42. In the spring and summer of 1943, Wings For Victory Weeks were in progress all over Britain, followed by Salute the Soldier

Weeks in 1944. As the titles given to these festivities suggest, the same kind of economic nonsense as had bolstered the Spitfire Funds was repeatedly instilled. One propaganda film showed a small boy discovering some coins in a forgotten money box and spending them on Savings Certificates. The official historian of financial policy acidly observes: " 'Little Albert' was thus, the film purported to tell the public, helping the war effort, although in truth he had merely, by abstaining from spending the coins on useful real resources, abstained from hindering the war effort."[26]

The real object of the campaign, as Whitehall saw it, was to combat inflation. But the War Savings Campaign was run for the Government by Sir Robert Kindersley as an extension of the National Savings Movement which he had led before the war. This had had some twelve hundred local committees, busy encouraging thrift and organizing savings groups. Its organization had provided the basis for the wartime drive which Sir John Simon had launched in November 1939 with a 15s. National Savings Certificate, rising to 17s. 6d. after five years and £1 0s. 6d. after ten years. Because the certificate was exempt from income tax, the maximum permissible holding was only five hundred. For small investors with more money, a new Three Per Cent Defence Bond had been offered at the same time, with holdings up to a thousand pounds.

On this basis, Kindersley's movement had waxed mighty. By 1943, there were nearly three hundred thousand individual savings groups – street groups, works groups, school groups, groups organized at wardens' posts and so on. The Treasury, though it sincerely disliked the campaign's misleading propaganda, did not dare to discourage the voluntary workers by removing Kindersley and his colleagues from leadership. To make matters worse, the later and more spectacular drives, such as Wings for Victory, cost a great deal to run, though it seemed quite likely that their effect was on balance to discourage small savers. Monstrous targets were set for the local Weeks, and were met without any trouble because insurance companies and other financial institutions were quite happy to exchange idle money for Government bonds, and this perhaps made potential small savers feel that they need not bother, since the Government was being "lent" all the money it needed. To cite only one manifest absurdity, the Hebridean Isle of Lewis raised no less than £270,000 in its Warship Week in 1942.

However, the parades and competitions for which thrift provided an excuse, did help to brighten wartime life in the provinces. And by 1943, a more sensible line of propaganda had been introduced, featuring a hairy and satanic Squander Bug whose leering cartoon shape cavorted through the newspapers inciting housewives to waste money and wearing a swastika to show which side he was on.[27]

At the height of the war, private individuals were saving something like a quarter of their disposable incomes (after they had paid direct taxes), as compared with a normal rate of saving before the war of less than five per cent.[28] Conspicuous consumption was impossible; one consumed luxuries furtively if at all. The production of many luxury goods had been prohibited and to compound their obloquy, a purchase tax of a hundred per cent had been heaped on the more luxurious of them. Even if the new rates of supertax permitted them to spend such sums of money, the wealthy could not readily lay hands on the domestic labour required for the upkeep of large households, nor (without ensuring the complicity of a coal merchant) acquire the fuel to heat them. In 1944, Marghanita Laski published a witty little novel called *Love on the Supertax*, parodying the title of Walter Greenwood's grim best-seller of the 1930s, *Love on the Dole*. She imagined the daughter of a noble family crushed by the war vainly seeking the hand of a Communist working man, a member of the new aristocracy of munitions workers.

Of course, it was not like that. Neither for the wealthy, nor even for the working classes, were the war years so unrelentingly sour and frustrating as earlier chapters may have suggested. *Britain's Wartime Revolution*, to quote the title of another popular book published in 1944 (when all books were popular), was certainly not joyless. Though commentators then and since have made too much of this proposition for its own good, it was really true that the existence of a common goal, to achieve which meant, increasingly, sharing and sharing alike, gave many people, young and old, a proud and even gay motive for existence. The suicide rate, it might be noted, fell from 12·9 per hundred thousand in 1938 to 8·9 in 1944. The People's War, which many articulate people believed might actually end, unlike all previous wars, in a true victory for the people, produced a distinctive culture of its own, even its entertainments had their political edge.

III

The spirit of the People's War was well represented by the B.B.C. On the one hand, there were restrictions of choice, formality of presentation, a great deal of patriotic worthiness and double-think. On the other hand, there was a mixture of good humour and progressive earnestness which matched both the manifest craving for light relief, and a new seriousness and curiosity among the listening public.

The B.B.C. was a unique institution, uniquely fitted to serve as the official voice of a united people at war. In 1922, the British Broadcasting Company had been given a monopoly of the new medium. John Reith, later Sir John Reith, later Lord Reith, a dour, austere Scot, had made his mark as its general manager. In 1926, the General Strike, which had prevented the publication of all but a few newspapers for more than a week, had established the importance of radio. It had also established the importance of Reith, who had successfully resisted the strong wish of Churchill and other well-placed class warriors that the B.B.C. should be made a vehicle for official propaganda against the strikers. Later in that year the B.B.C. had become a corporation, with its monopoly reaffirmed in a public charter, maintaining its independence though supported, via the licensing of radio sets, from public funds.

Reith's autocratic regime as director general had lasted until 1938, and he had imposed his personal world view on the new medium. He had given the public what he had thought they should learn to like, not what they had actually liked. He had kept the sabbath holy, free from dance music and low "variety". He had let symphony concerts, which the B.B.C. had propagated with a fruitful but priggish zeal, overrun into the time allotted for favourite programmes. Inevitably, the B.B.C. had acquired a reputation for stuffiness, and listeners in search of gayer fare had increasingly tuned in to rival commercial stations operating from foreign soil. The war had destroyed these rivals, though it created new ones in the diverse forms of Lord Haw Haw and the American Forces Network. The total number of licensed sets had fallen slightly from its peak of nearly nine million in 1939, but was rising again after 1942. Listening had increased greatly, since the blackout kept people indoors and communal sets in shelters, army camps and other wartime centres served a vast public.

"Auntie B.B.C." herself had been thoroughly shaken up. In the early months of war, before the evacuated departments had settled down, programmes had been improvised out of chaos, often with success. Foreign language broadcasting had expanded enormously; the B.B.C., given an almost unlimited budget by the state, retained its formal independence yet became, in a more real sense than before, the "Voice of Britain". By the end of 1943, it was broadcasting in forty-seven foreign languages, as compared with eight before the war.

Air raids, the supreme challenge, had been met with superb efficiency. In Germany, raids halted the broadcasts. In Britain, stations were grouped so that if one closed down, listeners went on receiving the same programme (with a different quality of reception) from another station. The news was still read in London, and in spite of bombs which damaged Broadcasting House itself on three occasions, it had always gone out on time, though at one stage the news readers had performed in a basement protected by an iron door and armed men, and had lived, eaten, worked and slept in a lavatory. Two hundred and fifty pallets on the floor of the concert hall had accommodated broadcasters and technicians sleeping shoulder to shoulder; but as Reith would have wished, an immense curtain had segregated the sexes.[29]

So Reith, vicariously, had had his finest hour. The B.B.C. had entered the war with a staff of 4,233 and twenty-three transmitters with a total power of 1,620 kw. broadcasting for fifty hours a day. When the war ended, it had 11,417 staff and a hundred and thirty-eight transmitters with a total power of 5,250 kw. broadcasting for a hundred and fifty hours per day.[30] Reith, however, had been bested by Churchill at last, and had lost his job as Minister of Works in the cabinet purge of February 1942. To his own astonishment, he was not thereafter required to serve in high office.

The public knew and cared little about Reith, or his less distinguished wartime successors in the director generalship. But those were the days when a voice, artfully or authentically sincere, was enough in itself to make one man the friend and idol of millions. "I found myself tied," recalls J. B. Priestley, "like a man to a gigantic balloon, to one of those bogus reputations that only the mass media knows how to inflate . . . Voices cannot be disguised, and if I went into a crowded shop or bar all the people not only had to talk to me, but also had to touch me – I had thousands of hands laid on me – as if to prove to themselves I was more than a disembodied voice." Yet the "stars" were not grandly paid. Dr Charles Hill, whose impact as "the Radio Doctor" will be discussed shortly, has remarked that he had received five guineas for a five-minute broadcast before the war, and continued to draw the same fee until 1950, when he gave up his regular series. "They had no competitor," he points out, "and there was a clamouring queue of applicants for every vacant minute on the air."[31]

Amongst those whose position as stars was secure were the regular announcers and news readers. Even before the summer of 1940, when they had begun to give their own names, there had been listeners who had tuned in to certain programmes, not for their own sake, but because they doted on the voices which introduced them. Now, Frank Phillips, Alvar Liddell, Bruce Belfrage, Joseph McLeod, Alan Howland, Stuart Hibberd, Frederick Allen were better known than all but a handful of cabinet ministers. Their art was not, of course, as simple as it sounded. Apart from their sometimes controversial attempts to pronounce an ever greater range of foreign place-names, they were required, Reith-wise, to recite the direst and happiest tidings without showing the slightest sign of emotion. Their craft had become still more taxing in the autumn of 1941, when an "enemy voice" had begun to cut into the pauses in the bulletins with sardonic comments; thereafter, the readers had been told to fill their time as closely and accurately as possible.[32]

The readers up to September 1939 had performed in evening dress. This consorted with the fact that their voices, while pleasant, were all southern English and impeccably upper middle class. In mid-war, this convention was broken when a Yorkshire character actor named Wilfred Pickles was called south from the B.B.C.'s northern headquarters in Manchester to become a regular "front line" newsreader. There was a press furore over the prospect of a reader who pronounced his "A's" short in the northern manner. Excitement increased when he ended the midnight news by saying a special "Good Neet" to all northerners. Though his voice was very popular (especially in the south), Pickles himself asked to return to Manchester. But his name had become magical, and he quite soon found less dignified, but much more lucrative, work as a music-hall comedian and star actor.[33]

Joseph McLeod, an intellectual and a rebel with left-wing views, has written sourly of the "factitious" fame which he and his colleagues enjoyed. Their star status, he says, went to their heads. "This has happened to almost every successful regular broadcaster. Some listened to their own voices, and became vain.

Some listened to their own souls, and became pontifical. Either meant the end of that directness which makes the good broadcaster . . ."[34] It was one factor in the success of Tommy Handley, the star of radio stars, that he never lost his homeliness, his intimacy and his "directness".

Handley's rise to a peak of fame had coincided, during the Bore War, with that of Lord Haw Haw. Haw Haw had slipped rapidly from his sinister eminence, though he seems to have retained a sizable public in Scotland, where reception of the Home Service was sometimes poor, until well into 1941. By the middle of the war the Ministry of Information was little concerned about the scanty audience which he still found.[35] But ITMA, which in June 1941 had returned to the air from the Variety Department's new centre at Bangor in North Wales, after nearly seventeen months' absence, proceeded to stamp itself indelibly on the life of the war years.

Handley was, in radio terms, a veteran. In the 1920s, he had been one of the first comedians to make a name in broadcasting. He was a Liverpudlian, now in his late forties, who had gone to work as an office boy at fifteen and had for a time been a salesman of baby carriages before he had gone on the stage in 1917 to commence a career which was to end, at his death in 1949, with a national memorial service in St Paul's Cathedral. He became an institution, and his friendly north country voice, which could deliver dialogue very rapidly without tripping and with perfect timing, was the basis of that institution.

When ITMA had first been launched in the summer of 1939, its format had been relatively novel. Radio comedy series based on a situation and a story of some sort, however fatuous, had been popular in the U.S.A. for some time, but the first example in Britain had been heard only shortly before – "Band Waggon", featuring "Big-Hearted Arthur" Askey and "Stinker" Murdoch, which had continued, rivalling ITMA in popularity, for a while after the outbreak of war. ITMA's formula, as developed by Handley, his script writer Ted Kavanagh and the producer Francis Worsley – a team which held together for ten years – was to set Tommy himself up as presiding dignitary of some zany but just recognizable institution, and to surround him with a troupe of funny voices; the handful of supporting mimics could produce more than twice their number of characters, though amongst them perhaps only the weirdly versatile Jack Train became a top celebrity in his own right. Each of the established characters would figure for at most two or three minutes of each programme.

Handley was there all the time, in a unique role combining those of comic, "feed" and "link man". He reappeared as His Washout the Mayor of the seaside resort of Foaming at the Mouth ("Other mayors are talking about after-the-war plans but mine are in hand already. I intend to dehouse the whole population of the borough. My motto is – Loosen the Green Belt, tuck in the blue prints and paint the town red."[36] In subsequent series, he was manager of a war factory, keeper of a hotel, squire of the manor of Much Fiddling, and so on.

Kavanagh aimed, with mathematical nicety, at a hundred potential laughs in the eighteen and a half minutes of actual dialogue which were possible in a half-hour show, including music to make it "variety". That was one laugh every eleven seconds, a cheetah-like rate sometimes stepped up to one every eight seconds. Kavanagh deftly blended up-to-the-minute topicalities, and mild political satire, with timeless and outrageous puns, crazy situation comedy, and grotesque sound effects. The result was always and essentially good radio. As Kavanagh himself has put it, "the ITMA characters, unlike good children, were designed to be heard and not seen."[37]

Funf, the German spy with feet of sauerkraut who had been the star supporting voice of the first series, was less prominent in the later ones. But there was a galaxy of new stars, each with a catchphrase which caught: Ali Oop the pedlar ("I go – I come back"); the Diver, with two memorable utterances, "Don't forget the diver, gents, don't forget the diver" and "I'm going down now, sir"; Claude and Cecil, the polite brokers' men ("After *you*, Claude." "No – after *you*, Cecil."); the Commercial Traveller ("GOOD morning, NICE day"); and Signor So So, his Tomship's Foreign Secretary, much troubled by the English language. One ITMA character who will clearly retain immortality in dictionaries of that language was Mrs Mopp, the Corporation Cleanser, introduced triumphantly in the autumn of 1941, with her invariable opening gambit "Can I do you now, sir?" and a flow of lavatorial *double entendres*.

In the autumn of 1942, the fourth ITMA series introduced the fruity, bibulous Colonel Chinstrap, the most famous of all Jack Train's voices. One need only cite his memorable lament when the 1943 budget increased, yet again, the duty on drink. "Why must the Chancellor always tax necessities? Another penny a pint, sir – that's an extra five shillings a day. It's a terrible burden." His catchphrase "I don't mind if I do" is still commonly enough heard from people accepting drinks.

These familiar yet, somehow, never predictable absurdities were manna for young and old, rich and poor, forces and civilians. In any one week, more than sixteen million people would listen to ITMA. R.A.F. pilots shouted "I'm going down now" as they dived to attack; a small boy trapped under a pile of rubble in Bath piped out to the rescue squad, "Can you do me now, sir." When ITMA was off the air for a few weeks, the public could work its magic for themselves by repeating the catchphrases. Capable, by some alchemy, of making fun out of Dame Austerity herself (on her second appearance, Mrs Mopp presented the mayor with a jar of "carrot jelly", strained, as she proudly declared, through her own jumper), ITMA sparkled through the life of the nation like bubbles through soda water.[38]

ITMA was by no means the B.B.C.'s only contribution to national gaiety, and there were probably some who perversely preferred Vic Oliver, Bebe Daniels and Ben Lyon in "Hi Gang". The Forces Programme, offering chiefly light entertainment, regularly attracted some six listeners out of ten, while the Home Service, more varied and serious, mustered the remainder. (After February 1944, however, the former was replaced for technical reasons by a General Forces Programme which confined itself to thin material suitable for mass listening in service canteens, and this drove the civilian audience back to the Home Service.) The American Forces Network, which had low-powered transmitters supplying the chief U.S. camps in Britain, attracted some following after it opened in July 1943, with its more or less continuous stream of swing music and comedy, but not more than one Briton in ten could receive it, and London itself was not within range.[39]

Two new features of the B.B.C.'s own lighter broadcasts were the growing proportion of programmes broadcast from factories, army camps and so on – there was even one in the blitz called "Helter Shelter" – and the increase in request programmes such as "Forces Favourites", where the playing of chosen music provided a sentimental link between scattered relatives and lovers. One of the most successful series of the war was "Ack Ack – Beer Beer" which made use of talent found on A.A. and Balloon Command sites; while "Works Wonders" featured lunch-time concerts given by talented workers for their fellows and broadcast "live". As this celebration of the common life became an accepted feature of wartime listening, it was inevitable that the B.B.C. should produce, in 1941, its first soap opera, the saga of a "front line family" called the Robinsons, who gathered a devoted audience and paved the way for those staples of post-war listening, the "Dales" and the "Archers".

The Home Service regularly included all types of music, and literary talks, as well as comedy. At five twenty on September 7th, 1940, when the Luftwaffe were firing the London docks, younger listeners elsewhere were enjoying "Children's Hour". After the six o'clock news bulletin came, at this stage of the war, news in Norwegian, which could not be fitted in anywhere else. At six forty-five, "Women in Wartime" featured the voices of girls in the W.A.A.F. The comedian Cyril Fletcher was followed by a Beethoven concert which was succeded, as the raiders returned to London, by another variety programme until the nine o'clock news introduced graver topics. But afterwards, an eminent man of the theatre was presenting "Picture Postcard Beauties", described as "a recollection of their charms, their lives and their favourite songs", while the timber blazed in the Surrey Docks. After the religious programme at ten fifteen came the news in Gaelic, specially for Highland listeners; then, as the night's destruction neared its climax, those who did not know that the code word CROMWELL had gone out might have enjoyed "PIG HOO-O-O-O-EY", a presentation of the most famous of P. G. Wodehouse's Blandings Castle stories, set in that never-never aristocratic England which he had invented.

There were devoted Home Service listeners who could enjoy more or less everything, and would cook their meal during the news in Norwegian and make their late night cocoa during the news in Gaelic so as not to miss a word in English. But most found the other wavelength more reliable. On the day that Singapore fell, the Forces Programme offered, before lunch, the comedy of Jack Benny, in a recording from America. After the one o'clock news came music hall, when "Accent on Rhythm" (so much for Reith's sabbath) and later "Music While You Work" (so much for the sabbath in general). The early evening included ice hockey from Canada, community hymn singing and more comedy from Arthur Askey. After the nine o'clock news and Churchill's sombre broadcast (not scheduled) there was "SINCERELY YOURS – VERA LYNN", "a sentimental half-hour linking the men in the forces with their womenfolk at home".[40]

Miss Lynn was another institution. With her plangent mid-Atlantic voice, she had made her most famous song,

> We'll meet again, don't know where, don't know when,
> But I know we'll meet again some sunny day,

Keep smiling through just like you always do
Till the blue skies drive the dark clouds far away . . .

express the loneliness of millions. She was the "Forces' Sweet-heart", but their sweethearts liked her too. That other virtuoso of good clean sentiment, Wilfred Pickles, has paid her sincere tribute. "When Vera visited hospitals and then, on the Forces Programme, told the fighting men about their new babies, she was not merely reading a script; she really saw every child she talked about – and took flowers to all the mothers."[41]

The Forces Programme that grim Sunday included another item of immense popularity, more significant than Vera Lynn's because much more unexpected; at four in the afternoon, the weekly session of "The Brains Trust".

During the war, the educational ambitions of the Reith era reached astonishing fulfilment. It was not just that serializations of such classics as *Cranford* and *Vanity Fair* provided a soothing accompaniment to some of the darker passages of the war; nor that the B.B.C. characteristically overreached itself with a pro-duction of *Hamlet* on the Home Service which was allowed to run for forty-five minutes over the scheduled time before it was cut off at the graveyard scene. There was a real increase of public interest in serious drama, and there was a growing avidity for general knowledge of all kinds which gobbled down the Brains Trust week after week after week. "Favourite topic on Mondays seems to be the previous day's Brains Trust session," a worker in a great chemical factory noted in his diary in November 1941; "hardly anyone ever confesses that he didn't hear it, or if they do, take care to give adequate reason for so doing."[42]

In the autumn of 1940, the Forces Programme planners had noted a growing demand from servicemen for information of all sorts (no doubt largely inspired by the wish to settle barrack-room arguments). A newcomer from commercial radio named Howard Thomas had been invited to help devise a new programme, and he had borrowed a "brand name", "Brains Trust", from Roose-velt's nickname for his circle of advisers. There was a significant modulation of Reithian doctrine. The aim, as Thomas saw it, was education by stealth, "to give listeners not what *you* wanted them to hear but what *they* wanted to hear without always realizing they did". In short, a soft sell. The "Question Master", another Thomas brand name which became universally current, was also an advertising man, the quick-talking Donald McCul-lough. The "Trust" had three basic members; the zoologist

Julian Huxley, a brilliantly lucid popularizer of science; the philosopher Professor Cyril Joad; and a retired naval man, Commander A. B. Campbell. These became as well known as Mrs Mopp and the Diver. The supporting cast of two other distinguished "Brains" varied from week to week.

When the saga of the Three Wise Men began on New Year's Day 1941, they were scheduled to give six broadcasts of half an hour each at the non-peak time of five thirty on Wednesday. After the first programme, they were sent fifteen questions; by the end of the month they were getting thirty a day. The first series was extended for eighty-four weeks without a break, and the Brains were promoted to the peak Sunday time of four o'clock and given forty-five minutes.

The contests which developed between the regular Brains, as Thomas had hoped, generated much of the popular interest. The cool Huxley clashed with the volatile Joad in philosophical argument, and the cheerful Campbell would make some man-in-the-street remark to bring them back to earth. They too had their catchphrases. Huxley would begin, "Surely, Joad . . ."; Joad would greet a philosophical teaser with "It depends what you mean by . . ." and Campbell would launch into a yarn, more or less apposite, with "When I was in Patagonia . . ." (or somewhere equally unlikely).

Joad, tweedy, bearded and bright eyed, the epitome of the *New Statesman* intellectual, made the running at first. His popularity, based on dazzling width of reading and brilliant eloquence, was such that in one Yorkshire town police had to force a way for him through a milling mob who could not get into the hall where he was due to speak. But his high-pitched voice and his tendency to monopolize the sessions soon irritated many loyal listeners, and it was the non-intellectual, Campbell, who took over the lead, with a huge following based on exotic anecdotes which reflected all too accurately the plain man's superstitions. Campbell claimed, for instance, to have dreamed the name of a Derby winner before the race and, when the question of allergies came up, he cited a friend who was so allergic to marmalade that when he had it for breakfast steam rose from the top of his head.

Most of the eight or ten questions which the Brains got through in a normal broadcast were serious scientific or philosophical teasers, but Thomas habitually selected a light-hearted one to ward off boredom. "How does a fly land on the ceiling?" was a famous one which stirred up much argument. Though all answers were unscripted and spontaneous, only about two questions in a

THE PEOPLE'S WAR

hundred stumped the Brains, among them "Why can you tickle other people but you can't tickle yourself?" Controversy could not be avoided; indeed, it was the programme's main attraction. There were outcries from time to time, as when Huxley expounded the case for scientific humanism so brilliantly that thereafter religious questions were excluded.

Rested in July 1942, the Brains Trust came back with several new features in October. The regulars were increased to nine by six distinguished additions, including some of the notabilities who had come well out of the ordeal of appearing as a guest, which had damaged several formidable reputations. Amongst them was the conductor, Malcolm Sargent, who soon equalled the original trio in popularity. Despite grumbles from those who lamented that they could now hear Campbell or Joad only once every three weeks, the programme was more popular than ever.

In 1943, the Brains Trust had a regular audience of ten to twelve millions every week. Just before Christmas in that year, three out of ten listeners were tuned in for one Brains Trust at its new time on Tuesday evening; and perhaps one in six would hear, for the first or second time, the repeat broadcast on Sunday. Only a few variety programmes, the news bulletins and the outstanding "Postscripts" could rival this popularity.[43]

Howard Thomas himself ruminated that "There was something historic and representative of our day when the Brains Trust opened its second season, in September 1942, with five such men as Dr Gilbert Murray, O.M., Dr Julian Huxley, Colonel Walter Elliott, Sir William Beveridge and Dr Malcolm Sargent, assembled to answer the ordinary man's questions."[44] And also, though Thomas did not add this point, there was "something representative" in the fact that any one Brain, on the most serious philosophical question, would be lucky to speak for one minute.

IV

Radio apart, people in Britain were spending a greater proportion of their incomes on entertainment. Official figures which adjust personal expenditure in wartime to the price levels of 1938 gave only a crude picture, since they include the use which G.I.s made of their pay. But it is roughly true to say that consumption of food had fallen by one-eighth between 1938 and 1944, expenditure on clothing by over one-third, and expenditure on household goods by nearly two-thirds. Certain pre-war pleasures, also, were much restricted. Not only was week-end motoring virtually impossible, the Government devoted much effort, largely unavailing, towards persuading people to accept the idea of "Holidays at Home", and local councils promoted a wide range of entertainments during holiday periods.

Pub-going was a custom, to a greater or lesser degree, with perhaps three-quarters of the nation's men and half its women. Overall, consumption of alcohol had not risen much, though the big increases in price meant that much more was spent on it. Spirits were harder to come by. During the war, only three short periods of distilling for Scottish whisky were allowed, and what was then made was designed for export. The pre-war stocks which remained were in shorter and shorter supply. But beer drinking had risen by twenty-five per cent though the brew was now adulterated, not only with more water, but with oats and potatoes in lieu of barley. Before the war, the end of the week had been the favourite time for drinking and the last hour before closing time had seen the peak of public house potations. But now that supplies of beer were erratic, people chose times when they were most likely to find it in stock; drinking was spread more evenly over the week, and the middle of the evening was the period when pubs were generally most crowded. A change in drinking habits with more permanent significance was the shift of working-class drinkers from the cheaper public bar to the saloon bar. It was not just that they now had more money; scarce supplies were increasingly allocated to the more expensive bars, and fuel shortage meant that the saloon might have a fire when the public did not. (This trend was reflected, after the war, in many newly built pubs which dispensed with the "public" altogether.[45])

Money spent on entertainments had risen by about a hundred and twenty per cent between 1938 and 1944. Since Entertainment Tax was another favourite standby of Chancellors of the Exchequer, the actual rise in "consumption" over pre-war had been only about forty per cent. Far and away the most popular entertainment covered by these figures was the cinema, where seat prices had risen steeply, but audiences had grown rather than diminished.

Every week in Britain, some twenty-five or thirty million cinema seats were sold. The habit was strongest of all among children, but three-quarters of the adult population were cinema-goers, and a third, overall, went once a week or more often still. Town dwellers went more than folk in the country, women more often than men, and the under forties much more than the over forties. The Wartime Social Survey found that four out of five adolescents between fourteen and seventeen went at least once a week, and two of these four would go twice a week or more. The young wage earner, especially in light engineering, was most likely of all to be a besotted addict. An observer in a west country war factory in 1943 noted that "The pictures is the one event in the week which the factory girls really do look forward to and enjoy." A young miner of twenty-one proudly revealed in a reply to a questionnaire, "In 1942 I saw 306 films, in 1943 I saw 382, and in 1944 I reached the grand total of 430, I hope I can beat that total in 1945." Probably, most people under forty saw at least fifty features every year.[46]

And on average no more than seven of these films would be British. The competition of English-language films from Hollywood had stunted the pre-war British film industry, both financially and artistically, as compared with those of Germany and France. A Quota Act of 1927 had compelled British cinemas to show a gradually increasing proportion of British films – twenty per cent by 1939 – but this had only encouraged the production of cheap and worthless second features which had discredited the native cinema.

The war, to begin with, had seemed likely to make matters worse. Call-up had stripped the studios of two thirds of their personnel. The Government had requisitioned many of those tempting floor spaces for war industry. In 1939 there had been twenty-two studios using sixty-five sound stages; in 1942, there were only nine with thirty sound stages. In an average pre-war year, a hundred to a hundred and fifty British feature films had been produced – say one-fifth as many as in the U.S.A. In 1941–42, only forty-six had been made; in 1943–44 there were only seventy.[47]

Yet the war saw a vast increase in the prestige of British films, both with the most severe critics and with the general public. "Everyone recognizes now", asserted the influential critic Roger Manvell, at the end of the war, "that there has been an extraordinary renaissance in British feature-film production since about 1940."[48]

Oddly enough, this renaissance was associated with the empire which J. Arthur Rank had established over the British industry. Rank was a wealthy flour miller, an ardent Methodist who had first been led to Wardour Street by an interest in religious films. During the war, when others were loth to find money to support

British pictures, he stepped in, and came to own half the studio space and two of the three biggest cinema circuits. Rank had no taste in films and little interest in how they were made. While he readily supported bad films, his lack of sophistication meant that he was equally ready to support daring ideas and good new directors; he could not tell the difference. Indeed, what films were made were of necessity created largely by new talent; besides those top British actors, writers and directors who had been in Hollywood at the outbreak of war and had stayed there, others had been called up for service. While a few veteran film-makers like Anthony Asquith and Michael Balcon were leading figures in the so-called renaissance, such newcomers as Carol Reed, David Lean, the Boulting brothers and Robert Hamer were given a splendid chance to establish themselves, mostly under the aegis of the Rank Organization.[49]

In this context, there was a remarkable flowering of the tradition of painstaking, didactic British documentary realism which had been planted and watered between the wars by John Grierson and others. The documentary film movement, though largely left-wing in inspiration, had been fostered by state patronage. Grierson had led a unit established by, of all things, the Empire Marketing Board; the secretary of the board, Sir Stephen Tallents, was a notable pioneer in the field of official propaganda and had taken the unit with him when he had moved on to the Post Office. During the war, the same unit, now without Grierson, became the Ministry of Information's Crown Film Unit, and the ministry produced several scores of films every year, mostly brief but some full length.[50]

Covert propaganda, the sugaring of the pill, was one motive force underlying the apotheosis of British documentary realism during the war. There were straightforward official documentaries of distinction, such as *Fires Were Started*, a film about the blitz directed by Humphrey Jennings for the Crown Film Unit. There were fictionalized documentaries like Carol Reed's *The Way Ahead* (1944), made in celebration of the common soldier. The more orthodox story lines of feature films based on the common life of wartime Britain often concealed Government instigation; thus, Thorold Dickinson's *Next of Kin* was made to discourage "careless talk" and Launder and Gilliat's *Millions Like Us* praised and inspired the effort of "mobile women" working in munitions.

The most famous example of the new realism was *In Which We Serve*, which, when it appeared in 1942, was probably given more fulsome critical praise than any British film before or since. It was made, as a somewhat daring venture, under Rank auspices, with its scriptwriter Noel Coward cast "out of type" as a naval captain and with a list of unknown actors, many of whom subsequently became major stars. The director, also unknown then, was David Lean. The film was based on flashbacks to life in Britain seen through the eyes of the survivors from H.M.S. *Torrin*, clinging to a float in the oily water after the ship had been dive-bombed and sunk in the Battle of Crete. The film, besides having real merits, was excellent propaganda for Britain and her navy, and it was a commercial success both in Britain and the U.S.A.[51]

Audiences preferred home-made products which reconstructed the boredom and banality, as well as the heroism, of the People's War, to uncomprehendingly romantic American films about life in Britain, Calif. (The notorious *Mrs Miniver*, the saga of middle-class courage set in an olde worlde utopia, provoked very mixed reactions from British audiences.) One survey of the taste of cinema patrons found that virtually all of them thought that British films had improved during the war, a compliment which only a quarter were prepared to pay to those from the U.S.A.[52] New British stars, given their chance, like the directors, by war-time conditions, had begun to encroach on the American hege-mony of dreams. Before the war, only a handful of British actors had had anything approaching international star status – notably Vivien Leigh, and Leslie Howard, the "typical" ill-dressed, pipe-smoking Englishman with mild good looks, who was mourned by millions in 1943 when the plane in which he was flying to Lisbon was shot down by Nazi fighters. Now there was a cluster of exciting newcomers – James Mason, Stewart Granger, Rex Harrison, John Mills, Deborah Kerr, Margaret Lockwood – most of whom, of course, found their way to Hollywood when the war ended.

Such stars, of course, did not acquire their glitter solely by impersonating able seamen or "mobile women". The British cinema turned aside from worthiness to produce melodramas, romances, comedies and costume pictures. The flashy Granger, the dark and sullen Mason and the glamorous Miss Lockwood confirmed their reputations in a notable figment of tushery called *The Man in Grey*. More spectacular, though much more seriously intentioned, was Laurence Olivier's *Henry V*, filmed in Eire in 1943 (when there were no "extras" for the Battle of Agincourt in the india-rubber island) at a cost which swelled to half a million pounds, without overheads, a record for any British picture up to that date. Yet Shakespeare ,with the help of some good Techni-colour, paid for himself.

But Hollywood still contributed the staple cinema viewing of the British, and the quota was now reduced to a mere fifteen per cent. Not even Olivier at Harfleur could match the impact of his wife, Vivien Leigh, in *Gone With the Wind*. David Selznick's epic had arrived in London with three simultaneous premiers during the Norwegian campaign, and it stayed in the West End until the spring of 1944, after going on general release in 1942. Its appeal was not entirely escapist; perhaps its most' memorable shots showed Vivien Leigh picking her way through a vast panorama of war-wounded men. But that war had finished three-quarters of a century before, and it is safe to conclude that for most of the film's three hours and forty minutes, the millions of war-weary minds which encountered it were content to be swept away by its colour, costume and glamour.

Indeed, the success of a few of the British documentaries ran counter to the general pattern of public taste, which lapped up Charlie Chaplin clowning as Hitler in *The Great Dictator*, but did not generally respond with much pleasure to war films as such until 1942, when the tide had clearly turned. Even after that many would have agreed with the woman who wrote to her local paper in 1944, "I've just seen Bette Davis's film *Now, Voyager*, and what enjoyment and what relief – *no war*. I have worked in a large office with other women in whose homes the war is ever present by the absence of husbands and sons on service, and who, like myself, snatch their bit of break in a couple of hours each week at the cinema. The general opinion is: 'We don't want to see war films; we've had it.' "[53]

Hollywood, however, had not grasped this point. There were splendid American films, of course, like Orson Welles's *Citizen Kane*; there were also miles of mediocrity dedicated, after their fashion, to democracy. Joan Crawford appeared as a notably well-dressed heroine of the French Resistance (in *Mademoiselle France*); Clark Gable, to the irritation of some of his *Gone With The Wind* admirers, was awarded the Victoria Cross in *They Met in Bombay*. The wittiest London critic of those years, C. A. Lejeune, remarked at the end of the war that the scriptwriters would now have to work harder for their stories. "Among the stories that are inexorably doomed," she noted, "are the follow-ing:

The story about the honest chorus girl, who rejects her millionaire suitors for a simple sailor, only to find that he is the richest of them all, having joined the navy to avoid publicity.

The one about the society woman who puts on knife-creased overalls, a chic bandeau, and a delicate smudge of oil, and goes into an aircraft factory for a little light war work.

The story, so popular with our British exiles, about the experiences of an American soldier in the London air raids.

The film in which Errol Flynn pops into occupied Europe to teach the beauties of fortitude to Czech, Polish, French, Norwegian or Belgian patriots.

The one about the beautiful spy in Lisbon, who is an anti-Nazi pretending to be a Nazi pretending to be an anti-Nazi.

The semi-documentary about (a) a bomber, (b) an aircraft carrier, (c) a submarine, that keeps on going somewhere for two hours and eventually gets there . . .

The story about the Camp or Canteen show, in which Five Great Bands and Fifty-Nine Famous Film Stars demonstrate the principles of Democracy to dazzled G.I.s.

Any film that ends with dewy eyes, celestial choir, the vicar in full canonicals, and a squadron of bombers flying into the sunlight.[54]

The tune most in request from cinema organists throughout the war appears to have been "The White Cliffs of Dover", sentimental and patriotic, which beat off challenges from time to time from such other topical songs as "Shine On Victory Moon". It was a symptom, perhaps, of the failure of the British light music industry to produce many songs with much vitality, that a German song, "Lili Marlene", is the best-remembered hit of the war. Celebrating the nostalgia of a German soldier for his girl, a forgotten pre-war recording of "Lili Marlene" by Lale Anderson was relayed to Rommel's troops in North Africa in mid-1941. Thereafter, it was played virtually every night for three years over German radio. It captured, not only Rommel's Afrika Korps, but also the Eighth Army (indeed, it was eventually parodied or adapted in every European language) and in 1942 the lyricist Tommy Connor was asked by Whitehall to provide it with acceptable English words. The success of his version, first recorded by the buxom Anne Shelton, did not stamp out innumerable bawdy variants improvised in every arm of the British forces.[55]

Bawdyness was a problem which greatly exercised the mind of

Basil Dean, the distinguished theatrical producer who was director of ENSA, the Entertainments National Service Association.
Dean felt so strongly that the troops wanted something more
noble than smut that he was known to sack an offending comedian more or less on the spot. ENSA was very much Dean's own
brainchild, which he had persuaded the Government to support
before the outbreak of war. By early 1946 ENSA had given over
two and a half million concerts to H.M. Forces and to industry,
and it had employed more than four-fifths of the entertainment
industry at one time or another.

A great part of ENSA's work lay in entertaining troops on
remote sites. ENSA had the distinction of taking the first film to the
island of Barra in the Hebrides. Local people were admitted.
When the Gaumont newsreel began with the figure of an old-time
watchman ringing his bell, the islanders "stampeded, bowled over
the operator, trod on his projector and vowed never again to enter
the haunted hut". ENSA accompanied the troops to every theatre
of war, providing blue jokes within sound of the enemy guns.
ENSA also, from mid-1940 onwards, became Bevin's ally in his
efforts to brighten the tedium of war work. Every factory on an
approved list of over a thousand now had one or two ENSA parties
every week, generally performing in the canteen during lunch
breaks.[56]

ENSA paid poor fees. Though an artiste's deferment from
national service had come to depend on the offer of six weeks'
service to ENSA, and some major stars – Gracie Fields with her
Lancashire schmaltz and George Formby with his ukelele – performed under ENSA auspices, ENSA relied heavily on low-grade and
near-amateur talent; it was the unsuccessful singers and comedians who relished the security of ENSA contracts, and the entertainments industry too was stretched to provide the manpower
necessary for its far-flung commitments. There were, of course,
some ENSA discoveries, notably Tony Hancock and Terry
Thomas, but in general the complaint from troops and workers
alike was not so much that ENSA, in spite of Dean's efforts,
was synonymous with smut, as that the smut was far from
funny.

Mass Observation printed a note from the works manager of
one war factory, revealing that the workers' committee had
"actually complained about the low quality of the humour in
many ENSA concerts, and requested more music and straight stuff.
Two CEMA concerts (classical, instrumental and vocal music) have
been very successful, and attempts have been made for more, as

well as for lunch-time gramophone recitals, which it is hoped to start very shortly."[57]

ENSA itself had a division concerned with classical music; in this field, it had a powerful rival: CEMA, the Council for Education in Music and the Arts. (Bevin confided once to Dean, in the hot room of the Turkish bath where the two men would sometimes meet, that he thought CEMA's efforts "too 'ighbrow".) CEMA had been set up in January 1940 to give the arts a fighting chance in wartime and had soon received twenty-five thousand pounds from the Government. Its activities ranged beyond concerts. It sponsored Art for the People Exhibitions which took the work of the best British painters to provincial towns. The Old Vic company made a triumphal tour of the Welsh mining towns, led by Sybil Thorndike; the Pilgrim Players took serious drama to village halls. The Ballet Rambert was sent out to tour factories and hostels, and Sadler's Wells, driven out of London by the blitz, presented "utility" opera in lesser industrial towns, with an orchestra of four and a company of only twenty-six. (The décor for *Marriage of Figaro* once consisted of two chairs and a sofa.)[58]

The warm response which all these activities met was only partly due to the dispersal of the intelligentsia from London to the previously benighted provinces. Certainly, classical music found a new audience, somewhat jealously disputed between ENSA and CEMA. Many regular orchestral players had been called up, but they found scope for their talents in the forces, where several Commands prided themselves on possessing their own symphony orchestras. At one period, Southern Command alone had as many as thirty chamber groups in practice, and Northern Command was providing some fifteen concerts a month for its men. Even more spectacular was the undergrowth of gramophone clubs which throve on ENSA's disc-lending service. The B.B.C. Symphony Orchestra broke a record for Saturday night takings set by Gracie Fields herself when it played for the troops at Aldershot.[59]

Besides CEMA's chamber music recitals, which received rapt attention in factory canteens, there were from 1943 onwards "ENSA Symphony Concerts for War Workers", arranged in the towns with the greatest concentrations of war industry. Pablo Casals played Elgar's cello concerto in Chester Cathedral for the ENSA standard fee of three guineas. And this bore fruit; Thomas Russell, the chief administrator of the London Philharmonic Orchestra, noted a few years after the end of the war that "some hundred centres are now enjoying regular concerts where, only ten years ago, nothing of the kind had ever been heard."[60]

Sir Malcolm Sargent, "Flash Harry", the star of the Brains Trust, who might be described as the Monty of classical music, pointed out one reason for the boom. People had been attracted to music for the first time "because it has been made available to them in the places they have been in the habit of visiting in search of entertainment – theatres, music halls, and cinemas". Thousands would always pack the auditoriums to hear him. It was he who took over London's famous series of cheap summer Promenade Concerts, when their originator Sir Henry Wood died in 1944. Between the wars they had been given in the Queen's Hall; when this was destroyed in a raid in 1941, they moved to the bigger, though acoustically inferior, Albert Hall, and filled it with audiences of up to five thousand for two months on end.[61]

People found it harder to use what spare time they had, and were willing to venture their new earnings on culture, to give it a try. And the war itself enhanced the escapist value of music, the most portable and adaptable kind of beauty. A famous vignette of the war was provided by the lunchtime concerts organized, from the autumn of 1939, by Dame Myra Hess in the deserted National Gallery. The admission price was nominal, and during the blitz Londoners had packed the concerts, which had transferred to a basement during daylight raids. (Once, an unexploded bomb had gone off in the gallery during a performance of Beethoven's F major "Rasoumovsky" quartet. No one had moved; the players had proceeded without missing a beat.) The most popular composers were Teutonic – Beethoven, Mozart and Bach. John Strachey has vividly described proceeding, at the height of the blitz, through the ruin and chaos of the West End, to hear Dame Myra herself take part in the Archduke Trio. "The first bars", he wrote, "struck the audience with unbearable force. The precision, the accurate, ordered, disciplined intricacy of the unrolling world of the music overwhelmed them. How could there exist such worlds as this, and as that?"[62]

V

A rather different species of escapism helped to explain the continued appeal of spectator sports, another world with its own rules and its own energies. But almost no national institution of comparable importance had been so badly hit by the outbreak of

war. Amateur clubs had been chiefly destroyed by the exodus of
young men to the forces and by the requisitioning of playing
fields. Professional sportsmen, conspicuous for their youth and
fitness, had been obvious candidates for the armed forces, and
when Raich Carter, probably English soccer's greatest inside
forward, had joined the A.F.S., he had grown so tired of the jibes
thrown at him by the press that after two years he had enlisted in
the R.A.F. (which gave him the dangerous post of P.T. instruc-
tor). Some professional soccer clubs had encouraged their
employees to volunteer *en masse* at the start of the war; one of
these was Arsenal, the leading English club of the 1930s, which
eventually lost all but two of its forty-four professionals to the
services. Furthermore, its ground at Highbury had been transformed by concrete and blast walls into a Civil Defence fortress,
and the "Gunners" had swallowed their pride and shared the
ground of their rivals, the Spurs.[63]

The headquarters of Rugby Union at Twickenham was given
over to allotments and Civil Defence. Home Guards drilled on
the playing area at Wimbledon. The Surrey cricket ground at
Kennington Oval became a prisoner-of-war camp, and the military also acquired Epsom racecourse. Horse racing had become a
favourite target for moralistic ire; not only did it foster gambling,
its continuance encouraged people to waste petrol and public
transport in travelling to its far-flung meetings. After the fall of
France it was banned for three months. In the spring of 1942, Sir
Stafford Cripps denounced it, and a poll showed that half the
public wished to see it prohibited. Meanwhile, bloodstock
breeders had to fight hard for land and food supplies, and the
number of foals fell by one-third. By 1943, there was no flat-
racing at all in Scotland and the six remaining courses in England
were restricted, on a regional basis, to locally trained horses –
though the substitutes for the great "classic" races, a Derby and
a St Leger run at Newmarket instead of at Epsom and Doncaster,
were exceptions to this rule. Races continued to attract gambling,
and sometimes large crowds, and by the end of the war the
B.B.C. was broadcasting commentaries again on most of the
major events.[64]

Boxing was a minor butt of public opprobrium, but almost no
one had anything to say against soccer, which was easily the
greatest of spectator sports. Its appeal to the working class went
far beyond the "pools" which, as we have seen, continued on a
Utility basis.

When professional football had restarted in September 1939,

the leagues had been completely remodelled on a regional basis to save travelling time. Crowds had been restricted by A.R.P. regulations to an eighth (later a quarter) of pre-war capacity. Fearing that they might not be admitted, keen supporters had stayed away, and in any case many now worked on Saturday afternoon or had to travel to see evacuated children. For a time it had seemed that the game had lost its hold. Receipts were insufficient for clubs to make ends meet and many famous teams, from Plymouth Argyle to Dundee United, were suspended temporarily, or even for the duration. A wartime substitute for the F.A. Cup had helped to raise interest, but clubs had continued to drop out, and further reorganization had been necessary. In the 1941–42 season, sixteen clubs in the London area had broken away from the Football League and founded their own, claiming that the distances involved in the official Southern League were too great.[65]

The game was not quite what it had been. Air raids sometimes interrupted play, though there were no major disasters at sports grounds and restrictions on crowds were relaxed as the danger decreased. The players were all youths, or part-timers from the forces and industry, turning out for a small match fee, and with the other likely calls on their time, the manager of a famous club often did not know before the kick-off which eleven men (and boys) would represent it that day. Norwich City on one occasion met a side purporting to be Brighton and Hove Albion, and in fact consisting of five Brighton men, a couple of Norwich reserves, and soldiers recruited on the ground. Norwich won 18–0; more frequent goals were a pretty general compensation for lower standards of play.[66]

Raich Carter was one of many famous players who might turn out unexpectedly as a guest for any local team, depending on where the R.A.F. decided to move him. The stars, indeed, played almost as much as ever. One of them, Denis Compton, has recalled that for him "Cup finals, League South matches, and army representative games followed one on top of each other in a seemingly endless stream." The Army and R.A.F. representative sides both consisted largely of internationals; playing regularly together, they developed a teamwork they could never have achieved in peace. The fruits (for one footballing race at least) were seen in 1944 when a superb England team overwhelmed the old enemy, Scotland, by 8–0.[67]

England–Scotland internationals attracted as many as sixty thousand spectators, and by 1943 the roar on the terraces on

Saturday afternoon had recaptured much of its peacetime volume. Other sports had also revived. The Rugby Union international between England and Wales at Swansea attracted twenty thousand fervent Welshmen that season. (It was a remarkable symptom of national unity that the amateur Rugby Union, which demanded a fifteen-a-side game, permitted its followers to play alongside men from the professional, thirteen-a-side Rugby League.) Greyhound racing, the major working-class sport after football, continued to attract good crowds to restricted fixtures. And in 1943, some quarter of a million spectators, less than a third fewer than in 1939, attended cricket matches at Lords.[68]

Although the G.I.s introduced baseball and played before large crowds – "Plymouth Yankees", for instance, took over a greyhound stadium and performed on Saturday evenings, with a running commentary on the finer points of the game relayed to the speculating masses over loudspeakers – cricket retained its quasi-religious hold over its following. The county tournament, with its three-day matches and processional pace, was abandoned, but first-class cricketers played in briefer fixtures for army sides, Civil Defence sides, and new wartime teams "representing" London Counties and the British Empire. In the later years of war, the Australian Air Force side reintroduced an element of international competition. While many major grounds were closed or bombed, Lord's provided what one ironic loyalist called "a farrago of cricket which varied pleasingly from the first-class, or near it, to that in which 'the players were remarkable rather for their enthusiasm than for their technical ability'". But in 1943, "even the most modest of fixtures found a cluster of enthusiasts in front of the Tavern or sunning themselves on the Mound . . ." Amongst those who turned out to watch the play were Ernest Bevin and – could alliance go further? – one Russian general.[69]

Even Lord's was not immune from the ravages of war; the R.A.F. took over the practice ground and the pavilion. But the redoubtable Sir Pelham Warner made it his war job to preserve the chastity and holiness of the place against all comers. ". . . I had the feeling," he declared later, "that if Goebbels had been able to broadcast that the war had stopped cricket at Lord's it would have been valuable propaganda for the Germans." It was in this spirit that he had written to a former test cricketer, Bill Edrich, during the blitz, "It was a bit close the other night. Several high explosives near by, a few incendiaries on the ground and an oil bomb at deepish mid-on, if you were bowling from the Nursery end. After a little clearing up we shall be all right to start

again soon."[70] Edrich himself was later the squadron leader of a
daylight bomber formation. He has recalled a match arranged
one Saturday between his squadron and a side from a village near
its base. The planes had been called out urgently to attack some
shipping off the Dutch coast, and two had been brought down.
When the men landed again at lunch time, the squadron side had
to find substitutes for players now at the bottom of the North Sea.

"At times it seemed like a bad dream . . ." he writes, "Both
cricket teams played well, and it was a hard and exciting game.
Every now and then would come the old, accustomed cry –
'OWZATT?' – and then one's mind would flicker off to the briefing,
and to joking with a pal whose broken body was now washing in
the long, cold tides, and one saw again his machine cart-wheeling
down flaming from nose to tail; and then a ball would roll fast
along the green English turf and in the distance the village clock
would strike and the mellow echoes would ring through the lazy
air of that perfect summer afternoon."[71]

VI

A somewhat similar spirit to Sir Pelham Warner's inspired those
women in Britain, of all classes, who did their best to keep smart.
It was patriotic to be chic. You mustn't disappoint your husband
by a sluttish appearance when he came home on leave. Adver-
tisers sedulously fostered the notion that female display was good
for the soul of the nation, like the Manchester beautician who
urged, "DON'T let the anxieties of wartime living spoil your
beauty by bringing wrinkles and taking the bloom from your
cheeks . . . A facial treatment is no idle luxury even in these days
of cautious spending [sic]. It is justified by the comfort it gives you
and the sense of well-being you experience."[72]

For those who had the time and money to seek high fashion in
the West End of London, the end of the trail would be a disappointment. There were still mannequins, but now that the
younger ones had been called up, it was mostly veterans who
displayed the attempts of the top designers to match quality with
the spirit of the times. Prices, one such seeker observes, "had
rocketed sky-high. The fourteen-guinea made-to-measure coat
and skirt was now forty-two pounds; the guinea handbag was
now six pounds; the guinea hat was now six to eight guineas; the
twenty-five shilling nightie was now twelve pounds to fourteen
pounds." (It is, of course, of more than incidental interest that

pretty things could still be sold at such prices.) Since the seam-
stresses had also been called up, one would have to wait seven or
nine months for a garment ordered from the best fashion house.[73]

On top of all this, there was clothes rationing. Sixty-six coupons
for fifteen months were provided as a detachable section of the
food ration book. Coupon "prices" fluctuated; in November
1943, a fully-lined overcoat made of wool would cost eighteen
points, a kilt sixteen, a woollen dress eleven, a dressing gown
seven or eight, a pair of knickers two. The ration gave adults
something like their pre-war consumption of clothing, if they
were lucky enough to qualify for one of the various supplements
conceded by the Board of Trade.

A rash of such special schemes had followed the introduction
of rationing as the claims of different sections of the community
had been pressed. Miners, in a fit of generosity, or appeasement,
had been given at first a ludicrous allowance of sixty extra
coupons. By 1943, the situation had been rationalized. All
manual workers had a supplement of ten coupons – this went to
over twelve million people, and about two million heavy workers
were eligible for a further "iron ration" from coupon pools established in mines and factories. There was still a proliferation of
special schemes – for civilians in uniform, for servicemen, for
stage productions, for certain sick people, for diplomats, for
prisoners, for teenagers, for outsize children. But there was no
special allowance for twenty-year-old admirers of Joan Crawford
or Margaret Lockwood; while about five civilian men in seven
qualified for the supplement, only one about woman in five did
so.[74]

With the famine of clothes, fashion sense expressed itself
increasingly in elaborate attention to the head and face. Such hats
as could be found were sported at jaunty angles – at the one
extreme, wide and shallow cloche hats, at the other natty berets
and pill-boxes. Under them flowed the time-consuming long locks
of the period, garnished with wreaths of sausage curls or, especially in 1943, arranged in the style of Veronica Lake the film
star ... "the hair hanging just on to the shoulder and curled
inwards to form a roll. The front off the forehead, with side
parting". Improvised headgear of varying degrees of fetchingness
were commonly seen – home-made turbans to protect the hair at
work, and garish patterned headscarves, some with regimental
badges.

The face was a still greater problem. Cosmetics had become the
subject of extraordinarily detailed manufacturing regulations.

Black marketeers and willing manufacturers wove a crooked course through the controls, while the P.X. gave widespread outdoor relief. Limitations on the supplies of cosmetics had been circumvented in some cases by disguising them as medicines; in others, manufacturers supplied small packets of unmixed ingredients in the proper proportion, so that women could make them up themselves.[75]

Beneath the neck, fashion was almost impossible. One despairing commentator concludes that "the real 'fashion' " of the war years was "to be unfashionable". Clothes were either Utility or utilitarian. The prevailing taste for wide shoulders, exaggerated by padding and puffed sleeves, gave a lean, hard effect akin to that of women's uniforms, and adds a spurious pathos to many photos of the period. The waist had disappeared, though it began to sneak back in the autumn of 1944. Skirts had crept up inch by inch, but mini skirts were not yet dreamt of, and even the increased use of trousers and slacks by women partly reflected the fact that they prevented accidental impropriety when bomb blast was around in air raids. A marked taste for loudness of colour, by the middle of the war, set off the sad increase in black mourning. Socks were worn in place of stockings, or legs went bare. Shoes were severely practical, with flatter heels and squarer toes than before the war. Coupon-free clogs for working women confirmed their traditional popularity in the north, but there was no acclaim for women's shoes with wooden soles, of which over a million pairs were made in 1944.[76]

The strangulation of fashion caused heartache chiefly among the wealthy, the young and the gay. Even well-to-do women of maturer years quite often secretly welcomed the disappearance of formal evening dress, and those who had formerly scrimped and saved to appear as "respectable" as their better-off neighbours, relaxed with joy now that shabbiness was socially acceptable. As for the working-class housewife, she had never had time or money for fashion anyway, and it was no novelty for her to obey the slogan of those salvage-conscious years, "Make Do and Mend."

When rationing had come in, one fashion writer had observed, "A jumble sale became a major social occasion with tickets for admission at the door and no favours for latecomers." The W.V.S. set up "clothing exchanges", where mothers bartered clothes for their growing children. Architects and engineers surrendered old drawings so that the linen base could be boiled off them; old stockings were cut into strips and made into rugs;

there were large exhibitions of ingenious conversions – silk scarves turned into children's frocks, plus fours made into overcoats. So far as is known, nor sows' ears became silk purses, but dogs and cats were certainly combed for their wool.[77]

The Board of Trade had to move fast to counter opportunistic customers who noticed the real "coupon bargains" very fast, or used goods exempted from rationing for unintended purposes. Worker's bib-and-brace overalls had been rationed perforce, after people had bought them for housework or gardening; and further action had been necessary to stop women turning furnishing fabrics into dresses. Nothing much could be done, however, by those women, outsize or working all day on their feet, who really needed corsets. Not only were corsets in short supply; the substitutes introduced to save steel and rubber abetted a catastrophic fall in quality. The Board of Trade had to step in, reserving the best of the scarce materials for those in greatest need.[78]

But few children seem to have suffered greatly from clothes rationing, and many men positively liked it; they had at once made it the excuse for slovenly, comfortable dressing. Before the war (Mass Observation found) many men had found clothes buying, especially for display purposes, an irritation. The outcry over Dalton's austerity regulations must be attributed to habit and a concern for comfort, not to baulked aspirations to smartness. However, few relapsed so far as Humphrey Lyttelton's eccentric Uncle Richard, a prominent executive in the steel industry, who "gave up wearing socks altogether, and travelled into the City on the Tube with a large area of naked skin showing below the bottom of his pinstripe trousers."[79]

VII

The "Make Do and Mend" philosophy even extended to food; the papers were full of unlikely hints. Why not use "turnip water" to provide baby with his Vitamin C? Why not experiment with unrationed sheep's heads? Why not fish the reservoirs for eels? Or use cormorants' eggs for making cakes? The Scottish press saw informed discussion, furthermore, of the merits of this scraggy and sinister seabird as poultry. "I have eaten boiled and roast cormorant," one correspondent swore. "There are different methods of getting rid of the salty, fishy taste. One old lady I know steeps them for a day or so in the sea. Others bury them in a piece of mossy ground, but on the whole I think the sea-steeping is the better way." London's Granada cinema chain, which provided restaurants in its picture palaces, and which had told its contacts north of the border that it would take literally any unrationed food which they could send, once offered on its menu "Roast Eagle and Veg".[80]

Odd meats, of course, were seized on. Horseflesh, it is sad to say, was now easy to sell. Uncouth American canned meats, with names like Tang and Prem and Mor and Spam, came over on Lend-lease and established their credentials, at least after it was realized that "sausage" in these cases did not mean "sausage". To save shipping space, meat from the Argentine and elsewhere was boned before despatch, and housewives now neither knew nor cared which part of the animal they were cooking.

Important foods like bread, potatoes, vegetables, fruit and fish were still unrationed. In 1944, it was estimated, nine shillings in every pound which the average housewife spent was going on unrationed foods, and two shillings more on points-rationed foods where there was a fair element of choice.[81] However, with most of the remainder, she was tied not only to particular foods but to particular shops (though rationed tea might be purchased anywhere). The retailer received supplies in accordance with the number of his registered customers. When presented with the ration books, he cancelled the coupons reserved for particular foods. Simplicity was a striking feature of the British system of rationing. In Germany, there was a range of differential rations, for children of various ages, for night workers, for heavy workers and for very heavy workers. In Britain, almost everyone over six got the same, though miners and agricultural labourers were given extra cheese and, from the end of 1944, over-seventies might buy an extra ounce of tea.

When the peak of rationing was reached in August 1942, every citizen was entitled to one shilling and twopence worth of meat per week. This covered beef, veal, mutton and pork, but not rabbits or poultry. It is roughly true to say that this ration gave nearly a pound of meat per person. Children under six might have sevenpence worth. Most other rations applied equally to adults and children. Each was entitled to four ounces of bacon and ham per week; eight ounces of sugar; eight ounces of fats, of which two might be butter, two might be cooking fats, and four must be margarine; and eight ounces of cheese. (Cheese was the most volatile of the rations; during 1943, it fell by stages to a mere two ounces in April 1944.) Over a four weeks' period, the consumer might purchase sixteen ounces of hard soap, and sixteen ounces of jam, marmalade or mincemeat. (Those who liked to make their own jam were entitled, in the early summer months, to transmute part of their preserves ration into extra sugar.) Over the same period, each consumer was allowed eight ounces of sweets. Over eight weeks, holders of adult ration books could get one packet of dried eggs equal to twelve eggs in shell. Children under six were allowed two packets. Dried-egg omelettes were possible, if not palatable.

For the month, each person had twenty points, which might go on goods ranging from tinned salmon priced at (say) thirty-two points for a pound, to dried peas for as little as one point per pound.

The distribution of eggs in shell was controlled so that most people might expect no more than thirty per year – but "priority consumers" got more, in some cases three per week. There was a similar system with milk. The priority classes – expectant and nursing mothers, children and invalids – had a guaranteed ration, a pint a day in most cases, while the general public got what was left, usually about two pints a week in winter (supplemented by National Dried Milk), but rising to three or four pints in the summer months.[82]

The administration of rationing was in the hands of the Ministry of Food, which in 1943 employed a peak of fifty thousand civil servants, an outstanding bureaucratic Leviathan. The local Food Offices, more than a thousand, whence the citizen obtained his ration books, his identity card, and, if he was very small, his free orange juice and cod-liver oil, vied with the post offices and the labour exchanges as the Government's chief beleaguered outposts among the governed. Behind the tired face of the girl on the other side of the counter loomed "the biggest shop in the world", with an annual turnover of some six hundred million pounds. The ministry was the sole importer of basic foodstuffs; its agencies all over the world made enormous bulk contracts. At home, it was the sole buyer of fatstock and milk, and it owned the former right down to the moment when it entered the hands of the butcher. With varying degrees of directness, sometimes through newly created autonomous wartime combinations of formerly independent manufacturers or wholesalers (of which MARCOM produced margarine, and BINDAL distributed imported bacon, but BACAL, confusingly, dealt with butter and cheese), the ministry controlled the manufacture and distribution of virtually all foods.[83]

Such a monster was in much need of personalizing, and it was personalized most successfully by Lord Woolton, formerly Sir

Frederick Marquis, boss of a big chain of department stores; formerly Fred Marquis, social worker in the slums. Woolton "Uncle Fred" to his colleagues (who found him somewhat ponderous in committee), has been described as "a philanthropic businessman inclined to make light of administrative obstacles". The businessman saw to it that the ministry's control of industry and trade never went so far that it must become permanent, striving successfully to ensure that the now functionless middlemen were kept artificially alive, and that, so far from civil servants controlling entrepreneurs, entrepreneurs occupied key positions in his department.[84]

The philanthropist radiated goodwill towards all. At his very first public appearance as minister, in the phoney war period, Woolton's homely phrasemaking had marked him out as a man on the people's side, when he had urged housewives, not, in so many words, to make weaker tea, but to give only "one spoonful for each person . . . and *none* for the pot". Woolton had been to Manchester University, not to Oxford or Cambridge; he was a man of the provinces, not a slick metropolitan personality; his somewhat potato-like face was suffused with earnest sympathy. In the words of one citizen (whose comments were passed on to Woolton by the postal censors), "When he harangues us on the radio, as he does now and again, we fancy we are back at dame school. He speaks with the firm precision of a talented schoolmarm and we all sit quiet and say, 'Yes, teacher.' "[85]

While Woolton's image-building was certainly made no harder by the colossal sums which his ministry spent on press advertising, it is of interest that he had once made a large part of his living out of free-lance journalism. He was one of the first truly "media-conscious" British politicians. Newspapers and magazines were pervaded with information and exhortation from the Ministry of Food. Some of it was covert – cookery correspondents submitted recipes to the M.O.F. public relations departments to make sure that they contained only ingredients which were available, or retailed others devised by the ministry itself. "And last of all, if Mother has time for it, here is a new sweetmeat invented by the Ministry of Food as a treat for the kiddies." enthused one cooking correspondent, somewhat unconvincingly. The "carrot stick-jaw" so proposed was, he added, "deliciously brittle". This was in the winter of 1941–42, when an unexpected glut prompted the most famous, or notorious, of the ministry's campaigns, in which the public was assured that eating carrots meant that you could see in the blackout. An incessant stream of M.O.F. advertise-

ments offered advice on such matters as the making of Christmas
puddings without eggs; preserving fruit without sugar; creating
Pilchard Layer Loaf (with the help of National Wheatmeal
Bread) or corned beef rissoles (with National Wheatmeal bread-
crumbs).

> Pat-a-loaf, pat-a-loaf
> Baker's Man,
> Bake me some Wheatmeal
> As fast as you can:
> It builds up my health
> And its taste is so good,
> I find that I *like*
> Eating just what I should.[86]

When new policies were initiated, Woolton made a point of
giving a personal explanation on the wireless – he would usually
spend at least eight hours preparing one twelve and a half minute
broadcast. Every weekday morning at eight fifteen, the B.B.C.
broadcast "Kitchen Front" to the nation. The most famous
contributor was "The Radio Doctor", who had arrived in 1941
to begin a series of talks which lasted unbroken for ten years.
Once a week, up to fourteen million listeners would shudder or
salivate as Hill's intimate, throaty tones assured them that liver
and kidneys were "very solid organs stuffed full of food", extolled
the virtues of "my old friend the dandelion leaf" as a salad vegetable or denounced sugar as "a menace". Hill's "vulgarity" was
notorious, though most of the indelicacy of which he was accused
amounted to no more than describing the stomach as "the belly"
and the bowels as "the bowels". In any case, it was essentially a
middle-class vulgarity, the voice of the self-made man (which he
was) in the genteel drawing-room, and much of what he said was
aimed at the reformation of middle-class prejudice ... "Don't
come over all superior at the mention of fish and chips. It's not
only very tasty and very sweet – it's first-glass grub. That's true
whether it's dished up with dignity to the duke in his dining-room,
or scoffed by the nipper from a newspaper spread out on his
knees."[87]

Much of the ministry's propaganda was directed at uprooting
the vices of English cookery, Hill exulted that the war was driving
out the habit of the Sunday joint ("Hot on Sunday – cold on
Monday – and if there's anything left, hashed or murdered on
Tuesday") and protested against the "assassination" of vegetables by over-boiling. But when the Wartime Social Survey, in

mid-1942, asked over eight thousand workers what they considered the most important foods for their health, it had to report that "The outstanding fact when interviewing on this question was that people did not understand it, and the investigator usually had to repeat it and explain what was meant. Even then, the answers were not forthcoming." It was found that people were not concerned much with what was good for them; the foods they considered essential to their well-being were the "items of their traditional diet which they missed most". So two-thirds of the men said "meat", few understood the value of cheese, and many more people attributed importance to tea than to beans or lentils. So much, one must say, for official propaganda.[88]

The twentieth century had seen a remarkable improvement in the national diet, thanks mainly, of course, to the general rise in earnings. But overall statistics concealed vast disparities between different sections of the population. Several surveys in the 1930s had stressed the intimate relationship between *Food, Health and Income*, to use the title of Sir John Boyd Orr's famous book, published in 1936. Orr had concluded that "a diet completely adequate for health according to modern standards is reached only at an income level above that of fifty per cent of the population." Between a fifth and a quarter of the nation's children were found in the lowest income group, of which the diet was very seriously deficient. Improvement could only come when more expensive foods were within easier reach of the poor. In 1940, Orr had pointed out trenchantly that "For a large part of the population foodstuffs have in fact always been rationed by price."[89]

Woolton himself had been deeply affected by an incident during his career as a social worker when his next-door neighbour in the Liverpool slums had unobtrusively died of starvation. His interest in nutrition was deep and sincere, and one of his first actions when he had arrived at the Ministry of Food had been to ask who his scientific adviser was. By 1942, the top officials of his ministry were, as the official historian puts it, "successfully indoctrinated with the need to refer even small decisions to a nutritional context". What had occurred, he adds, was "a revolution in the attitude of the British state towards the feeding of its citizens".[90]

This revolution was a victory for the pressure of events. ("For those we are about to deceive, may the Lord make us truly thankful.") To defeat Germany, citizens must be sufficiently well nourished to work harder and longer than in peacetime; food was therefore a factor in the production of heavy bombers. But there were also victories for idealism, as the special schemes for non-productive mothers, invalids and children showed.

Before the war, the average consumption of milk per head per day had been nearly one pint in the U.S.A., well over one pint in Switzerland, and only half a pint in Great Britain. By 1943, the production of milk in Britain had fallen, as an inevitable result of the "plough up" policy for agriculture. But direct consumption had risen, by thirty per cent, since far less was used in manufactured foods. While adult factory workers might now have less milk than before the war, there had been a marked rise in milk drinking among the poorer classes (who before the war had drunk only a third as much milk as the well-to-do). A regional breakdown showed that consumption in the pre-war depressed areas had multiplied twice or four times between 1935 and 1944, though it had increased only by a small fraction in the affluent south. Moreover, a lion's share of the nation's milk supplies now went to those who needed them most. The National Milk Scheme launched just after Dunkirk had provided for free milk for the poorest mothers and children – but with the wartime rise in wages, this had become virtually redundant. By September 1944, nineteen out of twenty of those entitled were taking part in the scheme, and the provision of one-third of a pint of subsidized milk daily to schoolchildren, which had covered about half the school population before the war, had been extended to nearly three-quarters by the time it ended.[91]

While the ministry could strive to ensure that adequate quantities of foods containing the vitamins necessary for a healthy diet were available at all times in the war – and after the worst period of 1941, it more or less managed to achieve this – it could not, of course, compel people to eat what was good for them. Several stratagems, however, were available. Unpopular as it was, the National Loaf was an immense nutritional advance. In 1943, a typical loaf would have contained eighty-two per cent wheatmeal flour, ten per cent white flour, five per cent barley flour, and three per cent oat flour, together with chalk and perhaps a little milk powder, and it was much better for people than the effete white stuff which they preferred.

The Vitamin Welfare Scheme for children, launched in December 1941, was intended to counter directly certain expected deficiencies in the diet. The scheme had begun with a free issue of blackcurrant juice and cod-liver oil for under-twos; the former had later been replaced by Lend-lease orange juice, and small charges were made. However, because of laziness and ignorance amongst the mothers, demand for the supplements ran far below the maximum potential issue. Only a quarter of the issue of cod-liver oil was being taken up in 1944.[92]

A third stratagem was communal feeding, where the Government could provide facilities for needy groups, and influence the dietary. By 1945, there had been a twelve-fold increase in the number of subsidized meals provided in schools. One child in three was now fed at school. About one school meal in seven (out of over a million and a half) was given free to a child from a poor home, and the rest cost the parents only fourpence or fivepence. The nutritional standard, at least theoretically, was high, and children were given extra meat through them which compensated for the fact that many fathers wolfed little Johnnie's meat ration as well as their own. Special provisions for shelterers, blitzed homeless and evacuated mothers have already been mentioned. Another innovation was the Rural Pie Scheme, launched in 1942, whereby W.V.S. ladies carried pies and other snacks out to agri-cultural labourers at work in the fields – at peak, an average of one and a quarter million snacks a week were being distributed in some five thousand villages.[93] But the British Restaurants formed the most famous innovation.

Early in 1940, the Chamberlain cabinet, prompted by its usual trepidation of middle-class opinion, had decided that restaurant meals as such should not be rationed. Instead, hotels and board-ing houses received supplies of food in accordance with the num-ber of ration books held by residents and restaurants, pubs, cafés and tea-shops in accordance with the number of meals they regularly served, on a scale which was adjusted to the housewife's provision for her family. (Thus, if Mother made do with one shilling and twopence worth of meat for fourteen main meals in a week, restaurants got a pennyworth per main meal served.) There was an obvious catch here; if restaurants snapped up good supplies of unrationed foods like fish, lobsters, chicken, rabbits and fruits in season, they could serve more meals and claim more meat. In the spring of 1942, the Government had pondered the question again, after widespread complaints about the con-tinuance of luxury feeding. All that had emerged was the restric-tion of restaurant meals to one main course and the imposition of a five-shilling maximum charge – though this latter regulation was waived for classy establishments with high overheads (such as those in which cabinet ministers tended to eat) and tipping clearly remained open to abuse.[94]

Now, if the better-off could eat relatively well "off the ration" in the city centres, what about the people who lived and worked in areas where the cafés were small and new workers had flooded in, or where many eating houses had been bombed? The British Restaurants were born in the blitz; their parent was the Londoners' Meal Service. Their name was an inspiration of Churchill's. Provision, on a non-profit-making basis, was left to local authorities, who were frequently sluggish or apathetic, although the Government guaranteed them against loss. The commercial catering trade was naturally vehement in its reaction to a state enterprise which could undercut it. The total of 2,160 which had opened by September 1943, after a very slow start, fell far short of the ten thousand the Government had had in mind, though they served six hundred thousand meals a day. But where they existed, their good food and friendly atmosphere made them very popular. The meals were extremely cheap, at tenpence or a shilling per head, and the self-service system which was used to save labour was copied by commercial caterers. In Cambridge, the whirligigs of time brought their revenges, and a British Restaurant was opened in 1942 in the Pitt Club, traditionally the resort of aristocratic young "bloods".[95]

"Eating out" had increased enormously as a result of the war to seventy-nine million meals a week in May 1941 and a hundred and seventy million in December 1944, when about eight or nine per cent of the sugar, meat and fats consumed by civilians were provided in this way outside the normal rations. Most of these meals were eaten in places specially organized during the war; besides the British Restaurants, there was the boom in factory canteens.[96]

The latter compensated, to some extent, for the absence of differential rations for manual workers. The Ministry of Labour compelled some employers, and encouraged others, to provide canteens. Where there had been about fifteen hundred industrial canteens before the war, there were eighteen thousand, five hundred in 1944. Ordinary canteens were allowed more meat, cheese, butter and sugar per meal than restaurants, while those for heavy workers were given twice as much again. (These "industrial scales" were also provided in some five thousand restaurants catering mainly for manual workers.) But the canteens were not universal, as a differential ration would have been. Even those which existed rarely had room for all the employees, and transport workers, police, shipyard workers and dockers, all enduring arduous conditions, were still notably short of feeding facilities. A large proportion of workers who could have used canteens did not; the quality of the food offered by inexperienced staff was often a discouragement, and it was found that not even meat and sugar "off ration" could wean certain people away from the habit of taking packed lunches to work.[97]

In a circular to local authorities in November 1940, in the first flush of enthusiasm for communal feeding, Woolton had suggested that "If every man, woman, and child could be sure of obtaining at least one hot nourishing meal a day, at a price all could afford, we should be sure of the nation's health and strength during the war." This modest aim was not fulfilled; nor were the more ambitious educational and nutritional intentions of the M.O.F. Efforts by well-informed caterers to widen the variety of the English diet and to brighten the wartime table with experiment were tacitly or loudly rejected. The Wartime Social Survey reported the peevish comments of an ex-hotel chef who, in the middle of the war, found himself managing a factory canteen. "He despaired of Birmingham's taste in food. He had been all round the world, and catering in Birmingham was the worst in the world. He said the workers at the factory only wanted fish and chips, cream cakes, bread and butter, and brown gravy over everything. They had protested when he had made white sauce with boiled beef and carrots. They would not eat salads, did not like savouries – 'Birmingham people do not understand food.' "[98]

VIII

Asa Briggs has remarked that, in the twentieth century, "Warfare has necessitated welfare . . ."[99] This is illustrated to a nicety by the new deal for disabled men. By 1941, the shortage of able bodies had made the forgotten men who had been crippled at work and play seem valuable enough to be worth special trouble; and of course, the armed forces were discharging a new spate of maimed derelicts. One of Bevin's junior ministers, George Tomlinson, a Labour M.P., was appointed to head a committee to report on the subject, and took the chance to improve matters with missionary fervour. As a result of the committee's reports, the Government extended the existing meagre rehabilitation services to cover all parts of the country and every class of disabled patient – the blind, the tubercular and the neurotic, as well as those with fractures. The Disabled Persons Act of 1944 made it possible to force employers to take a prescribed quota of rehabilitated workers. Although the Act was not applied until after the war, between July 1941 and December 1945, jobs were found for over three hundred thousand disabled people.[100]

Shortage of men had brought the E.W.O.s into being, and new managers complained that the E.W.O. had destroyed discipline in industry. In fact, full employment was the culprit; you could not sack a man if you could not replace him, as a pointed anecdote from the Sheffield buses illustrates. A driver, bored to death after two years on the job, attempted to goad the municipal transport department into sacking him. "On one occasion he refused to cut short a snack at the mobile van and told the inspector who had given him the order, '*Drive the bloody bus yourself.*' The inspector did so. Gleefully the driver wrote a long report to the management, maximizing his guilt, but they simply ignored it. And, perforce, he stayed."[101] It was very hard in such a context to deal with absenteeism.

In 1941 and 1942, while the left had shouted "Cost Plus", the right had retorted "Absenteeism". The resulting controversy provided many salutary examples of the misuse of statistics. As with "hold-ups" and "idle time", it was often forgotten that absenteeism had occurred in industry before September 1939. The leading facts were that few firms kept statistics, that these were rarely collated with those of other firms, that no reliable basis existed for comparing wartime rates with pre-war rates, and that most of what was said on the subject was therefore merely scalding hot air. Even when the Government began to collect fairly reliable figures in 1942, there remained the undrawable distinction between avoidable and unavoidable absenteeism. That of a youth who could get his doctor to certify him as unfit and went off for a day at the races was classified as unavoidable; that of a mother who took a day off to do her housework avoidable.

The most serious problem, it emerged from the more sober analyses, was that of the younger workers who had arrived on the scene in the days of full employment; especially girls who were prone to extend their week-ends by taking Saturday and Monday off. Other factors swelled the figures. Where hours remained long, workers would take time off as their own precaution against undue fatigue. Where conditions were bad, there was every incentive to slack. In some districts, absenteeism among bus and tram conductresses rose as high as thirty per cent in a day during the winter months; but this was a job where inexperienced girls might be called upon to work for broken periods stretching from six a.m. in the morning to ten p.m. at night.[102]

In 1942, the E.W.O. was amended so that a habitual absentee

could be prosecuted. But the Ministry of Labour, under Bevin's leadership, took the view that "a solution of the problem of avoidable absence from work is more likely to be found by those establishments which look for that solution within themselves, than by those which tend to rely more on external powers of discipline or punishment." In spite of all efforts, absenteeism did not notably decrease in the last three years of war, but it did not increase either, for all the cumulative strain. In 1943–44, according to Ministry of Labour statistics, about three-quarters of absenteeism was unavoidable and half was due to certified sickness. The rate fluctuated between six and eight per cent for men, and twelve and fifteen per cent for women.[103]

It was women, in fact, who above all necessitated welfare. In the first place, what could mothers do with their children when they went to work? The Wartime Social Survey found that war workers' children who were not at school were generally looked after by relations or neighbours, but a welfare officer in one industrial town told a horrified inquirer that mothers on night shift kept children up to school age in bed with them all day while they tried to get some sleep, and at night the child was in bed again with Father. While such a situation was exceptional, it reinforced the arguments in favour of state-sponsored day nurseries.[104]

From mid-1941 onwards, the provision of day nurseries had been greatly expanded; by the end of 1943 there were some fourteen hundred and fifty such nurseries under local authorities, with places for sixty-five thousand children, and more than double that number of under-fives had been given places in elementary or nursery schools, where they were yet another trial for the overworked teachers. While feminists saw the idea as a vehicle for the emancipation of the sex, most mothers were unwilling to send their children to the nurseries. Gran round the corner or Mrs Jones next door was one thing; strange young baby-minders were another. Staffing was difficult. If two women with five children between them decided to go to work, another woman, according to the officially prescribed ratio of minders to charges, would have to be found to care for their offspring – though one such minder has recalled that she was often left alone with forty children on her hands for a whole afternoon. As with so many promising experiments initiated during the war the conditions of the time hardly gave the nurseries a fair chance to show what they might do.[105]

Then, there was shopping. Housewives who had registered for

rationed goods at shops near home were sorely inconvenienced if
they were sent to work on the far side of town. About half of all
working women, it was found, were mainly responsible for the
family's shopping; but shops still generally opened and closed at
peacetime hours. A woman worker could shop in the lunch hour
and miss her own meal, or join the horde who jammed the
groceries on Saturday afternoon when the week's work had
ended. In either case, she had no time to queue for unrationed
goods. The problem drove many women almost to the point of
desperation, and was by itself sufficient to account for high rates
of absenteeism. The Government tinkered unsuccessfully with
piecemeal solutions, but special shopping passes to enable war
workers to jump queues created bad feeling amongst other
shoppers, and were not always recognized by tradesmen.

The Ministry of Labour called forcibly on managements to
"recognize frankly that many workers, especially women, cannot
be expected to work five and a half days a week, for long hours,
week in, week out, if they have to spend, in addition, two or three
hours a day or even more in travelling, possibly by a crowded bus
or train and in all weathers, or if they have homes and young
children to look after."[106] While most managements still failed to
see that to give women regular time off for shopping was better
than unpredictable absenteeism, there was some growth in awareness of the human factor in industry.

And so, from the influx of women, improvements resulted of
which men, too, reaped the benefit. It is extraordinary to find
those elderly members of parliament who composed the Select
Committee on National Expenditure (which was dedicated, after
all, to the pursuit of economy) turning aside from grander
matters to complain "that in many factories rest rooms are either
inadequate or non-existent. There may be a single couch in a
first-aid room available for the use of a large number of girls.
The decoration, as well as the furnishings of rest and recreation
rooms, is also a matter which should not be neglected. It costs
little more to wash the walls with light restful colours than it does
to whitewash them; and" (it added, mindful of its duty) "the
money spent in providing rest rooms might just as well be thrown
away if these do not provide a restful atmosphere."[107]

The psychological point is well illustrated from the diary of a
personnel manager:

January 16th: See two more girls sent down from London.
A striking blonde from a beauty parlour and a brunette from

a gownshop, both in the West End. Capstan shop foreman afraid to put them on his machines; said they were too good a type. I was seriously concerned myself as our factory is an old shabby place and its sanitary arrangements of a very low standard . . .

January 17th: Started blonde and brunette on their job. Myself, W.M. (works manager) and shop superintendent all seriously bothered about them, and always came back to our *bête noire*, the sanitary accommodation . . .

January 18th: . . . These girls only emphasize how much short of what they should be are some of the facilities provided for them. Our canteen is not good, and we are trying hard to get a new management in. Lavatory accommodation such as most factory hands use without a qualm will revolt these girls. But with staff and men and building materials and floor space all at a premium we don't know how we can put it right fast enough.

As this man remarked, the "local factory-class girls" were used to such factories; it was outsiders with well-manicured fingers who provoked remorse.[108]

The First World War had posed similar problems and had stimulated a new degree of managerial interest in the relationship between human comfort and industrial efficiency. A fistful of organizations had emerged – the Industrial Health Research Board and the Institute of Labour Management, inter alia – to press the work forward. The Factories Act of 1937 had established new standards for industry and the next year had seen the Holidays With Pay Act, covering at least eleven million workers.

But by the outbreak of the Second World War, only a thousand firms belonged to the Industrial Welfare Society. When the Ministry of Supply had been set up in 1939, it had had no section devoted to personnel and welfare problems. Trade unionists had learnt to regard "welfare" with suspicion; it was paternalistic, anti-union firms which tended to be most lavish with it. Managers, on the other hand, continued to regard solicitude for workers' comfort as an obnoxious symptom of creeping socialism. Mass Observation found in its survey of war industry that managements progressive in this respect were prone to be bashful and defensive. "Nearly all the 'enlightened' employers," it noted, ". . . once they had got talking freely, *apologized* for what they regarded as the extremeness of their views."[109]

The hero of the few, and often underpaid, welfare managers

employed in British industry might well have been Ernest Bevin. As soon as he had arrived in office, Bevin had insisted on bringing the factory inspectorate into his own ministry from the Home Office. While he constantly reminded firms that good welfare management would increase their profits, he gave the atmosphere of a crusade to developments which basically reflected the problems of discipline and exploitation of labour in an age of full employment. If firms could not get more workers to help them to fulfil more contracts, then they had to coddle those they had.

An order issued by Bevin in July 1949 had given factory inspectors power to compel establishments with more than two hundred and fifty employees to appoint welfare officers, and this had been reinforced by the E.W.O.s. But there was very little point in compelling reluctant firms to shunt one of their less efficient managers into welfare. The Ministry of Labour had accordingly promoted special three-month training courses for personnel managers; by August 1944, there were facilities for training a hundred students at a time. It was claimed in that year that about ninety per cent of the larger factories, with more than five hundred workers, now had some definite form of "welfare supervision"; whatever that meant.[110]

In fact, with the best will in the world, a woman taking such a job on as her war work would find it hard to make progress. Blackout regulations (for instance) were always detrimental. When the Select Committee on National Expenditure raised the topic of lighting very forcibly, it was told by the Government departments concerned that electricians were mostly employed now on vital work and that raw materials were short, so that it was "a difficult time for getting alterations made". Bad lighting and ventilation made medical attention more important. At the beginning of the war, there had been less than a hundred doctors employed full-time or part-time in industry, but this total was raised to just over a thousand by the end of 1944, and five times as many nurses then had jobs in factories as in 1940.[111]

Bevinism in industry was symbolized by the growing understanding of the value of music and entertainment in helping people to work faster. Besides peripatetic Ensatainments, there were the B.B.C.'s "Workers' Playtime" and "Music While You Work", which "progressive" managements relayed over loudspeakers several times a day. These novelties appealed greatly to J. B. Priestley, who had coined the slogan "Let The People Sing" which ENSA used as the title of its signature tune; new humanity, even new gaiety, emerged from the dourness and violence of war.

Bevin himself liked to put in an appearance at a works' concert (and to sample personally the food in the canteen). "Let The People Sing", it might be said, was the spiritual essence of Bevinism.

From one aspect, Bevinism was the most realistic of creeds; its practical results were seen here in a rise in wages, there in a new canteen, at a third place as a new sick room, everywhere in industry in individually small but cumulatively significant signs of progress. After the war, it would not be so easy as before to treat industrial workers badly, and if full employment took the main credit, Bevin's imagination and Bevin's skill at wielding both the carrot and the stick were also important. Yet, from another aspect, Bevinism was idealism and illusion. Bevin's vision of "Industrial Democracy", of a self-confident, fully-unionized working class taking an increasing share in the government of industry alongside ever more enlightened managers, was mocked by the central facts of capitalist economy. Industry remained the property of private owners, who would not share any real power with their wage-earners; and those "progressive" managers who had increasingly usurped the former functions of ownership in the increasingly dominant larger firms were most conscious of their managerial destiny, and were concerned to "lead", and to manipulate, the workers beneath them.

BUT SOME ARE MORE EQUAL THAN OTHERS

In a famine-stricken world the little fish restaurant dispensed in their seasons Colchester oysters, Scotch salmon, lobsters, prawns, gulls' eggs . . . and often caviar, obtained, only Ruben knew how, through diplomatic channels. Most surprising of all there sometimes appeared cheeses from France, collected by intrepid parachutists and conveyed home by submarine. There was an abundance of good wine, enormously costly, at a time when the cellars of the hotels were empty and wine merchants dealt out meagre monthly parcels only to their oldest customers. Ruben had for some years enjoyed a small and appreciative clientèle . . . There was also an increasing dilution of odd-looking men who called the proprietor "Mr. Ruben" and carried large quantities of bank notes in their hip pockets. That restaurant was a rare candle in a dark and naughty world. Kerstie Kilbannon, who had made noxious experiments with custard powder and condiments, once asked: "Do tell me, Ruben, how do you make your mayonnaise?" and received the grave reply; "Quite simply, my lady, fresh eggs and olive oil."

Evelyn Waugh, *Unconditional Surrender*[1]

I

Bevin's arrival in office symbolized the acceptance of the union bureaucracies as essential aides of good government. The First World War had anticipated the Second in strengthening the trade unions and giving them new status; but its aftermath had been a period of furious militancy, which had ended with the failure of the General Strike in 1926. The moderate trade union leaders had thereafter settled for compromise as a way of life. This policy flowered in the Second World War. The most recent historian of the trade union movement remarks that "The annual reports of the T.U.C. General Council began to read like the records of some special Government department responsible for co-ordinating policy in the social and industrial spheres." "Tripartitism" was the philosophy of the day; numerous advisory committees were set up representing unions, employers and Whitehall. Sidney Pollard has observed, of all this top-level sweetness and light, that the leaders of the large trade unions "became so eager to show a sense of responsibility for the economy as a whole, that they laid themselves open to legitimate attacks by their own members for neglecting their interests". (He contrasts them, aptly, with the tough men at the head of the National Farmers Union, who more or less held the Ministry of Agriculture as their fief.)[2]

The status of the unions was perhaps most clearly embodied in the shape of the new Control of coal-mining which was established in 1942. In this case, they provided the labour directors, whose job was to bully and cajole the miners into working harder. Nowhere did the unions dominate, but they were permitted to become the handmaidens of domination. By and large, their bureaucrats, increasingly satisfied with themselves, loyally performed their allotted role of restraining wage demands and preventing inflation. There were, of course, positive advances. A minor but instructive incident occurred in 1941, when the employers in the laundry trade became so desperate for labour that they beseeched Bevin to clap an E.W.O. on the industry. Bevin refused until guaranteed weekly wages were raised, and this was done by negotiation with two unions active in the industry – a poorly organized one in peacetime. Union membership in the laundries soared as a result.[3]

Indeed, one result of full employment was that overall union membership in Britain increased by over one-third between 1938 and 1943, to 8,174,000. The unions involved in war industry naturally registered the largest increases, while those in concentrated industries were actually weakened. Most sensational was the growth of the A.E.U. which had 909,000 members at the end of 1943, as compared with 413,000 in 1939. There were 308,000 new members in 1943 alone. Meanwhile, Bevin's old union, the Transport and General Workers', also recorded a six figure increase, and became the first to top the million mark. Such expansion made it harder than ever for the bureaucracies to exercise control over unruly elements. Former officials were now in the forces and had been replaced by inexperienced recruits. The same number of officials had to cope with all the new complexities of industrial life in wartime. The A.E.U. in 1943 had only a hundred and fifty officials to handle its vast membership; that was no way to run an army.[4]

The gulf between leaders and rank and file yawned wider than ever. The procedures for settlement of disputes slowed down until it seemed to impatient new recruits that they were halting altogether, though employers, and even union officials, were glad enough for the delays, which after all helped to hold wages back in accordance with Government policy. The shop steward stepped into the breach, as the elected representative of the workpeople who could air and settle problems on the spot.

The shop stewards' position vis-à-vis the bureaucracies was thoroughly ambiguous. Most unions had such "non-commissioned officers" and they were recognized under union rules. The shop steward now became the key man in maintaining the union's hold over its members. "It was he", a historian of the A.E.U. explains, "who became the chief figure in the aim to recruit all the workers in his shop or department; to see that they attended their branch meetings and kept up to date in payments of their dues. It was he who had to demonstrate the value of trade unionism to the workers, through his willingness and ability to deal with the varied problems of the members at home and at work."[5]

But neither the A.E.U.'s, nor any other union bureaucracy, could stomach the shop stewards in their potential, and sometimes real, role as an alternative leadership. The engineering shop stewards, especially on Clydeside, had played a dramatic role in the troubled industrial history of the First World War. When the C.P.-controlled Shop Stewards' National Council had leapt to fame after the invasion of Russia, the spectre of grass-roots leadership had been raised again. Union officials attempted to prevent shop stewards from different unions cutting across the lines and establishing their own local and national confederacies. They had been deeply indignant when Beaverbrook (doubtless partly for the pleasure of scoring off Bevin) had by-passed them and addressed the shop stewards directly.

It will be remembered that Order 1305 in the summer of 1940 had set up a National Arbitration Tribunal (which handed down over eight hundred decisions during the war, about two-ninths of all settlements). It had also illegalized strikes. Yet in 1943, 1,800,000 working days were lost in 1,785 strikes. The year 1944 actually set a new record for the aggregate number of stoppages, with 2,194 involving the loss of 3,700,000 days. While coal-mining was always the most strike-ridden industry, accounting for two-thirds of the days lost in 1944, engineering, that is, war industry, was its closest competitor. In fact, only two other industries, road transport and the docks, produced really important strikes during the war, both in 1943.[6]

But though there were more strikes, they were shorter strikes, and the figures for days lost bore no comparison to those for 1919–21, the heyday of union militancy. Nine out of ten strikes in engineering and allied industries in 1943 and 1944 lasted for less than one week. Throughout the war, only one important strike in munitions spread to more than one locality; most affected only one factory or yard. Six out of ten wartime stoppages were over wages; the typical "strike" was a swift outburst over piece rates.[7]

While shop stewards naturally assumed the leadership in illegal strikes, this did not in itself make them agitators. Only a minority were strongly political, and that minority was certainly under Communist influence. But the shop steward had to support his supporters. A plaintive doggerel in the *A.E.U. Monthly Journal* expressed his dilemma:

> If with the foreman he's agreed
> He's sold the men or been weak-kneed.
> When for the men he tries to cater,
> He's called a blinking agitator . . .[8]

K. G. J. C. Knowles's analysis of strikes in engineering disposes of much "reds in the bed" mythology by demonstrating that the C.P. failed to damp down industrial unrest after the invasion of Russia. However, it perhaps held the increase down somewhat, and one may guess that it helped to make strikes shorter. Mrs Katin describes the attitude of the "political" section of the Sheffield busmen during the big transport strike of 1943. "We came to these conclusions: we must continue to work against a strike decision, but, should the workers come out despite our efforts, we must avoid isolating ourselves by staying in. Instead we should join the strikers and urge return to work, together with united mass pressure on the union executive and the authorities."[9]

And where, it might be asked, was the mailed fist of Order 1305? During the war there were exactly seventy-one prosecutions under Order 1305 in Scotland (mostly against coal-miners), and thirty-eight in England and Wales. Some six thousand, three hundred individuals were involved. In 1944, there were only three prosecutions under the order in England and Wales, and in two of them the Ministry of Labour lost the verdict because a clever solicitor convinced the magistrates that the "strikes" were in fact "lock-outs". Fines of up to twenty-five pounds for strikers were recorded, but five pounds was more normal. It emerged that it was quite impossible to prosecute large numbers of much needed workers. (In only twenty-one prosecutions were more than a hundred men involved.[10]) A richly farcical case early in 1942 had exhibited the limitations of the order to a nicety.

A thousand and fifty underground workers at Betteshanger Colliery in Kent had gone on strike following a dispute over wages. They had all been summonsed, and the chairman, secretary and one committee member of the local trade union branch had been imprisoned, while the rest of the men had been fined three pounds or one pound. After the men had been out for nineteen days, the dispute had been settled in the miners' favour, and soon afterwards the prisoners had been released. Three months later only nine of the strikers had paid their fines. But there had not been enough room in the jails for the rest, and if individuals had been victimized, the result would have been another strike in sympathy.[11] When hundreds of thousands of miners came out on strike in 1944, prosecution was not, of course, attempted.

II

With full employment, not a few workers learnt that they could answer back. A joke current in industry told of a man over military age who registered at the labour exchange and said he wanted to find work as a labourer. The Ministry of Labour interviewer replied: "As a labourer? No fear. You'll start as a fore-

man and work your way down." The veteran Liberal social
scientist and industrialist, Seebohm Rowntree, observed near the
end of the war that "Employers and business executives will have
to learn to lead the workers, since they will no longer be able to
drive them, once the fear of unemployment is removed."[12]

It was in this spirit that the Joint Production Committees of
management and men, superficially one of the most striking
manifestations of the "wartime social revolution", were fostered
by the supply ministries. Again, the previous war had provided a
foretaste. The Government had then encouraged the so-called
"Whitley" works committees. These bodies had mostly passed
into limbo with the war, and had left few bright memories
behind, though a number were still in existence when the Second
World War began, concerning themselves with welfare matters
and sport. In 1922, during the famous engineering lockout, which
had involved 260,000 workers over thirteen weeks, one of the
A.E.U.'s claims had been that the union should have a say on
such questions as entry to the trade, manning of machines and
overtime. The employers had insisted on their rights to manage
their own establishments, but had conceded that works committees might be set up as part of the regional trade union negotiating machinery. Under that agreement, a few still existed.

The first gestures in the same direction in the Second World
War had been Pit Production Committees, set up in the mines
very early on, and Yard Committees in the shipbuilding industry
after March 1941. Neither experiment had commanded much
enthusiasm; the workers had correctly seen them as essentially a
device to be used against absentees, who it was hoped might be
cowed by the judgment of their peers on the committee. Those
peers who did pass judgment became highly unpopular.

But in mid-1941, the leaders of the A.E.U. and of the powerful
General and Municipal Workers had begun to call for the establishment of joint committees in war industry, and after the entry
of Russia into the war the cry had been backed by the Shop
Stewards' National Council. The winter of 1941–42 had seen a
spontaneous growth of "works committees" with various titles,
designed to produce co-operation in the production drive. That
noted monopolist, Lord McGowan, the chairman of I.C.I., had
already told the Prime Minister that there was nothing to fear
from such developments. ". . . Though there was a risk of their
getting into hands of extremist workers, his experience of the use
of such bodies was that they moderated the extremist by giving
him a place in the sun and at the same time weakened his in-

fluence amongst the other workers because they were taken into the confidence of the management on production questions." It was doubtless in this spirit that the employers' side of the Midland Regional Board of the Production Executive had unanimously agreed with the trade union side in September 1941 to foster such committees; provided they were divorced from "political or wages questions", and so made fangless. But in January 1942 the Engineering Employers' Federation had turned down a suggestion on these lines from the A.E.U. Its director's attitude had recalled the spirit of the 1922 lockout – he "was not going to be a party to handing over the production of the factory and the problems concerning production to shop stewards or anyone else".[13]

At this point, the Government had stepped in. The Ministry of Supply, in February 1942, had signed an agreement with the unions to set up J.P.C.s in the Royal Ordnance Factories. The agreement had been made on the ministry's initiative, and it forced the hand of the private employers. In March, the E.E.F. and the A.E.U. had signed an agreement providing for J.P.C.s in all engineering establishments with more than a hundred and fifty workers.

The T.U.C. had then called for J.P.C.s to be made compulsory, but the Government confined itself to exerting pretty strong pressure. It saw immediate benefits in the J.P.C.s, over and above any direct effects on productivity. They might, as Lord McGowan had put it, "neutralize" militants. They provided a channel whereby workers on the shop floor might be given to understand, however cryptically, the reasons for hold-ups, modifications and changes of policy. They might serve to break down the not unreasonable feeling among rank and file trade unionists that the war was being fought for purposes not wholly made clear, but which were probably against their own interests and in favour of those of the employers. It was no doubt with these considerations in mind that the Tory Reform Committee (of which more later) welcomed the J.P.C.s, and that the Conservative Party's *Industrial Charter* after the war paid lip service to them.

The trade union militants themselves saw the J.P.C.s as a victory for working-class pressure. The syndicalist feeling so strong in Britain around the First World War had withered, largely thanks to the failure of the General Strike; a vague enthusiasm for whatever it was they actually had in Russia had replaced it. The J.P.C.s, while clearly not exactly Uncle Joe's cup of tea, did seem to have the merit, as the president of the A.E.U. put it, of opening the eyes of the workers who sat on them "to the often inefficient and unscientific reality which lies behind the sacred words 'managerial functions' . . ."[14]

By the end of 1943, there were nearly four thousand, five hundred J.P.C.s known to be in existence in the engineering and allied industries. There were J.P.C.s in forty R.O.F.s, and yard committees in nearly all the shipyards. Eleven hundred pit production committees were in existence (though the Minister of Fuel and Power admitted that only one in four was "functioning really effectively"). There were joint site committees on most of the larger Government building sites, and there was a scattering of such institutions in other industries. Altogether, it was estimated that J.P.C.s and their equivalents covered more than three and a half million workers.[15]

Not all the federated engineering employers had bothered to implement the 1942 agreement, but it was in engineering that the committees were most publicized and, probably, most effective. The agreement provided that all workers over twenty-one could vote in ballot, but that only trade union members were eligible for election to the J.P.C. Ideally each shop, department and section of the factory would have its own representative, but the number of union members on the committee was limited to ten. The management nominated an equal number from its own ranks to confront them and appointed the chairmen. Each side would provide a joint secretary. The J.P.C. would meet at least once a month.

Those twixt-and-tween employees like the draughtsmen and scientific workers were usually squeezed out; though the draughtsmen's union fought hard for representation, the employers insisted on regarding them as "management", with the paradoxical result that the campaign for representation brought their union closer in sympathy to the manual workers, whose own unions backed its claim.[16]

The scope of the committees was confined by the agreement to "matters relating to production and increased efficiency", but an A.E.U. survey in the autumn of 1942 suggested that about one J.P.C. in five was going beyond the agreement to discuss such things as piece rates and output bonuses, and pointed out that where it could solve such problems, the prestige of a committee was greatly enhanced among the workers. That the J.P.C.s could achieve first-rate results was clear. Often, a suggestion from a worker which seemed obvious once it was implemented would save time, tools or materials, and the Government encouraged suggestion boxes in factories. But if the agenda stayed on to such matters as overall shortage of materials or machine tools, or the problems arising out of sub-contracts to outside firms, the J.P.C. could not settle them itself. If both sides agreed, it could raise them with the Ministry of Production's regional boards. That the boards received very few suggestions or complaints perhaps indicated some want of vitality in the J.P.C.s.

In some factories, the workers deliberately elected dead-heads. In others, the J.P.C.s aroused real interest and enthusiasm; it was found that excitement generally ran highest when there was a prospect of the workers' representatives attacking the management, and when the two sides were co-operating successfully, there were often cries that the former had "sold out". M.A.P. produced optimistic figures which indicated that nearly half the items discussed by J.P.C.s led to action of some kind, though this was more usual on welfare than on technical questions. The A.E.U., preening itself after its victory, made still more optimistic claims. As for the employers, it seems that few were prepared to say they were a waste of time, though they were better appreciated in large factories than in small ones.[17]

An authority writing some time after the end of the war concludes that "All that can be said with confidence is that many committees were generally regarded as successful, and perhaps almost as many as unsuccessful ..." By then, the post-war withering of the J.P.C.s had proved them to be hothouse plants forced out of the climate of industrial disharmony by wartime conditions. In 1948, only five hundred and fifty survived.[18]

III

Men were notoriously more equal than women. The First World War had prompted a grateful nation to give women the vote. No such large step towards equality resulted from the Second, though there were a few shame-faced concessions. For instance, there was an outcry over the fact that women were to receive rates of compensation twenty-five to fifty per cent lower than men for incapacitation resulting from "warlike operations", and in 1943 they were given equal rates.

Yet perhaps, in its effects on the attitudes of women themselves, the Second World War was more significant than the First. Early in the war, Richard Hillary had a letter from a university friend who had revisited Oxford. "Richard, whatever you do, don't go back. It would take a book to explain how it's changed;

but to sum it up in one sentence – in the Randolph Bar there is a notice saying: 'No unaccompanied ladies will be served with drinks.' " Unaccompanied sallies into public bars were the tip of an iceberg which emerged in the 1960s as the mini skirt and the pill. It seems that some of the unmarried mothers of the war years were of a "new type", which amazed the social workers to whom they were referred. They shunned preachifying moral welfare societies, and resented the punitive atmosphere of some of the voluntary homes. As the official historians put it, "Their spirit of independence was considerable, and there was little of the sinner and the penitent about them."[19]

The women's services took young girls, gave them a taste of the world, and yet taught them none of the skills and graces traditionally regarded as the woman's. Mass Observation found that "the wanderlust" was now "very widespread in the women's services. The uppermost feeling seems to be a negative one; 'I'll never be able to settle down again.' " Many planned to travel abroad "at all costs" after the war ended. While women in industry accepted the continuing inequality of the sexes, servicewomen tended to hope for equal competition with men.[20]

Domestic work, for her family or for others, had traditionally been the woman's job. In 1931, the census had recorded well over a million females employed in private homes in England and Wales (permitting their lady employers, if they so wished, to agitate for the rights of women). The numbers had probably declined through the 'thirties, with the increase in "all-mod-con" semi-detached and detached houses on the new modest scale suited to smaller middle-class families. Even so, private domestic service accounted for over six per cent of the occupied population (both sexes) in 1939.

The war accomplished a great winkling out of skivvies, chars and slaveys. (By 1950, the proportion had fallen to three and a half per cent.) Now they were in short supply, domestics had their rights too. Perhaps the quintessential product of the Bevin era was the report by two eminent women which successfully recommended the setting up of a National Institute of House-workers, which it was hoped, somewhat over-optimistically, would elevate domestic service to the status of a skilled trade. The war helped to weaken the vestigial feudalism which characterized the relationship between rich ladies and their ill-paid staff. Mass Observation published the remarks of a girl in a war factory who had worked as a parlour maid in a sizable country house. Her employer had tried to persuade her to pretend that she had

bad eyesight, so that she would not be "directed". When Molly
had been called to the labour exchange, her employer had rung
them up. ". . . When I went round there", Molly related, "the girl
said all right, they'd change it for me. But I told the girl, I said:
'Please don't change it . . .' So she wrote to Mrs B. that they
couldn't change it, I'd have to come, but she never told Mrs B.
I'd asked her to say so . . . I wrote to her the other day, and I told
her that for ruining my eyes, I do all my work here without looking at it. It was cleaning your silver, I said, ruined my eyes, not
this work. I told her that I'm ever so happy, and my board is tiny,
and I spend an average of ninepence a day in the canteen. I'm
putting away as much as I got altogether with her. Now the
cook's left too, she's gone to a factory in London, so I don't
know how she'll manage."[21]

There were other women who found in part-time war work a
release from bondage. The sheltered daughters of comfortable
homes, who had married, had had children and had slaved to
look after them might now, in their forties, escape into the life
which had passed them by. Mass Observation noted that "The
chance of spending her days outside her own home, of making
fresh contacts and seeing fresh people, is occasionally welcomed
by such women with something approaching an ecstasy, which
neither strain nor fatigue can spoil."[22]

Full-time factory work was another matter. The companionship, and still more the money, were compensations for boredom
and long hours. But endless repetition of the same unskilled or
semi-skilled task, of the kind which most women were given in
war industry, was hardly emancipation. In the same factory as
Molly, there was a pretty, lively twenty-year-old whose broken
drills were a standing joke and who collapsed with laughter after
the manager had told her that she would be sent to prison if her
indiscipline continued. "Where are we now, I wanted to ask him?
Isn't this a prison?"[23]

The Wartime Social Survey found that for about two-thirds of
women the money they earned was "the chief, in some cases sole,
advantage of work". But apart from solitary spinsters, widows
and wives of servicemen, most women saw their earnings chiefly
as a way of "topping up" what the man brought home. Man and
wife were assessed jointly for taxation, so that a woman earning
three pounds a week with a husband in well-paid work might
have to give a pound of it back to the Treasury. A young girl
living at home and earning about two pounds, fourteen shillings a
week in a war factory might see a pound of that as pure pocket

money, to be spent as she liked on pictures, dances and saving to get married.[24]

Such attitudes helped to explain the lack of interest which women showed in joining unions and agitating within them. Not more than half a sample of J.P.C.s, it should be noted, had any women members at all, and even in those they were generally under-represented. The woman, burdened with her housework, had always left such things to the man. A writer who, just before the war, had exposed the prevalence of bad health among working-class housewives had found it "little short of a miracle that some women, even some of the most hard worked, find time and mental energy to belong to such organizations as the Women's Co-operative Guild, the Salvation Army or a branch of their political party where they can hear and talk about the wider aspects of their own or other people's problems".[25]

Woman did relatively best in the buses and the railways – their average wage in those industries was over four pounds at the end of the war – but here too men took much more home. No great scandal was caused by the fact that women in Government Training Centres were paid more than one-third less than male trainees. When the railway companies were challenged by the unions to pay women clerks the "rate for the job", they replied that "since the managers had been unable to find any industry where the principle of equal pay for equal work was applied, they did not see why they should apply it on the railways."[26]

In the summer of 1940, when agreement had been reached between the two sides of the engineering industry to permit the "extended employment of women", the provision had been that the employers could sign on women to do work previously performed by men on condition that after they had worked for thirty-two weeks they received the full man's rate for the job. Comparable agreements had been reached in 1941 and 1942 in a long list of other important industries.

Inevitably, the words which had been signed left some ground for sincere misunderstanding, and a great deal more for wilful evasion. Towards the end of the war, the national organizer of the A.E.U. (Wal Hannington) made a list of the many ways in which the engineering agreement could be, and had been, circumvented. Employers could claim that the work had been "commonly performed" by women before the war, and this claim grew harder to contest as more and more skilled work was broken down by the advance of mass production. The employer could make a small alteration in the job and say there was no pre-war precedent. He could affect to believe that the agreement applied only to skilled work, which was quite untrue, or argue more plausibly that a woman who could do only one skilled job was worth less than a fully trained man. When the eight month period when lower rates might be paid had run out, the employer could make the fact that women still needed male help occasionally in lifting heavy fixtures into a pretext for claiming that they still worked under "extra supervision".[27]

Under the dilution agreement, there were undoubtedly a proportion of women who earned at male rates, even the occasional girl who in Russia would have been decorated as a Stakhanovite and who built up earnings at piece rates which exceeded those of many men. But in January 1944, women in metalwork and engineering earned on average three pounds, ten shillings a week, as compared with seven pounds for men.

The unions, of course, could not stand idle. While the general unions – the Transport and General Workers and the General and Municipal Workers – recorded ninefold and tenfold increases in their female membership, traditionally "craft-minded" unions of skilled men – the National Union of Foundry Workers, the Electrical Trades Union and above all the A.E.U. – swallowed their pride and admitted women to membership for the first time. It was, as Wal Hannington put it, "the force of inexorable circumstance" which compelled the A.E.U. to give way. In the first place, the general unions were grabbing large female memberships in engineering. Less narrowly, the step, which was taken in January 1943, was an admission of the fact that in this age of mass production techniques and narrowing differentials, the only way to preserve the position of the skilled man was to organize his semi-skilled sisters (and brothers) before they ousted him. In 1943, nearly a hundred and forty thousand women joined the A.E.U. The overall number of women in all trade unions had risen slowly before the war to about 970,000. By the end of 1943, it had nearly doubled, to 1,870,000.[28]

There were one or two showdowns. The huge new Rolls-Royce factory at Hillington, Glasgow, had been planned so that the work could be largely done by women and by mid-1943 was employing twenty thousand workers with only a tiny nucleus of skilled men. The A.E.U. wrangled with the management, and a court of inquiry found that Rolls-Royce had indeed evaded the 1940 agreement. When a settlement was reached in August 1943, the girls refused to accept it, and sixteen thousand women (and men) were out on strike for about a week with a call for wider application of men's rates. The dispute was settled by a new agreement which named, and accounted for, every individual machine; the work done on it, not the sex of the operator, would determine the pay.[29]

But the extent to which female inequality was taken for granted was illustrated in the spring of 1944, in a row over the position of woman teachers, who quite clearly did exactly the same jobs, for the same hours, as men, and had the same qualifications. The House of Commons voted in favour of amending R. A. Butler's new Education Bill to give them equal pay. Churchill denounced this impertinence, and the Commons, called on for a vote of confidence, sheepishly revoked their decision.

IV

And, in spite of everything, the upper middle class remained more equal than the working class. Food was the most obvious case in point.

The nutritional wastefulness of British cooking was only one of the things which made it very hard to judge the real adequacy of the national diet. From 1943, the Ministry of Food busied itself with measuring the "body-weights" of a cross section of the population at regular intervals, but the earnestness of these investigations far exceeded their scientific conclusiveness. And the figures produced at the time which purported to show that no real deficiencies in the nutrition of citizens existed, ignored or handled crudely the sociological factors which separated man from man and family from family in their needs and the ways in which they could meet them.[30]

The overall changes in the national diet were clear enough. By 1943, consumption of milk had risen by thirty per cent, of potatoes by over forty per cent, of other vegetables by thirty per cent, over pre-war levels. Consumption of meat, on the other hand, was down by over twenty per cent; of poultry and fish by forty per cent; of sugar and syrups by thirty per cent; of tomatoes and citrus fruits by fifty per cent; of other fruits by more than forty per cent. (Oranges were rare, and bananas were unheard of.) There had been a decrease of some five per cent in the consumption of eggs, and of about seventeen per cent in that of oils and fats. The average British citizen (whoever that abstraction was) would, before the war, have taken in about a third of his calories through grain products and potatoes and about one-sixth through meat; by 1943, approaching forty-five per cent would be coming from the former, and only one-eighth from the latter.[31]

According to one estimate, the average calorie level of the diet had fallen from three thousand per day pre-war to little more than twenty-eight hundred in 1940 and 1941, but had been restored by 1944. Indeed, the diet theoretically available to each citizen had actually improved since 1939, not of course in variety, but in nutritional content. Those "building bricks of protein" which the Radio Doctor extolled were found in potatoes as well as in meat. The average intake of vitamin B, calcium and iron rose.[32]

While several indices to general well-being had pointed to a deterioration in 1940 and 1941, the trend had been reversed in subsequent years. The death rate had fallen. In 1939 the rate of infantile mortality per thousand live births had been fifty-one in England and Wales, sixty-nine in Scotland. By 1945, the figures were forty-six and fifty-six respectively. The rates of tuberculosis, which had risen sharply early in the war, had been checked and turned downwards. These figures were a testimony to the value of the special nutritional schemes for mothers, babies and invalids.[33]

But they did not give the whole story. There are two myths about wartime rationing in Britain. On the one hand, the sedulous efforts of right-wing propagandists may have succeeded in convincing a younger generation that rationing was generally loathed. On the other, it is too often taken for granted that it provided "fair shares for all", in a practical application of the socialist doctrine "to each according to his needs . . ." Rationing was a popular policy, though very far from fair.

The limitations of its popularity will illustrate the limitations of its fairness. The Wartime Social Survey, in a 1942 sample, found that only one person in seven was dissatisfied with rationing, and its apparent fairness was widely applauded. In particular, nine housewives out of ten approved of it, and nearly half wanted it to go on after the war, including over half the middle-class women in the sample. But when men were taken into account, approval was far less marked. It was highest amongst white-collared and professional workers, and highest in London and the south. Rationing, in fact, was regarded as most fair in those sections of the population and regions where food had been plentiful before the war, and was least popular with heavy workers and those who lived in the pre-war depressed areas.[34]

There were good reasons for this. A coal-miner might need half as many calories again as the three thousand which were judged sufficient each day for a moderately active man of average build. The Wartime Social Survey found in 1943 that half the men and one-third of the women in a sample of industrial workers thought that they were not getting enough food to keep fit. Many of these may well have been right, as other surveys at this time confirmed that there were enormous variations in consumption of different important foods as between occupations and between regions. The general pattern was that dockers, miners, shipyard workers and iron and steel workers were less well nourished, absolutely, not just in relation to their much more arduous work, than clerks or workers in light industry. Agricultural workers were a notable, and easily explained, exception.[35]

The Ministry of Food itself had observed, in the privacy of internal Whitehall controversy, that the British system of rationing was "essentially inequitable", providing "the same quantity of an article for each person without any consideration of their needs or habits or of their capacity to secure alternatives."[36] Apart from favouring the middle class, it favoured those with large families, who could pool their resources and to some extent indulge the tastes of individual members, as against those living alone – provided, that is, that the former were not so poor that they could not afford to take up all their rations – and it favoured parents with very small children as against those with fast-growing teenagers.

Clothes rationing, with its elaborate system of special supplements, might seem to have avoided this basic inequity. Standards, what was more, levelled, not only because Utility cloths drove out bad, cheap cloths, but because people, when they were restricted in their buying, tended to invest in more expensive clothes which would last longer. But Board of Trade surveys into a cross-section of the nation's wardrobes in 1942–44 revealed a somewhat unexpected outcome of rationing. On average, the top twenty per cent of the population, in terms of income, had actually increased their wardrobes. The wardrobes of the next sixty-five per cent had diminished, though only slightly, while those of the bottom fifteen per cent were significantly down. In spite of the "industrial ten" coupon supplement for manual workers, men in white-collared jobs who qualified only for the basic ration had on average considerably larger wardrobes, and heavy workers, even with their special "iron ration", had the smallest wardrobes. The quantitative disparity between the wardrobes of well-to-do women and those of ordinary women had actually increased.[37]

Middle-class men with good quality jackets could patch them and wear them for months or years beyond their normal life. The poor, on the other hand, could afford to use their coupons only on the shoddiest goods, which had the same "coupon price" in most cases as the best ones, and so were bad coupon value. The Board of Trade recognized this in the autumn of 1943 when it reduced the pointing on low-grade clothes.

The lives of the really well-to-do were, of course, much diminished in glamour. Certainly, dining out for the upper classes might be a trial. One lady remarks that by the middle of the war "the stomach trouble" had become "a regular part of all restaurant service". "Canapé Cheval" appeared on the House of Commons dinner menu in 1943 (and even this candour was surpassed after VE Day, when "Chicken (literally) Ancienne" was offered).[38]

But even now, luxury feeding, in the words of the official historian, was "unlawful but not impossible". The conscience-racked J. L. Hodson continued to note the manifestations of this fact on his journeys. In 1943, he lunched with Lady Rhondda in Soho and had "a capital lunch with a little red wine" for twenty-eight shillings. "This", he commented, "is all right for me, but not much use to a poor housewife in the suburbs or to the driver of a bus."[39]

A cigar formerly sixpence might now cost nearer five shillings; grapes were on sale at a guinea a bunch. But delicacies might still be obtained. The wise shopkeeper, when salmon (say) came into his hands, reserved it for his richest clients and charged accordingly. The phrase "under the counter" was a significant wartime coinage. When people were away on holiday or newly dead, the shopkeeper might still claim rations for them. For other reasons, the full rations were not always taken up – cheese, particularly, repelled many who could have claimed it. The clever retailer did not dispose of little extras to strangers who might be M.O.F. spies; he whispered a word in the ear of his most valued customers.

"Under the counter" favouritism, the "grey market" as it has been called, shaded into the "black" market. How big the latter was, no one will ever know; it was in the nature of a successful black market transaction that it was left out of official statistics and evaded the courts of law. Much more or less innocent bargaining went on, and it was not only rich people who "knew a man" who could get them what they wanted when a child was ill or a radio broke down. There was a secret staff at the Ministry of Food which kept a lookout for signs of major, organized attempts to deal in the black market, and Woolton himself believed that its efforts, combined with orders which enabled the courts to impose fines of up to five hundred pounds, with or without two years' imprisonment, plus three times the total capital involved in the transaction, deterred offenders and ensured that most who transgressed went to jail for their pains. He suggests that the amount of food which went on the black market was insignificant in relation to total supplies. By the end of 1944, nearly nine hundred inspectors were employed on ensuring that the four hundred and fifteen statutory orders of the Ministry of Food were obeyed by customers, retailers and wholesalers.[40]

Meanwhile, the Board of Trade employed its own snoopers, who were up to little tricks like visiting clothes shops and trying to buy garments with loose coupons. But there seem to have been several rattling rackets in consumer goods. One had involved the circumvention of the Limitation of Supplies Orders by the production of bogus certificates entitling the forgers to claim supplies as "wholesalers". At the end of 1940, only a few months after the orders had been first imposed, Government accountants had calculated that goods worth millions of pounds had entered the market illegally in this way. Another profitable loophole had been found in the clothes rationing system. Originally, retailers passed back the coupons they had cut from customers' books as tokens of their entitlement to further supplies. To simplify matters, they had been able to exchange batches of five hundred at the post office for vouchers. Anyone could hand in an envelope, filled with spuriously certified waste paper, and make a good thing out of five hundred coupons' worth of black market clothes. The practice became remarkably common before it was checked by the introduction of a highly complex system of coupon banking. Meanwhile, lost clothing books had been replaced without much scrutiny – in the first year of clothes rationing no less than eight hundred thousand people who had claimed to have lost their books had been recompensed with no fewer than twenty-seven million coupons. Even after the procedure for replacement was tightened up, malpractices continued. By 1944, the black market value of one clothing book was around five pounds, or two shillings a coupon, a pretty clear indication of the class of customers with whom the black marketeers expected to deal.[41]

The loopholes in food distribution were easier to find. Unscrupulous farmers and small-holders were an obvious source of scarce or rationed foods for the black market; and the system of supplying restaurants was open to constant abuse. Here were two

obvious classes of potential black marketeers. But the identity
of the main villains was, naturally, surrounded in enigma. The
most conventional image was probably Evelyn Waugh's – a
strange man in smart but vulgar dress, to which popular anti-
Semitism would infallibly add the trace of a foreign accent. That
observant land girl, Shirley Joseph, reported an exciting lift from
three men driving a magnificent limousine of the type which in
theory only diplomats and the U.S. Army were now able to run:

> They all had black hair, smoothed to perfection like the
> smiling gentlemen in the hair cream advertisements. But they
> were not gentlemen and they looked as though they never
> smiled . . . They spoke in a sort of harsh whisper. "Here
> we've come all the way from Birkenhead and haven't done
> no business." "One thing, petrol's no object." "Did you fix
> that deal for the thousand tyres?"
> At the mention of tyres I pricked up my ears. I knew my
> father had badly wanted some new tyres for a long time.
> "What, can you get tyres?" I asked impulsively.
> For a moment there was silence. I think they had forgotten
> my existence.
> "Tyres? As many as you want – at the right price," one
> answered, laughing without smiling.[42]

V

The clearest area in which the rich stayed rich and the poor got
poorer as a result of wartime conditions was housing. The gap
was very wide to begin with, and the immense movements of population made it worse.

Billeting allowances had been raised, but not much, in 1940,
and there were further slight rises in 1942 and 1944. They
remained a cause for grievance, although unscrupulous people
were known to gather as many evacuees as they could and to
make a modest living out of them by keeping them at low
standard. If a war worker was taken in, the householder could
charge his own price, within reason, but even this was no temptation for the better-off.

Even in the earliest days of evacuation, there had been many
allegations that billeting officers, usually "respectable" people
themselves, had let other "respectable" people off lightly. As the
third year of evacuation had begun, the Ministry of Health's
senior officer in one of the larger reception areas had delivered his

verdict that "the real hard core" of the billeting problem was in the upper middle classes.

And it was indeed remarkable how often the large houses were spared. "In one town", records the official historian, "thirty-seven prominent citizens (including the vicar, the ministers of two churches, the town clerk, the deputy clerk, the chief billeting officer, the chairman of the billeting committee, the coroner and a bank manager) had not billeted an evacuee up to at least April 1942." In another case, the council protested that the town was full up and could take no more immigrants, but an official investigation showed that while the working-class districts were, indeed, full, twenty-three town councillors had between them no fewer than seventy-six rooms to spare.[43]

There is no doubt that most working-class children and adults were happier to stay with their own kind of people. But there were places where this literally meant sleeping in double shifts, an expedient to which few lord mayors can have been reduced. The moral was that status remained status, power remained power, and class remained class.

Housing was one field in which, although conditions everywhere grew worse, the pre-war depressed areas, less heavily bombed, and still further depopulated, were relatively better off. But it would have taken more than Ernie Bevin and Lord Woolton could have devised to redress the disparity between life in the Nineteenth-century England of declining heavy industry and life in the New England which was now preoccupied with the production of tanks and aircraft.

True, people had more wages. But they very often could not buy those necessities and near-necessities which they had previously lacked. In slum towns like Middlesbrough (where half the houses had no bathrooms and nearly four-fifths had no indoor sanitation) there were crying shortages of galvanized baths, heavy large kettles, oil stoves, wicks and chamber pots. The former depressed areas suffered from the persistence, the ossification in fact, of pre-war patterns of distribution. This was not checked by, and indeed often resulted from, the Government's control of distribution. Consumer goods, and even points-rationed food, generally went where the demand had previously been highest – so South Wales went short of canned fruit, which its people had been unable to afford before the war. Families which had been unable to pay for anything better than cotton blankets for their beds were now demanding woollen blankets and better clothes. In the summer of 1943, Board of Trade investigators compared the stocks of consumer goods in Bournemouth and the Durham town of Seaham Harbour. Bournemouth had, of course, been the most opulent of British seaside resorts, a favourite centre for wealthy and retired people. With its satellite suburbs (each of which had its own shopping centre), it had a population of about a hundred and twenty thousand people. Seaham Harbour was a coastal mining town with about twenty-three thousand, five hundred people, where unemployment had been rife; the nearest large town was several miles away. The stocks of all the eight drapers in Seaham Harbour were counted; as were those of only four drapers in Bournemouth, situated in just one of the main shopping streets. Bournemouth's four shops had nine hundred and forty-six woollen and four hundred and sixty-five cotton blankets; Seaham's eight had one and nought respectively.[44]

The Old England of agriculture also suffered unduly from shortages. Because of the shortage of time and the deterioration in transport services, rural housewives tended to shop less than before in the larger towns and cities. So the shops in the minor centres were overtaxed, especially when there were evacuees to provide for and service camps in the area from which Tommies and G.I.s sallied to make casual purchases. But in other respects, the countryside was drawing level with the standards of the south and the midlands. Almost inordinately prosperous, mechanizing itself at a furious rate, British agriculture had transformed itself so quickly that one might have said that there were now only two Englands.

Chapter Seven

Only Two Englands:
Agriculture, Coal and Aircraft Manufacture

PLOUGH UP

> Back to the Land, with its clay and its sand,
> Its granite and gravel and grit,
> You grow barley and wheat
> And potatoes to eat
> To make sure that the nation keeps fit . . .
>
> Women's Land Army song[1]

I

NOTHING could have prevented geographical and geological disparities between one part of the United Kingdom and another from producing rather different wars. Britain, mercifully, was not yet homogeneous.

At one extreme the Channel Islands – in peacetime the centre of profitable agriculture, holiday pleasures, and delectably low rates of taxation attributable to a large measure of local independence – suffered basically the same kind of war as the rest of Europe, a continent to which they were closer than they were to Great Britain. In the summer of 1940, the British Government had decided not to bother to defend them. They had been "demilitarized", and after one sharp experience of strafing and bombing, Jersey, Guernsey, and the smaller isles of Alderney and Sark had been occupied. When the Germans had arrived, practically every house had flown the white flag. The authorities, previously instructed to carry on their duties, as far as they could, as if normal conditions prevailed, had appealed for the peaceful acceptance of the invasion.

At first, the islanders had been as much amazed by the lenience of the Germans as the latter had been by the absence of resistance and sabotage. The tiny isle of Sark – still ruled autocratically by its feudal Dame – had been occupied by only eleven soldiers, who had soon found themselves sharing rounds with the local inhabitants in the pubs. Throughout the occupation – that is, until 1945 – there were only two cases of rape; the Royal Mail vans continued to carry the post; the teaching in the schools was little interfered with, except in the introduction of compulsory German. The autonomous States of Guernsey, like its counterpart in Jersey, continued to meet. The German commandant was in attendance, but the royal coat-of-arms and a portrait of King George V still hung on the wall. German soldiers were not allowed to marry islanders, and the girls who slept with them were nicknamed "Jerrybags". Guernsey, which had had the high illegitimacy rate of 5·4 per cent before the war, produced 21·8 per cent in 1944, after a steep rise; both unmarried and married women were included.[2]

The military commander-in-chief of the islands was a Silesian aristocrat, Colonel Graf von Schmettow, who pleaded for, and was to some extent able to secure, favoured treatment for the islanders as compared with the people of occupied France just across the waters. German civil administrators, also, struck up friendships in several cases with the islands' own officials. The German harbour boss and the Guernsey harbour-master drank and sang sea shanties together. Illicit listening to the B.B.C. was often winked at. But when the "V" campaign was launched in 1941, the results on the islands showed that not all was harmony and fraternization. Chalked Vs appeared on walls everywhere, cardboard Vs were pushed through letter boxes. The Bailiff of Guernsey, in peacetime its indulgent ruler, warned his fellow islanders against "these foolish acts, which accomplish nothing but merely bring grave consequences in their train", and when the culprits were not discovered, offered a twenty-five pound reward for information. A cartoon passed from hand to hand showed the Bailiff as Judas hanging from a tree.[3]

There were fewer than ten Jews on each island, but the Royal Courts both in Jersey and Guernsey were forced to pass anti-Semitic edicts, and several were dispatched to an obscure fate on the Continent. In June 1942, the confiscation of all wireless sets was ordered, a step not even taken in occupied France. In the

autumn of that year, two thousand islanders were sent to internment camps in the south of the Reich after Hitler had ordered
that all people born in Britain should be deported.[4]

These measures followed his decision to turn the islands into
fortresses, part of the "Atlantic Wall" raised against a second
front. The islands were crammed, eventually, with thirty-six
thousand Germans; also, with many thousands of foreign slave
labourers from the *Organization Todt* who arrived to build underground castles of concrete and massive anti-tank walls on the
beaches. They were dressed in tattered clothes; the islanders
glimpsed them fighting for soup and fishing in the sewage dis-
charges. Some islanders took great risks to help them; the
medical officer of health on Jersey provided fake ration books for
those who escaped. Alderney, however, had been virtually
deserted after the evacuation in the summer of 1940, and camps
for "political prisoners", run by the S.S., were established on the
island. A Frenchwoman conscripted to cook there wrote of Alderney as *"Aurigny: île du silence, du cauchemar et de l'épouvante"*.[5]

The priest of a Jersey church died in German hands after conviction for illicit wireless listening. A projectionist at a Jersey
cinema was sent to Buchenwald after wireless equipment had been
found there. Mrs Louisa Gould, who helped a young Russian
from the *Organization Todt*, died in the gas chamber at Ravens-
bruck. Her brother, a young schoolteacher, also found with a
wireless set, survived, although he was the only British citizen to
be lodged in Belsen. The five men who ran GUNS, the Guernsey
Underground News Service, which provided typewritten tran-
scripts of B.B.C. news, were also imprisoned after they had been
betrayed by one of numerous informers busy on the islands, and
two died.[6]

There were those who escaped, those who resisted, and those
who collaborated, and one guesses that the population of Great
Britain itself would have divided in much the same proportions
after invasion. For those who could afford it, there was a vigorous
black market. One Jerseyman openly boasted after the war that
he had never lacked a Sunday joint; though an official medical
report from the islands after their liberation commented that
"Lapses of memory of recent events were fairly frequent" and
suggested that "the causes were probably psychological." As the
occupation continued, basic necessities became scarce, and then
scarcer. The staple diet was reduced to root vegetables, coffee
made from acorns and tea made from blackberry leaves, while
smokers experimented with dock leaves and rose leaves. With the

shortage of soap, the tiniest cuts would fester. People fainted at work from hunger. At Guernsey in 1943, a packet of Orange Pekoe tea was publicly auctioned for £7 7s. 6d. At the end of that year, all British currency was finally withdrawn, and the reign of a tyrant more severe than austerity was confirmed by the issue of "occupation marks".[7]

At the other extreme was a second autonomous section of the United Kingdom, Northern Ireland, with about 1,300,000 inhabitants at the outbreak of war, a limb lopped off Eire in the aftermath of the Irish revolution and run ever since by a species of Protestant Mafia. Ulster, especially after the summer of 1940, was part of the front line; four divisions were stationed there by 1941 to guard against a bold German invasion of Ireland, it was an important base in the Battle of the Atlantic, and, over four years, it entertained some three hundred thousand G.I.s.

But, under its own Unionist (Conservative) Government for civilian matters, Ulster evaded much of the inconvenience, and some of the compensations, of the war effort in Great Britain itself. In April and May 1941, Belfast was bombed four times, twice daily. The shelters were probably fewer and worse than in any other British city. A hundred thousand trekkers, or "ditchers", as they called them over there, fled to the countryside after the first big raid. It was a striking result of the trauma that Protestants and Catholics joined in prayer at a public funeral for a hundred and fifty of the victims.[8]

There was, however, no conscription. Though the Unionist Government called for it, the United Kingdom War Cabinet believed, probably rightly, that the R.C.s and the active Irish nationalists would oppose it bitterly, and its effect would be to strengthen the underground Irish Republican Army and to outrage Irish feeling in the U.S.A. (an objection with which President Roosevelt concurred). So recruiting rallies were a feature of the war in Ulster. Some forty-two thousand Ulstermen and women volunteered; the peak periods, which would probably have matched those in England had there been no conscription there, were October 1939, the summer of 1940, and 1943 (when the war was clearly about to be won). Other young Ulstermen, however, earned good money in British factories, whither some sixty thousand workers transferred in the course of the war.[9]

Unemployment remained higher in Ulster than in the rest of the United Kingdom. There had been sixty-four thousand unemployed at the outbreak. The figure remained high until the middle of the war; it was not until mid-1942 that it fell below twenty thousand. The linen industry, which had employed about one-fifth of Ulster workers, had been cut off from most of its flax supplies by the German conquest of the Low Countries. The shipbuilding and aircraft industries expanded to absorb much of the surplus labour, but even in June 1943, one worker in twenty was unemployed in Ulster, as compared with one in two hundred in Great Britain. Just before that, the Unionist Prime Minister had been forced to resign by mounting political unrest, and his Unionist successor incorporated members of the hitherto negligible Labour Party into his cabinet.[10]

Part of the trouble was that the direction of labour was much less used in Ulster. Nor was rationing so strict. Half the population derived their livelihood directly or indirectly from the land. The Six Counties were a closely woven tissue of small farms, and provided the nearest equivalent in the United Kingdom to a peasantry. They produced, amongst other things, enormous quantities of eggs for export to Great Britain; but a careful scanning of the statistics showed that a great many eggs also found their way into the black market. The Eire border was impossible to police (whereas it was quite difficult to cross the sea to Britain). A busy black market traffic flowed in both directions; illegal fat cattle from the south, for instance, and tea and fertilizers from Ulster, which had, in fact, a decidedly Irish sort of war.[11]

The south-east coast of England, of course, had the bleakest war of all, with barbed wire on its promenades, constant tip and run raids, and troops everywhere. Dover could claim to be the most harried town in Britain. After Dunkirk, its population fell by more than half. Many of those who stayed (some seventeen or eighteen thousand in mid-1941) took to sleeping in caves in the famous white chalk of its cliffs, which were extended to provide accommodation for fourteen thousand people. There were no fewer than three thousand and fifty-three warnings, of bombing, and also of shelling. This was the nearest point to Europe; one would glimpse a flash on the dim smudge of France, count sixty or ninety, and wait for the shell to explode. The casualties – some six hundred killed or severely injured – were not overwhelming, but as one local man put it after the ordeal was over, "If London's raids were like a blow on the head, what we had was a sort of gnawing toothache all the time."[12]

One might contrast the Wye Valley. Its woods and hills provided an idyllic holiday for Mrs Robert Henrey in the spring of 1944. There were subtle traces of war there – children in isolated farms with East End accents, the occasional military aircraft overhead, G.I.s in the bar of the inn where she stayed. But petrol shortage had restored to the valley its ancient peace, banishing the motor-coach trippers who had taken to descending on it. "I even believe", Mrs Henrey wrote, "that some of the aged inhabitants were slipping back into their local jargon, and if this state of affairs went on long enough who could tell but they would end by reverting to the smock."[13]

Of course, this was whimsy; the internal combustion engine and the B.B.C. had spread the accent and ideas of the metropolitan south-east to all but the most aberrant corners of the island; to the once isolated fishing communities, for instance, still locked in their grim theological combat with the devils of the sea. Fishing ports, large and small, had suffered between the wars, especially the communities of inshore fishermen, and those who caught herring, for which Britain had largely lost her continental markets in 1914–18. Blasphemously, fish had been dumped overboard because they could not be sold.

The war had transformed the situation. The navy had naturally requisitioned many boats, and with them had gone fishermen for whom minesweeping was merely a specialization of their peacetime trade. Hull, with its modern deep-sea trawling fleet, had prospered before the war. Now virtually all the city's boats were in the hands of the navy. Fishing went on, with new dangers – wrecks scattered profusely, minefields and stray mines, which were sometimes washed up on the coasts to explode against a sea wall. Many boats had been armed with machine guns to fight the Luftwaffe planes which now bombed and strafed them as they went about their business. The west coast was safer, and thither went east coast boats to revive the prosperity, for instance, of Fleetwood in Lancashire, where the number of boats had fallen from a hundred and fifty-nine in 1927 to ninety-six in 1938.[14]

Even on the east coast, ancient ships which were of no use to the navy, and which were jokingly said to be held together by rust and paint, could bring uncanny rewards to their skippers. J. L. Hodson found in North Shields that one of these "scufflers", which in peacetime might have earned a hundred pounds with a good catch, had come in with fish which had fetched seventeen hundred pounds. Prices had soared; at this time (1941), a stone of prime haddock costing three or four shillings before the war was worth seventeen shillings and sixpence or eighteen shillings. The deckhands might have doubled their meagre pay. But it was the skippers who garnered astonishing profits. In Lancashire, where the Iceland trawlers were bringing home catches worth ten or even twenty thousand pounds, a skipper might make six hundred pounds from one voyage. Trawlermen were said to buy new trunks when they came home, which two of them would carry about the shops, filling them with whatever goods they could find. One skipper, it was related, had bought forty pairs of shoes; if you offered such a man a choice of four embrellas, he would take the lot, or twenty top hats, or six radio sets.[15]

But in the Mull of Kintyre, a pretty remote corner of western Scotland, a holiday-maker found about the same time that the fishermen were cannily putting their money into savings. "It seems to be a source of perpetual amazement to them to think of their present prosperity . . . and to compare this with only three years ago. They talk about the 1937 quota, which limited each boat to fifty baskets at a price of four shillings. And even then there was no market."[16]

The far northern county of Ross and Cromarty was another area which combined farming with fishing. With a population of only sixty-odd thousand before the war – a third of that of a London borough – this had been "the most seriously depressed of the Scottish counties". Unemployment, even in 1938, had run at nearly half the insured population.[17] Ross could have only a small part to play in the war, though there was a naval base at Invergordon and a fighter sector station at Tain.

The editorial with which the *Ross-Shire Journal* celebrated the New Year of 1941 recalls delightfully the style of local journalism which Dickens had parodied a hundred years before. "Croesus, the Lydian, in counsel with the conquering Cyrus, then at issue with the Queen of the Massagetae, reminded Cyrus that 'there is a wheel in human affairs, which, constantly revolving, does not suffer the same persons to be always successful' . . . Much blood may flow in 1941, but well-held now, the boasted conqueror of Europe is marching with his millions to a predestined fate."

As the writer admitted, after commenting on the heroism of the bombed cities. "Here in the Highlands, so far we have been somewhat in a backwash of war. Activity co-related to the conflict goes on, but the real blitzkrieg has not operated 'totally' in the North." He hinted, however, that the Home Guard would best the invaders if they came. And later that year there was what the same paper called a "realistic" exercise in the little town of Dingwall, where a practice was conducted to test the rest centre in the academy buildings. A "gas bomb" fell in the main street, an "H.E. bomb" in a side street, an U.X.B. in another street, whence householders were "evacuated", and, to complete the test, an incendiary "caused a fire" at a fourth point. As a final flourish of fancy, two "enemy parachutists" were captured, crowning a memorable affray.

Amongst other activities "co-related to the conflict", that of one Murdo McGregor, butcher of Dingwall High Street, should not pass unsung. The new year of 1941 found him advertising "large supplies" of VENISON (his capitals) for "the Festive Season". There were large deer forests in the area, now short of labour; and venison was off coupons. Mr McGregor appears to have handled the by-products of necessary slaughter. Before the autumn, he had opened a branch in Strathpeffer, had adopted temporarily the telegram address of "VENCON", to entertain "Wholesale Inquiries", and had bought up a rival in Dingwall High Street. At the fifth "festive season" of war, Mr McGregor was trading under the name of QUALITY. Prime geese and ducks, also off the ration, he offered in plenty. But, alas, the deer which, so to speak, had laid the golden eggs, had now been killed:

VENISON:
Poor quality. Supplies irregular.

Ross-shire's Spitfire Fund raised well over five thousand pounds. Later, the farmers in the peaceful Black Isle provided several hundred pounds in a month for the Aid to Russia Fund. Forty-three and a quarter tons of books were collected in a Ross-shire salvage week. Most of the men in the fishing villages had joined the navy or the mercantile marine. The county battalion had been part of the 51st Highland Division, surrounded and captured in France in June 1940, and the production of "comforts" for prisoners of war was a major preoccupation.

The G.I.s were about, however, and amongst the events of 1942 which the *Journal* felt obliged to highlight in its summary of that year was an exhibition of baseball at Dingwall. It was a portent, in these God-fearing parts, when the Dingwall town council came out in favour of permitting entertainments for the military on Sunday, though the Dingwall and Tain Free Church presbytery protested vehemently. But some of the young girls who might otherwise have got on well with the military had been sent south to work in war factories, and others wore the knee breeches of the Women's Land Army.

The *Journal* carried long lists of "Wanteds" on its back page. "Smart girl" for Strathpeffer bookstall; "Smart girl" for a grocers; "Experienced kitchen-maid", "Experienced head housemaid", "Smart maid" and, much more realistically, "Woman, over forty, to help with two children and do light housework". Croesus the Lydian's apophthegm applied to Ross-shire as well as to Hitler. While the silver in the big houses went uncleaned, the farms were crying loudly for every able-bodied labourer they could find, and even the prejudice against employing girls in the fields had broken down.

The hill sheep farmers were thriving on lavish Government subsidies. On the fertile plains of Easter Ross, every inch was valuable, and farmers were told to produce more and more and more milk, potatoes, wheat, oats and barley, in that order of importance. Because agricultural labourers were reserved at a very low age – twenty-one at first, raised to twenty-five in 1941, but with call-up postponed – many young men were spared from uniform, but those who remained had to work hard. Farmers who could not or would not increase their acreage under crops had their land requisitioned in several cases, by their own fellows who formed the County War Agricultural Executive Committee. The war had come to Ross-shire in dead earnest.[18]

II

"What a satisfactory job ploughing is," wrote Arthur Street in his diary on September 20th, 1939. ". . . I have not personally ploughed a furrow since 1928, but I find that I have not forgotten my old skill." All over Britain, as in Street's part of Wiltshire, farmers had brought out ploughing equipment which they had never expected to use again, or were competing briskly for gear at local sales. "Just now," Street observed a little later, "British farmers can be divided into five classes. One, those who are ploughing up grassland; two, those who are cultivating and sowing ploughed up grassland; three, those who are talking about their intention to plough up some grassland; four, those who are toiling and worrying on the local committees responsible for getting a certain acreage of grassland ploughed; and five, those who are objecting to any suggestions that they should plough up any of their grassland."[19] The British farmer, unlike most other civilians, was seriously at war from September 1939; plans to put agriculture on a war footing had been introduced in the previous spring.

In 1939, there were roughly twelve million acres of arable land in Britain, and over seventeen million acres of permanent grassland. In 1944, the position was neatly reversed; there were eighteen million acres of arable land, and only eleven million of permanent grassland. The acreage under potatoes had more than doubled, and that under wheat had increased by over two-thirds. The total arable acreage had nearly, but not quite, returned to its level in the 1860s, the heyday of British agriculture, before the invasion of cheap corn from the New World had set arable farming into retreat.

The First World War had reversed that retreat for a while. The years 1917 and 1918 had seen three million acres brought back under the plough to meet the threat of blockade. And then the farmers had been betrayed. The Government, during the war, had given guaranteed prices for wheat and oats and these, on a revised basis, had been part of the Agriculture Act of 1920. In 1921, the Act had been repealed. The price of wheat, eighty shillings and tenpence a quarter in 1920, had fallen to forty-seven shillings and twopence in 1922. The depression brought further woe. In 1934, wheat had stood at twenty shillings and ninepence a quarter, "the lowest figure in the record of wheat prices, which goes back to 1646".[20]

Farmers had developed persecution mania. While some had met the crisis by mechanization and improved systems of management, and had continued to do well, the average farmer had had no more than fifty to two hundred acres at his disposal, too few to be economic, and had suffered from lack of capital and lack of credit. Typically, he had come from a farming family; he had shared its limited perspectives and its distrust of education, and had tended to ignore the startling advances in agricultural science which were taking place. The powers of his landlord had been diminished almost to extinction by legislation, and most landlords had consequently taken little interest in farming, or in pulling their tenants out of the bog. (Though owner occupancy had increased greatly in the present century, it was still far less common than tenancy.)

Georgian poets and their associated cricket correspondents had dwelt nostalgically on the beauties of the English countryside and the virtues of the English yokel, while the former had decayed and the latter, if they had had much enterprise, had fled to the towns. Even during the war, many writers who should have known better implied that the soldiers and airmen were dying to preserve an essentially rural Britain, the fantasy world of Thomas Hardy's minor and more optimistic followers, of *Mrs Minniver* and of P. G. Wodehouse. In fact, as evacuated schoolteachers found, the more picturesque parts of Britain were inhabited by increasingly demoralized, and often remarkably incestuous, communities of near-paupers. One lady who tried her hand at farming during the war wrote in a debunking spirit near the end of it, "There are no crafts in the country and there is no culture. From the lowest to the highest the greatest ambition is a suite of furniture."[21]

The agricultural labourer's cottage might seem more attractive than a city slum, but with its small rooms, its old thatch, its lack of drainage, piped water or electric light, it was not really much to be preferred. The wages of farm labourers had been very low, their prospects of rising to prosperity in farming had been nil, and there had been a shortage of cottages, accentuated by rich town-dwellers who had converted many of them into week-end retreats from the trials and tribulations of conspicuous consumption. Agriculture had lost labour at the rate of ten thousand a year between the wars, and it had been largely the best and youngest who had upped and gone.

Nor was the boss much better off. In 1943, it was found that under half the farms in England and Wales had a piped supply of water. Only a quarter had a public or private supply of electricity. While the farmers of the home counties were relatively well provided in these respects, those of Wales and the south-west mostly lived and worked in conditions which were coming to seem unbelievably primitive.[22]

Faced with low prices for cereals, many farmers between the wars had turned their backs on cultivation and had bound themselves in servitude to the dairy cow, "a lowly, offensive taskmistress," A. G. Street called her, "who produces milk and mess on seven days in every week". They had ranched their livestock to save expenses, and had let good arable land go to waste. "To farm well in those days," writes Anthony Hurd, one of their leaders, "often meant to lose money; the importance of keeping the land productive and in good heart had little appeal to the bank manager." Drains, ditches and fences had been neglected. A report from the Sherwood Forest in 1936 indicates how bad the decline had been. "The farms, in general," an expert had noted, "are under-manned, under-cultivated and under-stocked. Lime deficiency is almost everywhere glaringly obvious. Many of the water meadows, costly projects of a century ago, are falling into disrepair and disuse. On some estates the carefully made roads and commodious farmhouses and buildings show only too clearly the effect of nearly a quarter of a century of neglect." In

almost every part of Britain, there were large tracts of total
dereliction, where bracken, gorse and briars had encroached on
good grassland, or where fertile soil had been abandoned because
it paid no one to cultivate it.[23]

The state had stepped in. Its prescription for a depressed agriculture had been much the same as for coal, steel and cotton;
taxation relief, import control and internal reorganization of the
industry. The producers' prices for sugar beet, cereals, milk,
bacon, cheese, sheep and fat cattle had been subsidized. Home
pig rearers, hen keepers and fruit, flower and vegetable growers
had been protected by import duties and import quotas against
foreign competition. Under Acts of 1931 and 1933, marketing
boards, elected by farmers, had been set up to dispose of milk,
bacon, potatoes and hops, with varying degrees of success. With
a guaranteed price of forty-five shillings a quarter, the acreage
under wheat had risen somewhat, and dairy farmers had done
pretty well out of the Milk Marketing Board. But the recovery
had not been even, and in 1939, farming in general had still been
a depressed industry.

III

For every acre of grassland which they ploughed in that first
winter of war, farmers received a subsidy of two pounds. The
County War Agricultural Executive Committees (C.W.A.E.C.s),
the "War Ags", were summoned into being, as in the First World
War, to supervise the execution of the Government's plan for two
million extra acres under the plough. The first plough-up achieved
its target by April 1940, despite a freezing January and February,
and a chilly spring. For seven days a week, in many cases, the
farmers ploughed, sometimes by moonlight or with the help of
lamps, by special permission of the A.R.P. authorities.

In 1940–41, nearly two million more acres of permanent grassland went under the plough; in 1941–42, another one and a half
million. When the shipping situation was at its worst in 1942,
farmers were told that they must now "put forward their maximum effort without regard to the effect on the crops obtainable in
1944 or subsequent years. The response", adds the official historian, "was magnificent." Because both grassland for ploughing
up and men to work were now running short, only 960,000 more
acres were asked for in 1942–43; 1,376,000 were given, and the
hot and glorious summer of 1943 saw a record harvest.[24]

Farmers who had turned to livestock for salvation between the wars had relied increasingly on cheap imported feeding-stuffs, to the tune of some 8·7 million tons annually. In 1943–44, only 1·3 million tons came in. Reduction in livestock was implicit in the plough-up policy, as the carnage of the autumn of 1940 indicated. Though the Ministry of Agriculture loyally defended the livestock farmers as far as possible against the indignant calls of the Ministry of Food (always insatiable for more potatoes), in the spring of 1942 it was compelled to point out to them that one acre of average arable crops fed far more human beings than one acre of average grassland, whilst one acre of average wheat saved "at least as much shipping space as seven acres of the best grass in England".[25] And the best grass in England was not immune, not even the lush grazing land of Leicestershire.

But outside the few acres of specialization, British farming was essentially mixed farming – to reduce livestock too drastically would destroy its balance, quite apart from jeopardizing the call for more milk which the war itself had helped to produce. In 1943–44, while milk production was only four per cent below its pre-war level, the output of beef and veal had fallen by one-sixth, that of mutton and lamb by one-fifth, that of eggs by half, and that of pigmeat by two-thirds. Pigs and poultry, which gave little back to the soil in return for what they ate, were subjected to holocaust. But there were actually more cows, and the fall in milk output was explained by a severe decline in the yield per beast caused by a shortage of concentrated feeding stuffs and an enforced departure from normal feeding practices. Yet the Ministry of Food's concern about standards led to improvements in the safety and quality of milk. Another advance was much more efficient use of grazing land; several hundred thousand more cattle fed on under three-quarters of the previous area of grazing. The Ministry of Agriculture encouraged farmers to "take the plough round the farm", improving their grassland by ploughing, cropping for a time and reseeding, while they restored their old arable by leys.[26]

Ley farming – the sowing of arable land with temporary grasses – had long been advocated by the eminent agricultural scientist Sir George Stapledon, and had already been much used in Scotland. It was now increasingly adopted, as a method of restoring tired soil. The stored up fertility of former grassland had helped to provide record yields of wheat and oats, but by the middle of the war, these reserves were being exhausted, while the disruption of normal rotations was bringing bad trouble from weeds, pests and diseases. Leys remained controversial, however, and veteran farmers were always writing to the papers to extol the unique virtues of old pasture. Another much debated subject was the increased use of ensilage to preserve the goodness of young green fodder through the winter. The bolder farmers took to experimenting with "recipes", and improvising silos out of wire and cardboard, or old iron tanks, or even railway sleepers lined with newspaper.

In 1943–44, another six hundred thousand acres of permanent grass were ploughed up, though the emphasis of Government policy was beginning to shift back towards the expansion of live-stock farming. The total area of crops other than grass stood at fourteen and a half million acres in 1944 – five and three-quarter million more acres than in 1939. The increase had been achieved in spite of the loss of eight hundred thousand valuable acres to aerodromes, factories, camps and other warlike purposes.[27] It had spelt doom for the rabbit, which provided meat and furs in place of its former nuisance value. It had involved the ploughing of golf courses and bowling greens, and also of the difficult fields of Galloway, where men and horses steered round jagged, jutting lumps of granite. In the orchards of Kent, Cambridge and the west country, farmers ploughed between the trees; the flower growers of Devon and Cornwall forsook their precious bulbs (though not all of them) to produce potatoes, of course, and carrots. The King's Great Park at Windsor became the largest wheatfield in Britain, and large tracts of the Sussex Downs carried their first crops since the days of the Saxons.

With lavish financial help from the Government, farmers were encouraged to improve their drainage and to eliminate thorns. Swamp and marshland in Cumberland and Cheshire, bracken land in Devon, forest acres in Wiltshire, were reclaimed for farming, or claimed for the first time. Two such projects became especially famous. In East Anglia thousands of acres of fenland, many of which had never been ploughed before, were subjected to a gigantic operation. Drainage revealed the remains of a primitive forest, long trunks of bog oak lying fifty or sixty to the acre just below the surface, and the Royal Engineers were called in to dynamite them. Corn and celery grew in place of scrub willow and reeds. At a very different altitude, large areas of the heights of Montgomeryshire were cleared of bracken and thorn, and pro-vided enough potatoes to feed the whole of Manchester.[28]

To accomplish these feats meant using machines on a grand scale – huge and lumbering gyrotillers which cleared forest, excavators which cut drainage canals, and, of course, tractors. The plough-up made it imperative to speed up a rate of mechanization which had been sluggish between the wars. Telling farmers to plough up two million acres, or over twenty per cent more land, did not, as the official historian puts it, "lengthen the hours of daylight by an hour and a half nor the ploughing or sowing seasons by one-fifth".[29] The Government had prudently placed an advance contract with Ford's to ensure that there were enough tractors to meet the inevitable demand.

There were still 545,000 farm houses in 1945 (as compared with 649,000 in 1939). But the number of tractors in use had risen dramatically. In spite of the competition for resources from armoured cars and aircraft, home output of tractors had doubled by 1941, and imports were then running at three times the pre-war level. There were fifty-six thousand tractors in use in 1939 and two hundred and three thousand in January 1946, though even at this date, horses were still far more numerous. Between May 1942 and January 1946, the number of disc harrows in use doubled and the number of milking machines increased by sixty per cent. Not only were there more machines in use, but the C.W.A.E.C.s saw to it that they were more fully used, moving from farm to farm as they were needed. A degree of modernization had occurred in six years of war which might have taken decades in peacetime.[30]

Farmers had more money to spend on fertilizers now. The War Ags propagandized in their favour, and the fact that phosphates and potash were now rationed convinced many farmers that they must be worth having. Very few farmers indeed (about three in a hundred) had taken any formal course in farming, and the attitude that Father knew best was still very strong, but agricultural science had put its foot in the door. Ocular proof convinced doubting Farmer Thomas that it had something good to sell.

A land girl describes the irruption of technology into the life of a Cambridgeshire village; in this case, the artificial insemination of cows.

> Village opinion was very mixed but those who approved were in the minority. For a few weeks the topic was to the fore at any village gathering. I went down to "The Plough" for some cigarettes one night and listened over my shoulder while I was waiting for my change.
>
> "No, I don't 'old with un," Bob was saying. "That's going

agin nature, come what may it can't lead to no good."

"They bin doing it in Roosia these many years, Ern were telling me," said George.

"Roosia!" said Bob, drawing viciously at his cigarette. "They may be good at fighting and I'll give 'em credit where it's due, but what do we know they knows about farming? Old bull's bin good enough for us up to now, why do we want to go traipsing about after new ideas like this'n for?"

In the event, the cow concerned gave birth to a "fine little heifer", and village opinion, also swayed by the fact that the innovation disposed of the unenviable task of driving the cow over to the bull, switched strongly in favour of it.[31]

IV

The farmer's life continued to obey the slow and sometimes stubborn rhythms of the seasons; there was nothing the scientists could do about that. There were some glorious summers, but also some foul winters, and record crops meant, in some places, that harvesting dragged on towards Christmas. Farmers contended with vast fires caused by incendiaries on their fields, or, more commonly, with soldiers who insisted unanswerably on training across their winter wheat, and tearing holes in the hedges into the bargain.

Yet to many people it seemed that the yeoman agriculturalist, already to some extent coddled by the state before the war, was now doing altogether too well as a result of his new importance. It was officially estimated in 1942 that, while net national income had risen by thirty-five per cent since 1938–39, weekly wages in manufacturing industries by forty-two per cent, and the agricultural wages by sixty-one per cent, farmers' net incomes had increased by no less than two hundred and seven per cent – and by over a hundred per cent even when it was admitted that 1938–39 had been a bad year for them. Over the war period, agricultural incomes rose faster and relatively further than wages, salaries, professional earnings or profits. While dairy farmers, on average, did about as well as before, arable farming had become immensely more profitable, and those poor relations, the hill sheep farmers, were now quite prosperous. So a "levelling up" within farming itself had made farmers, quite conspicuously, one of the most wealthy sections of the community. And even these startling figures had omitted the considerable potential of the black market.[32]

The farmers had indulgent masters at the Ministry of Agriculture. The first wartime minister, Sir Reginald Dorman Smith, had come to office straight from the councils of the National Farmers Union itself, which was now established as perhaps the most successful pressure group in British politics. Churchill had displaced him with Robert Hudson, with the Duke of Norfolk and Tom Williams as his junior ministers, and good relations were confirmed which lasted out the decade. Williams was an ex-miner who understood the farmers' persecution complex, relished his back-slapping popularity with them, and was somewhat obsequious to their wishes, and he became the first Minister of Agriculture after the war.

By the autumn of 1940, the farmer had guaranteed prices for all staple products, and guaranteed markets for most of them. Hudson then promised him that this security would continue for the duration of the war and for at least one year thereafter. Nevertheless, the farmers, not wholly for the purposes of bargaining, remained uneasy and suspicious. The First World War and its aftermath had shown the ease with which promises might be broken.

The authorities were realizing, moreover, that now that prices had been set to encourage the high-cost or marginal producer – for instance, the dairy farmer growing potatoes for the first time on not very suitable land – the established and successful producers were harvesting inordinate profits; and the fact that many farmers still did not keep proper accounts made it difficult to retrieve these windfalls through income tax. There were rumblings of discontent among farmers in 1942, when the third wartime "price review" failed to cover a recent pay rise for farm workers. In June 1943, there was another increase in wages and Hudson again refused to raise prices to match it. A storm of angry meetings and speeches followed, which Hudson, not the most tactful of men, was unable to pacify. The Government duly made certain concessions, while reassuring its critics that guaranteed prices and assured markets would extend up to the summer of 1948.[33]

Farmers were traditionally individualistic to a proud, if sometimes ruinous, degree. But the experience of depression, followed by this new lushness, converted them thoroughly to state control. They were told what to grow, how to sell it, and at what price. The ministry argued that the farmers were "trustees for the nation" for the land they used, which "like the factory, must be at the full disposal of the Government to be used in the way that is best for the war effort".[34] It would have taken little more than the dispossession of the redundant landlords to convert the wartime system to full nationalization. The farmer, like the businessman, hated filling in forms. (If he applied for a few yards of piping to lay water on to a field, he had to complete the same form as if he had wished to build a factory.) He grumbled, as he had always done, but he knew that state intervention had brought him real prosperity.

And its execution was supervised, not by civil servants picking their way through his mud in their pinstripes, but by fellow farmers. The Ministry of Information, with much justification, acclaimed the C.W.A.E.C.s as "perhaps the most successful example of decentralization and the most democratic use of 'control' this war has produced".[35] Each would number eight to ten men, including one agricultural trade unionist, and one lady representing the Women's Land Army. These were not elected, but appointed by the minister. They further devolved responsibility to district committees of four to seven local residents. There were nearly five hundred of these, and it was their members who had the job of visiting each farm regularly and giving detailed instructions or advice. Each D.C. member would be responsible for, say, fifty farms covering about five thousand acres.

All these committee members worked voluntarily, and all were residents of the county. Seed merchants, estate agents and milk retailers might be found on them, but most of the five and a half thousand C.W.A.E.C. and D.C. members were farmers. The progressive, intelligent and successful farmers now had their chance to restore the land, and they made their work a crusade. Thanks to the war, they could tell others to put the best methods into effect almost without counting the cost.

The War Ags had power under the Defence Regulations to send their own labour to work on any land, to take possession of any land, or any idle machinery, and to give directions as to the cultivation, management or use of agricultural land, which the tenant could disobey only at risk of dispossession. They allocated the more important farm requisites, including machinery, fertilizers, feeding stuffs, and of course, labour. They organized their own gangs of land girls, Irishmen, conscientious objectors and prisoners of war to execute drainage or reclamation and to farm requisitioned land.

Yet the operation of these vast powers met with general

acquiescence. The county quotas for the principal crops were
worked out by county, district and, in the last stages, parish committees which knew the land and the men well. Two recent students of the subject conclude that the committees, though encouraged by Hudson to put bashfulness behind them when they
dropped in on their neighbours or reported on them to the
authorities, "resembled over-indulgent parents, saving the rod
and spoiling the child, far more than some stone-hearted rural
gestapo trampling down the rights of British yeomen".[36]

From 1941 to 1943, the committees were busy compiling what
was modestly described as "a modern Domesday book". Every
farm in England and Wales was visited by committee members or
other experienced observers, who noted (or should have noted),
the types of soil, the state of the buildings and cartroads, and so
on. The statistics so produced therefore represented the opinions
of various observers rather than unquestionable fact, and there
were those who were very ready to question the classification of
farmers according to merit, as "A", "B" or "C". Twelve farmers
out of every twenty, in the event, were adjudged "A" and had
nothing to complain about. Only one out of twenty was graded
"C", which meant that the investigator thought he was getting
less than sixty per cent of the maximum possible production out
of his land.[37] It was the five per cent of "C" farmers who, before
and after the survey, were likely to find themselves overwhelmed
with help by the committee-men, or deprived of their land.

By the end of 1943, the C.W.A.E.C.s had taken over nearly
four hundred thousand acres in England and Wales alone. Most
cases of dispossession involved non-resident occupiers, parts of
farms, or formerly non-agricultural land. Less than one-tenth of
ten thousand acres recorded involved a farmer having to quit his
house or a complete holding. About half the requisitioned land
was let to tenants, and the rest was farmed by the War Ags themselves, often badly because they were using inexperienced labour.
It was at the point of eviction, when the mailed first showed
through the velvet glove, that the committees did incur some local
unpopularity.[38]

In 1940, the Hampshire C.W.A.E.C. ordered a farmer called
Walden to plough, summer-fallow and prepare for cropping an
area of about four acres on his farm. He did not comply, and
when he was told to quit, he refused to do so. The committee sent
police to evict him. Walden bolted himself inside his farmhouse
and fired a sporting gun, wounding several policemen. Tear gas
was used unsuccessfully. The police broke in, and Walden, still

fighting, was shot down. The Farmers' Rights Association, set up later to expound the grievances of evicted farmers, acclaimed Walden as a martyr of civil liberty. The F.R.A. claimed that the official figures for evictions did not tell the whole story, and that many farmers withdrew voluntarily when given the option by the C.W.A.E.C.s. Cases of real or apparent corruption were quoted – of a Gloucestershire tenant farmer evicted in favour of his landlord's son-in-law, of one in Yorkshire whose farm was taken over by the brother of a C.W.A.E.C. member. It was certainly a somewhat questionable feature of the system that a good farmer victimized by a corrupt committee-man had the right of appeal only to the C.W.A.E.C. itself. But one may conclude that most of those who suffered genuine misery and hardship through eviction were, when all was said and done, bad farmers.[39]

V

The war, for reasons already given, had brought specially acute shortages to many rural areas, and the influx of soldiers, evacuees and land girls had overburdened the already inadequate housing. Of the three thousand new cottages for which the Government gave special permission in 1943, some two thousand, six hundred were actually built, but this was a drop in the ocean.

But the "drift from the land" was, forcibly, reversed for the duration. In the early months of war, people anxious to avoid conscription actually drifted in of their own free will. But by March 1940, agriculture in England and Wales had lost over thirty thousand men to the army (mostly Territorial volunteers called up at the outbreak) and some fifteen to twenty thousand to other occupations. The moral, for the Government, was clear. The average weekly wage in agriculture during the phoney war was thirty-seven shillings and tenpence, and unskilled labourers constructing camps and factories in rural areas were drawing double that. Bevin, in the summer of 1940, forced the Agricultural Wages Board to institute a minimum of forty-eight shillings before he would take any action to restrain the drift. In 1941, agriculture came under an E.W.O.

Farm workers, thanks largely to the vengeful hostility of many farmers towards the unions, had been weakly organized. Now that the dearth of labour made victimization very unlikely, the National Union of Agricultural Workers was able to double and triple its membership, from 47,000 in 1938 to 163,000 in 1947.

The national minimum for male workers was reset at sixty shillings in November 1941 and at sixty-five shillings in June 1943, while overtime rates also rose. By 1950, agricultural wages had tripled since 1938, while the national average had merely doubled, but the absolute disparity remained great.[40]

In June 1939, there had been 546,000 regular male workers in agriculture, and 55,000 regular female workers, together with some 111,000 casual workers of both sexes. By June 1944, there were only 522,000 regular men, but there were 150,000 more land workers than there had been five years before. The Women's Land Army then stood at 80,000, slightly short of its peak numbers.

The W.L.A. had operated, on a smaller scale, in the previous war, and had been reformed in June 1939. By the outbreak of war, there had been a thousand volunteers; by the harvest of 1941, there were nearer twenty thousand. Then conscription began to bring in more apathetic recruits, and the upward swing was checked only in the summer of 1943 when the aircraft industry won priority over girl-power. Land girls came from all classes, and though about one-third of those who volunteered had lived in London or other large industrial cities, many, of course, were countrywomen born and bred.

They were not really an "army". Land girls had to be mobile and work wherever they were sent, but there was no discipline except dismissal, which meant at worst direction to the auxiliary services or to war industry. Over a third of land girls, in December 1943, were employed in gangs directly under the C.W.A.E.C.s, but when girls from the north were sent to the home counties to thresh in these gangs, some grew homesick and simply went back. The members of gangs often lived in hostels, where officious care might be taken of their morals and behaviour. But most of the rest worked for individual farmers, and obeyed their employers' orders. If, as happened very often, the girl's bedroom was small and bleak, the hours were long or even virtually non-stop, and the pay was less than the official minimum of forty-eight shillings, she could appeal only to the W.L.A.'s Local Representative, a woman appointed on the basis of her local standing who might well side with her neighbour, the farmer.

Land girls had seven days' official leave a year, as compared with twenty-eight days for the real military. Their uniform – green jerseys, brown breeches, brown felt slouch hats and khaki overcoats – was not always worn, and those who assumed it were prone to make eccentric use of it. Land girls, their historian observes reprovingly, would "cheerfully go about in a flowery frock showing under their khaki overcoat, or a magenta jumper combined with dungarees".

The girls did a great variety of jobs. Thousands were employed in "horticulture", on the understanding that their time would be devoted to food production; and some even compensated for the shortage of gardeners in private houses until 1943, when they were mainly withdrawn and sent to farms. About a thousand land girls were employed as rat-catchers; in Lincolnshire, two such young ladies, aged twenty and nineteen, caught twelve thousand of the creatures in one year. About six thousand girls were in the W.L.A. "Timber Corps", felling trees, working in sawmills, or selecting trees for poles or timber. (Those on the last job might have had a strange, lonely war, walking thousands of miles through remote countryside, living in whatever billets could be found, and frequently under suspicion of being spies.) Other land girls worked at reclamation. For the C.W.A.E.C. gangs, threshing was the main job for eight months of the year; the work, performed in an atmosphere of dirt, dust and noise, was quite ruinous for the complexion. About a quarter of all land girls at the W.L.A.'s peak were engaged on milking, or milking combined with general farmwork.[41]

The farmer often found his girl, or girls, not the least of his added wartime burdens. Milking was the obvious job for such interlopers – repetitive, incessant and especially bothersome in its combination of hygiene and filth. Ladylike land girls took a horrrifying plunge into the muck and the routine swearing inseparable from farm work. Rachel Knappett, one of those who came to like the life, found that her presence at first inhibited the male labourers on the south Lancashire farm she worked at. "Bugger", in this part of the world, was a generally used term of friendliness, even of endearment. Soon after her arrival, a labourer stumbled into her. " 'Cum art road, yet gaupin' bugger,' said Alec. The men turned round in horror. Then, seeing that I was laughing and not flat on the floor in a swoon, they joyously received the word back into their vocabularies, their tongues were loosened and the sun shone more brightly. From that moment, for better or worse, I began to belong to Bath Farm. Instead of being addressed in a stiff and formal manner, I became 'Owd yaller 'ead', 'Owd Knappoo', 'the bloody wench', 'sparrer', 'the poot', 'gaupie', 'blondie', or 'oo' (she)."[42]

There were tales of land girl Stakhanovites; the press was tickled when a former hairdresser won a horse-ploughing competition against a field of men. But careful study showed that, while women could match or even excel men at certain light jobs, such as tending poultry or pulling peas, and were not too much less efficient at turning hay, milking and lifting potatoes, they were so far behind in performing shoulder-and-arm jobs that three women, to the farmer, were worth only two men.[43]

But farmers could not be choosers. By July 1943, there were nearly forty thousand Italian prisoners of war at work in the fields, many of them billeted with farmers. Soldiers stationed at home, and even G.I.s, also turned out to help with the harvest; and the general public discovered that farm work was a dignified, and notably cheap, way of taking a holiday in wartime.

In 1943, besides the camps for schoolchildren, there were one hundred and fifty-five for adults, occupied from April to October by volunteers ranging, quite literally, from dustmen to bishops. Volunteers paid a small charge for their accommodation, but mostly recouped that, and more, by what the farmers paid them. And there were two hundred week-end clubs as well, the members of which cycled out on Saturday afternoon and cycled home exhausted on Sunday evening.[44]

Meanwhile, the Englishman's passion for gardens and allotments was justifying itself on a grand scale. The "DIG FOR VICTORY" campaign had begun with the outbreak of war. Under a gigantic propaganda barrage – ten million instructional leaflets were distributed in 1942 alone – the number of allotments advanced from 815,000 in 1939 to 1,400,000 in 1943; a survey of manual workers about the middle of the war indicated that over half kept either an allotment or a garden. By 1943–44, domestic hen keepers were producing about twenty-five per cent of the country's officially known supplies of fresh eggs, and by the end of the war the Domestic Poultry Keepers' Council had over one and a quarter million members owning twelve million birds. Pig keeping was another craze – there were eventually six thousand, nine hundred "Pig Clubs" with hundreds of thousands of members, feeding their beasts on kitchen waste.[45]

So in various ways the war broke down the barriers between the producers and consumers of bacon and eggs, potatoes and greens. Agriculture was dragged, without the proverbial kicks and screams, into the twentieth century; the ploughman servicing his tractor and the farmer calculating his needs for fertilizers drew closer in spirit and attitudes to the engineers and managers who made, amongst other things, the new farm machinery.

In several rural counties, the farmer ploughed his fields and, beneath him, miners hewed at the coal face. But there were no "Coal Clubs", no "Hew for Victory" posters and, no Women's Mine Army. That was a job, as the war illustrated sharply, which only a class of men reared to the pits, shaped in their physique and in their minds by them, could now be expected to perform with much success. They were the living symbols, the living victims, of a Nineteenth-century England still decaying, still declining.

THE SINNERS IN HELL

> Farewell, our dear wives and our children,
> Farewell, our old comrades as well.
> Don't send your sons down the dark dreary pit;
> They'll be damned like the sinners in hell.

"The Gresford Disaster", a miners' song commemorating an explosion in a North Wales pit in 1934, which killed 265 men and boys.[1]

I

Before the war, the people of Britain had been burning over forty million tons of coal and anthracite a year in their grates. In the last year of war, they consumed only 35·8 million tons – a fall of nearly ten million as compared with 1939–40.

After the crisis of 1942, the public had loyally saved the situation by cutting back their use of fuel. But in the winter of 1943–44, the crisis returned. The month to month restriction on household deliveries which had been enforced from July 1941 to August 1942 was reimposed so stringently that in the south-east, in January 1944, the householder might officially receive no more than four hundredweight for the month, and that only if he had less than one ton in stock. The coal merchant's labour force, already much diminished, was further weakened by an epidemic of flu. The trains were in a muddle again. And the pits were not producing enough coal. January 1944 was benign, the public responded once more, and the coal budget was balanced.

The well-to-do, if they were patriotic, suffered with the poor. If they were not, they connived with the coal merchant. In any case, they tended now to use gas and electricity. As for the limit theoretically imposed on deliveries to people who had sizable stocks, the middle class had valiantly resisted official inspection of their cellars to the point where it had become unworkable. Meanwhile, people in working-class tenements without lifts could hardly stock at all.

II

How could this be, when Britain's abundance of coal had been the basis of her industrial greatness, the dusky backside of the Pax Britannica? Coal had blackened the centre of every city in England, had always until now poured from the delivery man's back in the quantities required, as George Orwell had put it, "like manna except that you have to pay for it".[2] The answer lay in the ruined valleys of South Wales, the mean villages of Durham and Lanark, even in the orchard county of Kent. It lay with the owners of well over a thousand mining companies, and with seven hundred thousand miners, or about one employed man out of every twenty.

Before the First World War, the mines had been riding a high wave of prosperity and profits. They had produced nearly half the European output of coal, and had provided Britain with a staple export trade. Towards the end of that war, the Government had assumed complete responsibility for the mines' finances, to stave off crisis; and after the war, the wave had smashed down on a desolate beach. The Government had dropped its control like a hot dish early in 1921, betraying the miners much as it betrayed the farmers. The coal-owners had applied their traditional specific, a savage attack on wages. The miners had put up an equally bitter resistance, culminating in the General Strike of 1926, when the rest of the Trade Union movement had come to their aid. Other trades had resumed work after the T.U.C. had surrendered. The miners had stayed out and had fought on for seven months, when privation had driven them back on the owners' terms. But the owners' terms could not revive the industry. Little new capital had come in; mechanization, in which Britain lagged far behind its rivals, had proceeded slowly. The slump had turned the raw wounds of 1926 septic. In August 1932, four out of every ten miners – in total, 435,000 men – had been unemployed. Between the wars, the number of mines worked and of men on the collieries' books had fallen. So had production, which had stood at 227 million tons in 1938.

Truly, the colliery owners were a lucky race of men. During the struggles of the 1920s, their obdurate insistence on lower wages

had forfeited the sympathy, though not the support, of Baldwin's
Conservative Government. The miners and the Labour Party had
made nationalization of coal a primary aim. Yet MacDonald's
minority Labour Government had thrown the owners a lifebelt,
the Coal Mines Act of 1930, which had instituted a national compulsory cartel. This limited sales in each region to an agreed quota
and gave the coal-owners the right to fix minimum prices. The
aim had been to restore profitability and to provide money for
much needed re-equipment. With control in the owners' hands,
it had become instead "a device by which the available business
was spread among weak concerns and strong, efficient and
inefficient; all enjoyed the benefit of fixed prices and restricted
output, while the expensive and systematic technical re-equipment of which the industry was beginning to stand badly in need
... was postponed indefinitely..." (Thus, the official historian.)[3]

So the industry had entered the war combining, as one critic
put it, "the worst features of decaying and restrictive monopoly
with the most brutal evils arising from cut-throat competition" –
the latter being seen, for instance, in the wastage of coal which
lay under the boundaries drawn between two pits. Hundreds of
firms mined drifts and outcrops on a petty scale, while the
twenty-five biggest companies and combines produced perhaps
half of the nation's coal. These large concerns were often linked
with metal and chemical industries, providing cheap coal on a
basis of low wages, and sharing in big profits. Most colliery companies were paying larger dividends as a result of the war.[4]

In the House of Commons, the owners' men confronted the
miners' men in a miniaturized and somewhat more polished
enactment of the trench warfare which prevailed in the coalfields.
That the Labour Party had survived the 1931 General Election at
all could be attributed to the miners of South Wales and Durham,
who had stood firm against "National" appeals. That bitterness
in Nye Bevan's attacks on Churchill which puzzled and appalled
his fellow members was a genteel refinement of the feeling still
latent in Bevan's own Welsh valleys. Churchill had sent the
troops in to break strikes; Churchill had fought the General
Strike as a war against the working class; and in a debate on coal
in October 1943, Alex Sloan, a Scottish miners' M.P., relieved
himself of a parody of Churchill's finest hour. "The vested interests were led by a great war leader and the fight was fought out
to the bitter end," he said, recalling 1926. "The miners were
defeated, but not without a struggle. They fought on the hills of

Scotland and on the beaches of the north-east coast, the valleys of South Wales and in the streets of the midlands, but it was all of no avail. They were defeated . . ."[5]

It was not for nothing that the miners had the richest corpus of living industrial folk-song of all occupations, grim, defiant ballads which recalled old strikes, old disasters, as if they had been yesterday. The attitudes of men, women and children in the coalfields were shaped by ever-present reminders of a century and more of class warfare, conducted in most areas in geographical isolation from less strenuous industries and blander ways of life. Wages made up as much as two-thirds of the price of producing a lump of coal. To the natural hazards of coal-getting had been added the cruelties of an unreliable market, and the determination of the owners to cut wages at the slightest temptation. Against the crudest exploitation known in British industry, the miners had erected unions of legendary solidarity. Through their union lodges, their co-operative societies, their elected Labour councillors, the miners had created islands of decency and fairness in the usually hideous villages constructed by the owners. The president of their National Federation insisted in 1944 that "Every penny on the wages, every minute off the hours, every improvement in housing conditions, every pit-head bath and welfare centre has had to be fought for and won by the miners themselves. The owners have never willingly given a single concession."[6]

These struggles could be charted in any pay-docket, which for the miner who received it was a sheet of living history. Each item in the rococo wages structure, which included wide variations between the districts, represented victory, compromise or defeat in the near or distant past. As late as 1940, Scottish miners had a minimum wage of nine shillings a shift based on an 1888 agreement.

State unemployment benefits had served the owners' turn in the depression years; they had held most of the labour force together until better days arrived. But the motor bus and the cinema had helped to acquaint the young with the possibilities of life beyond the stricken villages. Even when work was to be had in it, the pit would repel youth with its darkness, its danger, with its almost unbearable heat or its almost insufferable damp or its killing dust. Wounds filled with coal dust so that every miner wore blue scars like a brand. Disabled men stood at the street corners or did light work at the pithead, "a walking propaganda against recruitment for the pits", as one youngster put it.[7]

So the industry had an ageing and depleted labour force, clinging to its restrictive practices, reluctant to face the unknown
physical and economic perils of mechanization, and ready to
wreak any possible revenge on the colliery owners. One of the
miners' leaders had remarked of the president of the owners'
mining association, some years before the war, ". . . You might
as well tell the Sphinx of Egypt as say anything to him."[8] Not an
inch must be given, every chance to raise wages must be taken,
and only a strike was likely to wring concessions from the Sphinx.
The Miners' Federation had agreed in 1938 to a levy of two
shillings and sixpence per member in support of Republican
Spain; its members were far too political to accept a Nazi victory
now. But their history predisposed them to attitudes which struck
the toiling poor in the West End clubs as unpatriotic. The coal
crisis emerged inevitably from an industry with such a history;
which is not to deny that the Government could have done much
more to master the situation.

Quite apart from the political objections to nationalization of
Churchill himself and the majority of his colleagues, Whitehall
had sobering memories of the period of state intervention and
state subsidies which had culminated in the General Strike, and
was anxious not to involve itself again in the finances and the
quarrels of the industry. The Government, of course, had ample
powers to control the mines and all to do with them, but it used
them timidly. The Mines Department was a feeble limb of the
Board of Trade, and the control established early in the war was a
weak one; the supplies officers in the mining districts were the
chairmen of the owners' district executives, now paid by the
Government. Even the new system of "dual control" introduced,
with the new Ministry of Fuel and Power, in 1942 merely formalized the Government's growing involvement in a situation
which it was not prepared to dominate effectively.

The 1942 White Paper announced boldly that the Government
had "decided to assume full control over the operation of the
mines, and to organize the industry on the basis of national
service . . ."[9] But this formula of "operational control" left the
owners in charge. The manager of any individual pit, still paid by
the owners, could refuse to execute any order which he deemed
incompatible with its safety, and in practice most demands which
the owners did not like could be resisted on such grounds.

The ministry's policy was to concentrate work on those pits
where coal was easiest to win; to encourage mechanization; and
to make the scanty supply of really first-rate colliery managers

and technicians go further by "grouping" all pits for supervision and technical advice. The first plan was soon dropped after negligible results had been achieved; the third broke on the rock of the owners' opposition. The second met with some success, and the proportion of coal cut and conveyed by machinery increased significantly during the war, but mechanization was a long-term matter, not really a way of boosting production overnight.

A year after the new control had been established, the Minister of Fuel and Power, David Lloyd George's son Gwilym, who was in effect a Conservative, criticized it strongly in the privacy of the War Cabinet. He told the Cabinet that the control had "too little influence upon the day to day management of the pits", and that the managers "were trying to serve two masters, the companies and the state, and even the best of them tended to lose single-mindedness". The answer, in his opinion, was a complete state takeover. Churchill would have none of it, and in the Commons debate in October 1943 finally knocked on the head all hope that the coalition would introduce this, the only rational solution. A miners' leader commented bitterly and typically on this speech that the capitalists were now "crawling out of their funk-holes and claiming their position for the post-war world".[10]

So dual control, with a little tinkering, remained. One or two collieries were in fact directly taken over by the ministry – at the Priory pit in Lanarkshire, this came about because the owners locked out the men until they accepted new rates, and the manager was fined fifty pounds for a breach of the E.W.O. But overall, the ministry had grievous responsibility without full power, and the owners made an excellent thing out of Government intervention. A new device, the Coal Charges Account, had been introduced, whereby the more profitable districts subsidized the weaker ones, and unprofitable pits were kept in business. By the end of 1944, the owners owed the Treasury some twenty-five million pounds via this account, and the Government was helping a great many collieries through its Necessitous Undertakings Scheme. Many collieries abused Government support, increasing their profits by fiddling the Coal Charges Account and using the Necessitous Undertakings Fund as a means of introducing improvements which would stand them in good stead against post-war competition.[11]

III

In spite of Gwilym Lloyd George's efforts, production of deep-mined coal continued to fall – 204 million tons in 1942, 194 millions in 1943, 184 millions in 1944, 175 millions in 1945. Hence the curious fact that opencast mining on a large scale appeared in the precious countryside, and American machines were used to dig coal where it lay near the surface. (Afterwards, the top soil was carefully replaced and sown for the farmer.) The excavations exceeded those for the Panama Canal. The results – over eight and a half million tons in 1944 – were better than expected, but such relatively small proeeeds from such a grand operation merely served to emphasize the seriousness of a situation which they could barely alleviate.

The owners had a simple explanation for the crisis. The miners were shirkers who had used their sudden access of indispensability to renounce discipline and indulge in mass absenteeism. One Conservative parliamentary candidate deplored the lenience shown to certain miners' strike leaders: "Without the least hesitation I say I would never have released these men from prison, except for one purpose – to put them against the wall and shoot them."[12]

"The trouble with coal", according to Hugh Dalton's rather different version, "was simple . . Too many miners had joined the army and the average age of those who were left was too high." This was true; yet the facts of the case were also very complex, and their complexity was not diminished by the over-simplification implicit in statistics of absenteeism. Such statistics showed that the miners were not, in fact, very much grosser offenders than workers in other industries. When the rates were at their highest, in 1944–45, "voluntary" absenteeism accounted for between four and a half and seven per cent of "possible" shifts. The word "possible" indicates a factor often disregarded at the time. Because of the wartime demand for coal, more shifts were offered, and miners who were habitually working a longer week than before the war took most unkindly to suggestions that they were slacking.[13]

In fact, the line between voluntary absenteeism or slacking, and involuntary absenteeism or bad health was impossible to draw accurately. The code of the miner was that if he felt in the least ill, he should not work – it would be unfair to his mates, as a mistake by one man could mean death for many. The ill-favoured birds of the depression years had come home to roost. The nation paid now for its neglect of coal between the wars. Almost frantically, the Government tried to redress this neglect now, and simply reinforced the miner's feeling that no one understood him but his mates. Miners were given a huge supplementary clothing ration – which struck them only as a belated admission by society that they had very special needs. Deprived of their usual quantities of bacon, and suffering like other heavy workers from the inequity of rationing, they were insulted rather than placated by an extra allowance of cheese, which was far from being a popular food with them.

In the 'twenties, the birth rate in the mining villages had fallen in reflection of their hunger and misery. In 1941, forty per cent of miners were over forty years old. Absenteeism, whatever adjective you gave it, was bound to increase as middle-aged men who had suffered, in many cases, from years out of work, filled more shifts and contended with increasingly run-down equipment. Good steel, good rubber, the right wood for pit props, were in short supply. In the older coalfields, in Wales, Scotland and the north-east, where the best seams had largely been worked out, thinner and poorer ones were now hewn, with increasing danger and discomfort. The rate of accidents, already alarming, rose horribly. In each of the years 1943–45 it was higher than one serious accident (involving disablement for more than three days) per every four employees. A fall in output per shift was inevitable.[14]

In the Bevin era of industrial relations, such facts could not be ignored. A growing regard for miners' welfare must, paradoxically, have had the effect of increasing involuntary absenteeism. The scanty medical services on the coalfields were greatly improved. The early stage of the terrible disease of silicosis, which almost literally turns men's lungs to stone, was identified and, sufferers were allowed to leave the pits. Abe Moffat, the Scottish miners' leader, puts it that during the war his men "were for once treated as human beings", and instances that part of the "very posh" Gleneagles Hotel, which had cost five guineas a day, became a rehabilitation centre for injured miners.[15]

In March 1942, the Secretary for Mines, David Grenfell, told the House of Commons that over eighty thousand of "the youngest and strongest men in the industry" had entered the army and sixty thousand had gone into other jobs. M.P.s from both sides pressed for the recall of miners from the forces, but as

Dalton pointed out in May, the Government could not recall them all as it would "pick the eyes out" of some of the army's best regiments – the Northumberland Fusiliers, the Durham Light Infantry, the South Wales Borderers. Miners, for obvious reasons, made good soldiers. And for equally obvious reasons it was hard to find ex-miners to return willingly to the pits, and harder still to find adequate recruits elsewhere. Of a hundred thousand ex-miners registered on Bevin's orders, only a quarter were fit and willing to go back.[16]

Bevin had, of course, applied an E.W.O. to the industry. The Miners' Federation, at a special conference, had accepted the order in a blazing fury. The miner's son, or even his daughter, might well be earning better wages in munitions, a bitter slight to his manhood, when his own low wages had risen only with the cost of living. One miners' leader cried that "There are thousands of skilled miners in Government jobs, some sweeping floors, for higher wages than they can get as skilled colliers."[17] But as usual, the E.W.O. included the guarantee of a minimum wage; and the miner became more and not less militant as he realized that after twenty years of oppression, full employment gave him a chance of making the enemy run.

By a variety of more or less resented shifts and devices, manpower, which had stood at 766,000 in 1939, was stabilized around 710,000 from 1942–45, in spite of the high fall-out of aged men. Young men were found and bound; in 1945, the proportion was higher than pre-war. Bert Coombes, a remarkable miner-writer, described his own feelings when his boy went down. "I thought, as do thousands more, why should our boy have to work in this unnatural place? Had he not the right to walk the land and see the sky every day? Why should his body be battered and his skin blemished, or his lungs choked?"[18]

But more attention was attracted by the "Bevin Boys", those extraordinary symbols of the democratization forced by total war. There was an option to enter the mines rather than the forces, but few had taken it. In July 1943, Bevin warned that, unless more "optants" were forthcoming, compulsion would be used. In December, the hated system of balloting for Bevin Boys began. As youngsters came of age for National Service, the ballot picked out the unlucky numbers, one in ten. It was no use protesting that you wanted to fly the new jet fighters instead. Some boys refused and were jailed. About forty per cent of the unlucky boys appealed against the decision, but only a few petitions were accepted. It was hoped to get fifty thousand boys a year in this way, but the estimate did not allow for the need to train, and to weed out, youths who were going into specialized and dangerous work. In the end, only twenty-one thousand ballottees entered the mines in 1944–45, together with sixteen thousand optants. The boys, mostly seventeen, had a month's physical training, blackboard instruction and introduction to underground work, followed by two weeks' further training at the pit. Only about a third were up to the exacting requirements of work at the face itself – though it was here that the need for strong young men was greatest, since dilution in mining, the upgrading of men to the face, had contributed largely to the fall in productivity. Most Bevin Boys worked on haulage or maintenance underground.

The press had a field day. Here were the scions of professional families directed to work for the miserable wages allotted to juveniles in mining; together, of course, with working-class boys whose case was almost equally bizarre. The Bevin Boys' reports of their crucifixion may have helped to bring home to the public what those wicked striking coal-miners really had to contend with. But their direct contribution to solving the crisis was small. They were a minor component of the hundred thousand or so men working in the coal industry in October 1944 who had been compelled in one way or another to enter or re-enter it. Compelled men were generally, and understandably, prone to deliberate absenteeism and resentment of what the colliery owners called discipline. The young strangers were likely to be the least co-operative of all. Their example was bad for the young miners, already less scrupulous about absenteeism than their fathers. There were notorious cases of Bevin Boys who rarely appeared at the pit, or deserted entirely. They had the wrong muscles and the wrong attitudes.[19]

J. B. Pick, himself a volunteer miner, reports that in the midlands coalfield where he worked, "The miners regarded them with good-natured aloofness, the volunteers with lofty amusement. The miners were kindly but non-committal, and watched them with a half-humorous, half-bitter smile. Here they were, conscripting people for the pits, said the miners, after all these years throwing colliers on the scrap heap and leaving them to rot! . . . It would do the Bevin Boys no harm to see what the pits were like, but as for increasing production – a fat lot of difference they would make. Why, it would be more trouble to teach them than to do the work yourself!"[20]

IV

Pit Production Committees were not the answer either. Even when the new system of dual control rid them of the odium of dealing with absentees, they still had no power to discuss wages, which was in the miners' eyes the key to the problem. Some achieved striking improvements in output, following up suggestions made by the men. More usually, they became a kind of grumbling appendix of the class war. Mark Benney described a P.P.C. meeting in the north-east. "The workmen in the group called attention only to shortcomings in the equipment or layout of the pit. The officials called attention only to shortcomings in the workmen."[21]

Of course, no pay was enough for what the miner did. The Miners' Federation insisted, however, that more pay was the only answer to the crisis. Its members at rank and file level were seized with fits of impatience which could find an outlet only in strike action. Arthur Horner, the Communist firebrand who led the men of South Wales, found himself being denounced as a traitor to his class "because I refused to support strike action to remedy every grievance".[22]

Not all strikes were about wages. Some were about conditions in the pits, the sending underground of miners' sons, the preservation of restrictive practices (which would be most necessary when the next slump came). Many strikes were incomprehensible to an outsider ignorant of an industry where even the pit ponies had their practices so deeply ingrained that they would refuse to pull one tub over their usual load (this zoological phenomenon is well attested); and where, in 1941, twenty-five Northumberland face workers were asked by the management to increase their output, achieved and held the required increase, and were then asked to accept a cut in wages.[23]

In the summer of 1942, the Government appointed the independent "Greene Board" to arbitrate on wages in the industry. It reported rapidly and unanswerably in favour of a large increase and the establishment of a national minimum wage (£4 3s. for underground workers). Though their federation had not received all it had asked for, this was a triumph for the miners. This and later work by the board restored the national basis which had been lost in 1926 and paved the way for the amalgamation of the many district unions which composed the Miners' Federation itself into one National Union in 1944. An independent national tribunal of three was set up, following the Greene award, to pronounce finally on unresolved disputes.

And its first action was disastrous. As the Greene award slipped behind the still-rising cost of living, the Miners' Federation continued to press for better wages. The tribunal made the so-called "Porter Award" early in 1944, raising the national minimum rate. The new rate was still only five pounds for underground workers, and the tribunal had refused to raise piece-rates, so that cherished distinctions between degrees of skill were abolished and Bert Coombes, a miner of thirty years' standing, found himself earning no more than a portly and incompetent optant. As the miners nursed their resentment, the Government announced that the national average earnings for manual workers were now six pounds, ten shillings. There was a storm of strikes.

That morning (Coombes relates) we heard that many South Wales collieries had ceased work and the others in our valley were idle. A meeting of our men was arranged between the day and afternoon shifts, and I was there in the crowded hall . . . The argument that a strike would let our soldiers down was countered by men who had brothers and sons in the forces who, so they claimed, had urged them to fight and maintain their customs or privileges. They argued that they must retain something for those absent ones to come back to, whilst the suggestion that we should wait for further negotiations was swamped by the reply that we had already waited a long while and that we had disputes still unsettled after twelve months' negotiations – and that is still very true. Feeling ebbed and flowed whilst outside the sun shone and the buses waited to see what the men would do. The scales were loaded against continuing work, because all around us collieries were idle and we felt their fight must be ours. Yet it was only a small majority that decided we would not work. Once taken, however, that decision was accepted by all without the least quibble. They streamed out, and homewards. The miners have an extraordinary loyalty to one another in matters like this. Nothing would have induced any man to work in defiance of that decision . . .
Things became quiet. With the colliery idle the local folk could do their washing and even see green leaves emerge from the grey dust mass near the colliery screens. The air was sweet for a few days.[24]

About a hundred thousand men came out in South Wales, and more than that number in the Yorkshire field. As the cold spring winds bit a nation short of fuel, while everyone knew that an invasion of France must come soon, the miners felt the familiar lash of the press. The Government stepped in. The cherished differentials were restored. A new national minimum was accepted in April, and the miners emerged with the highest minimum wage in the country. In a list of average earnings in about a hundred industries, the miner had come eighty-first in 1938; now he stood fourteenth, below only certain munitions trades paying extensive overtime.[25] So far as money went, the miner could now look his escaped son in the face; but he would see no blue scars there.

The pot of strikes, which had overboiled, now returned to its usual simmer. But Bevin was convinced that the furore which had struck at the invasion plans had been the work of Trotskyite agitators. Nothing would satisfy him but a new regulation which would severely penalize those instigating unofficial strikes. The General Council of the T.U.C. accepted it. On April 17th, 1944, Regulation 1AA was unveiled, whereby an agitator might win himself five years in jail or a fine of five hundred pounds. The left was outraged, and Aneurin Bevan was very nearly thrown out of the Labour Party again for leading a revolt against Bevin. In a less hectic time, these ludicrous tales of Trotskyites would have been laughed to death; and in fact, after a split in the Labour Party had been narrowly averted, Regulation 1AA was never used.[26]

The British Trotskyites were a tiny body, whose genuine enterprise was not matched by any noticeable success. Two infinitesimal warring fragments, both of which had claimed to be the true British section of the Fourth International, had fused as recently as March into the Revolutionary Communist Party. The larger of the two bodies, the Workers' International League, had with great efforts raised its membership to two hundred and fifty, under the vigorous leadership of Jock Haston.

Haston, an ex-sailor endowed with immense resourcefulness and a pungent sense of humour, had kept his troops together through a series of unsung and anticlimactic adventures. At the outbreak of war, the W.I.L. had anticipated suppression, and a section of the leadership had evacuated to Ireland, only to return when it found that the Government had no interest in gagging it. Indeed, Haston had later been able to persuade the Paper Control that the W.I.L.'s *Socialist Appeal* had had a pre-war circulation of twenty thousand, and had duly been given a paper quota sufficient to print that number. Its columns had unswervingly denounced the imperialist war and had prophesied more or less instantaneous revolution.

Haston seems to have enjoyed his sudden notoriety, solemnly assuring a *Daily Mail* reporter, "Hitler drops me the money packets when he raids London." In the summer of 1944, he was prosecuted, with three associates, and imprisoned, for assisting a recent strike of Tyneside engineering apprentices. Bevin did not deploy 1AA against them; he invoked the 1927 Trades Disputes Act, a vindictive Conservative reprisal for the General Strike and so hardly an apt instrument for a Labour minister. The trial vastly increased the R.C.P.'s self-importance. But in September, the convictions were quashed on appeal. Regulation 1AA acquired a further ironic footnote when Haston stood in a South Wales by-election in 1945. He received 1,781 votes, well below a Welsh Nationalist, and his Labour opponent won with 31,000.[27]

V

Absenteeism continued to rise and output continued to fall. No one, of course, had any right to cast stones. Colliers' wages were now more than adequate to maintain the traditional, communal standard of living of the pit villages, where everyone knew his neighbour's earnings and the status race was so remote that housewives might all deliberately buy the same wallpaper from the local Co-op store. (In any case, shortages were particularly acute in mining areas; no use having enough money for woollen blankets if you couldn't buy them.) Men could now take their "wages" not as money, but as leisure, as freedom from the dark and the dirt. Young miners especially tended to earn what they needed and then stay away to enjoy their money.

The fact was that mining was not civilized. The old pits of Durham, damaged irreparably by generations of managers looking for short-cuts to quick profits rather than to the husbanding of precious natural resources; the mentality of owners who deliberately saved the better seams for after the war and refused to mechanize in case they were nationalized; such things were anomalous in the new world of Spitfires, radar and light metals (though these depended on the precious black stuff). They belonged to Nineteenth-century England.

So did other industries with similar problems. In the iron

mines, too, fathers would not let their sons follow in their foot-steps, and only direction and the use of optants halted a decline in manpower. Even so, many who had taken the option decided soon that they would rather face death in the army. Zinc smelting was another option, also because its conditions were repulsive in an age of full employment; and it was difficult to hold men in hot noisy work with antiquated plant in the drop-forging industry.

Shipbuilding was a half-way house to the new world of modern engineering. The shipyards had suffered as badly as the pits between the wars. The number of workers had fallen by a hundred thousand, yet as late as July 1939, twenty per cent of the remainder were still unemployed. With this history went an unappeasable suspicion of the bosses, and also restrictive practices, designed to spread work as far as possible, which not even the Battle of the Atlantic could root out. Here, too, workers were ageing, wages were low, and the work might be very cold and dirty, or conducted in small compartments filled with the fumes of red lead. Dilution proved difficult; like mining, the work called for trained muscles, and raw memories enhanced the suspicion that dilutees would take veterans' jobs when the bad times came again with peace. "Whenever dilution is raised", complained a Ministry of Labour official, "we seem to be brought up short against this ghostly squad of unemployed boilermakers."[28]

What is much more astonishing to think of than the prevalence of disputes in coal-mining is the fact that essential work was never brought to a stop for lack of coal except on a small scale, and then as a result of transport problems, in the later winters of the war. Enormous quantities of black manna were still hewn from the ground at the expense of broken limbs, ruined lungs and lives, young and old, spent chiefly in darkness, often in circumstances which one observer said reminded him "more of work in the galleys which is portrayed in the films than modern conditions of industrial labour".[29]

Afterwards, the men would gather at their club to regain, in enormous quantities of beer, what they had lost in sweat during the shift, and would turn again and again to the work which obsessed them. "They loved and hated it," noted Mark Benney, "were proud and ashamed of it, fascinated and repelled by it. They noticed their own confusion of feeling about it and laughed helplessly. 'They's more cowels won in t' club than they is in t' pit,' they would confess of their inability to leave work behind them at the end of the shift." The miner, as many observers have pointed out, has seen his life as a metaphysical drama, the good

community against the callous employer, the hewer embattled
with nature herself. This war, for the men who waged it, was in no
sense subservient to the battles of North Africa. When the pits
were nationalized after the war, the north-eastern miners in their
massed choirs celebrated the event with a song so old that, as
A. L. Lloyd tells us, when it was first printed at the end of the
eighteenth century it had long been corrupted almost to inco-
herence. "The Colliers' Rant" describes how a miner, pick in
hand, fights with the Devil in the dark of the pit and emerges
victorious.[30]

BIRTH OF A WHITLEY

The Ministry of Aircraft Production's demands could be cut; but after
they had been cut it was essential that they should be met. This was the
salient conclusion of the manpower discussions of mid-1943 . . . According to the Prime Minister, the greatest shortcoming threatening the
war effort was [the] falling off in the planned supply of aircraft.
Somehow or other, the labour must be found for aircraft production
. . . Intake into the women's services would have to be reduced to a
minimum; women up to the age of fifty inclusive would have to register
for employment; the Ministry of Aircraft Production would have to
keep the mechanics loaned to them by the R.A.F.; the services would
have to postpone, for the time being, their claims on men employed on
aircraft production; the Ministry of Supply must so far as possible
make its releases of men in areas where the Ministry of Aircraft Production needed them; the highest preference must in effect be given to
the filling of vacancies in aircraft production. These measures were
willingly approved by the War Cabinet.

Sir Keith Hancock and Margaret Gowing, *British War Economy*[1]

I

If modern warfare had any glamour for the people of Britain, it
rested in the clean lines of the fighter planes which won the Battle
of Britain, and later in the huge dark silhouettes of the four-
engined bombers which set out in their hundreds at night to
destroy German lives and, hopefully, German industry. Even the
designers were adulated. Leslie Howard impersonated R. J.
Mitchell, designer of the Spitfire, in a popular film. When the
nation learned, in January 1944, that a dour Lancastrian named
Frank Whittle had perfected a jet engine, he was, in his own

words, "besieged by reporters and snowed under with mail . . . I found it was virtually impossible to move about in public without being accosted by complete strangers who recognized me from the published photographs . . ."[2]

Figures tell the story of a monstrous growth, in which Churchill's reliance first on Fighter Command, then on Bomber Command, was the main leaven. Britain made 3,000 warplanes in 1938; 8,000 in 1939; 15,000 in 1940; 20,000 in 1941; 24,000 in 1942; 26,000 in 1943; a peak of 26,461 in 1944. And the planes themselves changed constantly in the direction of greater heaviness and complexity. According to M.A.P.'s index, based on man-hours and structure weight, production trebled between January 1940 and January 1942, and doubled again by March 1944. In that last month, 2,715 planes were delivered, and M.A.P. contracts were employing 1,700,000 people in the engineering, chemical and metal industries.

Over a thousand different types of material were used in the production of aircraft, some of them arcane and precious. Sailors braved the U-boats to bring cryolite from Canada, balsa wood from Ecuador, farina pine from Brazil. At the other extremes, many elementary shortages which harried civilians in such banal substances as paper, cotton and glue could be largely explained by the imperious demands of the plane-makers. A light alloy industry was created virtually from nothing to serve aircraft production; and between 1940 and 1944, the production of fabricated aluminium and aluminium alloys tripled. The manufacture of aircraft was by then the pre-eminent concern of the New England.

II

The beginning of rearmament in the mid-thirties had created a boom in aircraft shares, with many well-taken opportunities for speculators. But before that the industry had been a small-scale affair, kept alive by the enthusiasm of its pioneers more than by any rich pickings. Aircraft had been big business for a while in the First World War, but afterwards the restriction of military spending and the disappointing progress of civil aviation had meant that "most of the aircraft factories were little more than experimental aircraft shops built around their design establishments". Such enterprises could often trace their origins directly to a pioneer flyer who had assembled a few mechanics around him in the Homeric epoch before the First World War. Even in 1935, the industry had employed only about thirty-five thousand workers, and the Vickers factory at Weybridge, with seventeen hundred, had been a large one by the stands of the time.[3]

The Air Ministry had looked for its planes to a group of sixteen aircraft firms and four engine firms known to its friends as "the family" and to its critics as "the ring". The lesser firms which had mushroomed in the late 1930s in the hope of sharing in the rearmament boom had complained bitterly at this "favouritism", but war showed that even twenty firms were too many. The small design departments competed for a limited supply of draughts-men. Factories were small, and the shortage of floor space made it difficult to begin work on new types while the old ones were still needed. Managements were used to handling small bodies of skilled craftsmen; when war came they were often incompetent to deal with masses of inexperienced workers.

In 1940, the efforts of the plane-makers had seemed to set the example for the rest of industry; in 1941–42, the malaise of the aircraft industry seemed to symbolize that of war production as whole.

Above all, the big new heavy bombers were the problem. In May 1942, production of fighters was above target, but that of heavy bombers fell short by fifty-two on a target of a hundred and ninety-three – that is, by well over twenty-five per cent.[4]

The war played unmercifully on the weaknesses of the straggling, ramshackle industry which it had created. One thinks first of the large factories – A. V. Roe at Manchester, "making Lancaster bombers"; Vickers Supermarine at Castle Bromwich, "making Spitfires". If "making" an aircraft was seen as assembling the plane for delivery, only some twenty-one or twenty-two thousand workers were "making" Spitfires at peak; of twenty thousand delivered, all but a few hundred were "made" at two Vickers factories. But from the outset of the Spitfire's production in the rearmament period, Vickers had subcontracted for about three-quarters of the aircraft's parts. The Merlin engine which the Spitfire used was "made" by Rolls Royce – who used three hundred subcontractors. From 1936 to 1945, the Government spent nearly four hundred million pounds on buildings and plant for the aircraft industry; this included both "shadow" factories made from scratch and extensions to existing firms, and the expense was spread over nearly two thousand, eight hundred premises. But at peak some fourteen thousand engineering works were employed on M.A.P contracts.[5] "Aircraft industry" covered a multitude of metamorphoses.

The great motor-car firms had, of course, been brought in very early to employ their similar engineering skills on more deliberately offensive weapons. But the wooden Mosquito, the most remarkable British plan born during the war itself, made use of more unlikely branches of industry, right down to housewives like Mrs Hale of Welwyn Garden City who made components in her own home with a group of neighbours. Among the four hundred and more subcontractors who worked on the Mosquito in Britain and the Dominions were firms of furniture makers, church pew carvers and pianoforte makers. Littlewood's, the famous football pool firm, made floors for Halifax bombers, fuselages for Lancaster bombers, and even complete Wellington bombers. Paper manufacturers helped to make disposable "drop tanks" for petrol which increased the range of fighters.[6]

The Government, of course, encouraged subcontracting as a way of increasing capacity. But it reached riotous proportions. A motor dealer with a few good mechanics could wax great on the production of components. At one point, an M.A.P. inquiry into the subcontracting arrangements for the Lancaster "revealed at one firm that they had subcontracted some work to another firm which had in turn passed some on to another, and so on along a chain of subcontractors, one of whom had subcontracted some of the work back to the original parent firm itself!" By 1943, when the Select Committee on National Expenditure undertook one of its periodic surveys of the industry, some forty-two per cent of construction and assembly work was subcontracted, and the position was disquieting. Subcontractors rarely took advantage of the technical advice offered by M.A.P. to those who were struggling to produce delicate and vital components. The bottom of the barrel was staring through the lees, and the "little men" still free to take on subcontracts were often "unsatisfactory in regard to quality, delivery or price". Gross overcharging seems to have been common.[7]

The deliberate "dispersal" of the main firms in 1940-41 had added its own complexities. The aircraft firms had had little or no experience of large-scale production until the rearmament period and even then what Professor Postan calls "stubbornly persisting small workshop methods" had maintained themselves in many quarters. Now their very limited expertise was spread thinly over thousands of subcontractors and dispersal units, and previously small main factories had swollen. The industry had outgrown its capacity to organize itself; the image is one of a brawny parent in nappies. Nineteen main aircraft firms had, in January 1938, been

managing forty-five factories with more than a hundred workers.
Exactly five years later they were managing three hundred and
twenty-three such units, and one group which ran eighty-five of
these larger factories also had "some two hundred and sixty-five"
smaller groups of workers under their control. Many young
managers and potential managers were in the forces. Elderly
foremen suddenly found themselves in command of whole "dispersal units". "The enormous expansion of the industry has
entailed the up-grading of large numbers of men with relatively
little experience", reported the Select Committee, "and it is freely
admitted by managements that they have had to promote many
men whom they would not normally so promote."[8]

But at least the "professional" firms understood the design of
their machines, and their experience must be transmitted somehow to their motley complement of "daughters". The most
developed form which this tutelage took was the "group" system
used for the big four-engined bombers as they lumbered slowly
into production in 1940–42. The Halifax bomber was undertaken by a group which included the parent firm, Handley Page,
together with English Electric (which emerged after the war as an
aircraft designing firm in its own right), Fairey Aviation, the
Rootes motor-car firm, and an enterprise combining the London
Passenger Transport Board with several London car firms. The
theory was that the parent supplied drawings, with lists of tools
and gauges, and freely gave advice to other firms which in peacetime had been, or might yet be, its competitors.

Some daughters of course were giants in their own fields, most
able to learn. Ford – naturally enough among the leading
exponents in Britain of mass production – were called in to work
with Rolls Royce, the most prestigious practitioners of "old
fashioned" workshop methods, who handed over the blue prints
of their magnificent Merlin engine ("most patriotically", as the
historian of Ford's war effort observes). Ford broke the crafts-
man-tailored machine down to suit their own methods, and by
the end of the war they were employing seventeen thousand
workers in a big new factory in Manchester, of whom not more
than a hundred had had anything to do with an aero engine
before the experiment had begun. Yet Ford's Merlin parts had to
be, and were, interchangeable with those from Rolls Royce.[9]

But often the harassed parents neglected their daughters or the
daughters were too wilful to accept advice. Mark Benney, who
worked as a fitter in several London bomber factories, gives a
vivid portrait of a smallish "quality" car firm involved in the

group system. The managing director owed his job to his ability to sell cars, not making them; he was now lost, but he would not admit it. During the tooling-up, the drawings sent by the parent were often inaccurate, and "sometimes whole sets of tools were designed round a drawing error and had to be scrapped". The parent firm was soon blamed for all blunders. Benney observes that while much of the new labour supply had been trained at G.T.C.s before entering the industry, "there was no such institution for managements. The manufacturers who were called in to take the main strain of the expanded aircraft programme received not so much as an official booklet warning them of some of the difficulties confronting them . . . Instruction was left to the parent aircraft firms, and inevitably, as the demands on their technicians multiplied, became sketchier. Even the most modest managements were therefore reduced to unprofitable methods of trial and error; while the more complacent and arrogant and pigheaded (and the successful car manufacturer taking over the products of an industry much smaller than his own is likely to become such) was given free play for all his more violent preconceptions and vanities."[10]

And even the aircraft firms themselves, as the Select Committee on National Expenditure found, were slow to learn new managerial methods from each other and still in some cases too individualistic to call on each other for time-saving technical help.

M.A.P.'s contracts with the "family" or "ring" firms in the Society of British Aircraft Constructors were governed by the so-called McLintock Agreements which seemed to avoid a crude Cost Plus basis. During the period of the first production of a new plane, it was recognized, Cost Plus could not be avoided; but once production had got into its stride, a price would be fixed in advance. In practice, however, wrangles between M.A.P. and its contractors ensured that even in 1943 a large proportion of orders were completed before a final price had been agreed, which weakened the incentive to economy in labour and materials, and the urge to harry profiteering subcontractors.[11]

On top of these numerous factors making for "idle time" and newspaper scandals, there was the necessary flow of new designs and modifications. When the Metropolitan Vickers factory in Manchester switched over in May 1941 from the Manchester bomber to the much improved Lancaster, no less than 9,276 new jigs and tools were needed. A further 256 modifications called for a further 2,000 jigs and tools, and when the Lincoln replaced the Lancaster in July 1943, 7,000 more were needed.[12] Such switches could cause demoralizing hold-ups. Had the factories themselves been larger, these need not have occurred. As it was, the biggest British aircraft factories had three thousand to fifteen thousand employees at a time when their American counterparts commonly had twenty thousand to forty thousand workers, and along with this went a dire shortage of floor space, which was compounded by the failure of aircraft managements to introduce full double-shift working.

III

After Beaverbrook left M.A.P. in the summer of 1941, his successors established a more formal system of functions and designations in its upper reaches, but it retained a reputation for unscrupulousness and unorthodoxy.

M.A.P., with twenty-one thousand staff at peak, was smaller than the Ministries of Supply, Labour and Food, but it reflected the general bureaucratic elephantiasis. Retired civil servants were brought back and the retirement age was raised to sixty-five. The expertise of university teachers, professional men, and, of course, imported businessmen was used at the highest levels, while lower down large numbers of women were brought in to swell the clerical staff; but permanent civil servants retained almost all the key posts. In any case, dons and lawyers shared the background and the attitudes of the doges of Whitehall, and were happy to abide by the traditions. Businessmen tended to fret more about red tape and ancestral caution, but they too grew used to them as the war went on, even in M.A.P. where their influx had been most dramatic and riotous.

M.A.P. had six directorates general, with special responsibility for aircraft; for engines; for equipment and armament; for raw materials; for repair; and for planning, programmes and statistics. The first included separate directorates for bombers, for fighters, and for naval aircraft. Each of these was subdivided into deputy directorates, and below the deputy directors were found the assistant directors who were responsible each for a specific type of aircraft. At this level, every factory of every contractor had someone specially charged with overlooking its work. In the factories themselves, the Air Ministry, long before the war, had installed resident technical officers, who now came under M.A.P., and in many of the larger firms M.A.P. also had overseers, usually senior R.A.F. officers with plenipotentiary powers, and aircraft production officers with lower status but a good deal of influence. So the tentacles of bureaucracy spread downwards and outwards. M.A.P., of course, controlled allocations of raw materials and labour to its contractors. Under the system of "embodiment loans", M.A.P. itself placed all the contracts for certain vital components – engines, propellers, turrets, guns, radio and so on – and supplied them to firms as it saw fit.[13]

When Sir Stafford Cripps went to M.A.P. in the autumn of 1942, he completed the ousting of the crude "carrot" planning which had been Beaverbrook's unfortunate legacy to M.A.P. The publication of the ministry's new "Minimum Programme" in January 1943 was designed to exorcize illusions. It proposed 4,250 fewer aircraft in 1943 than the previous programme – yet it still called for an increase of thirty per cent over the actual output of 1942. The new theory was that M.A.P. set a realistic minimum programme for each firm based on its past record and the firm's own views of its likely performance. Since the inefficiency of backward firms could not merely be endorsed, a small "carrot" element had to remain, with M.A.P. revising firms' own estimates upwards. Shortfalls continued to occur, and although the new programme gave the R.A.F. a more reliable picture than before of what it was likely to get in the near future it had, like its predecessors, to be adjusted downwards.[14]

However, Sir Stafford's tenure of office at M.A.P., which concluded only with the war, has generally been depicted as an immense success. War, and the full employment which it had brought, placed an ever growing premium on efficient management in all spheres of industry, but nowhere was the new ideology preached with more sound and fury than by Cripps at M.A.P. In March 1943, he rudely nationalized the important firm of Shorts on the grounds of inefficient management, expelling its board of directors. Certain other firms were forced to change managerial personnel. Soon after his arrival, Cripps created a Production Efficiency Board to ginger up laggard firms with advice on management techniques. Personnel management, in which aircraft firms were notoriously backward, was given special attention – regional personnel officers were appointed and four courses were established at universities to train personnel managers for the aircraft industry. Cripps was a tireless visitor of factories, averaging eighteen such pastoral calls per month during his period at M.A.P. Everywhere, he took the gospel of managerial efficiency and goodwill to all men. Extolling the work of the joint production committees, he called, with the home-made lemonade, as it were, boiling more briskly than ever in his veins, for the obliteration of the barriers between "we" and "they", workers and management. For the sake of reducing German cities to rubble, that class war which he had preached with equal fervour in the 1930s must be put aside. In Manchester and Coventry at least, there must be human brotherhood. Nevertheless, in the remaining years of war, shortfalls and absenteeism continued, and strikes increased. Management, like patriotism, was not enough.[15]

M.A.P., like the rest of Whitehall, was now given over to an adoration of statistics. A guilty conscience had gripped the civil service around 1941, when M.A.P. had set up its own statistics and programmes department under Professor Jewkes of Manchester University (later to become better known as a bitter opponent of "socialist" planning). One of Jewkes's assistants has written impishly that "once the figures were called 'statistics', they acquired the authority and sanctity of Holy Writ. The veneration paid to figures increased when they were neatly presented in well laid out tables, and reached its height if these tables were printed."[16]

The worship of statistics helped to produce a frame of mind in which the production of useless aircraft was preferred to the production of no aircraft at all. If a factory was making an obsolescent plane, and could not for the moment be transferred to producing the latest type, M.A.P. kept it hard at work. Hence the Whitley bomber, which had been obsolescent almost as soon as it had been ordered (although it had become one of Beaverbrook's five "priority types" in May 1940), was produced in numbers six times as great as had originally been planned, and continued in production until the middle of 1943, the peak of the war effort. The official historian solemnly records that "At the time when it was rolling out in highest numbers it was no longer usable as a bomber and was employed chiefly for glider towing, paratroop dropping and Coastal Command work. But many, perhaps most, of the Whitleys produced during the war scarcely left the Aircraft Storage Units."[17]

M.A.P.'s repeated demands for more, and more, and more manpower and womanpower assumed, with appropriate blind faith, that the planned aircraft programme would actually be achieved. Further, there was known to be a difference between the number of men required to make an aeroplane of a given type after the design had been established in long-term production, as compared with the period of its introduction. Thus, in a firm making Halifax bombers, 487 men were needed per aeroplane in April 1942; a year later, only 220 were needed. But could 267 surplus men be uprooted and sent where they were most wanted? The overall central estimates gave no picture of local needs. In any case, firms worked their own version of the carrot principle and pitched their demands for labour as high as they dared; if they asked for a hundred men they might, they reasoned, be given the seventy-five they thought they really needed. Furthermore, they could then blame their own shortfalls and shortcomings on M.A.P. or Ernie Bevin; if only, they could lament, they had been given the extra twenty-five workers they had asked for, all would have been different. Similarly, one school of thought in M.A.P. was terrified that the ministry would actually get all the workers it demanded, for then M.A.P.'s own alibi would be shattered. There would always be a let-out however, since a favourite qualifying clause stipulated that the labour must be "of the right type and available at the times and in the places required" – though what these latter were, none of the eminent social scientists in M.A.P.'s statistics department could be sure. So the firms bluffed M.A.P., M.A.P. bluffed Bevin, and the matter was finally settled when Anderson or Churchill took a round figure and subtracted several hundred thousand. Then girls of twenty were extracted from Scottish villages and the production of Whitleys was nobly maintained.[18]

The main instruments of planning in M.A.P., the most august expression of faith, were the programmes. For all the saintly assurance of their statistics, the changing pattern of the war, new demands from above, new failures in the factories, together ensured that the programmes were always in flux. In the case of engines, we are told, ". . . The final stages of getting out the programme were always a mad scramble. The maximum amount of agreement was secured by frantically telephoning to the firms to obtain their compliance with some last-minute change, and pressure was exerted on the typists and printers to ensure that the programme was issued before some new change in circumstances rendered it out of date."[19]

So Sir Stafford achieved his apotheosis, as the High Priest of subtly organized, dexterously managed, and even, under his influence, deeply dedicated, inefficiency.

IV

For those who worked in it, the aircraft industry shared, and
usually exaggerated, the trends of war industry as a whole.
M.A.P. led, for instance, in the field of propaganda to workers.
Between mid-1941 and mid-1942 over a thousand visits to factories by pilots were arranged, and two hundred thousand posters
and bulletins were distributed to M.A.P. contractors; thereafter,
this type of thing actually increased, in spite of sardonic remarks
about the paper shortage.[20] M.A.P. led also with dilution, which
was relatively easy, because aircraft work was mostly light, and
women could perform most types of job. Eventually, fifty per cent
of all workers in aero-engine factories, and a considerably higher
proportion in the aircraft factories proper, were women and girls.

But it was in wages, above all, that aircraft work went furthest
and fastest. Even in the rearmament period, wages in the industry
had been high compared with those paid in engineering at large.
Its rapid expansion had ensured that it had set the pace in forcing
up wages in competition for skilled labour, and it had had no
foreign competition for the favours of the R.A.F. to keep its
notions frugal. Its heartland in the midlands was also the centre
of the car industry, which had already paid exceptional wages,
and against which it had competed directly for labour.

Furthermore, the rapid extension of payment by results, which
was a feature of war industry in Britain, had peculiar consequences for wages in aircraft factories. It was relatively easy to
fix "realistic" piece rates for an uncomplicated item like a shell,
which was run off in large numbers, each one identical. But with
aircraft, there was a great difference between the first exploratory
months when a factory began to produce a new type in small
quantities, and the time when planes dashed off the assembly line
in considerable numbers. The trade unions, naturally, took
unkindly to any lowering of prices. "Prices fixed, efficiently or
inefficiently, when the flow of materials was irregular, the number
of jobs required limited and the workers relatively new or inexperienced at the job remained the same when the flow was
smooth, numbers increased and the workers had invented and
applied numerous gadgets and improvements for speeding
production."[21]

And some firms paid huge bonuses to attract labour. The
Eldorado of the engineering worker was the aircraft industry in
the west midlands. Here, two M.A.P. inquiries in 1942 found

bonuses up to five hundred and eighty-one per cent of the regional standard rate being paid, and the *average* bonus in one factory was three hundred and seventy-two per cent. Certain factories were paying as much as four pounds, ten shillings a day – more than an agricultural labourer or railwayman was likely to earn in a week. Even women might take home three pounds a day, and both these figures exclude overtime, which was generally the cause of high earnings in war industry.

However, all the plagues which managers and ministers complained of as inevitably attendant on super-high earnings had not accumulated in a black flood to overwhelm the midlands. Cripps's Production Efficiency Board, when it investigated the situation in Coventry, claimed there was a waste of labour. "In each factory there was evidence of slackness and lack of discipline. Operators were slow in starting work at the beginning of each shift and after each break, and there was complete stoppage of work from fifteen to thirty minutes before each break. The Board's discussions showed that managements were aware of these weaknesses but felt powerless to remedy them."

Yet, taking Bristol aero engines as an example, the evidence showed that the cost of producing them, either in manpower or in money, was no higher in this Sodom than in other parts of the country. "Indeed", adds the official historian, "indications were to the contrary." Little progress was made in rooting out these sinful practices, and the earnings position in Coventry was officially regarded as "unsatisfactory" as late as June 1944.[22]

Most of the relatively few firms which paid big money were in the midlands. It was in the aircraft industry in general and in the midlands in particular that the shop stewards' movement had gathered momentum in the rearmament and early war period. At the famous meeting of shop stewards in London in October 1941, the list of factories from which delegates came "compared closely with the list of the main M.A.P. contractors and shadow factories". That conference was markedly under C.P. domination, and when C.P. membership expanded rapidly in the first three months of 1942, it was surely no coincidence that the greatest increases occurred in the midlands. High wages, paradoxically, went with class consciousness.[23]

Mass Observation, in its peregrination through war industry in 1941–42, concluded that "The least satisfied section of the community engaged in war industry is probably the highly skilled male worker, who is in a stronger position than ever before and is getting relatively high pay and prestige." He could afford to laugh away threats of dismissal; when no other was forthcoming to replace him, few managements would invoke the E.W.O. against a lazy but gifted worker. As one director glumly put it, "The tool maker is the complete boss of industry today, and he knows it." But the skilled man had many problems, which helped to explain the bitterness with which he viewed "idle time", He was liable to transfer to worse paid areas, by order of Bevin, unless he was constantly employed on important work. If piece rates were high, earnings might fluctuate considerably, and a modification in design or a halt in the supply of components might shrivel them.[24] The skilled worker was vividly conscious that the management needed him more than he needed them, and that boards of directors which after the war might amputate his wages, as in 1922, were now conspiring to pay him as much as they dared so as to keep him with them. Yet such straw dictators claimed the right to rule his life, to take the best of the sanitary facilities, and to eat in a separate place with napkins tucked in their white collars.

There was no counterpart in the Second World War to the acutely political, largely syndicalist shop stewards' movement of the First World War, yet in those Coventry factories which so appalled the Production Efficiency Board, the employees had arrived at a position where they could set their own hours and work as they wanted to, thrusting an impotent management to one side, and getting on with the job at their own pace, perfectly well.

V

Altogether, some one hundred and twenty thousand planes were built in Britain during the war. Many were unglamorous, if useful – little Tiger Moth biplanes for elementary training, Austers for observation and light air transport. Others were operational failures. But the best British aircraft were feats of design and engineering which inspire respect even in the later age of long-range missiles: Mitchell's Spitfire, Camm's Hurricane, Wallis's Wellington, Chadwick's Lancaster, Bishop's Mosquito – evocative names for oddly beautiful creations.

For all the Wellington's "geodetic" construction, which meant that it could limp home miraculously after severe punishment, and for all the wooden frame of the Mosquito, these planes did not represent fundamental revolutions in design. Until the Gloster Meteor jet fighter, with its Whittle jet engine, went into action in July 1944, the most advanced planes were still based on technical innovations of the early 1930s. In the field of jets, the Germans had a lead of sorts – their first jet had flown in August 1939, two years before the test Meteor, and they had the first jet fighter in service, though it was so unreliable that it took an improvident toll of pilots' lives. In the field of rocketry, the Germans were years ahead.

Yet British planes were probably better than German ones for most of the war. The basis of this success was not a rapid flow of new types, though the Mosquito and the Lancaster were both designed during the war itself. It was, rather, the adaptation and modification of proven ones. No satisfactory naval types existed (though the quaint Swordfish biplane did contrive to rout the Italian navy). But the Hurricane deputized as a naval fighter, and the Spitfire begat the Seafire. The Spitfire, after continuous modification, ended the war over two thousand pounds heavier and nearly one hundred miles per hour faster than when it had begun; its advance depended on the Merlin engine, which likewise increased greatly in horsepower through successive mark numbers. With these, and the other "great" planes, it was the basic soundness or brilliance of the original design which made them so versatile.

The aptest case in point was the Mosquito, which Sir Wilfred Freeman had ordered from De Havillands "off the drawing board" at the end of 1939. Originally designed as a fast unarmed bomber, it was adapted for reconnaissance, as a night fighter, as a meteorological plane, and as the fastest passenger aircraft in the world, whisking V.I.P.s from Britain to neutral Sweden and back. And so on; at the end of 1943, there were about fifteen different "marks" of the Mosquito simultaneously in service. The advance of British aircraft during the war is summed up neatly by a comparison of the twin-engined Mosquito bomber of 1943 and the twin-engined Wellington of 1939. The Mosquito could carry an equal bomb load – but 170 miles per hours faster, 300 miles further and 21,000 feet higher.[25]

Except for Beaverbrook's first hectic months at M.A.P., when research and development were obstructed by the overriding demand for more planes at once and at all costs, the doctrine of the R.A.F., with which M.A.P. complied, was that modifications and new equipment should be introduced as soon as possible, whatever the effect on the production figures. Cripps told both sides of the aircraft industry in September 1943, ". . . Quality is more important than quantity. Nothing but the best and most up-to-date is good enough for our magnificent airmen."[26] This makes the case of the Whitley more bizarre than ever. Yet, from one angle, the story of the aircraft industry from 1935 to 1945 was a success story. Out of lies, bungles, profiteering and chaos, emerged a large number of superfine planes. And then, many of them were deployed uselessly in Churchill's efforts to destroy urban life in Germany.

Chapter Eight

War on the Mind:
Science, Religion and the Arts

The Ministry of Truth – Minitrue, in Newspeak – was startlingly different from any other object in sight. It was an enormous pyramidal structure of glittering white concrete, soaring up, terrace after terrace, three hundred metres into the air. From where Winston stood it was just possible to read, picked out on its white face in elegant lettering, the three slogans of the Party:

—WAR IS PEACE
—FREEDOM IS SLAVERY
—IGNORANCE IS STRENGTH

The Ministry of Truth contained, it was said, three thousand rooms above ground level, and corresponding ramifications below. Scattered about London there were just three other buildings of similar appearance and size. So completely did they dwarf the surrounding architecture that from the roof of Victory Mansions you could see all four of them simultaneously. They were the homes of the four ministries between which the entire apparatus of government was divided. The Ministry of Truth, which concerned itself with news, entertainment, education, and the fine arts. The Ministry of Peace, which concerned itself with war. The Ministry of Love, which maintained law and order. And the Ministry of Plenty, which was responsible for economic affairs. Their names, in Newspeak: Minitrue, Minipax, Miniluv, and Miniplenty.

George Orwell, *1984*

THE PLAYING FIELDS OF MALVERN (I)

... All facts are good: they may be facts about bad things, but if they are facts they are good and valuable.

Sir Robert Watson Watt[1]

I

In 1943, the Select Committee on National Expenditure found it necessary to warn that "The aeronautical industry in this country is suffering from an acute shortage of scientific and technical men, and there are not enough adequately qualified men available to maintain the industry at the proper level of efficiency."[2]

The R.A.F., the pampered prodigy of this new war, was an inherently technical and scientific service, quite obviously depending for its efficiency on the most advanced equipment. So M.A.P. found itself involved in the two most dramatic scientific and technical developments of the war: radar and the atomic bomb. It was the Air Ministry's Tizard Committee which initiated work on radar in the mid-'thirties. When the Maud Sub-committee was set up in 1940 to promote work towards a nuclear bomb, it came under the aegis of M.A.P. Yet in that same year, Beaverbrook summoned the main midwife of radar, Watson Watt, from his bed and told him that he was stopping the development of the invention, which was "grievously cramping the freedom of action and the success of the fighter pilots".[3] Like many others, he was reluctant to admit, or incapable of understanding, that science had "spoiled war".

However, no one, "in the know", could fail to recognize the essential part which airborne radar played in the growing success of the night fighters early in 1941. Their pilots ostentatiously swallowed Vitamin A tablets "for night vision" in front of journalists, and paraded before visits to air bases in smoked glasses, but in fact the ace night fighter, "Cat's-eye" Cunningham, privately attributed all but one of his score of confirmed victims to radar. A distinguished Oxford physicist was among the observers who flew with him. "These special pilots and observers", it has been pointed out, "were more like men working in a laboratory than ordinary aircrews operating standard equipment."[4]

Matters went further. One of the scientists who developed the OBOE target-finding device for bombers was personally responsible, when the equipment was first used, for bombing the *Scharnhorst* and *Gneisenau* in Brest harbour. But he was sitting in front of equipment in England by which he gave the signal to release the bombs over the target. The Air Ministry realized with horror that a civilian was dropping bombs, and sent an officer in blue uniform to replace him.[5]

Yet an indignant group of scientists calculated after the war that during 1944 the time given to science in the Home and Forces Services of the B.B.C. worked out at about half an hour a week. This compared with six or seven hours for religion, ten or twelve hours for non-scientific talks, and sixty or so hours for the various types of music.[6] Of the members of the British cabinet, only Anderson, Cripps and Cherwell had had the scientific training which could give them swift insight into current developments. Science had changed, and was changing, the nature of war and peace, yet was hardly stirring the consciousness of the most avid saloon bar politicians.

Conversely, war had taken a dominating grip over certain fields of science. J. D. Bernal had remarked that even the definition of pure mathematics by its great practitioner G. H. Hardy – "This subject has no practical use; that is to say, it cannot be used for promoting directly the destruction of human life or for accentuating the present inequalities in the distribution of wealth" – has been belied by developments during and since the war.[7]

II

It was radar, swiftly extending its domain in all three services, which spearheaded the renewed incursion of science into war. The fundamental principles of radar had been known in 1924, when Edward Appleton had used them in his work on the atmosphere. But it had been the threat of war which had brought their practical application. The R.A.F.'s exercises over London in 1934 had revealed that present methods were giving Britain no defence against the bomber – both the Air Ministry and the House of Commons had been easily "obliterated". The current British early warning system, merely a giant concrete acoustic screen in Kent, had been patently ineffective. The Air Ministry had appointed the Tizard Committee, which had met to deliberate on air defence for the first time in January 1935. Its chairman, Sir Henry Tizard, the Rector of Imperial College, London, was the prototype of the "boffin" (a whimsical term later universally applied to scientists working with the services). His committee had included a younger scientist, P. M. S. Blackett, who was to make a great individual contribution to British victory over Hitler. Later that year, under pressure from Churchill, Lindemann had been admitted as a member. In their youth, he and Tizard had been close friends. But on the committee they had quarrelled so violently that Blackett and another member had resigned. It had then been reconstituted as before, but without Lindemann.[8]

Meanwhile, radar had been born. The Air Ministry had asked Robert Watson Watt, then director of the Government's Radio Research Station, whether he could make them a "death ray" to burn bombers out of the sky. It had been the work of minutes for Watt to dismiss the idea, and it had taken barely longer for one of his assistants, A. F. Wilkins, to show that Appleton's techniques could be used to detect raiders at a considerable distance. The Tizard Committee had moved swiftly, the Air Ministry had provided the necessary money, and so the Battle of Britain had been won before Chamberlain had become Prime Minister or Hitler had invaded Czechoslovakia. As early as 1936, on Tizard's initiative, civilian scientists had been attached to the fighter station at Biggin Hill to study the art of controlled interception – the first admission, as Blackett points out, that modern war had become so complicated that the traditional training of service personnel themselves was inadequate. "The Biggin Hill experiment", he remarks, "was the first step towards the fully fledged Operational Research Sections attached eventually to all the major commands of all three services."[9]

The coastal chain of radar stations had been maintaining a vigil for some months before the outbreak of war, when the research establishment, of which A. P. Rowe was superintendent, had been evacuated first to Dundee, then, in May 1940, to Swanage in Dorset. At Swanage, its scientists, supplemented now by brilliant men from the universities, had perfected and invented a stream of new devices: A.I., the airborne radar for night fighters; GEE, the grid navigational system; OBOE, the pinpoint target finder used with great effect in the second half of the war by low-flying Mosquito "Pathfinders"; and H²S, "the most brilliant of the infants of radar", a magic eye which enabled a pilot to pick out ground features in the dark and permitted precision bombing out of range of ground assistance.[10]

Its most fertile period was over when, in May 1942, Rowe's establishment was moved to Malvern College, the famous public school in Worcestershire. But it is with Malvern that the Telecommunications Research Establishment (a deadpan name which it received late in 1940) is now chiefly associated. It was said that the Napoleonic Wars had been won on the playing fields of Eton; Rowe joked that the Second World War would be won on the playing fields of Malvern. Malvern, however, was perhaps more distinguished for its cricket than Eton, and while "The junior playing fields, scattered with various ground radar devices, looked like the coming or going of a circus . . .", the hallowed senior cricket pitch was spared. By the end of the war, T.R.E. had a staff of three thousand, and Malvern was a centre for pilgrimage for military brasshats, ministers and American notables.[11]

Radar secrets were among the treasures of British science which Tizard took with him in his famous "Black Box" to the U.S.A. in the autumn of 1940, hoping, as the blitz began in Britain, to enlist American scientific help for the war effort. The "Black Box" was described by the official American historian of the scientific war as "the most valuable cargo ever brought to our shores". Here was Whittle's jet engine; and here, above all, was a sample cavity magnetron, "probably", C. P. Snow remarks, "the most valuable single device in the Hitler war".[12] For the cavity magnetron was the key to the use of shorter and shorter wavelengths in radar. With the compact power which it provided, radar devices could be disseminated in great numbers through all the fighting services.

But the control over nuclear power, for good or ill, which the development of the atom bomb implied, now seems more important even than shortwave radar. The later work on the bomb took place in America, whither key British scientists were exported. But for more than a year, it had been very much a British story. Without the decisive research of Professor Peierls and Dr Firsch at Birmingham University early in 1940, it is unlikely that nuclear weapons would have been used in the Second World War; and the work of the Maud Committee in co-ordinating research towards the bomb in several British universities in 1940–41 was also crucial. But Britain simply had not the industrial capacity available to develop the bomb herself. "Tube Alloys", as the project was called, would have needed "a peak labour force of about twenty thousand men, a quarter of it skilled, and probably in difficult labour areas", together with half a million tons of steel and half a million extra kilowatts of electricity (and hence, more coal). The india-rubber island could not stretch so far.[13]

Sadly, the story of penicillin, the great life saver, at the other extreme of intention, provides a counterpart. Fleming had discovered the effect long before the war, and it had been in Britain that further research had been undertaken. But penicillin was, for Britain, a casualty of the war economy. When it was first used in 1941 in an attempt to save the life of a policeman with blood poisoning, he died because supplies ran out. Britain suffered from an acute shortage of the microbiologists needed for the drug's large-scale development, and from lack of specialized factories or resources to build them. So the patents were lost to America. Though the Government began building six new factories at its own expense before the end of the war, it was not until 1945 that home production of the drug, now seen as a vital requirement for the services, exceeded imports from the U.S.A.[14]

But the provision of medical stores in general had been called "the most remarkable achievement" of British war production "outside the conventional range of weapons". Huge increases in output were squeezed out of the limited supplies of specialized factory space and technical management which were available. New drugs were developed and produced; drugs previously imported were replaced. "Between 1942 and 1945 the yearly rate of output of 'Sulphanilamide', the original drug of the sulphonamides group, was raised from a hundred and fifty-three tons to more than five hundred tons."[15] Advanced science and technology strove to heal what advanced science and technology had wounded.

III

The First World War had proved that "scientific research" and "national defence" were now synonyms. Britain's rulers had found that her industry had lagged so far behind in the application of science that she had depended on Germany for countless drugs, for magnetos, for tungsten, for smelted zinc. In 1915, the Government's Department of Scientific and Industrial Research (D.S.I.R.) had been established, to encourage and assist co-operative research organizations in individual industries, to give grants to students and post graduates, and to control its own laboratories, research stations and research boards.

This work had continued on a modest scale between the two wars, and D.S.I.R. laboratories did important work in the Second in such matters as the construction of concrete runways, the preservation of food, and advanced aerodynamics (where Government research establishments provided the theoretical backbone for the achievements of British aircraft design). But whereas the First World War had confirmed the importance of scientific research, the Second established the importance of the scientist and his questioning, irreverent outlook.

It had seemed by no means certain at the outset that this transformation would happen. In 1938, it had been the initiative of the then President of the Royal Society which had prodded the Government into crystallizing the idea of a central register of men with administrative, executive – and scientific – qualifications. In practice, administrative experience had proved to be a highly elusive entity, and after the register had tried to cope with a surge of amiable muddlers who believed themselves equipped to direct great enterprises, it had settled down to its main work, directing scientists and engineers where they were most needed. In the autumn of 1939 the universities had been emptied suddenly of many of their most brilliant men, who had largely gravitated to radar. But a serious dearth of further technically qualified recruits, especially for telecommunications, had soon emerged, so that in July 1940, all people qualified as engineers, chemists, physicists and quantity surveyors had been required to put their names on the register.[16]

However, it seemed clear to many that not all the available talent was being used, and that much of it was being misused. Years before, a brilliant group of scientists had set up a small dining club, called the "Tots and Quots" (*quot hominies, tot sententiae*) to mark their diversity of viewpoints. Amongst these men, now malcontent, were Solly Zuckerman and J. D. Bernal. At one of their meetings in the summer of 1940, Allen Lane, the founder of Penguin Books, was present, and suggested that their bitter criticisms of the inadequate mobilization of science for the war effort should be published in his series of "Specials". The book took a fortnight for its twenty-five authors to put together, and within a month, anonymously, it was on the bookstalls.[17] It is a most important document, as Zuckerman, Bernal, and others who helped with its writing, found jobs of key national importance where they put their ideas into practice.

Science in War complained roundly that "A large proportion of the scientific brains in this country are not being used at all and, due to defects of organization, most of those that are being used are not working at anything like their possible efficiency." Scientific method, the authors argued, must be applied in every field of battle and every corner of the war economy. Their point was not that scientists should be used as consultants merely – indeed, the trouble was that this was the limited role to which business and the civil service assigned them at the moment. They must be brought right into the crucial discussions of policy; they must be there when decisions were made. The book predicted "a revolution in strategy far greater than that introduced by Napoleon" when scientists were directly involved in warfare; and

subsequent events showed that this arrogance was justified.
Scorn was poured on the "verbalism" of the arts graduates
trained in classics and the humanities who still dominated British
public life. The authors quoted an editorial from the famous
journal *Nature* which pointed out that at the Civil Defence
Camouflage Establishment, "Of some sixty-five technical officers,
all but four are either professional artists or, at the time of
recruitment, were students at art schools. Not one member of the
establishment is a qualified biologist." But only a biologist could
advise on the principles underlying visual concealment or decep-
tion. Paint was, therefore, splashed on with ignorant abandon.
"An extravagant example of this foolishness was the decoration
of the cooling towers of a large works to represent a grove of tall
trees. It should scarcely be necessary to point out that the result
of light and shade is such as absolutely to kill this piece of stage
scenery at bombing range."[18]

And beyond the obvious applications of science, the authors
pleaded for the use of applied psychology in the forces, for the
involvement of social scientists in the assessment of morale and
the construction of propaganda, and for "scientific management"
in industry, gloomily remarking of the seven-day week recently
introduced into war factories that "The ministers responsible
were probably acting in ignorance rather than deliberately
sabotaging the war effort."[19] Lo and behold, these things came to
pass.

For *Science in War* was pushing at a door which was already
half open, and which would soon be torn off its hinges by the
pressure of events. Scientists, even in their role as consultants, had
already shown themselves capable of influencing events. As
Zuckerman points out, the original suggestion that radar should
be explored had come from Watson Watt himself; and when
Peierls and Frisch early in 1940 had shown that it was possible to
exploit nuclear fission in the development of a bomb with unprecedented destructive potential, there had been no staff requirement for such a weapon. The Tizard Committee itself had in effect
drawn scientists into the process of decision making at the most
crucial level (though during the war Sir Henry Tizard himself
experienced the other edge of the blade when, as a member of the
Air Council, he was involved in the inspection of various designs
of W.A.A.F. underwear).[20] The position which Tizard's arch
rival, Lindemann, now occupied in the counsels of Churchill was
more than a portent – it was already an important political fact.
And the famous clash of opinions between the two men, in which

Lindemann, in 1942, was victorious illustrated the uncomfortable truth that when the scientist became involved in Government, his claim to objectivity was jeopardized by the ambience of top-level politics.

The story of the arguments between the humourless, vain and often cruel Lindemann and the gentlemanly, witty, balanced Tizard has often been told in such a way as to exaggerate their differences over specific questions of policy. Where the use of the R.A.F. was concerned, their disagreement in effect boiled down to one of emphasis; though it was Blackett's view that Lindemann was fanatical, besotted with the idea that "any diversion of aircraft production and supply to the anti-submarine campaign, to army co-operation or even to fighter defence – in fact, to anything but bombing" would be "a disastrous mistake".

The battle was over sums. Lindemann maintained that German war production could be disrupted by the wholesale destruction of working-class districts. He produced cost efficiency calculations which Tizard claimed were wrong by an order of five and Blackett, independently, said were out by an order of six. All three were eventually shown to have been wrong; Lindemann's figures were wrong by a factor of about ten to one. It would be absurd to regard the controversy as a metaphysical clash between Compassion, played by Tizard, and Sadism, represented by Lindemann. Like all top defence scientists, both men assumed that practically any idea which would bring victory, and bring it quickly, was acceptable. But Tizard wanted to concentrate aircraft on the destruction of U-boats. Blackett maintains that if this had been done, and more aircraft had been made available to support land fighting, the war could have been won "half a year or even a year earlier". While this is open to argument, it is abundantly clear that the offensive launched on the basis of Lindemann's figures was a costly failure.[21]

The whole controversy, then and since, has illustrated the degree to which major strategic decisions, in the middle of the war, might be influenced by academic scientists working in secret. The same penetration had been achieved by experts in other fields. It will be remembered that the distinguished Scientific Food Committee had proposed, after Dunkirk, a rock-bottom but adequate "basal diet" which had been spurned. The official historian of food policy suggests that the committee's weakness stemmed from its remoteness from the practical work of the administrators who would have had to implement such a diet. "... It was only possible for scientists to influence food policy if they were behind the scenes and privy to the innermost counsels of the Ministries of Food and Agriculture." They soon were; the same historian later points out that by mid-1941 "the influence of scientific advice could be said to penetrate to every corner of ministry activity."[22]

Still more striking was the permeation of all three services with boffins which is summed up by the phrase "operational research". *Science in War* provides a definition. "The waging of warfare represents a series of human operations carried out for more or less definite ends. Seeing whether these operations actually yield the results expected from them should be a matter of direct scientific analysis."[23] There had been some work of this kind done in the First World War, but the term "operational research" and the attitude which it represented became widely current only in the Second. Its rise is associated above all with the name of "Pat" Blackett who, a few years before, had been one of Rutherford's astonishing galaxy of young scientific stars at the Cavendish Laboratory at Cambridge.

Blackett advocated that operation research would "help to avoid running the war on gusts of emotion". In August 1940, he was called in by General Pile to assist the A.A. staff in making the best use of the new gun-laying radar sets. He collected a group of young scientists in several fields to work with him. While his group was not the first body of civilian scientists to study operations, it was one of the first to be given, as Blackett puts it, "both the facilities for the study of a *wide range of operational problems*, the freedom to seek out these problems on their own initiative, and sufficiently close personal contact with the service operational staffs to enable them to do this".[24]

After success in A.A. Command, Blackett went on, first to Coastal Command, then to the Admiralty. His groups confirmed the scientists' new role. From now on, they would analyse the performance of guns and bombs on the spot, make notes over the corpses in the field, fly in night fighters and hobnob with generals. One of the more spectacular jobs of work was that done by the Communist biologist, J. B. S. Haldane, whose investigations of the dangers to which divers and men trying to escape from submarines might be exposed took him repeatedly into a compressed air chamber, where he and other volunteer "guinea-pigs" courted burst ears, lung collapse and nitrogen poisoning. Calmly, he took notes of his own behaviour under oxygen poisoning. "Even after I had had two severe fits and crushed some vertebrae I remained more resistant than the average," he wrote. One of his teeth exploded, because of a cavity, when he "decompressed" too fast.[25]

Less arduous work was called for in every field of war. Solly Zuckerman, an expert on the physiology of apes, was called in to examine the effects of bomb blast on human beings. Later, he made one of the greatest contributions to the success of D Day with his well calculated "Transportation Plan" for the bombing of German communications. But he was greatly irritated by persistence of superstition among the "brass hats", the professional military planners, who insisted on tinkering with the most carefully prepared figures and who "as a guide to decision, preferred intution rather than the methods of science".[26]

The marriage of the military mind with scientific common sense was far from complete when the war ended. This was not always because the boffins themselves were naive about war. Blackett said in 1958 that "During nearly twenty years of my lifetime of sixty years, I have been either training for war, fighting wars, or studying and thinking about them. In between, I became an experimental atomic physicist."[27] He had served in the navy in the First World War, when Lindemann had been a daring experimental pilot and Tizard had served in the Royal Flying Corps.

But the immediate background from which most of the boffins came was the university laboratory, where they had been great men in their own fields (and had known it), and had been used to judging others by different standards from those of rank and seniority which applied in the civil service and the armed forces. They were the only outsiders whom it proved impossible for Whitehall to digest into its traditional way of doing things. After all, in their scientific work, if the youngest of their colleagues had a good idea, it was still a good idea.

A. P. Rowe records the influx of university men into radar research at the beginning of the war. "A very few were hopelessly unfitted for work on applied science and other spheres of effort had to be found for them. Nearly all found difficulty in adapting themselves to the atmosphere of Government research. Few understood that there was a reasonable method of obtaining a screwdriver, for which the taxpayer paid, other than by walking out and buying it . . . Few of these men cared about promotion or recognition and the sole object of most was to get the war over and to return to fundamental scientific work in their universities."[28] Such men brought unorthodoxy, and sometimes genius, to the service of Stuffy Dowding and Bomber Harris. The scientists who developed centimetre wavelengths in radar deliberately chose this field because they were not interested in following other people's work and wanted a project which would really tax them.

At T.R.E. at least, such newcomers found an excellent relationship with the R.A.F. which had been established years before at Biggin Hill. Simply because radar was so novel, military men "necessarily came as learners, as well as prospective users". What they learnt was that the scientists could give them near-miraculous new toys to play with. The scientists, by their success, commanded respect, and, as the historian of M.A.P. puts it, "As monopolists they could impose their own conditions."[29]

The result was a creative two-way flow of question and answer, need and response, which was very different from the cavalier fashion in which the Nazis treated their scientific hirelings. It is paradoxical, perhaps, to think of the development of the atom bomb as "creative", but a similar absence of formality and red tape – due to the light regard at first paid to the project in official circles – brought results in the early days. The few M.A.P. officials concerned were given, Margaret Gowing relates, "a pretty free hand". This meant that, as compared with the corresponding work in America, there was a free interchange of ideas between the teams of scientists working at the Universities of Birmingham, Cambridge, Liverpool and Oxford, and very efficient co-ordination.[30]

At T.R.E., a remarkable brasshat-to-boffin give and take persisted into the Malvern days; indeed, it flowered there in a famous symbol of the continued freedom of British science, the "Sunday Soviets", which had begun long before the move to Worcestershire, but are best remembered from that phase. The idea was that visiting officers of high rank, pilots, development engineers, scientists, and anyone indeed, however junior, whose views might help to solve a current operational problem, could join in free discussion. The sessions became legendary. Cabinet ministers and commanders-in-chief took part. An air marshal remarked, "You can say anything in Rowe's office on a Sunday," and this was quoted to excuse all sorts of frankness.[31]

The nickname "Sunday Soviets", so hypertypical of the period, serves as a text for a further point about the arrival of science in the corridors of power. While the older generation of boffins – Lindemann, Tizard, A. V. Hill – were generally right-wing in politics, the young men who had made their reputations in the 1930s were often ardent Marxists. That old-fashioned radical H. G. Wells had satirized this new strain of scientists as "the Martians". *Science in War* interspersed its more specific criticisms with general assaults on capitalism and traditionalism. Amongst other unthinkable feats, the war hoisted a Communist boffin, J. D. Bernal, into the highlands of the military establishment.

Science, by tradition, was pacific and internationalist. Now political anti-Nazism went hand in hand with annoyance at the disruption of their work to break down traditional inhibitions among British scientists. The dictators had broadcast to the world their contempt for intellectual standards by the persecution of Jewish and left-wing scientists – many of whom were now doing vital work in Britain. From the wall of Rowe's room, a photograph of Goering looked down, with much inspirational force, on the Sunday Soviets.

Yet scientists who had seen the free passage of ideas between the nations as an essential basis for achievement could not always settle down happily into the atmosphere of ultra-security imposed by total war. The atom bomb troubled the peace of mind of some, at least, of those who pressed the work on it forward. Britain's greatest nuclear physicist, Sir James Chadwick, told two American scientists, "I wish I could tell you that the bomb is not going to work, but I am ninety per cent certain that it will."[32]

And in the case of the atomic bomb, the limits of the influence of scientists were illustrated. Niels Bohr, the great Danish nuclear scientist, was smuggled out of Europe in a high-speed Mosquito (nearly perishing from lack of oxygen en route). He was flown, first to Britain, then to America, to assist in the development of the bomb. In 1944, he tried desperately to convince Roosevelt and Churchill that international control of this terrible new force was essential from the outset, and that the Russians must be brought in. He had struck up a curious friendship with Sir John Anderson, who had done research work on the chemistry of uranium before the First World War. Anderson, convinced by Bohr's arguments, pressed on Churchill that "no plans for world organization which ignore the potentialities of Tube Alloys can be worth the paper on which they are written." Churchill peppered Anderson's minute with disapproving remarks and "wrote at the end simply 'I do not agree.' " He continued to keep Tube Alloys secret, not only from Stalin, but from the Labour members of the cabinet.[33]

Some scientists had resisted the idea of an atom bomb from the very beginning. One was Professor Max Born, of Edinburgh University, who, in spite of some distinguished work on the atom, was never invited to take part in Tube Alloys. "My colleagues", he said years later, "knew that I was opposed to taking part in war work of this character which seemed to me horrible. My wife is a Quaker and an absolute pacifist. I cannot say that at that time I was a pacifist, since I wished the downfall of Hitler with all my heart. But I could never reconcile myself to the methods used . . ." Two of Born's assistants were Germans, and were interned in the summer of 1940. One of them, Klaus Fuchs, after returning to Edinburgh, was invited by Peierls to join in secret work. Born advised him not to go. "But," he recalled, "he was filled with a tremendous hatred of the Nazis, and accepted."[34] Fuchs later "betrayed" nuclear secrets to the Russians; which was what Niels Bohr, after all, had not unreasonably wished the allies to do. Did science recognize frontiers, or not? Did the nation which interned Fuchs as an alien have the right to object when he acted as one? These, of course, were never easy questions.

Total war against a totalitarian state had a logic of its own, a logic one, one might say, of the *Catch 22* variety, which overrode qualms. If Germany got the atom bomb first, the results would be unthinkable. The allies must anticipate the Germans and possess a weapon such as Hitler would use if he could. And when the time came, there was only one way to justify the labour and the money, or, for that matter, to find out if and how the bomb worked. That was, to use it.

It is argued sometimes that research undertaken for war purposes (for "defence", in the terminology of 1984) indirectly benefits peaceful industries and serves mankind; which, of course, begs the question whether it was necessary to bomb Hiroshima to find out about nuclear power for electricity. Sir Solly Zuckerman, who went on to become Chief Scientific Adviser to a post-war British Government, concedes that "a state of war can stimulate the scientists to great feats of the imagination and to great practical achievement." He goes on to point out that when scientists "abandoned, or slowed down, the basic researches they had been carrying out in peacetime" to devote themselves to the demands of war, "most of them enjoyed resources on a scale they had never dreamt of in peace . . . But I do not know", he adds, "of any of these wartime researches yielding results as far-reaching as those which had been revealed in years of peace . . . The fundamental scientific discoveries on which the great technical achievements of the Second World War were based were made well before the war."[35] And he might have added that those discoveries, directly or indirectly, had belonged jointly to scientists of more than one of the combatant nations.

IV

For the moment, in spite of everything, the public optimism of men of science served to colour the millenarian visions of the war years. Just before the war, the British Association for the Advancement of Science had bowed to the pressure of enthusiasts, "Wellsian" and "Martian", and had set up a new division for "Social and International Relations of Science". One of the prime movers had been the veteran scientific publicist and educationalist, Sir Richard Gregory, who was president of the B.A. during the war. In September 1941, the new division sponsored a conference on "Science and World Order", in London, where scientists from twenty-two nations met to "demonstrate the common purpose of men of science in ensuring a post-war order in which the maximum benefits of science will be secured for all people". It lasted for three days. There was a huge demand for tickets, the B.B.C. publicized the conference at home and abroad, and it was filmed by the Ministry of Information. The speakers included Herbert Morrison, as well as an impressive array of Fellows of the Royal Society. But "perhaps its most notable feature was the audience. Young men in flannels and hatless girls outnumbered the die-hards of science, to applaud the suggestion of Professor A. V. Hill . . . that scientific advisory bodies should be established for each department of the cabinet." There were messages from Churchill and the King, and all present enthusiastically endorsed a Seven Part Scientific Charter, replete with noble aims, which stressed the need for freedom of speech and for international interchange of ideas. The ultra-Tory *National Review* fulminated against "papers read by the group of socialist partisans and their cortege of political cheapjacks . . ." Though Hill was a Conservative M.P. as well as a former member of the Tizard Committee, it was correct in identifying the conference as yet another distasteful manifestation of the left-wing idealism which provided the Spirit of the Age.[36]

As scientists themselves progressed through a maze of appointments and committees towards some real authority, the rapprochement of science and society had its parallels at the level of research itself. Operational research could not stop short at analysing the performance of machines; it was inevitably concerned with the people who handled them.

The authors of *Science in War* regarded "social science" as a complement to their own work in physics, biology and chemistry. In the early 1930s, a group of progressive experts and businessmen had set up Political and Economic Planning (P.E.P.) which continued to publish influential reports on industrial and social questions during the war. A P.E.P. broadsheet of 1934 had spoken of the need to make heard in the circles of Government the views of "those on whose service technical civilization depends – the administrators, the managers, the engineers, scientists, teachers and technicians". One of P.E.P.'s early members had been Julian Huxley, whose contention that political planning should "always be in touch with scientifically ascertained fact" sums up part of its credo.[37]

In 1937, Huxley had been one of the sponsors of a new social survey organization, Mass Observation, a name often seen in these pages. It did more than any other body to popularize "social science" in the weeklies and illustrated papers. Its enthusiastic "observers" all over the country were instructed to watch their fellow humans with the closeness, and detachment, of an anthropologist or biologist. Also in the late 1930s, the Gallup Poll had made its first appearance in Britain.

Yet survey techniques had been so little understood in higher administrative circles that when, in October 1939, the War Cabinet had pondered the introduction of rationing, its chosen method of ascertaining public opinion had been to ask the then Minister of Labour to make "soundings" among bodies "representative of public opinion". Of nineteen contacts, only two had been actively hostile, and inquiries on Fleet Street had elicited what had seemed to the cabinet the "significant fact" that rationing was not in the forefront of the public mind. The old notion that public opinion was an aggregation of the views held by pressure groups and journalists still survived; and the fact that the decision then taken actually accorded with wider public opinion was merely good luck.[88]

However, it was soon recognized that the Government must, in a war which depended so greatly on civilian morale, make use of the techniques already well known in market research. In the spring of 1940, the Wartime Social Survey was set up, under the Ministry of Information, yet such was "the doubt and hesitancy which were prevalent among the heads of the ministry as to its necessity and value" (as the S.C.N.E. found), that the enterprise was kept secret. Other ministries objected to its criticisms. When the press found out that Government employees were going about asking people questions on topical matters, a fear arose that the Government intended to set up its own news-collecting agency. After a parliamentary storm, the survey was reorganized and restricted in its scope so that it could be used only for work directly commissioned by other ministries.[39]

Yet its value was obvious, even before the independent Madge survey of working-class attitudes to money persuaded the Treasury that it might safely go ahead with the superficially intolerable Keynes-Wood budget of 1941. When clothes rationing came in, the scheme depended from the outset upon "market research" into what people actually wore. The Ministry of Food also relied on surveys of various kinds. The Ministry of Health called for research on disease (and found, to its surprise, that public opinion had no objection to the open discussion of V.D.). The Ministry of Agriculture, through the Social Survey, studied the impact of "Dig For Victory" propaganda. All the private survey firms, including Mass Observation and Gallup, were used by the Government to assess morale and to provide statistics.

The Ministry of Information itself was a relevant example of the use of social science. On the accuracy of its understanding of the public rested the Government's chance of success in handling the mass media, or, to apply the word which the British reserve for the activities of lesser Governments without the law, its propaganda. Here, there had been a gradual development. The establishment of a Ministry of Information in the First World War had been followed by the pioneer work, already mentioned, of Sir Stephen Tallents at the Empire Marketing Board and the Post Office – where an inquiry into "customer dissatisfaction" had resulted in full inkwells and pens which actually wrote being installed in the local post offices. It was natural that the one Government department which actually sold things to the public should have taken the lead in surveys and in the allied field of propaganda. It was natural, too, that the Post Office should have been followed by the Ministries of Health and Food, the Home Office and the services, which could not avoid direct contact with the public.

The Second World War made it imperative that the Government should find the best ways of selling to people the commodities and attitudes which it thought were good for them. Information had to be collected to find out if propaganda had been effective. Further propaganda must be produced, tailored ever more closely to the prejudices of the public. The Ministry of Information had three thousand staff at its peak, excluding postal censorship workers, and other Government departments employed seventeen hundred people on "information" work in January 1944. The advertising industry, one might say, was nationalized for the duration.[40]

On one level, this was good "People's War" activity; how sublimely democratic that Government departments should worry constantly about their relationship with ordinary people. But the overall effect, of course, was quite the opposite. Having found out what people thought and how they behaved, the rulers of the country could manipulate them more efficiently, while simultaneously conforming themselves to the lowest common denominator of public opinion. The old gentlemanly notion that the Government was doing all right if the habitués of London clubs approved of it was superseded by the obsession of politicians with the opinion polls and their increasing use of the soft sell, the below the belt advertisement and what Daniel Boorstin called the "pseudo event". Ancient superstitions were still very much alive when the war ended, and the contemporary assessments of the 1945 General Election result have considerable antiquarian charm. But the straws were there in the wind, and the largest of them was Woolton's success as Minister of Food. After the war, which had given him much useful experience, he undertook the first sustained and methodical exercise in image building known to British politics, as organizer of the Conservative Central Office.

Equally ambiguous was that development of psychiatry in the armed forces which so much displeased Churchill. (" I am sure it would be sensible to restrict as much as possible the work of these gentlemen, who are capable of doing an immense amount of harm with what may very easily degenerate into charlatanry," he minuted to Anderson in December 1942. ". . . There are, no doubt, easily recognizable cases which may benefit from treatment of this kind, but it is very wrong to disturb large numbers of healthy, normal men and women by asking the kind of odd questions in which the psychiatrists specialize.") The "trick cyclists", as they were widely nicknamed, were in the most curious position of deciding which members of the forces were insufficiently sane to perform or assist in the action of killing other men, which would normally have indicated madness. Nevertheless, they were now found indispensable in officer selection and aptitude testing, as well as in the more negative task of treating those judged to be sick. By the end of the war, one of their leaders and inspirers, Dr J. R. Rees, was able to write of the army, "It is very striking how few cf the really intelligent and valuable leaders fail to appreciate the contribution of psychiatry . . ." In fact, the better generals must have grasped that it was an essential technique for accommodating totalitarian military institutions to the well-educated and independent minded people whom they had recruited.[41]

Of course, the motivations which have led to the acceptance of "scientific management" have been very similar. The First World War, by bringing British management close to collapse, had stimulated interest in such techniques as F. W. Taylor had pioneered in the U.S.A. Their advance between the war had been slow; Britain had no institution to compare with the Harvard Business School, and only three universities had small departments teaching management. But the considerable American invasion of British industry had created colonies of modernity. General Motors, Ford, Goodyear, Monsanto, Proctor and Gamble, Hoover and Remington Rand had bought British businesses or built their own factories. At the same time, the balance of the British economy had been shifting towards the newer and lighter forms of engineering, and within the engineering industry itself the old skilled jobs were being increasingly broken down to semi-skilled level. To maintain a smooth and peaceful flow of work through increasingly large factories of increasingly interdependent workers, skilled management was essential. In 1939, its practitioners had remained rare in Britain. The war made them the heroes of the hour, the demigods of a new ideology.

Ernest Bevin voiced what it was hoped was the nation's gratitude towards these "new men". "Calculation of profits", said Bevin, "and all the other things that have cluttered up progress in the past has to go [sic], and the great genius of our managers and technicians is being given full play – and never in the history of our country has it had a greater opportunity. It is not to satisfy a dividend that they are working, it is for the greater contribution they are glad to make for the benefit of us all." Those currently planning a New Jerusalem fell over themselves to prophesy that management would more gladly serve nationalized industry than private owners, in spite of the evidence freely gathered by Mass Observation that top managers hated working under the supply departments and were jealously obsessed with the post-war interests of their own firms. But it was true that the war had made financial matters less important. As one Labour intellectual put it, "In many firms the salaried managers have become for the first time more important than the financial directors, the advertising agents, the sales promoters and so on."[42]

The efficient use of raw materials was vital now that they were in short supply. The shortage of labour made it essential to handle carefully, "scientifically" what there was of it. The Government itself set an example in the R.O.F.s. Besides this, it increasingly provided an excellent argument for improved management in the manner in which it distributed its contracts. Professor Postan, stressing this point in his official history, remarks that "The better-managed firms were singled out and loaded with contracts to the point of overloading . . . Indeed, on more than one occasion the existence of a manager of proved quality was sufficient to attract munitions contracts, however remote might be the field of the manager's pre-war activities." Littlewood's Pools landed one war job after another on the strength of its experience in handling large numbers of young girl workers.[43]

Partly for similar reasons, partly for still more obvious ones, the war increased the prestige of the technician in industry. The small paint industry will serve as an example. It was called on to do vital, and even secret, work for the armed forces, while manufacture of paint for civilian purposes almost ceased. Because the flow of imported raw materials had been reduced to a mere dribble, substitutes had to be found; and meanwhile the industry was called on to develop new paints for camouflage and highly refined ones for aircraft finishes. Small wonder, then, that a *Times* correspondent was able to write at the end of the war that it had "at any rate taught the British paint industry the importance of the chemist and of research. There will be no return to the salary level of pre-war days, when the value placed by many manufacturers on their chemists might be gathered from advertisements of posts carrying as little as three hundred pounds a year. Today a competent paint chemist can command a salary around eight hundred pounds, and it is not grudged."[44]

Between the wars, D.S.I.R. had found it hard to maintain the interest of British firms in the industrial research which it had been established to promote. During the war, it could sit back and relax; economic and military intransigences did its work for it. By 1945 the amounts spent by Government and private firms through co-operative research associations for various industries had risen by two hundred and sixty per cent to eighteen million pounds, and the number of such associations increased from twenty-one in 1939 to thirty-eight by 1948. Furthermore, as the big modern corporations waxed greater as a result of the war, they were more than ever able to support lavish laboratories.

Even the industries of nineteenth-century England, cotton and coal, were compelled to contemplate pulling themselves up by their technological bootstraps. A mission from the British cotton industry which visited the U.S.A. in 1944 startled everyone by revealing how low productivity was in Lancashire, compared with that of American workers, and published an influential report. The Reid Report on the coal mines, issued by the Government in 1945, was equally devastating.[45]

But the new demand for technicians arose most obviously from the very nature of the newer industries which the war thrust to the fore, and which were based on up to the minute scientific research. Aircraft manufacture was a case very much in point, as was electrical engineering, so closely involved with the development of radar. British valve production tripled between 1940 and 1944 and even so, heavy imports from the U.S.A. were necessary.

The chemical engineering industry went through a still more startling growth in size and importance. The large demand for synthetic rubber put it on its mettle. A new call for coke created a great deal of tar which could be turned into plastics, insecticides, soaps, and, of course, nylon. Plastics were substituted widely for scarce materials – replacing wood, for instance, in the furnishings of naval ships. PVC was first developed on a large scale to meet the shortage of rubber for insulating wire and other vital requirements. The use of nylon for ropes and parachutes revealed new possibilities for synthetic fibre. The war laid the industrial basis, in fact, for the mass production of television sets which symbolized Macmillan's affluent society and for the records and gear clothes which later typified swinging Britain.[46]

And all this, of course, meant more work, even a new role, for technical colleges and universities.

V

The First World War had denuded the universities of pupils. The Second was kinder to them. Even so, by 1944 they had lost a third of their teachers and over a quarter of their pre-war number of students. These figures cloaked an uneven pattern of disruption. The numbers of women students had actually increased, by one eighth, while the arts faculties had been reduced to a quarter of their pre-war strength.[47]

From September 1940, the Ministry of Labour employed

officers to tour the universities, looking for potential candidates for key jobs. University students reading physics and mathematics were encouraged to take a special crash course in radio. In spite of special deferments for students of technical subjects, their numbers were tending to fall, so in June 1941 a scheme was announced for state bursaries in science, which were given to schoolboys ready to study radio, engineering, chemistry, and later metallurgy. Conflicting claims upon people qualified in such subjects led to the appointment, in August 1941, of a Technical Personnel Committee under Lord Hankey, which allocated the bursaries so that half were given for radio, forty per cent for engineering, and ten per cent for chemistry; no better index to the importance of radar is needed. Altogether, about six thousand state bursaries were awarded in 1942–45, covering, in a novel fashion, the full cost of fees and residence at universities, without any means test for parents.

Simultaneously, Hankey's committee initiated a six months' intensive training course at technical colleges for the Higher National Certificate in several branches of mechanical or electrical engineering. Here also, the Government paid fees and maintenance grants. The courses were recognized by the relevant professional institutes and some four thousand service trainees and young men from industry passed through them. Before the war, the technical colleges (which were primarily concerned with training skilled workers) had been for the most part somewhat stagnant backwaters of education, catering chiefly for evening students, so that their buildings were virtually unused during the day. Even by 1940 the situation had been transformed. "Some institutions", reported H. C. Dent, "are working twenty-four hours a day; shift succeeds shift of khaki-clad boys in endless procession; course succeeds course with barely a breathing interval between."[48] The surge forward of the "techs" was to continue after the war.

Meanwhile, the universities, under the thumb of Dame Austerity, were beginning to look oddly like techs. Even Oxford and Cambridge were forced to accept the function of vocational training; the "vocation", of course, being a call from society rather than one felt by the individual student. "British universities", Dent lamented in 1944, "have almost ceased to function as universities." What he meant can be illustrated from the wartime activities of Southampton University College – one of the "Redbrick" civic universities which, unlike "Oxbridge", had a deposit of utilitarianism in their bones already. It ran short courses for R.A.F. cadets selected from schools, nearly five hundred of them, each of whom had only six months in "residence". It provided emergency training for war workers, lectures in foremanship, full-time courses in radio, correspondence courses in navigation and marine engineering for prisoners of war, and assistance with adult education in the forces. The engineering department undertook nearly forty research projects connected with weapons and military equipment, while the physics department worked on the degaussing of warships, and the chemistry department on aspects of chemical warfare. The college's machine shops, furthermore, turned out a steady flow of mortars, gun components and other warlike products.[49]

During the first couple of years of war, arts students could stay at university until they were twenty. But when the age of call-up was lowered to eighteen, the intake of arts students was almost completely restricted to men judged unfit for service, and to women, who were only allowed to complete their courses if they were going on to professional training. Students who were called up after somehow completing the requisite number of terms of residence could, if they wished, accept a B.A. (War) degree; otherwise, they must return after the war. Boys of sixteen began to go up to university so as to qualify for a B.A. (War), and in some places a fourth academic term was instituted. While teachers of arts subjects seethed quietly and cited hard cases – a brilliant history student snatched away to do a routine office job in the army, superb linguists wasting their talents in the P.B.I. – they could not argue against Dame Austerity, who prudently ensured that some science departments actually registered more students than ever before, and permitted them to finish their courses. Towards the end of the war, the authorities relented a little, and eventually many of the service cadets who arrived for brief courses to improve their officer potential were allowed to study the humanities.[50]

As A. S. F. Gow, a Cambridge classics don, remarked, it was psychologically difficult to carry on research in the arts in wartime. ". . . It is not obvious", he added, "whether it is ultimately more important to clarify the observations of a Greek poet or to discover a means of locating aeroplanes in the dark. But whichever of these problems is ultimately the more important, there is no doubt which is at present the more urgent: and with such inky clouds ringing the horizon the task of kindling farthing dips on my tiny sector of the darkness front must needs be less engrossing."[51]

Undergraduate life of the traditional, relaxed mode had also become a luxury, to be consumed somewhat furtively if found at all. Undergraduate societies and magazines showed surprising stamina under taxing conditions. But over all explorations and pleasures hung the demands of war, the shadow of mortality. The poet Keith Douglas, called up from Oxford in 1940 at the end of his second year, foresaw his death from that traditional undergraduate habitat, a canoe on the river:

> Well, I am thinking this may be my last
> summer, but cannot lose even a part
> of pleasure in the old-fashioned art of
> idleness. I cannot stand aghast
> at whatever doom hovers in the background . . .[52]

Douglas was perhaps the only member of the generation of writers who emerged during the war to maintain his courage and with it his probing intellectual, moral and aesthetic curiosity, in the face of the anonymity and complexity of technological warfare. Several of the leading boffins – Blackett, Zuckerman, Haldane and Bernal spring to mind at once – wrote excellent prose, but literary intellectuals, who could have read without difficulty what such men had to say about their subjects, showed a nearly universal lack of curiosity where science was concerned.

The man in the street, of course, did not ignore the jet plane and the atom bomb, nor the interest which his small son took in these things. With a vague awareness of science, however, there went an instinctive distaste; the blitz had shown what the boffins were up to. Mass Observation, during the war, found that only one in five of its voluntary national panel, who were after all, *ipso facto*, committed to social science, had an unqualified favourable reaction to science, and the main feeling expressed was that it had "got out of control". The use of the atom bomb, of course, strengthened such feelings; a widespread reaction was summed up by an elderly man who told an investigator, "The heathen with his bow and arrow; we used to laugh at him, but now he's got the laugh of us."[53]

THE PLAYING FIELDS OF MALVERN (2)

B.B.C. Board. We discuss whether the clergy should use the microphone to preach forgiveness of our enemies. I say I prefer that to the clergy who seek to pretend that the bombing of Cologne was a

Christian act. I wish the clergy would keep their mouths shut about the war. It is none of their business.

Harold Nicolson, Diaries and Letters, 11.6.42[1]

I

In the prolonged dialogue between religion and science-based secularism which has been a feature of the last hundred years, the 1930s, on balance, marked a phase where the theologians had withdrawn their forces. The humanist theology of "Modernism" which had been dominant in the 1920s had been supplanted by a reaction in the next decade largely inspired by Karl Barth. A writer in a theological journal soon after the outbreak of the war pointed out how paradoxical it was that "the older men are to a greater or lesser degree liberals, while the younger are demanding a return to dogma." A more recent commentator has suggested that "The gulf which Barth opened between God and man, eternity and time, served to feed the sense of impotence which was widespread between the wars."[2]

The decline of the Protestant faith in Britain was one good reason for feelings of impotence. It should not be exaggerated; the godlessness of the urban masses had been apparent long before the opening of the twentieth century, and while only six adults in a hundred took communion in Anglican churches on Easter Day 1940, the figure in 1900 had been no more than nine in a hundred. The Established faith had long ceased to play an important part in the lives of most of those over whom it was established. In many respects, the waning of Nonconformity, so much more a matter of active adherence, was of greater significance. After a dramatic revivalist period in the first decade of the century, the Methodist, Baptist and Congregationalist churches had gone into a chronic decline. It was not just that membership had fallen (though the number of Sunday scholars in Congregationalist churches in 1939 was, at two hundred and sixty thousand, almost exactly half what it had been thirty years before). The fervour, even wildness, of the turn of the century had abated. After 1910, a historian of Methodism records, the characteristic social expressions of the sect, the class meetings, the love feasts, the Sunday night prayer meetings, the camp meetings, had "silently disappeared".[3]

Mass Observation, in a survey at the end of the war, found that about two-thirds of men and four-fifths of women, in a London suburb, said they believed in God, and only about one person in twenty was ready to profess atheism. But six out of ten said they never went to church. A third of the under-forties were non-believers. And of those who had, within the previous six months, attended an Anglican church (where a typical congregation would now consist chiefly of ageing women), less than one-third confidently accepted three cardinal points of church dogma – that there was life after death, that Christ had been more than a man, and that He had been born to a Virgin. On the other hand, two-thirds of the Nonconformists questioned were orthodox; and so were virtually all the Catholics.[4]

From the Roman Catholic point of view, Britain was steadily becoming not less, but more Christian. The Catholic priests had found converts at a steady rate of eleven or twelve thousand a year in the mid-'thirties, "spread fairly evenly over the cities, industrial and suburban areas and country towns and . . . found at all economic levels".[5] During the war, every labourer from Eire and every Italian prisoner of war who decided to settle in Britain was more grist to the Papist mill. Though the mobility of manpower threatened the hold of the priests, especially over younger people, the estimated Catholic population of Britain increased in the 1940s by over four hundred thousand, to nearly four millions (and in the 1950s it waxed by another million).

A very different type of Old Time Religion also had its successes, seen in the mushrooming of the Pentecostal Elim Four Square Gospel Church between the wars and the remarkable rise of the Jehovah's Witnesses, some six thousand in 1938, who multiplied sevenfold in the next two decades. Dogma, on the one hand, and millenarianism on the other, maintained and even increased their attraction; while war promoted a wider interest in Spiritualism, and the heretical doctrines of Christian Science continued to flourish amongst a small section of the more prosperous classes.[6]

But for Protestantism, the war made matters worse than ever. A gloomy significance was read by the faithful into the silencing of the parish church bells. Another portent of the advance of secularism was the complacency with which ministers encouraged factories to work on Sundays. After the blackout had made it necessary for many churches to hold evensong in the afternoons, the blitz came to smash many of the buildings. The Methodists suffered particularly severely; two thousand, six hundred of their nine thousand churches were damaged, and eight hundred had to be written off. It is estimated that altogether over fifteen thousand ecclesiastical buildings of all denominations were damaged.[7]

Still more serious was the slackening of the church-going habit which vast movements of population brought in their train, and the growing shortage of manpower within the churches themselves. The voluntary ladies had gone over to the W.V.S., leaving the dwindling body of clergy and ministers shorter of help than ever. The latter were immune from call-up, but thousands went as chaplains to the forces, while newcomers in training mostly enlisted. The Church of England found its supply of ordinands drying up completely, and this exacerbated a chronic fall in the numbers of Anglican clergy. There had been 6,095 curates in 1905, and 4,554 in 1938; in 1948 there were only 2,189. The shortage was worst in the great industrial cities. The diocese of Birmingham, a somewhat extreme case, had 178 curates in 1938, and only 38 in 1948.[8]

Although the faithful saw the war's horrors as the clearest signs yet of the harm which secularism had done to humanity, for the less committed believers, it seemed that they must call God's goodness in question. But faith in reason and science was also violated by the brutalities hourly heard of. The more observant clerics were pleased to witness signs that the war had put their rival humanism, and its most virulent and dogmatic manifestation, Marxism, at an equal disadvantage. The most extraordinary symptom of their retreat was the revolt against Communism, in 1940, of John Strachey himself, that Jesuitical figure who had done more than any other man to spread Marxism in the universities. At the end of 1940, he wrote a tract called *A Faith To Fight For*, in which he argued that "the moral approach to human problems" was "by no means obsolete. On the contrary, as the world sinks in havoc, and the continents are piled with the bodies of dead nations, two ideals, truth and love, emerge as fixed stars." Only a moral revival, he went on to argue, could enable Britain to defeat Nazism.[9]

While Strachey did not become a convert to Christianity, his personal crisis illustrated the impossibility of explaining how and why Nazism was different from monopoly capitalism in orthodox Marxist terms. Unless one could prove that Nazism was in some way more evil than British capitalism, the C.P. was right to denounce the war as "imperialist". No less a pundit than Professor Joad himself, writing in the *New Statesman*, pointed out how the diabolical evil which must be attributed to Hitler and Goering sapped the bases of scientific humanism and economic determinism; it was, he suggested, very difficult to believe that the

Nazis were "*all* the victims, and *wholly* the victims of unwise psychological training and economic injustice". Meanwhile, the journal's editor, Kingsley Martin, had opened its pages to a running debate on religion. To his surprise, "the argument lapsed almost at once into a discussion about the value, not the truth, of Christian teaching. One after another, apparently serious people wrote saying that, true or not, Christian doctrines were important as a means of saving us from the immoralism of Fascism or Communism."[10] H. G. Wells, who had been as great an influence as any in establishing the claims of science and faith in a purely human progress, collapsed into pessimism during the war and summed up his crisis with the title of the last but one of his many books: *Mind at the End of its Tether*.

Nor was it only thoughtful intellectuals on the left who were encouraged by the events of the period to reopen their minds to the serious consideration of religion. "It is curious what a lively interest most of us had taken in God during these last few weeks," a society lady has written of the summer of 1940. "People who hardly knew of His existence before suddenly began to ask each other what God could be thinking about to allow such awful things to happen to the British Empire." Fear, of course, on the side of the angels. A hymn composed and circulated widely during the blitz began:

> God is our refuge, be not afraid,
> He will be with you all through the raid . . .

Even disbelievers, Mass Observation found, were prompted to prayer by constant danger and worry. This phenomenon was clearly related to the quickening of interest in astrology. In 1941, when only sheer faith could support the hope that Britain would win, four or five out of every ten people questioned admitted to having some belief in astrology. The proportion fell in inverse ratio to the likelihood of victory, and by the end of the war was under twenty per cent.[11]

It seems that very few people "lost their faith", though Mass Observation detected a trend away from religion amongst those previously without strong beliefs. Firm believers were generally strengthened in their faith, and this, without adding to church attendances, produced certain tokens of religious revival – for instance, a much livelier and more widespread response to religious broadcasting.[12]

his chairmanship to "consider from the Anglican point of view what are the fundamental facts which are directly relevant to the ordering of the new society that is quite evidently emerging, and how Christian thought can be shaped to play a leading part in the reconstruction after the war is over". There are curious divergencies as to the number of people present; the higher count gave fifteen bishops and nearly four hundred clergy and laity.[17] They assembled, oddly enough, at that same Malvern College which within a year and a half was to house T.R.E. The gathering was mixed, but not strictly representative. The distinguished list of speakers included Canon V. A. Demant, T. S. Eliot (on religious education); Dorothy Sayers, the detective novelist; and that vatic literary pacifist, Middleton Murry.

The papers were long, numerous and disparate. There was very little time for debate. On the third day, Sir Richard Acland brought passions to life by using his paper to denounce the profit motive, root and branch, and to claim that "Common Ownership" was a matter of fundamental Christian principle. Temple, with his habitual aplomb, sat down on the last night and drafted a series of "Conclusions" which (his biographer relates) "he informed an astonished conference on the next morning, expressed its 'common mind'". This concise statement of Temple's own views became known as the "Findings" of the conference. They attacked materialism, urged congregations to participate in social work, and advocated certain internal reforms in church organization. But at one point, Temple's conclusions were challenged by Acland, who proposed an amendment directly condemning private ownership, and after some horse-trading, this emerged as the most sensational part of the Findings. While it was admitted that the Church could never commit itself to any proposed change in the structure of society as being a "self-sufficient means of salvation", it could point to "stumbling blocks" which made it harder for men to lead Christian lives. "In our present situation we believe", the Findings went on, "that the maintenance of that part of the structure of our society, by which the ultimate ownership of the principal industrial resources of the community can be vested in the hands of private owners, may be such a stumbling block . . ."[18]

The last sentence had the unsatisfactory effect of appearing to commit the conference to an attack on capitalism, and in fact committing it to nothing whatever. "There is nothing in the least novel in the Malvern resolutions," protested a former editor of the *Church Times*. "They have been accepted a score of times by earnest and uncomfortable Christians, and they have not had the smallest practical results." Nevertheless, T. S. Eliot, amongst others, hastily dissociated himself from the Findings. The two pamphlets containing them had a joint circulation of over a million. Temple himself declared that Malvern had " 'put the Church on the map' again for many who had ceased to regard it as having any relevance".[19] And in many circles, on the right and even on the left, it gave Temple a bright red aura.

But what was the Church of England, that crumbling pillar of the Establishment, that it could play a part in the People's War? In October 1940, the bishops had met to discuss whether they should hold a conference to "give a lead". Dr Garbett, then Bishop of Winchester, had remarked wrily in his diary, "If we have a conference, it will only mean that we shall deliver to one another the speeches we have heard time after time, and then issue a statement. Of this a third of the Church people will speak with enthusiasm, another third with disappointment as the loss of a great opportunity, and the rest will describe it as dangerous. The great public outside will not know it has been issued unless we say something about Bishops' Palaces, Divorce, Birth Control, or Reprisals." When the conference of bishops duly assembled in the summer of 1941, the public, as Garbett had foreseen, paid no attention whatsoever. The whole question was a trial for Archbishop Lang of Canterbury. "How wearisome", he had exclaimed during the blitz, "is the constant and petulant cry for 'strong leadership'."[20]

Cosmo Gordon Lang had been at Canterbury since 1928, and was now in his late seventies. He was an accomplished politician and courtier, who had handled the abdication crisis with great prowess. He moved at ease among the great of the land, and the man in the street knew and cared little about him. In the summer of 1941, Lang himself decided that he was really too old to continue, but he held on avidly to Lambeth Palace until January 1942, when he announced his resignation at last. He then made a public statement which brought to the fore the contempt which many laymen felt for the Church of England. He dwelt on how much it meant to him "to contemplate a sudden withdrawal to some obscure place in the circumference, and to face the restraints and inconveniences of very slender means". The *Daily Mirror* went to town, pointing out that Lang's pension of fifteen hundred pounds a year was not bad at all for a single man of seventy-seven, and maliciously quoting, "Blessed are the meek, for they shall inherit the earth."[21]

There was more than one possible successor. Bishop Bell of Chichester had been regarded, quite seriously, as Lang's rival for the succession thirteen years before. But now, as that detached veteran Bishop Henson observed, Bell's prospects had worsened "as his sympathies with Jews and Germans have been more openly declared".[22] Temple had long been regarded as the heir-apparent.

However, Temple's "political" aura had raised the hackles of the Conservative Party. An influential section of that party pressed the claims of the "safe" Bishop Fisher of London. Lang himself wanted Temple to succeed him. Churchill, in whose hands the appointment lay, reacted with annoyance to Lang's suggestion; this man Temple "went about talking of Christian revolution and stuff of that kind". However, this was the least of his preoccupations in the political crisis of January and February 1942, and in the latter month, almost simultaneously with the cabinet changes, William Ebor became William Cantuar. Churchill's misgiving had been allayed by the stratagem of sending the "safe" Garbett to York to keep an eye on Temple. Garbett himself was not altogether pleased with this view of his political bias; he was, if anything, drawn towards the Labour Party, and privately regarded himself as a much more dangerous reformer than Temple. A saintly man of wide human sympathies, Garbett in effect joined Temple in a tandem of People's Archbishops.[23]

Except in Conservative circles, Temple's appointment was universally popular. Amongst the unbelievers, George Bernard Shaw spoke for others besides himself when he declared that "an archbishop of Temple's enlightenment was a realized impossibility". And a Free Church leader assured Temple that ". . . Nonconformists in England do in fact accept you as the spokesman of the whole Church in a way which is quite new in our experience."[24]

Physically, Temple was just right. He looked exactly like one of Dickens's true philanthropists; a portly, chubby-faced, twinkling eyed, bespectacled figure with a gusty laugh, exuding goodwill to all from every pore. Buoyantly self-confident, utterly serene in his acceptance of his mission of leadership, Temple himself had never known doubt or want. He was the son of a former Archbishop of Canterbury; the easy brilliance of his mind had taken him swiftly to the top. That mind showed a phenomenal capacity for dialectically relating opposite positions, and so far from being an impassioned extremist, Temple was the quintessence of compromise. In the dispute between the different factions of the

Church, he took sides neither with High nor with Low, though he inclined High-wards as he grew older. He was irreproachably orthodox in theology, to balance the apparent unorthodoxy of his political stands. Though he had for seven years been a card-carrying Labour Party member, that had been a long time ago. What impresses the contemporary student, coming to Temple without preconceptions, is how firmly in the centre of British politics he stood; while he outraged certain people by offering detailed political proposals, these proposals were in fact the commonplaces of consensus.

Being the People's Archbishop, he published a best-selling Penguin Special called *Christianity and Social Order*. Being a man of the centre, he consulted J. M. Keynes before ending the book with a series of practical proposals to which almost no one, reading them closely, could have taken exception – family allowances, better housing, holidays with pay, a higher school-leaving age. While he was careful to produce the most orthodox theological arguments for his social prescriptions, he stressed whenever he produced them that he uttered them as a private citizen, not as Archbishop of Canterbury. ". . . We must be very careful", he wrote once to a clerical supporter, "that we do not give the impression that the Church is an agency for supporting left-wing politics which are often based on presuppositions entirely unChristian." He quoted approvingly to the Malvern Conference the saying that "It is the duty of Lambeth to remind Westminster that Westminster is responsible to God; but this does not mean that Westminster is responsible to Lambeth." The Church's role, as he argued, was to provide a theological foundation for the actions of Christian politicians of all parties; and he himself insisted that the significance of Malvern had been theological[25]

In short, the Church itself could not assume social leadership; and the rare gifts and appeal which Temple brought to Canterbury merely emphasized how impossible it was that it should. So did the series of public meetings which he launched in the autumn of 1942. Temple, Garbett and Sir Stafford Cripps spoke at the first of them, in the huge Albert Hall in London. All tickets had been sold two months beforehand. Temple was at his most provocative, announcing that he thought all monopolies in essential industries should be taken over by the state. There were loud grumblings from the City of London. The provincial meetings which followed attracted thousands; large crowds waited outside the Guildhall in Birmingham to glimpse this prodigy, the People's

Archbishop. Churchill's son, Randolph, said mockingly in the House of Commons, "Now that the Archbishop of Canterbury has entered the sphere of party politics and the Lord Privy Seal (Cripps) is changing places with him and offering spiritual guidance to the Church of England, I am not sure that it will not be considered very bad taste for a mere politician to make a speech on a political subject." He need not have worried. Cripps himself at the Albert Hall had insisted, "It is not the function of the Church, as an organized body, to enter the lists of the political parties. To do so would be to confuse matters and jeopardize the power of religion". In any case most of the other bishops, even Garbett, were dubious about all this open politicking on Temple's part.[26]

Temple, as archbishops went, had been a young man, only sixty-one, when he ascended his throne. But he had struggled from his childhood against gout, and to the amazement and dismay of the nation, he died very suddenly in September 1944. One clergyman has recalled sharing the soap with some labourers, just afterwards, in the toilet of a London Tube station, and being overwhelmed by their reaction to Temple's death. "They clamoured to make it plain that they had seen in him their hope for better things, and had personified that hope in him."[27] That, indeed, was Temple's significance. Partly because he was above politics, he symbolized very exactly, for many people who did not really know what he was saying, the social aspirations of the People's War, the vision of a decent society. He was so obviously a nice man.

Yet a high-powered Committee on Evangelism which Temple had appointed was forced to report in 1945 that "a wide and deep gulf" still existed between the Established Church and the people. The report, dedicated to Temple's memory, showed that the Bourbons of the Church which he had briefly led had learnt almost nothing. Its more or less explicit aim was to reverse history. It stressed that the decline in religion was most apparent in the south-eastern urban complex – that is, in the New England – and deplored the "mechanical thinking" of the new technical classes, who, it said loftily, lacked "the necessary apperception for apprehending abstract ideas". (One of the most grotesque features of the Church of England at this time was its repeated cries of "back to the land". The Malvern Findings themselves had called for a deliberate revival of agriculture, a revival of "true community, which is possible in a village as it is not in the great cities".) The committee deplored the trend towards the sciences in

education, because it would tend to destroy faith. It waxed
vehement on the subject of "sexual laxity" – "the present
depravity can cause no surprise when we recall the sex obsession
that has demented a disillusioned people since the last war" – but
it did not question the morality of area bombing. A pregnant
W.A.A.F. seemed to cause the Church more alarm than the
attitudes of Cherwell and Bomber Harris.[28]

Temple was succeeded by that "safe" man, Bishop Fisher.
Bell of Chichester, after Temple the Church's most striking
leader, was by-passed again. Indeed, he could not even be considered seriously. "There is no doubt", his biographer concludes,
"that his speeches on the war had destroyed his chances of
succeeding to the primacy."[29]

III

The Churches were in a very vulnerable position whenever their
leaders expressed an attitude to war itself. Even those of their
critics who believed most passionately that the war must be
fought were liable to retort in disgust when Christians said openly
"Thou Shalt Kill". It was of course a most difficult question, and
it was not one which religious leaders could, or did, take lightly.
Bishop Henson explored the dilemma in his diary when he was
asked to preach to the troops in August 1939. "What can I say to
these young soldiers which is fitting, helpful and definitely Christian? The conventional patriotic tub-thumping is out of the
question. We have got past that phase. As Nurse Cavell said,
'Patriotism is not enough.' Pacifist sentiment is so widely diffused
that probably most of my hearers will be more or less uncomfortable in their consciences... The Sermon on the Mount
haunts the mind, though it does not, and cannot, control the
life." Henson decided that he might fairly say that the British
cause was a good one.[30]

That granted, it seemed obvious to some prelates that it was
perfectly in order to pray for victory. Lang did; and to Temple's
horror, he associated Ebor with Cantuar's prayers. Temple's
view was typically subtle. He was a staunch defender of the
minority which practised conscientious objection, but himself
justified killing in this war. "We are involved in an entanglement
due to the sin of mankind, including our own, in which the best
thing we can do is still a bad thing. None the less, it is right to do
it because it is the best possible. And so we have got to do it and

be penitent while we do it." While it would be gross to suggest that he was ever guilty of "trimming" on moral questions, there was in the last analysis a trace of glibness in Temple's answers which is faintly disturbing. Garbett, who favoured direct prayers for victory, put his finger on it. Temple told him that he thought one should pray for victory only with the qualification "if it be thy will", or "for the victory of righteousness". "I disagree entirely", Garbett wrote in his diary: "unless we thought it was God's will that we should war against the Nazis, we ought to have opposed the war: if it is His will, then we may pray for victory."[31] Yet clearly, one must love one's enemies. This was a far from simple matter, when the British people traditionally regarded foreigners as quite different from themselves.

The Japanese war impinged remarkably little on the consciousness of the British people, except of course in those families which had members serving in the Far East. Save at the time of the fall of Singapore, its advances and reverses meant little in Britain. Only thirty thousand British servicemen died in the war against Japan, as compared with two hundred and thirty-five thousand in the war against Germany. To people in Britain, and even to some of the troops who fought them in Burma, the Japanese were "little yellow men", or even "monkey men". When Eden made a statement in the House of Commons, in January 1944, on the treatment of prisoners of war by the Japanese, the *Daily Mail* expressed a widespread revulsion in a quite preposterous editorial. "The Japanese have proved a sub-human race ... Let us resolve to outlaw them. When they are beaten back to their own savage [*sic*] land, let them live there in complete isolation from the rest of the world, as in a leper compound, unclean." All trade, all travel, all communication should be broken, the writer argued. All Japanese subjects in other parts of the world should be sent home. "We will keep and guard the cleanness of the seas between us."[32]

"Hari Kari", the Jap in ITMA, was no more than a gabbling zany. Conversely, the impossibility of hating the Italians was demonstrated when Signor So-So appeared in the programme. The intention had been to make him fatuous but sinister; it broke down with the warm response to his falsetto, querying voice. ("A Meestair Handpump, I am diluted! To me you are indescribable.") Duff Cooper had set the tone, even the Government's tone, when the Italians had entered the war and he had prophesied that they would be a liability to the Germans. A somewhat excessive contempt for their military potential had made the appearance of a few Italian planes over London during the blitz peculiarly galling. "... That was the last word, that was," one man said; "we can stand anything but the idea of Wops coming over London ..." A. P. Herbert, at this stage, attempted to whip up a little "healthy" hatred against the "Wops".

> SOCK THE WOPS, and knock their blocks;
> Sock the Wop, until he crocks;
> Slosh the Wop because he's mean;
> WASH the Wop – he isn't clean ...

But when Italy joined the allies' side, Herbert vowed, in further verses, that he would never use the word "Wop" again, and added "I think you never really liked the Germans." Which summed up the attitude of many Britons.[33]

The Germans were, first and always, the real enemy. Yet the hysterical propaganda of hate which had been directed against the "Boche" in the First World War had rebounded; the men from the trenches had brought home fellow-feeling for their enemies. This time, the "Hun" actually attacked British civilians in their homes. Yet the effect of putting civilians in the front line was to bring many of them to share the soldier's attitude to his opponent, whom he called "Jerry", "Ted" or "Kraut" more often than he called him "Hun". The Britons who wanted reprisals most, as we have seen, were those in areas safe from bombing. Meanwhile, firemen sometimes slaved to rescue a building, only to see it knocked down the following night. Yet, Stephen Spender reports, " 'It's all in the day's work' expressed their ideology. This functional view could get to a pitch where the war no longer seemed a conflict between Germany and Britain, but simply an inter-relationship of jobs within a system."[34]

Of course, there was also much bitterness in the bombed cities. In London in 1940, the inhabitants of one shelter so much enjoyed a recording of *The Magic Flute* in German that it was repeated the next night. But in Bristol in 1943, one resident wrote to the local paper complaining that all-German programmes of music were still played in the concert hall, to 'clamorous expressions of applause', and that the B.B.C. had broadcast over a hundred and twenty programmes featuring German music during the previous six weeks. It was later claimed, probably with optimism, that Lord Vansittart's Win The Peace movement had more than ten thousand members in Bristol alone; certainly, the Lord Mayor chaired its public meetings.[35]

Vansittart was a most distinguished veteran of the Foreign

Office, who before the war had warned repeatedly, in diplomatic circles, that Hitler must be resisted. He was still Chief Diplomatic Adviser to the British Government, in the autumn of 1940, when Duff Cooper permitted him to make an extraordinary series of broadcasts on the Overseas Service of the B.B.C. The theme of *The Black Record*, as Vansittart called his talks, was that throughout their history the Germans had been brutal butchers. Ignoring the origin of the "Anglo-Saxons" themselves, he quoted Julius Caesar and Tacitus on the behaviour of the Germanic tribes to prove his point. He diagnosed "envy, self-pity and cruelty" as basic elements in the German character; the first quality, he suggested, was largely prompted by the existence of the British Empire. He agreed, somewhat grudgingly, that there were good Germans, but "Unfortunately they are never there on The Day ..." He attributed all wars in Europe over the past seventy years solely to this "breed which from the dawn of history has been predatory and bellicose". Hitler, he said, "gives to the great majority of Germans exactly what they have hitherto liked and wanted ..."[36]

Even if Vansittart had been retailing truths, instead of half-truths, it was bizarre that he should have been allowed to make these, and later, broadcasts at a time when political circles in Britain quite seriously hoped for a rising of the German people. Goebbels plastered the walls of the chief German cities with huge posters containing extracts from Vansittart's *Black Record*, which drew the moral that the whole race was criminal and must be punished accordingly. "After the war", wrote the little Doctor in his diary, "a monument ought to be erected to him somewhere in Germany with the inscription, 'To the Englishman who rendered the greatest service to the German cause during the war.' "[37]

Vansittart, of course, was not the only prominent public figure in Britain to express such sentiments. The Beaverbrook press indulged in such headlines as "Why all this bosh about being gentle with the Germans after we have beaten them when ALL GERMANS ARE GUILTY!"[38] Trade union leaders and civic dignitaries joined in the chorus. "Vansittartism" was, however, the name commonly given to all such outbursts, by those others who still insisted on drawing an emphatic line between the guilty minority and the mass of the German people.

Yet where should the line be drawn? Virtually everyone wanted to see the top Nazis punished. To them, one might add the entire Nazi Party, or (like Vansittart) the entire German army, which meant in effect the whole people. The press mostly argued against extreme Vansittartism. But then, what did "punishment" mean? Suggestions varied from the notion that strong moral disapproval might be sufficient, to that of "complete political annihilation", a reversion to the Germany of agriculture and petty states, or a permanent occupation by the peoples it had maltreated. Somewhere in between the extremes lay the notion of punishment for the few and "re-education" for the many. No one attitude emerged from right, left or centre of British politics, though liberal opinion was strongly "anti-Vansittart".[39]

Mass Observation, in eight surveys between 1940 and 1944, found consistently that about a third of those questioned, when asked what should be done with Germany after the war, based their ideas on revenge, and a similar proportion felt that Germany should be prevented from ever making war again. But "vengefulness" might be theoretical or fiercely impassioned. When Londoners were asked at the beginning of 1944 whether they approved of British raids on Germany, about six out of ten gave "unqualified verbal approval", two had qualms, and only one felt that they were too terrible to be fully condoned. However, a positively gloating attitude ("Lovely – smash 'em up") was rare even amongst those giving unqualified assent. People thought that the raids would shorten the war, so they accepted them, though very few actually liked the idea. And only one person out of ten was aware that the British were not aiming solely at military targets – three-quarters affirmed positively that they were. "Few people", Mass Observation concluded, "think that the crimes of war should be visited on the ordinary citizens of Germany . . ." Vansittartism, at least in its cruder forms, was the creed of a vocal minority.[40]

Temple spoke out strongly against "reprisals", an idea which clearly reflected the ethics of the Old Testament rather than the New. So did other church leaders. But Churchill, from the summer of 1940, accepted the idea. Arguing over the matter in the House of Commons in October 1940, he indicated that he considered accurate bombing of military targets to be the only reprisal necessary. "Our object must be to inflict the maximum harm on the enemy's war-making capacity. That is the only object that we shall pursue." Two months later came the first indiscriminate attack on a German city by British bombers. In April 1941, Churchill revealed himself as something of a Vansittartite with the remark (in a world broadcast), "There are less than seventy million malignant Huns – some of whom are curable and others killable . . ." When Russia was invaded, he promised that Britain would make "the German people taste and gulp each month a sharper dose of the miseries they have showered upon mankind". Another world broadcast, in May 1942, contained a jeering suggestion as to how the Germans should escape from the havoc which the British bombers were supposedly wreaking. "All they have to do is to leave the cities where munitions work is being carried on – abandon their work, and go out into the fields, and watch their home fires burning from a distance."[41]

These threats should have made it clear that German civilians were regarded as a legitimate target. There were many who deplored this, in public and in private. But Bishop Bell is now remembered as the leader of the opposition.

George Bell was fifty-six when the war broke out. The blunt monosyllables of his name expressed the man well. He was a notable advocate of church patronage for the arts, and had done much to bring about the revival of religious verse drama which was then in progress. His tastes were refined, his manner was mild. But he had a way, which secretly irritated his episcopal colleagues, of turning every issue he touched into a moral issue; he "was by nature a protagonist, and seemed to make every subject controversial when he spoke on it".[42]

In the 1930s, he had annoyed people with his passionate concern for German refugees at a time when most Christians had preferred to ignore the problem. Then, in 1940, he had taken up the cudgels for the interned enemy aliens; he had gone to their camps and made a fuss about the conditions. The worldly Lang had written to him at that time in a most fulsome vein: "I should feel," he had said, "that the Church had been wanting in an obvious duty if you had not been able with your exceptional knowledge and your indefatigable zeal to take it up."[43] So that was Bell's role; to espouse the causes with which no one else could be bothered.

Meanwhile, Bell had been deeply involved in the ecumenical movement which, in 1938, had produced a provisional constitution for the World Council of Churches. He entered the war with "a vision of the Church across the frontiers, with a Gospel for Mankind", and with the personal friendship of such famous opponents to Hitler amongst the German Protestants as Martin Niemoller and Dietrich Bonhoeffer. In the first winter of war, he had written that the Church's function now was "at all costs to remain the Church . . . It is not the nation. It is not the state's spiritual auxiliary with exactly the same ends as the state." He had gone on to urge that the Church must set itself firmly against "the propaganda of lies and hatred", and even against attempts to destroy enemy morale.[44]

Speaking from a Sword of the Spirit platform on, of all days, May 10th, 1941, he called the night bombing of non-combatants "a degradation of the spirit for all who take part in it". He had already suggested, in a letter to *The Times*, that the British should offer to refrain from night bombing provided the Germans recriprocated. Lang reasoned with him privately. Hitler, Lang said, would not respond; if he did, his word could not be trusted; and such an offer would suggest to the Nazis that their blitz on Britain had been effective. "I fear all this means that – to use the language of the day – you are an optimist and I am a realist." He tried to prevent Bell's raising the matter at the Canterbury Convocation. Bell raised it all the same; though he agreed that what he had said should be kept from the press.[45]

In 1942, he threw himself into another unrealistic campaign. Children in Europe were starving because of the British economic blockade. An interdenominational Famine Relief Committee was set up under Bell's chairmanship, and proposed that dried milk and vitamins for mothers, children and invalids in Belgium and Greece should be shipped through the blockade. The Government thwarted its schemes at every turn, and although large sums were collected for the cause, very little relief was actually sent to the Continent.[46]

Bell was still considered "safe" enough to be sent on an official mission to the Swedish Churches in May 1942. In Stockholm, at the end of that month, he met unexpectedly with Dietrich Bonhoeffer, now deeply involved in the German resistance to Hitler, who had flown there specially to see him. Bonhoeffer described the opposition group led by General Beck and by Goerdeler, the former mayor of Leipzig, and on Bell's return to England, he passed his information to the Government. Eden and Churchill were uninterested. Then, in January 1943, Roosevelt and Churchill, meeting at Casablanca, announced that they would not make peace except on terms of "unconditional surrender".

The announcement was dictated by temporary expediency; in the end, both Italy and Japan were allowed to surrender on elaborate conditions. The unconditional surrender policy was intended to avoid dissent among the allies, to provide safeguards against another Darlan episode, and to reassure Stalin. But it made the work of British "political warfare", aimed at encouraging a German rising, virtually hopeless. In March 1943, Bell was able to extract from Simon, in the House of Lords, what amounted to the first repudiation of Vansittart; the Lord Chancellor stated "that we agreed with Premier Stalin, first that the Hitlerite state should be destroyed, and, secondly, that the whole German people is not (as Dr Goebbels has been trying to persuade them) thereby doomed to destruction". But the damage had been done.[47]

Bell continued to fret about the night bombing of civilians. In July 1943, he asked Temple to request in the House of Lords a Government statement on the aims of British bombing. Temple refused. "I am not at all disposed", he said, "to be the mouthpiece of the concern which I know exists, because I do not share it." By this time, Bell's outspokenness had brought him trouble in his own diocese. The organizers of a Battle of Britain Commemoration service, held in his own cathedral in September 1943, disliked his pronouncements so much that the dean had to ask him to withdraw from preaching at it. At last, in February 1944, Bell himself asked, in the Lords, for a Government statement on bombing policy with reference to civilians and non-military objectives. Lord Woolton told Bell, as he sat on the bench of bishops waiting to speak, "George, there isn't a soul in this House who doesn't wish you wouldn't make the speech you are going to make." Bell, however, accepted the legitimacy of attacks on centres of transport and war industry; it was, as he made clear, the obliteration of whole towns, of people and of cultural monuments, which he rejected. "How can the War Cabinet fail to see that this progressive devastation of cities is threatening the roots of civilization?" Lord Cranborne, for the Government, argued that great cities could be paralysed industrially only if all life there was brought to a standstill. The attacks, he promised, would increase.[48]

Military historians have since produced ample justification for Bell's stand. Yet to say this, paradoxically, exposes the weakness of Bell's position. His arguments, on what he himself saw as a moral issue, were often couched in those very terms of military expediency which he rejected; obliteration bombing was a waste of effort. He was deeply committed to the war itself, and several times agreed, in response to the arguments of Lang and Cranborne, that it would be inopportune to raise his favourite questions at such and such a juncture. As his biographer puts it, "Fundamentally he believed that war was wrong . . . Yet he refused to become a pacifist and continued to maintain that Great

Britain went to war for a just cause . . . As the struggle dragged on, he deplored the retreat from the original high ideals; yet the war itself made such a retreat inevitable."[49]

The most authentic protest, of course, came from the pacifists. There were only seven or eight in the House of Commons; among them Dr Alfred Salter, the veteran Labour M.P. for Bermondsey, who had seen his life's work in the borough devastated by bombs, and the members of his own local party turning away from the pacifism which he had taught them. He had himself suffered a thrombosis of the brain, and when he recovered sufficiently to make a last appeal to a small scattering of members in the House of Commons, he was, aptly, almost inaudible. Of the bombing of civilians, he said, "All this is founded on the great and terrible fallacy that ends justify means. They never do – never, never . . . Is there no pity in the whole world? Are all our hearts hardened and coarsened by events? . . . Will not somebody, for the love of God, for the sake of Christ, demand sanity and peace?"[50]

Yet if Bell was trapped in the logic of *Catch 22*, so were Salter and his fellow pacifists.

IV

In the First World War, manifestly a struggle between rival imperialist powers, it had been philosophically easy to make a pacifist stand, but physically arduous for many who did so. Abuse from society, persecution and even torture in the army, had cemented those socialists, Liberals and Christians who had opposed the war into a fellowship of martyrdom, and the events which had followed the war had seemed increasingly to justify their behaviour.

In the Second World War, by contrast, the authorities had softened in their attitudes, and were even rather proud of their pacifists. But it was far harder for a man to justify a pacifist position to himself.

". . . I was too conscious of the evil of Nazism and Fascism to be completely pacifist", writes Fenner Brockway, a veteran of the movement of 1914–18. "Yet I could not be pro-war. It would have been utterly against my nature and my philosophy. I was in the dilemma of seeing everyone around me supremely engaged and I could neither join in nor actively oppose."[51] As the tribunals were fond of reminding the conscientious objectors who came before them, if a pacifist so much as bought a postage stamp, he was aiding the war effort; if he tended a sick soldier, he was helping to send him back to fight. Yet the pacifist could not opt out of society except by going to prison, where the authorities were now very reluctant to put him. Except for the most determined objectors to the institution of the state itself, pacifism was a matter of uneasy compromise.

"... Where scruples are conscientiously held we desire that they should be respected and that there should be no persecution of those who hold them", Neville Chamberlain had said when introducing the new deal for C.O.s in the Act of 1939 which had brought back conscription. In the summer of 1940, cabinet ministers and M.P.s attended the memorial service for the greatest of Labour pacifists, George Lansbury, in Westminster Abbey, while six Peace Pledge Union organizers were on trial at Bow Street police court for putting up a poster which said, "War will cease when men refuse to fight. What are YOU going to do about it?" The magistrate dismissed the case, saying, "This is a free country. We are fighting to keep it a free country, as I understand it ..."[52]

The local tribunals were constructed differently from those of the First World War. Of the five members, one would be appointed after consultation with trade unions. There was no War Office representative present, and this removed a widespread abuse of the First World War, when such men had made it their business to inflame prejudice against the objectors. The objector had the right of appeal to a higher tribunal. There were still a few cases where the judges who chaired the tribunals hurled abuse at those who came before them; one, told by a C.O. that passive resistance was more effective than fighting, exclaimed, "I am not prepared to sit here and be talked to by an infant of twenty on these sort of lines indefinitely." But such outbursts were exceptional and most tribunals were patently anxious to be fair.

Of 59,192 people who claimed conscientious objection (a number almost four times as great as in the First World War), only 3,577 were given unconditional exemption. Nearly half (28,720) were registered as objectors only on condition that they took up approved work, generally in agriculture, or stayed in their present jobs; 14,691 were registered for non-combatant duties in the armed forces, and 12,204 were turned down altogether, and so remained liable to call up.[53]

Public opinion, which had been notably tolerant of C.O.s during the phoney war, swung sharply against them in the hysterical atmosphere of the summer of 1940. Many private employers sacked pacifists; by July, a hundred and nineteen local authorities had decided to dismiss all C.O.s from their service or to suspend them for the duration, thirteen to put such men on soldiers' pay, and only sixteen had ruled against dismissal. The L.C.C., perhaps mindful of the fact that its former boss Herbert Morrison had been a "conchie" in the First World War, set a lead by allowing them to remain; Temple and one or two other bishops denounced victimization; and Churchill himself made it known that he felt that "anything in the nature of persecution, victimization, or man-hunting" was "odious to the British people".[54]

Naturally, prejudice persisted. Vera Brittain, a prominent pacifist of long standing, reports that friends who had known her for years cold-shouldered her at public gatherings, and that she received a spate of abusive letters. But many well-publicized reports of incidents in which C.O.s, serving in civil defence and in ambulance and bomb-disposal units, had shown conspicuous courage, served to mitigate prejudice. In one remarkable case, a pacifist working in a vegetable nursery in Devon was post-humously decorated for shielding another man with his body when the area was bombed and strafed.[55]

Cripps had a C.O. with him in Moscow as his personal secretary. Well-known pacifists were allowed to lecture to troops and prisoners of war, with full freedom of speech. They might not broadcast, but even this rule was broken when the well-loved James Maxton was allowed to take part in a transatlantic discussion over the air. A special Non Combatant Corps in the army, founded in the spring of 1940, eventually had nearly seven thousand members. Scores of C.O.s in the Parachute Field Ambulances were among the first soldiers to land on the Continent on D Day, all refusing to carry revolvers, and it was a right-wing newspaper, the *Sunday Graphic*, which proudly printed the remarks of a German prisoner. "And what happened when I found my first Englishman is the reason why I say you people are mad. I lifted my revolver and fired at him twice. The two shots missed. The British paratrooper dodged behind a tree and instead of firing back . . . he cried out in German, 'Tell me, Herr Officer, have you fellows any blankets I can borrow?'"[56]

So the vast majority of registered C.O.s in fact served their country well, both as tokens of British tolerance and freedom, and by doing jobs which somebody had to perform. The C.O. drafted into a coal mine was, in effect, in the same position as a Bevin Boy who had wanted to fight. Official tolerance blunted pacifism as an effective force, whereas persecution would have strengthened it.

There was, in fact, no single pacifist movement, though various interested bodies came together to form a Central Board for Conscientious Objectors. This acted as a pressure group on behalf of all C.O.s, and became closely involved with Whitehall, to the point where it obtained departmental approval in most cases for the broadsheets which it issued to explain the manpower regulations. Here was another catch; those who rejected the actions of the state sought justice from the state. A more extreme example was provided by the small religious sect of Christadelphians, who tempered their traditional opposition to state power and treated for special privileges of conscientious objection, rendering unto Caesar that tribute which they had previously held was God's alone.[57]

Besides the Society of Friends, which employed the wealth of its members on the energetic provision of ambulance units and other social services, there were small pacifist groups in most of the Churches; there was the Peace Pledge Union which had claimed 113,000 supporters at the outbreak of war and, although this estimate was ludicrously optimistic, remained by far the largest group in the field; there was the I.L.P., whose members were divided over the issue of pacifism; and there were multifarious small political and religious groups, and individual postures. While it seems that the great majority of objectors specified religious grounds for their stands, they were probably in many cases no more activated by purely religious zeal than the men who registered as C. of E. in the army. It is interesting that, in proportion to their weight in the population as a whole, professional people, above all, and also men providing personal services (such as barbers) were much more likely to be C.O.s than manual workers; miners were amongst the least prone. Objection was, therefore, most common amongst those individualists who worked on their own account, relying on their wits and skills. Artists frequently pleaded for exemption on the grounds that they had a vocation for their work which must not be gainsaid. Victor Pasmore, one of the best of English painters, and Benjamin Britten, the leading young composer, were unconditionally exempted on such grounds. (Though Michael Tippett was jailed for three months for refusing to comply with an order to work in Civil Defence or on the land.) Probably the most unusual grounds for objection were advanced by a woman whose conscience revolted against wearing trousers in the Land Army.[58]

In the First World War, three C.O.s out of ten had been imprisoned. In the Second, only three out of a hundred went to jail for their principles. Only about four thousand amongst those who were told they must enter the army, as combatants or non-combatants, maintained their objection to the length of prosecution or court-martial. Some hundreds of these were court-martialled and jailed two or three times, and one man was brought up six times. Jehovah's Witnesses were often unlucky with the tribunals, which resented their anti-social stance, and they frequently courted and suffered a series of imprisonments.

Every extension of conscription and direction brought in a new crop of objectors; two hundred and fourteen women were jailed for refusing on conscientious grounds to be directed to civilian work, and there were nearly five hundred prosecutions of women C.O.s for this and other offences. Numerous men and women objected to fire-watching, and these produced five hundred and fifty-five prosecutions. The case of George Elphick, a church sidesman in Lewes (Sussex), who was imprisoned five times for refusal to fire-watch, was taken up by a galaxy of eminent people.[59]

But the principles, religious or personal, involved in such isolated hard cases, seemed remote from the great revulsion of feeling against war in the early 1930s. Some of those who had led that revulsion – notably Bertrand Russell and C. E. M. Joad – had now decided that Nazism must be resisted by force. Other distinguished men and women – the Bishop of Birmingham, Dame Sybil Thorndike, the Methodist leader Donald Soper – maintained their pacifism throughout the war. Yet their choice was uncomfortable to sustain, as news came from Europe of the fate of the Jewish communities.

V

Nazi anti-Semitism, above all else, provided moral justification for the prosecution of the war with the utmost ferocity. Yet no serious observer could have pretended that Britain was free from anti-Semitism. Zelma Katin reported that in the bus depots of Sheffield, "Jews were blamed for the war, black markets, high prices and most other universal ills." Yet, paradoxically, "when a group of us went round collecting signatures for the re-internment of Sir Oswald Mosley, we had no difficulty in obtaining a roll of nearly a hundred per cent." It would seem, from this witness and others, that the connection between Nazism-Fascism and anti-Semitism was not widely grasped in Britain. ". . . It is generally admitted", wrote George Orwell in 1945, "that anti-Semitism is on the increase, that it has been greatly exacerbated by the war, and that humane and enlightened people are not immune to it."[60]

As Orwell pointed out, part of the trouble was that the nation's 430,000 Jews were largely concentrated, occupationally, in trades which were bound to bring unpopularity to those who pursued them at such a time, selling or making clothes, food, furniture and tobacco. Most of the "enemy aliens" in Britain were Jews. Coming from a frightful situation to a largely hostile environment, they were bound to behave in furtive or neurotic ways which British citizens disliked, and they had brought with them the queuing habits of the Continent, or, rather, a reluctance to keep their places in queues. Because the East End had so many Jewish inhabitants, the prejudice against London evacuees, after the blitz had started, might easily become anti-Semitic in tone.

Further, as James Parkes put it, Nazi propaganda had helped to make Britain "Jew-conscious". Much mud had been thrown; some had stuck. Certainly, it was no longer possible to be detached where Jews were concerned, least of all if you were Jewish. It is said that Chaim Weizmann found Lord Rothschild vainly trying to calm his three small children in the shelter of the Dorchester Hotel during the blitz, and asked him why he did not send them to the U.S.A., as other rich people had done. Rothschild replied, "Why! Because of their blasted last name. If I sent those three miserable little things over, the world would say that seven million Jews are cowards." Parkes quoted an editorial in *The Times*, in November 1944, deploring the recent assassination of the British Minister in Cairo by Palestinian terrorists. "The Jews", said *The Times*, "have been the principal victims of the Nazi doctrine of the glorification of violence and, as such, have won the eager sympathy of men of good will throughout the world. They would stand to lose all if they seemed to become in the least degree contaminated by the villainies from which they have suffered." Like Hitler, *The Times* presumed that the Jews were a single force.[61]

There was little overt anti-Semitism in British publications during the war. The right-wing journal *Truth*, to which Sir Ernest Benn was the leading contributor, indulged lavishly in it. As late as 1943, the *Catholic Herald* was insisting that mass baptism was the Jews' only refuge from Hitler; and when, in the following year, there was a furore over reports of anti-Semitism among Polish troops in Britain, which had driven over two hundred Jews to desert, the same paper detected a "conspiracy" against the Poles. But Cardinal Hinsley attacked Nazi anti-Semitism with great vigour. Polls taken three or four years after the end of the war suggested that extreme anti-Semitism was confined to a small minority, but that about half the population, working class and middle class alike, were capable of making anti-Semitic statements; and this probably underestimated latent anti-Semitism.[62]

The British press had had, on balance, an honourable record of reporting the violent results of Nazi anti-Semitism in the 1930s. The White Paper issued by the British Government in October 1939, which gave details of outrages in Buchenwald and other concentration camps, said little or nothing that was not known already. By 1942, however, it was clear that Nazi brutality had acquired new dimensions. In January 1942, leading British newspapers reported that over a million Jews had been killed since the outbreak of war. Word of the extermination of Jewish prisoners with a new gas, Zyklon B, had soon filtered through to Britain. In September 1942, the *Manchester Guardian*, a paper with a magnificent record in this field, published an amazingly accurate report of Hitler's "model" camp at Theresienstadt.[63]

The British and American Governments had reacted only slowly to clear signs that the systematic extermination of the Jews was in progress in Europe. In 1942, they set up a joint War Crimes Commission to collect evidence. A week before Christmas in that year, a new White Paper gave a detailed account of recent happenings, and Eden made a public statement to a shocked House of Commons. At the suggestion of an obscure Labour M.P., not Jewish, every M.P., including the Speaker, rose in tribute to the Jews and stood, head bowed, for two minutes' silence.[64]

In the following weeks, the rising in the Warsaw ghetto was given some prominence in the British press. Many ideas for helping the Jews in Europe, or for helping them to escape from Europe, were ventilated. On the day that the Germans launched their final assault on the sixty thousand Jews remaining from the original half million inhabitants of the ghetto, an Anglo-American conference convened at Bermuda. It met, officially, to discuss not the special problem of the Jews, but the general problem of European refugees. The *Observer*, not at that time a radical newspaper, commented bitterly that here were "well-dressed gentlemen" assembling in "leisurely beach hotels" to "assure each other in the best Geneva fashion that really nothing much can be done". The Bermuda conference authorized only one definite action; the transfer of twenty-one thousand refugees, including five thousand Jews, from Spain to North Africa. Bishop Bell, predictably, launched into the attack in the House of Lords. But that, effectively, was that.[65]

The manner in which the issue was handled reflected backwards most interestingly to the Hore Belisha episode in 1940. Chamberlain had originally intended, not to sack Hore Belisha, but to shift him from the War Office to the Ministry of Information. This idea had been vetoed by the Foreign Office, on the grounds that such an appointment would have a bad effect on neutral countries, not solely because of Hore Belisha's flashy approach, but because the man was a Jew.[66] Like the unconvincing attempt by the allies to disguise the fact that the Bermuda conference was prompted by the special situation of the Jews, this veto had reflected a morbid fear of anti-Semitism, in foreign countries, especially in Arab countries, but also at home in Britain and America. This fear resulted in virtual anti-Semitism.

If Nazi propaganda had thus succeeded in making the British "Jew-conscious" the propaganda of all combatant nations in both world wars had weakened awareness of the full horror of the situation, by robbing the world of credence in horrible stories, and of language in which to describe them if it believed them. When Temple described the attempt at genocide as "the most appalling horror in recorded history", and when Eden spoke of "barbarous and inhuman treatment", they were using words which no longer had any force.[67] The atrocity stories which had churned out of the propaganda machines of both sides in the First World War, and which had seemed ridiculous soon after it had ended, had made all intelligent people extremely sceptical. Journalists and orators had expended all their strongest adjectives – barbarous, inhuman and the like – to describe the German bombing raid on Rotterdam in May 1940. (And that, incidentally, had been a classic "atrocity". Civilians had been killed, but in only a tiny fraction of the numbers supposed.)

So when people heard about Zyklon B and the reduction of human beings to soap, they only half believed in them. The obliteration of the finer shades of language, a task to which the British Ministry of Information, amongst others, had busily applied itself in the interests of propaganda, served to reduce the sense of horror, the sense of urgency. It was partly from the desensitized prose of most of the British press during the war, from the desertion of subtleties of meaning in favour of slogans, that George Orwell derived the notion of Newspeak, the vocabulary of totalitarianism.

WHERE ARE THE WAR POETS?

Progress and reaction have both turned out to be swindles. Seemingly there is nothing left but quietism – robbing reality of its terrors by simply submitting to it . . . Give yourself over to the world process, stop fighting against it or pretending that you control it; simply accept it, endure it, record it. That seems to be the formula that any sensitive novelist is now likely to adopt.

George Orwell, *Inside the Whale*, 1940[1]

I

Indeed, the invention of Newspeak, the realization that technology and total warfare, working together, must impose a new language as hard and vicious as society, was Orwell's great advance over previous practitioners of futurist fiction. The purges of Uncle Joe Stalin, and the calculated perversions of his propaganda hacks, provided the main inspiration for 1984. But the background of the book – rocket bombs and diluted beer, ersatz chocolate and citizens expected to devote their waking hours to the service of the state – was a projection of the Britain of 1944.

In that Britain, considerable cultural and political freedom still existed. One might still express quite openly heterodox views on any subject from salvage drives to Winston Churchill; though "defeatism" or open praise for the Nazis, earlier in the war at least, had landed people in jail. One might still publish pacifist and Trotskyist views; though if one's publication had become widely influential it would, like the *Daily Worker*, have been suppressed. One might be compelled to fire-watch, but one could read Bakunin, or even *Mein Kampf*, while one was doing it.

Yet history, some history, was rewritten. Mention of the crimes of Stalinism was as unfashionable and contemptible, as, ten years later, would be any suggestion that Marxism was not identical with Nazism or that not all Russians were robots. "Bloc thinking" was the rule of the day, and long memories were discouraged. Like the Germans, the British devised "black propaganda" – the creation of fake "underground radios", the forgery of documents, the fabrication of rumours – justifying this on the grounds that such lies were necessary if a Nazi regime based on lies was to be defeated. At home, letters and telephone conversations were censored. Propaganda lurked in many guises – "It interests me to find you control even the stars in their courses," said J. L. Hodson when a newspaper director told him that he had instructed the paper's astrologer to take the line that Britain must expect heavy knocks now, but was sure of ultimate victory.[2]

And that illustrated the prevalence of voluntary self-censorship. Because Britain was fighting a regime which burnt books and suppressed the truth, journalists and other intellectuals in Britain consented to the suppression of the truth, and gladly took part in the fabrication of mendacious propaganda, arguing with themselves that the ends must justify such means.

II

The Ministry of "Information", and Government departments in general, had three broad methods of imposing their ideas on the public through the mass media. One was to suppress news and views which should not be known. A second was to release, or to invent, news which should be known. A third was to give writers special facilities to report what was happening, on paper or on screen; with concomitant restrictions on the liberty both of the chosen few, and of those who were not given special privileges.

All three operated in the case of films. State sponsorship of films, and state influence with their makers, have already been mentioned. Censorship in this field was nothing new. While the British Board of Film Censors had chiefly concerned itself with preventing the adult treatment of sex on the screen, it had also tackled politics; in the 1930s, a March of Time documentary called "Inside Nazi Germany" had been banned. Until June 1940, the Board, with this distinguished record, was deemed sufficient; but in that month the Ministry of Information set up its own Film Censorship Division.[3]

The cinema offered exceptional scope for the manufacture of irrefutable lies. Some propagandist devices were clumsy, perhaps even unintentional. On July 19th, 1940, the Defiant two-seater fighters went into action over British soil for the first time. Of

nine planes, only three came back; the Germans claimed that
twelve had been shot down. The British newsreel commentator,
on the other hand, as one of the Defiants came whining down over
Dover and blew up, screamed excitedly, "There goes another
Messerschmitt."[4] Other types of falsification were more positive.
Factory workers might be annoyed to find their machines taken
over for the morning by a troop of glamorous young women in
ministry-approved war worker outfits, who performed for the
benefit of the cameras and were subsequently used to illustrate
the mobilization of women.

The control of radio was still simpler. Not only did the B.B.C.
monopoly make it easy to ensure that only "safe" people were
heard on the air, the use of pre-recording made assurance doubly
sure. Scripts of live programmes were vetted by the censors in
advance. When live talks were delivered, the announcer would sit
in the studio, carefully comparing what the speaker said with the
censored script in front of him, with a special switch to hand by
which he could cut the speaker off instantly if he strayed. A similar device was used for essentially spontaneous programmes like
the Brains Trust; it had the disadvantage that if a trusted per-
former had suddenly gone berserk and shouted "Peace at any
price!" or "The Germans are here!", the damage would have
been done before the switch could be used. But there were few
security leaks in unscripted discussions.[5]

There were two types of radio censorship. Security censorship
was intended to ensure that the enemy received no information
which would be of any use to him; it covered such matters as
details of new weapons, and the movements of Winston Churchill. Weather was always top secret; the commentator covering
one of the wartime boat races between Oxford and Cambridge
had to refrain from admitting that he could not see how far
Cambridge were ahead because the sun was in his eyes. The
B.B.C. ran its own censorship. Its chief censor claims that the
Americans who broadcast from London found British security
censorship "kindly and sensible" compared with that of the
Germans and the Russians. As for the second type of censorship,
policy scrutiny, he "can remember few, if any occasions on which
we interfered with anything critical which the Americans wanted
to say about us". Whereas security censorship was governed by
long lists of "stops" and "releases" from the service ministries,
policy censorship had no set rules. It was designed to prevent the
broadcasting of anything which might give comfort to the enemy,
cause despondency among the troops, or alienate neutrals and

allies. Thus, one must not call the Americans "Yankees", or refer to anti-war movements in Britain.[6]

The Government, without taking over the B.B.C. directly, reserved the right to order the B.B.C. to broadcast anything it wanted to be heard, and the B.B.C. on occasion fought jealously against orders from the Ministry of Information. This was the first war in which it was technically possible for one combatant power to relay its propaganda directly into the homes of the citizens of another, and the British did not neglect the opportunity. Every twenty-four hours, the Political Warfare Executive broadcast a hundred and sixty thousand words over the air in twenty-three languages, and nearly a quarter of this went to Germany itself. This was, of course, propaganda; but "white" British propagandists prized the B.B.C.'s reputation for objectivity, and the news which was broadcast to Occupied Europe was as accurate as it could be. High-mindedness, of course, was part of the Reithian tradition, and the "black" propagandists, who ran their own studio, resented this characteristic heartily.[7]

But British civilians, of course, were also subjected to covert propaganda. Wilfred Pickles, who certainly believed quite sincerely that the British were marvellous folk and that this was really their war, made a hit as "Billy Welcome", touring the country and talking to ordinary but interesting people. After a time, the B.B.C. decided, in Pickles's words, "to turn us over to the war factories and make propaganda of the programme. It disturbed me to have to go into canteens of great industrial firms and ordnance works and work up a frenzy of patriotism, national fervour and 'go-to-it' spirit among the overalled, grease-stained men and women. I hated the job. There were marching songs and sentimental melodies and I would interview these folks about their war jobs. I had to ask such questions as: 'Are we afraid of Hitler?' and 'Can we lick him?', which would be followed by a united decisive roar. And there were the personal endeavour stories in which a young mother told us about her own effort. 'Looking after three children and still doing a grand job in the factory. Good lass,' I would say, giving her a pat on the back. How I loathed it, and how embarrassed I felt."[8]

The British were well known to be the world's most avid newspaper-readers. In 1943, the number of newspapers bought per head of the population was even higher than before the war. It was estimated by the Wartime Social Survey that four men out of five and two women out of three saw a newspaper on any one day.[9] Excellent though the B.B.C. news was, only the printed word could be studied so as to form the basis of a considered opinion.

In this connection, it was somewhat dismaying that the sales of newspapers were maintained only at the cost of a great reduction in size. In 1938, newspapers and periodicals had been using up to twenty-three thousand tons of newsprint weekly. The total fell, first by a third, and then, after the summer of 1940, much further. In June 1940, newspapers were pegged at their current circulations and limited in their number of pages. At rock bottom, in February 1943, only 4,320 tons of newsprint were consumed weekly; thereafter, the demand for newspapers from the forces prompted a slight increase. The effect of this stringency was to reduce a typical London daily from between sixteen and twenty-four pages to six, or later four, pages. The "quality" newspapers, *The Times*, the *Telegraph* and *Manchester Guardian*, maintained larger issues, up to eight or even ten pages, but only at the cost of deliberately restricting their own circulations; a gesture which worthily represented the honourable traditions of the best British journalism.[10] There was more news than ever before, from many unfamiliar parts of the world, much of it making immense demands on the understanding of the most sophisticated reader. Even when the sports pages had been virtually abolished, the crime news had been cut, and kiddies' corner had been banished, there were inevitably many important items of news which could not receive detailed treatment.

And even if the press had been quite free to gather news, the call-up of journalists would have made it hard for them. By the end of 1943, well over a third of the nation's nine thousand journalists were in the forces, and a substantial proportion of the rest were engaged on non-journalistic work. Most newspapers lost about three-quarters of their staff photographers, and even without the activities of the censorship in this field, they would have been compelled to use more or less identical photographs. Only official service photographers were allowed to work in overseas theatres of war. The position of war correspondents was rather different. There were over a hundred of these in theatres of action at the end of 1943. Their papers had to receive War Office permission to send them out, and they were then given a uniform with distinctive insignia which permitted them to move freely. Fifty such men, from Britain and the Empire, were killed or wounded in action. Much of the reporting was excellent, and Alan Moorehead's accounts of the desert war were republished, with acclaim, twenty-five years later. But the best men could not be everywhere at once. Where it was impossible to give equal facilities to all accredited war correspondents, one or more would be selected by rota. In that way, a *Daily Herald* reporter came to cover the 1942 raid on Dieppe for the whole London press.[11]

In less exciting fields, such as agriculture, specialist correspondents of quality were hard to come by. The Ministry of Agriculture's press officer recalls that those newspapermen with whom he dealt consisted largely of "youngsters who for one reason or another were not needed by the fighting services or the wartime industries, a few earnest women who had turned over from household hints and cookery columns, with a sprinkling of veterans who had emerged from retirement with the laudable object of helping to keep the old rag going, even if it meant grubbing about in a turnip field at Dithering Parva". Clearly, such novices would find it hard to make sensible criticisms, and would be under great temptation to accept what the ministry told them. Still further down the scale of prestige came the small local newspapers which now had to rely on a skeleton staff of ageing men, invalids and teenagers. In one extreme case, that of a small weekly paper, the proprietor-editor also acted as chief reporter, and helped to make up the pages. His printing staff comprised four youths aged between fourteen and eighteen.[12]

The position of the press *vis-à-vis* censorship was a complicated one. Under the emergency regulations of the summer of 1940, the Home Secretary, as he showed in the case of the *Daily Worker*, could close down a newspaper summarily. Apart from this, newspaper editors were left in the same position as other British citizens; under Defence Regulation 3 they were prohibited from "obtaining, recording, communicating to any other person or publishing information which might be useful to an enemy", and four cases of infringement of the regulation were tried in court at the instigation of the Ministry of Information's press censorship.[13]

In theory at least, press censorship only affected news; comment was always free. The suppression of the *Worker* and the *Mirror* incident showed the practical limitations of this admirable doctrine. However, the press, unlike the radio, had security censorship without policy censorship. Every editor had been given a copy of a document known as the Defence Notices, which listed subjects on which it was thought that no information should be published without advice from the censorship. There were myriad borderline cases; one might not mention the locality of a power station, but what about reporting the matches of the station's football team? The Defence Notices were supplemented by a stream of memoranda and letters to editors (one of whom ruefully guessed that he received about five thousand during the war). These added new items to the list of banned topics. There were also letters which gave the real, and often unpublished facts behind current news topics, to ensure that the press at least knew what it was leaving out; these sometimes went so far as to suggest, without compulsion, that the matter might be treated in such and such a fashion. The Ministry of Information had a Scrutiny Division which aimed to read through everything published in Britain; but the censorship itself, under this wary eye, remained voluntary. If newspapers wished to handle items where security was, or might be, involved, they submitted them on their own initiative. The articles thus submitted might be cut, held up, or banned altogether, but they might not be rewritten at the ministry.[14]

The Ministry of Information was violently unpopular with Fleet Street just after the outbreak of war, but good relations were established later. Rear Admiral Thomson, the chief press censor, earned himself a name for siding with Fleet Street against Whitehall. The last word, however, always rested with the Government department. The Admiralty was especially furtive, and suppressed most naval news, except for the results of actions or the losses of ships, until long after it had ceased to be topical. So determined was the navy that the Germans should not know where its ships were that ignorant and nervous censors at various times deleted mentions of H.M.S. *Pinafore* and the *Marie Celeste* from press items.

At one extreme, the lists of deaths and marriages in the smallest local papers were carefully scrutinized lest references to servicemen would reveal to the enemy the movements of regiments or ships. (This was not petty; the British black propagandists derived invaluable information from such material.) At the other extreme, the reports of parliamentary debates in Hansard were censored, and even, on one occasion, a Bill before parliament which gave away the location of an R.O.F.[15]

With the best of reasons, the public was left in ignorance of many of the most important developments of the war. The existence of radar, then called "radiolocation", was revealed only in June 1941, as part of the campaign to recruit radar operators for the R.A.F. Security, paradoxically, had the effect of encouraging gossip and rumours, about which the Government was almost equally concerned. The most famous of all wartime rumours was that in August or September 1940, an attempted German invasion, or at least a rehearsal for it, had been destroyed in the Channel, and that corpses in German uniform had been washed up prolifically on the south and east coasts of England. The story was current in American, in Lisbon and in occupied Europe. Many people on the Continent claimed to have spoken to "survivors", many people in Britain had "witnessed" it, so they said; and in 1941, the Free French Information Service made an official statement (which was suppressed in Britain) that thirty thousand Germans had been drowned. In Britain, it was very widely believed that the issue of the code word CROMWELL on September 7th, 1940 had really been prompted by an abortive invasion.[16]

The blitz, as we have seen, fostered dangerous crops of rumours, especially in the provinces. The Air Ministry permitted the press to name bombed cities only when they were certain that the Germans knew which place they had raided; this meant that the news generally reached the papers on the second day after the raid. It was forbidden to give the names and localities of damaged buildings for twenty-eight days after the raid in question, though to alleviate the boredom caused by vague references to "a" church or "a" cinema, Admiral Thomson decreed that a random scattering of well-known buildings from different towns might be released after a variable lapse of four to seven days, which sustained the object of keeping the Germans in the dark. All references to factories, especially to say that they had *not* been hit, were taboo. The lists of casualties were posted locally, but not published; and this in particular gave rise to pessimistic rumours. The work of the bomb disposal units received no publicity, because it was forbidden to mention U.X.B.s except in the vaguest terms, and any reference to parachute mines was kept out of the press for the duration of the war. Censorship of blitz stories strayed far from the bounds imposed by security precautions; the terrible catastrophe at Bethnal Green Tube station in 1943 was reported, at Morrison's request, not only without reference to the district in which it had occurred, but without any suggestion that panic had been involved.[17]

The attitude of newspaper editors made the efforts of the Censorship Division remarkably easy. According to Thomson, an editor would frequently ring him up to point out that in his opinion the censors had passed an item which would give information to the enemy. Editors were generally amenable to suggestions that such and such a passage, although not trespassing against security, should be omitted out of regard for the "national interest". There were, of course, journalists who defied such warnings, and those who were duly quoted by Goebbels referred to themselves, without sheepishness, as "the Goebbels Club", arguing that the negative aim of yielding no comfort to the enemy would jeopardize the positive aim of winning the war, because complacency in certain fields was dangerous.[18]

The News Division of the M.O.I. issued a daily average total, at peak, of thirty-five thousand words, consisting of official Government releases and advance copies of B.B.C. broadcasts. Inevitably, much of this was reprinted as it stood. After the night in September 1940 when the A.A. barrage over London opened up in full strength for the first time, the "popular" Labour *Daily Herald* and the "quality" Conservative *Daily Telegraph* carried front-page reports which were almost identical except that the *Herald*'s phrasing was more dramatic, referring to "a ring of exploding steel" rather than a "ring of bursting shells".[19]

Further pressure to conform must have been exerted by the new reliance on official advertising. Newspapers, which had drawn their chief source of revenue from private advertising before the war, now found that source drying up. The Government stepped into the breach, sometimes buying as much as thirty per cent of a national paper's advertising space. At a peak at the end of 1942, Government departments were spending over two hundred thousand pounds a month on advertising.[20]

Eventually, behind all velvet gloves, lurked the mailed fist of coercion. The authorities had no great hankering to resort to it. Paul Einzig, the lobby correspondent of the *Financial News*, was eventually "muzzled" by the paper's board of directors after Anderson had objected strongly to a controversial scoop. But Anderson had previously asked Morrison to intern Einzig, and this approach had been rejected. And on a previous occasion, in 1941, when Einzig had been in dispute with the Ministry of Economic Warfare, the leader of the lobby correspondents had warned Dalton "in no uncertain terms" that if one journalist was victimized, the entire lobby and the whole of Fleet Street would make trouble. The Government needed the support of the press, in the last resort, as much as the press needed the complaisance of the Government.[21]

III

The same paradox applied to other forms of creative and intellectual activity. As George Orwell argued, "The ideal, from the official point of view, would have been to put all publicity into the hands of 'safe' people like A. P. Herbert or Ian Hay; but since not enough of these were available, the existing intelligentsia had to be utilized, and the tone and even to some extent the content of official propaganda have been modified accordingly." He also pointed out, shrewdly, that "the bigger the machine of government becomes, the more loose ends and forgotten corners there are in it."[22]

It was certainly true that in this war the right hand, of which Churchill himself was the index finger, did not know what the left hand was doing. As Duff Cooper complained aggrievedly, Churchill was "not interested in the subject" of propaganda. If he had been, he would have noticed the remarkably radical tone which had crept into official publications. Here was the Ministry of Information in a pamphlet on "Manpower", designed for circulation abroad as well as at home, referring to shipyard workers building ships "for a Britain that had once allowed them to be thrown on the scrap heap", and speaking of the benefits of "a planned peace". Here were many Government departments, in 1943, assisting Paul Rotha and Eric Knight to make an angry film about world poverty called *World of Plenty*. The fact was, as one sad Conservative put it in 1944, that Conservatism had "allowed itself to be deprived of the intellectual leadership of the nation . . . If you spend the week-end with an educated man, with a university don, a barrister, a higher civil servant, the odds are you will find that the *New Statesman* is the only weekly taken. Your host may affect to laugh at its politics; he may say that he only takes it for its literary articles or its film criticism; but the point remains that he does take it and that he and his like have been reading it and its predecessors since the last war."[23]

But Orwell also pointed out the other half of the bargain. Intellectuals might now be permitted to express the message of propaganda in their own way; but it remained propaganda. "Everything in our age", Orwell wrote, "conspires to turn the writer, and every other kind of artist as well, into a minor official, working on themes handed to him from above and never telling what seems to him the whole of the truth." What was worse was

the mass *trahison des clercs*, in which Orwell himself was implicated, which embraced this new role for the creative worker. The
leaders of Mass Observation were intellectuals, with radical
views; yet in 1941 an M.O. publication went so far as to deplore
the fact that "Among the hundreds of people on the Ministry of
Information staff, not one is responsible for music, not one for
novels."[24]

The establishment of CEMA, and the remarkable spate of official
hand-outs to music and the theatre, reflected, it should be
stressed, a quite disinterested desire on the part of the Establishment that war should not crush beauty and the arts which
expressed it. This was seen in the exemption of books from purchase tax in 1940 and in the discrimination in favour of the
"living theatre" by which the Entertainment Tax on theatre seats
increased far less than that on cinema stalls.

A borderline case between disinterested state patronage and
propaganda was seen in the position of composers and artists.
The pacifism of Britten and Tippett has already been noted.
Britten's opera *Peter Grimes* (1945) was an impressive portrait of
the persecution of a sensitive individual by a conformist society,
and Tippett's oratorio *A Child of Our Time* (1944) was deeply if
vaguely pacifist in feeling; that both were acclaimed showed that
tolerance flourished still. The doyen of English composers,
Vaughan Williams, sprang to Tippett's defence when he was
imprisoned. But he himself was "desperate" to help the war
effort, and besides collecting salvage, taking on a war savings
round, and undertaking fire-watching (all this in his late sixties),
he composed music for the M.O.I. film about *Coastal Command*.
William Walton, perhaps his most distinguished contemporary,
devoted himself to providing soundtracks for official films; of his
best-known works of the time, *Spitfire Prelude and Fugue* is self-
explanatory, and his *Sinfonia Concertante* had its first London
performance at an ENSA concert. Lesser composers also contributed many patriotic scores, while Sir Arnold Bax, the Master of the
King's Musick, wrote an *Ode to Russia* for chorus and orchestra.[25]

Painters were more obviously conscripted; indeed, many of
those who became official War Artists enjoyed a military status
much like that of the war correspondents. But the propagandist
value of painting was throughly obscure, if it had one, and few
compromises were involved. The War Artists' scheme followed a
precedent set, with remarkable success, in the First World War,
and Paul Nash, amongst others, "served" with distinction in both

conflicts. A War Artists Advisory Committee, under the sensitive chairmanship of Sir Kenneth Clark, was established with ten thousand pounds of Government money in the third month of war. A hundred or so artists were asked to do specific work or sent on special assignments; about twice that number of others sold their work to the committee by submitting it independently, and thirty artists were employed full-time, and given a salary. Nine remained civilians; the rest were attached as "officers" to one or other of the services. Sir Kenneth Clark's remark is richly symptomatic; he says that it enabled the men concerned "to go on painting with a clear conscience". Edward Ardizzone, who was a "captain" with the Eighth Army in North Africa, has recalled that "You could do your own jobs, you were as free as air. Quite frankly if I'd disappeared for six months no one would have noticed."[26]

The exhibitions of the work of war artists, which were held in London and the provinces, were remarkably popular. In effect, this meant that characteristic work by good modern painters was introduced to a wider public than would have noticed it in peacetime. War, indeed, provided ideal subjects for the leaders of the main current tendency in painting, loosely called neo-romanticism, and influenced by Continental surrealism and by the English tradition of Blake and Palmer. Blitzed ruins and forlorn wrecks – ghostly, fragile and evocative – suited the decadent line of John Piper and Graham Sutherland. The lovely shapes of aircraft inspired several effective compositions from other artists. Paul Nash was attached to the R.A.F., and some of the best work of his career was based on the surreal topography of air war. Painters who centred their work on human figures were more likely to convey outrage. Henry Moore found an ideal subject for his drawings in the London Tube shelters. Ordinary, troubled faces, joined to the heroic torsos typical of his sculpture, made for a grinding, ironic dissonance. Or his figures were wraithlike, so that the infamous Tilbury shelter in Stepney emerged as a phantasmagoric landscape reminiscent of Magnasco. The more direct response to violence in the work of Edmund Burra and Francis Bacon resulted, unlike Moore's, from an enduring obsession; the war did no more than to confirm it.

IV

Of the publishers' many worries, the least was censorship. Only security censorship applied to books, and while pacifists might not express themselves over the radio, or in most of the press, Vera Brittain's book *Humiliation With Honour* sold ten thousand copies in four or five months in 1942–43.[27]

The limitation of paper supplies was much more serious. Publishers were limited, first to sixty per cent, then to forty per cent, of the paper they had used before the war. At the peak of the war effort, when official publications were accounting for a hundred thousand tons of paper a year (and the War Office alone was using twenty-five thousand tons), less than twenty-two thousand tons were available for books. On the one hand, many well-loved children's comics had disappeared entirely; on the other, important publishers of serious books found it hard to keep them in print. The blitz made matters worse. Twenty million unissued volumes were lost. A species of black market publishing arose. Mushroom firms which, because they had not existed before the war, had no quota and need not declare their stocks, found stray sources of paper in the hands of jobbing printers, and published much trash. Meanwhile, a thirst for classics was impossible to slake; new copies of novels by Trollope and Jane Austen were eventually quite unobtainable.[28]

New books, generally, became shorter. While the typical war-time publication, a hundred and fifty pages of thin paper, was a suitable format for political tracts and modest documentary writing, it could not suit works of scholarship or ambitious novels. War books were easy to write, and easy to sell. Several of the Ministry of Information's pamphlets which extolled the People and their War became best-sellers. Tom Harrisson, in the cause of social science, undertook the ordeal of reading sedulously every book about the war published between the outbreak and the end of 1941; all the evacuation novels; all the diaries written by people who assumed that anything which happened to anyone at this time was of intrinsic interest; all the blitz books; all the spy thrillers (*Death to the Fifth Column*), and all the R.A.F. romances (*Winged Love, Wellington Wendy* et al.). Much of this output, of course, consisted of low-grade fiction. Harrisson was taken aback by the right-wing sympathies of most of the authors, and by the prevalent anti-Semitic tone. Nearly half the books, by his count, included a Jew somewhere, "and only in one case was the reference not unfavourable".[29]

So the increase in *per capita* sales of books by fifty per cent between 1938 and 1944 did not in itself necessarily indicate greater cultural awareness, nor did the increased use of libraries (marked even in the depopulated East End borough of Hackney). The fact that over four hundred libraries had been blitzed was enough in itself to account for an increase in book buying, since they needed replacements for over a million lost volumes. The three services had a huge demand for books, largely met by donations, and everyone changing his job was liable to seek out a manual of some kind or other. With reading for pleasure, as with religion, the war made the addicts keener, while reducing the calls for "good light reads" among housewives of all classes, now much overworked. The longueurs of war, and the blackout, encouraged the addict. The shortage of books increased their attraction for the kind of mentality which believed in snapping up whatever other people wanted. Books remained exempt from purchase tax while other forms of entertainment rocketed in price, and people found it hard to buy more basic necessities.[30]

The historian of Churchill's own publishers observed that "So great was the demand for books that many comparatively minor titles sold out their entire edition as quickly as a really great book, the deserved success of which could not be followed up for lack of further paper supplies." But there were encouraging signs. There was a clear trend towards more serious reading, and increased book buying was most marked among the young. These developments had been emerging before the war; one of the most significant events of the 1930s – comparable in its way with the birth of the B.B.C. in the previous decade – had been the arrival of the cheap paperback. Allen Lane had issued his first batch of Penguins in 1935, and had soon followed up their success by moving from reprints of best-sellers to new titles, and to "serious" books – educational Pelicans and political Penguin Specials. Penguins grew scarcer with the paper shortage, but the eighty-seven titles published in 1941 averaged well over a hundred thousand copies sold. The extraordinary success of the Specials was among the political portents of the war years. In the summer of 1940, a new work of left-wing political theory, Laski's *Where Do We Go From Here?*, easily sold eighty thousand copies as a Special, and it was far from being the biggest seller among these little red and white books, which were almost all socialist or radical in tone.[31]

Yet in all this, the serious creative talent was in the position of the host at a crowded reception with a sore throat and doctor's orders not to drink. "Ach! What was the good of writing a long novel when I couldn't see the way into the next day?" protested Alun Lewis in a letter to a friend in the autumn of 1939; sure enough, he was soon called up. The imminence of death further encouraged brevity. Those young writers who acquired reputations during the war specialized in documentary, in short stories, or in poems.[32]

With the call for propagandists and cultural impresarios, no writer of proven merit needed to starve in a garret; one might say, indeed, that the problem was the shortage of garrets where he might find a little quiet. In the centre of London, the Ministry of Information, the B.B.C., and the various official and semi-official film companies provided a range of employment, of a kind. A closely knit literary society emerged at this focus; for the first time, perhaps, English literary intellectuals began to see themselves as a class, an intelligentsia on the Continental model. Orwell, William Empson and Louis MacNeice were amongst those who found a relatively tolerant mistress at the B.B.C.; though Orwell, who resigned more in sorrow than in anger in 1943, described it as "a mixture of whoreshop and lunatic asylum."[33] At the M.O.I., other good writers produced propaganda which often achieved elegance and even distinction. Besides the army, Civil Defence claimed many. T. S. Eliot and Graham Greene both served as full-time air raid wardens. Henry Green and William Sansom found time to write well in and about the Fire Service. The most extreme case of personal immolation naturally came from that habitual extremist Hugh McDiarmid, who deserted the utter seclusion of the Shetlands, at the age of forty-nine, to take on heavy manual labour in a Clydeside factory.

Not surprisingly, very few memorable works of fiction or drama emerged during the war itself; though of course, many writers were able to bank experiences which they drew on heavily later. The theatre had long suffered from a dearth of native talent which the war did nothing to remedy; new plays by Priestley, Bridie and Noël Coward, and the emergence of Peter Ustinov, were the most remarkable novelties in a period otherwise marked by distinguished revivals of Shakespeare, Webster, Sheridan and Oscar Wilde. The only new novelist of much note was an interesting, but coarse writer, Nigel Balchin. The most impressive fictional achievement of the war years was probably Joyce Cary's trilogy, *Herself Surprised, To Be A Pilgrim* and *The Horse's Mouth* (1941–44); but these were not war novels. Henry Green, however, revealed all his strange talent in his novel of the A.F.S., *Caught* (1943); Evelyn Waugh's *Put Out More Flags* (1942) is still the funniest book about the phoney war, and Graham Greene's *Ministry of Fear* (1943), set in the blitz, is perhaps the most underrated of his metaphysical thrillers.

Waugh and Greene had the advantage that their Catholicism remained valid. The leaders of the literary "movement" of the 1930s had espoused, with somewhat comic ferocity, a communist faith which the Nazi-Soviet pact, coming after the purges, had quickly subverted. The leader of leaders, W. H. Auden, had migrated to America with his friend Isherwood several months before the war started; he remained there, jeered at by the right-wing press in Britain (which liked to pretend that the war had been caused by the young intellectuals and their famous vote in the Oxford Union in 1933), but still influencing British poets of his own and a newer generation. His influence now pointed in the direction of scepticism, quietism, a desertion of the big battalions, Marxist or Nazi, in favour of an individual morality. "We must love one another or die."

Large, confident generalizations of the kind which Auden's weaker followers had indulged in to a fatal extent now clearly stood condemned. Yet how else could the writer, made intensely political by the events of the era, hope to influence events, if not by propaganda? The nature of the new war, its immense scale, its technological complexity, its ramifying bureaucracies, increased the resulting feeling of helplessness. "Everyone", writes Stephen Spender of that time, "had shrunk in his own mind as well as in the minds of his fellow-beings, because his attention was diverted to events dwarfing individuals."[34] Not only influence, but adequate interpretation, seemed impossible. ". . . Accept it, endure it, record it" was the formula which Orwell suggested in "Inside the Whale", not himself wholly approving of the abdication of the writer from politics. In practice, one might do all three; but the three verbs pointed eventually in somewhat different directions. Acceptance led one to the state to which Cecil Day Lewis was reduced; work for the M.O.I. and patriotic verse about the Home Guard and the moral superiority of Britain. Of the two new periodicals which became the focus of literary aspiration during the war, it would be crudely true to say that Cyril Connolly's *Horizon* was preoccupied with endurance, John Lehmann's *New Writing* with the tasks of the recorder.

Lehmann had founded *New Writing* in 1935, at the heyday of political poetry, as a series of hardbacked miscellanies. In 1940, when its existence was threatened by paper shortage, Lehmann was able to sell to Allen Lane the idea of a monthly periodical, *Penguin New Writing*. In mid-1942, further restrictions of paper forced it to become a quarterly; but every issue sold as many copies as could be printed, seventy-five thousand or even a hundred thousand, an unprecedented circulation for a purely literary magazine.[35]

Lehmann himself was somewhat colourless, both as a writer and as a man, but he was an able impresario. He cast his net so wide that *Penguin New Writing* published new work by most of the leading talents of the period. While his own politics moved sharply from left to right during the war, Lehmann deplored the "ivory tower" attitude of *Horizon*, and maintained the stress on the social role of the writer which had been fashionable in the 'thirties. Along with that stress had gone a faith in documentary; the writer, immersing himself in the life of the unemployed or in the Spanish Civil War, could not merge with the proletariat, but he could describe it; and whoops of delight had hailed the appearance of a few genuinely proletarian descriptive writers, most notably B. L. Coombes. The war transmuted the ethos of documentary from dissent to conformity. Since the war was politically right, and since all the People were involved in it, irrespective of class, the young writer kept faith by his commitment if he merely described, in lame prose or bald verse, exactly what he himself was doing. Contributions poured into Lehmann's office, he recalls, "from all the services, from every front". *New Writing* made a point of introducing young aspirants to its relatively vast public, and the staple fare which it provided was largely mediocre rapportage.[36]

Cyril Connolly, on the other hand, spurned such cultural equivalents of Lord Woolton's potatoes. Stephen Spender, his assistant, compared him with "a cook, producing with each number a new dish with a new flavour", and his taste was refined, even precious. *Horizon*, he wrote loftily in one of his editorials, "does not exist to give young writers their first chance". He did launch some promising new talents, among them Julian Maclaren-Ross, who describes Connolly sitting, when he first met him, in the bar of the fashionable Café Royal with the proofs of an article by Somerset Maugham on his knees. Connolly told him he proposed to reject it. " 'I have the greatest respect for Maugham as a novelist,' Connolly said in his soft bland voice, 'and I don't say this is a *bad* article. It's good enough to be accepted for *Horizon* but not quite good enough for me to publish.' "[37]

Horizon had been launched in January 1940, with the declared object of maintaining cultural standards in spite of the war. "Our standards are aesthetic, and our politics are in abeyance," proclaimed the first editorial. The second provocatively praised Auden and Isherwood for deserting "the aesthetic doctrine of social criticism", and for saving their own skins by abandoning "what they consider to be the sinking ship of European democracy". This blistering cynicism was not sustained. Connolly later poured praise on Winston Churchill and described the war as "a necessary evil". But *Horizon* maintained its stand against cultural austerity; this was a magazine which in November 1940 could publish an article called "Some Notes on English Baroque" from an address in London W.C.1 where the ruins of English Georgia lay all around it.[38]

Connolly was certainly an escapist, and proud of it. From one angle, *Horizon* can be seen as a distressing portent of the reactionary, decadent trend of British culture in the 1940s and early 1950s. But Connolly was an intelligent escapist, who retained the respect even of such a determined anti-escapist as George Orwell. Orwell, indeed, found his first adequate platform in *Horizon*, which published several of his longest, best and most heterodox essays. The contributors to *Horizon* did not have to accept the editor's views, and many who disagreed with them helped to maintain the magazine's high standards of craftsmanship and intellectual integrity. Connolly denounced all signs of state control in the arts. "We are becoming a nation of culture-diffusionists. Culture-diffusion is not art. We are not making a true art. The appreciation of art is spreading everywhere, education has taken wings, we are at last getting a well-informed inquisitive public. But war artists are not art, the Brains Trust is not art, journalism is not art, the B.B.C. is not art, all the Penguins, all the discussion groups and M.O.I. films and pamphlets will avail nothing if we deny independence, leisure and privacy to the artist himself."[39]

This was grudging and ungrateful. Yet it was also true and pertinent. J. L. Hodson, a novelist and a journalist with high standards, wrote exasperatedly in 1943, "I have worked on and off for ministries for the past six months, on books and films. I feel that no artist ought to be required to go within a thousand miles of any government department . . . Men who can only write jargon, and who never use one word when they can find three have the effrontery to alter pieces of writings, or rather to attempt to alter them. Plain, direct statements are anathema to them."[40] Civil service jargon, of course, reflected the pressure on bureaucrats to play safe. It was not that they wished to suppress the truth; it was rather, that they were afraid that direct statements might trespass against some obscure dictate of security they had never heard of.

Which makes it all the more remarkable that it was in the issue of *Horizon* for October 1941 that Arthur Calder Marshall, Connolly himself, Bonamy Dobrée, Tom Harrisson, Arthur Koestler, Alun Lewis, Stephen Spender and, of all people, George Orwell, called for the formation of an official group of "war writers", with the same facilities as approved journalists, who could stimulate the war effort by interpreting events in Britain for the outside world. But it was still more extraordinary that Sir Herbert Read, who supported the war in spite of his anarchism, should produce the suggestion that there should be official war poets.[41]

V

That remarkable woman Christina Foyle, owner of London's largest bookshop, explained to a Mass Observer in the spring of 1940, "Poetry, as I expect you know, has not sold at all for the last twenty years but wars usually do create an interest in poetry".[42]

There were certain commercial reasons why young poets now found it easy to publish their work. Poetry normally meant a loss for the publisher. But now that any book could be sold, a form of writing which was highly economical in print and paper was bound to commend itself. Stephen Spender observed that "even less known poets could reckon their sales as between two and four thousand instead of in hundreds, as would have been their circulation before the war."[43]

Poetry was light to carry in the pocket, and could be read in small gasps between wartime chores. But much of the new interest in it came from that repeated query, "Where are the war poets?" The public expected to find startling new genius between the covers of the slimmest of volumes by the slimmest of talents; who knew where he might lurk, that prophet, that Messiah, the War Poet? There were hundreds of young men, in and out of uniform, writing poems about the war, but the critics rejected most of them; they had in their minds a prototype of a War Poet to which these did not correspond. He was young, he was handsome, he was precocious, he was doomed; he was propaganda. He would tell the Younger Generation what it ought to think, and his elders would hearken and applaud him.

Right and left had different prototypes, or perhaps one might say different mark numbers of the same type. The First World War had seen two manifestations of the War Poet, and the Spanish Civil War had produced a third.

In 1914, Rupert Brooke had sounded a call to volunteer which had expressed the idealism of his generation. His patriotic sonnets were still universally familiar, and culturally backward elements believed that someone should do the same job again. As late as 1944, a Conservative M.P. (Beverley Baxter), writing in the press under the inaccurate headline "Our Poets Are Silent", announced no less inaccurately that the P.B.I. had rediscovered Brooke and were "turning to the dead Adonis of the last war for the solace denied to them by living poets".[44] As the word "solace" suggests such people saw poetry as a sedative for the conscience rather than as a stimulant to thought.

By contrast, the left remembered the protest of Wilfred Owen, writing from the vileness of the trenches, believing that the poet's function was "to warn", and dying in action just before the Armistice in 1918. In the 'twenties and 'thirties, his poems had deeply influenced Auden's generation, and had been a potent force making for pacifism. But John Cornford, the undergraduate martyr of the Spanish Civil War, had left a few war poems of a different sort, proclaiming his faith in the world revolution of which current violence was a part. So the literary intelligentsia, if they were foolish enough to join in the hunt for the war poets, expected to find either passionate rejection of the war or sophisticated affirmation. Either stand, of course, would demand that the young man who took it must know whether the war was good or evil, right or wrong, and this was the news the world wanted to hear. The fervour with which it was sought is suggested by the fact that in 1944 the *Times Literary Supplement* devoted two full page articles in successive issues to the literary remains of Stephen Haggard, killed the year before; a slender talent, rapidly forgotten.

Except that he was not a poet, Richard Hillary came close enough to the specifications to satisfy the quest for a symbol. He was a genuinely talented writer, and in *The Last Enemy* (1942) he told the enthralling story of his part in the Battle of Britain, of the fearful burns which he had suffered when he had been shot down, and of the patching up of his skin by the great surgeon McIndoe, all with real distinction of style and manner. He had then completed the requirements by insisting that he must return to the R.A.F., and by dying in an accident during a training flight at the age of twenty-three. Hillary was easily made to serve as propaganda for the courage of his generation. Yet his own explanation of the motives of his book clearly showed why no symbolic martyr in this war could be as clear and stirring in his outline as Brooke or Owen. "I got so sick," he wrote in a letter, "of the sop about our 'Island Fortress' and 'The Knights of the Air' that I determined to write it anyway in the hope that the next generation might realize that, while stupid, we were not that stupid, that we could remember only too well that all this has been seen in the last war, but that in spite of that and not because of it, we still thought this one worth fighting."[45]

Few of the better poets in uniform engaged in action which was anywhere near as dramatic and significant as the Battle of Britain. They shared, to a still greater degree, Hillary's sceptical confusion. "The first war", one of them (Robert Conquest) has written, "was deep in the family consciousness of many. At the same time, Nazism appeared a monstrous evil, and we had in principle no anti-war views as regards our own war. Thus, our opinions and our feelings were not well-adjusted to each other."[46] In any case, whichever way you felt, Owen or Cornford had been there before you, and the war poems had already been written.

Robert Graves, who had himself been acclaimed as a war poet in 1914–18, gave a radio talk in 1941 in which he attempted to explain the dearth of successors in this war. He pointed out that the introduction of conscription before the outbreak had made "volunteer pride" like Brooke's "irrelevant". Then, the British army had not been engaged on a grand scale; the soldier, he said, "cannot even feel that his rendezvous with death is more certain than that of his Aunt Fanny, the fire-watcher". Graves suggested further, that "no war poetry can be expected from the R.A.F. . . . The internal combustion engine does not seem to consort with poetry."[47] This was over-confident, but he had hinted at an important point. Owen's protest had arisen from combat, in the most appalling conditions, with enemies who were close and recognizably human. Technology had made blitzkrieg possible; the man in the tank moved fast, largely independent of others, dependent on his machine, and distant from his enemy. The pilot high in the air could not imagine what life he was destroying on the ground. Machines, in fact, had made the morality of war less clear-cut; and there was no need to follow up Owen's prescription and "warn" the public when the public itself was liable to violent death.

In fact, the most violent verse of professional standard which was published during the war was written by civilians. Some major poets – Graves for one – were conspicuous by their silence on the war itself. T. S. Eliot's *Four Quartets*, the poetic event of the war for many readers, were mostly remote from the immediate struggle, though the blitz provided a famous scene in *Little Gidding*. But the raging imagery and strained tone of the best known wartime poems by Edith Sitwell and Dylan Thomas illustrate the point; it was civilians now who proclaimed their sufferings.

A number of young writers, some of them pacifists, had banded together in a movement called the "New Apocalypse". Henry Treece was then the best known Apocalyptic, though Norman McCaig had the greatest potential. The name even then gave rise to jokes about apoplexy and epilepsy, but the group was taken fairly seriously as the "latest thing" in English verse. It represented, at an extreme, two common features of the period; the retreat from politics in poetry, and the reversion to romanticism in this and in other arts. The painting of Sutherland, the music of Tippett, the poetry of Dylan Thomas were perhaps the outstanding examples of the latter trend. In the case of poetry, it represented a retreat to wild, clotted imagery which yielded only with difficulty any meaning which it happened to have and also, in essence, a retreat from reason. The Marxists had failed, politically and poetically; now let madness have its head.

One of the ringmasters of the Apocalypse, G. S. Fraser, explained peevishly, "The obscurity of our poetry, its air of something desperately snatched from dream or woven round a chime of words, are the results of disintegration, not in ourselves, but in society; we have not *asked* to be thrown back on to our own imaginations for comfort and consolation, or to exercise our function in quite this isolated way." The crucifixion was a favourite symbol with them (and it was used also at this time by Edith Sitwell and Dylan Thomas; as Ian Hamilton has remarked, these neo-romantics liked to assume a "quasi divine posture" of prophecy, taking upon themselves, with unregarded generosity, the pangs of the whole race). The offerings of the Apocalyptics are quite fairly represented by this:

> In spring we cross our foreheads with the holly,
> Heigh ho the blood and berry,
> And nail the merry squires to the trees.

On which Fraser commented enthusiastically, "It arouses all sorts of obscure impulses, not only in the head: we feel our muscles tensing for that effort of nailing the merry squires to the trees . . . There is joy, perhaps of a rather dark and sinister sort, in nailing the merry squires to the trees."[48]

The Apocalypse, as one might guess, rapidly disintegrated, and towards the middle of the war there was little trace of it. But the rejection of reason was implicit in the attitudes of other young poets, and quite explicit in the theorizings of Meary J. Tambimuttu, the editor of *Poetry London*. The third month of blitz found him launching into an assault on the doctrines of the "'Thirties poets". "In art, in politics, in religion," he complained, "we made ourselves believe what we really did not believe . . . In other words, we lost our self-consistency, our spontaneity."[49]

"Tambi" himself was certainly an impressive living example of spontaneity, more so in the flesh than in his own verse which was wild, disordered, but surely rhetorical. He was the high priest of a kind of literary underground which flourished in Soho at the height of the war; there were troops of would-be literary figures whom he led round the pubs night after night, an affront to the fastidiousness of Cyril Connolly as well as to John Lehmann's sense of responsibility. "Tambi's blue-black hair", one of his followers relates, "was bobbed like a woman's and curled up at the corners; his extraordinary hands, with fingers that bent right back, apparently boneless and like a lemur's only longer, flickered mesmerically as he talked in rapid tones with an accent that on the wireless sounded Welsh, white teeth and eyeballs flashing meantime in the dusk of his face." Around him legends collected; he was the son of a prince in Ceylon; he had arrived in England penniless and had been befriended by T. S. Eliot; none of this was quite true, but he was certainly Oriental, most notably in his attitude to the eager young poetesses who sought him out. Another admirer records that "His manic eagerness after two pints of bitter (through eating so little he became drunk very easily) and his Elephant Boy sex appeal were enough to secure him most of the literary girls of wartime London."[50]

Yet in *Poetry London*, Tambi, besides scores of unknowns who were destined to remain unknown, managed to publish many of the best poets of the time. The magazine appeared erratically (at

one stage there was no issue for nearly a year and a half); but
Henry Moore and Graham Sutherland contributed covers for it,
and Tambi could somehow produce a sixty-four page issue in the
barest days of austerity. And he included much work by the best
of the new soldier poets; Alun Lewis and Keith Douglas.

For war poets had been found, and acclaimed, though attempts
to make prophets of them were doomed to failure. In the navy,
Roy Fuller expressed, better than anyone, the boredom of long
periods of waiting for action, and the sense of futility which they
engendered. "The trouble is I seem to have escaped the war
again," he wrote to John Lehmann from Kenya, – "it must be
fated that there shall be no war poets. I just have the disadvan-
tages of noise and gregariousness without the stimulant of
action." Attempting, as a Marxist, to understand the process of
history which had set him where he was, he recoiled into pessimism:

> The years of war pile on our heads like lime
> And horrors grow impersonal as engines;
> Nor can I think in discipline and slime.
> Perhaps besides some blue and neutral lake
> Another Lenin sorts the real from fake.[51]

The "perhaps" was the key word; the machines had taken over,
and an inscrutable, pitiless history was the largest of the machines.

In the R.A.F., Squadron Leader John Pudney had established
himself as a bard with quasi-official status. His books sold hugely,
and conscientiously reflected the scenery of the service. His banal
celebrations of "The lonely ones who each to each/By intercom
report" came close to sentimental patriotism, but, the times being
what they were, Pudney shied away. He produced one poem
almost as famous (at the time) as Brooke's "Soldier":

> Do not despair
> For Johnny-head-in-air;
> He sleeps as sound
> As Johnny underground . . .

Instead of going to an early grave, Pudney achieved an official
post in the R.A.F.'s Public Relations Branch. On a tour of
Africa and the Middle East, he received, at Malta, a signal with
priority "Important", regarding the Twenty-fifth Anniversary of
the R.A.F. on April 1st, 1943: "POEM REQUESTED FROM PUDNEY
FOR 25TH ANNIVERSARY. 30 TO 36 LINES LONGISH METRE SUGGESTED
. . . SIGNAL IF POSSIBLE IF NOT FASTEST." Pudney set to work at

once and was soon able to signal back ". . . FITTERS AND RIGGERS
COMMA DRAUGHTSMEN AND ENGINEERS COMMA NEW LINE ALL YOU
COMMA NAMED AND UNKNOWN COMMA WHO FASHIONED THIS
FORCE COMMA LINE . . ." And so on.[52]

More fastidious readers preferred Sidney Keyes, who added
death in Tunisia at the age of twenty-one to his other qualifications. Keyes first attracted attention as an undergraduate in the
tantalizing, barely real world of wartime Oxford. His imaginative
world was neo-romantic to an extreme, dominated by Rilke and
Yeats, and he wrote almost nothing directly on the war. It was
only an obsession with death and a pervasive sense of disenchant-
ment which linked him with his contemporaries in the forces:

> There's no hope in hoping now:
> God has left us like a girl.

It has been said, fairly, of Keyes, that "the work he left really was
'war poetry' . . . in the sense that these poems would have
received little attention except during a war. Only in wartime
could one critic have discovered 'austerity' in a verse notable for
its self-indulgence, and another have claimed that he was the first
English poet 'effectively to marry Continental symbolism to the
English Romantic tradition.' "[53]

Alun Lewis was older, twenty-eight, when he died mysteriously
in India in March 1944, and he was obviously struggling towards
important achievements, both in poetry and fiction. His friendliness, seriousness and sincerity left a deep impression on those
who knew him. Even so, the praise given to him seems somewhat
hysterical. His first book ran through six impressions in four
years. While much of his poetry expresses poignantly the loneliness of a young man separated from his wife, it remains technically rather lame, and his language has heaviness and staleness
about it.

At the time, Keith Douglas was less famous than Lewis or
Keyes. Though both *Horizon* and *Poetry London* acclaimed him
as the best of the war poets when he died in Normandy in June
1944, he was not widely recognized until the 1960s, when he came
to assume the dimensions of a major figure in twentieth-century
literature. What marks him out from all his contemporaries is the
almost complete technical mastery of his poetry, from his early
teens onwards. He was only twenty-four when he died, yet his
work was complete in itself.

His prose account of the North African war, *Alamein to Zem
Zem*, consummated and transcended the documentary style. So

complete is Douglas's mastery of descriptive writing that the contest between observer and things observed which mars so much in the genre is wholly absent; while preserving wit and grace, Douglas conveys the ugliness of what he saw with an exactitude which matches the objectivity of a naturalist or doctor. He describes a dead Libyan soldier: "There were no signs of violence. As I looked at him, a fly crawled up his cheek and across the dry pupil of his unblinking right eye. I saw that a pocket of dust had collected in the trough of the lower lid."[54]

His poetry is equally uncanny. He sought rhythms which would, in his own words, "enable the poems to be *read* as significant speech", and he succeeded so well in his best work that a poem of immense complexity reads with the utmost fluency. His dexterously involved syntax ensures that his vocabulary, always fresh and surprising, catches the mind differently on different readings; the poems are like diamonds with many facets, seen in a shifting light. A superb intelligence radiates through everything he wrote, and controls everything, even the fear of death. A zest for experience made him desert a desk job in Cairo and rejoin his regiment at El Alamein. He enjoyed soldiering, its techniques and excitements. He saw his comrades clearly for what they were, describing their behaviour closely, neither idealizing nor satirizing them, though in his poem "Aristocrats" he brilliantly played off the two inadequate attitudes against each other:

> Peter was unfortunately killed by an 88:
> it took his leg away, he died in the ambulance.
> I saw him crawling on the sand; he said
> It's most unfair, they've shot my foot off.
> How can I live among this gentle
> obsolescent breed of heroes, and not weep?...[55]

He expressed his notion of his own role in a letter replying to a friend who had called on him to write in a more lyrical style. "To be sentimental or emotional now", commented Douglas, "is dangerous to myself and to others. To trust anyone or to admit any hope of a better world is criminally foolish, as foolish as it is to stop working for it. It sounds silly to say work without hope, but it can be done; it's only a form of insurance; it doesn't mean work hopelessly." He had previously introduced his friend to the word "bullshit". "It symbolizes what I think must be got rid of – the mass of irrelevancies, of 'attitudes', 'approaches', propaganda, ivory towers, etc., that stands between us and our problems and what we have to do about them."[56]

There was an intellectual rigour and a cold courage in Douglas which remind one of J. B. S. Haldane in the compressed air chamber. He was surely right to suggest that nothing was going to do much good now save an unremitting clarity of vision, a refusal to be fooled, the concentration of a curious gaze on a desperate reality which could only so be mastered.

Chapter Nine:

Never Again?:
December 1942 to August 1945

... The nearer victory comes in sight, the clearer the character of the war reveals itself as what the Tories always said that it was – a war for national survival, a war in defence of certain conservative nineteenth-century ideals, and not what I and my friends of the left said that it was – a revolutionary civil war in Europe on the Spanish pattern.

Arthur Koestler, January 1943

CMD 6404

I feel quite exhausted after seeing & hearing so much sadness, sorrow, heroism and magnificent spirit. The destruction is so awful, & the people so *wonderful* – they *deserve* a better world.

Queen Elizabeth to Queen Mary, in a letter, 19.10.40[1]

I

OTHER decisions emerged from the meeting of Churchill and Roosevelt at Casablanca in January 1943 besides the policy of unconditional surrender. The policy of strategic bombing was maintained. Although Churchill and Roosevelt had agreed that the war against the U-boats in the Atlantic must have the first claim on resources, big planes were still committed to ineffectual raids on the U-boat bases and building yards rather than to their destruction at sea. But improvements in radar equipment, and new tactics for guarding convoys at last tipped the scales decisively against Germany in the Battle of the Atlantic. By the second half of May, U-boat losses were so heavy that Admiral Doenitz called back his boats; and no merchant ships at all were sunk in the main convoy routes in June. However, the need for shipping to transport men and military equipment from America to the Old World meant that the British public had no increase in its rations, no slackening of its belts.

The tide was flowing towards an allied victory; the keynote of popular discontent was no longer fear, but impatience. Rommel was still fighting in North Africa; but at last he was displaying his brilliance and cunning in retreat. In February, he reached Tunisia, where the fighting was severe; not till May 12th did the British public hear, on the midnight news, that the arduous, controversial North African campaign had finished at last. Tunis had fallen, and with its fall two hundred and fifty thousand troops had been captured by the Allies.

After a lull of several weeks when news from the Mediterranean was, for once, unexciting, allied forces landed in Sicily on July 9th. As is now well known, while the British cut a bloody passage up the east coast of the island, the Americans in the centre and west had a much easier time; they had enlisted the help of the Mafia. While this was not, of course, publicized, knowledge of it would merely have confirmed the lesson of the Darlan episode. The ideals for which Britons had believed themselves to be fighting were hopelessly compromised as soon as enemy territory was captured.

The fighting in Sicily ended on August 18th, but long before that, on July 25th, political opposition in Italy had brought down Benito Mussolini. The King replaced him with the former Italian commander-in-chief in Ethiopia, Marshal Badoglio, who soon began to stretch peace feelers towards the Allies. They proved far from averse to treat with him.

In the Far East, the front in Burma was stagnant, and otherwise there were only squabbles over obscure islands in which the British people could take little interest. In Russia, a successful German counter-attack postponed for a brief period the total collapse of Hitler's fatal venture. But in the summer, a new German offensive against the Russian salient at Kursk was broken, and in August the Russians began to thrust the Germans back towards the Fatherland. Yet there was irritation and sadness for Uncle Joe's admirers. Poland was clearly becoming an issue again, and here right and left, Catholic and Communist, disagreed violently. The dream of world harmony after the war began to fade.

How near victory seemed depended on the latest news in the papers – in April 1943, one person in twenty-five thought the war in Europe would be over in less than a year; in September, three out of four. Yet people were gloomier, rather than brighter, as the military position improved. While fears of mass unemployment after the war were receding, as people grew used to the new security at work, it seemed clear to many that the future would be little better than the past. In this despondency, the toll of three, nearly four years of war strain clearly played its part; it was fashionable for women to have a flash of grey in their hair. Another factor was the Government's reception of the Beveridge report.[2]

II

The first impetus for the Beveridge report had come from the T.U.C., which in February 1941 had sent a deputation to lobby the Minister of Health on the inadequacy of the existing provision for health insurance. Since health insurance could not be treated in isolation, the committee appointed by Arthur Greenwood on June 10th, 1941, with Beveridge as its chairman and eleven civil servants representing the Government departments concerned, had been entrusted with a comprehensive survey of all existing social insurance schemes.

The need for such a survey was obvious. In 1938–39 nearly twenty-one million people had been covered by the state's old age pensions scheme; fifteen and a half million workers by unemployment insurance; and twenty million people – but no more than half the population – by National Health Insurance.[3] The benefits given under the different schemes were theoretically meeting the same need – for enough money to live on when earning ceased – but in fact varied greatly. Wives and families of those insured under the National Health scheme were not covered by it. Because so many people were privately insured against sickness, benefits under the scheme were meagre, and prolonged illness might drive even a well-paid and thrifty member of the working class into the hard hands of the poor law.

Beveridge had as long an acquaintanceship with the problems of poverty and unemployment as almost any man living. From social work in the slums of London, he had proceeded to important posts in the civil service before and during the First World War. Between the wars, he had been Director of the London School of Economics. He was the outstanding combination of public servant and social scientist. He was also vain, humourless and tactless.

Beveridge, as soon as he could find the time from his many other duties, had presented his interdepartmental committee with a memorandum which contained all the essentials of his famous scheme. "Once this memo had been circulated," he himself remarks emphatically, "the committee had their objective settled for them and discussion was reduced to consideration of means of attaining that objective." But this scheme of which Beveridge was Onlie Begetter raised what then seemed to be fundamental and controversial issues, and if the assembled civil servants endorsed it, they would commit their ministers to it, and with them the Government as a whole. The cabinet became aware of the case and in January 1942, Greenwood wrote to Beveridge that "In view of the issues of high policy which will arise, we think that the departmental representatives should henceforward be regarded as your advisers . . . This means that the Report, when made, will be your own report . . ."[4]

Yet the scheme was nothing like so revolutionary as Beveridge, and some of his admirers, liked to pretend. In the first place, in A. J. P. Taylor's words, he "finally rejected the socialist doctrine of a social security provided by society". His scheme was contributory, of course, and the contributions involved were to be paid on a flat rate, applying to all income levels, which was essentially a retrogressive arrangement. The scheme provided a minimum level of security for those who could afford no better; but the well-to-do classes could still buy better provision if they wished. Secondly, it was abundantly clear by 1942 that the existing social insurance schemes must somehow be rationalized and co-ordinated, and there was a wide measure of agreement on the left and centre of British politics that the elimination of poverty must be an aim. Beveridge's scheme expressed this consensus. The civil service experts who advised him generally sympathized with his ideas. From January to October 1942, the committee took evidence from no less than a hundred and twenty-seven individuals and organizations, and Beveridge himself emphasized that witnesses as far apart in their interests as the T.U.C., the employers in the Shipping Federation, and the social scientists of P.E.P., made proposals of their own agreeing on "practically all" the main principles of the report.[5]

Beveridge was not an obscure grey eminence; he kept himself well in the public eye with his broadcasts, notably on the Brains Trust. "Everybody has heard of Sir William Beveridge," wrote a

Picture Post journalist in March 1942, under the title "BEVERIDGE, THE MANPOWER EXPERT, IS BEING WASTED HIMSELF", going on to ask whether this boring looking job with the committee on social insurance was "worthy of him". This may well have reflected Sir William's own views; he was still smarting after a bout with Ernest Bevin. But those who gave evidence before his committee began to whisper it around that something very large was afoot. Expectations began to build up in Westminster and in Fleet Street. In mid-November 1942, just before his report was completed, Beveridge produced a signal example of his ruinous lack of political tact. He permitted a journalist from the right-wing *Daily Telegraph* to interview him; he was quoted in the paper as saying that his proposals would "take the country half way to Moscow".[6] This, if nothing else, would have put Beveridge in bad odour with the War Cabinet, and would have ensured a hostile reception for the report from the right wing of the Conservative party and its associated vested interests.

The report, Cmd 6404 in its official numbering, was published on December 1st, 1942. It contained three hundred very closely printed pages and was priced at two shillings. All the leading newspapers summarized it. The staunchly Conservative *Yorkshire Post*, illustrating the prevalence of confused high spirits and goodwill to all men at that psychological turning point just after El Alamein, praised Sir William's "pioneering vision" and said that a prompt decision to implement its main features "would be a most heartening affirmation of faith in the future of Britain . . ." Tommy Handley appeared on ITMA as "His Fatuity the Minister of Social Hilarity", explaining, "I've been up the last three days and nights reading the first chapter of a book called 'Gone With the Want', by that stout fellow Beveridge."[7] The Minister of Information, Brendan Bracken, for a brief moment whipped all the horses of publicity.

Outside the shops of His Majesty's Stationery Office, the most significant queues of the war lined up to buy the report. A brief official summary was issued, and sales of the two combined eventually ran to at least 635,000 copies. Within two weeks of its publication, a Gallup Poll discovered that nineteen people out of twenty had heard of the report, and nine out of ten believed that its proposals should be adopted.[8]

The "Plan" took all the existing social insurance schemes and gathered them into one overall scheme covering, it was said, every crisis of life from the cradle (maternity grants) to the grave (funeral grants). Beveridge, explaining his three guiding principles, married the doctrines of Liberal individualism to the revolutionary sentiments of the People's War.

> The first principle is that any proposals for the future, while they should use to the full the experience gathered in the past, should not be restricted by consideration of sectional interests established in the obtaining of that experience . . . A revolutionary moment in the world's history is time for revolutions, not for patching.
> The second principle is that organization of social insurance should be treated as one part only of a comprehensive policy of social progress. Social insurance fully developed may provide income security; it is an attack upon Want. But Want is one only of five giants on the road of reconstruction and in some ways the easiest to attack. The others are Disease, Ignorance, Squalor and Idleness.
> The third principle is that social security must be achieved by co-operation between the state and the individual. The state should offer security for service and contribution. The state in organizing security should not stifle incentive, opportunity, responsibility; in establishing a national minimum, it should leave room and encouragement for voluntary action by each individual to provide more than that minimum for himself and his family.[9]

Besides his three principles, Beveridge based his plan on three assumptions. That family allowances would be given for all children, was one. That a National Health Service would be provided was a second. Thirdly, he assumed that mass unemployment could be avoided. This granted, his plan would cover all citizens without any upper income limit. There would be a flat rate of contribution and a uniform rate of benefit. Every contributor – here was the most striking innovation, the beguiling simplicity at the heart of the plan – would be covered for all his needs by a single weekly contribution. Any who fell "through the meshes" of the scheme would be given National Assistance. Integral to the plan was the idea of a national minimum, an income which would ensure a decent level of subsistence to the poorest citizens, below which no one should be allowed to fall. Speculating as to the post-war value of money, Beveridge set this as forty shillings a week for an adult, and this, he suggested, would be the basic rate for social insurance benefits of every sort; family allowances would provide the necessary "topping up" for those with children.

A tempting comparison was drawn, showing the provision for a man with a wife and two children "before and after" the implementation of the Beveridge proposals. Under existing schemes, such a man would receive thirty-eight shillings a week for twenty-six weeks when he was unemployed; under the plan, he would get fifty-six shillings per week for an unlimited time. As a disability benefit, he would currently receive eighteen shillings per week for twenty-six weeks, followed by ten shillings and sixpence per week. After Beveridge, he would be given fifty-six shillings a week in this case also.[10]

But there was a significant and sinister qualification of the principle of the national minimum when Beveridge came to old age pensions. The number of old people in Britain was great, and growing. While their pensions would eventually reach the national minimum, Beveridge said that this part of the scheme was so expensive that it could not be fully implemented for twenty years if the plan was to be financially viable. The public certainly spotted this cloud over the Brave New World; one in every four adults was currently helping to support an old age pensioner, and two-thirds of those questioned by the Gallup Poll thought that Beveridge's transitional rates were too low. Indeed, there was also widespread feeling that the sickness and unemployment benefits were inadequate. The greatest public acclaim was given to a proposal which was outside the report's field, but which Beveridge made one of his three assumptions – the setting up of a comprehensive National Health Service. One must conclude that it was not the details of the plan which appealed so greatly to so many; it was the fact that it was a "plan", and also the aura of millennium with which Beveridge surrounded it.[11]

The plan would involve a large increase in social insurance contributions by individuals – from one shilling and tenpence a week to four shillings and threepence a week for the family postulated earlier. It was calculated, however, that the average household was already paying out so much towards private, voluntary schemes and private medical services which the plan would make redundant, that no great increase would be involved for those content with the national minimum.[12]

Contributions by employers and by the state would also increase, but Beveridge swept aside any objections based on the cost of the scheme, as "defeatism without reason and against reason". The extra cost to the state would be considerable, but not crippling, even allowing for Britain's shrunken overseas investments and her lost export markets. Beveridge called for immediate steps towards implementing his plan; the acceptance by parliament of its fundamental principles and the establishment of a new Ministry of Social Security to organize the unified scheme ". . . The purpose of victory," he concluded, "is to live into a better world than the old world . . . Each individual citizen is more likely to concentrate upon his war effort if he feels that his Government will be ready in time with plans for that better world . . . If these plans are to be ready in time, they must be made now."[13]

The right wing of the Conservative Party was unimpressed. That somewhat extreme organ, the *National Review*, described Beveridge, inaccurately, as a "well-known socialist bureaucrat" – in fact, he soon joined the Liberal Party, and became a Liberal M.P. in the autumn of 1944 – and observed gloomily that "The dole is to be greatly increased, so greatly that thousands of people will greatly prefer to do nothing. And an immense scattering of public money under the name of 'social security' is to take place on every sort of occasion." The line of more moderate Tories, as Harold Nicolson observed it developing immediately after the report's publication, was "to welcome the report in principle, and then to whittle it away by detailed criticism. They will say that it is all very splendid and Utopian, but we can only begin to know whether we can afford it once we have some idea what our foreign trade will be like after the war." Moreover, some canny socialists saw clearly enough that the plan was far from being revolutionary; and one veteran Labour Party agent described its ecstatic reception as "a deluge of slush".[14]

But in December, the National Council of Labour, representing both the Labour Party and the T.U.C., endorsed the report in general; so did the Liberal Party; and soon the British Council of Churches followed suit. A good many Conservatives, mainly younger ones, welcomed it as enthusiastically as anyone. Quintin Hogg, M.P., remarked, significantly, that "It was not that it was a bible or a panacea, but it was a flag to nail to the mast, a symbol, a rallying point for men of goodwill – above all, an opportunity to re-establish a social conscience in the Tory Party."[15]

An American edition of the report was published at great speed. News of the plan roused hopes in the Resistance in occupied Europe. The German press were instructed to avoid mentioning it, "as no indirect propaganda should be made for the plan". The *Manchester Guardian* summed up the situation accurately on February 15th, 1943, when the House of Commons was about to debate the report. "As the weeks have gone on it has become more and more clear that unless we get the Beveridge plan, or something at least as comprehensive and bold, we shall not escape without injury to our national reputation abroad and without far-reaching political reactions at home . . . The truth is that the Government when it published the report delivered a hostage to political fortune. Its credit, external and internal, has become bound up with the putting through of a great scheme of social security."[16]

In fact, the cabinet had been embarrassed, rather than delighted, by the report's popular success. Churchill seems to have seen the report as a distraction from the task of winning the war, not as something which might help to win it. Bevin, who might have argued back, disliked Beveridge, and had originally suggested him as an apt head for an inquiry into social insurance because he had wanted to get him out of his way in the Ministry of Labour. In spite of its overwhelming popularity, the report could not be implemented without a controversy which would jeopardize the coalition itself; the private insurance firms, a formidable bloc of vested interests, were mounting a bitter campaign against its "thriftlessness". But Bracken, by permitting the initial spate of publicity, had fathered this one-man plan on the whole Government.

So after the first glare of limelight, the Government went to extraordinary lengths to stifle all official publicity for the report. A summary, by Sir William himself, was issued as an ABCA pamphlet on December 19th, 1942 – and then, two days later, the War Office withdrew it. The War Minister explained to indignant M.P.s that he could not permit ABCA discussion groups, which were compulsory, to discuss such a controversial subject. In the absence – for more than three months – of any decisive pronouncement by the Government, increasingly angry sections of the press and public saw the ABCA affair as a clear sign that the Government disapproved of the report.

The cabinet eventually decided to accept sixteen of Beveridge's twenty-three recommendations "in principle", and rejected outright only the proposal that industrial assurance should be nationalized. When the House of Commons debate began on February 16th, the cabinet was ready to commit itself to a start on the work of preparing necessary legislation; but at Churchill's insistence, any decision as to whether this legislation should be implemented or not must be left to a new Government elected after the end of the war.[17]

The cabinet had a plausible case, but presented it in exactly the manner best calculated to enrage their opponents and dismay public opinion. Churchill himself was ill, and Anderson was put up to introduce the Government's position, which he did in a manner which made clear that he lacked, not only any enthusiasm for the plan, but also any understanding of the depth of interest taken in it by the people. On the second day of the debate, Sir Kingsley Wood lingered, with apparent satisfaction, over the financial perils of the plan. The result was a revolt by its backbenchers which perhaps did as much as anything to bring about the Labour Party's electoral victory in 1945. Only one member of the parliamentary party who was not actually a minister voted with the Government at the end of the debate. Amongst a total of a hundred and nineteen rebels ninety-seven Labour M.P.s voted against the Government, and Arthur Greenwood headed the revolt in person.[18]

Equally significant was the action of a group of young Conservatives, led by Quintin Hogg and Lord Hinchingbrooke, who had threatened to revolt also, but changed their mind when Herbert Morrison made a brilliant face-saving speech on behalf of the cabinet during the third day of the debate. The group shortly constituted itself as the Tory Reform Committee, and achieved a membership of fifty M.P.s.

III

The younger and more intelligent Conservatives were moving from reaction against the tendencies of the war to an acceptance of them. Hogg, the leading ideologue of the Tory reformers (who had the sympathy, in private, of such young ministers as Harold Macmillan, R. A. Butler, and Eden himself), called on his fellow Conservatives to follow the example of Benjamin Disraeli, who had "hit upon the role of Conservatism in revolutionary times – to lead and dominate revolution by superior statesmanship, instead of to oppose it, to by-pass the progressives by stepping in front of current controversy instead of engaging in it . . ."[19]

From the consensus which was now developing sprang the ideology which was to govern the practice of both parties in office after the war. Capitalism, and with it a system of powerful private interests, must be preserved; but the state would take a positive role in promoting its efficiency, which would include measures of nationalization. In effect, this consensus included the whole of the centre of British political life; Cripps and Eden,

Herbert Morrison and R. A. Butler, the Liberal Action Group and the Tory Reformers, William Beveridge and William Temple and many influential members of the Fabian Society.

A distinction between the major parties was maintained by their different social bases. Labour's working-class base made it emphasize nationalization, whereas the Tory reformers emphasized "rationalization"; in practice the two would be little different. What Woolton called a "shandy gaff" of Conservatism and socialism was beginning to emerge. Emanual Shinwell co-operated happily in an informal group which included the Liberal Action leader Clement Davies and also Hinchingbrooke and Hogg. All these men accepted the idea of a "planned peace", and they met amicably to discuss its details. Superficially, party strife was reviving from 1942 onwards, and the Beveridge debate came to symbolize in the mind of the public the difference between Labour and Conservatives. Yet at the same time, the coalition was laying the foundations of a post-war policy which both parties accepted, but which it later fell to Labour to execute. Captain Randolph Churchill, M.P., the Prime Minister's son, suggested in a public speech in September 1942 that a "Centre Party" might emerge, "based around all the best political elements" in the Liberal, Tory and Labour Parties, which would fight the "vested interests"[20] of both left and right. But it was really much better for business to maintain two centre parties, as post-war history has shown.

Hogg, a frothing, bubbling, mockable but curiously clever young man, defined the Tory Reformers' position in the House of Commons: "We mean that social and economic policy is as much a matter for intelligent participation and the conscious direction of Government as diplomatic and military affairs. We believe that that is the true doctrine for the future. It may very well be that it will take us in some directions along the lines of public ownership and in other directions it will not." In practice, the committee pondered the nationalization of power, and perhaps of gas and water, but stopped short of advocating a state takeover of coal, advancing the quaint argument that "of all industries, coal with its infinite variety and complexity is the last on which the experiment of nationalization should be tried." Its own prescription for the coal industry – reducing the number of undertakings slowly to a mere two or three score and bringing them under a national authority – bears a strong resemblance to the answer with which the colliery owners themselves came up about the same time (and also to that proposed in May 1945 by

Churchill's brief "Caretaker Government"). Nor were the Reformers prepared to clarify their position on independence for India, though they hoped that "many" of the colonies would eventually become independent. But on social security, the committee was able to pose effectively as a "progressive" body. "Social justice requires", declared its manifesto, "that basic human needs should be ascertained and that it should be a first charge upon society to meet them."[21]

The respect of the Tory Reformers for Herbert Morrison was symptomatic. Morrison, bidding as always for the leadership of the Labour Party, had insisted, in spite of Churchill's opposition, on making "political" speeches in 1942 and 1943 which adumbrated his views on the new society and the direction he thought Labour's policy should take. Labour, he said, should nationalize, not in the name of socialist doctrine, but in the name of the community. And it should no longer seek to nationalize the whole of private industry (a policy which it had never at anytime favoured for immediate application, but which most of the party's members believed to be its ultimate goal). Morrison offered a new formula – "a practical mixture of genuine socialism and genuinely free enterprise, the whole resting upon and in turn supporting national policies of social and industrial welfare . . . Public ownership where it is appropriate, stimulating public control elsewhere." Such speeches drew enthusiastic comments from other Conservatives beside the Tory Reformers; even from the *National Review*, which applauded Morrison's "new found faith in the Empire made by our countrymen . . ."[22]

Then, with obvious boredom and reluctance, Churchill himself groped his way towards the head of the consensus. On March 21st, 1943, he made an important broadcast in which he recognized what he called a "duty to peer through the mists of the future to the end of the war". And what he saw there was a continuation of the coalition into the peace, or failing that a "National" Government of "the best men in all parties" who were "willing to serve", which would implement his own "Four Year Plan". He made no direct reference to the Beveridge report – and at that time, such an omission could only be deliberate. He warned, however, against "attempts to over-persuade or even to coerce His Majesty's Government to bind themselves or their unknown successors . . . to impose great new expenditure on the state . . ." Which was curious, because he himself stressed that plans for the "five or six large measures of a practical character" which comprised his Four Year programme would need "prolonged, careful, energetic preparation beforehand". His own plan included "national compulsory insurance for all classes for all purposes from the cradle to the grave", as well as an end to unemployment, continued state aid for farmers, a National Health Service, equal opportunity in education, and much rebuilding. He too saw a "broadening field for state ownership and enterprise, especially in relation to monopolies of all kinds."[23]

Already, in July and August 1942, the Scott and Uthwatt reports had attracted great attention. The former, on *Land Utilization in Rural Areas* (Cmd 6378), had denounced the uncontrolled development of land in the inter-war years and had made many recommendations for improving the standard of living in the countryside while preserving its charms. The Uthwatt report on *Compensation and Betterment* (Cmnd 6386) was more topical. A committee of experts had been set up to advise on steps to be taken "now or before the end of the war" to prevent the work of physical reconstruction, notably in blitzed areas, from being prejudiced by the high price of land. It recommended that the rights of development in all land outside built up areas should be vested in the state immediately, and that within the towns and cities, authorities should have wider and simpler powers to purchase areas as a whole, at prices not exceeding the value of the land in 1939. The manner in which this report was shelved, following Conservative opposition, endeared it to the left so much that "Uthwatt now" was bracketed with "Beveridge now" in its litany of demands. Eventually, in 1944, a compromise emerged in a Town and Country Planning Act which pleased neither side very much, but which extended the power of local authorities to acquire private property, and met the immediate needs of the blitzed cities to some extent.

The creation of a Ministry of Town and Country Planning early in 1943 was followed, in November of that year, by the transfer of Lord Woolton from the Ministry of Food to the new post of Minister of Reconstruction, with a seat in the War Cabinet. He had a small department only, which was intended to co-ordinate the efforts of various Government departments.

Beveridge, nursing a deep resentment against Churchill and Bevin, had launched, in April 1943, a private inquiry into full employment, which eventually issued in a book, *Full Employment in a Free Society* (1944) and became a best-seller. But if he hoped to outpace the Government, he was disappointed. In 1944, it caught him up and passed him in what he contemptuously called the "White Paper Chase".[24]

In March 1944, exactly a year after the adumbration of his Four Year Plan, Churchill went to the microphone to point out that legislation had already been made or prepared in several of the fields which he had named. On the most immediate problem of all, rehousing, he had large promises to make. The Government, he announced, was already preparing the construction of up to half a million prefabricated "Portal" houses, so named after the Minister of Works, Lord Portal. Their manufacture would be "treated as a military evolution handled by the Government, with private industry harnessed to its service". Quite apart from this emergency scheme, which resulted after the war in no more than a hundred and sixty thousand utilitarian but serviceable "pre-fabs"), the Government promised two hundred thousand to three hundred thousand permanent houses within two years of the defeat of Germany; "ample land", Churchill said, would be forthcoming, and at 1939 prices.[25]

Eight months later, in December 1944, Eden was able to claim in the House of Commons that the Government had already set its hands "to a great social reform programme, and even though there be an interruption it is the intention of each one of us who are members of the Government to carry that programme through." He did not doubt, he added, that "if a Labour Government were returned, that Government would put through what was outstanding in this programme." Both parties, he stressed, were now fully committed to it.[26]

A White Paper on social insurance had emerged in September 1944 from a committee of civil servants set up over eighteen months before to consider the Beveridge proposals, and foreshadowed the lines of the Act passed in 1946 by the post-war Labour Government. The authors rejected the "subsistence principle" of Beveridge's national minimum, on the grounds that it would involve incessant fluctuation of benefits in time with the cost of living. But they accepted the idea of the universal scheme based on a single weekly contribution with flat rates of payment and benefit, and the White Paper was welcomed by a spokesman for the Social Security League which had been set up in May 1943 to press for "Beveridge in Full".[27] In November 1944, a Ministry of National Insurance was set up. In February 1945, a bill to provide universal family allowances, payable to the mother for the second and all subsequent children, was presented to parliament and it became law that summer.

The two other assumptions which Beveridge had made were also on the way to being justified. In 1943, a small committee of officials had been set up to consider full employment. In May 1944, it reported in a White Paper called *Employment Policy* (Cmd 6527). The *Economist* pointed out that it really represented a greater revolution in state policy than the acceptance of Beveridge would have done. Yet while Cmd 6404 had been greeted with a "chorus of hosannas", Cmd 6527 had caused "hardly a ripple", though the latter, while hedged with qualifications, marked the acceptance of Keynes's approach at the highest levels. The White Paper proposed sufficient state intervention in the economy to ensure a "high and stable level of employment", and argued that wartime controls must be continued to tide over the transition from war to peace.[28]

Beveridge's second assumption, a National Health Service, was the subject of a White Paper in February 1944. Meanwhile, Butler's major Education Act was passing into law. Both these developments deserve detailed consideration. But before they receive it, the paradox of their reception must be stressed. In December 1942 the public had gone wild over a scheme put forward by a single private individual. This enthusiasm, it may be said quite confidently, spurred the coalition forward on its plans for reconstruction; it made a comprehensive health service and the institution of family allowances politically inevitable; it probably forced Churchill to make promises on social policy which he would not otherwise have made. And yet, as a programme of social reform materialized on a scale of which no Government since the First World War had dreamt, the public remained cynical, sure that its hopes would be betrayed, certain that everything was being "watered down" from the high Beveridge proof.

IV

"The British have a socialized medical service," an American authority has remarked, "simply because of the deplorable state of the old medical system."[29]

Confronting the dangers of aerial bombardment, the Chamberlain Government had organized an Emergency Hospital Service, involving initially 2,378 of the nation's three thousand hospitals, to co-ordinate hospitals in the danger areas with each other and with those elsewhere. Before 1938, statistics and information about the hospitals had been in remarkably short supply. The Government survey which preceded the scheme provided shocks which, war or no war, must have prompted reorganization.[30]

In the first place, there was a serious shortage of beds. Secondly, the existence side by side of two contrasting systems had contributed to a maldistribution of the facilities which existed. On the one hand, there were over a thousand voluntary hospitals, independent of public control, ranging from the great teaching hospitals to many tiny, impecunious institutions. On the other hand, there were the hospitals provided by local authorities.

The former had traditionally depended for their funds on private donations. As the costs of medical provision had increased, and as private charity had failed to keep pace with them, many voluntary hospitals had been reduced to ignominious means of raising money – to flag days, even to the selling of advertising space on their walls to patent medicine manufacturers. Even so, they had tended to compete wastefully with each other in the installation of prestigious but expensive new equipment. Shabby though many of them were, they were the aristocrats among the nation's hospitals, attracting an unfair proportion of nurses. They could choose whom they treated, and their senior medical staff gave their part-time services free, for the sake of the prestige. Naturally, they preferred to take spectacular cases who might be honorifically cured, rather than long-term sick who would threaten their precarious finances.

The results can be illustrated from a report made for the Government in 1938, on the hospitals of the Sheffield and east Midlands area. In the voluntary hospitals, the authors found that "short stay cases" were the rule, and an average stay exceeding twenty days was rare. Chronic cases were almost always transferred to municipal institutions, if they were lucky enough to be admitted at all. "The great majority of the local authority general hospitals remain institutions for the treatment of the chronic sick . . . Many of the buildings are antiquated and unsuitable for hospital accommodation with bare, overcrowded, large wards, cheerless, uncomfortable day rooms and primitive facilities for nursing . . . We have visited institutions where the ratio of patients to trained nurses is sixty or over." To make matters worse, there was a form of class warfare between voluntary and municipal hospitals. "Opposition occasionally is carried to such lengths that a patient who has once entered one hospital will have small chance of ever subsequently securing admission to the other."[31]

In London, conditions were better; but in South Wales they were far worse. Many of the nation's public hospitals were still poor law infirmaries, receivers of the destitute who must not ask for more. ". . . When the time came to organize the emergency scheme," relates Richard Titmuss, "many municipal hospitals and public assistance institutions were found to contain in their general wards an unholy and unhygienic collection of nursing mothers, infants with gastro-enteritis, healthy new born babies, and aged and chronically sick women."[32]

The best qualified doctors generally shunned the public hospitals, where salaries fell far below what might be earned by a man combining private practice with free service in a voluntary hospital. Specialists were generally in short supply, but especially in the unprestigious fields normally covered by public hospitals, and especially in the poorest areas. "The chief determining factor", remarked an official survey of the north-west, also made in 1938, "is not whether there is enough work to keep a specialist busy, but whether there is enough private practice to make it worth his while to settle in the place concerned . . ."[33]

The same maldistribution was found among general practitioners. The wealthy London suburb of Kensington had seven times as many doctors per head of population as South Shields, in the north-eastern depressed area.[34] Under the National Health scheme, the G.P.'s practice was divided into three compartments. He had panel patients – insured workers – and received a capitation fee for attending them. He treated their dependants, who were not covered by National Health Insurance, either as private fee-paying patients or under the aegis of local clubs which used subscriptions to retain him. Finally, he took fees from well-to-do patients. The last were the most profitable. Doctors, especially young ones, and especially those serving poor districts, were often far from well paid; but a genial G.P. in a rich suburb did very nicely indeed.

The call-up of doctors, the bombing of hospitals, the strains created by the emergency scheme, made matters worse, especially for the commonplace civilian sick. Waiting lists for entry into the voluntary hospitals, which had been running at or near six figures before the war, grew even longer. Though the blitz taxed local resources in some areas severely, elsewhere beds stood empty waiting for bomb victims who would never arrive. This suited some of the voluntary hospitals perfectly. Under the Emergency Scheme, the Government was paying them to keep beds empty, so they both made money and saved it. Since high taxation was likely to cut off many sources of charity, and since bomb damage would be costly to restore, their financial position was potentially worse than ever, and they clung shamelessly to the lifebelt which the Government had handed them, dumping more patients than ever on the public hospitals. In February 1941, official figures showed that in London's voluntary hospitals, empty beds now outnumbered occupied ones – while the proportion in municipal hospitals coming under the Emergency Scheme was only one to eight.[35] It was clear that the great voluntary tradition had failed, and that solvency and common sense could come only through a unified state system.

What this could achieve was illustrated by the more positive features of the Emergency Scheme. By October 1939, the Government had provided hospitals with nearly a thousand completely new operating theatres and many millions of bandages, dressings and fitments, to make up for quite appalling shortages of equipment which the planning of the scheme had brought to light. Many thousands of new beds were provided in "hutted annexes". A national blood transfusion service was created (and during the war, self-sacrificing civilians added to the strain on themselves by making repeated donations of blood). By the end of 1940, the Government was taking measures to ensure that specialized facilities were more widely available, and that patients were directed to those hospitals which could best treat them. The free treatment given under the Emergency Scheme, at first reserved for civilians and military war casualties, was gradually extended to more and more classes of patients – war workers, evacuees, people with fractures, firemen and so on – until a sixty-two page booklet was needed to define the different eligible classes. While conditions bore hard on the remainder of the nation's sick, especially old people, a growing section of the population enjoyed the benefits of the first truly "national" hospital service.

As early as August 1940, the various bodies representing the medical profession had combined to set up a Medical Planning Commission, and in May 1942 this came out in favour of a unified, centrally planned public medical service under state control. The powerful British Medical Association, which represented the doctors in a partial and limited way, accepted this scheme in broad outline; largely, one must presume, because its leaders expected nothing to come of it.[36]

Then came Cmd 6404. The Beveridge report made a National Health Service practical politics, because its reception showed clearly that the public wanted such a thing more than any other reform of the social services. Three months after its publication, the Minister of Health (Ernest Brown, leader of the Liberal

Nationals) initiated discussions with the medical profession on the future shape of the service. He put up, purely for discussion, the idea that doctors should be salaried servants of the public. The leaders of the B.M.A. reacted with a violence which made further amicable explorations impossible. The Radio Doctor, cherubic Charles Hill, was then deputy secretary of the B.M.A. He started the flare-up by warning a mass meeting of doctors that they must be ready "for a fight" against the "translation of a free profession into a branch of the local government services". The doctors' leaders, who only a few months before had been equally divided over the idea of a "hundred per cent service", now came out fighting in favour of a "ninety per cent service" which would exclude, to the profit of the doctors, the wealthiest section of the population.[37]

When the White Paper on *A National Health Service* (Cmd 6502) was published early in 1944, it defined the objects of the proposed service clearly and nobly:

> (1) To ensure that everybody in the country – irrespective of means, age, sex, or occupation – shall have equal opportunity to benefit from the best and most up-to-date medical and allied services available.
> (2) To provide, therefore, for all who want it, a comprehensive service covering every branch of medical and allied activity . . .
> (3) To divorce the care of health from questions of personal means or other factors irrelevant to it; to provide the service free of charge (apart from certain possible charges in respect of appliances) and to encourage a new attitude to health – the easier obtaining of advice early, the promotion of good health rather than only the treatment of bad.[38]

The service would be non-contributory, financed by taxation, and would cover dentists and opticians as well as doctors and surgeons. The panel, the means test and the poor law would be swept out, and all hospital treatment would be free.

Parliament welcomed the scheme; so did almost everyone. The chief dissenters were the leaders of the B.M.A., who tried frantically to discredit it, finding sinister implications of bureaucratic control lurking everywhere under the idealistic promises of the White Paper. Yet when they conducted a survey of the association's members, it was found that on every single important issue raised by the White Paper, a clear majority of doctors were in favour of the Government's proposals; and nearly forty per cent of the profession were in favour of the scheme, "lock, stock and barrel". Six doctors out of ten wanted a "hundred per cent service". Almost the same proportion favoured the White Paper's suggestion that a Central Medical Board should be empowered to keep doctors out of relatively over-doctored areas, which the B.M.A. leadership had denounced as tyranny. Hill and his colleagues were stunned by this outcome, and hinted, most implausibly, that the diminutive Socialist Medical Association had rigged the ballot. But the fact was that the constitution of the B.M.A. ensured that the wealthy G.P.s from the suburbs and spas dominated its leadership, drowning the more numerous voices of struggling doctors in working-class areas, ill-paid salaried men in the public hospitals, and young doctors in the armed forces.[39] What followed the survey is one of the most famous episodes in the history of pressure groups in Britain; the B.M.A. kept up an unedifying racket until the very eve of the new service's creation.

V

In education, as in health, there had been significant and deleterious divisions, first between the independent "public" schools and the state system, and secondly, within the state system, between the best facilities, which were largely a middle-class preserve, and the lower standard which came the way of most of the nation's children. The National Union of Teachers, in a report on *Educational Reconstruction* published in 1942, called it a "caste system", observing that "The type of school determines the standards of accommodation, the character of the amenities provided, the normal length of school life, the salaries of teachers engaged and even the fees which have to be paid."[40]

Only one child in ten in England and Wales was educated outside the state system. Of the other ninety per cent, five out of six were educated up to the age of fourteen in elementary schools. A proportion of the remainder went after the age of eleven to selective central or technical schools where the bias of the curriculum was vocational. Secondary education, in the full meaning of both words, was given only in grammar schools. The policy of the Board of Education since 1902 had systematically favoured this elite secondary education over the elementary system. Between 1930 and 1936, the capital expenditure per pupil approved for county and municipal secondary schools had been four times that approved for elementary schools. While the average number of children in a secondary school class before the war had been about twenty-five, classes of more than sixty had been known in elementary schools, and a very large proportion had been over forty.[41]

Under the system created in 1902, the elite had been broadened, and a small proportion of working-class children had scaled the golden ladder to universities, even to Oxbridge. But in 1938, the proportion of children eligible by age for secondary education who had actually obtained admission to secondary schools had been only fourteen per cent. Just under half of secondary schoolchildren had been "scholarship boys" or girls, whose education was paid for wholly by the local authorities. But as Jean Floud has remarked, "... Not only a child's chances of getting to a secondary school at all, but also his chances of doing so *as a holder of a free or special place* were startlingly higher the higher his place in the social hierarchy . . ."[42]

In 1926, the Hadow report had proposed secondary education for all, urging the reorganization of the elementary schools into junior (or primary) and senior (or modern) schools, with a break at eleven. By 1938, about two-thirds of the children over eleven had been in schools reorganized on Hadow lines. But the so-called "dual system" had helped to retard progress. Over one-third of schools in England and Wales had been provided originally, not by local authorities, but by religious bodies, chiefly the Church of England. Since the 1902 Act, these schools had been maintained by local authorities, but they had kept their denominational character, and they had to provide capital for building and rebuilding out of their own voluntary funds; hence many were in bad condition, and reorganization had usually been difficult or impossible for them.

The Board of Education, such were the values of society, was regarded as a political backwater. As the ravages committed upon the educational system in 1939–40 had shown very clearly, its President carried little weight against other members of the Government. Occupants of the post had usually been very glad to move on to something more prestigious; between August 1931 and July 1941, there had been six Presidents with an average tenure of just over eighteen months. The last of these, before R. A. Butler assumed the office, was one Herwald Ramsbotham, unknown to fame.

Butler, still only thirty-eight, had held junior office before the war, and his reputation had somehow survived his stonewalling defences of appeasement in the House of Commons. Rich and

extremely intelligent, Butler showed an attractive capacity for
deadpan unorthodoxy; and he made that uncomely maiden, the
Board of Education, his bride for the rest of the war. His junior
minister, Chuter Ede, was a Labour man and a former schoolteacher. They formed together an energetic team; and they
operated in an atmosphere highly favourable to comprehensive
educational reform.

Evacuation had made education a burning political issue. How,
people asked, could things have been so bad? By the middle of
the war, general agreement amongst leaders of opinion had
emerged on a number of important points. There should be
equality of educational opportunity as between class and class,
town and country. All forms of post-primary education should be
regarded as secondary, and equal in status. The school-leaving
age should be raised to fifteen and then, as soon as possible, to
sixteen. But the future of the dual system, and the place of religion
in schools, remained highly controversial, and discussion of these
issues sidetracked and obscured the more fundamental controversy over whether all secondary schools should be multi-
lateral, catering for all children in a given area; or whether
specialized grammar and modern schools should continue to seg-
regate children with "different types of aptitude" – that is, the
middle class from the hoi polloi.

Future policy in these matters was, by default, decided by the
notorious Norwood committee on curriculum and examinations,
which Butler appointed in 1941. It reported in 1943, and its
authors proclaimed their discovery that the existing system provided for three broad categories of children, and concluded that
these corresponded, with extraordinary exactitude, to three
broadly but neatly separate types of human beings. There were
the natural scholars, who should enjoy a grammar school curriculum on their way to the top jobs; there was the "technical"
type, who often had an "uncanny insight into the intricacies of
mechanism", whereas the "subtleties of language construction"
were "too delicate for him"; and there was the "modern" type
[sic] who could deal with "concrete things" more easily than with
"ideas" and who was interested "only in the moment". This
latter simple materialist would clearly be happiest if he were
absolved from undue speculation, and for him, after the war, the
elementary schools were renamed "secondary moderns". One
educationalist has commented, without undue harshness, on this
document, "Seldom has a more unscientific or more unscholarly
attitude disgraced the report of a public committee .. The sugges-

tion of the committee seems to be that the Almighty has bene-
volently created three types of child in just those proportions
which would gratify educational administrators."[43] Nevertheless,
the Norwood committee, besides establishing the principles of a
division at "eleven plus", forecast and influenced the entire shape
of British education which emerged, mouselike, from the moun-
tains of idealistic blather which preceded the Education Act of
1944. The tripartite (or as the cruel joke had it, tripartheid)
system ensured that privilege was perpetuated behind a façade
of democratic advance.

Another blow on behalf of the "caste system" was struck by the
Fleming committee, also appointed by Butler, which reported in
1944. Its brief had been to consider means whereby the public
schools might be more closely "associated" with the state system.
The public schools seemed about to enter a fatal sickness akin to
that of the voluntary hospitals. Surely high income tax, cutting
away at the capacity of wealthy parents to pay high fees, would
thrust them, impoverished, upon the mercies of the state? The
Fleming committee ingeniously proposed that the schools should
take a limited number of boys, up to twenty-five per cent of their
number, from within the state system. Without affecting the
essential exclusiveness of the schools, this arrangement would
ensure that the local authorities subsidized them. In fact,
"Flemingism" never caught on. But the report, by arriving at
superficially quite "democratic" conclusions, ensured that the
basic issue of the schools' invidious position could be shelved for
another two decades or so. Meanwhile, thanks to officially sanctioned tax evasions, the public schools were able to raise their
fees and simultaneously retain their clientele.[44]

However, in the middle of the war, hopes were high that a
genuinely democratic educational system might emerge from the
current chaos. Even before Butler had arrived at the Board, his
civil servants had drawn up a tentative scheme for reconstruction,
which served as a basis for talks between the Board and various
interested parties – local authorities, teachers and so on. In the
light of their response, the Government issued a White Paper in
July 1943. In a two-day debate on it, the House of Commons, as
The Times observed, "showed itself of one mind, to a degree rare
in parliamentary annals . . . Not a single voice was raised in
favour of holding up or whittling down any one of the proposals
for educational advance embodied in the White Paper . . ."[45]

The spirit in which progressive educationalists accepted these
proposals was probably well represented by the most eminent of

them all, R. H. Tawney. He told the annual conference of the Workers' Educational Association in 1943, "When we feel exasperated by the omissions, or outraged by the provisions, of an educational measure, the question, I submit, which we should ask ourselves is not whether it is in accordance with our personal preferences and private convictions. It is whether on the balance, with all its imperfections on its head, and when due allowance has been made for the existence of persons so perverse as to cherish preferences and convictions different from our own, it will, or will not result in a happier and more fruitful life for the boys and girls whose future will be affected by our attitude to it . . . If we decide that it will, we ought not to allow our annoyance or disappointment with particular parts of it to prevent our according it our general support."[46]

So, not without reservations, the left gave consistent and even fervent backing to the White Paper, which was the basis of the Bill which Butler introduced into parliament in January 1944. There was a good deal of controversy in parliament provoked by the Bill's provisions concerning the dual system and the smaller educational authorities, but it emerged, after tactful pilotage by Butler and Ede, more or less unscathed. In May 1944, it became an Act, the most impressive ever passed in the field of British education.

Under the Act, the President of the Board of Education was renamed "Minister of Education", confirming a new status for his department. He would have far greater powers to impose national policy on the mass of local authorities, which it was hoped might help to obliterate the disparities between different areas. Furthermore, a hundred and sixty-nine out of three hundred and fifteen local education authorities in England and Wales now lost their powers. Those affected were chiefly small municipal boroughs with inadequate resources.

Previously, L.E.A.s had been obliged to provide only elementary education; secondary and further education were matters for their own discretion. The Act now defined these three stages and laid down that secondary education, whatever that meant in practice, was now to be provided for every child in the country. No L.E.A. was to be allowed to charge fees in its schools, though all would have power to buy places in public schools or in the "direct grant" grammar schools which took up to fifty per cent of fee-paying pupils though receiving public support direct from the ministry. The school-leaving age was to be raised to fifteen in March 1945 (though this was later postponed for two more years) and then to sixteen (a development still awaited a quarter of a century later).

A compromise preserved the dual system. Church schools could become either "controlled" – in which case the L.E.A. took over financial responsibility but the Church concerned preserved some of its power over the content of the curriculum – or "aided". Aided schools would go on much as before, and would have to meet only half the cost of necessary repairs and improvements. The Roman Catholic schools, of which there were approaching two thousand, all opted for "aided" status, but under half the Church of England schools were able to do so. The Churches were rewarded for this settlement by the introduction, for the first time, of compulsory religious education. In every school, the Act ruled, the day must begin with "collective worship on the part of all pupils in attendance" (though atheists would be permitted to opt their children out). While the Church schools would continue to provide sectarian instruction, local authority schools would give non-denominational religious teaching as the only compulsory part of the curriculum. Future historians of the decline of religion may well conclude that the making compulsory of the joyless and perfunctory morning service in schools was all that was needed to consummate the process. However, it seemed at the time to be a triumph for the Churches.

Education in Scotland remained distinct, in its traditions, which were in some respects superior to those of the south, and in its practical organization, which was not now more impressive. However, Scotland had avoided a dual system, and its schools were already organized in primary and secondary stages. A further Act of 1945 brought the Scottish system into line with the English one on certain important points.[47]

This, then, was the most signal measure of social reform which became law during the war itself; indeed, it was potentially the most important gesture towards democracy made in the twentieth century, a fitting product of the People's War. In practice, however, it confirmed and legitimized the existence of class distinction in education. Butler had obeyed Quintin Hogg's injunction that Conservatives, confronted with an apparently irresistible tide towards fundamental change, should keep cool and seek to divert it.

VI

Post-war planning was not merely a necessary precaution of Government. It became a kind of universal craze with institutions great and small. Even the Jockey Club appointed a small committee to consider the whole future of horse racing, composed of a duke, three other peers and a knight, which made sweeping recommendations in 1943 in favour of cheaper and better accommodation for the race-going public.[48]

Through all this forward-looking thought ran the theme, "Never Again". A new Britain must arise like a phoenix from the ashes of the fire raids. And never again must there be a war like this; never again must great nations fall out and fight; never again must a new Versailles produce a new Hitler.

Those who stayed at home, no matter how hard they worked, could never forget that sons, grandsons, brothers, cousins were living in improvised conditions in strange places, fighting and laying down their lives for the nation which had reared them with little to hope for. The eagerness with which the public had embraced austerity, the hope with which so many had turned to Cripps, and which others now vested vaguely in William Temple – these had indicated a new unselfishness in popular attitudes to politics. With this had come a new political awareness, prompted and educated by the war. When Mass Observation had asked people in 1938 what they thought of the Government's foreign policy, a third had been unable to answer, and forty per cent of the remainder had expressed ignorance, uncertainty or bewilderment. In 1944, seventeen people out of twenty had an answer, and the overwhelming majority were in favour of international co-operation.[49]

To this new spirit, the Beveridge report appealed as the first clear indication that life really could be much better after the war. Its proposals, and still more its assumptions, clarified for the public what exactly it was that it wanted. The new idealism emerged most significantly in the response of the middle class to the Gallup Poll on the question. Only three people out of ten in the highest income group thought that they would gain if the report was implemented – but three-quarters thought it should be adopted. Under half the professional and white-collared section of the population thought they would gain – but nine out of ten supported the scheme.[50]

Mass Observation reported that "There was an unprecedented

surge of optimism, hope, and faith in the goodwill of leaders and parliament after the publication of the report. After the debate, feeling sank to a lower level of pessimism and cynicism than before the report." The views of a young scientist were quite typical. "At the time they were first put forward I felt certain that Scott, Uthwatt, Beveridge, Barlow etc. reports were pure propaganda to try and stimulate people to further interest in the war, at a time when there was little or nothing doing. Immediately we made the first move away from Alamein, the brake was applied to all these great social schemes and as long as the war is favourable in our eyes the dust will continue to pile up on them. In fact, if we win the war we shall lose every stronghold of the home front."[51]

The attitude of "once bitten, twice shy" underlay the lukewarm public response to the advances promised, or even achieved, in health, town planning, education and housing. On one level, the reaction was irrational; but in so far as the party leaders in the Government did not propose to try to realize the millenarian dreams of the populace, cynicism was not misplaced.

As parliament was debating Beveridge, the new Common Wealth Party was involved in contesting a range of by-elections. Besides supporting bona-fide independent socialists in two constituencies, it was fighting on its own account in four more. In each of these four contests, it polled a considerably higher proportion of the vote than Labour had done in 1935. The most striking of these results were at North Midlothian, where Tom Wintringham, one of the heroes of the Home Guard, came very close to winning a formerly safe Conservative seat, and Watford, where a young serviceman stood, propounding what he called Common Wealth's "great new spiritual message".

Common Wealth proclaimed its support for the immediate implementation of Beveridge, and for many voters the two words became almost synonymous. The Conservative candidate at Watford referred to the Beveridge report early in his campaign as a "poet's dream", but recovered in time from this lapse to issue a poster which emphasized that he wished to see it "put into *immediate* operation without any unnecessary tinkering or modification". This by-election, like others at the time, illustrated the difficulty which many Conservatives had with Beveridge. They could not share the general enthusiasm, yet felt bound to defer to it; the public, quite correctly, judged them to be insincere.[52]

Common Wealth had been founded in July 1942 by a merger of the 1941 Committee led by J. B. Priestley with Sir Richard Acland's Forward March movement. Its creation at that time had reflected the widespread dismay and trepidation after the fall of Tobruk. Priestley, never very patient with organized politics, had resigned from the new party's presidency in the autumn, and the turning point at El Alamein had robbed "C.W." (as its members were soon calling it) of its immediate role; it had urged at its inception that Britain must change rapidly in the direction of socialism if she was to win the war, and now the war was clearly being won without the degree of socialism which C.W. considered essential. But the publication of Beveridge gave Common Wealth a new role. While receiving very little publicity in the curtailed newspapers, and without achieving wide fame and support in the country as a whole, C.W., in by-election after by-election, represented the refined essence of "Beveridgism" – the revolutionary zeal, the millenarian dream, the unselfishness.

After Priestley's departure, Sir Richard Acland was the figurehead of the new party. Tall, lean, bespectacled and earnest, his repeated calls for social revolution were a subject for laughter rather than admiration in the House of Commons. But as a public orator he could pack almost any hall in almost any town in Britain. In front of one of the very worried, very earnest, very idealistic wartime political audiences, his revivalist fervour was irresistible, as he painted on the one hand the Hell of the Old Order, on the other the Heaven of the New. One of his admirers wrote later of "The burning sincerity of his enthusiasm, his obvious joy, amounting to something like exaltation, in his 'discovery' of socialism, his acute insight into the 'middle-class' approach to moral and political problems . . ." His appeal was essentially to the middle class. He remained a Liberal M.P. until 1942, long after his conversion to socialism, and Labour and trade union stalwarts remembered Mosley and regarded this rich landowner with suspicion. He called on the middle class to renounce its privileges and its snobberies, and to join in the creation of a classless New Jerusalem. As an earnest of his good faith, he made his hereditary estates in Devon over to the National Trust early in 1943.[53]

The three principles of Common Wealth, as Acland expounded them and his followers accepted them, were "Common Ownership" of all major industrial resources, and of land; "Vital Democracy", a vague term implying, inter alia, proportional representation, regional parliaments in Scotland and Wales, and joint consultation in industry; and "Morality in Politics", an end to public lying, to secret diplomacy and to the subservience of politics to expediency. In practice, C.W. ran up against the problem of identity which had destroyed the I.L.P. a decade before. Between the Labour Party and the Communist Party, there was no room in British politics for a third socialist party. C.W.'s policies were like those which Labour still professed, only more so; while it preached revolution as the Communists had done, it insisted that this must come through the ballot box. But C.W.'s members, like their leader, believed that it was something quite new. They identified themselves with a world revolution. Russia was already living through the New Order. The resistance movements in Europe were socialist, and would lead their nations after the war. Chiang Kai Shek in China and Gandhi in India were prophets of the New Order. Even in the U.S.A., the New Deal and the internationalist pronouncements of Wallace and Willkie suggested a red dawn. Come the end of the war, a socialist world was possible, and C.W. was its harbinger in Britain.

"The most important thing to understand about Common Wealth is this," Acland told the party's conference in 1943. "When we say that we have come to the end of an age and that a new society must emerge from the present world chaos WE MEAN IT . . .Other individuals, other organizations, may say with their lips that we 'have come to the end of an age', in much the same tone of voice as one might say that 'his trousers are worn out' and with about the same degree of inner disturbance. Immediately these other individiausl and organizations go on to propose relatively gradual alterations in the structure of the old order . . ." C.W., as Acland said quite explicitly, rejected consensus and the middle way. "The structural changes in the shape of society which we propose, though they are of course important in themselves, are much more important in that they will lead to the emergence of a new kind of man, with a new kind of mind, new values, a new outlook on life, and, perhaps most important of all, new motives."[54]

At its peak, C.W. never had more than fifteen thousand members, about one-fifth of them in the forces, where the notion of a new party had great attraction for the less cynical of the P.B.I. Its three hundred-odd branches were spread unevenly over the country, with the greatest concentrations in London and on Merseyside. They tended to be found in the wealthy suburbs rather than the working-class areas; and C.W. was very weak in Wales and Scotland, where Labour was traditionally strongest. Its base was the professions, major and minor – solicitors, doctors and clergymen on the one hand, local government officers, salaried scientists in industry, schoolteachers and journalists on the other. Young men in the forces could not take part in politics, but C.W.'s appeal was essentially to the young, and both its national and its local leaders were predominantly men and women in their thirties, just above the age for conscription. The typical C.W. member, it might be said, was a comfortably off schoolteacher living in one of the pleasanter suburbs of Liverpool, who had never been active in politics before, and quite likely would never be active in them again.

A feature which made C.W. representative of the orthodoxies of the age, as well as critical of them, was its faith in the new managerial class. The salaried managers of private industry, in Acland's view, were ready for revolution, and would gladly serve the community, even for lower salaries. A prominent member of the class was Alan P. Good, director of a score of companies, a very wealthy man who believed that Acland's ideas were good for labour relations. He became treasurer of the party, and gave well over thirty thousand pounds to C.W., over a period of two and a half years. Since Acland also made a major contribution, C.W. was able to spend twenty-five thousand pounds at headquarters alone in 1944 (roughly equivalent to the amount which the Liberal Party, with twenty times the membership, was spending in 1960). Its London office employed twenty-five or thirty people, though it found it hard to get secretaries in days of female conscription. C.W.'s propaganda, while unremittingly earnest in tone, was lavishly produced, brightly written, and copiously distributed.[55]

But in practice, there was not much that C.W. could do to promote the bloodless revolution which it wanted, except to fight by-elections. Other leaders had a more realistic view of its role than Acland. Wintringham, a Marxist who remained unconvinced by Acland's talk of "new motives", hoped that C.W. would take its place beside the trade unions, the Communist Party and even the radical elements in the Liberal Party, in a Popular Front. R. W. G. Mackay, who came in as boss of the C.W. headquarters in the spring of 1943, was a staunch, though left-wing, Labour Party man who saw C.W. quite simply as a stand-in for Labour. It might fight by-elections until Labour came out of coalition; still more important, it must stand on guard in case Labour accepted Churchill's hinted offer in his broadcast of March 21st and decided to remain in coalition after the war. If such a betrayal occurred and, as after the last war, the two major parties went to the polls together and endorsed each other's candidates, C.W. must be ready to fight every constituency for socialism. Such is the power of bureaucracy in any political party that Mackay, the master of the machine, imposed his view over that of Acland, the hero of the members. He began to whip the C.W. branches to canvass in advance for the election which would come when the war ended; not too successfully, since so many members had fire-watching or the Home Guard or the W.V.S. making great inroads into their spare time – and in any case, canvassing was rather vulgar.

But the routine tediousness of party politics was far from the minds of party members in April 1943, when C.W. won its first, and most remarkable, by-election victory in the almost completely rural constituency of Eddisbury, in Cheshire. The C.W. candidate, calling for a second front, for "Beveridge in Full Now", and for the nationalization of agriculture, was a handsome young pilot who had fought in the Battle of Britain. He was greatly helped by a split in the Government side. But his supporters, pouring in from Merseyside at the week-ends with the image of the New Order in their eyes, created, in this sleepy agricultural backwater, the atmosphere of a religious revival. In one tiny village, the locals waited until ten thirty at night for the chance of hearing the C.W. candidate; in the dusk, with a cold March wind blowing, more than a hundred people listened attentively to him on a village green. Labour had never contested this seat, it had seemed so hopeless. There was not even a branch of the Agricultural Workers' Union. But the Common Wealth candidate was put in, by a small majority. "Beveridgism" had made its potency clear, though the papers, with the news from Tunisia to talk about, virtually ignored the result.[56]

VII

In mid-August, Badoglio, one of the bitter pills which idealism would have to digest, began to sue for a negotiated peace. But by the time agreement was publicly announced on September 8th, the Germans had swooped down on their late ally and had taken control of the situation. The Allies had landed at Taranto on September 2nd and Reggio on September 3rd. On the 9th, there was a third landing at Salerno, east of Naples. On October 1st, the Americans entered Naples; but the Germans were falling back, to establish themselves strongly on a line through Monte Cassino on the route to Rome. Thereafter, the Allies' progress was minimal, exasperatingly slow for the public at home. The newspapers said that "the weather" was holding the Eighth Army up. This seemed a thin excuse, when the Russians were still moving forward.

In December, the news that Churchill was seriously ill with pneumonia in North Africa caused much dismay. When he reappeared in the Commons in mid-January, there were heartfelt cheers of relief from the Labour benches. But his Government was still unpopular. Fretful, tired, impatient, the British people in that winter produced a wave of strikes, already mentioned, and a notable outburst of feeling. In November 1943, Herbert Morrison released Sir Oswald Mosley from prison. Mosley was suffering from thrombophlebitis, and Morrison had been told that his life was in danger. The wealthy Fascist leader was allowed to return to his Oxfordshire home, though he had to report regularly to the police and was allowed to travel only within a radius of seven miles. Coming after Darlan, Beveridge and Badoglio, this was too much. About nine people out of ten felt that Mosley should not have been released, and a wave of angry demonstrations followed the announcement. Even after Morrison had explained himself in the House of Commons, most people were far from appeased.[57]

Morrison, of course, was a Labour man. It would appear that a general loss of faith in all parties accounted for the answers to a Gallup Poll about this time which asked people whether they would prefer coalition or party government after the war. Four out of ten said "coalition", and this was the most popular reply. Only one person in eight wanted a Labour Government, and only one person in twenty wanted a Conservative Government. But when people were asked how they would vote if there were a general election "tomorrow", forty per cent answered "Labour" (and six per cent said "Communist" or "Common Wealth", ten per cent said "Liberal"). Only twenty-seven per cent said "Conservative". Added to previous polls which had shown (in 1942) that three people thought it would be a bad thing if Churchill were Prime Minister after the war, for every two who would welcome it, these results made up a formidable weight of evidence.[58]

Yet politicians of all parties, as yet unused to the accuracy of Gallup Polls, and beguiled by the sycophancy of the press, assumed that Churchill and the Conservatives must romp home in an election. In January 1944, the *Political Quarterly* printed an article by Tom Harrisson of Mass Observation, in which he listed the proofs, from by-elections as well as from polls, that the received idea was innocently, wildly wrong. As a new spate of by-elections yielded further evidence, a few people began to pay attention.

In January an exciting campaign built up in the Yorkshire dales, where the local livestock farmers, already peeved by the plough up, were especially angry with Hudson over farm prices. Common Wealth sent in a highly efficient new "election team", which the press came to call "Acland's Circus", and scores, even hundreds of young supporters flocked to Skipton constituency to support the candidature of a young army officer, Lieutenant Hugh Lawson. The local Labour Party, robbed of members and activity by the war and the electoral truce, boiled over at the idea of supporting the Conservative, and courted trouble with party head-quarters by giving Lawson open support. He won by two hundred votes.[59]

At the end of January, the loyal press was dismayed when Churchill himself intervened in a further by-election at Brighton, and was bested. A section of the local Conservative Party was unhappy with the candidate wished on them by the "caucus". A well-known local man, brother of the mayor of the town, stepped in to contest the seat at the last moment. Churchill at once issued an open letter describing this independent intervention as "an attempted swindle", because the man claimed to be a supporter of the Prime Minister and yet opposed his nominee. Briant, the independent, suggested that Churchill himself could not have written anything so high-handed – Conservative Central Office must have issued the letter in his name. But Churchill insisted that the phrase was his own – "The words were not chosen lightly or impatiently by me." In spite of this, Briant took forty-five per cent of the poll.[60] Meanwhile, another contest in West Derbyshire was already set fair to provide entertainment worthy of ITMA itself. News of its bizarre events brightened weeks otherwise marred by gloomy tidings from Anzio.

From 1571 onwards, the Cavendish family of the Dukes of Devonshire had had an almost unbroken record of parliamentary representation of one or other part of the country of Derbyshire, where they had great estates. West Derbyshire itself was one of the most remarkable feudal survivals in Britain. Since the con-stituency had been created in 1885, a member of the ducal family had always been its M.P., save for a short interregnum between 1918 and 1923, when a cobbler named White had held it for the Liberals. The current M.P., Colonel Hunloke, was the duke's brother-in-law; it was probably not without bearing on the event that he was divorced from his wife, the duke's sister, in 1945. In

any case, he resigned, in January 1944. On January 26th, M.P.s
who had only just learnt this fact from *The Times* were amazed to
find that Eden, as Leader of the House, was soliciting their
approval for the issue of the writ for the by-election. Such haste
would have been extraordinary in peace, and was unearthly in war.

It transpired that the Duke of Devonshire's son, the Marquis of
Hartington, had been adopted as Conservative candidate two
days before. The selection conference had fallen with extraordinary convenience at a time when he was on special leave from
the army. The duke, announcing Hunloke's departure to an
emergency meeting of the council of the local Conservative Party,
had asked for nominations for a successor. Hartington's had been
the only name suggested. The new candidate, who had been
waiting outside in anticipation of a summons, had at once been
called in to make a speech. The haste with which the writ was then
issued was widely attributed to the fact that the Conservative
Chief Whip, in whose hands such matters lay, was Hartington's
uncle, and it was presumed that the Cavendish family in general
had decided to give C.W. and other independents as little time as
possible to muscle in on their fief.

But the People found their champion; bluff Charlie White,
Labour candidate for the division, and son of the only man who
had broken the Cavendish hold within living memory. He resigned from the Labour Party to stand as an independent, and
launched a series of personal attacks on the Cavendish family.
A richly traditional contest ensued. On the one hand there was the
elegant, attractive young marquis, touring the division in a pony
trap and calling out the tenantry to vote in the old way. (Hartington knew nothing much about politics, and his remark that he
thought the coal mines were already nationalized became
legendary, but some of his opponents had a sneaking affection for
him.) On the other hand, there was the round-faced, angry White,
inflaming the prejudices of the quarrymen and the townspeople.
Between them, the jibes flew back and forth. Hartington was so
provoked by the slurs which White's supporters cast on his
knowledge of farming that he challenged his opponent to a muck-
shovelling race in any farm in the constituency. White declined.

To surpass Ted Kavanagh himself, the gods had created one
Robert Goodall, a farm bailiff who arrived from his remote village
on nomination day and put himself up. He made one speech to
the crowds around, announced that he would issue no address,
and fled back to his native hills for the rest of the campaign.
Reporters, naturally, tracked him down. They discovered that his

highest ambition was to play the cornet, and that his candidature had been spurred on by the people of his own tiny hamlet, where the village blacksmith had "penned crude verses in his honour".

All this, and the Acland circus too. While Conservative M.P.s flocked down to help Hartington out of his fix (and a couple of Labour M.P.s consented to perform a like service) almost all the opposition elements rallied behind White – Denis Kendall, George Reakes, the Radical Liberals, one brave Labour M.P., and even, wonderful to relate, the Communist Party, so soured by the Mosley episode that it broke temporarily with its former policy of supporting Government candidates. Reporters spoke of the emergence of a "coalition of the left". The hub of the coalition was Common Wealth, whose fervent workers arrived in multitudes to do their bit for the People. The appearance of a Russian-born woman among them attracted breathless interest in the popular press, which increased when the Russian embassy disavowed her and she turned out to be an experienced trick cyclist.

A *Daily Mail* headline read "By-Election Comedy Speeds Up". An officer reported from his mess, "The sensational discuss it as once they talked of the Dionne quins and the latest murder: the sporting lay bets on it as once they did on a Derby of a different nature."

Through the hubbub was heard the voice of Churchill himself, rashly intervening in Hartington's favour. "I see", he wrote in an open letter, "they are attacking you because your family has been identified for about three hundred years with the parliamentary representation of West Derbyshire. It ought, on the contrary, to be a matter of pride in the constituency to have such long traditions of constancy and fidelity through so many changing scenes and circumstances." But the Churchillian sense of history no longer swayed his subjects. The Government took the election seriously, and for the first time a minister of cabinet rank was sent down to defend a coalition nominee. All to no avail. When polling day came in the third week of February, White transformed a Conservative majority of five thousand, five hundred votes to an independent socialist one of four thousand, five hundred. Goodall scored two hundred and thirty-three votes, and professed himself well repaid for his lost deposit by the pleasure which the contest had given him. As one outraged Conservative M.P. put it, "Democracy was at its worst."[61]

The truce, it was now clear, was breaking down. Tory M.P.s, seething with fury, turned on the inoffensive Liberal leader, Sinclair, and blamed him for not keeping his insignificant forces in better order. Labour organs openly exulted in Churchill's discomfiture. ("This is merely the immortal tragedy of all public life", mused Aneurin Bevin, "that the *hero*'s need of the people outlasts *their* need of him.") The Labour leaders seriously considered the idea of abandoning the truce and permitting by-election contests, while remaining in coalition, but they dismissed it. However, party headquarters issued a circular in March which told local Labour parties to begin to build up their organization for a general election. Simultaneously, the Conservatives poured their organizers into the Bury St Edmunds constituency where the next by-election was to take place, and successfully defended it against the advancing Common Wealth hordes. Speeches by Conservative leaders took on a more partisan character. A spate of anti-nationalization posters appeared on the hoardings. Any dream of continued coalition which Churchill had cherished was shattered in October, when both the Labour and the Liberal Parties announced that they would fight the next election independently of all other parties.[62] And as party warfare flowed slowly back into its former channels, Common Wealth lost its role. In the same autumn, it applied unsuccessfully for affiliation to the Labour Party. After its rebuff, it decided to remain in active existence, but its fate was assured.

D DAY, V 1, V 2, VE DAY

> Actors waiting in the wings of Europe
> we already watch the lights on the stage
> and listen to the colossal overture begin.
> For us entering at the height of the din
> it will be hard to hear our thoughts, hard to gauge
> how much our conduct owes to fear or fury.
>
> Everyone, I suppose, will use these minutes
> to look back, to hear music and recall
> what we were doing and saying that year
> during our last few months as people, near
> the sucking mouth of the day that swallowed us all
> into the stomach of a war. Now we are in it
>
> and no more people, just little pieces of food
> swirling in an uncomfortable digestive journey.
> What we said and did then has a slightly
> fairytale quality. There is an excitement
> in seeing our ghosts wandering.
>
> Keith Douglas, "Actors Waiting in the Wings of Europe"[1]

I

In 1943, Londoners had heard the voice of the sirens, still quite often sounded, like that of an old friend. On January 21st, 1944, the first of a new series of heavy raids made their "warble" as menacing as ever. From then until the end of March, London had thirteen major attacks, far more dispiriting, after the long lull, than regular raids had been in November 1940. The Germans used bigger, more destructive bombs, and against their planes the new rocket guns were in action, their crash and swoosh drowning all the other sounds of the night. The sheer din was unprecedented. The attacks were short, sharp and concentrated, and involved a high proportion of incendiaries. In one case, nearly three hundred aircraft took part. The London Fire Guard had their first major test. Operating the new plan, they came out of it very well; they extinguished three-quarters of all the fires created. But once again, there were blazes calling for thirty, fifty, even seventy pumps.

The "Little Blitz", as it was soon called, ranged far outside London; Hull, Bristol and South Wales had sharp attacks. But London bore the brunt again. Nearly a thousand people lost their lives in the seven major raids in February. Five of these took place between the 18th and the 24th, and in that period, three thousand houses in the borough of Battersea alone were made uninhabitable. There were four more large attacks in March, and a final sally on April 18th. By then it seemed that the Luftwaffe had shot its bolt; as spring wore into summer, enemy activity over Britain sank to its lowest ebb yet.[2]

But Churchill, broadcasting at the end of March, warned his subjects that they might be the object of "new forms of attack" from the enemy. "Britain can take it," he added curtly. In the same speech he referred, temptingly, to plans for demobilization which Bevin had prepared, but he refused to divulge any details. "This is no time to talk about demobilization. The hour of our greatest effort and action is approaching . . . The flashing eyes of all our soldiers, sailors, and airmen must be fixed upon the enemy on their front. The only homeward road for all of us lies through the arch of victory."[3]

The second front was coming; everyone knew that now. But nobody knew how, when, or even where; and elaborate censorship precautions prevented speculation in the press. Of course, preparations for the most complex and highly organized operation in military history could not be screened entirely from the public. There was no hysteria now about "fifth columnists", no scare about "careless talk" or "silent columns", though those whose relatives' lives were at stake in the invasion were naturally anxious that security should be maintained. Many people knew about PLUTO, the "pipeline under the ocean" prepared in the summer of 1943, which was to carry oil to the beachheads; many others were making landing craft or amphibious tanks. The island was crammed with soldiers, Poles, Frenchmen, Czechs, Americans, black and white, with strange accents and strange names, but no Home Guards now fired wildly at unco-operative strangers. Industry was now totally geared to war; there was annoyance in some circles with the rash of strikes, but little real fear that production at home would let the boys down. From such immense exertions in Britain, it seemed success must stem.

The most remarkable of these exertions, highly secret, was observed nevertheless by thousands of puzzled citizens. From October 1943, boatmen on the Thames saw odd things happening on the quiet Kentish marshes near London dock; crowds of men working amidst forests of iron poles. The W.V.S. was called in to provide hot food for them; many members were asked to stand by night and day for this duty. When they reached the sites, they must have eyes and ears for nothing; and they must not gossip about what they found there. The Fire Service was called in to clear channels with their hoses through the soft silt of the foreshore. The same work went on elsewhere – on Merseyside, at Portsmouth, Southampton and Goole. At the cost of banning civilian building in these areas, twenty thousand builders and civil engineers were employed. Eventually, there materialized huge, enigmatic concrete caissons, two hundred feet long, fifty-six feet wide and sixty feet high. And, wonder to relate, they floated, appearing suddenly in the docks, first one, then many of them. Rumour held that they were supporters for colossal nets to trap submarines.

Meanwhile, twelve hundred skilled men had been quietly drafted from vital jobs all over the country and sent to Leith, to Dartford, and to the smaller harbours of Conway in North Wales and Wivenhoe in Essex. Fifteen thousand workers elsewhere had been engaged on manufacturing prefabricated parts; and the chosen few now assembled them as pierheads and buffer pontoons. At Southampton, two thousand men, including three hundred and twenty scarce and very valuable steel erectors, were employed on making shelters, which would eventually protect ships unloading in deep water outside the huge concrete caissons. For these three projects, known to the initiated few as "Phoenix", "Whale" and "Bombardon" respectively, were part of the grander MULBERRY project for the provision of prefabricated, floating harbours to be towed across the Channel for use in the invasion.'

In the spring of 1944, traffic poured in incessant streams along the roads and railway lines to the south coast. Rivulets flowed to every port from Falmouth to Tilbury; the main torrents converged on Southampton, a stricken ghost town in 1941, a busy port again after 1942 when it had been reopened to ocean traffic and Lend-lease shipments had made it almost as active as in peacetime; now, in the words of a proud local historian, "the largest naval and military base of all time". By the beginning of May 1944, its docks were almost choked with military and commercial shipping. Vessels were berthed up to seven or eight abreast. Houses, shops and all kinds of business premises had been taken over by the military for billeting and storage; so had every school in the town. For miles in every direction, every by-road converging on the city was crowded with warlike goods in transit to the docks – guns, tanks, bridging material, jeeps, cranes.[5]

On the east coast, an elaborate and successful hoax was being played on the German reconnaisance planes which, now that the R.A.F. had total command of the air, could photograph only what the Allies wanted them to see. Serried flotillas of dummy landing craft appeared in the creeks of Essex and Kent. Dummy gliders made of plywood were assembled on redundant airfields. Inflatable rubber tanks were manifested in such a manner as to suggest that the invaders would strike at the Pas de Calais. Meanwhile, screened by the trees of the New Forest, formerly insignificant little stations in Hampshire were all but choked with warlike stores. Sidings and depots had multiplied beside the lines. "At every turn of every glade", writes Vera Brittain, who visited her cottage there that spring, "we found waggons and ammunition dumps, vainly sought by the Nazi observers, which the late-budding trees concealed – Our nights echoed to the ceaseless clatter of heavy tanks lumbering down the Bournemouth–Southampton road."[6]

The public accepted readily the sly curtailment of civilian railway services, undertaken as casually as possible. The Labour Party was one of several organizations which cancelled their Whitsun conferences to save rail transport. From April onwards, the coasts from the Wash to Land's End were banned to trippers.

On May 11th, Alexander, commanding the troops in Italy, launched an offensive against the Monte Cassino line. On May 18th, Monte Cassino itself fell. But, eyes turned towards France, people in Britain cheered only perfunctorily. Ten thousand firemen and firewomen had been called south to guard the dumps of ammunition and petrol. Extra dockers and railwaymen had been scraped up from other industries. Many thousands of volunteers had come forward to help with the transport shortage, following an appeal over the radio in March. The brewers had been given extra bottlers by the Ministry of Labour to ensure that the men got their beer when the time came. Not far from the heart of London, the Thames was crowded with tank landing ships. "England is expectant, almost hushed," wrote J. L. Hodson in his diary on May 26th. "Every time we turn on the radio we expect to hear that the great invasion of Europe has begun. Every morning, when I am still abed, I am wakened by a dull roaring in the heavens which tells me our aircraft are going over – some days seven thousand of them go . . . I know there are men and women who lie awake at night and cannot sleep for worry as to whether their sons will be 'in it', and middle-aged men are sick that they should escape and their sons fall."[7]

The whole of southern England was now virtually one vast military camp. The assault troops had had their embarkation leave and had said their goodbyes, and barbed wire entanglements cut them off from the outside world. The allied servicemen who had formerly thronged the streets of London had disappeared. On June 4th, the Allies captured Rome. Even this was no distraction.

II

D Day was scheduled for June 5th. But stormy weather postponed it for one day. In the small hours of June 6th, British and American airborne divisions dropped in France. At about six thirty a.m., the first American seaborne troops went ashore; the first British troops followed an hour later. By breakfast time, the Germans had announced the invasion, and the B.B.C., independent as ever, was anticipating the official allied releases by quoting the German reports. By the end of the day, a hundred and fifty-six thousand troops had reached France.

In Shirley Joseph's Land Army hostel, "That night was the

first (and last) time that there was complete silence during the six o'clock news."[8] After the nine o'clock news, the B.B.C. broadcast the first of its war reports with an eye-witness account from the French beaches. That day, and thereafter, the newspapers were snapped up in the streets as soon as they went on sale. Soon there were queues outside the news cinemas showing the latest sequences from France; many of those who watched were close to tears, and some wept. The convoys of fresh troops rattled down the streets of the outer suburbs of London, and when they stopped at appointed places, women and girls rushed up with jugs, even pails of tea, thrust packets of cigarettes into "the boys'" hands, joked a while, and cheered as they drew away; a Dunkirk in reverse.

Then, on the night of June 12th/13th, an unusual, spluttering noise was heard over south-eastern England. Astonishingly powerful explosions took place in several parts of London and the home counties. As Churchill had warned, Britain had something worse in kind to suffer than it had endured before.

As early as April 1943, intelligence reports had alerted the British Government to the advance of German projects for long-range attack. Alarming reports had reached Whitehall; it was estimated that a single rocket of the type now expected might damage property over a radius of six hundred and fifty acres and produce eighteen hundred casualties. Later the threat of the pilotless plane, the V1, had also emerged. Elaborate active and passive defence preparations had been made; mass panic had been anticipated.

The first V1s produced no panic, but many rumours. Three days later, a heavy and sustained bombardment began from bases in the Pas de Calais. On the 15th, there was a general alert in London just after eleven thirty; the all clear did not sound until nine thirty. From the next morning onwards, a procession of V1s came over, by day and by night. On the 16th, Morrison announced the beginning of an attack by pilotless planes, and shortly afterwards the cabinet ruled that they should be called "flying bombs".

For a fortnight, the attack went on at the rate of about a hundred V1s a day. The fast new British fighters would bring down about thirty of these, the static defences would halt perhaps ten, but more than half reached the target, Greater London, nosing inexorably through all snares. In Croydon, the unlucky borough which lay on their route to the City, one might see nine V1s in the air at the same time.[9]

One of the frustrations of the battle against the V1s was that they caused as much damage if they were shot down over a built-up area as if they had been allowed to proceed on their way. On June 21st, the A.A. guns were moved out from London to the North Downs. On July 6th, Churchill described to the House of Commons the dimensions of the threat and the action taken against it. By this time, the citizens of London and the inhabitants of "Bomb Alley" in Kent and Sussex had formed a clear enough picture of this revolting novelty.

The fiery tails of the little planes, seen sharply at night travelling at great speed across the skies, had prompted cheering at first, when people had taken them for enemy fighters in flames. But soon they were all too easily recognized. There was the noise, variously described as "a grating sinister growl which increased as it approached to a most menacing roar"; a "disagreeable splutter, like an aerial motor bicycle in bad running order"; and "a terrific noise like an express train with a curious hidden undertone".[10] They were christened "doodle bugs" or "buzz bombs"; as the doodling or buzzing grew louder, those below waited tensely in case the engine cut out. When the V1 ran out of fuel it crashed to earth with a deep-throated roar, followed by a blinding flash and a tall, sooty plume of smoke. If the noise seemed to stop directly above them, people flung themselves on the floor, under the table, into doorways. Work, meetings, parties, sleep were subject to hectic interruptions; not the least of the Londoner's grudges against the buzz bombs was that they deprived him of dignity. Sometimes, however, they dived straight to earth without their engines cutting out; there was nothing one could do about that.

June and July were months of heavy clouds, driving rain, leaden skies, which made the buzz bombs all but intolerable. Because they fell in the day, when civilians could not take constant shelter, casualties were severe; but the worst of it was not the fear of death so much as the nature of the weapon which brought it, aimed unselectively, designed to destroy without risking the life of a pilot. "It was as impersonal as a plague", writes Evelyn Waugh, "as though the city were infested with enormous, venomous insects."[11]

"London", one West End resident observed, "was becoming once more the city of the brave and the few." She adds cheerfully that there were compensations; ". . . the shopkeepers were suddenly very cordial. The customer was coming back into his own." In the suburbs, J. L. Hodson noticed fresh salmon in his local fish shop for the first time in ages. The people who normally got it had packed up and fled; part of a huge private evacuation of London. Early in July, an official evacuation of schoolchildren, mothers and tots began, but by late August, when it was estimated that nearly a million and a half people had quit London, only one in five had gone in official parties. Production, for a time, suffered seriously from absenteeism, sheltering and loss of sleep. But those who remained, willy-nilly, adjusted. On July 29th, a buzz bomb narrowly missed Lord's cricket ground; that puckish Middlesex batsman, Jack Robertson, hit the first ball he received after the resumption of play for a six into the stands. The warning system was soon sophisticated so that roof spotters in the London boroughs sounded the alert only when it was clear that a bomb would arrive in the immediate area. Stocks of Morrison shelters were hastily brought in from the provinces, and after July 9th three of the specially built deep underground shelters were thrown open, and current Tube shelterers and homeless people were admitted by ticket.[12]

As London "took it" for the third time, every borough suffered. Those south and east of the centre suffered worst of all, and some lived through a phase as destructive as the worst days of the blitz; above all, Croydon.

A hundred and forty-two V1s altogether fell on Croydon. In the eighty days of the main V1 attack, the borough lost over a thousand houses completely, and fifty-seven thousand cases of house damage were recorded, more than the total of homes in the borough, since many were patched, hit, and patched again. The culprit was blast. Since the V1 did not penetrate the skin of the city deeply, it caused little disruption to public utilities, but its explosion flung spears of glass over a square quarter mile, shattering buildings on its way. There were relatively few trapped casualties for the Civil Defence service to cope with, but there were unprecedented proportions of people killed or maimed where they stood. Early in the siege, on June 18th, the most famous of all V1s scored a direct hit on the Guards Chapel in West London, when many distinguished officers were present for a service; a hundred and nineteen people were killed, and a hundred and two seriously injured.[13]

In mid-July, Air Marshal Roderick Hill, commanding the defences, changed his plan and massed all the A.A. guns on the coast. In the next seven weeks they destroyed well over half the V1s which came over – ninety out of ninety-seven on one day. By now, the worst of the tension was past. The beer supply to the stricken areas had been stepped up in the interests of morale; evacuees, not necessarily as a result of this, were filtering back; the shelters were emptying; London was "taking it" again.

III

The news, at any rate, was good enough. By the end of June, more than eight hundred and fifty thousand men and nearly a hundred and fifty thousand vehicles had disembarked in France. The British Second Army was involved in heavy fighting round Caen, drawing the German armour away from the Americans to the west of it. On July 9th, Montgomery's men entered Caen itself. At midsummer, the Russians had launched an immense offensive along a four hundred and fifty mile front, which took them into Poland within a month. The Japanese, who had belatedly invaded the north-eastern corner of India in March, were set into retreat from the decisive battle of Imphal early in July. On July 25th the Americans broke out in the west of France and began a mighty sweep through the country. Meanwhile, news of the attempt on Hitler's life by Colonel von Stauffenberg had reached the outside world.

On August 1st, the Polish underground rose in Warsaw, with the Russians no more than walking distance from the city. Disturbing news followed. As the Poles were massacred, the Russians did nothing. Stalin frustrated allied attempts to aid the rising. The news encouraged the "Cold War" attitudes which had long been latent on the right, but which now began to emerge on the left also, where many uneasily remembered the days of the Nazi-Soviet pact. On the 25th, the German commander in Paris surrendered to the Allies. Four days later, Montgomery began an offensive which took the British Second Army from the Seine to Antwerp in five days, and for once justified his reputation for dash. On the way, he overran the V1 launching sites in the Pas de Calais, bringing the first phase of the V bomb attack to a close. By then, 6,725 V1s had been seen over Britain (while many others seem to have gone astray entirely). Nearly 3,500 had been destroyed by the fighters, the guns or the balloon barrage, and only 2,340 had reached the London target area. Altogether, the bombs had killed 5,475 people, and had severely injured 16,000 more. On September 7th, Churchill's son-in-law, Duncan Sandys, the junior minister in charge of the V bomb problem, was bold enough to tell a press conference that the "Battle of London" was over "except possibly for a last few shots".

This was a little over-optimistic on two counts. Firstly, the Germans extended their practice of releasing V1s from piloted planes. More than seven hundred and fifty came over in the next seven months, of which a tenth (seventy-nine) reached London. There was relief for the inhabitants of "Bomb Alley", but the reduced danger was spread more widely. Isolated V1s fell as far north as Yorkshire and as far west as Shropshire. On Christmas Eve, a salvo was aimed at Manchester. Only one reached the city, but twenty-seven people died in the nearby town of Oldham.[14]

Secondly, on the evening of September 8th, a mysterious, shattering explosion was heard all over London, where everyone imagined that it had happened in his own borough. There was a thunderclap, followed by a noise like a faraway express train. A second explosion followed immediately. The areas affected were in fact Chiswick and Epping, at the western and eastern ends of the city. Thereafter the strange noises continued, and slowly increased; by November, an average of four, then six a day were heard in London. The press kept its mouth tightly shut. Word was passed down official channels that these were to be treated as town gas explosions; but Londoners guessed from the flashes of white light through the sky that this was a new secret weapon, and sardonically talked about "flying gas mains". On November 10th, Churchill broke the silence when he assured the House of Commons that this new attack by rockets had not been serious in its scale or results.

Certainly, it had no effect on the morale of those now pouring back to their homes in London. The V2, mercifully, was far smaller than the irresistible weapon which had long been expected at top level in Britain. It was fast enough, and monstrous enough (forty-five feet long, and weighing fourteen tons), and it was more destructive than any weapon yet seen. Four V2s which fell on Croydon damaged two thousand houses between them. But they travelled so fast that one could not hear them before they exploded (sometimes in mid air, with a huge flower of smoke). By that time, one was either dead or not, as the case might be. In total, eleven hundred V2s were observed, of which a couple of score were aimed not at London, but at Norwich. Only 518 reached London. In all, 2,724 people were killed, and over 6,000 badly injured, but this, after what had gone before, was not intolerable. In any case, the rate of arrival was falling by the end of the year.[15]

What the V bombs had achieved was not the collapse of British morale, but yet another aggravation of the housing problem. At the peak of the V1 attack, more than twenty thousand houses a day were being damaged. By the end of September, twenty-five thousand houses in London region had been totally destroyed or damaged beyond repair, to add to the eighty-four thousand written off after earlier raids. A million more had been less seriously damaged. The War Cabinet agreed to give the highest priority to repair. The armed forces released men to help. Forty-five thousand builders were drafted in from the provinces, many of whom, because of the very shortage of accommodation which they were there to correct, had to sleep in Wembley Stadium or in improvised camps. Altogether, a hundred and thirty thousand men were employed in repair work on London by January 1945. By the end of March, nearly eight hundred thousand houses had been repaired after a fashion, but many bombed out families were living in huts erected with the help of American troops and former Italian prisoners of war.[16]

IV

On September 18th, a British airborne landing behind the enemy lines at Arnhem miscarried, with heavy casualties. By the end of the month, the Germans had succeeded in stabilizing all fronts; neither in east, nor west, nor Italy were the Allies on the verge of a decisive breakthrough.

But the war on the home front was running down. George Orwell wrote bitterly in August, "I see that the railings are returning – only wooden ones, it is true, but still railings – in one London park after another. So the lawful denizens of the squares can make use of their treasured keys again, and the children of the poor can be kept out.' From September 1944, Civil Defence outside the London area was virtually disbanded (though the final standdown did not come until May 1945). On September 17th, the long tyranny of the blackout was ended, and a "dim-out" was allowed in its place. There was not yet a return to full peacetime effulgence, but Bristol that first night "seemed almost gay save for those pools of darkness where, as at the Centre, lamp standards had been lost in the blitzes, and this applied also to the former main shopping streets, which assumed a double gloom." However, many people did not bother for the time being to remove the blackout material from their curtains; in the City of Westminster itself, the streets remained unlighted for several weeks because of the shortage of manpower and of electric globes, while Croydon did not install the new "moon lighting" until November 13th.[17]

On December 2nd, the Lord Mayor of London gave a dinner in

the Mansion House to mark the standing down of the Home Guard. As one of the speakers arrived at the climax of his peroration with the word "Victory", a V2 exploded in the Thames only a few hundred yards away.[18] Amid such reminders of war, signs of returning peace peeped out like snowdrops.

Slowly war industry was releasing workers; slowly, a drive to produce consumer goods for export was resumed. But the winter was marked by the most severe fuel shortage yet. The Londoners were worst off. Those who had evacuated during the summer had not been able to build up their stocks, and houses opened to the wind and rain by the V bombs needed more fuel than before. But there was less coal than ever, distribution was as clumsy as ever, and soldiers had to be released from the army to help. Centres were opened up in the south-east from which citizens might take coal themselves in whatever prams or buckets they had to hand.

Before Christmas, came dismaying news. In the early autumn, the Germans withdrew from Greece. Churchill visited Stalin in Moscow in October, and came to an agreement with him over the political control of eastern Europe. As good as his word, Stalin stood by while sixty thousand British troops turned on the Communists who had dominated the Greek resistance movement and suppressed them by force. The protests in Britain itself were led by *The Times* and the *Manchester Guardian*. In the House of Commons, Bevan and Acland launched a bitter debate on December 7th and 8th. The vote was 281 to 32 in favour of the Government, but only twenty-three Labour members voted on Churchill's side. Ernest Bevin, however, was adamant in Churchill's defence. On Christmas Day, Churchill and Eden went to Greece themselves, and imposed a provisional Government on the Greek people. This, as some people bitterly remarked at the time, had once been a war on behalf of national self-determination. What exactly was it now?[19]

As feelings raged high over Greece, came news which for a time prompted talk of another Dunkirk among some habitual pessimists. The Allies in western Europe now held a long line stretching from the Channel to the Swiss border. On December 16th, the Germans opened a surprise offensive against the weakly-held sector in the Ardennes. In three days, they advanced forty-five miles, driving towards Antwerp. The British public heard only slowly of the real seriousness of the fighting. It took much of the pleasure out of Christmas – the coldest, it was reported, for more than fifty years – though small boys who were enjoying the war and wanted it to last a while longer found it hard to conceal their delight in this new turn of events; and that sporting instinct which had made Rommel a popular hero now prompted some un-grudging admiration for General Rundstedt. The "Bulge" was not finally squeezed off until January 16th, when it had cost about eighty thousand allied casualties.[20]

V

By throwing so much into a final gamble in the west, Hitler had opened his back door in the east. On January 12th, the Russians launched a new offensive. By the beginning of February, the Red Army was only forty miles or so from Berlin. At Yalta, the three allied leaders assembled to settle their outstanding differences, as the Americans and British still struggled hard to reach the Rhine.

The Yalta conference concluded on February 11th in a last blaze of mutual harmony among the Allies. The Polish matter had been settled; Britain and the U.S.A. accepted Stalin's nominees as the provisional Government of the country. In the House of Commons on February 27th, Churchill defended the settlement, but more than a score of Conservative M.P.s defied him and voted against a motion to approve it. Churchill, Harold Nicolson wrote in his diary, was "as amused as I am that the warmongers of the Munich period have now become the ap-peasers, while the appeasers have become the warmongers" – for those who now revolted had supported Chamberlain.[21]

Meanwhile, the logic of area bombing had proceeded to the point of manifest insanity. American planes were achieving good results by precision attacks on Germany's vital and dwindling oil supplies. But Bomber Harris was allowed to follow his own whim, which was to end the war swiftly by a shattering raid, "Thunder-clap", aimed at German morale. Dresden was chosen for this charitable effort, with notorious results. Many refugees who had fled there from the Russian invaders were amongst the unknown, but very large number of casualties in the fire storm which swept the city on February 14th. From this work, Churchill and his colleagues at last recoiled. After the strategic air offensive officially ended in mid-April, Bomber Command was slighted and snubbed and Harris, unlike other well-known commanders, was not rewarded with a peerage. The knife was blamed for the meat.

Early in March, the Americans crossed the Rhine. On the 23rd, Montgomery's men in the north passed over the river also, on their way to the Ruhr. On March 27th, the last V2 fell in Kent;

the last V1 was launched two days later. The sirens, after five years and seven months, had lost their occupation.

In April, the political pillars which had sustained for years the world view of the British people began to crumble. With them went some of the supports of optimism. On the 12th, President Roosevelt died – a man identified, in the last resort, with the cause of the common people of the world. The shock in Britain was stunning; the mourning sincere. Just before this, the Allies had overrun the Nazi concentration camp at Buchenwald, and Belsen followed a few days later. What was found in them was enough to undermine all faith in human nature. The language of popular journalism had exhausted itself – when the *Daily Mirror* described British soldiers "sick with disgust and fury" driving the "infamous" members of the S.S. to bury bodies in the "tainted earth", its phraseology was that of boys' fiction. Photographs were more eloquent; perhaps the most horrifying of all, splashed over the front page of the *Sunday Pictorial*, showed "Hitler's Beast Women", the leering female warders of Belsen. Most of the press insisted that the entire German people now stood convicted of crimes against humanity; a few left-wing journals gently reminded their readers that Germans, too, had suffered in the camps, and more would have done so had they spoken out.[22]

On April 25th, the Russian and American armies met at the Elbe. Now that the harmony of Yalta was giving way ever more obviously to discord, the event was ominous as well as triumphant. On April 28th, the first of the dictators came to an ignominious end; Italian partisans strung the bodies of Mussolini and his mistress head downwards from meat hooks in a petrol station in Milan. Next day, the German armies in Italy surrendered.

The Russians had encircled Berlin. On the 30th, Adolf Hitler and his mistress committed suicide in the ruins of the city. The first reports, which reached Britain from German radio, said that he had died bravely defending his post. With quaint formality, Admiral Doenitz was designated his successor. On the day that his hero perished, William Joyce, Lord Haw Haw, made his last broadcast. Roaring drunk at the microphone, he said, "You may not hear from me again for a few months", shouted "*Es lebe Deutschland*", then dropped his voice: "*Heil Hitler*. And farewell."[23]

Had those impossible creatures ever lived? Had Low imagined them, like Colonel Blimp? The ruins of Hamburg, from which Joyce spoke, proved otherwise. The stage was grandly littered

with corpses; but there was no Fortinbras to round off the drama
with dignity. Against a banal background of wrecked streets and
hungry children, the next act, which was to end with the Berlin
Wall, was opening quietly.

On May 4th, the German forces in north-western Europe
surrendered at Montgomery's headquarters on Luneburg Heath.
His old adversary Rommel, implicated in the July Plot against
Hitler, had long since died by his own hand; it was a little known
admiral whom Doenitz sent to complete the formalities. On May
7th, the German Supreme Command surrendered at Rheims.
Unbelievably, the war in Europe was over.

VI

Churchill, speaking in the previous October, had foreseen that the
war against Japan would take eighteen months to complete after
the victory over Germany. It was going well; in those early days
of May, the British re-entered Rangoon. But it concerned most
of the British people very little as they prepared to celebrate the
triumph in Europe.

The news of Germany's final, unconditional surrender was
picked up from the German radio about lunchtime on May 7th,
and even before the official announcement that next day would
be a national holiday to celebrate the victory, flags were sprouting
in the streets, and tradesmen began to shutter their shops against
the expected crowds. As midnight ushered in May 8th, VE Day,
one of the bigger ships in Southampton docks let out a deep-
throated V sign. Others, large and little, joined in cacophonously
with their raucous or piping notes, and searchlights flashed out V
in morse across the sky.[24]

But London had earned the honour, which would have fallen
to it in any case, of providing the centre of rejoicing. The weather
was dull in the capital next morning; a light rain, inappropriately,
fell. Many houses displayed Union Jacks, but some had produced
hammer-and-sickles. Each resident prepared to celebrate in his
own manner. The *Daily Mirror*, fulfilling a faith long held in the
fighting services, rejoiced by disrobing completely the hitherto
tantalizing "Jane". Crowds massed, on the other hand, at St
Paul's Cathedral, which was packed with worshippers all day.

In the afternoon, the sun came out to play over the dense
crowds in the main streets. Many were wearing red, white and
blue rosettes. Comic paper hats of all kinds abounded, police-

men's helmets, crowns and silver cones. A couple of soldiers were spotted wearing a badge, "Pity the poor unemployed." At three o'clock, Churchill broadcast to the nation, and the many crowding outside the House of Commons heard his familiar voice relayed over loudspeakers, and joined in fervently with "God Save the King" when it was played at the end. Immediately afterwards, Churchill proceeded from Downing Street to the House, and his car was pushed the length of Whitehall by the sheer weight of the mobbing people, all of whom seemed set on shaking his hand. After cabinet and M.P.s had joined in a Thanksgiving Service at St Margaret's Church, opposite Parliament, Churchill pressed on to address rapturous crowds from a balcony overlooking St James's Park. He enjoyed himself, it seemed to his bodyguard, "like a schoolboy on an outing". Chamberlain after Munich had been nothing to this.

The night scene was consummated by the exhilaration of full-powered, aggressively sported, lighting. The statues and public buildings were floodlit; the searchlights danced a ballet in the sky; from restaurants and cinemas poured a glow which seemed unearthly to the small children whose parents let them stay up late to wander in this unimagined fairyland of illumination.

There were drunks about, but none seemed violent or even unduly rowdy. King George let the young princesses, Elizabeth and Margaret, mingle with the throng in the streets near his palace. "Poor darlings," he wrote in his diary that night, "they have never had any fun yet." At first sight, when one emerged from the underground, the whole of central London, bare of wheeled traffic, seemed impassably thick with people; yet this was illusion, for the crowd had no centre, no real purpose, and everyone was aimlessly on the move. What could one do, after all, but drink, as one had drunk before, kiss familiar, or unfamiliar faces, join in the sporadic outbreaks of singing, stare at the brave souls shinning up the lamp-posts, and cavort for a while in the uncouth, impromptu dances which suddenly cleared a space for themselves in the throngs? In the Strand, Tom Driberg saw "a buxom woman in an apron made of Union Jacks and a man of respectable middle-class and middle-aged appearance," performing an exaggerated Latin American dance while a passing accordion played "South of the Border"; a symbol, perhaps, of the fellow feeling, purged of inhibitions, which would soon be as out of date as the posters on the hoardings.

Amongst the sea of people which massed in front of the Palace, a young Guards officer, Humphrey Lyttelton, a relative of the

Minister of Production, created something of a current. Inspired by a picnic champagne supper in St James's Park, he took out his trumpet and started to play, New Orleans style. A crowd gathered, dancing began, and soon other instruments appeared; a man with a big drum strapped to his chest, a soldier with a trombone, "and then," Lyttelton relates, "an extraordinary grunting noise heralded the arrival of a sailor carrying what looked like the horn of an enormous old-fashioned gramophone." Soon the wanderlust seized them, and they set off in procession, shouting out "High Society", with a huge crowd in pursuit. Someone produced a handcart, and Lyttelton, still blowing lustily, was lifted bodily on to it. The rest of the band padded along beside as he rode in triumph along the Mall, by St James's Street, to Piccadilly Circus, then to Trafalgar Square, and finally back to the Palace, where there was more dancing, until the Royal Family appeared on the balcony. "I dimly remember", Lyttelton concludes, "blasting a chorus of 'For He's a Jolly Good Fellow' in the direction of His Majesty." The New World, so to speak, sang out its appreciation of the Old.

But, as Tom Driberg noticed, "Here and there, in sheltering darkness, stood lonely, living ghosts – a repatriated prisoner, dazed by the garish clamour and by the sudden accessibility of women after years of celibacy; a young American, wounded in Germany and due for discarge, bitterly dreading his return to Maryland and the instability of civilian life." That night, there were still twelve thousand people squatting in the Tube stations and the deep shelters, from which the last bunk was removed only at the end of the month. And Harold Nicolson, proceeding, he was not sure why, to a party given by a rich Conservative M.P., was confronted with uglier spectres. "There in his room, copied from the Amalienburg, under the lights of many candles, were gathered the Nurembergers and the Munichois celebrating *our* victory over *their* friend Herr von Ribbentrop. I left early and in haste, leaving my coat behind me . . ."[25]

In other towns and cities all over Britain, there were similar scenes on a smaller scale. Bonfires, lawful and unlawful, lit up the skies with memories of the blitz. Church bells pealed in freedom. Fireworks delighted children who had never known a Guy Fawkes Night. The great crowds which had gathered in the afternoon to hear Churchill's broadcast over the loudspeakers, and perhaps some apt remarks by the lord mayor as well, stayed to move to the music of bands, to join in communal singing, to behave as if they had no cares until the small hours of the morning. In the borough of Croydon, so recently stricken, pink and yellow neon lights flooded a huge statue of "Peace" over the roof of a store in the main shopping street, and thousands of people danced underneath it.[26]

"Well, it certainly is a great day; a great historic day," Sir Henry Tizard mused in his diary that night, after the free port which had gone with the special dinner at the Oxford college to which he had retired as President following Lindemann's triumph over him. "It is hard to realize now, but we shall know better later on. I feel rather like a patient coming round after a severe but successful operation. Deep down there is a feeling that all is well, and that a great oppression has been lifted, but other feelings are not so pleasant, and the nurse who pats one on the arm and shouts that all is over is excessively exasperating."[27]

LANDSLIDES

I am worried about this damned election. I have no message for them now.

Churchill to his doctor, June 1945[1]

I

Some junketing continued on May 9th, which, wisely, had also been declared a holiday; but a mood of anti-climax was setting in. To adapt Tizard's metaphor, the patient flexed his muscles and found them sore and stiff, and he dreaded the effort of standing again. The effects of total war could not be whisked away in a day, a year, a lifetime. The urgency and excitement which had inspired common striving, had now evaporated. The fear of death was departing; the fear of life was returning.

A hundred and fifty thousand men entered the armed forces in the first six months of 1945 – and until the end of the 1950s, conscription would be the common lot. Those who had already served, in some cases for six years, looked anxiously towards the future. It had been all very well for their employers to promise them their old jobs back; would they remember that promise now? And then there were those many cases where the same job had been filled by a succession of men, each called up in turn. Ernest Bevin had been moved to tears, as he had stood watching the soldiers filing past on their way to embark on D Day, when someone had called out, "Ernie, when we have done this job for you, are we going back on the dole?" They were in safe hands. In that month of general relaxation, September 1944, Bevin had released the details of the Government's plan to cover the interim period between the defeat of Germany and that of Japan.

There was to be no chaos of priorities as there had been after the First World War. The plan created two classes for demobilization. Class B would cover builders and others urgently required for reconstruction work, who would have priority in release, but would be subject to recall if they left the vital work to which they were directed. The remainder, the vast majority of servicemen, would be formed into an orderly queue, with their position established according to an ingenious scale which combined simplicity with self-evident justice. Both age and length of service would be taken into account. Two months' service would be taken to equal a year of age, so that a man of twenty-two with four years' service would be released with the same priority as a man of forty with one year's service, while a man of twenty-four with four years' service would "equal" a man of thirty with three. Each "demobbed" man in Class A would get eight weeks' paid leave on his release.

Bevin had also sponsored a variety of schemes for ensuring that servicemen got the jobs they wanted, and were encouraged to resume or take up professional training or apprenticeships. There were to be grants for university and college education, and for training in skilled trades, and even in business methods. Millions of copies of a booklet advertising these schemes were handed out to servicemen, and "Resettlement Advice" offices were set up in the larger towns. Each demobbed man was to get twelve pounds' worth of civilian clothing, "off coupons" and free of charge – hence the famous "demob suits" which appeared everywhere soon after the end of the war. Women, who would resent uniformity, were to get coupons and cash to use as they wished.

In November 1944, details had been published of a similar scheme for industry, to cover the same interim period. First priority for release would be given to housewives needed at home, wives of demobbed servicemen, women over sixty and men over sixty-five. Meanwhile, men who had been deferred in reserved occupations would be taken into the services, as soon as they could be spared, to replace those who were demobbed, and registration of girls would continue so as to provide substitutes for older women in industry.

So it was all settled – well enough, as it turned out, though there were "demob strikes" later among R.A.F. men in the east. A week after VE Day, Bevin cut the suspense short by announcing that releases would begin on June 18th, forecasting that three-quarters of a million men would be out of uniform by the end of the year. In the later months of 1945, some thirty thousand men a week were turning to the Resettlement Advice Service, which answered questions on anything from domestic problems to those of men wishing to set up shops. And, as Bevin had prophesied, with startling confidence, there was no mass unemployment of returned warriors; few Spitfire pilots, if any, had to stand in dole queues. J. M. Keynes, and five years of wartime experience, had changed all that.[1]

It was far easier to set evacuation into reverse than to demobilize five million men and women. The process had been started in September 1944, and by the end of that year, the only official evacuees still in the reception areas had been those from Hull, from other east coast towns, and from London. By June 1945, when the officially organized movement back to the capital began, the vast majority of evacuees had returned. But there were some who could not. At the end of July, seventy-six thousand people were still officially billeted under the Government scheme, and when it was finally wound up in March 1946, thirty-eight thousand survivors became the responsibility of the local housing authorities. For housing was the problem which had kept them in the country.[3] And housing was a headache for the demobbed man too. The return to civilian life might mean a confrontation with a faithless wife, a scene with a frosty employer, weeks, months or years of disorientation. Stabbing Germans in the belly and flying sorties over Berlin were not ideal preparations for a return to university, or for the search for a comfortable detached house. Majors and wing commanders, used to deference and smart salutes, would have degree taken away from them, and when that string was untuned, discord might follow.

There was a world shortage of food, reflected in famine in India, hunger and even cannibalism in Europe. There was less meat on sale in Britain in 1945 than there had been in 1944, less in the second half of the year than there had been in the first, and the improved supply of fish which followed the release of trawlers and fishermen from naval service could not compensate psychologically. With coarse irony, Dame Austerity whittled the bacon ration from four ounces to three and the lard ration from two ounces to one in the victorious month of May 1945. Then, as the shortage of labour in the mills was causing a new crisis in textile production, she turned to and cut the clothing ration in September, to only thirty-six coupons per year. It was a muddled, despondent, preoccupied nation which reluctantly turned its mind, in May 1945, to the question of choosing a new Government.

II

At the Labour Party conference, staged belatedly in December 1944, a striking incident had confirmed that the rank and file of the party held by its old faith in common ownership. A parliamentary candidate (Ian Mikardo) had moved a resolution calling on the National Executive to include "the transfer to public ownership of the land, large-scale building, heavy industry, and all forms of banking, transport and fuel and power" in its electoral manifesto. No formal vote had been necessary; the motion had passed clearly on a show of hands.[4] In February, the party had readmitted Cripps to membership with a due flourish of trumpets.

In March, the Prime Minister addressed the conference of the Conservative Party, a rarer assembly, without any claims to direct the leaders' policy. He attacked the Labour Party for adopting "sweeping proposals" which would destroy the whole of the existing system of society, and impose another "borrowed from foreign lands and alien minds". But he dangled before the Labour leaders, fishing most obviously for Ernest Bevin, the prospect that they might desert their hot-headed followers and join him in a post-war coalition. Bevin, greatly provoked by press speculation on the subject, slipped his reins for the first time. Speaking to a Labour Party gathering in Yorkshire on April 7th, he denounced the pre-war record of the Conservative Party and indignantly rebutted all suggestions that he might follow the example of betrayal set thirteen years before by Ramsay MacDonald. He suggested that all monopolies were ripe for nationalization, and specified the coal, fuel and power, steel and transport industries by name. The Conservative press was now shouting for an end to all controls over property and manpower as soon as possible; Bevin challenged the Tories to say whether they would take such a risk, and accused them of wanting "to get rich quickly at the expense of the community".[5] Brendan Bracken retorted in kind for the Conservatives. Party warfare of the old kind was reborn again, much to the disgust of the electorate.

It was assumed by the leaders of both major parties that to hold an election as soon as possible after VE Day would make Churchill's return as Prime Minister quite certain. Lloyd George's "Khaki Election" of 1918 had set a precedent, and everyone assumed that the electorate was still as gullible as ever. The Conservatives, naturally, pressed Churchill to break off the coalition at once. The Labour and Liberal Parties, equally naturally, wanted to postpone the event as long as possible. But Attlee himself agreed with Churchill that the best course would be to maintain the coalition until Japan was defeated. It was not that Attlee was, in Labour terms, a Quisling. "I am sorry that you suggest that I am verging towards MacDonaldism," he had written to Harold Laski the year before, when the latter had accused him of enjoying coalition too much. "As you have so well pointed out, I have neither the personality nor the distinction to tempt me to think that I should have any value apart from the party which I serve." An election after final victory had been won seemed to him best both for the party and the nation. He now helped Churchill to draft a letter to himself, which he would present to the Labour conference, soon to assemble once more at Blackpool.[6]

In this letter, Churchill proposed that the coalition should either continue until the war in the Pacific ended (an event still expected to emerge some eighteen months later), or disband at once so that an election might be held in July. The one eventuality which he ruled out quite finally was the October election which both Labour and Liberals had wanted. He suggested that a referendum might be held on the subject.

Attlee and Bevin argued with the Labour N.E.C. that Churchill's offer of continued coalition should be accepted, but only three others supported them. The conference, eleven hundred strong, with only two dissentients, endorsed the N.E.C.'s rejection of the offer. Attlee replied accordingly, and urged Churchill to reconsider an October election. With his typical grave acidulousness he dismissed the idea of a referendum. The device, he said, had "only too often been the instrument of Nazidom and Fascism".[7] Attlee has been much praised for his restraint in the 1945 election; it is only fair to point out that this remark set the mud flying.

So Churchill, on May 23rd, tendered his resignation to the

King. A few hours later, he was called back to Buckingham Palace and asked to form a new Government, though the King agreed to dissolve the current parliament on June 15th. The result was the so-called "Caretaker Government", a kind of shop-window display of the talent still at Churchill's disposal, with a few theoretically "non-party" figures, notably Anderson and Woolton, studded among a prevailing mass of Conservatives like plums in a cake. R. A. Butler succeeded Bevin as Minister of Labour, and Harold Macmillan entered the cabinet, while Hore Belisha reappeared in a minor post. When the new cabinet met, Oliver Lyttleton was interested to see how hardy is the political tradition in many families". This was the "Old Gang" back with a vengeance; the gathering included two sons of Prime Ministers, one grandson of a Prime Minister, and several others related to distinguished ministers in former Governments.[8]

When the Commons reassembled on May 29th, the row was so great that at times speakers were inaudible. In the following three weeks, the slanging match continued while certain legislation left outstanding by the coalition was hastily passed into law. Meanwhile, the election campaign got under way.

The auguries were confusing. Just before VE Day, a young wing commander standing at Chelmsford for Common Wealth had swept the Conservatives out of a hitherto safe seat with a quite phenomenal turn-over of twenty-three thousand votes. This was the first by-election to be held in England on a new register, which enfranchised those who had moved or come of age since 1939. The first in Scotland, at Motherwell, had conveyed a quite different suggestion. Dr Robert McIntyre, a leader of Scottish Nationalism, had beaten out a Labour candidate by a small majority. The result reflected the impact of Bevin's electioneering speech on Conservatives, who now saw no reason to maintain the truce, and who must have voted heavily for McIntyre; and also great local discon.ent in Scotland over issues such as the Government's refusal to support the building of a road bridge across the Forth. McIntyre, the first ever Scottish Nationalist M.P., preceded his brief spell in parliament by creating a sensation when he presented himself in the House of Commons without the customary sponsors. His arrival seemed to confirm that Labour would profit little from a quick election.

III

As Mark Abrams wrote, reviewing the election in cold blood soon after its conclusion, "From an examination of the campaign literature officially provided by the headquarters of the parties it was difficult to discover any basic conflicts separating the left from the right."[9]

The Conservative leadership was now moving into the hands of younger men like Eden, Butler and Macmillan who understood that major advances in social policy must be made if it was to maintain any prestige with the people. The Labour leadership, mellowed by five years in office, convinced in their hearts that Churchill must win the election, and very nearly satisfied with the degree of "socialism" already achieved as a result of the war, was in no mood to preach revolution; indeed, as Churchill had suggested in March, it was unhappy with the extent of the party's commitment to nationalization.

However, there were significant differences in the emphases which the literature and speeches of the two parties placed on different aspects of their common programme. The programme implied planning; the joint commitment to full employment was meaningless if wartime controls were immediately scrapped. Yet many Conservatives still saw these controls as a distasteful wartime necessity, like the blackout.

The policy of the Conservatives was determined by Churchill's "Four Year Plan", which he assured the country in his *Declaration of Policy to the Electors* had now been shaped ready for use. The plan itself was never published; in fact, Churchill, much to his irritation, had had to apply himself hastily to the concoction, on the advice of his ministers, of plausible policies in such fields as the health service, in which he had little interest. His pronouncements in the *Declaration* not unnaturally had an *ad hoc*, opportunist look about them. On the one hand, he suggested a policy for housing very similar to that proposed by Labour, whose leaders, in spite of their annual conference, had no intention whatever of nationalizing the building industry. Churchill urged control of the prices of building materials, a rapid increase in the labour force, continued rent control and the "planned use of land". But on the issue of full employment, Churchill all but reverted to the doctrines of *laissez faire* which his supporters were gleefully propounding from platforms up and down the country. (Brendan Bracken had the gall to proclaim, as if Jarrow had never been an ulcer on the earth, that under free enterprise total employment had increased between the wars.) Churchill wrote: "To find plenty of work with individual liberty to choose one's job, free enterprise must be given the chance and encouragement to plan ahead. Confidence in sound government, mutual co-operation between industry and the state, *rather than control by the state** – a lightening of the burdens of excessive taxation – these are the first essentials." Read carefully, this worked out much like Morrison's formula, but the implication, surely not carelessly included, was that controls would be scrapped.[10]

And how precisely could the Conservatives implement Beveridge and introduce a National Health Service while reducing taxation? Rather than arguing out the implications of their promises, the Conservatives reverted to the cry which had sustained Neville Chamberlain in office – trust the all-wise, omnipotent leader. The basic Conservative weapon in the election, reproduced in hundreds of election addresses, was a photograph of the Man with the Big Cigar. Their most familiar poster bore such an effigy, with the slogan "Vote National [*sic*] – Help him finish the Job."[11] Like naked heathens, they proclaimed the unique virtues of their tribal idol, a man whom most of them had spurned and ignored in the 1930s. The irony was not missed.

The authors of the standard study of the election contrast forcibly the fashion in which the Conservative candidates' addresses propose all manner of agreeable policies "in terms so vague that they seem to imply that the Conservatives know no way of planning for such ends", with the "confident tone" of the Labour addresses. The consensus, while serving in the long run to preserve private capitalism, had shifted the debate on to ground which Labour had made its own. Labour's manifesto, *Let Us Face The Future*, was a cosy, unprovocative document. Most of the items which it contained had been thrashed out in the 1920s and 1930s; almost all the Labour leaders had done was to leave out some old faithfuls. The nationalization of land had not been dropped, but it was now postponed indefinitely. The list of industries to be nationalized was the short and obvious one which Bevin had outlined; with the single exception of steel, the case for public ownership had long been recognized outside the Labour Party itself. The Bank of England, also scheduled for takeover, was in effect a public institution already, and the pre-

Author's italics.

war Labour proposal to engross the joint stock banks had been shelved.

The Labour leaders, in recent speeches, had emphasized that the party would nationalize not for the sake of socialist dogma, but for the sake of efficiency. As for maintaining the ready-made wartime controls for the purpose of exterminating free enterprise, Bevin had dismissed the notion with horror. Cripps had said early in May, "we have no interest in preserving or destroying private enterprise except to create efficiency in our production", and this sturdy managerialism was the purport of *Let Us Face the Future*. But when Labour called its programme "a practical expression" of "the spirit of Dunkirk and of the blitz", when it invoked the achievement of the Mulberry harbours to suggest what might be achieved in peacetime also, when it promised to plan "from the ground up", it was digesting the ideals of "Beveridgism" into its own traditional rhetoric.[12]

With relief bordering on hysteria, the Liberals had taken up Beveridge as their political lifebelt, and Sir William himself was now the chairman of their campaign committee. (Otherwise, their main policy line was monopolies, which they argued should either be curbed or taken over by the state.) But the contest, for most electors, was a boxing match between two parties, of which Labour had the cleaner record. The Conservatives, still smarting from the damaging success of *Guilty Men* in 1940, now produced a pamphlet of their own with the same title, quoting ten instances in which Labour, under Attlee's leadership, had voted or protested against measures of rearmament in the 'thirties.[13] But the right could not escape the blame for what had happened during its almost uninterrupted tenure of power between the wars; and many hecklers were able to quote the flattering remarks of Conservative M.P.s about Mussolini or Hitler from Tom Wintringham's anonymous handbook, *Your M.P.*

IV

Another feature of the pre-war Conservative record on which Labour laid great stress was the manner in which stunts – the "Red Letter" of 1924, the "Post Office Savings Scare" of 1931, Baldwin's specious support for the League of Nations in 1935 – had been used to win elections. Labour propaganda on this subject had been well digested, and the services in particular were ready for almost any unsavoury trick. Nevertheless, the ineffable

Lord Beaverbrook was ready to create new "scares". During the campaign, he and his ally Bracken made the running for the Conservatives; their speeches were more widely noted, especially in the Beaverbrook papers, than the moderate pronouncements of Woolton and Butler.

Beaverbrook resumed direct control of his papers during the campaign, and whipped them up into a frenzy of jibing. His personal line was quite remote from Churchill's Four Year Plan. Of the Conservatives, he said on May 28th, "So far as I can persuade them they will abolish every form of personal control." The *Daily Express* insistently claimed that Labour could execute its policies only by maintaining state control of labour, and Beaverbrook recklessly dangled the bait of high wages in front of trade union members, if only they would vote Conservative.[14] His influence with Churchill was certainly greater than that of any other political colleague. But it seems that Beaverbrook did not directly inspire the notorious gaffe with which Churchill opened his own campaign.

A feature of the election was that radio was used more than ever before. Both Labour and Conservatives were allotted ten programmes of twenty to thirty minutes each after the nine o'clock news; the Liberals had four, and the Communist and Common Wealth Parties one each. The average audiences achieved by the three main parties were almost identical, standing around forty-five per cent of the adult population, a proportion rivalled by ITMA, but by very few other programmes. Churchill gave four broadcasts for the Conservatives, and these were the most widely heard of all; about half the population tuned in for them.[15]

When he opened the first party political broadcast of the election on June 4th, Churchill launched into an astonishing attack on his former Labour colleagues. "I declare to you," he said, "from the bottom of my heart, that no socialist system can be established without a political police." If the Labour leaders tried to carry out a fully socialist programme, "They would have to fall back on some form of Gestapo, no doubt very humanely directed in the first instance..." And he suggested that, whatever Labour said now, they would nationalize everything if they were given a large majority.[16]

Next morning, the *Daily Express* wore the proud headline, "GESTAPO IN BRITAIN IF SOCIALISTS WIN – They would dictate what to say and do, even where to queue." Attlee had opened this vein of abuse, but when that night he rebutted Churchill's allegations, as usual, the voice was mild, the words biting. He offered an explanation for Churchill's behaviour. "He feared", said Attlee, "lest those who had accepted his leadership in war might be tempted out of gratitude to follow him further. I thank him for having disillusioned them so thoroughly. The voice we heard last night was that of Mr Churchill, but the mind was that of Lord Beaverbrook."[17]

The picador aimed deftly at the neck of the charging bull. The effect of this broadcast exchange has been much exaggerated. To judge from the opinion polls, Labour would have won the election easily if neither man had spoken; indeed, one remarkable feature of the period up to and including the election was the swing to the Conservatives, who in February had had the support of only twenty-four per cent of a representative sample. Though Labour also gathered committed support, the gap between the parties had narrowed from eighteen per cent in February to twelve per cent in June.[18]

But Mass Observation, and many less systematic witnesses, remarked on "the disappointment and genuine distress" which Churchill's "Gestapo" speech caused. How could such a great man lower himself in this way? Churchill's broadcasts were still more highly praised by the public than those of any other speaker. But the episode confirmed the generally held opinion that Churchill was a war leader, not a suitable peacetime Prime Minister; and Attlee's calm dignity impressed many of his opponents, and reassured the middle classes.[19]

However, lesser Conservatives took up Churchill's theme and improvised gaily upon it. One candidate declared roundly, "Mosley and Cripps have the same policy. The socialist state of Cripps is to be the same as the Fascist state of the blackshirts."[20]

Foreign policy was not an issue in the election. The Labour leaders had accepted Churchill's line over Greece, none more staunchly than Bevin, who had emphasized more than once in the intervening months his belief that foreign policy should be a matter for agreement between the major parties. Both parties, in their election literature, advocated continued alliance between the Big Three, and support for the United Nations Organization launched at San Francisco in May. Bevin had coined the phrase "Left understands left but the right does not", and had thus crystallized a specious suggestion which both he and Cripps harped on, that Labour would find it easier to deal with Russia in a friendly fashion than the Conservatives.[21]

But it seemed perfectly sensible in Churchill, as well as mag-

nanimous of him, that he should invite Attlee, as a potential
Prime Minister, to accompany him to Potsdam at the end of
July, where he, Truman and Stalin were to discuss major questions. Attlee, of course, accepted. At this point, another bull
opportunity came charging from the leftward direction. The
beast in question was that well-known socialist theoretician,
Harold Laski, then chairman of the National Executive of the
Labour Party. On June 14th Laski issued a statement in which he
insisted that Attlee should attend "in the role of observer only".
The Labour Party, he argued, could not be committed to decisions on matters which the National Executive and the Parliamentary Labour Party had not been able to discuss. Attlee,
furthermore, must not be saddled with agreements reached by
Churchill.

This blow at the roots of bi-partisanship was brave but hopeless. While Labour leaders were, by one theory, accountable to
the party they led, this eminently democratic notion did not apply
to them when they reached high office, to which they were elected
by the people as a whole (it was argued) and appointed by the
King. Churchill and Attlee at once exchanged letters in public,
which established that Attlee would be more than a "mute
observer". But Attlee, deciding to soft-pedal the matter, did not
reprove Laski, who continued to argue his point on Labour
platforms all over the country. Bracken at once took up the attack.
The Conservatives claimed that Laski's constitutional position in
the Labour Party was a threat to the authority of parliament.
Barely veiled anti-Semitism crept into their assault; which made
it all the odder that so many Tory speakers used Harold Macmillan's phrase "Gauleiter Laski". Beaverbrook declared that
Laski was aiming at the destruction of the British party system
and that he hoped to set in its place "the dictatorship of something commonly called the National Executive". (In fact, it was
always called the National Executive, and had been for years.)[22]

While the incident may have swayed some "floating" voters
rightwards, most of the electorate was not interested in Laski. In
the middle of June, successive Gallup Polls were published, of
which the first indicated that four electors out of ten thought
housing the major issue in the election; only one in seven named
social security, and one in fourteen full employment, and the
rest of the field were nowhere. The second, five days later,
indicated that for every five people who thought the Conservatives would handle the housing problem best, eight (forty-two

per cent) said Labour would. The cause was not any significant difference in the policies of the two parties; it was the concern which Labour had traditionally shown for the welfare of ordinary people. Bevin, who declared that Labour would build four or five million houses, but refused to say how long it would take them, could speak on the subject with the fervour of a prophet. "The better the house, the better the people", he said; not only quantity but quality, not only size but the difference which extra space would make to people's lives, formed a theme which he could take to the heights of his oratory.[23]

Such as they were. Bevin, in the definition which embraces Churchill, was hardly an orator; he was bluntness and plain speaking personified. That suited the people. Everyone who watched the election unfolding, in every part of the country, was impressed with a strange calm which prevailed at the public meetings. There was very little of the hysterical talk about punishing the Huns and exacting draconian reparations which had disfigured the 1918 election. There was not much heckling – it was commonest, it seems, at the meetings addressed by leading Conservative ministers. Radio had in any case taken much of the interest out of meetings given by local candidates; and it had surely helped to encourage the quiet, studious weighing of points, and the eager, earnest questioning which seemed to characterize these war-weary audiences.[24]

Only one feature of the election exhibited any of the old mass fervour; this was Churchill's triumphal tour of the provinces at the end of June. Birmingham, Yorkshire, Lancashire saw cheering crowds, spontaneous applause, the fluttering of bunting in the streets. Towards the end, Glasgow, that sullen home of left-wing extremism, gave him its ovation on a grey and overcast day. At his open-air meeting, boys perched in the trees above the rostrum and men stood in serried ranks on the roofs of near-by houses. As Churchill departed, the Scots took up the mourning refrain of "Will Ye No Come Back Again?", composed for the lost cause of that somewhat less noble reactionary, Bonnie Prince Charlie. Churchill's thanks for such displays of affection, in the last of his broadcasts, were gallant enough for the Pretender himself. "It was wonderful to see the beauty of so many human faces lighting up often in a flash with welcome and joy . . . What can I say to you of the girls and women, whose beauty charmed the eye, or of the old ladies who were brought out in chairs, or waved encouraging flags from high-perched windows. All this I saw as I passed through the English countryside . . . and no less dazzling were the spectacles which Scotland, in all her splendour, presented."[25]

Had he strayed from the main streets of Glasgow to the slums of Bridgeton, which Jimmie Maxton represented in parliament, the splendours of squalid tenements would have caught his eye. The veteran Independent Labour leader, stricken with the disease which would soon kill him, had his own people there, who still loved him. On a night of pouring rain, they packed out a school hall to hear him, and the burden of his speech was, "Twenty years ago you sent me to parliament to protest. I have protested for you, and I will protest for you till I die." An academic witness was moved to write, "He was in very truth the father of his people."[26]

V

Nearly seventeen hundred men and women, when nominations closed, were in competition for six hundred and forty seats. The main parties contested virtually every one; the Liberals mustered candidates for under half. It would seem that over three-quarters of Conservative candidates had fought in one or other of the World Wars, and if khaki had been the colour of this election, the right must have won. Against an impressive array of colonels, admirals, generals and D.S.O.s, Labour could produce less than half as many fighting men. Businessmen, and people with private means, accounted for approaching half the Conservative candidates; no wonder they disliked high taxation and controls so much.[27]

In the last week of the campaign, Churchill ventured somewhat rashly into the suburbs of London. He was booed, more than once, and when he attended a mass meeting in Walthamstow greyhound stadium, there were empty seats and many angry shouts. Herbert Morrison, with notable courage, had given up a safe seat in the East End to contest Lewisham, where it seemed Labour would be very lucky to win. Churchill went down there on the eve of poll and attacked his former Home Secretary for cowardice, saying he had run away from a Communist candidate. Again, he had provocation. Morrison, challenged over a notorious V1 incident in the borough, had revealed that Churchill had been responsible for an order that no warning should be given of the approach of individual V1s, and that he himself had later cancelled it. With a further shower of mud, the campaign ended.[28]

Polling day was July 5th. It was remarkable that some of the British people, at the end of a war for democracy, still had not one vote, but two; these were businessmen, who might vote in the divisions where they had their firms, and university graduates, who could take part in the interesting postal elections for the twelve university seats. There were further limitations to democracy; in the event, they favoured Labour. Because of pre-war and wartime movements of population, the working-class centres of the cities contained many seats where a small poll was sufficient to put in a candidate, while some booming areas of the New England had succumbed to electoral elephantiasis. There had been no time for a proper redistribution, but twenty-five new seats had been carved from the most swollen constituencies. The new register, also, had suffered from shortage of manpower in its compilation, and accidental disfranchisement was quite common, especially amongst the many who had changed address in 1945. On the day, seventy-three per cent of the electorate voted, and under the circumstances this was a good turn-out.

Servicemen were entitled to claim a postal vote or to appoint a proxy. The scheme had been long debated. As early as the summer of 1944 there had been distressing signs of a low response for the form (B 2626 in the army) which those fighting men who wished to exercise their rights had to fill in. The following conversation had been reported:

> OFFICER: Got your voting form?
> GUNNER: What's that for?
> OFFICER: So that you can vote in the next general election.
> GUNNER: Is there going to be one, sir?

A well-known story, perhaps apocryphal, relates that Bomber Harris, or some other noted commander, was asked casually by Churchill whether he might count on the votes of his men. "No, sir," answered the warrior, "eighty per cent of them will vote Labour." Churchill, much displeased, said, "Well, at least that will give me twenty per cent." "No, sir, the other twenty per cent won't vote at all." Whoever provided the source of this anecdote was wrong; well over half the forces did not vote at all. In June 1945, there were 4,531,300 men and women in the forces over twenty-one years of age. Many, of course, were serving far overseas. Only 2,895,000 had their names on the special service register, and only 1,701,000 votes were cast by post or proxy. However, the collection of the service votes, from as far afield as

Burma, meant that the election results could not be announced for three weeks.[29]

Churchill and Attlee both returned to the Potsdam conference on July 17th. Those who watched them reviewing a victory parade in Berlin saw a strange portent. When they left the rostrum with other V.I.P.s, to walk along the processional way, the assembled British soldiery reserved their warmest cheers for the awkward, unobtrusive figure of Clement Attlee, shuffling along after Churchill with a shy grin fixed on his face.[30]

Some Tories in Britain already feared, in private, that their day was over. But the political correspondents of the press were agreed, nem. con., that Labour had not won the election; the main argument was over the size of Churchill's majority. The Gallup Polls were ignored, even by the newspaper which published them. The trend on the stock exchange was upwards.[31]

The public awaited the results with remarkable apathy. On July 26th, they were announced in a stupefying rush. The B.B.C. gave the news hourly, and when the first bulletin went out at eleven a.m., two cabinet ministers, Macmillan and Bracken, had already fallen, and Birmingham, the heartland of affluent working-class Toryism, was swinging solidly to Labour. Leo Amery's ejection from his safe seat there was announced before midday, and now it was the white-collared suburbs of London which were going left. Morrison, soon afterwards, was in at Lewisham with a sensational majority, and then it was learnt that an unknown farmer, standing as an independent at Woodford, where the Labour and Liberal Parties had decided not to oppose Churchill, had taken over a quarter of the poll from the Great Man. By the time the last result was in, at about ten p.m., thirteen Conservative ministers had fallen. At seven o'clock, Churchill had tendered his resignation to the King, and the amazing Attlee had followed half an hour later to kiss hands on his appointment as Prime Minister.[32]

Labour had gained two hundred and twelve seats, many of them for the first time, giving them a total of three hundred and ninety-three members of parliament. The Liberals had been reduced to twelve, and Sinclair and Beveridge were among their casualties. The Tories and their allies were reduced to a meagre two hundred and thirteen seats. The remainder of the six hundred and forty had gone to the gallimaufry of independents and minor parties. A record number of independents had stood, but of fourteen who had been elected, seven sat for the universities. Brown and Kendall had held Rugby and Grantham, but Reakes had gone down to a Conservative, and Driberg and Charles White had both stood as official Labour nominess. D. N. Pritt had held one of the London suburbs for Uncle Joe, as an independent; the I.L.P. had kept their three seats in Glasgow; and the Communists, impertinently, had captured a Stepney division from Labour, giving them two overt M.P.s, as well as a handful of colleagues in the Labour ranks. But Common Wealth had failed disastrously. In sixteen seats it had had competition from Labour, and in every one it had lost a deposit. In six others, all hopeless for the left, Labour had not interfered and C.W. had lost more creditably. Only at Chelmsford was their man elected, thanks to a Labour withdrawal, and he took the Labour whip in 1946. Acland and Lawson, fulfilling earlier pledges, had renounced their seats and had consigned themselves to the flames of Labour opposition in the London suburbs; and the victor of Eddisbury, who had quietly joined Labour in 1944, was now heavily beaten as a Labour candidate. The "movement away from party" had been reversed, the Liberals had lost still more ground, and the big battalions had triumphed.

Fifteen million votes were cast against Churchill's Government, of which 11,992,292 went to Labour and 2,240,000 to the Liberals. If the splinter groups were included, there was a small majority of the electors (some sixty-five thousand) who had voted for what Mr Churchill called "socialism". However, the Conservatives and their allies, with 9,950,809 votes, had recovered remarkably well. Three votes out of five had gone against them, and Labour had taken an unprecedented slice of the middle-class vote – one manager had voted Labour for every two who had plumped for Churchill. But the Labour victory was based above all on a great increase in working-class support, and enough working-class people had voted Tory to give Churchill twenty-nine per cent of the whole adult population, as compared with thirty-five per cent for Labour.[33]

The vagaries of the electoral system had exaggerated Labour's advantage into a landslide. For the party's supporters, this was a moment for joyful tears; many had waited for decades for the first Labour Government with a clear majority over all other parties. When one of the young middle-class newcomers who formed a high proportion of the victorious Labour champions addressed a victory meeting in his Birmingham constituency, "The hall", as he remembered it, "seemed to be full of shining eyes aglow with the sight of the promised land." "POWER!" exclaimed a columnist in Manchester's Labour journal. "The *revolution* without a single cracked skull. The pioneers' dream realized at long last. Nothing to stand in the way of laying the *socialist* foundation of the new social order."[34]

The Gallup Poll now asked the public whether it thought that the results meant that the British people wanted Labour to govern "along existing lines only more efficiently, or to introduce sweeping changes such as nationalization?" Fifty-six per cent made the second assumption, as compared with only thirty per cent favouring the first, and this indicates the extent to which Labour's most "extreme" intentions were accepted as the will of the people.[35]

But revolution was not on Attlee's agenda. Anthony Howard has remarked without exaggeration, that "the overwhelming Labour victory of 1945 brought about the greatest restoration of traditional social values since 1660."[36] For six years, Attlee would remain Prime Minister, presiding over a valiant economic recovery. Productivity would soar. Exports would exceed the dreams of the wartime planners. "Full employment" would be maintained. Dame Austerity's tyranny would dwindle slowly, until her grip relaxed in the early 1950s. The transition from war to peace would be made, in the short run, with conspicuous success.

Labour would fulfil its programme of nationalization; but the only major item which would prove sufficiently controversial to provoke the Conservatives into repealing it would be the takeover of steel. The coal mines and railways, physically weakened by the war, were not worth saving for private enterprise, which indeed would find them more useful in state hands. By contrast, the money-making engineering industry would slip from the trammels of the controls as Labour, without much sign of a coherent strategy, scrapped them as soon as possible. Jet engines would prove a good dollar-earning business. In 1943, the inventor Frank Whittle had pleaded that Cripps, as Minister of Aircraft Production, should take over his prodigy for the community, pointing out that apart from a little money from Whittle himself and his backers, the state had contributed everything towards its development. Now private firms were exploiting the invention. Surely the case for nationalization was clear-cut? Cripps had replied that the coalition gave him no power to do such a thing. Labour had the power after July 1945, and still did not do it.[37]

There was, of course, the welfare state, which would have its symbolic birthday on July 5th, 1948, when the new National Insurance scheme and National Health Service would come into operation simultaneously. It would seem, for ten years or more, that the war on Beveridge's Five Giants had been completed. Disease, certainly, would lose much of its vitality. Ignorance, for all the limitations of the 1944 Education Act, would continue in steady retreat. But Want, Squalor and Idleness would covertly maintain a grim empire in the midst of increasing affluence. In 1960, seven or eight million people, representing one Briton in seven, would be living below the standard of living on which National Assistance was based, and the numbers would not be dwindling, but growing. The syndrome of low wages, bad housing, poor health and bad schooling would endure, to assault the senses of teachers in the pre-war depressed areas, still relatively depressed, and the slums of the big cities, still slums. Unemployment would not be abolished, but stabilized around half a million; for reasons which economists and other plump men in expensive suits would never tire of explaining, the prosperity of the many would necessitate the idleness of the few. If it was a question of making weapons of destruction, every cripple and simpleton, the war had shown, could be used; but when inoffensive things were to be made, the labour exchange must give doles to the unemployed, still concentrated in the north and Wales, where nationalization would not check the inevitable decline of the coal mines.

Indeed, those to have best service from the welfare state would be the well-to-do. Under R. A. Butler's ingenious dispensation, one child in seven from the middle classes would proceed to university in the 1950s, as compared with one in sixteen before the war; the proportion of students from the lower-paid sections of the working class would remain the same. Free hospital treatment would be a boon for the middle-class budget, but after promotion, there would still be expensive private hospitals providing more exclusive standards.

Labour had been elected, above all, on the issue of housing. With crude irony, housing would be the party's greatest failure. Pre-war rates of construction would not nearly be reached. The shortage, in 1951, would still be estimated at between one and two millions. In the 1950s, Britain's housing problem would begin to assume international dimensions; for an increasing flow of coloured immigrants would compete with Britons for such dwellings as were to be had, and would begin to assemble in near-ghettos. Racialism would become a staple of British politics, as it had been in Germany in the 1930s.

In 1951, Churchill would return as Prime Minister, still with nothing to say to the people. His ministers, so far from reversing Labour's policies, would adapt and expand them, to serve the wealthiest population which Britain had ever carried. But the trend towards increasing social inequality would be maintained. A callous and hedonistic society would head pell mell towards economic crisis, and few of its citizens would care. Perched on the world's straining shoulders like a toothless old woman of the sea, Britain would preoccupy herself with the problem of ensuring that her rich people continued to grow richer, while the world's poor stayed poor.

All this, of course, was veiled from Winston Churchill when his doctor, Lord Moran, found him deep in gloom on the afternoon of that July 26th, and spoke to him of the ingratitude of the people. Churchill's reply revealed that generosity of imagination which was always the strength of his weakness. " 'Oh no,' he answered at once. 'I wouldn't call it that. They have had a very hard time.' "38

VI

To Potsdam, whence Churchill and Attlee had returned for the results, Attlee and Bevin now flew, to face the disbelieving stare of Joseph Stalin, who could not credit that Churchill had let a mere fifteen million people stand in his way. "Left" confronted "left" as Bevin had recommended, and deadlock resulted nevertheless. The conference ended with the hopes of the world in ruins.

On August 2nd, President Truman, the third party in the quarrel, sanctioned the use of the atomic bomb against Japan. Not until March 1945 had the scientists been able to promise a few of the new weapons by the end of the summer. The British cabinet, learning that they might be used some time in August, had acquiesced almost casually; the bomb, like the war against Japan, was really America's affair. At Hiroshima, on August 6th, a sequence of events which had begun in the disinterested intellectual excitement of Rutherford's laboratory in Cambridge, came to its first climax, with seventy thousand deaths. Three days later, a second bomb was dropped on Nagasaki.

Some of those who heard the news in Britain thought of these happenings as no more than large-scale versions of the blitz which they had endured themselves; so, in most respects, they were. Men and women who still possessed idealism and imagination were appalled; and Bishop Bell, of course, was among the foremost to protest. A mother who wrote down her feelings for Mass Observation was typical of many others. "I was happier," she declared, "when I lay listening to bombs and daring myself to tremble; when I got romantic letters from abroad; when I cried over Dunkirk; when people showed their best sides and we still believed we were fighting to gain something."[39]

The Japanese surrendered on August 14th. On that day, a minute for the cabinet emanated from J. M. Keynes in the Treasury. Britain, he said, was faced by a "financial Dunkirk"[40] Lend-lease, sure enough, was terminated abruptly. With external disinvestment amounting to four thousand million pounds; with her shipping, an important source of invisible exports, reduced by thirty per cent; with her civilian industries physically run down after six years of war and her visible exports running at no more than four-tenths of her pre-war level; with 355,000 of her citizens dead by enemy action at home or abroad; with bread rationing looming ahead and spirit and flesh rebelling against further effort, the nation could consider only wanly the good fortune which had spared her the destiny of Germany, or Russia, or Japan.

As for her imperial pretensions, they were finished. There was a precise symbolism in the scene chosen for the stroke which officially concluded the war on September 12th. It was at Singapore that Mountbatten accepted the formal surrender of all the Japanese forces in South-east Asia. Fortune's wheel would perhaps revolve on a world scale; and what had Jarrow been to Calcutta?

References

Publisher and date of publication are given at the first reference to each book named.

The following abbreviations have been used where books have been frequently mentioned or have unusually cumbersome titles.

Berwick Sayers	W. Berwick Sayers (ed.), *Croydon and the Second World War* (Croydon Corporation, 1949).
Bullock	Alan Bullock, *The Life and Times of Ernest Bevin*, vol. 2, *Minister of Labour 1940–45* (Heinemann, 1967).
Calder	A. L. R. Calder, *The Common Wealth Party 1942–45* (University of Sussex D. Phil. thesis, 1968).
Churchill	Winston S. Churchill, *The Second World War* (Cassell, 1948–54). Six volumes, of which four are separately listed as:
Churchill GS	*The Gathering Storm* (1950 edition, originally 1948).
Churchill TFH	*Their Finest Hour* (1950 edition, originally 1949).
Churchill GA	*The Grand Alliance* (1950).
Churchill HF	*The Hinge of Fate* (1951).
Churchill WS 1	Winston S. Churchill, *War Speeches*, vol. 1, ed. Charles Eade (Cassell, 1951).
Churchill WS 2 and WS 3	*War Speeches*, vols. 2 and 3 (Cassell, 1952).
Collier	Basil Collier, *The Defence of the United Kingdom* (H.M.S.O., 1957).
Court	W. H. B. Court, *Coal* (H.M.S.O., 1951).
Ferguson	S. M. Ferguson and H. Fitzgerald, *Studies in the Social Services* (H.M.S.O., 1954).
Fogarty	M. P. Fogarty, *Prospects of the Industrial Areas of Great Britain* (Methuen, 1945.)
Graves HGB	Charles Graves, *The Home Guard of Britain* (Hutchinson, 1943).
Graves WG	Charles Graves, *Women in Green* (Heinemann, 1948).
Hammond I	R. J. Hammond, *Food*, vol. 1, *The Growth of Policy* (H.M.S.O., 1951).
Hammond FA	R. J. Hammond, *Food and Agriculture in Britain 1939–45* (Stanford U.P., Calif., 1954).

Hancock	W. K. Hancock and M. Gowing, *British War Economy* (H.M.S.O., 1949).
Hargreaves	E. L. Hargreaves and M. Gowing, *Civil Industry and Trade* (H.M.S.O., 1952).
351 HCDeb (etc.)	House of Commons Debates (Hansard), fifth series, vol. 351 (etc.)
Inman	P. Inman, *Labour in the Munitions Industries* (H.M.S.O., 1957).
Knowles	Bernard Knowles, *Southampton – The English Gateway* (Hutchinson, 1951).
McCallum	R. B. McCallum and A. Readman, *The British General Election of 1945* (O.U.P., 1947).
MO no. I (etc.)	Mass Observation typescript report no. 1 (etc.), filed at M.O. offices.
MO PP	Mass Observation, *People in Production* (Murray, 1942).
MO WB	Mass Observation, *War Begins at Home* (Chatto & Windus, 1940).
Moran	Lord Moran, *Winston Churchill – The Struggle for Survival 1940–1965* (Constable, 1966).
Murray	K. A. H. Murray, *Agriculture* (H.M.S.O., 1955).
Nicolson	Harold Nicolson, *Diaries and Letters 1939–45* (Collins, 1967).
O'Brien	T. H. O'Brien, *Civil Defence* (H.M.S.O., 1955).
Parker	H. M. D. Parker, *Manpower* (H.M.S.O., 1957).
Postan	M. M. Postan, *British War Production* (H.M.S.O., 1952).
Sayers	R. S. Sayers, *Financial Policy* (H.M.S.O., 1956).
SCNE 1 (1939–40)	First (etc.) Report from the Select Committee on National Expenditure, 1939–40 (etc.) (H.M.S.O., (1940–45).
Stat. Dig.	Central Statistical Office, *Statistical Digest of The War*, (H.M.S.O., 1951).
Taylor	A. J. P. Taylor, *English History 1914–45* (O.U.P., 1965).
Titmuss	R. M. Titmuss, *Problems of Social Policy* (H.M.S.O., 1950).
Turner	E. S. Turner, *The Phoney War on the Home Front* (Joseph, 1961).
Wartime SS	Wartime Social Survey, various mimeographed reports found in the British Museum.
Worswick	G. D. N. Worswick and P. Ady (ed.), *The British Economy 1945–50* (O.U.P., 1952).

Notes

Chapter 1: Prelude

1. W. B. Yeats, from *Last Poems 1936–39*, in *Collected Poems* (Macmillan, 1961).
2. O'Brien, 7–11.
3. Titmuss, 12–15, 327.
4. O'Brien, 71–2, 100–101, 125.
5. Charles Madge and Tom Harrisson, *Britain by Mass Observation* (Penguin Special, 1939), 49–50.
6. Stuart Samuel, "The Left Book Club", *Journal of Contemporary History*, vol. 1, no. 2, 1966.
7. Madge, *Britain*, 63–77.
8. Ibid., 87–96, 100–101; O'Brien, 156–65.
9. C. L. Mowat, *Britain Between the Wars* (Methuen, 1955), 615.
10. Iain Macleod, *Neville Chamberlain* (Muller, 1961), 268.
11. J. B. Priestley, *English Journey* (Heinemann, 1934), 397–403.
12. Fogarty, 22–5.
13. Ibid., 1, 5.
14. Ibid., 26–30; Priestley, *English Journey*, 314.
15. A. L. Lloyd, *Folk Song in England* (Lawrence & Wishart, 1967), 365.
16. Mowat, *Britain Between the Wars*, 484.
17. David Lockwood, *The Blackcoated Worker* (Allen & Unwin, 1958), 56; Asher Tropp, *The Schoolteachers* (Heinemann, 1957), 226.
18. Mowat, *Britain Between the Wars*, 492–3, 512–13.
19. Ibid., 510, 514–16; Fogarty, 4, 26–30.
20. George Orwell, *The Lion and the Unicorn* (Secker & Warburg, 1941), 54.
21. Eric Hobsbawm, *Industry and Empire* (Weidenfeld & Nicolson, 1968), 180–82.
22. Taylor, 409.
23. Mowat, *Britain Between the Wars*, 625–9; Postan, 55–6, 71, etc.
24. MO WB, 30, 35.
25. John Lehmann, *I Am My Brother* (Longmans, 1960), 3; MO WB, 32.
26. Maurice Gorham, *Broadcasting and Television Since 1900* (Dakers, 1952), 161.
27. MO WB 34–5; Hugh Dalton, *The Fateful Years* (Muller, 1957), 264–5; A. Duff Cooper, *Old Men Forget* (Hart-Davis, 1953), 259; 351 HC Deb, cols 279–83.

28. Earl of Birkenhead, *Halifax* (Hamish Hamilton, 1965), 447; Tom Driberg, *Colonnade 1937–47* (Pilot Press, 1949), 169.
29. Alexander McKee, *Strike from the Sky* (Souvenir Press, 1960), 23.
30. Titmuss, 91; Turner, 113.

Chapter 2: "This Strangest of Wars"

A. *Evacuation*

1. Titmuss, 182.
2. Ibid., 102, 137.
3. O'Brien, 352–8, 362–3; Turner, 140–44.
4. Titmuss, 101, 193–5.
5. Ibid., 90; Constantine Fitzgibbon, *The Blitz* (Wingate, 1957), 26.
6. Norah Baring, *A Friendly Hearth* (Cape, 1946), 11.
7. Titmuss, 23.
8. Ibid., 35.
9. Ibid., 31–44.
10. Ibid., 103–104; Richard Padley and Margaret Cole (ed.); *Evacuation Survey* (Routledge, 1940), 46–7, 145.
11. Titmuss, 103.
12. William Boyd (ed.), *Evacuation in Scotland* (U.L.P., Bickley, 1944), 55–6.
13. Titmuss, 108; Padley, *Evacuation Survey*, 220.
14. H. C. Dent, *Education in Transition* (Kegan Paul, 1944), 6–7.
15. F. Le Gros Clark and R. W. Toms, *Evacuation – Failure or Reform?* Fabian Tract 249, 1940, 2.
16. Titmuss, 110; Padley, *Evacuation Survey*, 234.
17. Titmuss, 553.
18. Ibid., 111.
19. Women's Group on Public Welfare, *Our Towns* (O.U.P., 1943), xv.
20. Boyd, *Evacuation in Scotland*, 92–3.
21. Padley, *Evacuation Survey*, 236–7.
22. Bernard Kops, *The World is a Wedding* (MacGibbon & Kee, 1963), 54.
23. *The Memoirs of Lord Chandos* (Bodley Head, 1962), 152.
24. National Federation of Women's Institutes, *Town Children Through Country Eyes* (Dorking), 1940, 5, 11, 18, 21.
25. Ibid., 4; Women's Group on Public Welfare, *Our Towns*, xiii.
26. Boyd, *Evacuation in Scotland*, 62–5.
27. H. G. Wells, *The New World Order* (Secker & Warburg, 1940), 72.
28. Titmuss, 122.
29. Ibid., 125–31; Women's Group on Public Welfare, *Our Towns*, 67–8, 79.
30. Titmuss, 131–2.
31. Susan Isaacs (ed.), *The Cambridge Evacuation Survey* (Methuen, 1941), 19.

32. Titmuss, 115.
33. Ibid., 116–17.
34. Ibid., 437.
35. Isaacs, *The Cambridge Evacuation Survey*, 34–5; Boyd, *Evacuation in Scotland*, 31; Padley, *Evacuation Survey*, 43.
36. A. St. Loe Strachey, *Borrowed Children* (Murray, 1940), 11.
37. Richmal Crompton, *William and the Evacuees* (Newnes, 1940), 10.
38. Titmuss, 156–69.
39. Dent, *Education in Transition*, 39.
40. Isaacs, *Cambridge Evacuation Survey*, 37, 79, 129–42.
41. Padley, *Evacuation Survey*, 160.
42. Titmuss, 159–61.
43. Ibid., 174–6.
44. Berwick Sayers, 247–8.
45. Padley, *Evacuation Survey*, 247.
46. Barnett House Study Group, *London Children in Wartime Oxford* (O.U.P., 1947), 47–52.
47. Titmuss, 94; Padley, *Evacuation Survey*, 200, 211.
48. Dent, *Education in Transition*, 29, 61, 67–8.
49. A. S. F. Gow, *Letters from Cambridge* (Cape, 1945), 36.
50. Padley, *Evacuation Survey*, 124.

B. *Anti-climax*

1. Evelyn Waugh, *Men at Arms* (Chapman & Hall, 1952), 18–19.
2. Douglas Reed, *A Prophet at Home* (Cape, 1941), 187.
3. Parker, 150–60.
4. Dennis Hayes, *Challenge of Conscience* (Allen & Unwin, 1949), 12–13, 36–7.
5. Donald Johnson, *Bars and Barricades* (Johnson, 1952), 175.
6. H. H. Henson, *Retrospect of an Unimportant Life*, vol. 3 (O.U.P., 1950), 85.
7. Herbert Read, *Collected Poems* (Faber, 1966), 152–3.
8. Henry Green, *Caught* (Hogarth Press, 1943), 63.
9. O'Brien, 197–8, 289–90.
10. Knowles, 109–10; J. L. Hodson, *Before Daybreak* (Gollancz, 1941), 90; MO WB, 131.
11. Thomas Johnston, *Memories* (Collins, 1952), 136.
12. Leo Walmsley, *Fishermen at War* (Collins, 1941), 23.
13. J. Wheeler Bennett, *King George VI* (Macmillan, 1958), 407.
14. Fenner Brockway, *Bermondsey Story* (Allen & Unwin, 1949), 221; Patrick Gordon Walker, "The Attitude of Labour and the Left to the War", *Political Quarterly*, vol. XI, no. 1, 1940, 82.
15. Victor Gollancz (ed.), *The Betrayal of the Left* (Gollancz, 1941), 1–2; Douglas Hyde, *I Believed* (Heinemann, 1951), 70–71.
16. MO WB, 175–6; O'Brien, 316–18.

17. Taylor, 459; Leo Amery, *My Political Life*, vol. 3 (Hutchinson, 1955), 330.
18. Macleod, *Neville Chamberlain*, 281.
19. MO WB, 420; Tom Harrisson, "What Is Public Opinion?", *Political Quarterly*, vol. XI, no. 4, 1940, 371.
20. MO WB, 80–97.
21. Kingsley Martin, "Public Opinion During the First Six Months", *Political Quarterly*, vol. XI, no. 2, 1940, 252–3.
22. MO WB, 239–42.
23. Ibid., 156–8; Churchill WS 1, 145.
24. O'Brien, 319.
25. MO WB, 192–5.
26. Titmuss, 139; Laurence Thompson, *1940* (Collins, 1966), 21.
27. O'Brien, 321–3.
28. Vera Brittain, *England's Hour* (Macmillan, 1941), 27.
29. O'Brien, 323–4; Turner, 134–5.
30. Ibid., 68–9, 135–6.
31. J. A. Cole, *Lord Haw Haw* (Faber, 1964), 110–19.
32. Ted Kavanagh, *Tommy Handley* (Hodder & Stoughton, 1949), 116–17.
33. MO WB, 74–8.
34. Ibid., 128–30.
35. Ibid., 111–17; Mass Observation, *Home Propaganda* (Advertising Service Guild, 1941), 9.
36. Cecil Beaton, *The Years Between – Diaries 1939–1944* (Weidenfeld & Nicolson, 1965), 11–12.
37. O'Brien, 340–4.
38. F. H. Radford, *Fetch the Engine* (Fire Brigades Union, 1951), 115, 118.
39. Henry W. Stedman, *Battle of the Flames* (Jarrolds, 1942), 6.
40. Amery, *My Political Life*, vol. 3, 327–8; Hancock, 126; Taylor, 456.
41. Maurice Edelman, *Production for Victory, Not Profit!* (Gollancz, 1941), 11.
42. Joel Hurstfield, *The Control of Raw Materials* (H.M.S.O., 1953), 143–50, 385–99.
43. Hancock, 112–14, 176–8.
44. Turner, 137–8.
45. Sayers, 33–4.
46. Titmuss, 139; MO WB, 359.
47. Hancock, 166–7; Hargreaves, 78–83.
48. MO WB, 376–84.
49. Herbert Tracey, *Trade Unions Fight – For What?* (Routledge, 1940), 127–9, 133–9, 153–7.
50. Hancock, 163–5.
51. Parker, 72–3; Bullock, 9.
52. Parker, 60, 83–4; SCNE 2 (1939–40), 18.4.40, 19–21.
53. Inman, 31.

54. J. L. Hodson, *Through The Dark Night* (Gollancz, 1941), 113, 117.
55. O'Brien, 223, 320–21, 337–40.
56. Churchill GS, 498; Dalton, *The Fateful Years*, 293; Tom Harrisson, "Public Opinion About Russia", *Political Quarterly*, vol. 12, no. 4, 1941, 353–66; Amery, *My Political Life*, vol. 3, 346.
57. Churchill GS, 526; *Daily Express*, 5.4.40.

Chapter 3: Spitfire Summer

A. *The Man with the Big Cigar*

1. MO WB, 158.
2. Kavanagh, *Tommy Handley*, 194.
3. L. P. Lochner (ed.), *The Goebbels Diaries* (Hamish Hamilton, 1948), 25.
4. Macleod, *Neville Chamberlain*, 283–4.
5. "Southwark and Party Truce", *US* 4 (Mass Observation), 24.2.40, 29–32.
6. Sayers, 36–44.
7. Churchill GS, 451; Nicolson, 70.
8. Macleod, *Neville Chamberlain*, 287.
9. Nicolson, 77.
10. 360 HCDeb, cols 1075, 1081–3, 1093, 1125–30, 1150, etc.
11. Ibid., cols 1253, 1265–6, 1283, etc.; Nicolson, 78.
12. Nicolson, 78–9; Dalton, *The Fateful Years*, 306; Duff Cooper, *Old Men Forget*, 279.
13. Laurence Thompson, *1940*, 83–5; Taylor, 473–4; Churchill GS, 597–8; Birkenhead, *Halifax*, 453–5.
14. Colin Coote, *Editorial* (Eyre & Spottiswoode, 1965), 203.
15. Churchill GS, 661.
16. Churchill WS 1, 181.
17. Wheeler Bennett, *King George VI*, 450.
18. Paul Einzig, *In the Centre of Things* (Hutchinson, 1960), 208–19.
19. Michael Foot, *Aneurin Bevan*, vol. 1 (MacGibbon & Kee,1962), 319; Hugh Cudlipp, *Publish and Be Damned* (Dakers, 1953), 145.
20. MO no. 496, *Popular Attitudes to Wartime Politics*, 24.11.40, 5.
21. Churchill TFH, 15.
22. Churchill WS 1, 334–5.
23. Hammond I, 229
24. *Left News*, March 1941; *History of The Times*, vol. 4, pt 2 (*Times*, 1952), 981.
25. Birkenhead, *Halifax*, 459.
26. Kenneth Young, *Churchill and Beaverbrook* (Eyre & Spottiswoode, 1966), 40; Churchill, *My Early Life* (Thornton Butterworth, 1930), 79.
27. Isaiah Berlin, *Mr Churchill in 1940* (Murray, 1964), 13.

28. A. G. Gardiner, *Pillars of Society* (Nisbet, 1913), 57–8.

29. Moran, 123.

30. *The Memoirs of Lord Chandos*, 182–5; W. H. Thompson, *I Was Churchill's Shadow* (Johnson, 1951), 46–7.

31. Vernon Bartlett, "Churchill as Orator", *The Big Four* (Practical Press, 1943), 4, 6; Nicolson, 185.

32. Nicolson, 321; Churchill WS 1, 211–12.

33. Churchill WS 1, 266; Lochner, *The Goebbels Diaries*, 52.

34. George Mallaby, *From My Level* (Hutchinson, 1965), 29–30.

35. Churchill GS, 375; W. H. Thompson, *I Was Churchill's Shadow*, 21.

36. Raymond Blackburn, *I Am An Alcoholic* (Wingate, 1959), 204–5.

37. Quentin Reynolds, *Only The Stars Are Neutral* (Cassell, 1942), 11–12.

38. Nicolson, 258.

39. John G. Winant, *Letter From Grosvenor Square* (Hodder & Stoughton, 1947), 25–6.

40. *The Memoirs of Lord Chandos*, 293.

41. Vernon Bartlett, *And Now, Tomorrow* (Chatto & Windus, 1960), 89.

42. Churchill WS 1, 262, 332; Churchill WS 2, 299; Nicolson, 358.

43. *The Memoirs of Lord Chandos*, 183; Foot, *Aneurin Bevan*, vol. 1, 321, 407.

44. Moran, 12–13, 247.

45. Hadley Cantril (ed.), *Public Opinion 1935–1946* (Princeton U.P., 1951), 106.

46. R. J. E. Silvey, "Some Recent Trends in Listening", *B.B.C. Yearbook 1946* (B.B.C., 1947), 28.

47. Nicolson, 99, 102, 139, 143–4.

48. Churchill WS 2, 344.

49. Churchill, *My Early Life*, 9.

50. Churchill WS 1, 283; Churchill WS 3, 45–6.

51. Francis Williams, *A Prime Minister Remembers* (Heinemann, 1961), 37; Earl of Woolton, *Memoirs* (Cassell, 1959), 214.

52. Churchill WS 1, 338.

53. R. F. Harrod, *The Prof* (Macmillan, 1959), 179–80.

54. Churchill WS 1, 333; Young, *Churchill and Beaverbrook*, 185.

55. John McGovern, *Neither Fear nor Favour* (Blandford, 1960); 133–45; Young, *Churchill and Beaverbrook*, 49.

56. Ibid., 232.

57. Francis Williams, *Ernest Bevin* (Hutchinson, 1952), 12.

58. Ibid., 217.

59. Ibid., 226.

60. J. G. Lockhart, *Cosmo Gordon Lang* (Hodder & Stoughton, 1949); 429; J. B. Priestley, *Postscripts* (Heinemann, 1940), 27.

61. MO WB, 119.

62. Charles Smyth, *Cyril Forster Garbett* (Hodder & Stoughton, 1959), 450.

63. J. Wheeler Bennett, *John Anderson, Viscount Waverley* (Macmillan, 1962), 225.
64. Churchill WS 2, 215; Wheeler Bennett, *John Anderson*, 315–16; Williams, *A Prime Minister Remembers*, 40.
65. Graves HGB, 14.

B. *Dunkirk*

1. Nigel Balchin, *Darkness Falls from the Air* (Four Square edn, 1961 – originally 1942), 40.
2. Churchill TFH, 38.
3. Beaton, *The Years Between*, 23–4.
4. 361 HC Deb, col. 152.
5. Jane Gordon, *Married to Charles* (Heinemann, 1950), 114.
6. Walmsley, *Fishermen at War*, 209–17.
7. Priestley, *Postscripts*, 2–4; also on a gramophone record, *The Sounds of Time*, Oriole MG 20021.
8. Bernard Darwin, *War on the Line* (Southern Railways, 1946), 28–9.
9. Basil Dean, *The Theatre at War* (Harrap, 1956), 123.
10. Churchill WS 1, 195–6; Tom Johnston, *Memories*, 221; Hewlett Johnson, *Searching for Light* (Joseph, 1968), 254–5.
11. Churchill WS 1, 206.
12. Robert Henrey, *The Siege of London* (Dent, 1946), 100.
13. Charles de Gaulle, *The Call to Honour 1940–1942* (Collins, 1955); 62–3; Drew Middleton, *The Sky Suspended* (Secker & Warburg, 1960), 75; Turner, 300–301.
14. *Radio Times*, 14.6.40; George Orwell, "Notebooks", *World Review*, June, 1950; Knowles, 133.
15. Donald Johnson, *Bars and Barricades*, 182.
16. Verily Anderson, *Spam Tomorrow* (Hart-Davis, 1956), 74; Roy Fuller, "August 1940", *The Middle of a War* (Hogarth Press, 1942), 14.
17. Mass Observation, *Home Propaganda*, 9; O'Brien, 366.
18. O'Brien, 358–60.
19. A. P. Herbert, *The Thames* (Weidenfeld & Nicolson, 1966), 160; Wheeler Bennett, *King George VI*, 460.
20. Brittain, *England's Hour*, 60.
21. Hancock, 119–20, 327; Sayers, 45
22. Sayers, 45–57.
23. Hammond I, 93–4.
24. Ibid., 101–102.
25. Inman, 45–6.
26. Collier, 123–5.
27. Ibid., 127; Postan, 117.
28. Collier, 128.
29. Ernest Fairfax, *Calling All Arms* (Hutchinson, 1945), 95.
30. Frank Rowlinson, *Contribution to Victory* (Metropolitan-Vickers

[Manchester], 1947), 39–40; Maurice Webb, *Britain's Industrial Front* (Odhams, 1943), 6.

31. L. Urwick and E. F. L. Brech, *The Making of Scientific Management*, vol. 2, *Management in British Industry* (Management Publications Trust, 1947), 207–209; "Political and Economic Planning", *British Trade Unionism* (P.E.P., 1948), 89; SCNE 17 (1940–41), 19.12.40, 3–9; Parker, 442–3.

32. Collier, 85; Peter Fleming, *Invasion 1940* (Hart-Davis, 1957), 33.

33. Ibid., 55, 70.

34. A. S. Millward, *The German Economy at War* (Athlone Press, 1965), 11.

35. Fleming, *Invasion 1940*, 15, 42.

36. Hancock, 138; Ministry of Information, *Manpower* (H.M.S.O., 1944), 7.

37. Julian Maclaren-Ross, *Memoirs of the Forties* (Alan Ross, 1965), 82; Collier, 219.

38. Collier, 142.

39. V. Anderson, *Spam Tomorrow*, 75; Fleming, *Invasion 1940*, 98.

40. Collier, 142.

41. Ibid., 145; Turner, 251–2; Darwin, *War on the Line*, 149–50.

42. Turner, 254–7.

43. Graves HGB, 15; Churchill GS, 384.

44. F. H. Lancum, *Press Officer, Please!* (Crosby Lockwood, 1946), 76.

45. Graves HGB, 25; H. K. Wilson, *Four Years – The Story of the 5th Battalion (Caernarvonshire) Home Guard* (R. E. Jones [Conway], 1944), 20, 32.

46. Graves HGB, 26–7.

47. Ibid., 356.

48. Ibid., 38

49. Lancum, *Press Officer, Please!*, 77.

50. George Orwell, "London Letter", *Partisan Review*, July–August 1941, 318.

51. Darwin, *War on the Line*, 194–200.

52. Admiral Lord Mountevans, *Adventurous Life* (Hutchinson, 1946), 239–41.

53. Graves HGB, 47; Tom Wintringham, *New Ways of War* (Penguin, 1940), 86.

54. *The Story of the First Berkshire (Abingdon) Battalion Home Guard* (Astle [Manchester], 1945), 11; Graves HGB, 32–3.

55. Cambridgeshire and Isle of Ely Territorial Army Association, *We Also Served* (Heffers [Cambridge], 1944), 26; L. W. Kentish, *Home Guard – Bux 4* (Lock, 1946), 18–20.

56. Berwick Sayers, 32.

57. Graves HGB, 78–9.

58. Fleming, *Invasion 1940*, 271–3.

59. *The Story of the First Berkshire ...* Home Guard, 10; Graves HGB, 316.

50. Priestley, *Postscripts*, 31.
51. Titmuss, 243–5; Collier, 144.
52. Titmuss, 248–9; S. Isaacs, *The Cambridge Evacuation Survey*, 35.
53. Titmuss, 246–7; Geoffrey Shakespeare, *Let Candles Be Brought In* (Macdonald, 1949), 243–74.
54. Titmuss, 246; Graves WG, 69–77; Alan and Mary Wood, *Islands in Danger* (Evans, 1955), 22–50.
55. Fleming, *Invasion 1940*, 86–7; Marcel Jullian, *Battle of Britain* (Cape, 1967), 41.
56. Churchill WS 1, 232; Graves HGB, 71–2; Arthur Horner, *Incorrigible Rebel* (MacGibbon & Kee, 1960), 163; Graves WG, 55.
57. Dalton, *The Fateful Years*, 336–7; Nicolson, 84–5; Bartlett, *And Now, Tomorrow*, 65.
58. François Lafitte, *The Internment of Aliens* (Penguin, 1940), 36–9, 67–8, 70–76, 87–145, 167–77; Turner, 281.
59. Margaret Gowing, *Britain and Atomic Energy 1939–1945* (Macmillan, 1964), 53–4; L. Thompson, *1940*, 136.
60. 364 HCDeb, cols 1537–8.
61. Parker, 344–6; Eugen Spier, *The Protecting Power* (Skeffington, 1951), 248; Elizabeth Woolley, "Quartet", *Sunday Times Magazine*, 18.12.66.
62. Fleming, *Invasion 1940*, 57, 71; Colin Cross, *The Fascists in Britain* (Barrie & Rockcliff, 1961), 193–8.
63. "Aping the Apes", *Bristol Co-operative Citizen*, August 1940.
64. Churchill WS 1, 195; Fleming, *Invasion 1940*, 62; Graves HGB, 72–3; Turner, 226–7.
65. L. Thompson, *1940*, 137–8; Jullian, *Battle of Britain*, 78.
66. A. P. Herbert, *Siren Song* (Methuen, 1940), 53; Turner, 269–70.
67. Fleming, *Invasion 1940*, 183–6; Johnston, *Memories*, 140–41.
68. Fleming, *Invasion 1940*, 64, 66, 102–103.
69. J. A. Cole, *Lord Haw Haw*, 155–69.
70. Churchill WS 1, 228.
71. Advertisement in *Radio Times*, 26.7.40; Turner, 270–77.
72. Orwell, *The Lion and the Unicorn*, 68–9.
73. Lehmann, *I Am My Brother*, 68; "Cato", *Guilty Men* (Gollancz, 1940), 15.
74. *The Times*, 1.7.40.
75. G. K. A. Bell, *The Church and Humanity* (*1939–1946*) (Longmans, 1946), 107; Wintringham, *New Ways of War*, 121–3.
76. "This England", *New Statesman*, 14.2.42.
77. R. J. E. Silvey, "Some Recent Trends in Listening", *B.B.C. Year Book 1946*, 28–9; *Radio Times*, 18.10.40.
78. Priestley, *Postscripts*, 17, 37–8.
79. MO no. 496, *Popular Attitudes to Wartime Politics*, 20.11.40.
80. Churchill WS 1, 192; Priestley, *Postscripts*, 39–43.

C. *The Battle of Britain*

1. McKee, *Strike from the Sky*, 185.
2. Telford Taylor, *The Breaking Wave* (Weidenfeld & Nicolson, 1967), 188.
3. Transcribed from the gramophone record of Leslie Baily's B.B.C. feature, *Scrapbook 1940* (Fontana FDL 493 014).
4. William Shirer, *The Rise and Fall of the Third Reich* (Simon & Schuster [New York], 1960), 754.
5. Basil Collier, *A Short History of the Second World War* (Collins, 1967), 155–6.
6. Hodson, *Through the Dark Night*, 108–109.
7. Derek Wood and Derek Dempster, *The Narrow Margin* (Hutchinson, 1961), 74; Ronald W. Clark, *Battle for Britain* (Harrap, 1965), 47; Jullian, *Battle of Britain*, 151; Parker, 159.
8. Richard Hillary, *The Last Enemy* (Macmillan, 1942), 118.
9. J. A. Cole, *Lord Haw Haw*, 168.
10. Berwick Sayers, 35–9.
11. Churchill WS 1, 240; Hodson, *Through the Dark Night*, 344.
12. Fairfax, *Calling All Arms*, 13–34.
13. Gordon Beckles, *Birth of a Spitfire* (Collins, 1941), 50–51.
14. Collier, 121; Wood, *The Narrow Margin*, 201.
15. David Farrer, *The Sky's the Limit* (Hutchinson, 1943), 8, 35; J.D. Scott and R. Hughes, *The Administration of War Production* (H.M.S.O., 1955), 294.
16. Postan, 159–61; Parker, 97–101.
17. Farrer, *The Sky's the Limit*, 71–2.
18. Fairfax, *Calling All Arms*, 38, 44.
19. Inman, 47–8.
20. Beckles, *Birth of a Spitfire*, 62–3; Farrer, *The Sky's the Limit*, 81.
21. Farrer, *The Sky's the Limit*, 77–9; Beckles, *Birth of a Spitfire*, 57–9, 77–80, 109, 119–20.
22. Walmsley, *Fishermen at War*, 255; Drew Middleton, *The Sky Suspended*, 191.
23. Drew Middleton, *The Sky Suspended*, 88; W. E. Holl, *Civil Defence Goes Through It – Paddington 1937–1945*, ms. in British Museum, 1946, 34.
24. McKee, *Strike from the Sky*, 140–42, 278; Jullian, *Battle of Britain*, 127–8, 212–13; A. G. Street, *From Dusk to Dawn* (Blandford, 1947), 66–7.
25. Fleming, *Invasion 1940*, 216; Collier, 163.
26. Taylor, *The Breaking Wave*, 150–51.
27. Jullian, *The Battle of Britain*, 135.
28. Collier, 208–13; Taylor, *The Breaking Wave*, 155–6; Shirer, . . . *The Third Reich*, 778.
29. Shirer, . . . *The Third Reich*, 779–80.

30. Barbara Nixon, *Raiders Overhead* (Lindsay Drummond, 1943), 13.

31. W. R. Matthews, *St Paul's Cathedral in Wartime* (Hutchinson, 1946), 35.

32. McKee, *Strike from the Sky*, 219–20; Clark, *Battle for Britain*, 142.

33. Nixon, *Raiders Overhead*, 16–17; H. A. Wilson, *Death Over Haggerston* (Mowbray, 1941), 123; Kops, *The World Is a Wedding*, 63.

34. H. K. Wilson, *Four Years . . .* , 39–41.

35. Fitzgibbon, *The Blitz*, 62.

36. A. P. Herbert, *The Thames*, 163–5.

37. Sir Aylmer Firebrace, *Fire Service Memories* (Melrose, 1949), 168–9; Ministry of Information, *Front Line* (H.M.S.O., 1942), 25–6.

38. H. W. Stedman, *Battle of the Flames*, 8.

39. Titmuss, 258–9; Graves WG, 86–7.

40. Sir Harold Scott, *Your Obedient Servant* (Deutsch, 1959), 126–7.

41. Kops, *The World Is a Wedding*, 67.

42. Taylor, *The Breaking Wave*, 161–3.

43. Churchill WS 1, 255.

44. Clark, *Battle for Britain*, 148–55; Taylor, *The Breaking Wave*, 163–5.

45. Taylor, *The Breaking Wave*, 165; Millward, *The German Economy at War*, 188–9; Wood, *The Narrow Margin*, 356, 365–8.

46. Wood, *The Narrow Margin*, 364; McKee, *Strike from the Sky*, 124.

47. W. Hornby, *Factories and Plant* (H.M.S.O., 1958), 204–8; *The Memoirs of Lord Chandos*, 208.

Chapter 4: Blitz

A. *The Even Tenor of the Blitz*

1. Sir Harold Scott, *Your Obedient Servant*, 129.

2. Nicolson, 114.

3. Matthews, *St Paul's Cathedral in Wartime*, 36–7.

4. Titmuss, 271; Brittain, *England's Hour*, 215–16.

5. Titmuss, 257; Ritchie Calder, *Carry on London* (English Universities Press, 1941), 125.

6. Douglas Hyde, *I Believed*, 82–3.

7. Fitzgibbon, *The Blitz*, 108–11; Basil Woon, *Hell Came To London* (Peter Davies, 1941), 158–9.

8. Fitzgibbon, *The Blitz*, 98–102; Nixon, *Raiders Overhead*, 20.

9. Wheeler Bennett, *King George VI*, 467–70.

10. Collier, 256–7, 494–5.

11. Churchill WS 1, 266–7.

12. Churchill TFH, 210–13; J. T. Murphy, *Victory Production!* (Bodley Head, 1942), 23–34; Churchill WS 1, 259; Hilary St George Saunders, *Ford at War* (Ford, 1946), 29–30.

13. Ralph Ingersoll, *Report on England* (Bodley Head, 1941), 41.
14. Graham Greene, *Ministry of Fear* (Penguin, 1963 [originally 1943]), 25; John Strachey, *Post D* (Gollancz, 1941), 46.
15. Charlotte Haldane, *Truth Will Out* (Weidenfeld & Nicolson, 1949), 186; Evelyn Waugh, *Officers and Gentlemen* (Chapman & Hall, 1955), 1; Nicolson, 109; Berwick Sayers, 50.
16. J. L. Hodson, *Towards the Morning* (Gollancz, 1941), 31.
17. Strachey, *Post D*, 92–3.
18. Graham Greene, "The Londoners", *The Month*, November 1952, 286–7; Nixon, *Raiders Overhead*, 24.
19. Brittain, *England's Hour*, 239.
20. Lehmann, *I Am My Brother*, 79.
21. Inez Holden, *It Was Different at the Time* (Bodley Head, 1943), 69.
22. Elizabeth Bowen, *The Heat of the Day* (Cape, 1954), 85–6.
23. Strachey, *Post D*, 44.
24. Ed Murrow, *This Is London* (Cassell, 1941), 195; Borough of Hampstead, *Warden's Bulletin*, 1.12.40.
25. Francis Faviell, *A Chelsea Concerto* (Cassell, 1959), 125.
26. Nicolson, 116; Paul Rotha, *Portrait of a Flying Yorkshireman* (Chapman & Hall, 1952), 171.
27. McKee, *Strike from the Sky*, 249–50.
28. Jane Gordon, *Married to Charles*, 133.
29. Titmuss, 285–6, 358–60.
30. O'Brien, 397; Mark Benney, *Over to Bombers* (Allen & Unwin, 1943), 77.
31. Fitzgibbon, *The Blitz*, 244–65.
32. Guy Morgan, *Red Roses Every Night* (Quality Press, 1948), 13, 27–33, 79–81.
33. Nixon, *Raiders Overhead*, 21.
34. W. H. Thompson, *I Was Churchill's Shadow*, 62.
35. E. I. Ekpenyon, *Some Experiences of an African Air Raid Warden* (Sheldon Press, 1943), 8.
36. Willie Gallacher, *The Rolling of the Thunder* (Lawrence & Wishart, 1947), 218–19.
37. Murrow, *This Is London*, 200.
38. Ibid., 232–3.
39. Negley Farson, *Bombers Moon* (Gollancz, 1941), 69.
40. MO WB, 119.
41. O'Brien, 334–5; C. M. Kohan, *Works and Buildings* (H.M.S.O., 1952), 356–8.
42. W. E. Holl, *Civil Defence Goes Through It . . .* , 40–42.
43. Nixon, *Raiders Overhead*, 51, etc.; Peter Conway, *Living Tapestry* (Staples, 1946), 129.
44. O'Brien, 392; Ministry of Information, *Front Line*, 67–8.
45. Darwin, *War on the Line*, 81–3; Scott, *Your Obedient Servant*, 132.
46. H. A. Wilson, *Death Over Haggerston*, 25–8.

47. R. Calder, *Carry on London*, 39–42; Scott, *Your Obedient Servant*, 129; Farson, *Bombers Moon*, 88.
48. R. Calder, *Carry on London*, 42–9; F. R. Lewey, *Cockney. Campaign* (Stanley Paul, 1944), 124–30.
49. William Sansom, *Westminster at War* (Faber, 1947), 43–4; Fitzgibbon, *The Blitz*, 158–61.
50. Churchill TFH, 310; Ingersoll, *Report on England*, 117; Charles Graves, *London Transport Carried On* (London Transport, 1947), 43.
51. Selfton Delmer, *Black Boomerang* (Secker & Warburg, 1962), 22; Mass Observation, "The Tube Dwellers", *The Saturday Book 3* (Hutchinson, 1943), 102–105; Kops, *The World Is a Wedding*, 87.
52. Kops, *The World Is a Wedding*, 69.
53. Faviell, *A Chelsea Concerto*, 150.
54. Swiss Cottage Station Shelterers Committee, *The Swiss Cottager*, five issues in the British Museum.
55. Ingersoll, *Report on England*, 120–21.
56. O'Brien, 512–22; Conway, *Living Tapestry*, 162–3.
57. Sansom, *Westminster at War*, 136–8.
58. O'Brien, 532, 540; Graves, *London Transport Carried On*, 59–60.
59. O'Brien, 523, 527–9, 538; R. Calder, *Carry on London*, 60.
60. Sansom, *Westminster at War*, 70–71.
61. Conway, *Living Tapestry*, 21.
62. Jane Gordon, *Married to Charles*, 137.
63. Ferguson, 222.
64. Titmuss, 273, 295.
65. Ibid., 251.
66. Ibid., 259, 301.
67. Ibid., 260–61.
68. Ibid., 263–66.
69. Ibid., 263.
70. R. Calder, *Carry on London*, 155.
71. Ibid., 65.
72. Ibid., 73–8; Radford, *Fetch the Engine*, 114; Titmuss, 266.
73. Titmuss, 277–8; E. Doreen Idle, *War Over West Ham* (Faber, 1943), 123.
74. Lewey, *Cockney Campaign*, 39; Hilde Marchant, *Women and Children Last* (Gollancz, 1941), 71.
75. Kohan, *Works and Buildings*, 210–17; Titmuss, 295.
76. Ritchie Calder, *Lesson of London* (Secker & Warburg, 1941), 15–20; Idle, *War Over West Ham*, 63–4.
77. R. Calder, *Lesson of London*, 28.
78. Graves WG, 12–13, 23–5.
79. Ingersoll, *Report on England*, 239.
80. Rosalind C. Chambers, "A Study of Three Voluntary Organizations", *Social Mobility in Britain*, ed. D. V. Glass (Routledge, 1954), 383–92.

81. Graves WG, 61, 77–82, 120–2.
82. O'Brien, 372–7, 549–50; Borough of Hampstead, *Warden's Bulletin*, 1.8.40.
83. O'Brien, 72.
84. MO WB, 102–103; Nixon, *Raiders Overhead*, 11, 76, 79–88.
85. MO no. 447, *Interim Report on A.R.P. in Kilburn*, 9.10.40.
86. Lewey, *Cockney Campaign*, 61.
87. Reginald Bell, *The Bull's Eye* (Cassell, 1943), 49.
88. Faviell, *A Chelsea Concerto*, 108–10, 118.
89. Ian Bisset, *The George Cross* (MacGibbon & Kee, 1961), 24.
90. Scott, *Your Obedient Servant*, 109; Admiral Lord Mountevans, *Adventurous Life*, 243.
91. Hampstead Borough Council, *Hampstead at War*, 1947, 11–12.
92. Graves WG, 135–7.
93. Faviell, *A Chelsea Concerto*, 115.

B. *Coventration*

1. MO no. 683, *Third Report on Plymouth*, 4.5.41, 14.
2. I. L. Janis, *Air War and Emotional Stress* (McGraw Hill [New York], 1951), 168.
3. Churchill TFH, 341–4; Ronald W. Clark, *The Rise of the Boffins* (Phoenix, 1962), 120.
4. Collier, 263–5; O'Brien, 405; Charles Graves, *Drive to Freedom* (Hodder & Stoughton, 1945), 45–52.
5. Marchant, *Women and Children Last*, 131.
6. MO no. 495, *Report on Coventry*, 18.11.40, 1, 2.
7. Hammond I, 156; R. Calder, *Carry on London*, 91.
8. Collier, 264–5; Fairfax, *Calling All Arms*, 81–3.
9. Collier, 281, 506–507.
10. Rev. S. P. Shipley (ed.), *Bristol Siren Nights* (Rankin [Bristol], 1943) 24.
11. Fitzgibbon, *The Blitz*, 204–15; Sir Arthur Harris, *Bomber Offensive* (Collins, 1947), 51–2; David Irving, *The Destruction of Dresden* (Corgi edn, 1966), 256.
12. O'Brien, 591–2: MO no. 536, *Fire Spotters and Compulsory ARP*, 3.1.41; Stanley Tiquet, *It Happened Here* (Wanstead and Woodford Borough Council, 1947), 40–41.
13. O'Brien, 592–5.
14. Firebrace, *Fire Service Memories*, 173–9, 187; Fitzgibbon, *The Blitz*, 210.
15. Firebrace, *Fire Service Memories*, 177, 198; O'Brien, 501.
16. Radford, *Fetch the Engine*, 119–31.
17. Firebrace, *Fire Service Memories*, 184–5, 195, 202, 204, 210–11; Michael Wassey, *Ordeal by Fire* (Secker & Warburg, 1941), 138; H. P. Twyford, *It Came to Our Door* (Underhill [Plymouth], 1946), 68–9.

18. Firebrace, *Fire Service Memories*, 204–208.
19. MO no. 600, *Preliminary Report on Morale in Glasgow*, March 1942, 4–5, 6, 44–5.
20. Titmuss, 313–14.
21. Ibid.; MO, *Preliminary Report* . . . , 29–32.
22. O'Brien, 415–17; Titmuss, 271.
23. O'Brien, 414; Reynolds, *Only the Stars Are Neutral*, 27.
24. Twyford, *It Came to Our Door*, 35, 39–41, 112–30.
25. Titmuss, 307–308 ; MO no. 683, *Third Report on Plymouth*, 19–20.
26. MO, *Third Report on Plymouth*, 1; Twyford, *It Came to Our Door*, 124.
27. MO no. 626, *Second Report on Plymouth*, 1.4.41; *Third Report on Plymouth*, 4–8.
28. Firebrace, *Fire Service Memories*, 201; Titmuss, 308, 310–13; Graves WG, 138; *Liverpool Daily Post and Echo, Bombers Over Merseyside*, 1943, 16.
29. MO no. 706, *Report on Liverpool*, 22.5.41, 2–4, 14.
30. Titmuss, 308; Churchill GA, 39.
31. Richard Collier, *The City That Wouldn't Die* (Collins, 1959), 215–17, 224, 229, 233–6.
32. Winant, *Letter From Grosvenor Square*, 46; Churchill WS 1, 389.
33. Nicolson, 164.
34. Churchill GA, 43–9; Rear-Admiral G. P. Thompson, *Blue Pencil Admiral* (Sampson Low, 1947), 92–6.
35. MO no. 595, *Report on Swansea*, 1.3.41, 6–7, 10.
36. Twyford, *It Came to Our Door*, 91; *Sheffield Telegraph and Star, Sheffield at War*, 1948, 12–13.
37. Shipley, *Bristol Siren Nights*, 26.
38. Lord Morrison, *Herbert Morrison* (Odhams, 1960), 187; Collier, 506; O'Brien, 684; Knowles, 148–153.
39. Knowles, 154.
40. T. H. J. Underdown, *Bristol Under Blitz* (Arrowsmith [Bristol], 1942), 5; Twyford, *It Came to Our Door*, 113.
41. Knowles, 154–63; Smyth, *Cyril Forster Garbett*, 264–5.
42. Knowles, 163–78; MO no. 516, *Report on Southampton*, 4.12.40, 8–9; MO no. 529, *Aftermath of Town Blitzes*, 19.12.40, 3–4; MO no. 603, *Third Southampton Report*, 9.3.41, 1–2, 4, 23.
43. MO no. 606, *Second Portsmouth Report*, 15.3.41, 3, 5, 7, 8, etc.
44. MO, *Aftermath of Town Blitzes*, 2.
45. MO, *Second Portsmouth Report*, 4.
46. Collier, 280; Postan, 491.
47. Saunders, *Ford at War*, 30; Ian Hay, *R.O.F.* (H.M.S.O., 1949), 93; Titmuss, 341–2; MO, *Aftermath of Town Blitzes*, 4.
48. Taylor, 501; Churchill TFH, 322–3.
49. G. H. Ingles, *When the War Came to Leicester* (C. Brooks [Leicester], 1945), 19–20.

50. Twyford, *It Came to Our Door*, 133–4; Darwin, *War on the Line*, 78–9.
51. Ministry of Information, *Front Line*, 131–5.
52. Ibid., 129–30.
53. Idle, *War Over West Ham*, 51, 53, etc.
54. Anderson, *Spam Tomorrow*, 150.
55. J. M. Richards, *Bombed Buildings of Britain* (Architectural Press, 1947), 8.
56. Kohan, *Works and Buildings*, 386–90.
57. Titmuss, 320, 328–30.
58. Ibid., 340–41; Janis, *Air War and Emotional Stress*, 73–97.
59. Boyd, *Evacuation in Scotland*, 32; Titmuss, 355–69, 562.
60. Titmuss, 370–71, 404.
61. Ibid., 370–75.
62. Janis, *Air War and Emotional Stress*, 94; Jane Gordon, *Married to Charles*, 152.
63. Idle, *War Over West Ham*, 87–90.
64. C. S. Segal, *Backward Children in the Making* (Muller, 1949), 6.
65. Titmuss, 333–5, 340, 416–17.
66. Ibid., 515.
67. Ibid., 559–61, 335–6.
68. MO no. 844, *Hull*, 23.8.41, 5.

Chapter 5: Through the Tunnel

A. From Brown to Red

1. Maclaren-Ross, *Memoirs of the Forties*, 85.
2. Churchill GA, 3–4.
3. Churchill TFH, 320–22, 405–406; Taylor, 517–19; Collier, *A Short History of the Second World War*, 177.
4. MO no. 2000, *Vengeance*, 14.1.44; Hodson, *Before Daybreak*, 58; Janis, *Air War and Emotional Stress*, 126–33.
5. Taylor, 519.
6. MO no. 1095, *Opinion on America*, 16.2.42, 2.
7. Ibid., 4; Hancock, 235–47; Churchill GA, 111; Lord Woolton, *Memoirs*, 229–30.
8. Churchill GA, 120–28.
9. Bullock, 31–2; Turner, 190–91.
10. Bullock, 30–31.
11. Ibid., 42–4; SCNE 17 (1940–41), 19.12.40, 3.
12. Bullock, 50–51, 70.
13. Parker, 101–109, 146, 160–61.
14. Bullock, 76, 141; Parker, 223–4.
15. Parker, 137–41.
16. Bullock, 55; Parker, 283–4.
17. O'Brien, 550–51.

18. Sayers, 23.
19. Ibid., 67–90.
20. MO no. 1149, *Some Thoughts on Greyhounds and National Unity*, 10.3.42, 20; Bullock, 86–92; Parker, 428.
21. Hammond I, 185–7.
22. *The Memoirs of Lord Chandos*, 204–205.
23. Sayers, 92; Hammond I, 188–93.
24. MO, *Home Propaganda*, 35, 66.
25. Advertisement in *Housewife*, June 1941; MO PP, 149–55.
26. MO, *Home Propaganda*, 61, 73.
27. Ibid., 27–8.
28. Churchill GA, 177.
29. Ibid., 202.
30. Jane Gordon, *Married to Charles*, 170–71; MO, *Home Propaganda*, 9.
31. A. P. Herbert, *Let Us Be Glum* (Methuen, 1941), v; Walter Graebner and S. Laird, *Hitler's Reich and Churchill's Britain* (Batsford, 1942), 46–7.
32. John MacCormick, *The Flag in the Wind* (Gollancz, 1955), 97–100; MO no. 208, *The North Croydon By-Election*, 19.6.40.
33. MO no. 205, *The Bow and Bromley By-Election*, 18.6.40, 6, 8–10; Gollancz, *The Betrayal of the Left*, 65–70.
34. D. N. Pritt, *Autobiography*, pt 1, *From Right to Left* (Lawrence & Wishart, 1965), 247–50.
35. Gollancz, *Betrayal of the Left*, vi–vii.
36. Ibid., 126–37, 144–7.
37. Murphy, *Victory Production!*, 38–44.
38. Pritt, *Choose Your Future* (Lawrence & Wishart, 1941), 184; Gollancz, *Betrayal of the Left*, 154–72.
39. Hodson, *Towards the Morning*, 91; Claud Cockburn, *Crossing the Line* (MacGibbon & Kee, 1958), 79.
40. MO no. 543, *The People's Convention*, 13.1.41, 1–2; Pritt, *From Right to Left*, 260–61.
41. Pritt, *From Right to Left*, 261–2; People's Convention, *The People Speak*, 1941; Vigilans, "Ananias Also Ran", *Tribune*, 17.1.41.
42. Murphy, *Victory Production!*, 43.
43. Cudlipp, *Publish and Be Damned*, 149–53.
44. Pritt, *From Right to Left*, 263; J. B. Priestley, *Margin Released* (Heinemann, 1962), 221–2.
45. *The Times*, 15.1.41; Cassandra, *The English at War* (Secker & Warburg, 1941), 84–6; E. S. Turner, *Gallant Gentlemen* (Joseph, 1956), 301–302.
46. E. S. Turner, *Gallant Gentlemen*, 306, 327; Hodson, *Towards the Morning*, 206; Hodson, *Before Daybreak*, 39.
47. Lehmann, *I Am My Brother*, 107.
48. Eric Partridge, *A Dictionary of Forces Slang* (Secker & Warburg, 1948), x–xi, 29–30.

49. MO no. 887, *Civilian Attitudes to the Navy Compared with Army and R.A.F.*, 30.9.41, 7; MO no. 1485, *Fourth Report on Reconstruction: Basis of Political Trends in the Army*, 31.10.42, 23–5; Maclaren-Ross, *Memoirs of the Forties*, 104.

50. Lord Beveridge, *Power and Influence* (Hodder & Stoughton, 1953), 285; Parker, 153–4.

51. N. Scarlyn Wilson, *Education in the Forces 1939–1946* (Evans, 1949), 20; T. H. Hawkins and L. J. Brimble, *Adult Education – The Record of the British Army* (Macmillan, 1947), 168.

52. Ibid., 100–107; Wilson, *Education in the Forces*, 12–22, 125–7.

53. Hawkins, *Adult Education . . .* , 114–20.

54. W. E. Williams, "Adult Education", *Voluntary Social Services since 1918*, ed. H. A. Mess (Kegan Paul, 1948), 155–8; Hawkins, *Adult Education . . .* , 120–24, 139–44, 158–77, 279.

55. Woolton, *Memoirs*, 300; "Serving Soldier", "The Inarticulate Revolution", *Tribune*, 10.3.44.

56. Hodson, *Before Daybreak*, 80–81.

57. Kingsley Martin, "Letter to a Friend in the A.E.U.", *New Statesman*, 28.6.41.

58. MO PP, 65.

59. Calder, vol. 1, 50–64.

60. Hodson, *Towards the Morning*, 95, 116–17, 166, 189, 215; *Before Daybreak*, 24.

61. *The Times*, 1.5.41; J. P. W. Mallalieu, "The Pied Piper", *Rats* (Gollancz, 1941), 79–80; Hammond I, 310; MO, *Some Thoughts on Greyhounds . . .* , 16.

62. *Daily Telegraph*, 16.6.41; *Report of the Proceedings of the 23rd National Committee of the A.E.U.*, June 16th–23rd, 1941, 227.

63. Kohan, *Works and Buildings*, 469; Idle, *War Over West Ham*, 127–8.

64. MO PP, 308; Tibor Barna, *Profits During and After the War* (Fabian Society, 1945), 6–9.

65. Nigel Balchin, *Darkness Falls from the Air* (1961 edn), 116.

66. MO PP, 20.

67. SCNE 48 (1941–2), 26.3.42, 6–7.

68. Donovan Ward, *The Other Battle* (B.S.A. [Birmingham], 1946), 70–71; Postan, 164–6.

69. MO PP, 60–61.

70. Postan, 123–4; Ely Devons, *Planning in Practice* (C.U.P., 1950), 28–9.

71. Devons, *Planning in Practice*, 31.

72. Postan, 183–95; W. J. Seymour, *An Account of Our Stewardship* (Vauxhall [Luton], 1946), 29–37.

73. MO PP, 15.

74. Ibid., 30–48, 66–70, 306–307, 326–9; MO, *The Journey Home* (Murray, 1944), 103–104.

75. Nicolson, 175; Churchill WS 1, 137.

76. Churchill WS 1, 452, 454.

77. MO, "June 23rd", *Horizon*, 4, July 1941, 13–23.
78. MO, *Home Propaganda*, 27, 51.
79. Hyde, *I Believed*, 104–13; *Proceedings of the 23rd National Committee of the A.E.U.*, 129–30, 251–2.
80. Pritt, *From Right to Left*, 272–7; *Daily Express*, 30.7.41; *The Times*, 7.8.41; George Orwell, "London Letter", *Partisan Review*, 1941, 494.
81. Hancock, 359.
82. Young, *Churchill and Beaverbrook*, 206–207; George Bilainkin, *Maisky* (Allen & Unwin, 1944), 324, 349–50.
83. Darwin, *War on the Line*, 160; John Aplin, "Towards Left Unity", *Left*, March 1942, 59.
84. MO PP, 50–53; Murphy, *Victory Production!*, 105–109.
85. Bilainkin, *Maisky*, 291, 355–7, 366.
86. Ibid., 338, 342; Murphy, *Victory Production!*, 86.
87. Bilainkin, *Maisky*, 346–8.
88. Churchill GA, 392–4.
89. Taylor, 529–30, 534–5; Bullock, 69.
90. Churchill, GA, 539.

B. *The End of the Beginning*

1. Moran, 46.
2. R. H. Bruce Lockhart, *Comes the Reckoning* (Putnam, 1947), 146; Churchill WS 2, 141.
3. MO, *Opinion on America*, 5–8; Nicolson, 196.
4. Lochner, *The Goebbels Diaries*, 26.
5. Bullock, 72–3, 148.
6. Churchill WS 2, 187–96; Churchill HF, 62.
7. Parker, 109–15, 167.
8. Churchill GA, 455; Bullock, 139–41.
9. MO PP, 159.
10. Wartime SS, *Women's Registration and Call-Up*, 1942, 6, 21–2; Murphy, *Victory Production!*, 47.
11. O'Brien, 555.
12. Graves HGB, 142.
13. MO PP, 89–91.
14. Parker, 309–10.
15. Taylor, 513; MO PP, 91; Parker, 170.
16. Hancock, 452.
17. MO no. 1413, *Fifth Report on Sir Stafford Cripps*, 29.9.42.
18. J. L. Hodson, *The Sea and the Land* (Gollancz, 1945), 136; Bartlett, *And Now, Tomorrow*, 85.
19. Moran, 74.
20. Churchill HF, 69.
21. *Daily Mirror*, 29.1.42; Cantril, *Public Opinion 1935–1946*, 79, 106; Nicolson, 223.

22. Nicolson, 205; Beaton, *The Years Between*, 133.
23. Eric Estorik, *Stafford Cripps* (Heinemann, 1949), 291–4; MO no. 1166, *Sir Stafford Cripps*, 23.3.42, 3.
24. Ibid.; MO no. 1362, *Report on Who Likes and Dislikes Sir Stafford Cripps*, 28.7.42; no. 1375, *Second Report on Sir Stafford Cripps*, 6.8.42; no. 1413, *Fourth Report on Sir Stafford Cripps*, 29.9.42; no. 1389, *Second Report on Reconstruction*, 26.8.42; no. 1414, *Third Report on Reconstruction*, September 1942.
25. Bullock, 148–51; Young, *Churchill and Beaverbrook*, 215.
26. Churchill WS 2, 179; Churchill HF, 81.
27. Churchill WS 2, 241–2; Moran, 27.
28. Churchill WS 2, 206; Henson, *Retrospect of an Unimportant Life*, vol. 3, 234.
29. Churchill WS 2, 208–12.
30. Bullock, 152–3; Moran, 26–30; Churchill HF, 66; George Malcolm Thomson, *Vote of Censure* (Secker & Warburg, 1968), 134–6; Harold Macmillan, *The Blast of War* (Macmillan, 1967), 141–5.
31. MO no. 1111, *Opinion on the Cabinet Changes*, 24.2.42.
32. MO, *Sir Stafford Cripps*, 4; MO, *The Journey Home*, 100–104.
33. Combined Production and Resources Board, *The Impact of the War on Civilian Consumption* (H.M.S.O., 1945), 33–4, 88.
34. Hammond I, 161–9, 260–62, 284–8; *The Memoirs of Lord Chandos*, 246–7.
35. Wartime SS, *Food I – Food Schemes*, 1942–3, 2–6, 8, 11; Woolton, *Memoirs*, 246–7.
36. *Bristol Evening Post*, 20.1.43.
37. Freda Godfrey, "National Cooking", *Manchester Guardian*, 9.2.42.
38. Ministry of Food, *How Britain Was Fed in Wartime* (H.M.S.O., 1946), 21, 28–32; advertisement in *Daily Express*, 28.1.44.
39 MO no. 603, *Third Southampton Report*, 9.3.41, 11; A. P. Herbert, *Less Nonsense!* (Methuen, 1944), 3; Hargreaves, 533.
40 William Temple, *Some Lambeth Letters*, ed. F. S. Temple (O.U.P., 1963), 17–19, 33–5.
41. Hargreaves, 315.
42. Ibid., 431–5, 440–43, 458–9.
43. Ibid., 436–9; *Daily Express*, 28.1.44.
44. Hancock, 504.
45. Hargreaves, 498–511, 522–31.
46. Anderson, *Spam Tomorrow*, 151; Hargreaves, 512–13.
47. Hargreaves, 514–21, 335–7.
48. Ibid., 503–11; Hancock, 496.
49. Brittain, *Testament of Experience*, 294.
50. Dalton, *The Fateful Years*, 392–3.
51. MO no. 1243, *Fuel Rationing*, 6.5.42.
52. Bullock, 145–6, 167–8.

53. Court, 161.
54. Dalton, *The Fateful Years*, 398–9.
55. 379 HCDeb, 7.5.42., col. 1471
56. Dalton, *The Fateful Years*, 399.
57. MO, *Fuel Rationing*; Court, 162, 215.
58. Court, 216.
59. Nicolson, 224.
60. Collier, *A Short History* . . . , 309–12.
61. Harris, *Bomber Offensive*, 76, 105.
62. O'Brien, 428.
63. Ibid., 429–31.
64. Catherine Williamson, *Though the Streets Burn* (Headley, 1949), 248–80.
65. Cudlipp, *Publish and Be Damned*, 147–8, 170–71.
66. Ibid., 163–8.
67. Ibid., 172–82; Foot, *Aneurin Bevan*, vol. 1, 353–4.
68. Cudlipp, *Publish and Be Damned*, 188–190; J. L. Hodson, *Home Front* (Gollancz, 1944), 8.
69. Calder, vol. 1, 80–83, 97; *First Report of the Committee of Public Accounts*, 1942.
70. Calder, vol. 1, 84–5; W. J. Brown, *So Far* (Allen & Unwin, 1943), 251–83.
71. Calder, vol. 1, 86–8.
72. "The Future of Politics", *The Economist*, 4.4.42; "The Movement Away From Party", *Tribune*, 3.4.42; "The Politics of Frustration," *New Statesman*, 11.4.42.
73. Cantril, *Public Opinion 1935–1946*, 279; MO, *Report on Who Likes and Dislikes Sir Stafford Cripps*.
74. MO no. 755, *Faith in Parliament*, 24.6.41, 13–14.
75. MO no. 1443, *Seventh Report on Sir Stafford Cripps*, 20.10.42; *The Economist*, 4.4.42.
76. George Orwell, "London Letter", *Partisan Review*, 1941, 315–16.
77. *History of The Times*, vol. 4, pt 2, 984; *The Times*, 19.9.42; Sir Herbert Williams in 386 HCDeb, 18.2.43, col. 2017.
78. MO no. 1442, *Sixth Report on Sir Stafford Cripps*, 8.10.42.
79. *The Economist*, 4.4.42; Samuel Courtauld, *Government and Industry* (Macmillan, 1942), 6–7, 11–12, 16.
80. Charles Madge, *Industry After the War* (Pilot Press, 1943), 30–38.
81. Deryck Abel, *Ernest Benn: Counsel for Liberty* (Benn, 1960), 99–107.
82. Ibid., 110–25.
83. Asa Briggs, *Seebohm Rowntree* (Longmans, 1961), 310–13; *Liberal Magazine*, November–December 1941, 423–4, and March–April 1942, 87–8.
84. Foot, *Aneurin Bevan*, vol. 1, 493.
85. Labour Press Department, *Labour in the War Government*, n.d. (1943): Tom Johnston, *Memories*, 148–53.

86. Labour Party, *The Old World and the New Society*, 1942, 10
    Annual Conference Report 1942, 145–50.
87. *Onlooker*, March, May and July 1942.
88. MO no. 1297, *Second Front Feelings*, 1.6.42, 2; Bilainkin, *Maisky*
    368–70; Young, *Churchill and Beaverbrook*, 243.
89. Churchill WS 2, 265; G. M. Thomson, *Vote of Censure*, 156.
90. Henry Pelling, *The British Communist Party* (Black, 1958), 120–21,
    127–30, 192.
91. Bilainkin, *Maisky*, 372–4; Hodson, *Home Front*, 96.
92. Churchill HF, 344; *Manchester Guardian*, 27.6.42.
93. Calder, vol. 1, 93–6; Churchill HF, 346.
94. Bullock, 177–9; see also Arthur Salter, *Slave of the Lamp* (Weid-
    enfeld & Nicolson, 1967), 50.
95. Bullock, 174–5; Churchill HF, 351–67; Churchill WS 2, 280–301;
    Nicolson, 231; Foot, *Aneurin Bevan*, vol. 1, 371–7.
96. *Chips – The Diaries of Sir Henry Channon* (Weidenfeld & Nicol-
    son, 1967), 332–5; "Critics in Parliament", *Spectator*, 10.7.42.
97. Moran, 71–2; MO no. 1484, *Ninth Report on Sir Stafford Cripps*,
    13.11.42; Cantril, *Public Opinion* . . . , 279–80; Nicolson, 241;
    Churchill HF, 497.
98. Churchill HF, 497–502; G. M. Thomson, *Vote of Censure*, 221.
99. *National Review*, April 1943, 266.
100. Montgomery, in *Alamein and the Desert War*, ed. Derek Jewell
    (Sphere Books, 1967), 65–6.
101. Eleanor Roosevelt, *This I Remember* (Hutchinson, 1950), 209–10;
    Wheeler Bennett, *King George VI*, 550–51.
102. Nicolson, 256; Jane Gordon, *Married to Charles*, 195
103. Churchill WS 2, 343.

Chapter 6: The India-rubber Island

A. Stretched

1. MO PP, 407.
2. Churchill HF, 573–6.
3. Sansom, *Westminster at War*, 167–8.
4. J. W. Blake, *Northern Ireland in the Second World War* (H.M.S.O.
   [Belfast], 1956), 250–251, 271–2.
5. Knowles, 227–8; Twyford, *It Came to Our Door*, 62.
6. Maurice Gorham, *Sound and Fury* (Percival Marshall, 1948), 134.
7. Graves WG, 196; MO no. 2021, *Mass Observation – 1943*,
   16.2.44, 11–12.
8. David Lampe, "Over Paid, Over Sexed, Over Here", *Sunday
   Times Magazine*, December 1966.
9. Graves WG, 193–7; Shirley Joseph, *If Their Mothers Only Knew*
   (Faber, 1946), 89–90.

10. *Mass Observation – 1943*, 8–11.

11. Wells, *The New World Order*, 129.

12. S. P. B. Mais, "The Americans and Ourselves", *Bristol Evening Post*, 29.2.44; Letter in *Bristol Evening Post*, 2.3.44.

13. J. P. Mayer, *British Cinemas and Their Audiences* (Dobson, 1948), 20, 33.

14. Ferguson, 97–8.

15. R. M. and K. Titmuss, *Parents Revolt* (Secker & Warburg, 1942), 30, 36–7.

16. Ferguson, 18–20; Lampe, *loc. cit.*

17. Ferguson, 89–94.

18. Ibid., 14–16; Sydney M. Laird, *Venereal Disease in Britain* (Penguin, 1943), 9–10.

19. Joseph, *If Their Mothers Only Knew*, 51, 91–7.

20. Ferguson, 98.

21. Kay Allsop, ms. diary, June-September 1942.

22. Ferguson, 20, 99.

23. Ibid., 99.

24. MO, *War Factory* (Gollancz, 1943), 34–6.

25. Ferguson, 4; Hargreaves, 283–4; Fogarty, 40.

26. Fogarty, 41–4; Hargreaves, 284.

27. Bullock, 158–61.

28. Fogarty, 40–41; Hancock, 497.

29. Combined Production and Resources Board, *The Impact of the War . . .*, 43–4; Inman, 219.

30. D. Johnson, *Bars and Barricades*, 229; MO, *War Factory*, 13–14.

31. Hargreaves, 284; A. P. Rowe, *One Story of Radar* (C.U.P., 1948), 135–6.

32. M. D. Brock, *An Unusual Happening* (privately printed, 1947), 32; Barnett House Study Group, *London Children in Wartime Oxford*, 20.

33. MO no. 2068, *Wartime Inconveniences*, 24.4.44.

34. Fogarty, 51–2, 61–4; SCNE 35 (1940–41), 6.8.41, 13–14; Philip S. Bagwell, *The Railwaymen* (Allen & Unwin, 1963), 580; C. I. Savage, *Inland Transport* (H.M.S.O., 1957), 399–410.

35. Ibid., 435–8, 529–30; Graves, *London Transport Carried On*, 26.

36. Hargreaves, 265–6.

37. Liberal Inquiry Committee, *War and the Independent Trader*, 1942, 5.

38. Hargreaves, 275; Ministry of Food, *How Britain Was Fed . . .*, 33.

39. Hargreaves, 263.

40. MO no. 844, *Hull*, 15.

41. Combined Production and Resources Board, *Impact of War . . .*, 8–22.

42. Ibid., 23; Hargreaves, 369–70; Ministry of Information, *Manpower*, 32.

43. Stat. Dig., 8, 9; Ferguson, 3; Postan, 278.

44. Fogarty, 34–5.
45. Parker, 334–43, 347–8; Inman, 167–75; Arnold R. Watson, *West Indian Workers in Britain* (Hodder & Stoughton, 1942).
46. Parker, 175–9, 204–11.
47. Hornby, *Factories and Plant*, 149; Postan, 434.
48. Hornby, *Factories and Plant*, 89–91.
49. Ibid., 103–105; Inman, 351, 422–3, Bullock, 63.
50. SCNE 31 (1940–41), 10.7.41, 4; SCNE 47 (1941–2), 26.3.42, 10.
51. Hay, *R.O.F.*, 58–67; Hornby, *Factories and Plant*, 90; Inman, 183–4.
52. Hay, *R.O.F.*, 63, 76–9.
53. Inman, 201.
54. *Bournville Utilities – A War Record* (Bournville [Birmingham], 1945), 24; Postan, 391; Charles Graves, *Drive for Freedom*, 69–77.
55. Hargreaves, 222, 250; Hammond I, 322–34.
56. Hargreaves, 343–72.
57. Alan Fox, *A History of N.U.B.S.O.* (Blackwell [Oxford], 1958), 554.
58. *Guardian*, 4.2.65.
59. J. B. Priestley, *Daylight on Saturday* (Heinemann, 1943), 2.
60. MO PP, 210–11; Parker, 441–5; Inman, 293–306.
61. Fairfax, *Calling All Arms*, 119–21.
62. Postan, 217.
63. Parker, 372–82, 389–91; Ministry of Information, *Manpower*, 16–17.
64. J. B. Jefferys, *The Story of the Engineers* (Lawrence & Wishart, 1946), 201–208, 214; Inman, 57–62.
65. M.O.I., *Manpower*, 32; International Labour Office, *The War and Women's Employment* (I.L.O. [Montreal], 1946), 23–8.
66. Fogarty, 10, 20, 51; G. Thomas, *Women at Work*, Wartime SS, June 1944, 9–10, 32; Jefferys, *The Story of the Engineers*, 207.
67. Parker, 287–92; M.O.I., *Manpower*, 26–7; Bullock, 253–5.
68. Zelma Katin, *Clippie* (Gifford, 1944), 6–7.
69. Parker, 288, 295–7; MO PP, 108.
70. Kay Allsop, ms. diary, June–September 1942.
71. Bagwell, *The Railwaymen*, 580–81; Darwin, *War on the Line*, 174.
72. I.L.O., *War and Women's Employment*, 51.
73. R. M. Fox, "London in Wartime", *A.E.U. Monthly Journal*, May 1942, 130; Katin, *Clippie*, 60.
74. Benney, *Over to Bombers*, 105–106.
75. A.E.U., *Minutes of the First Annual Women's Conference*, May 20th–21st, 1943, 14; Murphy, *Victory Production!*, 52.
76. Hodson, *The Sea and the Land*, 254.
77. Emma Smith, *Maiden's Trip* (Putnam, 1948), 51.
78. Titmuss, 215.
79. R. H. Ahrenfeldt, *Pyschiatry in the British Army in the Second World War* (Routledge, 1958), 32, 273; Michael Sissons and

Philip French (ed.), *The Age of Austerity* (Hodder & Stoughton, 1963), 97.

80. Twyford, *It Came to Our Door*, 136–40.
81. MO, "The Tube Dwellers", *Saturday Book 3*, 107–109.
82. G. F. Vale, *Bethnal Green's Ordeal* (Bethnal Green Borough Council, 1945), 7.
83. MO, *The Journey Home*, 67–70.
84. Stephen Spender, *World Within World* (Hamish Hamilton, 1951), 269; Firebrace, *Fire Service Memories*, 261–83.
85. O'Brien, 595–606.
86. Driberg, *Colonnade*, 236–7.
87. Graves HGB, 138; Cambridgeshire Home Guard, *We Also Served*, 20–21.
88. Graves HGB, 168.
89. L. W. Kentish, *Home Guard – Bux 4*, 16–18.
90. John Brophy, *Britain's Home Guard* (Harrap, 1945), 8.
91. Wilfred Pickles, *Between You and Me* (Werner Laurie, 1949), 117.
92. *A History of the 44th London (London Transport) Battalion of the Home Guard* (Thorn's, 1948), 7–13.
93. Street, *From Dusk Till Dawn*, 77.
94. Simon Fine, *With The Home Guard* (Alliance Press, 1943), 70–71.
95. 2nd Edinburgh Battalion H.G., *Home Guardian*, March 1941.
96. *Sheffield Telegraph*, *Sheffield at War*, 42.
97. Dent, *Education in Transition*, 111–16, 120–29.
98. Murray, 209.
99. Graves WG, 203–10.
100. *Western Daily Press*, 22.2.43.
101. Taylor, 550.

B. *Let the People Sing*

1. Titmuss, *Parents Revolt*, 38.
2. *Manchester Guardian*, 9.2.43.
3. A. P. Herbert, *Less Nonsense!*, 8.
4. *Western Daily Press*, 22.2.43.
5. Dean, *The Theatre at War*, 304–10.
6. Hyde, *I Believed*, 120–26.
7. Ibid., 144–5, 200; MO, *Peace and the Public* (Longmans, 1947), 23; Wheeler Bennett, *King George VI*, 584–7.
8. Ivan Maisky, *Memoirs of a Soviet Ambassador* (Hutchinson, 1967), 347–8.
9. *National Review*, November 1942; 387–8.
10. *Manchester Guardian*, 17.3.43; MO, *Peace and the Public*, 23.
11. Charles Thomas, "Bogy, Bogy", *Bristol Evening Post*, 24.2.43.
12. Hamish Henderson, *Ballads of World War Two* (Lili Marlene Club [Glasgow] n.d.), 13–14.

13. Sidney Pollard, *The Development of the British Economy* (Arnold, 1962), 345–6.
14. Stat. Dig., 200, 204–208; D. Butler and J. Freeman, *British Political Facts 1900–1960* (Macmillan, 1963), 222.
15. Ministry of Food, *How Britain Was Fed* . . . , 37; Hargreaves, 91, 613–14; Hammond FA, 153–5.
16. Wal Hannington, *The Rights of Engineers* (Gollancz, 1944), 22–5; MO PP, 197–210.
17. Stat. Dig., 204–205; Fogarty, 36; G. N. Worswick, "Personal Income Policy", in Worswick, 320.
18. Bullock, 220–24, 235–7.
19. Alan Flanders, "Industrial Relations", in Worswick, 114–15.
20. MO PP, 8; " 'Asset's' Assets", *Labour*, June 1942; *The Economist*, 30.1.43; Dudley Seers, "National Income, Production and Consumption", in Worswick, 53–4.
21. Keith Hutchison, *The Decline and Fall of British Capitalism* (Cape, 1951), 279.
22. Sayers, 99–111.
23. Ibid., 96–8, 119–22, 508–12.
24. Worswick, 315.
25. Sayers, 492.
26. Ibid., 193.
27. Ibid., 188–97; *Ross-shire Journal*, 1.3.41.
28. Worswick, "The British Economy 1945–1950", in Worswick, 22.
29. Joseph Macleod, *A Job at the B.B.C.* (Maclellan [Glasgow], 1947), 112–14; Bartlett, *And Now, Tomorrow*, 65–6.
30. Gorham, *Broadcasting and T.V. since 1900*, 213.
31. Priestley, *Margin Released*, 221; Lord Hill, *Both Sides of the Hill* (Heinemann, 1964), 118.
32. Gorham, *Broadcasting* . . . , 174.
33. Pickles, *Between You and Me*, 131–47.
34. Macleod, *A Job at the B.B.C.*, 96.
35. Cole, *Lord Haw Haw*, 207; MO no. 600, . . . *Morale in Glasgow*, 9–10.
36. Script for ITMA, 20.2.42, found at B.B.C.
37. Kavanagh, *Tommy Handley*, 107–11, 130; Frances Worsley, *Itma* (Vox Mundi, 1948), 74–81.
38. Kavanagh, *Tommy Handley*, 135, 142–3, 148, 167.
39. Gorham, *Broadcasting* . . . , 193, 199–203.
40. *Radio Times*, 30.8.40, 13.2.42.
41. Pickles, *Between You and Me*, 162.
42. MO PP, 277.
43. Howard Thomas, *Britain's Brains Trust* (Chapman & Hall, 1944), vii, 6, 13–49, 52, 100, etc.
44. Ibid., 68.
45. MO, *Puzzled People* (Gollancz, 1947), 124; Tom Harrisson, *Britain Revisited* (Gollancz, 1961), 173–4, 186.

46. Wartime SS, July 1943, reprinted in Mayer, *British Cinemas and their Audiences*, 124–5, 251–75; Roger Manvell, *Film* (Penguin, 1946), 163; MO, *War Factory*, 81; MO, *Puzzled People*, 122–4.

47. Roger Manvell, "The British Feature Film From 1940 to 1945" in *Twenty Years of British Film*, ed. Michael Balcon (Falcon Press, 1947), 82–3; Manvell, *Film*, 133–4; Guy Morgan, *Red Roses Every Night*, 89.

48. Manvell, *Film*, 133.

49. Ibid., 135–6; Alan Wood, *Mr. Rank* (Hodder & Stoughton, 1952), 105–106, 121, 124.

50. Marjorie Ogilvy Webb, *The Government Explains* (Allen & Unwin, 1965), 52, 58.

51 Wood, *Mr. Rank*, 120, 131–3, 148.

52. Manvell, "The British Feature Film . . .", 84–7; Morgan, *Red Roses Every Night*, 71, 94–5, 98–9.

53. Ibid., 26, 68–73; *Bristol Evening Post*, 28.1.44.

54. C. A. Lejeune, *Chestnuts in Her Lap* (Phoenix, 1947), 157.

55. Morgan, *Red Roses Every Night*, 26–7; Jewell, *Alamein and the Desert War*, 147–56.

56. Dean, *The Theatre at War*, 52, 64, 128–38, 202, 541.

57. MO, *War Factory*, 77–8.

58. Dean, *The Theatre at War*, 134; Dent, *Education in Transition*, 148–9; Arnold Haskell, "Ballet Since 1939", and Rollo H. Myers, "Music Since 1939", *Since 1939*, vol. 1 (Phoenix, 1948), 41, 118.

59. Dean, *The Theatre at War*, 216–18; Hawkins, *Adult Education . . .*, 194–204.

60. Dean, *The Theatre at War*, 220–22, 224; MO PP, 275; Thomas Russell, *Philharmonic* (Penguin, 1953), 123.

61. Myers, "Music Since 1939", 112–14; "Music for the Masses", *Bristol Evening Post*, 25.3.43.

62. Myers, "Music Since 1939", 114–17; Strachey, *Post D*, 44.

63. Raich Carter, *Footballer's Progress* (Sporting Handbooks, 1950), 147–52; George Allison, *Allison Calling* (Staples, 1948), 215.

64. MO no. 1149, *Some Thoughts on Greyhound Racing and National Unity*, 10.3.42, 12; MO no. 1229, *Attitudes to the Continuance of Organized Sport in Wartime*, 28.4.42; Ernest Bland (ed.), *Flat Racing Since 1900* (Dakers, 1950), 27–8, 66–8, 125–6, 229; *Racing Calendar 1943* (Jockey Club, 1943), ix.

65. G. Wagstaffe Simons, *Tottenham Hotspur Football Club* (T.H.F.C., 1947), 141–6; MO WB, 257–69.

66. A. M. Fabian and G. Green (ed.), *Association Football*, vol. 4 (Caxton, 1960), 81; Ivan Sharpe, *The Football League Jubilee Book* (Stanley Paul, 1963), 190–91.

67. Carter, *Footballer's Progress*, 153–7; Denis Compton, *Playing for England* (Sampson Low, 1948), 210–11, 214.

68. O. L. Owen, *History of the Rugby Football Union* (Playfair, 1955), 283; Keith Macklin, *The History of Rugby League Football* (Stanley

Paul, 1962), 129–32; Sir Pelham Warner, *Lord's 1787–1945* (Harrap, 1946), 255.

69. Twyford, *It Came to Our Door*, 26; R. C. Robertson Glasgow, "Notes on Season 1942", *Wisden's Cricketers' Almanack 1943*, 49; E. W. Swanton, *A History of Cricket*, vol. 2 (Allen & Unwin, 1962), 142; Sir Pelham Warner, *Long Innings* (Harrap, 1951), 158.

70. Warner, *Lord's*, 245; W. J. Edrich, *Round the Wicket* (Muller, 1959), 1.

71. W. J. Edrich, *Cricket Heritage* (Stanley Paul, 1948), 96.

72. *Manchester Guardian*, 1.5.42.

73. Henrey, *The Siege of London*, 176–7; Jane Gordon, *Married to Charles*, 243.

74. Hargreaves, 317–22, 329, 339–40, 427.

75. C. W. Cunnington, *English Women's Clothing in the Present Century* (Faber, 1952), 264–82; Hargreaves, 531–6.

76. Cunnington, *English Women's Clothing . . .* , 264; Hargreaves, 494–5.

77. Ann Page, "Can I help you, madam?", *Housewife*, August 1941; Graves WG, 142–5.

78. Hargreaves, 466–7, 483.

79. MO, *Clothes Rationing Survey* (Advertising Service Guild, 1941), 38; Humphrey Lyttelton, *I Play as I Please* (MacGibbon & Kee, 1954), 23.

80. *Ross-shire Journal*, 3.1.41; Morgan, *Red Roses Every Night*, 85.

81. Ministry of Food, *How Britain Was Fed . . .* , 42.

82. Ibid., 56–62.

83. Ibid., 25–41.

84. Hammond FA, 144; Woolton, *Memoirs*, 214–15.

85. Hammond FA, 171, 247.

86. Ambrose Heath, "Wartime Teatime", *Housewife*, February 1942; advertisement in *Housewife*, June 1941.

87. Woolton, *Memoirs*, 250–51; Charles Hill, *Wise Eating in Wartime* (H.M.S.O., 1943), 7, 9; Hill, *Both Sides of the Hill*, 111.

88. Hill, *Wise Eating . . .* , 4; Hill, *Wartime Food for Growing Children* (H.M.S.O., 1942), 10; Wartime SS, *Food*, 1942, 29–31.

89. Sir John Boyd Orr, *Food, Health and Income* (Macmillan, 1936), 21, 38; Sir John Boyd Orr and D. Lubbock, *Feeding the People in Wartime* (Macmillan, 1940), 38.

90. Hammond I, 218.

91. Titmuss, 510–13.

92. G. Wagner and A. Reynolds, *Food Supplements*, Wartime SS, April 1944.

93. Titmuss, 509–10; Graves WG, 147–9; Ministry of Food, *How Britain Was Fed . . .* , 45.

94. Hammond FA, 208–12.

95. Ibid., 172–6; MO PP, 270–4.

96. Ministry of Food, *How Britain Was Fed . . .* , 45.

97. Ibid., 43; Wartime SS, *Workers and the War*, 1942, 29–33; Wagner, *Food*, Wartime SS, 1943, 14–16.
98. Hammond FA, 173; Wartime SS, *Food*, 1942, 48.
99. Asa Briggs in *The System of Industrial Relations in Great Britain*, ed. A. Flanders and H. A. Clegg (Blackwell [Oxford], 1945), 20.
100. Titmuss, 476–80; Parker, 267–70.
101. Katin, *Clippie*, 117.
102. SCNE 55 (1941–42), 8.10.42, 5.
103. Ministry of Labour, *The Problem of Absenteeism* (H.M.S.O., 1942), 1; Inman, 277–8.
104. G. Thomas, *Women at Work*, Wartime SS, June 1944, 6–7; Amabel Williams-Ellis, *Women in War Factories* (Gollancz, 1943), 83.
105. Jane Gordon, *Married to Charles*, 198–9.
106. Ministry of Labour, *Problem of Absenteeism*, 3.
107. SCNE 64 (1942–43), 17.12.42, 7.
108. MO PP, 164–5.
109. Ibid., 77–8.
110. M.O.I., *Manpower*, 40.
111. SCNE 39 (1940–41), 11.11.41, 21; Parker, 412–15.

C. *But Some are More Equal than Others*

1. Evelyn Waugh, *Unconditional Surrender* (Chapman & Hall,1961), 19–20.
2. Henry Pelling, *History of British Trade Unionism* (Penguin, 1963), 215; Pollard, *The Development of the British Economy*, 342.
3. H. A. Clegg, *General Union in a Changing Socie*ᵗʸ (Blackwell [Oxford], 1964), 159.
4. Pelling, . . . *British Trade Unionism*, 218, 262; Jefferys, *The Story of the Engineers*, 296–7.
5. Ibid., 261.
6. Pollard, *The Development of the British Economy*, 340; Pelling, . . . *British Trade Unionism*, 261–3; Parker, 504–505.
7. Inman, 392–9.
8. Jefferys, *Story of the Engineers*, 261.
9. Katin, *Clippie*, 80–81; K. G. J. C. Knowles, *Strikes* (Blackwell [Oxford], 1952), 54–6.
10. Parker, 466–70.
11. Ibid., 460–62; MO PP, 337–43.
12. MO PP, 130; Asa Briggs, *Seebohm Rowntree*, 317.
13. Inman, 378–9; Hannington, *The Rights of Engineers*, 87–8.
14. International Labour Office, *British Joint Production Machinery* (I.L.O. [Montreal], 1944), 190.
15. Ibid., 88–9, 184; Inman, 380–81.
16. Hannington, *The Rights of Engineers*, 90–92; James Mortimer, *A*

History of the A.E.S.D. (Association of Engineering and Ship-building Draughtsmen, 1960), 215–16.

17. I.L.O., *British Joint Production Machinery*, 178–82, 185–6.
18. H. A. Clegg, in *System of Industrial Relations in Great Britain*, 339; Political and Economic Planning, *British Trade Unionism* (P.E.P., 1955), 181.
19. Hillary, *The Last Enemy*, 92; Ferguson, 95–6.
20. MO, *The Journey Home*, 59–64.
21. Roy Lewis and Angus Maude, *The English Middle Classes* (Penguin, 1953), 210–11; C. N. Ward Perkins, "The Structure of the British Economy", in Worswick, 74; MO, *War Factory*, 38.
22. MO, *Journey Home*, 37–8.
23. MO, *War Factory*, 34.
24. G. Thomas, *Women at Work*, 21–4; Sayers, 112–13.
25. Margery Spring Rice, *Working Class Wives* (Penguin, 1939), 95–6; I.L.O., *British Joint Production Machinery*, 125.
26. Stat. Dig., 205; I.L.O., *War and Women's Employment*, 64–7; Bagwell, *The Railwaymen*, 582.
27. Hannington, *The Rights of Engineers*, 40–43.
28. Jefferys, *Story of the Engineers*, 260; I.L.O., *War and Women's Employment*, 96.
29. Inman, 364–6.
30. Hammond I, 368–9.
31. Combined Food Board, *Food Consumption Levels* (H.M.S.O., 1944), 14, 52–3.
32. Ministry of Food, *How Britain Was Fed . . .*, 49; Hammond I, 369.
33. Titmuss, 517–25.
34. Regional Organization of the Wartime SS, *Food I – Food Schemes*, 1942–43, 8, 13–14, 23–32.
35. Combined Food Board, *Food Consumption Levels*, 32; Wagner, *Food*, 9–10; Wartime SS, *Food*, 1942, 4–11.
36. Hammond FA, 232–3.
37. Hargreaves, 329–31.
38. Jane Gordon, *Married to Charles*, 202; Driberg, *Colonnade*, 242, 286.
39. Hammond FA, 210; Hodson, *The Sea and the Land*, 100.
40. Woolton, *Memoirs*, 230–31.
41. Hargreaves, 325–8.
42. Joseph, *If Their Mothers Only Knew*, 98–9.
43. Titmuss, 392–4.
44. Hargreaves, 284–92.

Chapter 7: Only Two Englands

A. Plough Up

1. V. Sackville West, *The Women's Land Army* (Joseph, 1944), 112.
2. Wood, *Islands in Danger*, 64–72, 246.
3. Ibid., 111–14.
4. Ibid., 67, 133–8.
5. Ibid., 118–28.
6. Ibid., 151–2, 171–80, 215–16.
7. Ibid., 8, 81, 101–102, 156–61.
8. J. W. Blake, *Northern Ireland in the Second World War*, 206–49.
9. Ibid., 194–200, 424.
10. Ibid., 380–82, 386–90, 418–21.
11. Ibid., 36, 100–101, 415–16, 427–8.
12. Darwin, *War on the Line*, 47–53; Hodson, *The Sea and the Land*, 246–9.
13. Henrey, *The Siege of London*, 41–5.
14. Fogarty, 132–4, 214–15, 273–6, 384–5.
15. Hodson, *Towards the Morning*, 121–6, 165–6, 197.
16. MO no. 616, *The Mull of Kintyre*, 21.3.41, 5.
17. Fogarty, 6, 30 and Table 9.
18. *Ross-shire Journal*, 3.1.41, 15.8.41, 22.8.41, 19.9.41, 7.11.41, 28.11.41, 1.1.43, 17.12.43.
19. A. G. Street, *Hitler's Whistle* (Eyre & Spottiswoode, 1943), 15, 16–17.
20. Murray, 371; Sir A. Daniel Hall, *Reconstruction and the Land* (Macmillan, 1941), 14.
21. Frances Donaldson, *Four Years' Harvest* (Faber, 1945), 108.
22. Ministry of Agriculture, *National Farm Survey of England and Wales (1941–43) – A Summary Report* (H.M.S.O., 1946), 59–69.
23. Street, *Hitler's Whistle*, 29; Anthony Hurd, *A Farmer in Whitehall* (Country Life, 1951), 10; Hall, *Reconstruction and the Land*, 51–2, 61.
24. Murray, 183–4, 373.
25. Ibid., 238, 356.
26. Ibid., 239–40, 260–71, 367.
27. Ibid., 204–208, 230.
28. Hurd, *Farmer in Whitehall*, 56–71; Ministry of Information, *Land at War* (H.M.S.O., 1945), 38–48.
29. Murray, 86.
30. Ibid., 274–7.
31. E. M. Barraud, *Set My Hand Upon the Plough* (Littlebury [Worcester], 1946), 58–9.
32. Murray, 165, 290–92.

33. Ibid., 165–8, 211–17.
34. Ibid., 357–8.
35. M.O.I., *Land at War*, 12.
36. Murray, 324–9; Hurd, *Farmer in Whitehall*, 35–40, 124–7; Peter Self and H. J. Storing, *The State and the Farmer* (Allen & Unwin, 1962), 134.
37. Ministry of Agriculture, *National Farm Survey . . .* , 2, 52.
38. Murray, 302–303.
39. Farmers' Rights Association, *Living Casualties* (F.R.A. [Church Stretton], n.d.), 13–15, 22; Self, *The State and the Farmer*, 127–38.
40. Ibid., 167; Murray, 83–4; Reg Groves, *Sharpen the Sickle* (Porcupine Press, 1949), 229.
41. Sackville West, *The Women's Land Army*, 17–18, 23–5, 30–31, 38–9, 47, 56–66.
42. Rachel Knappett, *Pullet on the Midden* (Joseph, 1946), 14.
43. Sackville West, *The Women's Land Army*, 97; Lancum, *Press Officer, Please!*, 117.
44. Ibid., 98–105.
45. Murray, 245–8.

B. *The Sinners in Hell*

1. A. L. Lloyd (ed.), *Come All Ye Bold Miners* (Lawrence & Wishart, 1952), 81.
2. George Orwell, *The Road to Wigan Pier* (Gollancz, 1937), 34.
3. Court, 22.
4. Margot Heinemann, *Britain's Coal* (Gollancz, 1944), 108, 111–12, 124–5.
5. R. Page Arnot, *The Miners in Crisis and War* (Allen & Unwin, 1961), 391.
6. Will Lawther, foreword to Heinemann, *Britain's Coal*, 6.
7. Ferdinand Zweig, *Men in the Pits* (Gollancz, 1948), 103.
8. Arnot, *The Miners . . .* , 47.
9. *Coal*, Cmd 6364 (H.M.S.O., 1942), 4–5.
10. Court, 238–50; Arnot, *The Miners . . .* , 393.
11. Court, 333–50.
12. *Staffordshire Evening Sentinel*, 7.2.42, quoted in *Liberal Magazine*, May–June 1942, 185.
13. Court, 309–11.
14. Court, 117–24, 300.
15. Court, 302; Abe Moffat, *My Life with the Miners* (Lawrence & Wishart, 1965), 74.
16. 378 HCDeb, 17.3.42, col. 1355; 379 HCDeb, 7.5.42, col. 1461; Court, 144.
17. Arnot, *The Miners . . .* , 317.
18. B. L. Coombes, *Miners Day* (Penguin, 1945), 79.
19. Court, 302–308; Parker, 252–5.

20. J. B. Pick, *Under the Crust* (John Lane, 1946), 100.
21. Mark Benney, *Charity Main* (Allen & Unwin, 1946), 142–3.
22. Horner, *Incorrigible Rebel*, 164.
23. *Daily Express*, 26.9.41.
24. Coombes, *Miners Day*, 24–5.
25. Court, 266; Foot, *Aneurin Bevan*, vol. 1, 446.
26. Ibid., 440–63; Bullock, 268–70, 298–309.
27. Jim Higgins, "Ten Years for the Locust – British Trotskyism 1938–1948", *International Socialism 14*, 1963; private information.
28. Inman, 130.
29. Court, 163; Zweig, *Men in the Pits*, 63–4.
30. Benney, *Charity Main*, 100; A. L. Lloyd, *Folk Song in England*, 336.

C. Birth of a Whitley

1. Hancock, 448.
2. Sir Frank Whittle, *Jet* (Muller, 1953), 260–61.
3. Nigel Balchin, *The Aircraft Builders* (H.M.S.O., 1948), 15; M. M. Postan, D. Hay and J. D. Scott, *Design and Development of Weapons* (H.M.S.O., 1964), 36–7; J. D. Scott, *Vickers* (Weidenfeld & Nicolson, 1962), 209–10.
4. Postan, 305–306, 477, 485.
5. Scott, *Vickers*, 212, 281–2; Hornby, *Factories and Plant*, 211, 379–80.
6. E. Bishop, *The Wooden Wonder* (Parrish, 1959), 27–8, 75, 158–64; *From this Pool a Sword* (Littlewoods [Liverpool], 1946).
7. Devons, *Planning in Practice*, 114; SCNE 71 (1942–43), 4.8.43, 13–16.
8. Ibid., 13; Postan, 408.
9. Saunders, *Ford at War*, 59–70.
10. Benney, *Over to Bombers*, 68–9, 233–4.
11. SCNE 71, 18–19.
12. Rowlinson, *Contribution to Victory*, 57–8.
13. Scott, *Administration of War Production*, 319–330, 515; Devons, *Planning in Practice*, 59–63.
14. Scott, *Adminstration of War Production*, 398–400.
15. Inman, 229–30; Colin Cooke, *Life of Richard Stafford Cripps* (Hodder & Stoughton, 1957), 308–15.
16. Devons, *Planning in Practice*, 155.
17. Postan, *Design and Development . . .*, 12, 491–4.
18. Inman, 204; Devons, *Planning in Practice*, 125.
19. Ibid., 107.
20. Inman, 369–70.
21. Ibid., 324.
22. Ibid., 325–7.
23. Ibid., 377–8; D. F. Springhall, "Fifty Thousand Communists", *Labour Monthly*, May 1942.
24. MO PP, 106.

25. Balchin, *The Aircraft Builders*, 47.
26. Postan, 323.

Chapter 8: War on the Mind

A. *The Playing Fields of Malvern (I)*

1. R. Watson Watt, *Three Steps to Victory* (Odhams, 1957), 17.
2. SCNE 71 (1942–3), 4.8.43, 13.
3. Watson Watt, *Three Steps to Victory*, 231.
4. J. G. Crowther and R. Whiddington, *Science at War* (H.M.S.O. 1947), 29.
5. Clark, *The Rise of the Boffins*, 190.
6. Association of Scientific Workers, *Science and the Nation* (Pelican, 1947), 211.
7. J. D. Bernal, *Science in History* (Watts, 1954), 8.
8. P. M. S. Blackett, *Studies of War* (Oliver & Boyd [Edinburgh], 1962), 105–106.
9. Ibid., 103.
10. Crowther, *Science at War*, 60.
11. A. P. Rowe, *One Story of Radar*, 137, 141, 197.
12. C. P. Snow (quoting James P. Baxter), *Science and Government* (O.U.P., 1961), 45.
13. Gowing, *Britain and Atomic Energy 1939–1945*, 162–3.
14. Ritchie Calder, *Profile of Science* (Allen & Unwin, 1951), 203–205, 235–7; Postan, 357–8.
15. Postan, 356–7.
16. Clark, *The Rise of the Boffins*, 56–8; Parker, 319–22, 331–3.
17. Sir Solly Zuckerman, *Scientists and War* (Hamish Hamilton, 1966), 148–9.
18. *Science in War* (Penguin, 1940), 8, 35, 44–5, 138.
19. Ibid., 101.
20. Zuckerman, *Scientists and War*, 15–16; Blackett, *Studies of War*, 109.
21. Ronald W. Clark, *Tizard* (Methuen, 1965), 305–13; Earl of Birkenhead, *The Prof in Two Worlds* (Collins, 1961), 245–55; Blackett, *Studies of War*, 124–5, 223–8.
22. Hammond I, 96, 220.
23. *Science in War*, 34.
24. Blackett, *Studies of War*, 206.
25. J. B. S. Haldane, "Life at High Pressures", *Science News 4* (Penguin, 1947), 9–29.
26. Zuckerman, *Scientists and War*, 21.
27. Blackett, *Studies of War*, 73.
28. Rowe, *One Story of Radar*, 48.
29. Crowther, *Science at War*, 85; Scott, *Administration of War Production*, 328.

30. Gowing, *Britain and Atomic Energy*, 82–4.
31. Rowe, *One Story of Radar*, 83–4; Crowther, *Science at War*, 84–7.
32. Gowing, *Britain and Atomic Energy*, 85.
33. Ibid., 350–352.
34. R. W. Clark, *Birth of the Bomb* (Phoenix, 1961), 82–3.
35. Zuckerman, *Scientists and War*, 47–8.
36. W. H. G. Armytage, *Sir Richard Gregory* (Macmillan, 1957), 182–6, 188; *National Review*, November 1941, 483–4 and December 1941, 670–72.
37. W. H. G. Armytage, *The Rise of the Technocrats* (Routledge, 1965), 273–4.
38. Hammond 1, 113.
39. SCNE 42 (1941–2), 17.2.42, 4.
40. M. Ogilvy Webb, *The Government Explains* (Allen & Unwin, 1965), 49–66.
41. Ahrenfeldt, *Psychiatry in the British Army . . .* , 13–28.
42. Ernest Bevin, *The Job To Be Done* (Heinemann, 1942), 35–6; MO PP, 296–305; Austen Albu, *Management in Transition* (Fabian Society, 1942), 13.
43. Postan, 394–5.
44. *The Times, British War Production 1939–1945* (1945), 169.
45. Sir H. Melville, *The D.S.I.R.* (Allen & Unwin, 1962), 79–84; Hargreaves, 371–2; Court, 288–91.
46. Postan, 358–70; W. H. G. Armytage, *A Social History of Engineering* (Faber, 1961), 304–305.
47. H. C. Dent, *Growth in English Education 1946–1952* (Routledge, 1954), 164.
48. Parker, 325–30; Dent, *Education in Transition*, 130–33.
49. Parker, 144; Knowles, 194–6.
50. Dent, *Education in Transition*, 140–44; Bruce Truscot, *Redbrick University* (Penguin, 1951), 255–66.
51. Gow, *Letters from Cambridge*, 100.
52. Keith Douglas, "Canoe", *Collected Poems* (Faber, 1966), 73.
53. MO, *Puzzled People*, 132, 134.

B. *The Playing Fields of Malvern* (2)

1. Nicolson, 228.
2. F. A. Iremonger, *William Temple* (O.U.P., 1948), 607–8; E. D. Allen in G. S. Spinks (ed.), *Religion in Britain Since 1900* (Dakers, 1952), 184–5; R. Tudur Jones, *Congregationalism in England, 1662–1962* (Independent Press, 1962), 451–2.
3. Tudur Jones, 387, 390; R. F. Wearmouth, *Social and Political Influence of Methodism in the Twentieth Century* (Epworth, 1957), 57.
4. MO, *Puzzled People*, 21–2, 42–52.

5. David Mathew, *Catholicism in England* (Eyre & Spottiswoode, 1948), 258.

6. Tudur Jones, *Congregationalism in England*, 462; Bryan Wilson, *Sects and Society* (Heinemann, 1961), 56–8, 152–4.

7. Spinks, *Religion in Britain . . .* , 217.

8. Ibid., 38; Smyth, *Cyril Forster Garbett*, 358.

9. John Strachey, *A Faith to Fight For* (Gollancz, 1941), 23.

10. C. E. M. Joad, "Prospect for Religion", *New Statesman*, 22.8.42; Kingsley Martin, *Father Figures* (Hutchinson, 1966), 48–9.

11. Jane Gordon, *Married to Charles*, 116; MO, *Puzzled People*, 53–61.

12. Jane Gordon, 23; Archbishop's Commission on Evangelism, *Towards the Conversion of England* (Church Assembly, 1945), 15.

13. L. John Collins, *Faith Under Fire* (Frewin, 1966), 67–90.

14. Sir Harold Scott, *Your Obedient Servant*, 151–2.

15. Mathew, *Catholicism in England*, 263; R. C. D. Jaspers, *George Bell* (O.U.P., 1967), 249–55.

16. *The Times*, 21.12.40.

17. F. A. Iremonger, *William Temple*, 428–30.

18. Roger Lloyd, *The Church of England in the Twentieth Century*, vol. 2 (Longmans, 1950), 101–107; *Malvern 1941* (Longmans, 1941), 3–4; Iremonger, *Temple*, 430–31; Industrial Christian Fellowship, *The Life of the Church and the Order of Society*, 1941.

19. Sidney Dark, *The Church – Impotent or Triumphant* (Gollancz, 1941), 50, and letter to *New Statesman*, 5.9.42; *Malvern 1941*, 224.

20. Smyth, *Garbett*, 268; Lockhart, *Cosmo Gordon Lang*, 430.

21. Ibid., 441, 457–8; *Daily Mirror*, 22.1.42.

22. Henson, *Retrospect of an Unimportant Life*, vol. 3, 233.

23. Smyth, *Garbett*, 270–77, 466–7; Moran, 21–2.

24. Iremonger, *Temple*, 475; Temple, *Some Lambeth Letters*, 57.

25. Iremonger, *Temple*, 433; Temple, *Christianity and Social Order* (Penguin, 1942), 6, 75–90; *Malvern 1941*, 15.

26. Industrial Christian Fellowship, *The Church Looks Forward*, 1942, 6, 24–5; 483 HCDeb, 30.9.42, col. 832; Smyth, *Garbett*, 292–3.

27. Lloyd, *The Church of England . . .* , 100–101.

28. Industrial Christian Fellowship, *The Life of the Church . . .* , 12; *Towards the Conversion of England*, 2–3, 4, 10–11, 13.

29. Jaspers, *Bell*, 285.

30. Henson, *Retrospect . . .* , vol. 3, 47–8.

31. Lockhart, *Lang*, 436; Iremonger, *Temple*, 232; Smyth, *Garbett*, 291.

32. *Daily Mail*, 29.1.44.

33. Kavanagh, *Tommy Handley*, 141; MO no. 194, *Attitudes to Italy*, 12.6.40; Inez Holden, *Night Shift* (Bodley Head, 1941), 105; A. P. Herbert, *Let Us Be Glum*, 14, and *Less Nonsense!*, 59.

34. Partridge, *Dictionary of Forces Slang*, 22, 107–108; Stephen Spender, *World Within World*, 267.

35. Dean, *Theatre at War*, 223; *Bristol Evening Post*, 17.9.43, 29.11.44.

36. Sir Robert Vansittart, *The Black Record* (Hamish Hamilton, 1941), viii, 4, 5, 18–20.
37. Lochner, *The Goebbels Diaries*, 267.
38. *Sunday Express*, 7.3.43.
39. Andrew Sharf, *The British Press and the Jews Under Nazi Rule* (O.U.P., 1964), 133–6.
40. MO no. 2000, *Vengeance*, 14.1.44.
41. Churchill WS 1, 268, 396, 453; Churchill WS 2, 264.
42. Smyth, *Garbett*, 434.
43. Jaspers, *Bell*, 151.
44. Bell, *The Church and Humanity*, 23, 26–7.
45. Ibid., 49; Jaspers, *Bell*, 262–4.
46. Ibid., 264–6.
47. Ibid., 267–75.
48. Ibid., 276–8; Bell, *The Church and Humanity*, 129–41.
49. Jaspers, *Bell*, 283.
50. Brockway, *Bermondsey Story*, 232.
51. Fenner Brockway, *Outside the Right* (Allen & Unwin, 1963), 32.
52. Hayes, *Challenge of Conscience*, 5; Brittain, *England's Hour*, 42–51.
53. Hayes, *Challenge of Conscience*, 31–51; Parker, 155–7.
54. Hayes, *Challenge of Conscience*, 203–205.
55. Brittain, *Testament of Experience*, 289; Lancum, *Press Officer, Please!*, 85–6.
56. Hayes, *Challenge of Conscience*, 76, 122–4, 128–9.
57. Ibid., ix–x; Bryan Wilson, *Sects and Society*, 264.
58. Hayes, *Challenge of Conscience*, 26–30, 44–6, 49, 202.
59. Ibid., 68–70, 118, 170–73, 318–25.
60. Katin, *Clippie*, 72; George Orwell, "Anti-Semitism in Britain", *Collected Essays* (Mercury, 1961), 288.
61. James Parkes, *An Enemy of the People: Antisemitism* (Penguin, 1945), 138–9; Frederick Morton, *The Rothschilds* (Penguin, 1964), 18.
62. Sharf, *The British Press and the Jews* . . . , 26, 90–92, 117–19, 137, 200–201.
63. Ibid., 84–5, 91–100.
64. Nicolson, 268; Arthur D. Morse, *While Six Million Died* (Random House [New York], 1968), 35.
65. Ibid., 53–9; Jaspers, *Bell*, 156–7.
66. L. Thompson, *1940*, 40.
67. Morse, *While Six Million Died*, 35, 47; Sharf, *The British Press and the Jews* . . . , 70–72.

C. Where are the War Poets?

1. Orwell, *Collected Essays*, 158.
2. Hodson, *Towards the Morning*, 210.
3. Manvell, *Film*, 168–71; G. P. Thomson, *Blue Pencil Admiral*, 66–7.

4. McKee, *Strike from the Sky*, 44.
5. Macleod, *A Job at the B.B.C.*, 67–70; Gorham, *Sound and Fury*, 113–14.
6. Ibid., 112–14; Roger Eckersley, *The B.B.C. and All That* (Sampson Low, 1946), 206.
7. Gorham, *Broadcasting and T.V. Since 1900*, 183–4; Delmer, *Black Boomerang*, 78–81; Lockhart, *Comes the Reckoning*, 157.
8. Pickles, *Between You and Me*, 126.
9. *Newspaper Press Directory 1945* (Mitchell, 1945), 51; Mayer, *British Cinemas and their Audiences*, 272.
10. *Newspaper Press Directory 1945*, 48–51.
11. Ibid., 53–6.
12. Ibid., 57; Lancum, *Press Officer, Please!*, 10.
13. G. P. Thomson, *Blue Pencil Admiral*, 6, 65.
14. Ibid., 6–7, 25–9; Arthur Christiansen, *Headlines All My Life* (Heinemann, 1961), 210.
15. G. P. Thomson, *Blue Pencil Admiral*, 12, 67, 96–8, 102–106.
16. Ibid., 70–75.
17. Ibid., 77–91, 181.
18. Ibid., 176; private information.
19. *Newspaper Press Directory 1945*, 52–3; MO no. 397, *Special Note on Press Stories on Air Raids*, 12.9.40.
20. *Newspaper Press Directory 1945*, 58–61.
21. Einzig, *In the Centre of Things*, 228, 243–5.
22. Orwell, "Poetry and the Microphone" (1945), *Collected Essays*, 306–7.
23. Duff Cooper, *Old Men Forget*, 288; M.O.I., *Manpower*, 19, 20; "B", "The Age of Innocence", *National Review*, April 1944, 286–7.
24. Orwell, "The Prevention of Literature" (1946), *Collected Essays*, 310; MO, *Home Propaganda*, 46.
25. Ursula Vaughan Williams, *R.V.W.* (O.U.P., 1964), 229–31, 250, 253, 255; Myers, "Music Since 1939", *Since 1939*, vol. 1, 126–39.
26. Coote, *Editorial*, 211–14; Susan Raven, "The Canvases of War", *Alamein and the Desert War*, ed. D. Jewell, 177–81.
27. Sir Stanley Unwin, *The Truth About a Publisher* (Allen & Unwin, 1960), 392; Brittain, *Testament of Experience*, 293.
28. Unwin, *The Truth About a Publisher*, 256–8, 278, 394; John Hayward, "Prose Literature Since 1939", *Since 1939*, vol. 2 (Longmans, 1949), 178–80.
29. Tom Harrisson, "War Books", *Horizon IV*, December 1941, 416–37.
30. Combined Production and Resources Board, *The Impact of the War . . .*, 56; Unwin, *The Truth About a Publisher*, 271–3; Wilson, *Education in the Forces*, 109; MO no. 1332, *Books and the Public*, 15–16, 32, 71–4.
31. Ibid., 179–83; S. Nowell Smith, *The House of Cassell* (Cassell, 1958), 225; *Penguins – a Retrospect* (Penguin, 1951), 1–10; MO no.

2545, *Penguin World*, December 1947, appendix; information from Penguin Books Ltd.

32. Ian Hamilton (ed.), *Alun Lewis – Selected Poetry and Prose* (Allen & Unwin, 1968), 19.

33. Letter to Alex Comfort, 11.7.43, in *The Collected Essays, Journalism and Letters of George Orwell*, vol. 2, ed. Sonia Orwell and Ian Angus (Secker & Warburg, 1968), 305.

34. Spender, *World Within World*, 284.

35. Lehmann, *I Am My Brother*, 40–44, 91–105, 160–63.

36. Ibid., 212–13.

37. "Comment", *Horizon IV*, December 1941, 76; Spender, *World Within World*, 292–7; Maclaren-Ross, *Memoirs of the Forties*, 78.

38. "Comment", *Horizon I*, 5 (January 1940), 68–70 (February 1940); *Horizon II*, 283 (December 1940).

39. "Comment", *Horizon VI*, 371 (December 1942).

40. J. L. Hodson, *The Sea and the Land*, 130.

41. "Why Not War Writers?" *Horizon IV*, 236–9 (October 1941); Brian Gardner (ed.), *The Terrible Rain* (Methuen, 1966), xix.

42. MO no. 46, *Book Reading in Wartime*, 10.

43. Spender, "Poetry Since 1939", *Since 1939*, vol. 2, 112.

44. Beverley Baxter, "Our Poets Are Silent", *Bristol Evening Post*, 18.4.44.

45. Quoted in Arthur Koestler, *The Yogi and the Commissar* (Cape, 1945), 50.

46. Ian Hamilton (ed.), *The Poetry of War* (Alan Ross, 1965), 159.

47. Robert Graves, "War Poetry in This War", *Listener*, 23.10.41, 566–7.

48. J. F. Hendrey and Henry Treece (ed.), *The White Horseman* (Routledge, 1941), 14–15; Ian Hamilton, "The Forties IV", *London Magazine*, January 1965, 85.

49. *Poetry London I*, no. 3, 1940, 66.

50. Maclaren-Ross, *Memoirs of the Forties*, 137, etc.; Gavin Ewart, "Tambi the Great", *London Magazine*, December 1965, 60.

51. Roy Fuller, "Winter in England", *A Lost Season* (Hogarth, 1944), 56.

52. John Pudney, "Air Crew" and "For Johnny", *Ten Summers* (John Lane, 1944), 50, 51; Pudney, *Who Only England Know* (Bodley Head, 1943), 139.

53. "The Glass Tower in Galway", *Collected Poems of Sidney Keyes*, ed. Michael Meyer (Routledge, 1945), 38; "War Wounds", *The Times Literary Supplement*, 21.9.67, 840.

54. Keith Douglas, *Alamein to Zem Zem* (Faber, 1966), 38.

55. Keith Douglas, *Collected Poems* (Faber, 1966), 124.

56. Ibid., 149–50.

Chapter 9: Never Again?

A. *Cmd 6404*

1. Wheeler Bennett, *King George VI*, 470.
2. MO, *The Journey Home*, 21, 33, 42–4; MO no. 2022, *Notes on Public Opinion in 1943*, 25.2.44, 1; Hodson, *The Sea and the Land*, 94.
3. G. D. H. Cole, *Beveridge Explained* (*New Statesman*, 1942), 10.
4. Sir William Beveridge, *Social Insurance and Allied Services*, Cmd 6404 (H.M.S.O., 1942), 19–20.
5. Taylor, 567; Beveridge, *Power and Influence*, 302–3.
6. *Picture Post*, 7.3.42; Beveridge, *Power and Influence*, 315.
7. M. A. Gibb and P. Beckwith, *The Yorkshire Post: Two Centuries* (Yorkshire Conservative Newspaper Co. 1954), 99; Kavanagh, *Tommy Handley*, 164.
8. Janet Beveridge, *Beveridge and His Plan* (Hodder & Stoughton, 1954), 114; British Institute of Public Opinion, *The Beveridge Report and the Public*, 1943, 4, 14.
9. Beveridge, *Social Insurance . . .* , 6–7.
10. Ibid., 113.
11. British Institute of Public Opinion, *The Beveridge Report and the Public*, 12.
12. Cole, *Beveridge Explained*, 35–6.
13. Beveridge, *Social Insurance . . .* , 167, 171.
14. *National Review*, January 1943, 19; "The New Jerusalem", *Labour Organizer*, December 1942; Nicolson, 264.
15. Janet Beveridge, *Beveridge and His Plan*, 124–5; Quintin Hogg, *One Year's Work* (Hurst & Blackett, 1944), 53.
16. *Manchester Guardian*, 15.2.43.
17. Bullock, 224–9; Janet Beveridge, *Beveridge and His Plan*, 132–7.
18. Bullock, 229–31.
19. Hogg, *One Year's Work*, 43.
20. Woolton, *Memoirs*, 276; Emanuel Shinwell, *Conflict Without Malice* (Odhams, 1955), 161; *Liberal Magazine*, October 1942, 277.
21. 395 HCDeb 8.12.43, col. 1022; Tory Reform Committee, *Forward – By The Right!* (Hutchinson, 1943), 5–6, 10–12, 16; Hugh Molson, "How A Young Tory Would Reform Britain", *Bristol Evening Post*, 2.7.43; Tory Reform Committee, *A National Policy for Coal* (Hutchinson, 1944), 6, 12; W. A. Lee, *Thirty Years in Coal* (Mining Association, 1954), 185–203.
22. Morrison, *Herbert Morrison*, 232–3; Morrison, *Looking Ahead* (Hodder & Stoughton, 1943), 129; *National Review*, February 1943, 102–3.
23. Churchill WS 2, 425–37.
24. Beveridge, *Power and Influence*, 330.

25. Churchill WS 3, 112–13.
26. Quoted in K. Hutchison, *Decline and Fall of British Capitalism*, 285.
27. Joan S. Clarke, *Social Security Guide* (Social Security League, 1944), 1.
28. Bullock, 320–21; Hancock, 539–40.
29. Harry Eckstein, *The English Health Service* (Harvard U.P., 1958), 44.
30. Titmuss, 64–5.
31. L. G. Parsons, *et al.*, *Hospital Survey: The Hospital Services of the Sheffield and East Midlands Area* (H.M.S.O., 1945), 3, 5–6, 8.
32. Titmuss, 72.
33. Sir E. R. Carling and T. S. McIntosh, *Hospital Survey: The Hospital Services of the North Western Area* (H.M.S.O., 1945), 14.
34. Titmuss, 71.
35. Ibid., 73, 450–58, 490–91.
36. J. M. Mackintosh, *The Nation's Health* (Pilot Press, 1944), 46–50; Eckstein, *The English Health Service*, 118–22.
37. Ibid., 140–43; Hill, *Both Sides of the Hill*, 84–5.
38. *A National Health Service*, Cmd 6502 (H.M.S.O., 1944), 47.
39. Eckstein, *The English Health Service*, 143–55.
40. National Union of Teachers, *Educational Reconstruction* (N.U.T. [Cheltenham], 1942), 2–3.
41. W. O. Lester Smith, *Education in Great Britain* (O.U.P., 1949), 135–6.
42. D. V. Glass (ed.), *Social Mobility in Britain*, 105, 107, 109, 130.
43. Board of Education, *Curriculum and Examinations in Secondary Schools* (H.M.S.O., 1943), 2–4; S. J. Curtis, *Education in Britain Since 1900* (Dakers, 1952), 144–5.
44. W. O. Lester Smith, *To Whom Do Schools Belong?* (Blackwell [Oxford], 1942), 169; R. Lewis and A. Maude, *The English Middle Classes*, 187–9.
45. *The Times*, 31.7.43.
46. R. H. Tawney, *Education: The Task Before Us* (W.E.A., 1943), 12.
47. See Dent, *The Education Act 1944*, *passim*.
48. Bland, *Flat Racing Since 1900*, 28–9.
49. MO no. 2067, *The Mood of Britain – 1938 and 1944*, 20.4.44, 5.
50. British Institute of Public Opinion, *The Beveridge Report and the Public*, 9–11, 14.
51. MO, *The Journey Home*, 11, 21; MO no. 1783, *Social Security and Parliament*, 17.5.43, 9.
52. Calder, vol 1, 129–30.
53. Ibid., 25–32; Mark Forster, "How It Can Be Done", *C.W. Review*, August, 1946.
54. Calder, vol. 1, 152–3.
55. Calder, vol. 2, 77–91, 109–15, 121–30, 135–64.
56. Calder, vol. 1, 133–40.

57. Colin Cross, *The Fascists in Britain*, 197–8; MO no. 1990, *Mosley and After*, 1.1.44, 6.
58. H.. Cantril, *Public Opinion 1935–1946*, 195, 277; MO no. 1442, *Sixth Report on Sir Stafford Cripps*, 8.10.42.
59. Calder, vol. 2, 223–71.
60. *The Times*, 27.1.44, 29.1.44, 1.2.44, 2.2.44, 5.2.44.
61. Calder, vol. 1, 241–7; *Manchester Guardian*, 19.2.44.
62. Calder, vol. 1, 233–7; Aneurin Bevan, "A Labour Plan to Beat the Tories", *Tribune*, 11.2.44.

B. *D-Day, V 1, V 2, VE-Day*

1. Douglas, *Collected Poems*, 143.
2. O'Brien, 439–43; Henrey, *The Siege of London*, 21.
3. Churchill WS 3, 115.
4. Parker, 242–5; Darwin, *War on the Line*, 112–13; Firebrace, *Fire Service Memories*, 240; A. P. Herbert, *The Thames*, 183–5; Graves WG, 201–2.
5. Knowles, 201–40.
6. John Baker White, *The Big Lie* (Pan Books, 1958), 171–2; Darwin, *War on the Line*, 108–21; Brittain, *Testament of Experience*, 337.
7. Parker, 245–8; Hodson, *The Sea and the Land*, 145.
8. Joseph, *If Their Mothers Only Knew*, 106.
9. O'Brien, 645–53.
10. Berwick Sayers, 95; Nicolson, 380; John Lehmann, *I Am My Brother*, 279.
11. E. Waugh, *Unconditional Surrender*, 245.
12. Henrey, *The Siege of London*, 75; Hodson, *The Sea and the Land*, 168; Godfrey Evans, *The Gloves Are Off* (Hodder & Stoughton, 1960), 44–45; O'Brien, 653–6; *Hampstead at War*, 22.
13. Berwick Sayers, 104; Sansom, *Westminster at War*, 184–97.
14. O'Brien, 657–8, 665; Basil Collier, *A Short History . . .*, 422–3, 454.
15. O'Brien, 665–7; Brittain, *Testament of Experience*, 346–7; Berwick Sayers, 111–14; Sansom, *Westminster at War*, 197–9.
16. Parker, 248–52; Kohan, *Works and Buildings*, 222–35.
17. Orwell, "As I Please", *Tribune*, 4.8.44, in *Collected Essays, Journalism and Letters . . .*, vol. 3, 200; *Bristol Evening Post*, 18.9.44; Berwick Sayers, 116; Henrey, *Siege of London*, 107.
18. Firebrace, *Fire Service Memories*, 239.
19. Taylor, 588–9; Bullock, 340–47.
20. Hodson, *The Sea and the Land*, 275; Nicolson, 419–22.
21. Nicolson, 437.
22. *Daily Mirror*, 20.4.45, 21.4.45; Sharf, *The British Press and the Jews . . .*, 140–44.
23. Cole, *Lord Haw Haw*, 232–3.
24. Knowles, 244–5.
25. Driberg, *Colonnade*, 276–9; Graves, *London Transport Carried On*,

43, 95; Hodson, *The Sea and the Land*, 367–9; Lehmann, *I Am My Brother*, 293; Lyttelton, *I Play As I Please*, 97–8; Nicolson, 456–9; W. Thompson, *I Was Churchill's Shadow*, 157–9; Wheeler Bennett, *King George VI*, 625–6.
26. Berwick Sayers, 118–19.
27. Ronald Clark, *Tizard*, 367.

C. *Landslides*

1. Moran, 254.
2. Bullock, 318–20; Parker, 258–72; Hargreaves, 324.
3. Titmuss, 431–8.
4. Labour Party, *Annual Conference Report 1944*, 163.
5. Bullock, 366–70.
6. Ibid., 374–5; Kingsley Martin, *Harold Laski* (Gollancz, 1953), 162.
7. Bullock, 376–7; McCallum, 14–15; Williams, *A Prime Minister Remembers*, 64–7.
8. *The Memoirs of Lord Chandos*, 324–5.
9. M. Abrams, "The Labour Vote at the General Election", *Pilot Papers I*, January 1946, 16.
10. Moran, 251–2; McCallum, 51–3, 59.
11. Ibid., 45–7.
12. Ibid., 52–3, 100–101; Labour Party, *Let Us Face The Future*, 1945, 3–7, 9; Estorick, *Stafford Cripps*, 327; Bullock, 356.
13. McCallum, 61–4.
14. Ibid., 209, 211.
15. Ibid., 140, 154; R. J. E. Silvey, "Some Recent Trends in Listening", *B.B.C. Year Book 1946*, 30.
16. Churchill WS 3, 479–88.
17. McCallum, 143, 206–8.
18. Cantril, *Public Opinion 1935–1946*, 195.
19. MO no. 2268, *The General Election, June–July 1945*, October 1945, 10–15.
20. McCallum, 144.
21. Ibid., 49–50; Bullock, 349, 384.
22. McCallum, 144–9.
23. Bullock, 360, 388; McCallum, 237, 241–2.
24. Ibid., 95, 150–4; MO, *The General Election*, 54–71, 85–7.
25. McCallum, 156–8, 167–9.
26. Ibid, 167.
27. Ibid., 69–87.
28. Ibid., 172–7.
29. Ibid., 30–32, 258; D. E. Butler, *The Electoral System in Britain since 1918* (O.U.P., 1963), 100–101; MO no. 2135, *The Forces Vote*, 19.7.44, 17; Stat. Dig., 10; Dalton, *The Fateful Years*, 464.
30. Mallaby, *From My Level*, 51.
31. McCallum, 155–6, 240–42; Nicolson, 469, 477.

32. McCallum, 244–6.
33. Ibid., 247–52; John Bonham, *The Middle Class Vote* (Faber, 1954), 129, 154, 163, 168.
34. Blackburn, *I Am an Alcoholic*, 56; Mancunian, "The Rendezvous", *Labour's Northern Voice*, August 1945.
35. Cantril, *Public Opinion 1935–1946*, 277.
36. Anthony Howard, "We Are The Masters Now", *The Age of Austerity*, ed. M. Sissons and P. French, 31.
37. Whittle, *Jet*, 262–4.
38. Moran, 286.
39. MO, *Peace and the Public*, 8–11.
40. Hancock, 546.

Bibliography

An exhaustive list of all the books which have something to say about
life in Britain during the Second World War would, no doubt, make a
long book in itself; and more may be expected. This is a one-man
travelogue, pointing out some of the prominent landmarks and explor-
ing a few byways, rather than an atlas or gazetteer. All books listed
were published in London, unless it is otherwise stated.

IN GENERAL

The most famous source for the military history of Britain's part in the
war is, of course, Churchill's *The Second World War*, in six individually titled volumes (1948 to 1954). They will always be indispensable,
but besides some well-known errors of fact they contain misleading if
picturesque generalizations about life on the home front. His references to home politics should be read with special caution. A useful
recent synopsis of the military history of the war is Basil Collier's *A
Short History of the Second World War* (1967). A. J. P. Taylor's *English
History 1914–1945* (1965) is a *tour de force* which is open to correction
at many points; but the present writer has paid the sincere flattery of
copying many of its general judgments. Arthur Marwick's *Britain in
the Century of Total War* (1968) appeared after the present book was
completed; other readers should find its fresh emphases as stimulating
as this writer did.

During and after the war, a number of historians were enlisted to
work in Whitehall on histories of the work of various Government
departments. The results, not yet fully published, together form the
United Kingdom Civil Series of the official *History of the Second World
War*. The authors were given full access to the archives, though they
do not state their sources in detail. These works, around thirty in
number, are not panegyrics, and indeed are often sharply critical,
though their criticism is muffled by the practice of omitting names of
civil servants, and even ministers, and by the ponderously formal
presentation. Their findings are open to challenge now that the records
have been thrown open to independent venturers, but one may doubt
if they will ever be generally superseded. In the chapter-by-chapter lists
which follow, they are indicated by an asterisk.

There are three key volumes. *British War Economy* (1949),* by Sir
Keith Hancock and Margaret Gowing, provides a most readable
general introduction. M. M. Postan's *British War Production* (1952)*
introduces a series within the series. R. M. Titmuss's *Problems of Social*

Policy (1950)* stands out above all other volumes in its combination of immense scholarship, literary style, warmth and passion.

Two other official histories outside the civil series which are very relevant to the home front are Basil Collier's *The Defence of the United Kingdom* (1957) and J. W. Blake's *Northern Ireland in the Second World War* (Belfast, 1956). For the occupied Channel Islands, Alan and Mary Wood's *Islands in Danger* (1955), is the best study, a most disturbing one.

The Central Statistical Office's *Statistical Digest of the War* (1951) provides nearly two hundred officially compiled tables, though there are some irritating gaps. *Public Opinion 1935-46* (Princeton, 1951) includes Gallup Polls for the period. Several books by Mass Observation together provide a trajectory of public feeling over the war years: *War Begins At Home* (1940); *Home Propaganda* (1941); *People in Production* (1942); *The Journey Home* (1944) and *Peace and the Public* (1947).

John Wheeler Bennett's *King George VI* (1958) is a solid portrait of a likeable and quite important man. Other books which cover the war from the point of view of single individuals are mentioned in the appropriate places later, but Alan Bullock's second volume of the *Life and Times of Ernest Bevin* (1967) shoud be listed here as the best introduction both to wartime manpower policy and to wartime politics. Of the diaries published during and just after the war, most are marked by voluntary self-censorship, but J. L. Hodson's several volumes are still worth reading for their interesting vignettes of the life of the time. Harold Nicolson's *Diaries and Letters 1939-45* (1967), superbly edited by his son, give the most candid and best written picture so far of the reactions from day to day of an intelligent and well-placed observer. Finally, *Years of Wrath* (1949) is a selection of classic cartoons by the great David Low.

CHAPTER 1: PRELUDE – MUNICH AND THE 'THIRTIES

C. L. Mowat's *Britain Between the Wars* (1955) provides a magisterial introduction to the period, with very full references and bibliography. G. D. H. and M. Cole's *The Condition of Britain* (1937) still provides a most useful statistical background. For the sights and smells of depression, see J. B. Priestley's *English Journey* (1934) and George Orwell's *Road to Wigan Pier* (1937). The most vivid introduction to the ideas of the clever young men of the 'thirties is probably P. Stansky and W. Abrahams's *Journey to the Frontier* (1966). But the good books of and on the 'thirties would take pages to list.

For Neville Chamberlain, see the biographies by Keith Feiling (1946) and Iain Macleod (1961). *The Appeasers*, by Martin Gilbert and Richard Gott (1963), deals with them sharply. Mass Observation's *Britain* (1939) contains a day-by-day account of popular reactions to Munich and the crisis which preceded it.

Ronald Seth's *The Day War Broke Out* (1963) is based on the personal reminiscences of a wide range of citizens.

CHAPTER 2: "THIS STRANGEST OF WARS"

Evacuation policy and practice over the whole war are magnificently covered in Richard Titmuss's *Problems of Social Policy* (1950).* The rural householders' first horror is illustrated in *Town Children Through Country Eyes* (1940), published by the National Federation of Women's Institutes. *Evacuation Survey* (1940), edited by Richard Padley and Margaret Cole, is a collection of essays of varying merit by a wide range of observers. *The Cambridge Evacuation Survey* (1941), edited by Susan Isaacs, *Evacuation in Scotland* (1944), edited by William Boyd, and the Barnett House Study Group's *London Children in Wartime Oxford* (1947) are painstaking and authoritative sociological studies. *Our Towns* (1944), by the Women's Group on Public Welfare, is a most useful synthesis, directly prompted by the shocks of evacuation, of facts relating to social conditions in the cities. For a lively account of the experiences of an evacuated school, see M. D. Brock, *An Unusual Happening* (1947). Norah Baring's *A Friendly Hearth* (1946) is an absorbing memoir by a well-to-do woman who ran a home for "difficult" evacuees. The most notable fictional account of evacuation is, of course, Evelyn Waugh's *Put Out More Flags* (1942); very funny, very snobbish, and not to be relied upon. *The Evacuees*, edited by B. S. Johnson (1968), provides reminiscences of more than thirty of them.

The military and political history of the Bore War are covered in the first volume of Churchill's history, *The Gathering Storm* (1948). E. S. Turner's *The Phoney War on the Home Front* (1961) is a light-hearted survey of the oddities of the period. Mass Observation's *War Begins at Home* (1940), a long and detailed study of many aspects of the home front, was written before the phoney phase ended, and is free from the distortions of hindsight. J. L. Hodson's *Through the Dark Night* (1941) is an account of travels and talks in France and Britain.

Margery Allingham's *The Oaken Heart* (1941, reprinted 1959) contains a pleasingly written and perceptive account of the impact of war on an Essex village. Leo Walmsley's *Fishermen at War* (1941) deals with coastal life in Yorkshire and elsewhere. Evelyn Waugh's *Men At Arms* (1952) portrays life in the upper class and the army. Another novel which should not be missed is Henry Green's brilliant *Caught* (1943), which gives a delicate picture of life in the A.F.S.

CHAPTER 3: SPITFIRE SUMMER

A. COALITION

Churchill's account of the fall of Chamberlain in *The Gathering Storm* is misleading. Halifax's part in the crisis emerges from the Earl of

Birkenhead's *Halifax* (1965). There is a good account synthesizing the available sources in Laurence Thompson's *1940* (1966). Leo Amery's famous version in *My Political Life*, vol. 3 (1955) must now be treated cautiously.

The literature by, on and around Winston Churchill is already enormous, but there is still no biography to supplant his own *Second World War* as a record of his doings at this time. The standard biography, started by his son Randolph Churchill, will be completed in five volumes as *Winston S. Churchill* (1966–   ). Churchill's own *My Early Life* (1930) is essential to our understanding of him. His *War Speeches*, edited by Charles Eade, were published in three volumes (1951–2). The memoirs of his bodyguard, W. H. Thompson, *I Was Churchill's Shadow* (1951) prove that a man may be a hero to his valet and supply a description of his personal habits. His doctor, Lord Moran, in *Winston Churchill – The Struggle for Survival 1940–65* (1966) provides perceptive and often critical comments and a record of Churchill's conversation. Isaiah Berlin's essay *Mr. Churchill in 1940* (1964) provides the most sophisticated version of the conventional picture of the Great Man's relationship with his people.

Beaverbrook still awaits an adequate biography; while A. J. P. Taylor is writing it, Tom Driberg's *Beaverbrook* (1956) is a sharp portrait. Kenneth Young's *Churchill and Beaverbrook* (1966) is a well-documented record of their friendship. Bevin has been splendidly served by Alan Bullock. The first volume of *The Life and Times of Ernest Bevin* (1960) deals with his career as a union leader; the second (1967) is subtitled *Minister of Labour 1940–1945*; the third, not yet out, will cover his work as Foreign Secretary after 1945. Two earlier biographies – *Bevin*, by Trevor Evans (1946) and *Ernest Bevin* by Francis Williams (1952) – were written from personal acquaintance, and remain interesting. Bevin's early wartime speeches are brought together in *The Job To Be Done* (1942). *John Anderson – Viscount Waverley* (1962) is an excellent biography by John Wheeler Bennett; does the tongue of the writer often creep into his cheek? Attlee gives almost nothing away in his autobiography, *As It Happened* (1953), and not much more in his conversations with Francis Williams, *A Prime Minister Remembers* (1961). Morrison's autobiography, *Herbert Morrison* (1960), is much more personal but not very informative. The relevant volume of Eden's heavy record of his own career is *The Reckoning* (1965).

Hugh Dalton's *The Fateful Years* (1957) is full of sharp comment and is soundly based on diaries. Lord Woolton's *Memoirs* (1959) also have the merit of being informative about the author's own work as minister. *The Memoirs of Lord Chandos* (1962) form a gracefully written volume by the former Oliver Lyttelton. Among lesser ministers, there are meritorious memoirs by Duff Cooper, *Old Men Forget* (1953); Tom Johnston, *Memories* (1952); Lord Reith, *Into the Wind* (1949); Sir James Grigg, *Prejudice and Judgment* (1948); and Harold Macmillan. *The Blast of War* (1967). Two books by Labour junior ministers –

Time's Winged Chariot (1945) by Ernest Thurtle and *Digging for Britain* (1965) by Lord Williams of Barnsburgh – spill one or two small beans.

The best picture of life on the back and front benches of the Commons during the war years is found in Harold Nicolson s *Diaries and Letters 1939–45* (1967). A more gossipy saga is provided in *Chips – The Diaries of Sir Henry Channon*, edited by R. Rhodes James (1967). For the opposition to Churchill, there is Michael Foot's passionate biography of *Aneurin Bevan*, vol. 1 (1962). Emanuel Shinwell's *Conflict Without Malice* (1955) and Earl Winterton's *Orders of the Day* (1953) provide the apologias of two other rebels. For the view from the fringe, see *And Now, Tomorrow* (1960) by the Independent M.P. Vernon Bartlett.

Many extra-parliamentary figures observed Churchill and his ministers at close quarters. There are excellent portraits of Churchill and Attlee in George Mallaby's *From My Level* (1965). Robert Bruce Lockhart in *Comes the Reckoning* (1947) writes in a friendly way about Bracken, Eden and others. Bracken also figures memorably in Paul Einzig's *In the Centre of Things* (1960). An outsider's view of the War Cabinet is found in John G. Winant's *Letter from Grosvenor Square* (1947), by the U.S. Ambassador.

B. DUNKIRK AND THE BATTLE OF BRITAIN

Churchill's history of the summer and autumn of 1940 is *Their Finest Hour* (1949). Basil Collier's *The Defence of the United Kingdom* (1957) deals with both the preparations against invasion and the Battle of Britain. Peter Fleming's *Invasion 1940* (1957) is an elegant, witty and still useful survey of the improvisations of the period and the German plans of attack; the latter are more fully described in Ronald Wheatley's *Operation Sea Lion* (1958). Laurence Thompson's *1940* (1965) synthesizes political, military and social history, and makes many shrewd points.

Churchill's speeches are on gramophone records; and there is also an evocative disc of the B.B.C. programme *Scrapbook 1940*, edited by Leslie Baily (Fontana FDL 493 014). J. B. Priestley's *Postscripts* (1940) were immediately published. For the man himself and his own feelings about them, see his *Margin Released* (1962). George Orwell's *The Lion and the Unicorn* (1941) discusses the mood of 1940 from a heterodox socialist viewpoint.

The Home Guard seems not to have received sound overall treatment. Charles Graves's quasi-official *The Home Guard of Britain* (1943) is anecdotal and confusing; but its second half consists of fascinating unedited reports from the commanders of a good proportion of battalions. The resistance organization recruited against invasion is described in David Lampe's *The Last Ditch* (1968). A. G. Street's *From Dusk to Dawn* (1947) is an expert documentary based on the Home Guard in

Wiltshire. Many battalions published their own histories, usually pretty staid. Among the best are L. W. Kentish's unpretentious *Home Guard – Bux 4* (1946); H. K. Wilson's *Four Years* (Conway, 1944); and a magisterial volume from Cambridgeshire, *We Also Served* (Cambridge 1944). Those curious about the Home Guard's military notions may consult John Brophy's *Home Guard Handbook* (1940 and subsequent editions) and Tom Wintringham's *New Ways of War* (1940).

François Lafitte's *The Internment of Aliens* (1940) is an exhaustive and dismaying contemporary study. Eugen Spier's *The ProtectingPower* (1951) is the memoir, fully detailed, of one Jewish internee.

The Beaverbrook regime at M.A.P. is well described in *The Sky's the Limit* (1943) by David Farrer. Gordon Beckles's *Birth of a Spitfire* (1941) is informative about the "stunts". Ernest Fairfax's *Calling All Arms* (1945) describes the work of civilians on salvage and repair. The story of the Royal Observer Corps is told in *Forewarned is Forearmed* (1948) by T. E. Winslow.

The literature on the air battles is immense; there is no shortage of memoirs by pilots. Of these, Richard Hillary's *The Last Enemy* (1942) remains outstanding for its literary quality. Of the overall accounts, Basil Collier's *The Battle of Britain* (1962) is based on full knowledge of the British side. The most trenchant summary of the strategy, tactics and implications of the battle is found in Telford Taylor's *The Breaking Wave* (1967). Alexander McKee's *Strike from the Sky* (1960) assembles many eye-witness accounts from air and ground and describes the conditions of battle very well. Derek Wood and Derek Dempster, in *The Narrow Margin* (1961), provide an exhaustive compilation of facts and figures. Other books worth reading are Ronald Clark's typically sharp and sensible *Battle for Britain* (1965); a French viewpoint from Marcel Jullian, *The Battle of Britain* (1967), and Drew Middleton's *The Sky Suspended* (1960), by an eye-witnessing American journalist. The best-known account from the German side is Adolf Galland's *The First and the Last* (1955).

CHAPTER 4: BLITZ

The official story of the blitz is told movingly in R. M. Titmuss's *Problems of Social Policy* (1950),* which concentrates on the post-raid services; more drily in T. H. O Brien's *Civil Defence* (1955),* which covers A.R.P., the Fire Service and shelter policy in exhaustive but somehow unimpressive detail. C. M. Kohan's *Works and Buildings* (1952)* deals with shelter construction and house repair; R. J. Hammond's first two volumes on *Food* (1951 and 1956),* with blitz feeding. The military aspects are covered in Collier's *Defence of the United Kingdom* (1957), which may be supplemented with General Pile's *Ack Ack* (1949).

There is no good book devoted to the blitz which covers all aspects of it in London and the provinces, but the Ministry of Information's

BIBLIOGRAPHY

731

Front Line (1942) is a long, useful, and well-written propaganda tract, which does deal with Yarmouth as well as London, Falmouth as well as Coventry.

For the London blitz, there is Constantine Fitzgibbon's admirable *The Blitz* (1957), usually accurate and well researched. It makes much better use of first-hand reminiscence from ordinary people than Richard Collier's *The City That Wouldn't Die* (1959), an honest but ill-written attempt to reconstruct the great May 10th raid. A good book which, although it covers only one borough, gives a wealth of atmospheric general detail, is William Sansom's *Westminster at War* (1947). W. Berwick Sayers's *Croydon and the Second World War* (1949) is a less inspired but equally exhaustive work. Other worthwhile local accounts are F. R. Lewey's overwritten but vivid *Cockney Campaign* (1944), which is surprisingly honest about Stepney, and Doreen Idle's *War Over West Ham* (1943), an objective but absorbing sociological study.

W. R. Matthews's *St Paul's Cathedral in Wartime* (1946) is a model specialized study. So are Guy Morgan's *Red Roses Every Night* (1948), a loving and almost pedantic account of Granada cinemas at war, Bernard Darwin's stylish *War on the Line* (1946), which recounts Southern Railways' blitz experiences, and Hilary St George Saunders's *Ford at War* (1946). Charles Graves's *London Transport Carried On* (1947) is, inappropriately, more pedestrian.

Sir Harold Scott's *Your Obedient Servant* (1959) is most engaging on the inner workings of London Region Civil Defence, for which see also Admiral Lord Mountevans's *Adventurous Life* (1946). Reginald Bell's *The Bull's Eye* (1943) gives a very good account of the system of civil defence from lower down the hierarchy.

The more personal literature of the London blitz is so copious that it can be given only short shrift here. The best journalist's account is found in Ritchie Calder's *Carry on London* (1941) and *Lesson of London* (1941), two angry books. Hilde Marchant's *Women and Children Last* (1941) is also critical. Of the books by numerous friendly American journalists, Ed Murrow's *This Is London* (1941) is probably the best. Negley Farson's *Bomber's Moon* (1941) is more sickly. Ralph Ingersoll's *Report on England* (1941) is, from the point of view of the postwar generation, rewardingly naive; he noticed things that others took for granted.

Peter Conway's *Living Tapestry* (1946) is an interesting but somewhat over-ambitious attempt to analyse shelter life from the inside. H. A. Wilson's *Death Over Haggerston* (1941) gives the story of an East End parson. For the blitz in the West End see Vera Brittain's *England's Hour* (1941) and Jane Gordon's *Married to Charles* (1950). Francis Faviell's excellent and vivid *Chelsea Concerto* (1959) and Bernard Kops's *The World Is a Wedding* (1963) give notably more scaring pictures than most of the books published during and just after the war.

There are two outstanding contemporary books by air raid wardens, however, which make the best reading of all; John Strachey's *Post D* (1941), which contains definitive accounts of two incidents, and Barbara Nixon's dry-eyed, funny and harrowing *Raiders Overhead* (1943). Two novels also stand out for their atmospheric quality: Graham Greene's *Ministry of Fear* (1943) and Inez Holden's documentary *Night Shift* (1941).

The literature of the provincial blitz, alas, is almost non-existent. Most towns promoted at least a photographic account of the damage, and local newspapers often produced pamphlets. But only Bernard Knowles's thorough account in *Southampton: The English Gateway* (1951) and H. P. Twyford's *It Came to Our Door* (Plymouth, 1946) have much to say between hard covers. *Bristol Siren Nights*, edited by S. P. Shipley (Bristol, 1943), has first-hand accounts by local people. Catherine Williamson's *Though the Streets Burn* (1949) deals at immense and parochial length with A.R.P. in Canterbury and the town's big raids in 1942. For a good account of a blitzed Birmingham arms factory, see D. M. Ward, *The Other Battle* (Birmingham, 1946).

On the Fire Service in London and elsewhere the best book is Sir Aylmer Firebrace's *Fire Service Memories* (1949), a well written account from the very top. Two interesting books by A.F.S. men are Michael Wassey's critical *Ordeal by Fire* (1941) and H. W. Stedman's highly coloured *Battle of the Flames* (1942).

Ian Bisset's *The George Cross* (1961) has many stories of individual heroism. Charles Graves, in *Women in Green* (1948), catalogues the good works of the W.V.S. *ad nauseam*. Two other books which range over the whole nation are J. M. Richards's lavish photographic record of *The Bombed Buildings of Britain* (second edition, 1947) and I. L. Janis's *Air War and Emotional Stress* (New York, 1951). The latter draws together reports by psychiatrists and others on morale in Britain, and compares the result with morale under bombing in Germany and elsewhere.

CHAPTER 5: THROUGH THE TUNNEL

For a wide range of sights and activities in Britain in 1941 and 1942, J. L. Hodson's war diaries, published as *Towards the Morning* (1941), *Before Daybreak* (1941) and *Home Front* (1944), provide an honest commentary. An American viewpoint is found in Walter Graebner's contribution to *Hitler's Reich and Churchill's Britain* (1942), where he compares notes with Stephen Laird. Mass Observation's *Home Propaganda* (1941) shows how the national mood accepted, or more usually resisted, the Government's appeals. A. P. Herbert's *Let Us Be Glum* (1941), one of several volumes of ultra-light verse which he published during the war, reveals what the middle class was still prepared to laugh at.

The relevant volumes of Churchill's memoirs are *The Grand Alliance* (1950) and *The Hinge of Fate* (1951). The most solid summary account of the government of the home front and the controversies which it aroused is Alan Bullock's enviably lucid and authoritative second volume of *The Life and Times of Ernest Bevin* (1967). A sharper version of the political crisis of 1942 is found in George Malcolm Thomson's *Vote of Censure* (1968).

M. M. Postan's official history of *British War Production* (1952)* takes an eagle's-eye view and proves that everything was really going quite well. For the very different conclusions of well-placed observers at the time the *Reports* of the House of Commons's Select Committee on National Expenditure, published in many volumes from 1939 to 1945, and the annual *Proceedings* of the National Committee of the A.E.U., still make surprisingly good reading. Mass Observation's *People in Production* (1942) is a lengthy, tendentious and very readable survey of the national malaise. It quotes and summarizes most of the common criticisms; for a specimen of those from the left, see Maurice Edelman's *Production for Victory Not Profit* (1941). Also left-wing, but with his ear closer to the ground, is J. T. Murphy, whose *Victory Production!* (1942) adds to the controversy, but relates it shrewdly to life in a London factory. Mark Benney's *Over to Bombers* (1943) gives a fictionalized, but earnest and convincing portrait of the neurotic aircraft industry.

To take the politics of the early war years from left to right: Henry Pelling's *The British Communist Party* (1958) is a dull standard work on its subject. *The Betrayal of the Left* (1941) is an agonized exposure of the C.P. line edited by Victor Gollancz and including contributions from Laski, Strachey and Orwell. Among the memoirs of ex-Communists, *I Believed* (1951) by Douglas Hyde, who recanted and became a Catholic, gives a more exhaustive but perhaps less convincing impression than *Crossing the Line* (1958) by Claud Cockburn, who became a Cockburnite. The "official" account of the People's Convention is given in D. N. Pritt's first volume of autobiography, *From Right to Left* (1965). For his views at the time, see *Choose Your Future* (1941).

The C.P. line after the invasion of Russia is immaculately defined by R. Palme Dutt, *Britain in the World Front* (1942). George Bilainkin's *Maisky* (1944) gives a useful survey of the attitudes to the Soviet Union of British newspapers and top people, before and after. Maisky has written his own interesting *Memoirs of a Soviet Ambassador 1939–43* (1967).

A masochistically candid view from the outside-left position is found in volumes 2 and 3 of *The Collected Essays, Journalism and Letters of George Orwell*, edited by Ian Angus and Sonia Orwell (1968).

Cripps has so far defeated biography. Eric Estorick's *Stafford Cripps* (1949), written before the death of its subject, may still be preferred to Colin Cooke's tedious *Life of Richard Stafford Cripps* (1957), commissioned by the family after his death.

The atmosphere of the wartime *Daily Mirror* is perfectly evoked in Hugh Cudlipp's punchy but well documented *Publish and Be Damned*

(1953). Cassandra was in full cry when he wrote his short book, *The English at War* (1941).

There are some entertaining memoirs by independent parliamentary candidates, several of whom are well described in *Bars and Barricades* (1952), by Donald Johnson, a Liberal who joined their number in 1943. W. J. Brown's *So Far* (1943) is self-assertive but solid. George Reakes gives himself away in *Man of the Mersey* (1956). There is also *Half Term Report* (1954) by William Douglas Home, a brother of Sir Alec, who innocently put himself forward on several occasions.

G. D. H. Cole's *History of the Labour Party from 1914* (1948) is still the most exhaustive. Kingsley Martin's *Harold Laski* (1953) is important for the party's internal politics at this time. Of several poor biographies of R. A. Butler, Francis Boyd's (1956) is briefest. Butler's father-in-law, Samuel Courtauld, produced in *Goverment and Industry* (1942) one of the most discussed pamphlets of a pamphlet-ridden war. Charles Madge in *Industry at War* (1943) summarizes post-war plans by businessmen and others. On our far right, the arch-individualist is touchingly limned in Deryck Abel's *Ernest Benn: Counsel for Liberty* (1960).

A number of topical or theoretical books published in the field of politics during the war have symptomatic importance or lasting interest. They may be listed chronologically. The German émigré, Peter Drucker, excited religious as well as political thinkers by *The End of Economic Man* (1939), H. G. Wells, in *The New World Order* (1940), was as cantankerous and influential as ever. Evan Durbin, in *The Politics of Democratic Socialism* (1940), provided a definitive statement of the right-wing Labour ideology, by contriving to avoid almost any reference to the fact that Britain had an empire. The year 1942 saw E. H. Carr's *Conditions of Peace*, an important and much discussed mutation of liberalism, and also the British publication of James Burnham's *The Managerial Revolution*. Harold Laski elaborated his doctrine of "Revolution by Consent", in *Reflections on the Revolution of Our Times* (1943). Except for Burnham's, these books were all "progressive", or superficially so, and their message of change was reinforced by the voice of Roosevelt's America, Wendell Wilkie's *One World* (1943) and Henry Wallace's *The Century of the Common Man* (1944). The right-wing backlash now emerged; it was much inspired by F. A. Hayek's *The Road to Serfdom* (1944), and was abetted by disillusioned Communists, notably Arthur Koestler in *The Yogi and the Commissar* (1945).

Finally, to revert to one sizeable offshoot of "progress", the achievements of ABCA and army education in general are detailed in T. H. Hawkins and L. J. Brimble, *Adult Education – The Record of the British Army* (1947) and N. Scarlyn Wilson's *Education in the Forces 1939–46* (1949).

CHAPTER 6: THE INDIA-RUBBER ISLAND

W. K. Hancock's and Margaret Gowing's *British War Economy* (1949)* is the official survey of the whole field. Sidney Pollard's *The Development of the British Economy 1914–50* (1962) gives a useful summary of wartime changes. Several valuable essays are collected in *Lessons of the British War Economy* (Cambridge, 1951), edited by D. N. Chester. *The British Economy 1945–50* (Oxford, 1952), edited by G. D. N. Worswick and P. Ady, casts much light backwards on the war, summarizing the available knowledge of *The Levelling of Incomes Since 1938*, which is the title of a detailed survey by one of its contributors, Dudley Seers (Oxford, 1951).

A. CONSUMPTION

Consumers'-eye views from the upper middle classes will be found in A. S. F. Gow's *Letters from Cambridge* (1945); in Jane Gordon's *Married to Charles* (1950) and in Verily Anderson's *Spam Tomorrow* (1956). The Combined Production and Resources Board's *Impact of the War on Civilian Consumption* (1945) covers the U.S.A. and Canada as well as Britain, and the figures are probably as good as can be got.

The Combined Food Board's parallel studies of *Food Consumption Levels* (1944, 1946), however, are more suspect in the conclusions which they draw as to the adequacy of the national diet. The Ministry of Food's booklet *How Britain Was Fed in Wartime* (1946) is a useful compendium of administrative facts and figures. At an opposite extreme of scale, R. J. Hammond's three volumes on *Food* (1951, 1956, 1962)* together run to over two thousand pages and form the most detailed of all the official histories. The first volume deals with the growth of policy, while the second and third provide detailed studies of many areas of the M.O.F.'s activities. Plugging the gap in terms of length, R. J. Hammond's *Food and Agriculture in Britain 1939–45* (Stanford, 1954) offers a lively 240-page summary of the author's conclusions. Lord Woolton's *Memoirs* (1959) are frank and informative. Sir John Boyd Orr's *Food, Health and Income* (1936) gives a background to wartime nutritional thinking.

Clothes rationing, Utility, shortages and the problems of the shop-keeper are covered in E. L. Hargreaves and Margaret Gowing's compact and lucid *Civil Industry and Trade* (1952).* Mass Observation's *Clothes Rationing Survey* (1941) deals with the first impact of rationing.

B. PRODUCTION

H. M. D. Parker's *Manpower* (1957)* is comprehensive though uninspired. M. P. Fogarty's *Prospects of the Industrial Areas of Great Britain* (1945) and *The Times's British War Production 1939–45* (1945) are

useful general surveys. Joel Hurstfield in *The Control of Raw Materials*
(1953)* shows how industry was rationed. This is one of nine volumes
in the War Production sub-series of official histories, which contains,
besides others mentioned elsewhere, William Ashworth's *Contracts
and Finance* (1953).* Civilian industries, on the other hand, are covered
in Hargreaves and Gowing's *Civil Industry and Trade* (1952);* in
C. M. Kohan's *Works and Buildings* (1952)* and in C. I. Savage's
Inland Transport (1957).*

J. D. Scott's *Vickers* (1962) is a history of the most famous British
arms firm. Ian Hay's *R.O.F.* (1949) is a cheerful official account of that
phenomenon. V. S. Pritchett's *Build the Ships* (1946) does the same job
for the shipyards and Charles Graves's *Drive For Freedom* (1945) is a
survey of its own activities sponsored by the car industry. Many individual firms also commissioned books on their war efforts, evoking
an oddly Arcadian industrial scene in which absenteeism and strikes
have little place. Among the best are Donovan Ward's on B.S.A., *The
Other Battle* (Birmingham, 1946); Ernest Fairfax's of Nuffield, *Calling
All Arms* (1945) and H. St. G. Saunders's *Ford at War* (1946).

A more realistic picture of labour relations emerges from Mass
Observation's *People in Production* (1942) and from P. Inman's *Labour
in the Munitions Industries* (1957),* one of the most readable and
suggestive of the official histories. K. G. J. C. Knowles's *Strikes* (Oxford,
1952) and *The System of Industrial Relations in Great Britain* (Oxford,
1954), edited by Alan Flanders and H. A. Clegg, both have much to say
on the war.

The second volume of Lord Citrine's memoirs, *Two Careers* (1967),
by the then General Secretary of the T.U.C., reveals more, perhaps,
than its author realizes about the T.U.C.'s relations with the Government. Two books which deal with the early growth of that relationship
are John Price's *Labour in the War* (1940) and Herbert Tracey's *Trade
Unions Fight – For What?* (1940). Two relevant general studies published just after the war are N. Barou's *British Trade Unions* (1947) and
P.E.P.'s *British Trade Unionism* (1948). The Joint Production Committees are examined in *British Joint Production Machinery* (Montreal,
1944), published by the International Labour Office.

J. B. Jefferys's *The Story of the Engineers* (1946) is an excellent history
of the A.E.U., for which see also Wal Hannington's illuminating little
book *The Rights of Engineers* (1944). For a mixed bag of other unions
of various types, one might take H. J. Fyrth and Henry Collins's *The
Foundry Workers* (Manchester, 1959); Philip Bagwell's *The Railwaymen* (1963) and Alan Fox's *A History of the National Union of Boot and
Shoe Operatives* (Oxford, 1958).

The I.L.O.'s *War and Women's Employment* (Montreal, 1946)
provides the fullest general picture of its subject. Zelma Katin's
Clippie (1944) is an engaging memoir. Inez Holden's *Night Shift* (1941)
gives a polished account of women at work in a small London factory,
and Mass Observation's *War Factory* (1943), based on the shrewd

observations of a female novice, gives a most illuminating picture of a larger concern.

C. SOCIAL LIFE

The birth rate, promiscuity and V.D. are among the subjects well handled in S. Ferguson and H. Fitzgerald's *Studies in the Social Services* (1954).* For a contemporary view of the birth rate, see R. M. and K. Titmuss's *Parents Revolt* (1942). Sydney M. Laird's *Venereal Disease in Britain* (1943) was part of the taboo-breaking which went on.

While the third volume of Asa Briggs's definitive history of the B.B.C. is still awaited,* Maurice Gorham's *Broadcasting and Television since 1900* (1952) remains useful. The same author's *Sound and Fury* (1948) is among the best of many "inside stories". The announcers, for instance, have been prolific in memoirs. Joseph Macleod's *A Job at the B.B.C.* (Glasgow, 1947) is a clever, somewhat bitter book. Stuart Hibberd's *This Is London* (1950) is more loyal, and less interesting. Wilfred Pickles's amiable *Between You and Me* (1949) falls between the two. Edna Nixon's *John Hilton* (1946) is an interesting biography of one notable broadcaster. J. A. Cole's *Lord Haw Haw* (1964) and Rebecca West's *The Meaning of Treason* (revised, 1965) deal fully with a more unorthodox personality.

Ted Kavanagh's *Tommy Handley* (1949) and Francis Worsley's *Itma* (1948) give the inside story of the war's gayest phenomenon. More serious matters are dealt with in Val Gielgud's *British Radio Drama 1922–56* (1957). For the Brains Trust, there are two books by Howard Thomas: *The Brains Trust Book* (1942) and *Britain's Brains Trust* (1944).

The last word on ENSA and all that has been supplied by Basil Dean himself, in his enormous but absorbing volume, *The Theatre at War* (1956).

Dilys Powell, in her contribution to *Since 1939* (1948), gives a survey of the war-time cinema, as do *Twenty Years of British Film* (1947), edited by Michael Balcon, and Alan Wood's amusing study of *Mr. Rank* (1952). The funniest film criticism of the period was collected in C. A. Lejeune's *Chestnuts in Her Lap* (1947). Guy Morgan's *Red Roses Every Night* (1948) is a very worthwhile portrayal of a cinema chain at war, with much of interest to say on the taste of audiences. This is explored more ponderously in J. P. Mayer's *British Cinemas and their Audiences* (1948).

Naturally, the histories of various sports, and even the innumerable memoirs of sportsmen, have little to say about the war period. For cricket, the annual *Widsen's Cricketers' Almanacks* (1940–46) include most things worth knowing. *Flat Racing in Britain Since 1900* (1950),

* It has now appeared as *The History of Broadcasting in the United Kingdom*, Vol. III, *The War of Words* (1970).

edited by Ernest Bland, and *Association Football* (four volumes, 1960), edited by A. H. Fabian and Geoffrey Green, contain pertinent articles.

CHAPTER 7: ONLY TWO ENGLANDS

A. AGRICULTURE

The Ministry of Information's *Land at War* (1945) is a readable survey, while Sir Keith Murray's *Agriculture* (1955)* is a compact, if somewhat lifeless official history. *The National Farm Survey of England and Wales 1941–3 – A Summary Report* (1946) was published by the Ministry of Agriculture. Two useful, if controversial, books by experts were Sir Daniel Hall's *Reconstruction and the Land* (1941) and C. S. Orwin s *Speed the Plough* (1942).

The character of wartime control is lightly but informatively sketched by Anthony Hurd in *A Farmer in Whitehall* (1951). *The State and the Farmer* (1962), by Peter Self and H. J. Storing, comments incisively on the wartime situation. F. H. Lancum's *Press Officer, Please!* (1946) is an anecdotal memoir by the Min. of Ag.'s press officer.

A. G. Street's *Hitler's Whistle* (1943) was the work of an experienced farmer who was also a popular writer. Of the books by people who went back to the land in wartime, Clifton Reynolds's *Glory Hill Farm* tetralogy (1941–45) was probably the most popular; Frances Donaldson's *Four Years' Harvest* (1945) is probably the most sensible; and Ronald Duncan's *Journal of a Husbandman* (1944), the tale of a pacifist's experiments in community life on a Devon farm, is certainly the most off-beat and opinionated.

The Women's Land Army was given an unusually graceful official history by V. Sackville West (1944). The character of each of the numerous memoirs by land girls can be judged by its title. *Pullet on the Midden* (1946), by Rachel Knappett, is clear-eyed and well-written. *If their Mothers Only Knew* (1946), by Shirley Joseph, is snook-cocking and sharp. *Set My Hand Upon the Plough* (1946), by E. M. Barraud, and Jean Iddon's *Fragrant Earth* (1947) are more solemn.

B. COAL

W. H. B. Court's *Coal* (1951)* is most trenchant and readable. Margot Heinemann's *Britain's Coal* (1944) was a well researched survey from the left. The contrasted views of the Miner's Federation and the Mining Association are found in R. Page Arnot's somewhat ponderous *The Miners in Crisis and War* (1961) and W. A. Lee's apologia, *Thirty Years in Coal* (1954). J. E. Williams's *The Derbyshire Miners* (1962) is the most exhaustive of many local histories.

Ferdinand Zweig's *Men in the Pits* (1948) gives a panoramic view of conditions and attitudes in the various coalfields. Mark Benney's *Charity Main* (1946) is an excellent documentary job by a Coal Control official. J. B. Pick's *Under the Crust* (1946) describes the experiences of a middle-class volunteer. D. Agnew's *Bevin Boy* (1947) is vivid but superficial. B. L. Coombes's *Miners Day* (1945) contains delicate descriptions of wartime conditions by a lifelong collier.

C. AIRCRAFT

Nigel Balchin's official booklet, *The Aircraft Builders* (1948) is a lively account of the bright side. The most vivid insights into life in the wartime industry come from the protean Mark Benney's *Over to Bombers* (1943) and from J. T. Murphy's *Victory Production* (1942). J. B. Priestley's *Daylight on Saturday* (1943), one of his topical war novels, tells one less about making aircraft, but is of interest for the author's enthusiastic view of the New Technical Man.

David Farrer's account of the Beaverbrook period at M.A.P. in *The Sky's the Limit* (1943) is surpassed in style and entertainment value by Ely Devons's *Planning in Practice* (1950), a memoir-*cum*-academic-study. The official version of M.A.P.'s workings, much more sober, is found in J. D. Scott's chapters in *The Administration of War Production* (1955).*

For the expansion of the industry, see William Hornby's *Factories and Plant* (1958),* and for the problems of design see M. M. Postan's section in *The Design and Development of Weapons* (1964).* There are many books about individual planes, some technical, some sentimental. Among those sampled, E. Bishop's *The Wooden Wonder* (1959) is a good popular account of the genesis and feats of the Mosquito. Sir Frank Whittle's *Jet* (1953) is a dour but informative account of the progress of his invention, and his relations with M.A.P.

CHAPTER 8: WAR ON THE MIND

A. SCIENCE

Perhaps the quickest way of digesting the contrasts between "before", "during" and "after" is found through two Penguin "Specials": *Science in War* (1940); *Science and World Order* (1942), by J. G. Crowther, O. J. R. Howarth and D. P. Riley, based on the 1941 British Association conference on the subject; and a Pelican, *Science and the Nation* (1947), by the Association of Scientific Workers.

Ronald Clark's *The Rise of the Boffins* (1962) is a good introduction to the stories of radar and operational research. The wartime inventions are clearly explained in J. G. Crowther and R. Whiddington's *Science at War* (1947) and Ritchie Calder's *Profiles of Science* (1951).

The Lindemann-Tizard rivalry is illuminated in two studies of Lindemann – *The Prof* by R. F. Harrod (1959) and the Earl of Birkenhead's *The Prof in Two Worlds* (1961) – and by Ronald Clark's *Tizard* (1965), as well as by C. P. Snow's famous essay on *Science and Government* (1961). Sir Solly Zuckerman's *Scientists and War* (1966) contains some pertinent meditations, as does P. M. S. Blackett's *Studies of War* (1962), which deals at some length with operational research.

The inside story of radar is told drily and informatively in A. P. Rowe's *One Story of Radar* (1948), and over-excitably by Sir Robert Watson Watt in *Three Steps to Victory* (1957). Margaret Gowing's *Britain and Atomic Energy 1939–45* (1964) is already established as a classic; probably, no more important work of history has been published in this century. See also Ronald Clark's *The Birth of the Bomb* (1961). C. P. Snow's *The New Men* (1954) is a fictional version of part of the same story.

Government support for science, before, during and after the war is sketched in Sir Harry Melville's *The Department of Scientific and Industrial Research* (1962). For the public face of science, see W. H. G. Armytage's *Sir Richard Gregory* (1957).

Robert H. Ahrenfeldt's *Psychiatry in the British Army in the Second World War* (1958) brings together the history and findings of the subject. Marjorie Ogilvy Webb's *The Government Explains* (1965) charts the development of official use of surveys and mass media; see also Mass Observation's detailed *Home Propaganda* (1941). The second volume of L. Urwick and E. F. L. Brech's *The Making of Scientific Management* (1946) is a good introduction to pre-war and wartime developments.

Wartime life in the universities is described in A. S. F. Gow's *Letters from Cambridge* (1945), Bruce Truscott's *Redbrick University* (1951) and E H. Warmington's *Birkbeck College 1939–45* (1954).

B. RELIGION

Religion in Britain Since 1900 (1952), edited by G. S. Spinks, is a useful overall survey. Amongst more specialized studies might be mentioned: Roger Lloyd's *The Church of England in the Twentieth Century*, of which the second volume (1950) is most pertinent; R. Tudur Jones's *Congregationalism in England* (1962) and Bryan Wilson's *Sects and Society* (1961). The report of the Archbishop's Commission on Evangelism, *Towards the Conversion of England* (1945), describes the popular status of religion at that time, and Mass Observation's *Puzzled People* (1947) is an independent survey of the subject.

The biographies of bishops form a delightful genre of their own; lengthy, amply documented, and often casting some light on political life in general. J. G. Lockhart's *Cosmo Gordon Lang* (1949) and Charles Smyth's *Cyril Forster Garbett* (1959) are both good examples, especially the latter. Hensley Henson's third volume of his *Retrospect of an Unimportant Life* (1950) is one of the best published diaries of the war.

William Temple (1948) by F. A. Iremonger is immensely detailed; it may be supplemented by *Some Lambeth Letters* (1963), edited by F. S. Temple, and by the archbishop's book *Christianity and Social Order* (1942). The official report of the Malvern Conference was published, by various hands, as *Malvern 1941* (1941). The findings seem to be available in full only in a pamphlet, "The Life of the Church and the Order of Society" (1941), published by the Industrial Christian Fellowship.

Ronald Jaspers's *George Bell – Bishop of Chichester* (1967) is another good biography. Bell's wartime pronouncements are collected in *The Church and Humanity* (1946); see also his *Christianity and World Order* (1940). Sir Robert Vansittart's "Black Record" was published as a pamphlet in 1941. Andrew Sharf's *The British Press and the Jews Under Nazi Rule* (1964) is a careful account of an intricate subject. Arthur D. Morse's *While Six Million Died* (1968) describes the reaction of the allied governments to the Final Solution.

The story of conscientious objection in the war is told, in a thorough if pedestrian fashion, in Denis Hayes's *Challenge of Conscience* (1949). For leading individual pacifists, see Vera Brittain's *Testament of Experience* (1957) and Fenner Brockway's *Bermondsey Story* (1949), on Alfred Salter.

C. THE ARTS

The effects of the war on British journalism are succinctly described in the *Newspaper Press Directory 1945*. The chief press censor, Admiral G. P. Thomson, provides an engaging memoir in *Blue Pencil Admiral* (1947), which should certainly be read by anyone proposing to make use of wartime newspapers.

Just after the war, the British Council sponsored a series of pamphlets on the arts, *Since 1939*. These were later issued in two bound volumes (1948) of which the first includes Dilys Powell on films, Arnold Haskell on ballet, Rollo H. Myers on music and Robin Ironside on painting. (Perhaps the most enduring work of war art is found in Henry Moore's *Shelter Sketch Book* [1945].)

The second volume of *Since 1939* includes surveys, of various quality, by Robert Speaight on drama, Henry Reed on the novel, Stephen Spender on poetry and John Hayward on prose literature. The last covers the problems of wartime publishing, which are also described, with statistics, in Sir Stanley Unwin's *The Truth About a Publisher* (1960).

The files of *Horizon* are in most good libraries, and odd copies of *Penguin New Writing* are often found second-hand. *Poetry London* is more fugitive. Several pertinent articles on the condition of the writer are included in George Orwell's *Collected Essays* (1961). John Lehmann's autobiography *I Am My Brother* (1960) is extremely informative. If this provides a kind of "official" history of wartime writing, the "unofficial" side is hilariously recalled in Julian Maclaren-Ross's remarkable *Memoirs of the Forties* (1965). Jenni Calder's *Chronicles of Conscience* (1968) surveys and analyses the "documentary" style of Orwell and other writers.

Three anthologies of war poetry have appeared in quick succession. At one extreme, Ian Hamilton's *The Poetry of War* (1965) is a fastidious selection with a fascinating appendix of comments by the poets themselves. At the other, Charles Hamblett's *I Burn for England* (1966) prints almost everybody, good and bad. In between the two comes Brian Gardner's *The Terrible Rain* (1966). Many anthologies, especially of servicemen's writing, appeared during the war itself. John Lehmann's *Poems From New Writing* (1946) came out a little later, but is of special interest.

Two other anthologies, *The New Apocalypse* (1940) and *The White Horseman* (1941), edited by J. F. Hendry and Henry Treece, provide all one needs to know about the "apocalyptics".

John Pudney's *Selected Poems* (1946) come from several wartime volumes. Roy Fuller's work is found in *In the Middle of a War* (1942) and *A Lost Season* (1944). Alun Lewis's books are still in print; *Ha! Ha! Among the Trumpets* (1944) is the more mature of the two. Ian Hamilton has edited, with a biographical introduction, *Alun Lewis – Selected Poetry and Prose* (1966). *The Collected Poems of Sidney Keyes* appeared in 1945; see John Gunther's *Sidney Keyes: A Biographical Inquiry* (1967). An interesting Oxford contemporary of Keyes and Douglas, also killed, was Drummond Allison, whose one book was *The Yellow Night* (1944). Keith Douglas's entire work was republished in 1966, in two volumes: *Collected Poems* and *Alamein to Zem Zem*.

CHAPTER 9: NEVER AGAIN?

The relevant volumes of Churchill's memoirs are *Closing the Ring* (1952) and *Triumph and Tragedy* (1954). J. L. Hodson's *The Sea and the Land* (1945) is the last of his war diaries. Mrs. Robert Henrey describes West End life in 1944 in *The Siege of London* (1946).

For Beveridge and his plan, see, besides the report itself (*Social Insurance and Allied Services*, 1942), his collection of speeches and writings, *Pillars of Security* (1944); his second report, *Full Employment in a Free Society* (1944); his autobiography, *Power and Influence* (1953); and *Beveridge and His Plan* (1954), a loyal study by his wife, Janet Beveridge.

The hospitals in wartime are covered in Titmuss's *Problems of Social Policy* (1950),* while Sheila Fergusson and Hilde Fitzgerald deal with the Emergency Maternity Services and the nursing profession in *Studies in the Social Services* (1954).* The ten regional hospital surveys initiated before the war were issued separately in 1945 and summarized in *The Hospital Surveys* (1946), published by the Nuffield Provincial Hospitals Trust. J. M. Mackintosh's *The Nation's Health* (1944) is a useful illustrated survey of the British system before the National Health Service, the origins of which are trenchantly summarized in Harry Eckstein's *The English Health Service* (1959). Lord Hill's *Both Sides of the Hill* (1964) casts light on the doctors' attitudes.

For the Tory Reform Committee, see its manifesto, "Forward – By The Right!" (1943) and Quintin Hogg, *One Year's Work* (1944), a collection of speeches and articles. The present writer's doctoral thesis on the subject (University of Sussex, 1968) is so far the only detailed survey of the Common Wealth Party, but its ideas can be examined in Sir Richard Acland's *What It Will Be Like* (1942) and *How It Can Be Done* (1943), and in Tom Wintringham's *The People's War* (1942).

In the absence of an official history of education during the war, three books by H. C. Dent provide an informative though sometimes impressionistic substitute; *Education in Transition* (1944); *The Education Act 1944* (1944 and many subsequent editions) and *Growth in English Education 1946–52* (1954). W. O. Lester Smith's *To Whom Do Schools Belong?* (1942) is a most valuable introduction to the educational controversies of the period. See also S. J. Curtis's *Education in Britain Since 1900* (1952) and Asher Tropp's *The Schoolteachers* (1957).

Those official histories which deal with the blitz mostly deal also with the V bomb attacks. Basil Collier's *The Battle of the V Weapons 1944–45* (1964) is the standard military history.

The 1945 general election results are given in full, with a useful summary of the campaign, in *The Times*'s *House of Commons 1945* (1945). The Nuffield College survey of *The British General Election of 1945* (1947), by R. B. McCallum and A. Readman, suffers from a lack of statistical sophistication consequent upon its being the first of its kind, but is lively enough. John Bonham's *The Middle Class Vote* (1954) is of great interest and importance.

ndex